D1105807

UNDERSTANDING GLOBAL MIGRATION

Edited by James F. Hollifield and Neil Foley

STANFORD UNIVERSITY PRESS
Stanford, California

STANFORD UNIVERSITY PRESS
Stanford, California
Published in cooperation with the William P. Clements Center for Southwest Studies,
Southern Methodist University

Printed in the United States of America on acid-free, archival-quality paper

Library of Congress Cataloging-in-Publication Data

Names: Hollifield, James Frank, 1954– editor. | Foley, Neil, editor.
Title: Understanding global migration / edited by James F. Hollifield and Neil Foley.
Description: Stanford, California : Stanford University Press, 2022. | Includes
    bibliographical references and index.
Identifiers: LCCN 2021026176 (print) | LCCN 2021026177 (ebook) | ISBN 9781503614772
    (cloth) | ISBN 9781503629578 (paperback) | ISBN 9781503629585 (ebook)
Subjects: LCSH: Emigration and immigration—Government policy—Case studies. |
    Emigration and immigration—Political aspects—Case studies. | Emigration and
    immigration—Economic aspects—Case studies.
Classification: LCC JV6038 .U64 2022 (print) | LCC JV6038 (ebook) | DDC 325—dc23
LC record available at https://lccn.loc.gov/2021026176
LC ebook record available at https://lccn.loc.gov/2021026177

Cover design: Kevin Barrett Kane
Cover image: Adobe Stock
Typeset by Newgen North America in Minion Pro 10/13

CONTENTS

by Andrew Selee, MPI

Understanding Global Migration by James Hollifield and Neil Foley is both a timely and important book. For too long, comparative migration studies have focused on Europe, North America, Australia, and New Zealand as the paradigmatic cases of migration states, while in fact much of the world's migration has always been to countries in Asia, Africa, the Middle East, and the Americas.

This volume looks at how different countries around the world, in every region of the globe, have become migration states, and the result is illuminating. The notion of a single model of migration state, primarily tied to postwar economic globalization and the extension of rights, looks different in other parts of the world. Geographic location, colonial histories, ethnic politics, state capacity, insertion in global markets, and even particular understandings of national interest turn out to shape the way that states define their roles and set their priorities for migration decision-making in ways that defy easy categorization.

This book pulls together a truly exceptional group of scholars from around the world to look at how these differences have unfolded and what they tell us about how state formation and migration policies interact. As a result, this book provides original re-search on countries in regions of the world that have been understudied, and also puts Western countries, which have been extensively studied, under a different comparative microscope.

One of the great advantages of this book is that the editors took great care from the beginning to ask a set of common questions about state formation and migration policy to all of the contributors. As a result, each of the chapters explores a series of coherent and consistent themes that allow the reader to make comparisons across the different cases studies and to put them in historical perspective. Because of this methodological consistency and careful coordination, the volume often feels more like a single-authored book than it does a collection of separate essays. Yet within a common methodological and theoretical approach, the editors also manage to keep the distinct perspectives and textures that come from pulling together people who are nurtured by scholarly debates and on-the-ground-realities in different parts of the world.

In the end, one of the most important lessons that emerges from this book is that we should not assume that the migration state as it developed in Western democracies is the model for the rest of the world and that other regions will slowly converge to this model. Indeed, the priorities, institutional structures, and policy repertoires that other countries have for making migration decisions often differ notably in their foundations.

This book provides the first systematic attempt to compare the migration state across regions and to explore migration interdependence. As such, it will be a foundational work for future discussions about how policies are made in sharply different contexts around the world.

This book started as a conversation circa 2016 between Jim Hollifield and Neil Foley about how to study migration as a global phenomenon while recognizing that population movements are driven by deep historical, cultural, and (more often than not) regional ties. Our goal was to bring together a group of scholars, each specializing in a particular region or country, to study the evolution of migration corridors and interdependence, with a focus on issues of governance and economic and human development. The first challenge in a project of this magnitude was to find like-minded scholars who could agree on the research questions and a framework of analysis, but with a critical eye and a willingness to engage in the kind of give-and-take that would produce an original work of scholarship. We were lucky to convene such a group, first in 2017 at a workshop and retreat at the SMU campus in Taos, New Mexico, where we began to hash out the argument and present the first drafts of the work. Taos is a fantastic setting for a scholarly retreat to clear the mind in the high desert and cool mountain air. It was in Taos that we forged something of a consensus on the "migration state" framework, recognizing that all states, whether in the global South or North, face the dilemmas of migration management and that migration and mobility are vital for human and economic development in every region of the globe. We reconvened on the beautiful SMU campus in Dallas in 2018 to hone the second drafts of the chapters, and in the intervening years many panels and workshops grew out of the original project to refine the concept of the migration state and to delineate the varieties of migration states.

Using the "migration state" framework, we developed a typology that is reflected in the layout of this book, which is divided into five parts. In Part I we define the migration state in comparative and historical terms and trace the development of migration interdependence in the post–World War II era, showing how migration has become the third pillar of globalization alongside trade and money/finance, under the umbrella of liberal internationalism and in the wake of decolonization, the dismantling of the old imperial orders, wars of independence and liberation, and the rise of neoimperial and neocolonial orders. Part II looks at the emergence of "postcolonial migration states," specifically in Africa and the Middle East, presaging a discussion in Part III of developmental migration states in South and East Asia. In the twenty-first century it is imperative to understand migration from the perspective of the global South, where countries have evolved from sending to transit and receiving states. In Part IV we return to the global North to look first at the classical settler, colonial societies, under the rubric of what Hollifield calls "liberal migration states," with all of the paradoxes and contradictions that the term "liberal" implies. In Part V we turn our attention to "postimperial migration states" in Europe, including Turkey, before concluding with discussions of migration governance and development "beyond the state" in the European Union. Most of the contributors take a critical view of the migration state, which leads to a creative tension in the book. We view this as a positive attribute, and it is our hope that the book will serve not only as a scholarly reference but also as a text where teachers and students can go to learn about migration in a truly global context: its roots, its tensions, and the prospects for migration, mobility, and human development in the twenty-first century.

This work has benefited from exchanges with scholars around the globe and from anonymous reviews commissioned by Stanford University Press. The manuscript workshop in Taos and the public symposium in Dallas were organized and hosted by the William P. Clements Center for Southwest Studies and the John Goodwin Tower Center for Public Policy and International Affairs at SMU, with support from the Center for Presidential History at SMU and the Marian Tower International Conference Fund. We must thank all who participated in the workshop and symposium, and especially the staff of the Clements and Tower Centers: Ruth Ann Elmore, Luisa del Rosal, Ray Rafidi, and Bora Laci. The editors and contributing authors are solely responsible for the information and views presented in this book, which do not necessarily represent those of the underwriters.

Special thanks go to Nicole Rafidi, assistant to the director of the Tower Center, for her tireless work on the project and to Alan Harvey, director of Stanford University Press, and his colleagues, especially Caroline McKusick, the assistant editor. Without the extraordinary patience, skill, and support of the contributors, the staff of the centers, and the press, this book would not have been possible.

James F. Hollifield

Neil Foley
DALLAS, TEXAS
FEBRUARY 2021

CONTRIBUTORS

Fiona Adamson is Professor in International Relations at SOAS, University of London. Her research interests are in International Relations theory, transnational identity politics, international peace and security, global governance and migration, and diaspora. She has also written on the sources of foreign policy decision-making in Turkish politics, as well as on Kurdish politics, political Islam, and Cyprus. Her published work has appeared in leading journals in international relations as well as in a number of edited volumes. She is a co-investigator in the European Union Horizon 2020 research project Migration Governance and Asylum Crises (MAGYC) and is a co-convenor of the London Migration Research Group (LMRG). She also serves on the Governing Council of the International History and Politics Section of the American Political Science Association. Prior to joining SOAS, she was Director of the Programme in International Public Policy at University College London (UCL). Adamson holds a BA from Stanford University and an MA, MPhil, and PhD from Columbia University. She has held research fellowships at Harvard and Stanford Universities, as well as at Humboldt University, Berlin, and University of Basel, Switzerland.

Pieter Bevelander is Professor of International Migration and Ethnic Relations (IMER) and Director of MIM, Malmö Institute of Migration, Diversity and Welfare, and a senior lecturer at the Department of Global Political Studies, Malmö University, Sweden. His main research field is international migration and different aspects of immigrant integration and attitudes toward immigrants and ethnic minorities. He has a doctorate in economic history from Lund University. His publications include the labor market situation of immigrants in a regional setting and the effects of labor market policy measures directed toward immigrants in Sweden. His research topics also include the labor market integration of men and women in the Netherlands, the ascension to citizenship of immigrants in the Netherlands, and a comparison of ethnic social capital in Canada and the Netherlands. He has published in a number of international journals as well as co-edited books, including with Don DeVoretz, *The Economics of Citizenship* (2008); with Mirjam Hagström and Sofia Rönnqvist, *Resettled and Included? The Employment Integration of*

Resettled Refugees in Sweden (2009); and with Bo Petersson, *Crisis and Migration, Implications of the Eurozone Crisis for Perceptions, Politics, and Policies of Migration* (Nordic Academic Press, 2014).

Yves Charbit is Doctorat d'Etat ès-Lettres of the Sorbonne and PhD, University of Oxford. He is Professor emeritus of demography and development at the University Sorbonne Paris Cité and Associate Senior Research Fellow, School of Anthropology, Oxford. He was founding Director of the Centre on Population and Development. He has published 22 books and 74 chapters of books or peer-reviewed articles on international migration, family structures, nuptiality, reproductive health, and theories and doctrines of population. He has been a visiting lecturer in many countries and consulted for international organizations, including OECD, UNDP, and the World Bank. He was a founding member of the editorial board of the Revue européenne des migrations internationales and served as Senior Social Scientist advising governments in several Caribbean, African, and Southeast Asian countries on issues of migration management and research in the field of population and development, and design and implementation of training programs.

Erin Aeran Chung is the Charles D. Miller Associate Professor of East Asian Politics in the Department of Political Science at Johns Hopkins University. She previously served as Director of the East Asian Studies Program and Co-director of the Racism, Immigration, and Citizenship (RIC) Program. She has been a Mansfield Foundation U.S.-Japan Network for the Future Program Scholar, an SSRC Abe Fellow at the University of Tokyo and Korea University, an advanced research fellow at Harvard University's Weatherhead Center for International Affairs Program on U.S.-Japan Relations, and a Japan Foundation Fellow at Saitama University. She is currently co-editor of the Cambridge University Press Elements Social Science Series on the Politics and Society of East Asia. Chung specializes in East Asian political economy, international migration, civil society, and comparative racial politics. She is the author of *Immigration and Citizenship in Japan* (Cambridge University Press, 2010; Japanese translation, Akashi Shoten, 2012) and *Immigrant Incorporation in East Asian Democracies* (Cambridge University Press, 2020). She was awarded a five-year grant from the Academy of Korean Studies (AKS) to support the completion of her third book project on "Citizenship, Social Capital, and Racial Politics in the Korean Diaspora."

Neil Foley holds the Robert and Nancy Dedman Endowed Chair in History at Southern Methodist University and is Associate Director of the Clements Center for Southwest Studies. His current research centers on the politics of migration and citizenship in North America and Europe; nativism/xenophobia and ethno-nationalist movements; changing constructions of race, citizenship, and transnational identity in the US-Mexico borderlands; and comparative civil rights politics of African, Asian, and Latinx Americans. He is the author of *The White Scourge: Mexicans, Blacks, and Poor Whites in Texas* (University of California Press, 1997); *Quest for Equality: The Failed Promise of Black-Brown Solidarity* (Harvard University Press, 2010); and *Mexicans in the Making of*

America (Harvard University Press, 2014), which was nominated for the Pulitzer Prize in history in 2015. He is the recipient of fellowship awards from the John Simon Guggenheim Foundation, National Endowment for the Humanities, Woodrow Wilson International Center for Scholars, American Philosophical Society, American Council of Learned Societies, the Ford Foundation, and the Fulbright Scholars Program (Germany, Mexico, Spain). Before receiving his PhD from the University of Michigan, Foley lived for six years in Latin America, Asia, and Europe. He also spent two years teaching sailors aboard aircraft carriers of the US Navy's Sixth Fleet in the Mediterranean Sea.

Andrew Geddes is Professor of Migration Studies and Director of the Migration Policy Centre. During his career, he has led and participated in a number of major projects on aspects of international migration, working with a wide range of academic and non-academic partners. For the period 2014–19 he was awarded an Advanced Investigator Grant by the European Research Council for a project on the drivers of global migration governance (the MIGPROSP project; see www.migrationgovernance.org for further details). He has published extensively on global migration, with a particular focus on policy-making and the politics of migration and on regional cooperation and integration. Recent publications include *The Politics of Migration and Immigration in Europe* (Sage, co-authored with Peter Scholten); *The Dynamics of Regional Migration Governance* (edited with Marcia Vera Espinoza, Leila Hadj-Abdou, and Leiza Brumat); *A Rising Tide? The Salience of Immigration and the Rise of Anti-Immigration Political Parties in Western Europe* (*Political Quarterly*, with James Dennison); and *Governing Migration beyond the State* (Oxford University Press, 2021). Prior to joining EUI Geddes was Professor of Politics at the University of Sheffield, UK, where he served as Head of Department.

Charles P. Gomes holds the Sergio Buarque de Holanda Chair at Instituto Mora in Mexico City, is Senior Researcher at Fundação Casa de Rui Barbosa, and is Director of CEPRI, a pro bono legal clinic for refugees and migrants in Rio de Janeiro, Brazil. He has a PhD in political science (2001) from the former IUPERJ (University of Rio de Janeiro Research Institute), currently the IESP. During his doctoral studies, he was a visiting researcher at the European University Institute in Florence, Italy, and at the Institut d'études politiques in Paris, France. He was a visiting professor at the Université Paris I in 2006 and 2007 and at the Center for Forced Migration Studies at Northwestern University in Chicago in 2012. His research focuses on constitutional and supranational courts, international law, immigration, and refugee policies. Gomes is currently leading a comparative study in immigration policies and politics in major countries of Latin America. He has published several books, articles, and reports on the topics of refuge and international migration.

Miryam Hazán is a migration specialist at the Organization of American States, working currently at the Inter-American Commission on Human Rights. Previously, she was a senior consultant with the Inter-American Development Bank, where she led a major research project on international migration in Central America, Mexico, Haiti, and the Dominican Republic. Hazán is also a senior fellow with the Tower Center for Public

Policy and International Affairs at Southern Methodist University, and she has held research and scholarly positions at Demos, Ideas in Action, the Migration Policy Institute, the University of Pennsylvania, Rutgers University, and the Tomas Rivera Policy Institute at the University of Texas, Austin. Hazán holds a PhD in government from the University of Texas, Austin, an MA from Georgetown University, and a BA from the Autonomous University of Mexico. She is the author of numerous policy reports, journal articles, book chapters, and blogs on topics related to international migration and refugees in the Americas, migration and development, immigrant integration in the United States, Latino politics, and US-Mexico relations.

Charles Hirschman is Professor Emeritus of Sociology at the University of Washington. Hirschman received his BA from Miami University (Ohio) in 1965 and his PhD from University of Wisconsin–Madison in 1972. He was appointed Boeing International Professor in 1998 and held a joint appointment in the Daniel J. Evans School of Public Policy and Governance from 2002 to 2017. In addition to his academic appointments, Hirschman worked for the Ford Foundation (in Malaysia) in 1974–75, and was a visiting fellow at the University of Malaya (1984), Australian National University (1985), the Center for Advanced Studies in the Behavioral Sciences (1993–94), the Russell Sage Foundation (1998–99), and the Population Reference Bureau (2005–6), and was Fulbright Professor at the University of Malaya (2012–13). He has authored or edited four books (most recently, *From High School to College: Immigrant Generation, and Race-Ethnicity* [Russell Sage, 2016]), more than 125 articles/book chapters, and 50 book reviews/comments. He has been elected President of the Population Association of America (2005), Chair of Section K (Social, Economic, and Political Sciences) of the American Association for the Advancement of Sciences (2004–5), and is an elected fellow of the American Academy of Arts and Sciences and of the American Association for the Advancement of Science.

James F. Hollifield is Ora Nixon Arnold Chair in International Political Economy, Professor in the Department of Political Science, and Director of the Tower Center at SMU. He also is a Global Fellow at the Woodrow Wilson International Center and a Fellow at the Institut zur Zukunft der Arbeit (IZA) at the University of Bonn. Hollifield is a scholar of international and comparative politics, and he has written widely on issues of political and economic development, with a focus on migration. Before joining the faculty at SMU, Hollifield taught at Brandeis and Auburn, was a research fellow at Harvard's Center for European Studies, and Associate Director of Research at the French CNRS. In addition to many scientific articles and reports, his recent works include *Controlling Immigration* (Stanford University Press) and *Migration Theory* (Routledge), both now in fourth editions, and *International Political Economy: History, Theory and Policy* (Cambridge University Press, forthcoming). Hollifield has served as an advisor for governments around the world and for many international organizations on matters of migration and human and economic development. In 2021–22, he was named a Fellow of the French Institute for Advanced Study in Paris.

Audie Klotz is Professor of Political Science in the Maxwell School at Syracuse University. She has a BA from Oberlin College and PhD from Cornell University. She is a leading scholar of international relations and has published widely in this field, including works on *Qualitative Methods in International Relations*, edited with Deepa Prakash (Palgrave Macmillan, 2008) and *Strategies for Research in Constructivist International Relations*, with Cecelia Lynch (M. E. Sharpe, now Routledge, 2007). She is an expert in the politics of Southern Africa and author of *Migration and National Identity in South Africa,1860–2010* (Cambridge University Press, 2013) and *Norms in International Relations: The Struggle against Apartheid* (Cornell University Press, 1995). Klotz has served as Vice President of the International Studies Association and was co-founder and Chairperson of the Society for Women in International Political Economy.

Leo Lucassen is Professor of Global Labour and Migration History and Director of the International Institute of Social History (IISH). His research focuses on global migration history, integration, migration systems, migration controls, gypsies and the state, state formation and modernity, and urban history. He wants to stimulate interdisciplinary research on migration history and contribute to the public debate on migration. He is the co-editor of numerous books, including *Globalising Migration History: The Eurasian Experience (16th–21st Centuries)* (Brill, 2014), with Jan Lucassen; *Migration and Membership Regimes in Global and Historical Perspective* (Brill, 2013), with Ulbe Bosma and Gijs Kessler; *Living in the City: Urban Institutions in the Low Countries, 1200–2010* (Routledge, 2012), with W. H. Willems; *The Encyclopedia of Migration and Minorities in Europe: From the 17th Century to the Present* (Cambridge University Press, 2011), with Klaus J. Bade, Pieter C. Emmer, and Jochen Oltmer; *Migration History in World History: Multidisciplinary Approaches* (Brill, 2010) with Jan Lucassen and Patrick Manning; and author of *The Immigrant Threat: The Integration of Old and New Migrants in Western Europe since 1850* (University of Illinois Press, 2005).

Philip L. Martin is Professor Emeritus of Agricultural and Resource Economics at the University of California, Davis, whose research focuses on international labor migration, farm labor, and economic development. He is editor of the quarterly *Rural Migration News*. His recent books include *Merchants of Labor: Recruiters and International Labor Migration* (Oxford University Press, 2017). Martin has earned a reputation as an effective analyst who can develop practical solutions to complex and controversial migration and labor issues. He served on the Commission on Agricultural Workers to assess the effects of the Immigration Reform and Control Act of 1986 and evaluated the prospects for Turkish migration to European Union between 1987 and 1990, and the effects of immigration on Malaysia's economy and labor markets in 1994–95. Martin was a member of the Binational Study of Migration between 1995 and 1997.

Kamal Sadiq is Associate Professor of Political Science at the University of California, Irvine, having received his PhD from University of Chicago. His research focuses on the processes of political inclusion and legal membership of immigrants, refugees, and the urban poor in developing countries, specifically in South Asia (India, Bangladesh) and Southeast Asia (Malaysia, Indonesia). He is the author of *Paper Citizens: How Illegal Immigrants Acquire Citizenship in Developing Countries* (Oxford University Press, 2009; reprinted 2010) and a recent co-edited book, *Interpreting Politics: Situated Knowledge,*

India, and the Rudolph Legacy (Oxford University Press, 2020), with John Echeverri-Gent. His articles on illegal immigration, regional and national identity, and postcolonial citizenship have appeared in top journals and presses, and his research has been funded by the Smith Richardson Foundation, the Harry Frank Guggenheim Foundation, the MacArthur Foundation, and the Mellon Foundation. Sadiq served as Chair of the Ethnicity, Nationalism, and Migration Studies (ENMISA) section of the International Studies Association (2013–15) and as Co-president of the Migration and Citizenship section of the American Political Science Association (2015–17). He serves on the editorial board of the journal *Citizenship Studies* and the advisory board of the journal *Migration Politics*.

Zack Taylor is Assistant Professor of Political Science at Western University, where he specializes in urban political economy and Canadian and comparative politics and policy-making, with an empirical focus on historical and contemporary multilevel governance of cities. He also pursues parallel interests in municipal campaigns and elections, local public finance, and political geography. Taylor is Director of Western's Centre for Urban Policy and Local Governance and Director of NEST's Canadian Communities Policy Observatory. He is a Fellow at the Institute on Municipal Finance and Governance in the University of Toronto's Munk School of Global Affairs and Public Policy and a nonpracticing Registered Professional Planner.

Hélène Thiollet is a CNRS permanent researcher, specializing in the politics of migration and asylum in the global South, with a focus on the Middle East and sub-Saharan Africa. She teaches international relations, comparative politics, and migration studies at Sciences Po, Paris. Thiollet is a graduate of the Ecole Normale Supérieure and holds a PhD in political science from Sciences Po. She has been a board member of *Critique internationale*, a French language IR journal, since 2009. She is the editor of *Migrations en Méditerranée* (CNRS, 2015) and *Migration, Urbanity and Cosmopolitanism in a Globalized World* (Springer, 2021).

Daniel J. Tichenor is the Philip H. Knight Chair of Social Science and Director of the Program on Democratic Governance of the Wayne Morse Center for Law and Politics at the University of Oregon. His research interests include immigration and refugee policy, presidential politics, social movements and interest groups, children and politics, and American political development. He has published seven scholarly books and volumes. His most recent book (with Sidney Milkis) is *Rivalry and Reform: Presidents, Social Movements, and the Transformation of American Politics* (University of Chicago Press, 2018). *The Politics of International Migration* (Oxford University Press), with Marc Rosenblum, has recently been published in paperback. His book *Dividing Lines: The Politics of Immigration Control* (Princeton University Press) won the American Political Science Association's Gladys Kammerer Award for the best book on US public policy. Tichenor has been a Research Fellow in Governmental Studies at the Brookings Institution, a Visiting Scholar at the Center for the Study of Democratic Politics at Princeton University, a Faculty Scholar at the Eagleton Institute of Politics at Rutgers University, and the Abba P. Schwartz Fellow of Immigration and Refugee Policy at the John F. Kennedy Presidential Library.

Phil Triadafiloupoulos is Associate Professor of Political Science at the University of Toronto. He teaches courses in political science and public policy at the University of Toronto Scarborough and the Munk School of Global Affairs & Public Policy and conducts research in the areas of immigration and citizenship policy in Europe and North America. Triadafilopoulos received his PhD in political science from the New School for Social Research and is a former Social Sciences and Humanities Research Council of Canada Postdoctoral Fellow. He is the author of *Becoming Multicultural: Immigration and the Politics of Membership in Canada and Germany* (UBC Press, 2012), the editor of *Wanted and Welcome? Policies for Highly Skilled Immigrants in Comparative Perspective* (Springer, 2013), and the co-editor of *Segmented Cities? How Urban Contexts Shape Ethnic and Nationalist Politics* (UBC Press, 2014) and *European Encounters: Migrants, Migration and European Societies since 1945* (Ashgate, 2003).

Gerasimos Tsourapas is Senior Lecturer in International Relations at the School of Social and Political Science, University of Glasgow. His research examines the politics of migration in the Middle East and the broader global South via non-Western perspectives. He is the author of *The Politics of Migration in Modern Egypt: Strategies for Regime Survival in Autocracies* (Cambridge University Press, 2019) and *Migration Diplomacy in the Middle East: Power, Mobility, and the State* (Manchester University Press, 2020). His work has appeared in leading journals of international relations, and his books and articles have received numerous awards. *The Politics of Migration in Modern Egypt* was awarded the 2020 ENMISA Distinguished Book Award by the International Studies Association. He also received the inaugural 2021 ENMISA Emerging Scholar Award by the ISA. Tsourapas was a Fellow at the Center for European Studies, Harvard University (2019–20) and the American University in Cairo (2013–14).

Understanding Global Migration

INTRODUCTION

PART 1

INTRODUCTION

James F. Hollifield and Neil Foley

UNDERSTANDING GLOBAL MIGRATION looks at the rapidly evolving trends in international migration in the twenty-first century, the root causes, the drivers and dynamics of migration, its consequences for human and economic development, and the challenges and opportunities that the movement of people presents for states and regions. The book covers major topics in global migration: the exodus of refugees from the Middle East and Africa to Europe; the surge in child migration from Central America through Mexico to the United States; the exodus of Venezuelans in Latin America; the fluid populations and boundaries of South and Southeast Asia; the displacement of populations in Africa resulting from climate change, failed states, and other natural and man-made disasters; the effects of pandemic on mobility and migration; and the rise of new migration states and regimes. A principal takeaway from this book is that there is not a single "migration state," following the classic Western, liberal, and settler model, but rather a range of ways in which states grapple with migration in different historical and geographical contexts.

The book is based on a series of propositions. The *first proposition* of the project is that **the state matters**. International migration and mobility raise a host of economic, humanitarian, and security concerns for states in the global North and South. The garrison state was linked with the trading state in Europe in the eighteenth and nineteenth centuries. The twentieth and twenty-first centuries have seen the emergence of **the migration state** (Hollifield 2004a, 2012), where managing migration is vital for national development. The migration state is an "ideal type" that takes different forms in various regions of the globe, from the "liberal" state in classic settler nations to the "postimperial" state in Europe (evolving into a liberal type) and Turkey, to the "postcolonial" migration states in Africa, the Middle East, and South Asia, to the "developmental" migration state in East and Southeast Asia.

The *second proposition* is that we must put contemporary migrations into a **historical and comparative perspective**: Looking at recent migration "crises," it is important to keep in mind *la longue durée:* The migration "crises" of the late twentieth and early twenty-first centuries pale by comparison with the upheavals associated with imperialism, the Industrial Revolution, the two world wars, and decolonization, which resulted in genocide, irredentism, the displacement of tens of millions of people, and the radical redrawing of national boundaries, not only in Europe but around the globe (Lucassen 2005).

Since the 1940s, international migration has been increasing in every region of the globe, feeding the fears of some who give voice to a sense of crisis—a crisis that is more political and social than economic. We know that migration is *not* a new phenomenon in the annals of human history (Gabaccia 2015). Indeed, for much of recorded history and for many civilizations, the movement of populations was the norm. Only with the advent of the nation-state in sixteenth- and seventeenth-century Europe and the imposition of the nation-state system through European imperialism did the notion of legally tying populations to territorial units (sovereignty) and to specific forms of government become commonplace. In the nineteenth and twentieth centuries, passport and visa systems developed and borders were hardened and closed to nonnationals, especially those deemed to be hostile to the nation and the state (Torpey 2000). Almost every dimension of human existence—social-psychological, demographic, economic, and political—has been reshaped to conform to the dictates of the nation-state (Kohn 1962), which in "settler societies" resulted in the displacement and dispossession of Indigenous peoples and in genocide (Dauvergne 2016).

The *third proposition* is that since 1945 **human rights** have become a central feature of migration governance: Do the recent waves of migration rise to the level of a crisis that threatens the political and social order in various states and regions of the globe? What are the drivers and dynamics of migration in a world that, until the global pandemic of 2020, was relatively open in market terms, with human rights playing an increasingly important role in human mobility? What are the consequences of population movements and forced displacement for human development? How can states manage the flows in light of the fact that there are strong economic pressures for openness and strong political, legal, and security pressures for closure—what Hollifield (1992) has called "the liberal paradox"? The global pandemic has heightened the dilemmas of migration governance, making trade-offs between openness and closure more difficult.

The *fourth proposition* is that migration has contributed to **greater interdependence** among states and regions: Migration is a force driving interdependence between regions and states. As states and societies became more liberal and open, migration increased, contributing to political and economic interdependence. With the strong nativist backlash against immigration in "the West," migration is seen to be contributing to resurgent nationalisms and to a backlash against globalization (Norris and Inglehart 2019). How long will this backlash persist, will it spread around the globe, and will it undermine any chance for global governance and the ratification of the UN global compact on migration and refugees? Will the closure of borders and restriction of human mobility due to the global pandemic become permanent, reinforcing trends toward greater closure to protect public health? Will the pandemic and the populist backlash lead to the "end of liberalism" and the collapse of the rules-based, international liberal order?

The *fifth proposition* is that in the twenty-first century, **migration is more vital for sustained economic and human development than at any time in history**: Will migration be destabilizing, leading the international system into greater anarchy, disorder, and war; or will it lead to greater openness, wealth, and human development? Much will depend on how migration is managed in the core liberal democracies, and on whether there is a return to global migration governance in the post-Trump era. One takeaway from this book is that to avoid a domestic political backlash against migration in liberal societies, the rights of migrants must be respected and states must cooperate in global migration governance. Even as many states innovate and become more dependent on migration, they continue to face the challenges of the liberal paradox with its rights-markets dynamic and the need for societies to be economically open and politically closed (to protect the social contract). Does the liberal paradox apply in countries and regions where liberalism never took root? The authors in this volume seek to address these questions from a comparative, historical, theoretical, and policy standpoint, looking across regions and countries.

The Challenge of Migration Governance

International migration and mobility have been steadily increasing since the end of the Second World War, under the umbrella of an international "liberal" order (Ikenberry 2012). According to UN data, in 2019 approximately 272 million people resided outside of their country of birth for one year or more (barely 3.5 percent of the world's population). Even at the height of the postwar liberal order (in the 1980s and 1990s), emigration remained the exception, not the rule (see figure 1.1). Until the global pandemic of 2020, tens of millions of people crossed borders on a daily basis, which added up to roughly two billion border crossings per year. Human mobility was part of a broader trend of globalization, which includes trade in goods and services, investments and capital flows, greater ease of travel, and a veritable explosion of information. While trade and capital flows are the twin pillars of globalization, migration is the third leg of the stool on which the global economy rests. Yet until recently, migration, not to mention citizenship, has received little attention in the field of international relations (Hollifield 2012).

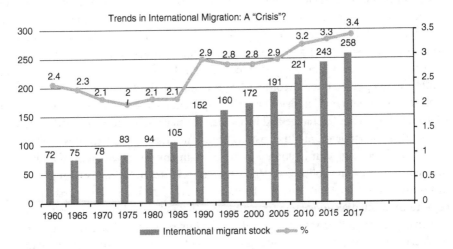

Figure 1.1. Trends in international migration: A "crisis"?

The COVID-19 pandemic calls these liberal trends into question, changing the trade-offs involved in managing migration and mobility, as states move to close their borders, to stop mobility in its tracks, to tighten migration and citizenship policies, and to roll back the rights of migrants, refugees, and asylum seekers. These developments pose the biggest challenge to the international "liberal" order since the 1930s and the Second World War. Could the pandemic be the fateful cataclysm that puts an end to roughly seventy years of globalization and the rights-markets dynamics of the international liberal order itself? Or will the legal and institutional edifice of globalization, which was under stress even before the pandemic, hold?

Like trade and foreign investment, migration has been a defining feature of globalization, and human mobility has been taken for granted, especially in the wealthier (Organization for Economic Cooperation and Development [OECD]) countries of the Northern Hemisphere. Migration and mobility are in many ways connected to trade and investment, yet they are profoundly different. *People are not shirts*, which is another way of saying that labor is not a pure commodity. Unlike goods and capital, individuals have agency and become actors on the international stage whether through peaceful transnational communities or violent terrorist and criminal networks. In the numerically rare instances when migrants commit terrorist acts, migration and mobility can be a threat to the security of states, and during a time of pandemic, the movement of people can endanger public health. This is especially true when foreign workers are concentrated in production-line work (like food processing and meatpacking in the United States) or confined in factories and dormitories, in crowded conditions and closed quarters, as in the sweatshops of South and Southeast Asia, in labor-intensive service industries and construction in Singapore, and in the oil sheikdoms of the Persian Gulf.

Yet migration remains vital for human and economic development, and it reduces global inequalities. The benefits of migration outweigh the costs, according to the most recent study of the US National Academy of Sciences. The NAS study demonstrates a tight correlation between successful immigrant incorporation, economic and social mobility, naturalization, and citizenship. Immigrants bring much needed labor and human capital, new ideas and cultures (diversity), and in liberal democracies they come with a basic package of (human and civil) rights that enables them to settle, to become productive members of society, and to acquire citizenship. Conversely, emigrants may return to their countries of origin where they can have a dramatic impact on economic and political development, often becoming "transnationals" shuttling between countries of origin and destination (Hollifield, Orrenius, and Osang 2006). Remittances remain a vital source of foreign exchange and investment in many developing countries, despite the fact that the pandemic and the ensuing economic crisis jeopardized this capital flow.

Lest we forget, not all migration is voluntary—in any given year, tens of millions of people move to escape political violence, hunger, and deprivation, becoming refugees, asylum seekers, or internally displaced persons. In 2019, the number of "persons of concern" to the United Nations High Commissioner for Refugees (UNHCR) was 70.8 million, including 26 million refugees, 3.5 million asylum seekers, and 41.3 million internally displaced people. Wars in the Middle East (especially Syria and Iraq), East and West Africa, and instability in South and Southeast Asia (Afghanistan and Pakistan, Rohingya in Bangladesh) and Central (Northern Triangle) and South America (Venezuela) continue to feed a growing population of forced migrants. Europe (as in the European Union) and Germany in particular struggled to cope with waves of forced migration from the Middle East and South Asia—almost 1 million asylum seekers arrived in Germany in 2015 alone. In 2018–19, tens of thousands of Central Americans fled the Northern Triangle countries, heading north to seek asylum in the United States. Because it is so complex and multifaceted, migration of all types (voluntary and forced) poses a challenge for liberal states, for regions like the European Union (EU) and North America (NAFTA), and for the international community as a whole.

International migration is likely to increase in coming decades, unless there is some cataclysmic international event, like a world war or global economic depression, or another global pandemic. Despite the 9/11 terrorist attack on the United States and the great recession of 2007–9, followed by the sovereign debt crisis in Europe, liberal democracies remained relatively open to immigration. From 1990 until 2016, the US admitted an average of 1 million migrants annually, and in 2018 roughly 2.4 million people emigrated to the EU from non-EU countries. Growing demand for basic manpower and competition for the highly skilled, coupled with stagnant or shrinking populations in the receiving countries, have created more economic opportunities for migrants. Transnational networks (family and kinship ties) are more dense and efficient than ever, linking the sending and receiving societies. Networks help to reduce risk and lower the transaction costs of migration, making it easier for people to move across borders and over long distances. Moreover, when legal migration is not an option, migrants (especially asylum seekers) have turned to professional smugglers, and a global industry of migrant smuggling has flourished. In 2016, almost 4,000 migrants perished at sea while trying to enter the EU to seek asylum. The US Border Patrol has recorded 6,915 migrant deaths along the border from 1998 to 2016, although humanitarian groups estimate the figure to be much higher.

In migration states, four factors drive migration and citizenship policy—security, cultural and ideational concerns, economic interests (markets), and rights (figure 1.2).

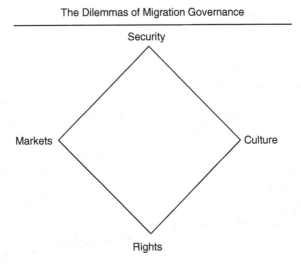

Figure 1.2. The dilemmas of migration governance.

National security—the institutions of sovereignty and citizenship that safeguard the social contract—economics (markets), and rights are all part of a multidimensional game
in migration policy-making. In "normal" times (like the 1980s and 1990s), the debate
about immigration and citizenship revolves around two poles: markets (numbers) and
(status) rights, or how many immigrants to admit, with what skills, and what status?
Should migrants be temporary (guest) workers, or should they be allowed to settle, bring
their families, and be put on a "path to citizenship"? Is there a trade-off between rights
and numbers (markets), as Martin Ruhs (2013) and others (Ruhs and Martin 2008)
suggest?

These are all good questions, but cultural, identity, and ideational concerns—what
regions of the globe should immigrants come from and with what ethnic characteristics
believed to be conducive to integration?—are often more important than markets and
rights, and the trade-offs are more intense in some periods and in some countries than
in others. Throughout much of US history, for example, immigrants were selected on the
basis of race and cultural compatibility: from the Chinese Exclusion Act of 1882 and the
Gentleman's Agreement of 1907–1908, which effectively halted Japanese immigration to
the United States, to the race-based National Origins Quota Act of 1924 to limit immigration from eastern and southern Europe and ban virtually all immigration from Asia.
It was only in the 1950s and 1960s that the US began to move away from selection by
race—the definitive break came with the repeal of the national origins quota system and
the passage of the Immigration and Nationality Act of 1965, known as the Hart-Celler
Act (King 2000; FitzGerald and Cook-Martín 2014; Foley, this volume).

With the September 11, 2001 terrorist attacks (9/11) in the United States and again
with a series of horrendous attacks in Europe in the first decades of the twenty-first
century, immigration and refugee policy-making shifted to a national security dynamic.
The reframing of migration and citizenship policy occurred with a deep cultural sub-
text, fear of Islam, and the concern that liberal migration policies pose a security threat
to the nation and to civil society (Rudolph 2006; Adamson 2006; Lucassen 2005). The
COVID-19 pandemic of 2020 reinforced the security dynamic, affording populist leaders an opportunity to pursue illiberal, xenophobic, and nativist policies. In times of war
and pandemic, the dynamic of markets and rights gives way to a culture-security dynamic and finding equilibrium (compromise) in the policy game is much harder—this
is the policy dilemma facing leaders in every migration state and it has opened the door
to a new and virulent nationalism.

In "normal times," such as the 1980s and early 1990s when the last major immigration
laws were passed in the United States and the EU was pushing to implement the "four
freedoms" of the Single European Act, the debate about immigration revolved around
markets—how many migrants should be admitted and with what skills?—and **rights**—
what status should the migrants have and how quickly should they be allowed to naturalize (figure 1.2)? Even in the best of times, from a liberal standpoint, these questions—
which define who belongs—are politically fraught and difficult to address. They become
infinitely more complex when a country is physically threatened, as happened in the
aftermath of the 9/11 terrorist attacks and with the public health emergency of the
COVID-19 pandemic. If a threat is perceived to be "cultural" as well as physical, debates

about markets and rights give way to **symbolic politics** that paint all immigrants from a specific religion (Muslim) or nationality (Mexican) as an existential threat, as happened in the US presidential campaign of 2016 and again with the debates over Islam and *laïcité* in France in 2020. Shifting the immigration debate away from interests (economics and security) and law (process, policy, and rights) to values and culture, race, ethnicity, and religion, accentuates the ideological dimensions of policy and intensifies the symbolic dimension of politics. This is what happened during the Trump administration when the pandemic made it easier to conflate the COVID-19 virus (the invisible enemy, which Trump referred to as the Wuhan or China virus) with immigrants and refugees, and to reinforce the nativist (and mercantilist, beggar-thy-neighbor) idea that immigrants are taking jobs from native-born Americans.

The four-sided game (see figure 1.2) is difficult at the national, state, and local levels, and it is made more complex because migration control has important foreign policy implications. The movement of people affects international relations and security in myriad ways (Rudolph 2006; Adamson 2006; Hollifield 2012). Hence, political leaders often are engaged in a two- or even three-level game (Putnam 1988), seeking to build local and domestic coalitions to maximize support for immigration policy but with an eye on the foreign policy consequences and implications for international security and stability. In the case of the United States, for example, foreign policy played a vital role in immigration and refugee policy to help win the ideological battles of the Cold War, including a refugee policy that favored those fleeing communism, and the repeal of the national origins quota system to bring US policy into line with rapidly shifting values on race and ethnicity (FitzGerald and Cook-Martín 2014; also Rudolph 2006; Zolberg 2006; Adamson, Triadafilopoulos, and Zolberg 2011; Joppke 2005).

If we accept the Weberian definition of sovereignty, a state can exist only if it has a monopoly on the legitimate use of force in a given territorial area. In this way, states have some protection from interference in their internal affairs (Weber 1947; Krasner 1999), and it is easier to manage religious conflicts. It would then follow that the ability or inability of a state to control its borders and hence its population is the *sine qua non* of sovereignty (Hollifield 2004b, 2012; Klotz, this volume, for a contrasting view). With some notable exceptions—such as the international refugee regime created by the 1951 Geneva Convention in the aftermath of the Second World War (Goodwin-Gill 1996; Betts 2009b, 2011, 2013)—the right of a state to control the entry and exit of persons to and from its territory is an undisputed principle of international law (Hollifield 2004b; Shaw 1997). But this principle, which is one of the cornerstones of the international legal system, immediately raises a puzzling question: Why are some states willing to accept rather high levels of immigration (or emigration) when it would seem not to be in their interest to do so and when public opinion is hostile (Hollifield, Martin, and Orrenius 2014; Freeman 1995; Joppke 1998; Boswell 2007)?

The Emerging Migration State

Notwithstanding the UN system of collective security, the most basic function of the modern state, providing security for the territory, the population, and the government, has not changed much since the creation of the garrison state and the evolution of the

Westphalian system of nation-states in Europe in the sixteenth and seventeenth centuries. But the eighteenth and nineteenth centuries also saw the rise of what Richard Rosecrance (1986) called the *trading state*, in which economic considerations (free trade and a stable international monetary system) often took precedence over crude power maximization. The eighteenth and nineteenth centuries were "the age of imperialism" during which the European model of the nation-state (and the trading state) would be violently exported around the globe, with the subjugation of Indigenous populations and colonization. From a strategic, economic, and demographic standpoint, trade and migration go hand in hand: in the twentieth and twenty-first centuries the wealth, power and stability of the state is dependent on its willingness *to risk both trade and migration* (Hatton and Williamson 1998; Hollifield, Orrenius, and Osang 2006; Peters 2015); and *international security and stability are dependent on the capacity of states to manage migration* (Hollifield 2012). Yet it is extremely difficult, if not impossible, for states to manage or control migration unilaterally or even bilaterally. Migration interdependence (more on this below) has increased sharply since 1945.

The latter half of the twentieth century gave rise to the *migration state* (see figure 1.3) where states are constrained by "embedded liberalism" and rights-based politics (Hollifield 1998, 2004a; Hollifield and Faruk 2017). The conceptual advance made by using the migration state framework lies in recognizing the importance of regulating migration for all nation-states, across regime type, region, and history, even though the Westphalian nation-state is in many ways by definition a migration state, because the legitimacy of nation-states depends upon their ability to control migration (entry and exit) (Weiner 1995; Krasner 1999; Hollifield 2004b). Thinking about the range of migration states in the world allows us to include considerations of forced migration, transnationalism, and diasporas. The expulsion of minorities, such as the Orthodox Christians/Greeks of Turkey or Jews of Germany, marked a loss of economic actors in both places, as did the expulsion of the Rohingya from Myanmar to Bangladesh. The decision to expel (or exterminate, in the case of the Jews in Germany) was based on membership considerations in the nation-state. Similar dynamics are present in myriad cases. With respect to diaspora and transnationalism, we can distinguish among nation-states that have moved to

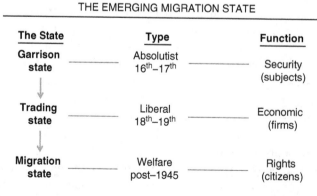

Figure 1.3. Changes in type and function of the nation-state.

enhance contacts with members abroad for economic, surveillance, consular, and symbolic purposes, and those (like Cuba) that seek to sever ties with diasporic communities. States can seek to improve contacts with diasporic communities to improve their bottom line (through remittances) and keep track of critics, or they can enhance protections for citizens abroad, or simply give the impression that they care about citizens abroad. High capacity / low rights states do the former, while lower capacity / higher rights states limit themselves to symbolic politics and policy.

Even though it is difficult to quantify rights—some like Martin Ruhs (2013) have attempted to score rights on an ordinal scale—there is a growing body of empirical work on migrant rights (for example, Block and Bonjour 2013). States that confer rights across critical dimensions (political participation, family reunification, labor market access) perform well when it comes to immigrant outcomes, education, health, and upward mobility (National Academy of Sciences 2017). While more analysis needs to be done (and more data collected), there is a connection between how a state manages its migration population and how successful that migration population is across a number of material dimensions. Success of a state's migrant population can be linked to a state's performance overall as measured by political stability, levels of social capital, and long-term economic performance.

The migration state must inevitably engage with other nations, and almost all states with the exception of a few, like North Korea in autarky, have migrant inflows and outflows. To manage migration effectively, multilateral or regional regimes are needed, similar to what the EU has constructed for nationals of its member states. The EU model points the way to future migration regimes, because it is not based purely on *homo economicus*, but incorporates rights for individual migrants and even a form of citizenship, which continues to evolve (Geddes 2003; Lahav 2004; Block and Bonjour 2013). The problem in this type of regional migration regime is how to deal with third country nationals (TCNs). As the EU expands and borders are relaxed, the issue of TCNs, immigrants, and ethnic minorities becomes ever more pressing, and new institutions, laws, and regulations must be created to deal with them (Guiraudon 1998). In the 2010s, the entire EU system of freedom of movement and open borders came under pressure because of the exodus from countries in the "arc of instability" from North Africa through the Middle East to South Asia (Geddes and various other chapters, this volume). Protests against globalization and nativist or xenophobic reactions against immigration have been on the rise throughout the OECD world (Bhagwati 2004; Mudde 2007; Norris and Inglehart 2019), and the vote by Great Britain to leave the European Union is a major setback for European integration, and especially for the principle of free movement. The EU system for refugee management has buckled with the surge of asylum seekers in the 2010s and the concomitant rise in ethnic nationalism and xenophobia. In Japan ethnonationalism is on the rise as immigration has increased, marked in particular by anti-Korean hate speech (Hollifield and Sharpe 2017; Chung 2010 and this volume).

The developmental scenario (garrison to trading to migration state) is understood largely as a Western (European and American) story that does not apply to non-Western countries and regions; but no state or region can escape the dilemmas of migration control and its consequences for human development. The migration state must reconcile the need for migration to meet economic ends against demands for nation-building and legitimacy, which makes some migrant groups unwelcome, because they deviate too greatly from the national ideal. This book offers a typology of migration states identifying several ideal types, ranging from the most liberal, like Canada, which balance markets, rights, security, and cultural concerns through a well-established national immigration policy, to the more illiberal, like Saudi Arabia and the Gulf states, which run strict guest-worker policies that are basically the modern equivalent of indentured servitude. High capacity liberal-democratic states like the United States and Canada (see Foley and Triadafilopoulos/Taylor, this volume) rationed rights according to racial criteria to shift migration in a way that complemented their nation-building prerogatives. These prerogatives shifted again in the post-1945 period, because of changes in the broader normative context in which these states operated (driven by reactions to the Holocaust, the discrediting of scientific racism, the civil rights movement, and—in Europe—decolonization).

Liberal openings to previously excluded groups have been accompanied by moves toward restriction that are based on security considerations and perceived demands of anti-immigration publics (see figure 1.1 and Huysmans 2006). An additional, distinctively legal concern has shaped migration politics and governance in the post-1945 period, namely, the emergence of the international refugee regime (Betts 2009a). States that have ratified it are bound by the Refugee Convention to consider asylum claims made on their territory. This legal obligation comes into conflict with security and democratic considerations, so that in high capacity / high rights (liberal) migration states, the turn has been toward preventing landing via offshore processing. High capacity / low rights (illiberal) states have sometimes violated their obligation to the convention altogether. Here and more generally, illiberal and authoritarian migration states face a different but related "migration-membership" paradox: How to exploit foreign labor for economic reasons while limiting migrants' access to membership, which ranges from secure residency and limited rights to highly precarious residency status and virtually no actionable rights (see Thiollet, this volume; Ruhs 2013).

Even though there are large numbers of economic migrants in Asia, especially South and Southeast Asia, the region remains divided into relatively closed and often authoritarian societies, with limited prospects of granting rights to migrants and guest workers (Fields 1994; Sadiq 2009; Hirschman, this volume). The more liberal and democratic states, like Japan, Taiwan, and South Korea, are the exceptions; and they have only just begun to grapple with the problem of immigration still on a small but expanding scale (Chung 2020 and this volume; Hollifield, Martin, and Orrenius 2014). In Africa and the Middle East, which have high numbers of forced migrants and refugees, there is a great deal of instability as a result of civil wars, as diasporas abound, and states are fluid (or failed) with little institutional or legal capacity for dealing with international migration (Lischer 2005; Adamson 2006; Salehyan 2009; Betts 2009a, 2011; various chapters, this volume).

Migration Interdependence and Global Governance

Migration is a force driving interdependence between regions and states. One way to see this is to plot migration dependence on two axes: remittances as a percentage of GDP

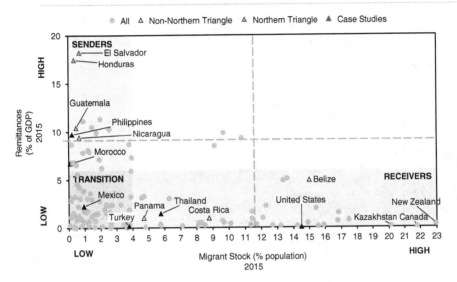

Figure 1.4. Migration interdependence and the "L-curve."

and migrant stock as a percentage of population. This produces an "L-curve" (figure 1.4) and shows that states tend to array on one of two poles, either sending or receiving, with some states in the transition category, neither sending nor receiving societies. The rates at which states change—some shifting from receiving to transition or transition to sending—vary significantly and are empirically correlated with not only the rate of economic and political development but also a state's willingness or ability to manage migration. For example, some states like the Philippines and Nepal have used migration as an explicit development strategy, while other states like Japan have limited the flow of migrants and the rights given to the small classes of migrants (low-skilled labor, university students, and temporary high-skilled workers and trainees) who are allowed into the country (Chung, Hirschman, and Sadiq, this volume).

In general, however, states cluster in terms of change in migrant stock and remittances (as a percentage of GDP) between 2005 and 2015. Some states are in transition, as migrants and/or remittances have increased over time; this increase could be the result of a concerted state policy (as in the case of the Lao PDR [People's Democratic Republic] to greatly increase its remittance flow; see figure 1.5) or it could be the result of a state's inability to manage its migration flows (as in the case of Iraq's inflow of refugees; see Tsourapas and Charbit, this volume). Moreover, the movement of countries along these axes over time suggests a degree of interdependence. While Mexico's overall change in migrant stock has increased, Guatemala's has increased at a far lower rate, a consequence of the inflow of Central American immigrants into Mexico (see Martin and Hazán, this volume). While some developing states, like the Philippines, Bangladesh, and Morocco, are highly dependent on remittances, the "nations of immigrants," like the United States, Canada, and Australia, along with countries of immigration, like Germany, France, and

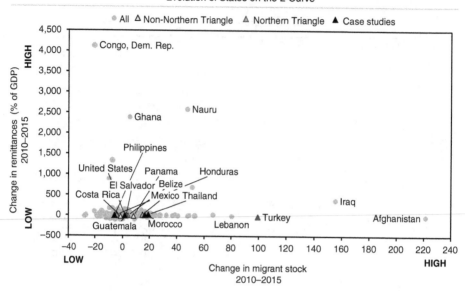

Figure 1.5. The evolution of states on the "L-curve."

other West European states, are dependent on immigrants for economic and demographic growth (on the distinction between nations and countries of immigration, see Hollifield, Martin, and Orrenius 2014).

One of the principal effects of economic interdependence is to compel states to cooperate (Keohane and Nye 1977; Milner 1988) and to pursue global public goods. Increasing international migration is one indicator of interdependence, and, until the pandemic of 2020, it showed no signs of abating. Still, global governance of migration is weak (Hollifield 2000). North America and Europe are among the most migration-interdependent regions in the world, with the Middle East and the "Arab world" not far behind. Will Japan and Asia follow this international trend? Will we see more regional cooperation in managing migration or less? We already have seen an example of the first strategy at the regional level in Europe. The EU and, to a lesser extent, the Schengen and Dublin regimes were built through processes of centralization and pooling of sovereignty. This was easier to do in the European context because of the symmetry (of interests and power) within the EU and the existence of an institutional framework (for the various treaties of European Union, see Geddes, this volume).

It is much more difficult to centralize control of migration in the Americas or Asia, for example, where the asymmetry (of interests and power) is much greater, and levels of political and economic development vary tremendously from one state to another. It is unlikely that regional trade regimes like the North American Free Trade Agreement (NAFTA), Asia-Pacific Economic Cooperation (APEC), or the Trans-Pacific Partnership (TPP, now Comprehensive Agreement for TPP) will lead to cooperation in the area of migration. Nevertheless, the regional option—multilateralism for a relevant group of states where migration governance can be defined as a club good—is one way to overcome collective-action problems and to begin a process of centralization of authority. However, most international regimes have had a long gestation period, beginning as bilateral or regional agreements. It is unlikely that an international migration regime could be built following the example of the International Trade Organization/GATT/ WTO. It is too difficult to fulfill the prerequisites of multilateralism: indivisibility, generalized principles of conduct, and diffuse reciprocity (Ruggie 1993). The norm of nondiscrimination (the equivalent of most-favored nation, MFN) does not exist for migration, and there are no mechanisms for punishing free riders and no way of resolving disputes. In short, the basis for multilateral governance of migration is weak, and the institutional framework is fragmented, notwithstanding existing IGOs (UNHCR, ILO, IOM) and the new Global Compacts for Migration and Refugees.

Changes in the international system with the end of the Cold War have altered the governance game in several ways. First, it has made defection easier. Since 1990, states have been more likely to pursue beggar-thy-neighbor policies by closing their borders and not cooperating with neighboring states in the making of migration and refugee policies. The Dublin process itself is a kind of beggar-thy-neighbor policy on a regional scale. Second, the new post–Cold War configurations of interests and power, at both international and domestic levels, make it more difficult to pursue a multilateral strategy for controlling international migration. Rights-markets coalitions have broken apart in the liberal states, especially in the United States (Hollifield, Hunt, and Tichenor 2008), increasing polarization and politicization over immigration and refugee issues. Yet liberalization and democratization in formerly authoritarian states to the east and south have dramatically reduced the transaction costs for emigration. Initially, this caused panic in Western Europe, where there was a fear of mass migrations from east to west (Fassmann and Münz 1994) and later from south to north, provoking a polemic about "The Great Replacement" (Camus 2011). Even though these massive flows did not materialize (with the partial exception of the surge in asylum seekers in 2015), Western states hunkered down and began to search for ways to reduce or stop immigration and to deter asylum seeking. The time horizons of almost all Western democracies became much shorter because of changes in domestic and international politics, and the terrorist attacks of the 2000s and 2010s exacerbated these fears, altering the trade-offs in migration governance (see figure 1.2), especially in the post-9/11 strategic environment.

If the US or the EU defects from the liberal refugee and migration "regimes," such as they are, it could mean the collapse of these regimes. One could argue that during the Trump administration the United States already had defected. In game theoretic terms, such defections fundamentally alter the equilibrium outcome, which is very costly to all states and to the international community (Hollifield and Takeuchi 2020). Moreover, with the pandemic of 2020, globalization of exchange and increased mobility have been quickly and dramatically reversed. To prevent the collapse of liberal migration and refugee regimes, the US and other liberal states must pursue an aggressive strategy of multilateralism, taking the short-term political heat for long-term political stability and economic gain, much as Chancellor Angela Merkel and Germany did in the face of the refugee crisis of 2015–16. This happened in the areas of international finance, with the collapse of the Bretton Woods system in the early 1970s and the creation of the G-7, and in trade, with the Single European Act (1986), Economic and Monetary Union (EMU) (1993), and NAFTA (1994). Without the kind of leadership exhibited in international trade and finance, irregular migrations will increase and become ever more threatening, leading more states to close their borders. Migration nevertheless continues to be a key element in strategies for national development, and how states manage migration varies from one region to another. In this book we offer a typology of migration states (Adamson and Tsourapas 2020), summarized in the following section, and review regional strategies for migration management.

Varieties of Migration States

As several of the authors in this volume point out, all states are to some extent migration states. No doubt, migration management is a core function of every state, but it has become more important in the post–World War II era marked by a rights-markets dynamic, increasing interdependence, and the growth of international labor markets, especially for the highly skilled. Migration played a vital role in the national development of the so-called "settler societies" in the eighteenth and nineteenth centuries (Dauvergne 2016). Recruiting colonists to the Americas, Australia, New Zealand, and South Africa (later the Dominions) was a key element in imperialism. Settlement and conquest in the Americas resulted in the dispossession and genocide of native peoples and their "assimilation" into European, colonial societies. Slavery was the cornerstone of plantation economies in much of the Western Hemisphere, as millions of Africans were enslaved and sent to the Americas in chains, what Leo Lucassen in this volume calls one of the largest "unfree" migrations in human history. At the same time—and with all the contradictions and injustices of colonial and racist legacies—the settler states evolved liberal forms of government with an emphasis on civil rights and citizenship (see Gomes, this volume), one of the ongoing schisms in Western liberal democracies. In the second half of the twentieth century, the United States, along with Canada and Australia, would become quintessential migration states with multicultural societies (Triadafilopoulous/Taylor, this volume).

The breakdown of imperial systems following World War I (the defeat and collapse of the Austro-Hungarian and Ottoman Empires) and World War II (the end of European and Japanese imperialisms) resulted in decolonization, the creation of many new states, and the displacement of large populations in different regions of the globe. Tens of millions of Germans were uprooted in Central and Eastern Europe, South Asians were expelled from East Africa, millions of Europeans and Jews were expelled from North Africa, and twenty million people were forced to move with the partition of India. New migration "corridors" would emerge after World War II, following the contours and legacies of imperialism, shaped in large part by the exigencies of global capitalism and a neoliberal, rules-based international order (Ikenberry 2012; Hollifield 2012). Of course, for much of this period (1945 through the 1980s) the world was divided between the "liberal" West (the US, Canada, and Western Europe) and the communist East (the USSR and the People's Republic of China), each with its own spheres of influence and particular rules governing migration, mobility, and citizenship. More migration corridors would emerge with the establishment of the European Community in 1957 and the integration of Europe, the pursuit of the "four freedoms," culminating in the EMU, the end of the Cold War, and the collapse of the Soviet Empire in 1990.

Migration would play a vital role in European reconstruction and development during the period of the *Trente Glorieuses* (1945–75; see Hollifield 1992 and this volume) and Europe would be transformed from a region of emigration into a "continent of immigration" in the last decades of the twentieth century. The settler societies, often referred to as "nations of immigrants" (Hollifield, Martin and Orrenius 2014), would evolve along liberal lines in the postwar period, overcoming de jure Jim Crow and segregation in the United States, dropping White Australia and White Canada policies in favor of more open immigration policies and greater multiculturalism (Foley, Tichenor, and Triadafilopoulous/Taylor, this volume). The US would enter the fourth great wave of immigration in its history, starting in the 1970s and continuing until the election of the nativist Donald Trump in 2016. Trump's anti-immigrant and anti-refugee policies— together with the suspension of immigration, the end of mobility, and the closing of borders because of the pandemic of 2019–20—cut legal immigration to the US almost in half. South Africa would throw off the yoke of apartheid in the 1990s to become a liberal and multicultural democracy, but with its own struggles to manage the southern African migration system (see Klotz, this volume). The Middle East, especially the oil-rich countries of the Persian (or Arabian) Gulf, came to rely heavily on (indentured) labor or guest workers from South Asia, Indonesia, the Philippines, and East Africa (see Thiollet and Sadiq, this volume). These migration corridors across Africa, the Middle East, and South and Southeast Asia would mirror in many respects the British imperial labor system, while new migration flows in East Asia would reflect legacies of the Japanese Empire and "co-prosperity sphere" (see Chung, this volume).

All states face trade-offs in migration governance between economic openness and political closure—what Hollifield (1992, 2004a) calls the "liberal paradox" (see figure 1.2). In the almost thirty years since he introduced the concept, international migration has become more central to how states regulate their labor markets (both high- and low-skilled) and how they respond to demographic trends and humanitarian crises, craft national security strategy, and shape public debates about citizenship and national identity. The migration state concept highlights the contradictory interests and trade-offs that states face in managing migration flows. The awkward compromises and strange bedfellow political coalitions contribute to inconsistencies and unintended consequences in migration policies and to gaps between policy outputs and outcomes (figure 1.2; Hollifield, Martin, and Orrenius 2014). The challenge for authors in this volume is to understand variations in migration governance across time and space. To reinforce a central point of the book, there is not a single "migration state," following the classic Western, liberal, and settler model, but rather a variety of migration states shaped by specific historical and geographical contexts.

This book improves our understanding of global migration in several ways. First, by bringing more regions and cases, especially in the global South, to the study of international migration, broadening our comparative framework to reconsider the relationship between migration, the state, and economic development in countries and regions well beyond traditional settler societies or "nations of immigrants." Second, by looking at historical antecedents of contemporary migration regimes, contributing insights into how states recruit migrant labor, how they manage migration and mobility during the process of state- and nation-building, and how various actors shape the institutions of migration states. Third, by bringing together scholarship across regions, from Asia, Africa, and the Middle East, to Europe and the Americas, which allows us to theorize about "varieties of migration states," proposing new typologies and applications of the migration state concept (see below) to develop a truly global approach to understanding migration. The book covers a wide range of migration states: major sending countries, recent countries of immigration, and countries that are simultaneously countries of origin, destination, and transition (see figures 1.4 and 1.5 above). We study liberal as well as illiberal migration states, former imperial powers (like Britain, France, Turkey, and Japan) and postcolonial states (like Morocco, the Philippines, Indonesia, and India), and some of the richest (Western Europe, the United States, and Canada) and poorest countries in the world (West and East Africa, Central America, South and Southeast Asia).

Africa, the Middle East, and the "Postcolonial" Migration State wrestles with the legacies of imperialism, which in the first instance are territorial but also legal and political, as many states reform, reshape, and adapt migration and citizenship regimes dating from colonial times, but responding to the dictates of nation- and state-building (Kohn 1962). Audie Klotz shows how South Africa fits as a node within three migration subsystems: Anglosphere, Indian Ocean, and Southern Africa. These patterns of population flows challenge conventional dichotomous labels of North/South divides, developed/ developing countries, and receiving/sending states. Stressing legacies of colonialism, her chapter traces the emergence and then evolution of the Southern African migration state. Prior to apartheid, segregation developed primarily as a reaction to Asians and Africans moving to cities and towns. During apartheid, increasingly draconian enforcement of segregated mobility sought to reconfigure patterns of urbanization. Even with the demise of official apartheid and a plethora of efforts to remedy its pernicious long-term effects, municipalities remain on the front lines, trying to cope with administrative, financial, and political pressures that result from ever-changing migration patterns and persistent antiforeigner protests (Klotz 2013). These long-standing and overlapping subsystems call into question how to demarcate "Africa" within the global migration system.

Hélène Thiollet offers an overview of Gulf migration systems from the early twentieth century to today. Mobility, motivated by trade, labor, politics, or religious devotion, whether permanent or temporary, has been central to the region's history. The first section of the chapter describes the changing geographies of immigration to the Gulf through three historical sequences. Gulf migration systems evolved from imperial geographies of colonial migration within the British Empire (1930s–1950s) to Arab regional integration during and after the oil-boom era (1960s–1991). In the 1990s and after, diplomatic interdependence with the Asian global South unfolded in the context of the diversification of Gulf economies, and the "second migration boom" of the 2000s took place. The second part of the chapter focuses on the contemporary era and unpacks the dynamics of migration governance in Gulf countries today. It describes the role of states, markets, brokers, and migrants in migration governance and illustrates the emergence of *illiberal* migration states, as a countermodel to *liberal* migration states in Western contexts.

Gerasimos Tsourapas explores how the "migration state" concept travels across the global South and, in particular, in the Middle East and North Africa region. This chapter has two aims: first, it introduces the reader to the history and politics of migration into, out of, and across the contemporary Middle East. The chapter's first part examines the historical evolution of migrants and refugees in the Middle East via a number of stages. Colonial and imperial exigencies initially shaped much of mobility throughout most of the region that constitutes the Middle East, leaving lingering legacies that continue to affect policy-making today. The rise of the modern nation-state in the post–World War I period of decolonization led to the emergence of *migration states* in the Middle East, which governed population mobility through *colonial* and *postcolonial* migration governance regimes, marked by periods of high- and low-skilled migrant recruitment by host states within and outside the region. The chapter's second part demonstrates how a closer examination of Middle East migratory processes and distinct migration corridors sheds light on existing debates within the field. It identifies the emergence of an *illiberal paradox* across Middle Eastern states' migration policy-making—namely, the contrast between the socioeconomic desire to allow mass emigration and the urge to maintain control over political dissent. The socioeconomic benefits of allowing citizens' "exit" contrasted with the political risks of enabling their "voice" abroad. The chapter draws on a range of case studies from across North Africa and the Middle East in order to detail how governments' attempts to resolve this illiberal paradox have arguably shaped the politics of migration in the Middle East across two levels. First, at the state level, the chapter identifies the emergence of *transnational authoritarianism*; namely, any effort to prevent acts of political dissent against an authoritarian state by targeting one or more existing or potential members of its emigrant or diaspora communities. Second, at the regional and international levels, it examines the manipulation of *migration interdependence* via coercion, as interstate rivalry encompasses the abuse, or expulsion, of migrant workers. Overall, the chapter demonstrates the empirical richness as well as the analytic utility of the Middle East as a crucial region of study for the politics of global migration.

Yves Charbit focuses on labor migration and development in North and West Africa. He shows how demographic dynamics enhance and hinder development. Migration plays the role of an adjustment variable, as emigration is the simplest and most immediate response in states faced with chronic poverty and political and economic crises, often linked to climate change. Charbit seeks to disentangle the impact of migration on development from those of the other aspects of demographic change, births and deaths. He examines the consequences of three major economic and demographic developments: first, the demographic context as a driver of migration; second, the remittances of migrants to their home countries; and third, the extent to which migration and remittances enhance human and economic development in the EU-Africa corridor.

Asia and the "Developmental" Migration State is related in many ways to the postcolonial migration state, in the sense that the focus of migration management is on economic development, often in a postimperial context, but with highly integrated national development strategies. Erin Chung's chapter extends Hollifield's migration state framework to Northeast Asian democracies, highlighting its generalizability as a frame of analysis and its limits. Despite labor shortages from the 1980s and impending demographic crises in all three countries, Japan, Korea, and Taiwan have maintained relatively

closed migrant labor policies. Immigration to East Asia has nevertheless grown exponentially over the past few decades, leading some to characterize East Asian democracies as "latecomers" to immigration (Hollifield, Martin, and Orrenius 2014) that will
eventually follow the trajectories of other former reluctant countries of immigration. As
non-Western countries with among the largest economies in the world that send *and*
host substantial migrant populations, East Asian countries do not fit easily into binary
categories such as global South/North, developing/developed societies, and countries
of emigration/immigration. Neither do they adhere to the liberal/illiberal migration regime framework. Rather than convergence toward a singular *liberal* migration state, the
East Asian cases suggest the emergence of a "developmental migration state" characterized by partially open borders and discrete institutionalized rights for specific subcategories of migrants. Chung argues that these states have become the exception to the
liberal convergence thesis as they have maintained exclusionary immigration policies
and low levels of immigration despite high levels of political economic development (cf.
Hollifield and Sharpe 2017).

Charles Hirschman argues that long-distance migration, particularly from China
and India, was a characteristic feature of Southeast Asian history during the precolonial
and colonial eras. Migration flows slowed to a trickle during the turbulence of the mid-
twentieth century (Great Depression, World War II) and was at low ebb in the nation-
building decades of the newly independent Southeast Asian countries from the 1940s
to the early 1970s. The latter decades of the twentieth century and early decades of the
twenty-first, however, witnessed a resumption of long-distance migration within and
between Southeast Asian countries. Uneven economic development, political upheavals, and demographic dynamics contributed to major flows of international migrants
to Thailand, Malaysia, and Singapore within the region and to significant emigration
of Southeast Asians, especially from the Philippines and Indonesia, to the Middle East,
Australia, North America, and Europe, and eventually to Northeast Asia. Although economic studies show that migrants generally contribute to economic growth in countries
of destination and their remittances help to sustain families and communities in countries of origin, there is widespread vilification and discrimination of migrants in many
Southeast Asian countries. These anti-immigrant perceptions, practices, and policies are
at odds with the region's history that was open to migrants from nearby and distant lands
and evidenced a remarkable ability to create syncretic cultures and religions that blended
indigenous and external beliefs and traditions.

Kamal Sadiq begins by pointing out that all states are migration states to some extent, but he asks, What is distinctive about variation in migration management policies
among states of the global South? Can the "migration state" concept explain a large,
developing, postcolonial, and non-Western state such as India? Although India often is
characterized as a major labor-exporting country, this chapter demonstrates the emergence of an Indian migration state as a response to major immigrations from neighboring Bangladesh, Nepal, and Sri Lanka. Consequently, it focuses on less visible immigration and refugees flows that mark India as *a major country of destination for survival
immigrants* from the broader South Asia region. First, India's alternative path to the institutionalized development of migration management is distinguished by a sequential

transition from a "subject state" to a "postcolonial state," followed later by the adoption of migration state features. Next, the chapter shows how India is unconstrained by a "liberal paradox" and is instead challenged by the "neighborhood effect" of thick, coethnic regional immigration flows amid weak state capacity. India emerges as a variation of the "classic" Western, liberal migration state model since historical legacies of partition and irredentism are key determinants of its institutional development. Finally, in this chapter, two state responses to regional immigration flows are identified: the narrowing and redefinition of Indian citizenship criteria and the enhancement of Indian border security. Taken together, these features of the Indian migration state underscore the tension between securing territorial sovereignty and realigning (and homogenizing) national identity across borders.

The Americas, the "Liberal" and Settler Migration States (Hollifield 1992, 2004a) are products of European imperialism and the "multiple traditions" of liberalism, as described by Rogers Smith (1993), which set the United States and the Dominions on a contradictory path. One marked by the subjugation of native peoples, slavery, violent racism, and white supremacy on the one hand, and variants of liberal democracy on the other. The liberal migration state is defined by a paradox—the commitment to an open, laissez-faire, market-based economy, including the need to attract immigrants for nation-building, but with the imperative of safeguarding the social contract and the institution of citizenship, often defined in racial terms (white Canada, white Australia, National Origins Quota in the US). The result is a long history of struggle to resolve the dilemmas of migration governance (see figure 1.2 above).

Daniel Tichenor's chapter highlights the power of nativist and liberal traditions in American politics, illuminating how each has shaped the development of a distinctive US migration state torn between competing interests and ideals. Since the late nineteenth century, nativist movements and xenophobic politicians have fueled the US government's capacities to exclude, marginalize, and remove immigrants—especially on a racial, ethnic, and religious basis. Yet pro-immigration groups and policy-makers since the 1960s have secured important gains for diverse immigrant admissions and greater democratic inclusion of noncitizens. Over time, the rivalry between nativist and pro-immigration forces in US politics has produced lasting conflicts and paradoxes in American immigration law and policy.

Neil Foley argues that many Americans live with a sense of cognitive dissonance about nationhood. The United States, unlike most European nations, claims to be a nation of immigrants, yet it also tries to keep out immigrants, refugees, and asylum seekers it deems undesirable. It welcomes immigrants when their labor is needed and turns them away when it is not. But this bipolar economic view of immigration over the last century fails to account for the interlaced politics of citizenship, immigrant exclusion, and unremitting nativism that lies at the very heart of American national identity. Culture and demography, more than economic and political developments, best explain the rapid growth of reactionary nationalist parties in Europe and xenophobic nativists in the US in the twenty-first century.

Phil Triadafilopoulos and Zack Taylor ask whether Canada has solved the liberal paradox. Whereas political winds in most liberal democracies are blowing in a restrictive direction, for the past thirty years Canadian governments have steadily increased annual immigration levels. Cross-party political consensus in support of an expansive immigration policy has endured economic slowdowns in the early 1980s and the 1990s and the recessions of 2001–2 and 2009–10. Consensus on immigration extends to support of Canada's policy of official multiculturalism and its liberal citizenship regime. Whereas multiculturalism has been judged a dangerous failure in many liberal democracies, it has retained pride of place in Canada, serving as an important source of Canadian national identity. And, despite some tinkering, Canada's liberal citizenship regime continues to transform immigrants into new Canadians at a high rate. Populist anti-immigrant politics in Canada are marginal.

In his chapter on trade, migration, and development in North America, Philip Martin points out that international migration involves the movement of people over national borders, while international trade deals with the production of goods or services in one country and their consumption in another. Migration and trade can be substitutes, so that lowering barriers to trade between countries with different wage levels can reduce economically motivated migration "naturally," as trade in goods narrows the differences in wages that prompt migration. However, migration and trade can also be complements, so that trade *and* migration rise together. NAFTA was promoted in the United States as a short-term substitute for migration, but turned out to be a complement, contributing to a decade-long Mexico-US migration hump between the mid-1990s and the 2008–9 recession. Martin states that most trade and migration is regional, between neighboring or nearby countries. US policy toward unwanted migration from neighboring countries calls for freer trade and investment to create jobs that keep migrants at home, while the European Union often provides aid and advice to induce changes in accession countries before their citizens gain freedom of movement rights, in the hopes that rising wages and opportunity at home translate into relatively little intra-EU migration. Recent fears of too much migration in Europe and the US have strengthened the hand of "restrictionists" who want to reduce immigration. Former president Trump moved away from trade-in-place-of migration policies with tariffs and other protectionist measures, and sought to reduce unauthorized migration and asylum seeking with a wall on the Mexico-US border and limits on asylum seeking. The outbreak of COVID-19 in 2020 closed borders to nonessential travel, and the Trump administration introduced measures to restrict immigration after the pandemic ends.

In her chapter on international migration and refugee movements in Latin America, Miryam Hazán reviews the turbulent history of the region, which is intricately bound up with migration and population movements. She points out that migration from Europe in particular was a dominant force in political, economic, and social change in Latin America, but over time emigration to the powerful and wealthier countries in the Northern Hemisphere became the norm, especially to the United States but also to Western Europe. Zeroing in on the experience of Mexico and Central America, she documents how Mexico went from being a source of surplus labor for the booming US economy, to a country of transit, and now destination. She explains the intricate relationship between political development in Mexico and the large Mexican diaspora in the US and how relaxation of dual nationality, the granting of voting rights to Mexicans abroad, and the opening of the Mexican economy to international trade and investment post-NAFTA helped to transform the country. She links developments in Mexico and North America more broadly with the failures of Central American countries to develop economically and to make the transition to democracy, leading to more pressures to emigrate, and widespread violence and violation of human rights. Finally, she returns (like Gomes, below) to the broader issue of the transformation of South America into a continent of immigration with its own dynamic of rights and markets leading to a convergence with liberal migration states in the Northern Hemisphere.

Charles Gomes argues that over the past four decades, since the end of military dictatorship and re-democratization in the 1980s, countries in South America have embraced greater economic openness and a rise in rights-based politics. As a result, South America has been transformed into a continent of immigration. He tests the argument by exploring how political pressures from economic actors propel governments in the region to adopt more liberal migration policies. He traces how rights-based politics led by civil society have pushed states toward more open borders under the aegis of new liberal constitutions, while free trade agreements have encouraged freedom of movement, rights of residence, and the consolidation of regional labor markets. He points out that new right-wing governments have moved to restrict migration and asylum seeking for security reasons, only to find that they are constrained by domestic and international human rights laws. Finally, he shows how the Venezuelan exodus illustrates the dynamic of emerging migration states in South America.

Europe, Turkey, and the Liberal and "Postimperial" Migration State is primarily a European type, because of the long involvement of imperial powers like Spain, Portugal, Britain, France, the Netherlands, Belgium, and (more briefly) Italy and Germany in various regions of the globe, leading to deep historical and cultural ties between European states and their colonies. Following the First and Second World Wars, European empires were dismantled, sometimes peacefully but often violently. As Lucassen points out, the First World War mobilized entire colonial armies to fight, especially on the French side, reinforcing cultural and linguistic ties between the metropole and the empire. In the 1950s, new migration corridors emerged, as foreign workers were brought from the former colonies to aid in the economic reconstruction of Western Europe. "*We are here because you were there*" would become a familiar refrain of postwar émigrés in Europe, and states, like Germany, that never considered themselves to be countries of immigration would face the reality of large-scale immigration and settlement. The same struggles over the rights of immigrants, over racial and ethnic diversity, and integration that were common in the settler societies of the Americas and Australia, would arise in Europe, as these states wrestled in turn with the liberal paradox (Hollifield 1997). On the periphery of Europe, Turkey, also a former imperial power, would become a major sending society with millions of Turks immigrating to Western Europe. Turkey also became a country of transit for migrants from Africa, the Middle East, and South Asia, linking networks and migration corridors from the Ottoman, British, and French Empires.

In her chapter, Fiona Adamson applies the "migration state" concept to the question of migration governance in Turkey. Taking a *longue durée* approach, she analyzes Turkey as a postimperial migration state. The chapter begins with a discussion of forced migration as a feature of postimperial nation-building, moving on to discuss the use of ethnic and religious immigration criteria during the early Republican period. She examines the role that both the Ottoman Empire and Turkey played as a destination for refugees and political exiles from Europe and elsewhere. Finally, she discusses Turkey's diaspora policies in light of its renewed foreign policy ambitions, in which the use of diaspora politics as a means of projecting state power has emerged as part of a "neo-Ottoman" resurgence. The chapter concludes with a discussion of future policy challenges surrounding migration in Turkey, and some thoughts on the strengths and limits of the "migration state" concept as applied to Turkey.

In Leo Lucassen's assessment, the political and societal debates about migration in postwar Europe, and the role of the state in controlling or facilitating it, are too limited to certain segments of migrants. To put it crudely, in general migrants only pop up on the political radar screen when they are low skilled and, rightly or wrongly, are perceived as posing a threat to jobs, housing, status, and identity. Especially higher-skilled migrants, a portion of whom are employed by international businesses and organizations, are excluded from the problematizing political migration discourse. For these "invisible migrants," new terms were invented like "repatriates," "returnees," and "Aussiedler" for the ex-colonial migrants and "expats" for high-skilled migrants. This conceptual apartheid affirms the self-fulfilling negative framing of migrants and reproduces the idea that migration is a problem that should be solved. Understanding and defining migration in much broader strokes, and adding internal, temporary, colonization, and seasonal migrations to the mix, helps us to put both optimistic and pessimistic views on current immigration into a long-term perspective. Furthermore, in Lucassen's view, a cross-cultural and historical approach can also help to understand better the nature of the migration state, which is prisoner to the narrow and statist obsession with "bad migrants" that fails to see how normal and essential migration is for human societies and how essential to understanding economic, social, cultural, political, and economic changes.

In his chapter, James Hollifield asks how states in Europe (and the EU) regulate migration, in the face of economic forces that push toward greater openness, while security concerns and powerful political forces push toward closure. States are trapped in a "liberal" paradox—in order to maintain a competitive advantage, governments must keep their economies and societies open to trade, investment, and migration. However, unlike goods, capital, and services, the movement of people involves greater political risks. In this chapter, Hollifield argues that rights are the key to regulating migration, as states strive to manage trade-offs among markets, rights, security and culture. He traces the evolution of migration states in Europe, which range from postimperial states to classic liberal and welfare states.

Pieter Bevelander points out that over the last five decades, the economic and structural changes in the European economy have coincided with a gradual increase in the low-skilled service sector as well as an increased demand for educated workers in the production of high-tech content. The increase in the number of humanitarian migrants being received by European states, as well as the subsequent family reunion migration, has further weakened the economic integration of migrants in Europe (Bevelander and Hollifield forthcoming). In addition to this, these new migrants have to overcome a number of hurdles, both individually and structurally, to be successful in the labor market. Policies addressing this problem have primarily focused on an individual migrant's shortcomings but have not addressed the structural barriers they face which hamper their economic integration. Bevelander contends that the continuation of this state of affairs will both increase marginalization and segregation as well as feed a growing anti-immigrant sentiment and a populist backlash.

In the last chapter of the book, Andrew Geddes develops an understanding of European Union (EU) migration governance that emphasizes not only the outputs or outcomes of governance (laws, policies, and the like) but also the understandings and representations of migration that inform it. The argument is that the EU actively contributes to "re-bordering," by which is meant that the perceived need to protect the internal European space and its project of market integration has seen limits both on free movement for EU citizens and efforts to more tightly regulate the external borders of the EU's member states. Geddes shows that migration governance is not just an *ex post* reaction to migration flows, but that governance systems through their actions, inactions, and interactions develop the categorizations that organize and manage international migration.

The populist and nativist backlash that has been building for decades in major receiving countries, together with the COVID-19 pandemic, has led many states to close their borders, severely curtailing migration and mobility. If the backlash persists and the pandemic leads to further closure of societies and to intensifying nationalism, the international system will descend into greater anarchy, disorder, and war. Human and economic development will suffer and global inequalities will rise. The more powerful states, like the United States and China, will set the trend for the rest of the world, and in both states, nationalism has surged to the fore, setting the stage for more conflict as new power blocs emerge and international cooperation recedes. It is too early to say with certainty whether these developments in world politics will lead to the end of liberalism. Clearly, however, the international liberal order is under siege, democracies are turning inward, and erstwhile open societies are closing. Yet states and economies are more dependent on migration than ever, and for decades to come states must face the challenge of managing migration in a way that simultaneously contributes to human and economic development and safeguards sovereignty and national security. This book shows how states in various regions of the globe manage the difficult trade-offs involved in migration governance.

References

Adamson, Fiona. 2006. "Crossing Borders: International Migration and National Security." *International Security* 31(1): 165–99.

Adamson, Fiona, and Gerasimos Tsourapas. 2020. "The Migration State in the Global South: Nationalizing, Developmental, and Neoliberal Models of Migration Management." *International Migration Review* 53(3): 853–82.

Adamson, Fiona, Triadafilos Triadafilopoulos, and Aristide Zolberg. 2011. "The Limits of the Liberal State: Migration, Identity and Belonging in Europe." *Journal of Ethnic and Migration Studies* 37(6): 843–59.

Betts, Alexander. 2009a. *Forced Migration and Global Politics*. Oxford: Wiley-Blackwell.

_____. 2009b. *International Protection by Persuasion: International Cooperation in the Refugee Regime*. Ithaca, NY: Cornell University Press.

_____. 2011. *Global Migration Governance*. Oxford: Oxford University Press.

_____. 2013. *Survival Migration: Failed Governance and the Crisis of Displacement*. Ithaca, NY: Cornell University Press.

Bhagwati, Jagdish. 2004. *In Defense of Globalization*. New York: Oxford University Press.

Block, Laura, and Saskia Bonjour. 2013. "Fortress Europe or Europe of Rights? The Europeanisation of Family Migration Policies in France, Germany and the Netherlands." *European Journal of Migration & Law* 15(2): 203–24.

Boswell, Christina. 2007. "Theorizing Migration Policy: Is There a Third Way?" *International Migration Review* 41(1): 75–100. doi: 10.1111/j.1747-7379.2007.00057.x.

Camus, Renaud. 2011. *Le Grand Remplacement, Introduction au remplacisme global*. Paris: Reinharc.

Chung, Erin A. 2010. *Immigration and Citizenship in Japan*. New York: Cambridge University Press.

_____. 2020. *Immigrant Incorporation in East Asian Democracies*. New York: Cambridge University Press.

Dauvergne, Catherine. 2016. *The New Politics of Immigration and the End of Settler Societies*. Cambridge: Cambridge University Press.

Fassmann, Heinz, and Rainer Münz. 1994. "European East-West Migration, 1945–1992." *International Migration Review* 28(3): 520–38.

Fields, Gary S. 1994. "The Migration Transition in Asia." *Asian and Pacific Migration Journal* 3(1): 7–30.

FitzGerald, David S., and David Cook-Martin. 2014. *Culling the Masses: The Democratic Origins of Racist Immigration Policy in the Americas*. Cambridge, MA: Harvard University Press.

Freeman, Gary P. 1995. "Modes of Immigration Politics in Liberal Democratic States." *International Migration Review* 29(4): 881–902.

Gabaccia, Donna R. 2015. "Time and Temporality in Migration Studies." In *Migration Theory: Talking across Disciplines*, edited by Caroline B. Brettell and James F. Hollifield, 37–66. Abingdon: Routledge.

Geddes, Andrew. 2003. *The Politics of Migration and Immigration in Europe*. London: Sage.

Goodwin-Gill, Guy S. 1996. *The Refugee in International Law*. Oxford: Clarendon.

Guiraudon, Virginie. 1998. "Third Country Nationals and European Law: Obstacles to Rights' Expansion." *Journal of Ethnic Studies* 24(4): 657–74.

Hatton, Timothy J., and Jeffrey G. Williamson. 1998. *The Age of Mass Migration: Causes and Economic Impact*. New York: Oxford University Press.

Hollifield, James F. 1992. *Immigrants, Markets and States: The Political Economy of Postwar Europe*. Cambridge, MA: Harvard University Press.

_____. 1997. "Immigration and Integration in Western Europe: A Comparative Analysis." In *Immigration into Western Societies: Problems and Policies*, edited by E. Uçarer and D. Puchala. London: Pinter.

_____. 1998. "Migration, Trade and the Nation-State: The Myth of Globalization." *UCLA Journal of International Law and Foreign Affairs* 3(2): 595–636.

_____. 2000. "Migration and the 'New' International Order: The Missing Regime." In *Managing Migration: Time for a New International Regime*, edited by B. Ghosh. Oxford: Oxford University Press.

_____. 2004a. "The Emerging Migration State." *International Migration Review* 38: 885–912.

_____. 2004b. "Migration and Sovereignty." In *Immigration and Asylum*, edited by Matthew Gibney and Randall Hansen. Los Angeles: ABC Clio, 2004.

_____. 2012. "Migration and International Relations." In *The Oxford Handbook of the Politics of International Migration*, edited by Marc R. Rosenblum and Daniel J. Tichenor, 345–79. Oxford: Oxford University Press.

Hollifield, James F., and Rahfin Faruk. 2017. "Governing Migration in an Age of Globalization." In *Migration on the Move*, edited by Carolus Grütters, Sandra Mantu, and Paul Minderhoud, 118–35. Leiden: Brill Nijhoff.

Hollifield, James F., Valerie F. Hunt, and Daniel J. Tichenor. 2008. "Immigrants, Markets and the American State: The United States as an 'Emerging Migration State.'" *Washington University Journal of Law & Policy* 27: 7–44.

Hollifield, James F., Philip L. Martin, and Pia M. Orrenius, eds. 2014. *Controlling Immigration: A Global Perspective, 3rd ed.* Stanford, CA: Stanford University Press.

Hollifield, James F., Pia Orrenius, and Thomas Osang, eds. 2006. *Trade, Migration and Development.* Dallas: Federal Reserve Bank of Dallas.

Hollifield, James F., and Michael Orlando Sharpe. 2017. "Japan as an 'Emerging Migration State.'" *International Relations of the Asia Pacific* 17(3): 371–400.

Huysmans, Jef. 2006. *The Politics of Insecurity: Fear, Migration and Asylum in the EU.* London: Routledge.

Ikenberry, G. John. 2012. *Liberal Leviathan: The Origins, Crisis, and Transformation of the American World Order.* Princeton, NJ: Princeton University Press.

Joppke, Christian. 1998. "Why Liberal States Accept Unwanted Migration." *World Politics* 50(2): 266–93.

———. 2005. *Selecting by Origin: Ethnic Migration in the Liberal State.* Cambridge, MA: Harvard University Press.

Keohane, Robert O., and Joseph S. Nye. 1977. *Power and Interdependence: World Politics in Transition.* Boston: Little, Brown.

King, Desmond S. 2000. *Making Americans: Immigration, Race and the Diverse Democracy.* Cambridge, MA: Harvard University Press.

Klotz, Audie. 2013. *Migration and National Identity in South Africa.* New York: Cambridge University Press.

Kohn, Hans. 1962. *The Age of Nationalism: The First Era of Global History.* New York: Harper & Row.

Krasner, Stephen D. 1999. *Sovereignty: Organized Hypocrisy.* Princeton, NJ: Princeton University Press.

Lahav, Gallya. 2004. *Immigration and Politics in the New Europe.* Cambridge: Cambridge University Press.

Lischer, Sarah. 2005. *Dangerous Sanctuaries: Refugee Camps, Civil War and the Dilemmas of Humanitarian Aid.* Ithaca, NY: Cornell University Press.

Lucassen, Leo. 2005. *The Immigrant Threat: The Integration of Old and New Migrants in Western Europe since 1850.* Urbana: University of Illinois Press.

Milner, Helen V. 1988. *Resisting Protectionism: Global Industries and the Politics of International Trade.* Princeton, NJ: Princeton University Press.

Mudde, Cas. 2007. *Populist Radical Right Parties in Europe.* New York: Cambridge University Press.

National Academy of Sciences. 2017. *The Integration of Immigrants into American Society.* Washington, DC: National Academies Press.

Norris, Pippa, and Ronald Inglehart. 2019. *Cultural Backlash: Trump, Brexit, and Authoritarian Populism.* Cambridge: Cambridge University Press.

Peters, Margaret E. 2015. "Open Trade, Closed Borders: Immigration Policy in the Era of Globalization." *World Politics* 67(1): 114–54.

Putnam, Robert. 1988. "Diplomacy and Domestic Politics: The Logic of Two-Level Games." *International Organization* 42: 427–60.

Rosecrance, Richard. 1986. *The Rise of the Trading State.* New York: Basic Books.

Rudolph, Christopher. 2006. *National Security and Immigration: Policy Development in the United States and Western Europe since 1945.* Stanford, CA: Stanford University Press.

Ruhs, Martin. 2013. *The Price of Rights: Regulating International Labor Migration.* Princeton, NJ: Princeton University Press.

Ruhs, Martin, and Philip L. Martin. 2008. "Numbers vs. Rights: Trade-Offs and Guest Worker Programs." *International Migration Review* 42: 249–65.

Sadiq, Kamal. 2009. *Paper Citizens: How Illegal Immigrants Acquire Citizenship in Developing Countries.* New York: Oxford University Press.

Salehyan, Idean. 2009. *Rebels without Borders: Transnational Insurgencies in World Politics*. Ithaca, NY: Cornell University Press.

Shaw, Malcolm N. 1997. *International Law*. Cambridge: Cambridge University Press.

Smith, Rogers M. 1993. "Beyond Tocqueville, Myrdal, and Hartz: The Multiple Traditions in America." *American Political Science Review* 87(3): 549–66.

Torpey, John. 2000. *The Invention of the Passport: Surveillance, Citizenship, and the State*. New York: Cambridge University Press.

United Nations Population Division. 2001. *Replacement Migration: Is It a Solution to Declining and Ageing Populations?* New York: UN Publications.

Weber, Max. 1947. *The Theory of Social and Economic Organization*. New York: Oxford University Press.

Weiner, Myron. 1995. *The Global Migration Crisis: Challenge to States and to Human Rights*. New York: HarperCollins.

Zolberg, Aristide R. 2006. *A Nation by Design: Immigration Policy in the Fashioning of America*. Cambridge, MA: Harvard University Press and Russell Sage.

PART 2

AFRICA, THE MIDDLE EAST, AND THE "POSTCOLONIAL" MIGRATION STATE

2   THE SOUTHERN AFRICA MIGRATION SYSTEM

Audie Klotz

SOUTH AFRICA FITS AS A NODE WITHIN three migration subsystems: Anglosphere, Indian Ocean, and Southern African. This chapter traces the evolution of these distinct yet overlapping subsystems since the mid-1800s. The Anglosphere subsystem mainly comprises Britain and its (former) colonies. The Indian Ocean subsystem encompasses areas that have relied on contract labor, including, historically, South Africa alongside the Caribbean and more recently the Middle East (see Sadiq and Thiollet, this volume). The Southern African subsystem emerged at the interface of British and Portuguese colonialism. Initially revolving around the mining industry and commercial agriculture, regional ties have extended, especially in the postapartheid era, farther north (Congolese), west (Nigerians), and east (Somalis) to make a nascent intracontinental subsystem.[1]

These patterns of migration call into question how to demarcate "Africa" within the global migration system, because they challenge conventional dichotomous labels of North/South divides, developed/developing countries, or receiving/sending states.[2] Therefore, building on Frederick Cooper's (2005, chap. 6) concept of the "empire state" alongside James Hollifield's (2004) "migration state," I stress the need to analyze global migration governance as inherently transnational, even after decolonization rewrote formal territorial borders. My hybrid theoretical lens of the "imperial migration state"

---

1   At the outset of the global coronavirus pandemic, South Africa quickly restricted cross-border travel and adopted strict domestic restrictions. At the time of writing, South Africa ranks among the countries with the highest number of infections. Whenever the region reopens, we will likely see only modest shifts in mobility patterns, however, since South Africa already restricts migration (as this chapter explains).

2   Tellingly, much of the comparative politics literature excludes South Africa from its universe of cases, including the migration literature on settler states and the debates over state formation in Africa (notable exceptions include Belich 2009; Vigneswaran and Quirk 2015). See Klotz 2013, chap. 1, for an extensive critique of these omissions.

highlights urbanization as a driving force in demographic shifts and policy responses. Acknowledging the legacies of imperialism also underscores that transnational mobility was the international norm until 1919, thereby denaturalizing the mythology of domestic jurisdiction over cross-border population flows as part of Westphalian sovereignty.

Imperial Migration States

Recognizing that the South African migration state emerged within an imperial context, this chapter employs an empire-state analytical lens to highlight urbanization as an underlying macro-historical force driving cross-border demographic shifts and migration policy responses. In essence, this (post)colonial framework takes transnationalism as normal rather than exceptional or anomalous, since governance within empires by definition spans territorial boundaries (Cooper 2005, 26–29; Ribeiro da Silva 2015, 39–40). This section outlines how I blend the empire state and migration state concepts into my hybrid notion of an imperial migration state. As prelude to the South Africa analysis, I illustrate with British imperial structures, but other empires exhibited comparable characteristics.[3]

Of course, the "state" is a thoroughly contested concept. Rather than revisiting basic controversies, I start with the Weberian definition upon which Hollifield (2004; Hollifield/Foley, this volume) built the notion of a migration state: a set of institutions that seeks to control cross-border human mobility. However, as Timothy Mitchell (1991, 82) notes, such classic claims rooted in a monopoly of legitimate violence or jurisdiction over borders remain amorphous. Instead, he urges analysis of how state practices articulate territorial space through the administrative frameworks that define geopolitical frontiers (Mitchell 1991, 94; also Caplan and Torpey 2001).

Yet Mitchell (among others, including Hollifield) too readily accepts the methodological nationalism embedded in his analytical goal of characterizing how a state governs geographically contiguous territorial space, because migration management is inherently transnational (Wimmer and Glick Schiller 2003, 590–92; also Vigneswaran 2013). Nor does control necessarily happen at borders (Breckenridge 2014, chap. 2). For example, states frequently employ both internal policing (such as workplace raids) and external delegation (such as visa determination). Formal borders mattered even less in Southern Africa, where fluid boundaries between colonial territories prevailed into the 1960s and then remained remarkably porous after decolonization (e.g., Kynoch 2005; Bakewell 2015; Klotz 2016).

Pushing any concept of the migration state even further analytically, Darshan Vigneswaran and Joel Quirk (2015, 2) challenge the core assumption that the state precedes migration management. In effect switching cause and effect, they open up the possibility that "*mobility makes states*," in addition to states channeling mobility (as in Hollifield's instrumental view). Thus attention shifts to characterizing variation in how

---

3   See, for example, Cooper 2005, 173–77, for a synopsis of the French system; Adamson, this volume, on Ottoman legacies; Ribeiro da Silva 2015 on Portuguese imperialism in Africa; and Lu 2019 on Japan.

states emerge and evolve as a set of institutions that respond to (both benefits and costs of) migration.

Their mobility-makes-states framework fits well with South African history, where the key components of the colonial-era administrative apparatus emerged to limit Asian mobility and profit from African contract labor, while also encouraging a particular sort of European settler (Bradlow 1978; Peberdy 2009; Klotz 2013; Breckenridge 2014; Klaaren 2017). Intra-imperial migration management preceded state formation. In the postapartheid period, laws and bureaucracies with roots in those histories—such as technologies of surveillance and reliance on detention—continue to manage migration.

To circumvent methodological nationalism, therefore, I build on Cooper's concept of the empire state, along with Vigneswaran and Quirk's stress on variation in state formation. Together, they challenge—both historically and analytically—commonplace reliance upon the assumption of a Westphalian nation-state. Generalizing from continental European history too easily leads to stereotypes of non-European regions, especially the characterization of states in Africa as deficient or deviant (Vigneswaran and Quirk 2015, 3–4). In contrast, by identifying the imperial migration states as historically specific transnational forms of governance over human mobility, I distinguish empire states from nation-states, while also leaving open the possibility of other types of (hyphenated) migration states (e.g., Adamson and Tsourapas 2019; Chung, this volume).

My framework is also rooted in historical reality. Crucially, I reject control of human mobility as inherent to sovereignty. Rather, my analysis acknowledges that the norm of domestic jurisdiction over transnational migration only consolidated in 1919, largely due to efforts by Australia and South Africa (assisted by Britain and the United States) in defense of racial exclusions (Brawley 1995; Lake and Reynolds 2008). Furthermore, empires recognized each other as legitimate actors in the international system, including through formal agreements such as the Berlin Conference of 1884 that divided up geographical spheres of control (Grovogui 2001). Similarly, empire states (not nation-states) designed the League of Nations, within which Britain played a hegemonic role (Pedersen 2017).

Within empire states, administrative power subordinates people differentially, including through regulation of mobility, while balancing the need for a degree of centralized legitimacy. Discourses of civilization or modernity play parallel roles to cultural claims that typically underpin nation-state narratives. For example, reaching its apex in the late 1800s, the British Empire encompassed a diverse range of territories through a complex administrative web, accompanied by civilizational claims rooted in a melding of racism and liberalism (Klotz 2012a). Invoking Benedict Anderson's classic, *Imagined Communities*, which characterized nationalism as a transnational elite phenomenon, Marilyn Lake (2005, 211) described politicians in South Africa and the other British self-governing settler colonies, as well as in California, as "an imagined community of white men."

As in any polity, debates over rights and responsibilities percolate across time and space within empires, violently on occasion but more often resulting in the co-optation of key elites (Cooper 2005, 172–73). Much like other forms of confederation, layers of hierarchy characterized British imperial governance. The avowedly civilized metropole ruled over supposedly unsophisticated peripheries, plus local elites often marginalized those defined as inferior. Within this basic hierarchy, British settler colonies (later known as the Dominions) carved out a degree of autonomy as semi-peripheral self-governing areas, not least because white men of Anglo descent could leverage claims of equal status. The imperial judicial system allowed for customary or religious local legal codes, nested within a centralized appeal process up to the Privy Council in London. For migration studies, this legal system mattered especially for disputes over citizenship.

In practice, British imperial administrative structures readily reveal such hierarchies (Lucas 1915). The Colonial Office in London appointed governors general to run their settler states, along with local legislative assemblies that incrementally gained autonomy. Canada led the way to substantial self-government in the 1840s (as it would again in the 1940s, the first to declare a separate citizenship). In contrast, the Colonial Office administered the other Crown Colonies without an intermediary layer of semi-democratic institutions. India remained an anomaly: the India Office in London worked with a governor general—decorously titled the viceroy—who ran the Indian government in Calcutta, which included some local representation.

Often, trading companies also played a role. The Hudson's Bay Company controlled vast swaths of North America into the 1900s. The East India Company lost such wide-ranging control in 1857. Personified by Cecil Rhodes, the British South Africa Company, with its operating base in Cape Town, played a critical regional role into the mid-1900s (Chanock 1977) and arguably continues through legacies in the mining industry.

Within this imperial migration state framework, I trace in the following sections the emergence and then evolution of the South African migration state. Confirming Vigneswaran and Quirk's claim that migration management might precede state formation, we see the creation of South Africa as an administrative unit through the union of four white-minority-ruled colonial territories, but still operating within the British empire state. First, a transnational network of white men, across the settler colonies and within the Colonial Office, sought to limit the mobility of nonwhite imperial subjects. The Union of South Africa consolidated these policies in 1910. During the apartheid era, especially, still-fluid regional borders exacerbated white fears of African mobility, which led to the formal demarcation of borders and decolonization of neighboring British territories in the 1960s. Finally, collapse of draconian migration management efforts in 1986 signaled the need for deeper reconfiguration, as partially implemented since the democratic transition.

Other British settler states, as well as the United States, followed a similar trajectory. Emergent white nationalism spurred barriers to nonwhite migration in the 1890s. By the 1960s, the former white Dominions, alongside the United States, grappled with global pressures to eliminate their racist laws, with South Africa the laggard (Klotz 2013, chap. 5; see also Foley and Tichenor, this volume). These processes also affected European metropoles, as Cooper (2005, 200) stresses. Contrary to conventional wisdom, he demonstrates that empires transformed into nation-states only by the 1950s and 1960s. Subsequent welfare state benefits generated new needs to restrict access through citizenship status, which shifted even intra-imperial migrants from subjects into problematic foreigners (also see Wimmer and Glick Schiller 2003, 583–84, 593–95). Consequently, post-1945 measures of migration flows often replicate flaws of methodological nationalism, because of ambiguities in who counts as a "foreigner."

Furthermore, imperial legacies explain why South Africa is not a node within the Mediterranean subsystem, to which most of the other regions of the African continent are linked (see Charbit and Thiollet, this volume). The absence of Francophone ties in the southern half of the continent, along with weak Lusophone linkages, reinforces the abiding significance of the Anglosphere and its South Asian influences on emigration, transit migration, and immigration. (The British ouster of the Dutch in the early 1800s severed the region's connections to Southeast Asia.) Similar reasons help to explain the anomalous position of Brazil as recipient, transit, and sending state within the global migration system (Acosta 2018; Gomes, this volume) or, frankly, southern European states, which also never fit neatly into conventional categorizations.

Origins of Segregation in Colonialism

Although born in disparate locales around the British Empire, governing elites nevertheless shared the racist assumption that democracy required the exclusion of nonwhites, and they circulated strategies for implementing their vision. In their eyes, Asians presented the gravest threat, because they defied dichotomous racial or civilizational categorization. Chinese migration garnered the most attention across the Pacific region, but in South Africa, the status of Indians as British subjects created crucial legal anomalies.[4] After decades of vociferous political battle, the resolution of this challenge, in the Immigrants Regulation Act of 1913, enshrined the physical and political exclusion of almost all Africans and Asians, with any ambiguities about assimilability among whites to be resolved through ad hoc procedures.

At the heart of this nineteenth-century immigration controversy was Natal's response to the settlement of previously indentured Indian laborers, who had been brought to work on sugar plantations in this southeastern African colony.[5] As elsewhere in the British Empire, the imperial government promoted contract labor as an alternative to slavery, which had been formally abolished in 1834. Responding to abuses in the indenture system, the India Office (in London) and the Indian government (in Calcutta) regulated destinations and recruiters. By 1860, the idea of importing indentured Indians had gained support as a source of plantation labor in Natal. Thus began a half century of intra-imperial negotiations over the rights of Asian migrants. The resulting restrictive

---

4   South Africa briefly imported Chinese labor for the mines, with abusive enforcement of residence in compounds and relatively successful repatriation (Breckenridge 2014, 79–82; Klaaren 2017, 39–45). Therefore, anti-Chinese sentiment played a smaller role in politics or legislation, as part of white animosity toward Asians generally, including people from the Middle East. A small number of deserters developed into a Chinese community, which has started to receive some scholarly attention in the postapartheid period.

5   This section distills Klotz 2013, chap. 2, which drew extensively on Huttenback 1971; Pachai 1971; Metcalf 2007 (among other sources, including primary documents). Also see Breckenridge 2014, chap. 3; Klaaren 2017, chaps. 4–5.

policies remained in place, with only minor modifications, throughout the twentieth century.

After the initial five-year contract, a worker could renew, return to India, or settle freely in Natal. A promise of paid return passage after ten years, intended as an incentive for repatriation, could alternatively be swapped for land, in order to reduce the costs of recruiting additional laborers in a competitive and volatile imperial market; tales of mistreatment in Natal also did not help recruitment. Over time the Indian population grew. Even those without land grants often opted to stay. Within a few decades, a local community took hold. Merchants expanded from specialty items into general merchandise, while free laborers worked in agricultural, transportation, and hotels, among other sectors. By the late 1880s, the number of British Indians in Natal nearly matched Europeans, although both groups remained modest minorities amidst the majority African population.

Local whites increasingly complained. Some focused on barriers to assimilation by Indians and harped on the preservation of so-called civilized standards, while others resented public expenditures on labor recruitment or worried about competition from traders. The intensity of this anti-Indian sentiment grew, along with stereotypes, but plantation owners continued to demand contract labor. As this political divide deepened, the legislative council tried to bolster voluntary repatriation and to ensure social segregation. In 1891, for instance, Law No. 25 ended land grants. White fears also concentrated on the potential for Indians to become voters, despite already high property qualifications. Although sympathetic to white fears, the Colonial Office in London did block attempts by Natal's legislature to restrict Indian franchise, due to its official, albeit often merely performative, commitment to racial equality. Thus their status as British subjects provided some protection from overt discrimination. However, other measures did pass, such as a requirement to keep shop records in English. Often municipalities enforced these laws, with little oversight.

These harsh disincentives to stay failed. Counterproductively, they sparked protests, culminating in the now-famous strategy of passive resistance created by Mohandas Gandhi. A London-trained lawyer, Gandhi first went to Natal temporarily in 1893, where he immediately encountered discrimination. Outraged, soon he was writing letters to newspapers and petitioning politicians, all the way up to the colonial secretary. His public pressure resulted in attention from the India Office, concerned about Indian nationalist sentiment. Founded by Gandhi and associates in 1894, the Indian National Congress of South Africa modeled itself on the National Congress of India, with regular contact between the two organizations, as well as with one Indian member of the British Parliament. Their concerted protests ensured persistent attention from London.

London repeatedly reaffirmed its responsibility for the welfare of its subjects in the self-governing colonies. Particularly salient in southern Africa, its commitment to non-discrimination went back to Indian incorporation into the empire, repeatedly reaffirmed by Queen Victoria, with oversight falling mostly to the India Office in London and the viceroy, who oversaw the Indian government in Calcutta. Yet self-governing white elites, often with sympathetic imperial governors, created clever ways to circumvent these constraints. For example, Natal restricted the Indian franchise in 1896 by using a generic disqualification of persons belonging to countries without parliamentary institutions. To no avail, both Gandhi and the viceroy pointed to municipal and provincial electoral systems in India. (Further efforts to restrict the rights of settled Indians in southern Africa, including disenfranchisement at the municipal level, eventually led to a halt in the flow of indentured labor in 1908 and its official end in 1911.)

Consequently, white legislators grew more daring, while their constituents grew increasingly vocal, as evident in petitions and protests. Inspired by the 1882 Chinese Exclusion in the United States and similar attempts to ban Chinese in New South Wales, the white legislators favored explicit exclusion of Indians. However, Natal's charter prohibited explicit discrimination based on race or nationality. And recent setbacks had proven that London could deliver on its threats to veto legislation by colonial parliaments. Seeking a compromise, the colonial secretary made clear to the governor of Natal that restrictions based on race would not be accepted, but targeting poor or uneducated immigrants would likely be allowed. Borrowing terminology about undesirable immigrants from legislation in the United States and its Jim Crow segregationist policies to restrict black franchise, Natal's Immigration Restriction Act (No. 14) of 1897 relied on a literacy test: prospective immigrants needed to write their names in a European language.

Viewing some sort of restriction as inevitable, London preferred this literacy test to an explicit ban. Furthermore, the Colonial Office approved Natal's use of a European language, rather than allowing the applicant to select a language, which would have enabled more Indians to qualify. Administrative discretion also allowed entry to less-literate Europeans. (Later versions granted greater authority to the examining agent.) This language-based approach proved so effective at resolving ambivalence in London that the colonial secretary subsequently promoted it as a model for its Australasian colonies and Canada, as well as the other southern African colonies. However, the status of Chinese and Japanese for colonies along the Pacific Ocean involved different diplomatic considerations. In the end, Australia (consolidated as a federation in 1901) and New Zealand (in 1899) did adopt a version of the literacy test. Only Canada continued to rely on head taxes until the 1920s (despite enthusiasm for a literacy test in British Columbia, which held little electoral sway).

Even with its ability to regulate transnational mobility, the literacy test did not resolve intraregional migration issues. With the discovery of gold in the Transvaal, to the north of coastal Natal, both demand for labor and opportunities for merchants expanded. Independent until 1900 (aside from a brief annexation that ended in 1881), the Transvaal (then known as the South African Republic, and also the neighboring Orange Free State, which adopted even harsher policies) did not fear a veto of its policies by London. The Transvaal did have treaty obligations that granted non-African persons equal treatment with citizens, but the 1884 London Convention had been signed with whites in mind, not British Indians. Laws required Asians to register and controlled their residency and property, in effect setting up so-called locations (or townships). After nearly a decade of diplomatic and legal disputes, implementation stalled until the Anglo-Boer War ended Transvaal's independence.

In 1902, the Indian community, again led by Gandhi, expressed its disappointment that contributions to the British war effort did not translate into alleviation of discrimination.

Just the opposite: the new postwar administration, ruling through martial law, sought to implement almost identical restrictions, including widespread uses of passes needed to forestall deportation. Once granted self-rule in 1907, the Transvaal legislation passed a supplementary fingerprint requirement that the Indian community found especially insulting, but which London tolerated because of unanimity in the white legislature. Even hoteliers had to keep records of visitors, subject to policy inspection. Transvaal also established a new Immigration Department, under the jurisdiction of its colonial secretary. Gandhi and his colleagues, disillusioned with ineffective legal processes, shifted to an innovative strategy of nonviolent protest campaigns, known as *satyagraha*, which created modest bargaining leverage.

While thus targeting Indian migration to Transvaal by restricting trade and prohibiting land ownership, the colonial government actively fostered settlement by English-speaking whites, through policies such as land grants to former soldiers or imperial bureaucrats. Even Yiddish was accepted for the literacy test contained in the 1907 Immigration Restriction Act (and thereafter). These policies in the Transvaal, which demoted Asians to the status of uncivilized masses in a dichotomous racial hierarchy, became the foundation for a consolidated approach when the four colonies (Transvaal, Natal, Cape, and Orange Free State) integrated as the Union of South Africa in 1910. Clarifying the ambiguous legal status of British Indians also made it easier to deny rights to Africans, since immigration enforcement had already established extensive policing powers (Chanock 2001, 19).

Retention of a literacy test in the Immigrants Regulation of 1913 signaled exclusionary intent, even for white immigration, despite a less exclusionary tradition in the Cape colony. While the history of white settlement in southern Africa is tied to religious persecution in Europe, any special consideration for refugees did not last into the twentieth century. Cape legislation in 1906 still reflected such concerns, but the 1913 Act did not. (Prior to Union, Cape policy dissuaded Indian settlement and practiced de facto segregation but did not use deportation or mandatory locations.) Influenced by Canada, Section 4 allowed ministerial discretion to exclude anyone viewed as having "unsuitable habits of life"—conversely desirable immigrants clearly meant European, preferably Christian—thereby overriding other protections. Due to this implicitly racist assimilation clause, few blacks could even attempt to be immigrants. Nor did the Cape's color-blind franchise (which allowed any highly educated or wealthy male imperial subject to vote, rules commonplace in both Britain and its colonies) become the law of the land at Union—even though stringent education and property qualifications already substantially limited nonwhite access to the vote. (More distinctively, African men could not use communal land ownership to qualify.)

Unchecked ministerial power, a trend found across the British self-governing colonies during this period, further deprived rights advocates of a basis for legal challenge. Plus, potential advocates for refugees lacked political resources, as evident in the 1920s.[6]

---

6   This section distills portions of Klotz 2013, chap. 4, which drew extensively on Bradlow 1978, Shain 1994, and Peberdy 2009 (among other primary and secondary sources). Also see Klaaren 2017, chap. 9.

Following upheavals in Russia and Eastern Europe, tensions over Jewish immigration intensified, even though Yiddish had been accepted as a Europe language for purposes of the literacy test. These newcomers posed an economic threat to low-skilled rural Afrikaners displaced by drought and depression. The conservative National Party used antisemitism as a mobilizing tool to counter class-based divisions among whites.[7] Even the centrist South Africa Party, governing from 1910 to 1924, applied the assimilation requirement and devised procedures to reduce Jewish immigration.

Yet some politicians did not want to lose Jewish votes, so they occasionally deflected criticism. For instance, prior to the 1924 election, the South Africa Party announced a temporary suspension of the assimilation requirement, while attempting to raise fears that the National Party would restrict immigration. Heightened controversy over immigration helped the National Party forge a coalition government with the pro-restriction Labour Party. Learning from the mistakes of its rival, the National Party waited until after winning the 1929 elections to pass the Quota Act of 1930.

Similar to quota policies in other settler states, South Africa capped inflows of less desirable whites. Such sentiments intensified in the 1930s, along with rising antisemitism around the world, to the point that South Africa sought to exclude even German Jews, who came from a desirable country according to the quota system, and typically could satisfy other requirements. Therefore, the 1937 Alien Act extended the scope of restrictions, only allowing unhindered entry by British subjects. In this hostile environment, Jewish organizations feared physical attack if they publicly voiced opposition. Without electoral leverage from an opposition party, and flexible procedures that enabled the government to filter the flows of desirable whites, rights advocacy around immigration issues was diminished even further during the apartheid era. Legal challengers focused on the broader issue of African rights.

Cities and Settlement under Apartheid

Early decades of South African immigration policy institutionalized a dichotomous hierarchy between whites and nonwhites, to which apartheid added draconian enforcement of employment restrictions, residency requirements, and appropriation of property (among other forms of discrimination). Afrikaner nationalists, through coalition governments or as intransigent opposition, had already successfully promoted their segregationist agenda for decades. What made election of the ultra-conservative National Party government truly distinctive in 1948 was its ambitious geospatial strategy, known as grand apartheid, which aimed to reconfigure structural patterns of mobility. By the 1960s, South Africa even converted select rural areas into nominally independent countries, mimicking decolonization in an attempt to legitimize the denial of African rights.[8]

---

7   Receiving scant attention in the literature of this period, gender also played a complex role, both among urbanizing whites and in demarcating class divisions; see Berger 1992, chaps. 2–3.

8   This section distills Klotz 2013, chap. 3, which drew extensively on Evans 1997 and Posel 1997 (among other primary and secondary sources). See also Klotz 2016 on the fluidity of intraregional borders.

Back at the time of Union, however, the government did not view African mobility as a crisis. Typically Africans lived in rural areas, variously on their own land, as renters, or by sharecropping. The Natives Land Act of 1913 sought to eliminate such farming in predominantly white areas by restricting Africans to communal land tenure and residency in so-called reserves. (In a controversial decision, London refused to intervene.) Since responsibility for enforcement was unclear, de facto tenancy continued. And others, no longer able to support themselves through agriculture, opted for towns and cities, where they could find jobs.

No white-minority government had ever seriously considered allowing a free market for African labor. In 1911, the Mines and Works Act consolidated existing restrictions, such as race-based job reservations that primarily protected unskilled and semiskilled whites from competition. Instead, major employers of unskilled workers satisfied the bulk of the needs through contracts. Displacement due to the Natives Land Act of 1913 destroyed peasant agriculture and thereby pushed many Africans into the cash economy, often through contract work in the mines. The mines also recruited aggressively in neighboring Mozambique, a Portuguese colony, as well as Malawi and Lesotho, both under British control.

Meanwhile, agriculture typically sourced its labor from nearby, either other rural regions within the Union or neighboring British colonies at a time when these territorial borders were nominal, in terms of Africans' physical mobility. Because so-called British Africans from neighboring colonies were imperial subjects, albeit not South African nationals, immigration legislation with its assimilation clause did not apply to them. These British Africans retained comparable mobility status to Union-born Africans until the late 1950s, providing them access to towns and cities. And in practice, if not in law, Mozambicans often integrated into local communities.

Increasingly, whites grew concerned about African movement to metropolitan areas. Segregationists, who worried about socially mixed neighborhoods, promoted the demarcation of African locations on the perimeter of towns or cities (whereas Indian locations tended to be nearer market areas of metropolitan centers). The Urban Areas Act of 1923 enshrined the demarcation of locations as national policy, but with local authorities responsible for enforcement. However, taxes generated insufficient revenue to hire enough police. Municipalities also faced a growing housing crisis, without resources or administrative capacity to provide promised accommodations for (supposedly) temporary workers, resulting in overcrowding and sanitation problems.

By the 1930s, the consensus among white political parties attributed many social ills to so-called urbanized Africans, who allegedly disregarded traditional social order linked to the jurisdiction of rural chiefs or native councils set up in urban areas (both of which relied on government funding). Family unification also undermined regulation of mobility. To encourage social stability, a (male) work-seeker could bring (his) family, which in turn reinforced permanent residency. White concerns escalated in tandem with an economic boom in the 1940s that drew more people (of all sorts) to towns and cities. Agriculture, mining, and a burgeoning industrial sector competed for labor, evolving into a complex web of formal and informal job reservations, intersecting race and gender (Berger 1992, chaps. 3–6). In the 1946 census, Africans outnumbered whites in urban areas for the first time, with about 40 percent arriving from white-owned farms (Posel 1997, 24–29).

Debates centered on how and where—but not whether—to regulate African mobility. All four provinces already had "pass" laws that allowed for removal of unemployed African men back to rural reserves if they lacked paperwork approving residency. Originally designed to control cross-border mobility of Indians between Natal and the Transvaal, this registration system provided administrative tools applicable to African men working outside the control of mining compounds. Initially, these laws merely required a work-seeker permit and did not apply to women, so they had little effect on African migration. Over time, however, these tools evolved into the notorious apartheid system, which produced an increasing complex number of permissions in a passbook that Africans needed to carry with them in order to avoid detention or deportation to a rural area. Both the scope and enforcement of the pass system, later known as "influx control," became ever more brutal.

Yet the ultimate goal of physical exclusion remained elusive. The economy relied fundamentally on African labor, whereas humans could not be distributed to employers as one might allocate commodities. Policy-makers failed to understand African motivations, including their persistence in the face of police brutality. At most, the administrative state could influence numbers and destinations. Thus the Native Laws Amendment Act of 1952 centralized the administration of influx control. And for the first time, women needed to carry passes—prompting one of the most famous mass protests, the Defiance Campaign. Conversely, efforts to decentralize industrial development away from the major cities failed to provide sufficient incentives to employers.

A crucial distinction between nationality and citizenship underpinned these restrictions on African rights. (Other empires exhibit similarly tiered degrees of citizenship.) People born within the Union of South Africa were British subjects, regardless of race, without any separate conception of citizenship until the Citizenship Act of 1949. Furthermore, British Africans from neighboring areas were treated as nationals rather than foreigners. In effect, only white British subjects could become South African citizens. Contrary to contemporary assumptions about citizenship, however, there had never been an automatic link between nationality and suffrage.

Apartheid may be most known outside South Africa for denying blacks the right to vote, but franchise had been a major stumbling block even back in the 1909 negotiations for Union. Some colonies allowed all white men to vote without restrictions, while others allowed nonwhite men to vote if they satisfied property or education conditions. (White women only got the right to vote in 1930, and all women finally in 1994.) Although optimists had hoped that a compromise, which allowed the Cape to retain its nonracial rules, would gradually lead to an expansion of voting rights, the opposite occurred. Africans residing in the Cape lost their right to vote in 1934 and so-called Coloureds lost theirs in 1956, leaving a whites-only franchise. Furthermore, when South Africa broke constitutional ties with Britain to become a republic, in 1961, even other residual rights as British subjects (of any race) evaporated. This legal shift instantly transformed anyone not born in South Africa (or if white, naturalized) into a foreigner.

Since most nonwhites born in Union territory were South African nationals who could not vote, governance fell to an increasingly authoritarian administrative state. Although established as a centralized (rather than federal) system, the government took decades to consolidate four provincial administrative systems. Even in 1927, a key point in the development of the administrative state, the Department of Native Affairs, lacked coherence or capacity. Revenue remained scarce. Already-limited resources mostly provided services for whites, and direct taxes on Africans did not generate much money.

Yet these direct taxes served another purpose: to create a need for African men to enter the cash economy, at least periodically. The Native Labour Regulation Act granted the mining industry control over its own recruitment infrastructure, whereas the Department of Native Affairs played a direct role in regulating agricultural labor. Legislation bolstered the notoriously abusive tenancy system, which civil servants did little to monitor. Desertion to the city provided an escape that also led to greater demands from farmers for tighter controls and stricter enforcement of tenancy contracts. From 1948 onward, the apartheid government sought to tighten decades of lax enforcement, in part by closing various loopholes.

By the early 1960s, foreign Africans received greater attention within overarching efforts to mute urbanization. Prior to 1961, British Africans from neighboring areas had readily worked in agricultural or mining without having to comply with laws that applied to foreign Africans. Then in response to concerns about apartheid, London conceded to independence for neighboring Botswana, Lesotho, and Swaziland (Spence 1964; Klotz 2016). Suddenly, the South African government wanted to know more about these (former) British Africans because immigration law now required their deportation as "illegal aliens" without passbooks. While some worked as contract laborers in the mines, or on nearby farms, many had integrated within urban communities, making them nearly impossible to identify. They become yet another problem for influx control.

Although apartheid-era rhetoric targeting foreign Africans as illegal aliens without passbooks far outstripped their numbers, white fears drove passage of laws to create formal borders with these former British colonies. Yet the full impact of decolonization reached much deeper into apartheid policy-making. Sensitive to intensifying domestic and international protests over apartheid, the government adapted with its own mimicry of decolonization as a purported solution for granting citizenship rights to Africans. As an extension of both influx control and decentralized industrial development policies, select rural areas (known as "reserves") were transformed into so-called ethnic homelands or Bantustans, eventually to be granted independence. According to this plan, Africans would be citizens of decolonized nation-states. Only four of these ethnically demarcated territories (the so-called TBVC states of Transkei, Bophuthatswana, Venda, and Ciskei) reached the stage of faux-sovereignty.

Instead of resolving problems, this shift toward putative decolonization of the Bantustans created its own contradictions and dysfunctions. The administrative state still wanted to remove Africans from urban areas, but the creation of these new territorial units created more regulations and thus greater need for enforcement. Nominal independence turned internal migration into international migration, so even more borders needed creation and control. That required duplicate bureaucracies to prop up the image of independent states, which cost money not covered by revenue (Development Bank of Southern Africa 1989). And Mozambican refugees, arriving in notable numbers by 1980, created additional problems. Although dislocated people often sought safety in not-yet-independent Bantustan territories, notably KwaZulu, South Africa officially denied their existence.

Most analysts point to South Africa's first universal suffrage elections in 1994 as the demise of apartheid, yet they typically overlook the failed Bantustan project as a crucial precursor. Fundamentally, this mimicry of decolonization acknowledged African subjectivity—blacks had rights, even if the white-minority government now claimed that those rights should be exercised outside of South African borders. In 1986, the pretense of influx control ended. Thus a key pillar of apartheid collapsed, even while Nelson Mandela remained in prison. Also in 1986, the government lifted the assimilation clause for immigration. These changes became the legal benchmark for many people with ambiguous residency or nationality status to claim a right to vote in 1994 (Klaaren 2000). Mobility, among other factors, had reconfigured the state.

Municipalities and Migration Challenges

Viewed as a system of migration management, the formal demise of apartheid took approximately a decade, from the end of influx control in 1986 to the adoption of a new constitution in 1996. During protracted negotiations in the early 1990s over the institutional redesign of the postapartheid state, the question of how to reincorporate the Bantustans intersected with the crucial choice of a unitary rather than a federal system. The decision to create nine new provinces reflected the extent to which apartheid had centralized administration—to the point that the original four provinces of the Union had been eliminated in 1986, displaced by nine development regions that more or less turned into the postapartheid provinces (Muthien and Khosa 1995, 305–13; Lodge 2002, chap. 2).

The momentum of reform reached its limits with migration policy, which remained mired in exclusionary legal legacies and administrative practices.[9] Even after two decades, many features of contemporary policy are rooted in the mindset embedded in the Aliens Control Act of 1991, one of the last pieces of legislation passed by the white-minority parliament. In turn, the Aliens Control Act drew upon core provisions of the Immigrants Registration Act of 1913. From that low baseline, it bolstered bureaucratic powers, such as indefinite detention and lack of judicial review. Initial attempts at greater reforms produced few results. Thus the Aliens Control Amendment Act of 1995 did little to alleviate concerns, although it did provide for some degree of judicial review, in line with the interim 1993 constitution.

One key legislative development did make a significant change. Prior to the Refugees Act of 1998, asylum seekers and refugees had no legal status, although that absence did not prevent their arrival through other channels. For instance, Mozambicans had found informal safety in Bantustans, among other places, while whites from Rhodesia (Zimbabwe since 1980) readily qualified as official immigrants. Although tied to the Aliens Control Act via conditions of residency and such, this new refugee law brought policy in line with the 1996 constitution and ratification of international refugee conventions in the mid-1990s, which provided claimants legal and procedural protections. These legislative and legal reforms provided leverage for rights-based challenges. Notably, the Constitutional Court affirmed that some provisions provide rights to denizens regardless of citizenship (Klaaren 2017, 212–16).

---

9   This section distills and extends the analysis in Klotz 2013, chap. 4.

When the Immigration Act of 2002 finally replaced the Aliens Control Act, after a remarkably convoluted political fight, many of its provisions still emphasized procedures for deterring, detaining, and deporting unwanted foreigners. Critics remained concerned about wide-ranging police powers and a formal role for the security forces. In effect, the Refugees Act has been a double-edged sword. In the absence of deeper reforms to immigration policy, granting protections inadvertently fuels perceptions (among both policy-makers and the public) that economic migrants falsely claim persecution. For instance, an ambivalent government established only a very limited number of Refugee Reception Offices to accept asylum claims. Furthermore, implementing regulations circulated in 2000 provided for the potential revocation of refugee status, which underscored its temporary nature, and foreshadowed proposals a decade later to limit rights of refugees to permanent residence status (Klaaren 2017, 221–22).

Such skeptical sentiments spiked when unrest in Zimbabwe, escalating dramatically by 2000, drove more people across the border (and to other destinations). Although antiforeigner attitudes and sporadic violence had already garnered negative attention, legal advocates lacked strong political allies even after extraordinarily widespread attacks in 2008.[10] Consequently, subsequent legislation made minimal reforms; a major focus continued to be the prevention of fraudulent asylum claims. Indeed, few policy-makers or commentators distinguished between those with official refugee status (including the right to work) and foreigners in general (portrayed as competing unfairly for jobs). Subsequent policies even sought to treat the status of accepted asylum seekers through the criteria of skills-based immigration priorities (Klaaren 2017, 219–20).

This conflation spills into public debate, but competition for jobs or housing does not automatically translate into or validate xenophobia. Circumstances can reinforce associations between migration and crime, for instance. Because of their reliance on the informal sector, immigrants often carry cash, making them likely victims who will, furthermore, not seek police assistance. Immigrants also tend to live in lower-cost, crime-ridden neighborhoods, with cheaper housing. Administrative delays in securing valid paperwork can drive even legal migrants to bribery and forged documents. Few immigrants can survive without, at some point, doing something of dubious legality. Not surprisingly, then, policy-makers and the media routinely recycle suspicions that economic migrants abuse an overly generous asylum system.

Although issues surrounding migrants living in the cities are not new, returning to 1986 as a critical juncture offers insights into some distinctive dynamics of the postapartheid era. Crucially, the demise of influx control marked only one component of a wider agenda of deregulation (in response to intensifying domestic and international pressures for the abolition of apartheid) that included lifting restrictions on African businesses

---

10   For the flavor of these attitudes and an overview of responses from civil society organizations, see Everatt 2011, as well as other contributions to that special issue of *Politikon*. Pugh 2014 provides more extensive analysis of the gap between civil society organizations and advocates for migrant rights. Meanwhile, the mining industry and unions continued to negotiate labor policies outside parliament (Crush and Tshitereke 2001).

(most visibly the minibus taxi industry) and property ownership (Simkins 1993, 324–39). Thus, increased population mobility in the early 1990s, from within South Africa and from neighboring countries, converged with nascent structural changes in previously segregated spheres directly impacted by competition from these urban newcomers—informal sector employment and access to housing.

Implementation of these efforts to remedy the pernicious long-term effects of geospatial fragmentation largely fell to local level governments, also radically restructured after the Group Areas Act (the legal keystone of urban segregation) had been rescinded in 1991.[11] Consequently, the distribution of basic infrastructure such as clean water and electricity offered additional political resources at the municipal level—coincidentally around the same time that Zimbabweans arrived in greater numbers. Indeed, local political dynamics explain much of the variation in the scope and intensity of antiforeigner violence (Steinberg 2008). Given the nature of media coverage, areas that actively suppressed attacks received less attention, publicly or analytically.

Unprecedented internal displacement due to widespread violence in 2008 demonstrated how unprepared South Africa was to cope with migration. Responsibility for protection fell to municipal governments, which relied mainly on emergency disaster assistance funds, along with help from the United Nations High Commissioner for Refugees (UNHCR). Not surprisingly, responses and effectiveness varied considerably. Furthermore, since municipal governments had often resisted national-level segregationist directives during apartheid (albeit with limited success), emergency responders had few institutional legacies or lessons upon which to build better coordination between local and national levels.

Municipalities are still trying to cope with administrative, financial, and political pressures that result from ever-changing migration patterns and persistent xenophobic protests. Some political leaders and policy-makers have gone so far as to express regret that South Africa signed international conventions in 1995. At that time, in keeping with growing skepticism internationally about putting refugees in camps, the postapartheid government adopted an integration-oriented policy, in consultation with UNHCR (Belvedere 2006). Ideally, once asylum claims were approved, refugees would support themselves and have access to basic services, such as medical care and schools.

Yet problems of bureaucratic inefficiencies and notorious detention centers highlight some less laudatory aspects of this integration approach. Notably, Refugee Reception Offices, mostly located in major cities, have been a central administrative feature. Persistent attempts by the Department of Home Affairs to relocate these registration offices to rural border areas—despite effective legal challenges to any relocation—suggest an apartheid-style reasoning: use of elusive paperwork requirements to keep migrants away

---

11   Simkins (1993, 323) skirts commonplace criticism of such market-based reforms as lightly veiled ways for whites to retain disproportionate economic power in whatever might be the new political dispensation. Market-based policies since 1994 often face similar criticism for failing to address structural inequalities (Lodge 2002, chap. 5). Similar debates continue over the question of land redistribution.

from cities. A century of experience in failed "influx control" style of migration manage-ment should make it clear that recent talk of a camp policy, based on a security rationale, would not disrupt the underlying dynamics of urbanization. People will find a way to get where they want to go.

In reverse, insights gleaned from the apartheid state's fundamental inability to regu-late human mobility—even with ample resources of authoritarian white-minority rule—underscore the need to include local-level governance into the analytical frameworks of migration studies. Methodological nationalism leads analysts to underestimate the role of urbanization as an underlying driver of migration (Wimmer and Glick Schiller 2003, 587, 599). In contrast, a view from below offers a valuable remedy to the prevail-ing naturalized vision of the world divided into nation-states (Vigneswaran 2008, 2013). Thereby removing the myth of Westphalia opens up possibilities for innovative forms in rights-respecting citizenship (Klaaren 2017, 225–28).

The macro-historical overview offered in this chapter illustrates how South African migration policies can be analyzed, like those of any migration state, as responses to a combination of domestic, transnational, and international pressures. Also, Australia and Canada followed similar trajectories, until the 1950s, providing ample material for comparative analysis.[12] Placed even deeper within an imperial context, the intersection of three migration subsystems within which South Africa fits as a node offers striking parallels to Britain. For instance, the fluid boundaries of the Anglo-Irish border allow for exceptionally flexible labor supplies on a par with (post)colonial relationships of (for-merly) "British Africans" in southern Africa (cf. Hollifield 2004: 894–95; also Paul 1997 and Lucassen 2005).

To what extent then can theoretical frameworks derived from Western European or North American countries provide insights into other liberal democracies, includ-ing postapartheid South Africa? Elsewhere, I have applied a migration state framework more systematically (Klotz 2012b, 2013): The notion of a liberal paradox draws analytical attention to courts and coalitions, but we should not presume their strength. In South Africa, rights advocates lack allies, thus limiting their successes. Meanwhile, the mining industry and unions continue to negotiate labor policies within a corporatist political system, reducing any potential incentive to form a political coalition through parties in parliament. These structural limits on any rights–markets synergy enable exclusionary practices to persist even after universal franchise.

Thus theories derived from North American and Western European contexts can be useful in other settings *and* in turn can provide lessons for that literature. For in-stance, placing South Africa back into the universe of comparative cases highlights omitted variable bias and the value of analyzing the absence, not only the presence, of

12   In my experience, South Africa has been systematically omitted from the universe of settler-state cases because Canadians and Australians do not like to admit their similarities and historical ties, but much can be learned from reclaiming the comparison (e.g., Klotz 2012a, 2013, chap. 5).

key factors. Expanding the range of cases also destabilizes geographical reification. For instance, South Africa still fits within three migration subsystems through abiding transnational links to other territories in the former British Empire. And even as intracontinental mobility increases, South Africa still does not fit in the Mediterranean subsystem that connects "Africa" to "Europe" (as typically labeled in the migration literature). To understand global migration governance, analysts need to move beyond such deeply Eurocentric conceptions of territoriality.

References

Acosta, Diego. 2018. *The National versus the Foreigner in South America: 200 Years of Migration and Citizenship Law*. Cambridge: Cambridge University Press

Adamson, Fiona, and Gerasimos Tsourapas. 2019. "The Migration State in the Global South: Nationalizing, Developmental and Neoliberal Models of Migration Management." *International Migration Review* (OnlineFirst, October). https://doi.org/10.1177/0197918319879057

Bakewell, Oliver. 2015. "Moving from War to Peace in the Zambia-Angola Borderlands." In *Mobility Makes States: Migration and Power in Africa*, edited by Darshan Vigneswaran and Joel Quirk, 194–217. Philadelphia: University of Pennsylvania Press.

Belich, James. 2009. *Replenishing the Earth: The Settler Revolution and the Rise of the Anglo-World, 1783–1939*. New York: Oxford University Press.

Belvedere, M. F. 2006. "Beyond Xenophobia: Contested Identities and the Politics of Refugees in Post-Apartheid South Africa." PhD diss., University of Minnesota.

Berger, Iris. 1992. *Threads of Solidarity: Women in South African Industry, 1900–1980*. Bloomington: Indiana University Press.

Bradlow, Emma. 1978. "Immigration into the Union, 1910–1948." PhD thesis, University of Cape Town.

Brawley, Sean. 1995. *The White Peril: Foreign Relations and Asian Immigration to Australasia and North America, 1919–1978*. Sydney: University of New South Wales Press.

Breckenridge, Keith. 2014. *Biometric State: The Global Politics of Identification and Surveillance in South Africa, 1850 to the Present*. Cambridge: Cambridge University Press.

Caplan, Jane, and John Torpey, eds. 2001. *Documenting Individual Identity: The Development of State Practices in the Modern World*. Princeton, NJ: Princeton University Press.

Chanock, Martin. 1977. *Unconsummated Union: Britain, Rhodesia and South Africa, 1900–45*. Manchester: Manchester University Press.

_____. 2001. *The Making of South African Legal Culture, 1902–1936: Fear, Favour and Prejudice*. New York: Cambridge University Press.

Cooper, Frederick. 2005. *Colonialism in Question: Theory, Knowledge, History*. Berkeley: University of California Press.

Crush, Jonathan, and Clarence Tshitereke. 2001. "Contesting Migrancy: The Foreign Labor Debate in Post-1994 South Africa." *Africa Today* 48(3): 49–70.

Development Bank of Southern Africa. 1989. *Statistical Abstract*. Halfway House (South Africa): Development Bank of Southern Africa.

Evans, Ivan. 1997. *Bureaucracy and Race: Native Administration in South Africa*. Berkeley: University of California Press.

Everatt, David. 2011. "Xenophobia, State and Society in South Africa, 2008–2010." *Politikon: South African Journal of Political Studies* 38(1): 7–36.

Grovogui, Siba. 2001. "Sovereignty in Africa: Quasi-Statehood and Other Myths in International Theory." In *Africa's Challenges to International Relations Theory*, edited by Kevin Dunn and Timothy Shaw, 29–45. New York: Palgrave

Hollifield, James. 2004. "The Emerging Migration State." *International Migration Review* 38: 885–912.

Huttenback, Robert. 1971. *Gandhi in South Africa: British Imperialism and the Indian Question, 1860–1914.* Ithaca, NY: Cornell University Press.

Klaaren, Jonathan. 2000. "Post-Apartheid Citizenship in South Africa." In *From Migrants to Citizens: Membership in a Changing World*, edited by T. A. Aleinikoff and D. Klusmeyer, 221–52. Washington, DC: Carnegie Endowment for International Peace.

_____. 2017. *From Prohibited Immigrants to Citizens: The Origins of Citizenship and Nationality in South Africa.* Cape Town: University of Cape Town Press.

Klotz, Audie. 2012a. "The Imperial Self: A Perspective on Anglo-America from South Africa, India, and Ireland." In *Anglo-America and Its Discontents: Civilizational Identities beyond West and East*, edited by Peter Katzenstein, 81–104. New York: Routledge.

_____. 2012b. "South Africa as an Immigration State." *Politikon* 39(2): 189–208.

_____. 2013. *Migration and National Identity in South Africa, 1860–2010.* New York: Cambridge University Press.

_____. 2016. "Borders and the Roots of Xenophobia in South Africa." *South African Historical Journal* 68(2): 180–94.

Kynoch, Gary. 2005. *We Are Fighting the World: A History of the Marashea Gangs in South Africa, 1947–1999.* Athens: Ohio University Press.

Lake, Marilyn. 2005. "From Mississippi to Melbourne via Natal: The Invention of the Literacy Test as a Technology of Racial Exclusion." In *Connected Worlds: History in Transnational Perspective*, edited by Ann Curthoys and Marilyn Lake, 209–29. Canberra: Australian National University Press.

Lake, Marilyn, and Henry Reynolds. 2008. *Drawing the Global Colour Line: White Men's Countries and the International Challenge of Racial Equality.* Cambridge: Cambridge University Press.

Lodge, Tom. 2002. *Politics in South Africa: From Mandela to Mbeki.* Bloomington: Indiana University Press.

Lu, Sidney Xu. 2019. *The Making of Japanese Settler Colonialism: Malthusianism and Trans-Pacific Migration, 1868–1961.* Cambridge: Cambridge University Press.

Lucas, Charles. 1915. *British Empire: Six Lectures.* London: Macmillan.

Lucassen, Leo. 2005. *The Immigrant Threat: The Integration of Old and New Migrants in Western Europe since 1850.* Urbana: University of Illinois Press.

Metcalf, Thomas. 2007. *Imperial Connections: India in the Indian Ocean Arena, 1860–1920.* Berkeley: University of California Press.

Mitchell, Timothy. 1991. "The Limits of the State: Beyond Statist Approaches and Their Critics." *American Political Science Review* 85(1): 77–96.

Muthien, Yvonne, and Meshack Khosa. 1995. "'The Kingdom, the Volkstaat, and the New South Africa': Drawing South Africa's New Regional Boundaries." *Journal of Southern African Studies* 21(2): 303–22.

Pachai, Bridglal. 1971. *International Aspects of the South African Indian Question, 1860–1971.* Cape Town: Struik.

Paul, Kathleen. 1997. *Whitewashing Britain: Race and Citizenship in the Postwar Era.* Ithaca, NY: Cornell University Press.

Peberdy, Sally. 2009. *Selecting Immigrants: National Identity and South Africa's Immigration Policies, 1910–2008.* Johannesburg: Witwatersrand University Press.

Pedersen, Susan. 2017. "Empires, States, and the League of Nations." In *Internationalisms: A Twentieth-Century History*, edited by Glenda Sluga and Patricia Clavin, chap. 6. Cambridge: Cambridge University Press.

Posel, Deborah. 1997. *The Making of Apartheid, 1948–1961.* Oxford: Clarendon.

Pugh, Sarah. 2014. "Advocacy in the Time of Xenophobia: Civil Society, the State, and the Politics of Migration in South Africa." *Politikon* 41(2): 227–47.

Ribeiro da Silva, Filipa. 2015. "Portuguese Empire Building and Human Mobility in São Tomé and Angola, 1400s–1700s." In *Mobility Makes States: Migration and Power in Africa,* edited by Darshan Vigneswaran and Joel Quirk, 37–58. Philadelphia: University of Pennsylvania Press.

Shain, Milton. 1994. *The Roots of Antisemitism in South Africa.* Charlottesville: University Press of Virginia.

Simkins, Charles. 1993. "State, Market and Urban Development in South Africa." In *State and Market in Post-Apartheid South Africa,* edited by Merle Lipton and Charles Simkins, 321–57. Johannesburg: Witwatersrand University Press.

Spence, J. E. 1964. "British Policy towards the High Commission Territories." *Journal of Modern African Studies* 2(2): 221–46.

Steinberg, Jonny. 2008. "South Africa's Xenophobic Eruption." Institute for Security Studies Paper 169. Pretoria: Institute for Security Studies.

Vigneswaran, Darshan. 2008. "Enduring Territoriality: South African Immigration Control." *Political Geography* 27(7): 783–801.

———. 2013. *Territory, Migration and the Evolution of the International System.* New York: Palgrave.

Vigneswaran, Darshan, and Joel Quirk. 2015. "Mobility Makes States." In *Mobility Makes States: Migration and Power in Africa,* edited by Darshan Vigneswaran and Joel Quirk, 1–34. Philadelphia: University of Pennsylvania Press.

Wimmer, Andreas and Nina Glick Schiller. 2003. "Methodological Nationalism, the Social Sciences, and the Study of Migration: An Essay in Historical Epistemology," *International Migration Review* 37(3): 576–610.

3 ILLIBERAL MIGRATION GOVERNANCE IN THE ARAB GULF

Hélène Thiollet

OF THE MIGRANT-RECEIVING REGIONS in the world, only North America and the European Union receive more migrants than the Arab Gulf (United Nations, Department of Economic and Social Affairs 2017a). The oil and gas–producing countries of the Gulf (Bahrain, Kuwait, Saudi Arabia, the United Arab Emirates, Qatar, Oman), in fact, host the highest proportions of foreigners in the world. Since most of these foreigners come from developing countries, the Gulf states are the epicenter of South–South migration dynamics—a quantitatively significant (Abel and Sander 2014) but largely understudied phenomenon. Gulf migration is also a blind spot in the study of migration governance. One reason for this oversight might be what Myron Weiner (1986) called the "illusion of impermanence," the fact that foreigners in the Gulf are called "foreign workers" or "expatriates," not "immigrants." This labeling suggests a limited period of time in the "transit states" of the Gulf ('Abd al-Hādī Khalaf, AlShehabi, and Hanieh 2014). Indeed, migrants have little prospect for formal integration in Gulf polities due to discriminatory citizenship regimes combined with exclusionary policies, institutions, and practices. Additionally, the Gulf states—like other Middle Eastern countries—are not parties to the 1951 Geneva Convention, which offers protection to statutory refugees and the forcibly displaced. As a result, Palestinians since 1949, Eritreans in the 1980s, Iraqis after 2003, and Syrians since 2011 have migrated to the Gulf but without legal protection. Regardless of whatever rights are given to foreign residents, recent qualitative studies have revisited the importance of immigration, long-term settlement, and diasporas in Gulf societies (Assaf 2017; Thiollet 2010; Thiollet and Assaf 2020; Vora 2013).

This chapter seeks to fill in existing gaps in migration-related scholarship by offering a comprehensive understanding of migration in the region. On the one hand, comparative studies on migration governance have generally failed to connect the dynamics observed in the Gulf to broader trends across the world and the Gulf Cooperation Council (GCC) countries rarely feature in general discussions on migration politics or migration governance.[1]

1 Gulf countries are absent from Rosenblum and Tichenor's handbook (2012), from the oft-cited edited volume by Betts and Loescher (2011), and from the main volumes on migration theories, such as Brettell and Hollifield (2008).

Although a few index-based comparative studies on migration policies include some Gulf monarchies (Miller and Peters 2018; Mirilovic 2010; Shin 2017), most quantitative research either does not include the region in the dataset (Beine et al. 2016; Bjerre et al. 2015; Haas et al. 2019) or seems to highlight the outlier status of oil rentier monarchies (Ruhs 2017). On the other hand, qualitative studies focus mostly on micro-level narratives of immigrant lives (Gardner et al. 2013; Longuenesse 1985; Longva 2005; Vora 2013). While a few deal with migration politics (Stanton Russel and al-Ramadhan 1994; Thiollet 2011), most of these studies highlight the exceptionalism of Gulf migration (Fargues and de Bel-Air 2015). As this volume's ambition is to understand *global* migration, this chapter locates the Gulf in global migration systems and exposes key features of migration governance outside Western contexts. It shows how immigration is embedded in long histories of foreign relations among the Gulf, the wider Middle East, the Ottoman and British Empires, the United States, and Asia and is tied to the political economy of labor-demanding, oil-producing countries and the sociopolitical structure of Gulf monarchies. As such, it not only offers an insight into the workings of migration governance in nondemocratic and illiberal contexts but also highlights the importance of historical interdependencies in contemporary global migration dynamics. It also opens up discussions of theories designed to analyze democratic (im)migration states and liberal paradoxes in migration management (Hollifield 2004; Natter 2018).

The chapter begins with a *longue durée* overview of how Gulf migration systems unfolded from the early twentieth century to today. Gulf migration systems evolved from dependency within the Ottoman and British imperial realms to regional integration in the pan-Arab era (1960s–1991) and diplomatic interdependence with the Asian global South. These systems, which varied across time, connected the Gulf to different regions: to India and Middle Eastern and East African colonies and Western imperial metropolises, to the pan-Arab Middle East, and, finally, to South and Southeast Asia again since the 1990s. The chapter links these varying migration geographies to the politics of migration governance, which shifted from colonial to regional to global migration systems.

The second part of the chapter unpacks the dynamics of migration governance in Gulf countries today. It describes the role of states, markets, and social institutions, including employers, recruiters, brokers, sponsors, families, and migrant networks. The section highlights the diversity of formal and informal institutions embedded in migration governance. It illustrates the recent emergence of *illiberal* migration states, in parallel to *liberal* migration states in Western contexts (Hollifield 2004), thus feeding into debates on the varieties of migration states across the world.

International Migration Systems and Gulf History

Permanent and temporary migration, motivated by trade, labor, politics, or religious devotion, are central to the Gulf's history. This section describes the changing international geographies and urban topographies of immigration to the Gulf through three historical sequences. The first sequence stretches from the colonial to the postcolonial era, tracing patterns of migration to the Gulf from the first "oil boom" of the 1930s. The second sequence describes the 1960s, leading to the second "oil boom" and first "migration boom" after 1973. The third sequence occurs from the 1990s onward, with new migration patterns emerging in the context of the diversification of the Gulf economies and the "second migration boom" in the 2000s.

Colonial Migration Governance and Imperial Geographies, 1930s–1960s

From the 1930s to the 1970s, most Gulf states were under colonial control within the British empire.[2] The Saudi kingdom, by contrast, was founded in 1932 as an independent state occupying central Arabia that progressively conquered former Ottoman territories in both the western (Hejaz and the Red Sea) and eastern (al Hasa oasis region and Dammam and the coastal area) regions. Although never formally colonized, Saudi Arabia fell under colonialism "by proxy" (Ochonu 2014), that is, indirect colonial domination by the United States through the influence of ARAMCO, the monopolistic American-owned oil company. British or American governments and firms, in collaboration with the rulers and elites of local sheikhdoms, thus operated colonial migration governance directly, indirectly, or by proxy. Migration systems under colonization were not only shaped by government policies but also by nonstate institutions that impacted the urban, local, regional, and international levels of migration management.[3] As such, Western, Arab, and Asian businessmen, together with diplomats and intermediaries, shaped Gulf colonial migration governance alongside vernacular or imported institutions, cultural and social norms, racial and class hierarchies.[4] The two central features of mobility in the region were incipient oil-related labor migration and Muslim pilgrimages.

The Discovery of Oil and Labor Migration under Colonial Rule

Through treaties signed from 1820 to 1916, the coast sheikhdoms surrendered sovereign control over immigration and granted oil and gas concessions in exchange for British protection. Labor migration systems were conditioned by imperial interests, channeled via oil companies partly or entirely owned by British or American firms (Seccombe and Lawless 1986). These exogenous determinants of migration governance were more potent than the oft-cited "endogenous" or "traditional" characteristics of Gulf societies or preexisting small-scale mobilities linked to slave trading and the pearling industry. In a nascent oil economy, as archival documents from British political officers confirm, "the demand for labour all along the Arab shores of the Gulf greatly exceeds supply" (Seccombe 1983, 5). The development of the oil industry led to large population movements of various kinds.[5]

2　Kuwait was under British control until 1961, Bahrain, Qatar, and the UAE—formerly the "trucial states"—until 1971. The sultanate of Oman was a British protectorate until 1971.

3　Given the recent downplaying of the role of states in world history (Osterhammel and Camiller 2014), looking at all types of migration institutions and their connection to governmental regulations and state power is particularly important to understanding global migration (Bosma, van Nederveen Meerkerk, and Sarkar 2013).

4　As Klotz showed for South Africa, colonial and postcolonial history offers powerful elements to understanding contemporary features of Gulf migration governance (Klotz 2012).

5　From the discovery of oil in 1932 to 1936, the number of employees in the Bahrain Petroleum Company (BAPCO) rose from 610 to 5,038. In Saudi Arabia, the first drilling camp was opened

1. Mobility of nationals and Gulf locals (domestic and intra-Gulf migration) from nonoil areas to oil areas for unskilled work, which can be termed *vernacular mobility*;
2. Recruitment of skilled, semiskilled, and unskilled workers for manual and crucial work from the Arab world and outside the region (the British Raj, notably), which can be termed *colonial mobility*;
3. Immigration of British and American skilled expatriates, such as engineers and managers, which can be termed *imperial mobility*.

Foreign oil companies directly managed these different types of mobility for the hydrocarbon industry and its necessary infrastructure, and they did so in close collaboration with local political elites and ruling families. The typology proposed above reflects the political and economic drivers of migration governance at the local level and, more globally, across the British Empire and the Saudi-American colonial relation by proxy.

The first type, *vernacular mobility*, characterizes local mobility systems within Gulf states. Domestic and intraregional migration in the 1930s was shaped by "nationality clauses" inserted in oil concession agreements, which allowed Gulf sheikhs to compel foreign-owned companies to hire locals (Errichiello 2012). Both in the colonial coastal sheikhdoms and in the recently created state of Saudi Arabia, nationality clauses were intended to compensate local economies for the decline in the pearl-fishing sector. However, securing jobs for nationals was a political concern for local sheikhs, who needed to maintain clientelist ties and ensure that their subjects remained loyal: the genesis of monarch-subject dependency within the contemporary "rentier state" can thus be traced to these early employment policies. But to staff the oil industry with locals, rulers and oil companies had to organize internal migration of workers across Gulf states, bringing subjects to the oil towns and settling Bedouins around the wells. In Saudi Arabia, these population policies were also a way to mitigate the influence of Shia Arabs in the kingdom's eastern provinces, as Sunni Saudi workers from other regions were brought to oil towns. But implementation proved difficult, with few locals possessing identity papers, and with workers from Gulf and other Arab countries forging certificates and circulating across the region. Gulf locals were mainly recruited as unskilled workers in low-paying jobs with difficult working conditions, mostly in construction rather than the oil sector (except for ARAMCO; see table 3.1).

Colonial mobility refers to the patterns of migration to the Gulf between the 1930s and the 1950s. As historian Ian Seccombe (1983) notes, the transfer of workers was organized across the empire from 1833 (when slavery was abolished in the British Empire) until the 1920s.[6] The number of British Indians for skilled and semiskilled work in Bahrain rose

---

in 1934 in Dhahran. The California Standard Oil Company (CASOC), and later its subsidiary Arabian-American Oil Company (ARAMCO), went from 150 employees in 1935 to 3,641 in 1939. The Anglo-American Kuwait Oil Company (KOC) and Qatar's PDQ (Petroleum Development Qatar) boomed slightly later.

6   Indentured migration was organized as a contract-binding relationship, creating enslaved or "unfree" labor conditions for wage-earning workers. This hybrid form of exploitation generally entailed surveillance, strict housing, and social segregation, and the integration of indentured immigrants depended upon the ethnic origin of immigrants, the period, and the host context. The colonial

Table 3.1. Composition of the SOCAL-ARAMCO labor force, 1933–1954.

	"Indigenous" *Laborers*	*US "Senior Staff"* *Employed*	*"Indians"*
1933	n.a.	n.a	n.a
1934	n.a	n.a	n.a
1935	120	c.30	n.a
1936	1100	c.60	n.a
1937	1550	c.50	n.a
1938	2745	236	n.a
1939	3178	322	n.a
1940	2688	226	37
1941	1647	107	c.40
1942	1654	87	n.a
1943	2692	116	c.50
1944	7585	961	n.a
1945	8100	1367	599
1946	5491	894	323
1947	12018	1855	602
1948	12226	4184	914
1949	n.a	4811	1063
1950	10767	2826	1122
1951	13786	3230	1813
1952	14819	4067	2430
1953	13555	3717	2406
1954	14182	3141	2451

from 450 in 1930 to 1,550 in 1939 (Seccombe 1983, 8). The British agent in Manama actively pushed for more recruitment from the Raj to balance the Iranian immigrants who were considered (by both the empire and local Sunni rulers) a dangerous Shia minority. However, Indian migrants proved to be less "docile" than expected, leading strikes and social movements in the 1930s. In Kuwait, Qatar, and the Emirates, Indian immigrants came to work in the oil industry, developed businesses, and filled the nascent state administration. Immigration also came from more populated Arab countries, even if massive numbers of Arab immigrants only began arriving in the 1950s.

---

migration industry at times fostered indentured migration of women or family reunion to persuade workers to prolong their indenture. Therefore, while indentured migration was conceived as temporary, South Asian and Chinese migrants did settle in their host colonies (see Klotz, this volume).

With a larger population than other Gulf territories, Saudi Arabia could draw more from a local labor force. Although Saudi Arabia was never formally colonized, ARAMCO directly managed labor recruitment and immigrant management in the territorial enclaves that hosted the oil and gas companies (Vitalis 2006). The absence of British imperial ties to South Asia meant that ARAMCO did not prioritize laborers from the Raj. Instead, when ARAMCO recruiters opened a recruitment office in Asmara in 1944, they sought to attract skilled and semiskilled Italian workers from the former Italian colony of Eritrea, alongside Americans and low-skilled workers from Yemen and other neighboring countries. In the late 1940s and early 1950s, the rising cost of labor, coupled with Italian workers' strikes from 1945 to 1949 (over the terrible housing conditions in oil camps and unequal pay compared to American expatriates), resulted in the termination of labor ties with Eritrea. ARAMCO officials turned to neighboring Arab countries, opening labor recruitment offices in Khartoum and Aden (between 1945 and 1947) and Beirut and the Palestinian Territories (in 1949). After the strike by Italian workers in 1947, new migration corridors were also opened with India.

Finally, *imperial mobility* was organized along the lines of colonial rivalries. British political officers sought to limit the recruitment of American skilled expatriates to minimize US influence in the industry (Seccombe and Lawless 1986, 555). In 1945, pressure from the British political agent led to the transfer of the American staff of BAPCO in Bahrain to ARAMCO. US expatriates composed the entirety of an exponentially growing "senior staff" in the American-owned CASOC and later ARAMCO, with no British staff in the company's rosters up to the 1950s (see table 3.2).

Companies did more than explore, drill, and extract oil and gas, or select laborers from abroad. They also fully organized the travel and legal conditions of employment, and regulated, to a significant extent, the daily lives of migrant workers (Seccombe 1983). Even after indentured labor was formally suppressed, immigration remained organized as a contract-binding relationship, creating unfree labor and exploitative relations between employees and employers. This was implemented through legal instruments like the sponsorship system or *kafala*. Stemming from religious and commercial local laws (Hassan 1986), the *kafala* regulated social interactions and foreigners' protection in Gulf societies. With the rise of oil immigration, sponsors (*kufala'*) became crucial intermediaries in the management of the arrival and presence of foreigners (Al-Shehabi 2019). The *kafala* thus became part of a general "policing" of migration that articulated imperial transnational institutions and vernacular regulations. This hybrid institution essentially worked as a local replacement for imperial indentured migration.

Oil firms provided daily transportation, housing, and leisure for foreigners and locals alike. They also built entire cities and designed roads. The urban fabric of oil towns along the Gulf shores followed the designs of British planners and American engineers in collaboration with colonial bureaucrats and local rulers. The housing policies of oil firms shaped homes and livelihoods through formal and informal rules of segregation and social control. These policies enforced national hierarchies among workers, not only pay and working disparities but also differences in material aspects of daily life. In Qatar and Kuwait, workers were segregated in the urban spaces according to nationality and employment status (contracted workers, month or day laborers). British employees lived

Table 3.2. Number of British and US expatriates in foreign-owned oil companies in the Gulf, 1933–1950.

Year	BAPCO		KOC		PD (Q)		CASOC/ ARAMCO
	British	US	British	US	British	US	US
1933	8	19	n.a	n.a	n.a	n.a	n.a
1934	15	24	n.a	n.a	n.a	n.a	n.a
1935	26	49	n.a	n.a	n.a	n.a	c.30
1936	157	153	13	17	1	n.a	c.60
1937	308	126	13	2	n.a	n.a	c.50
1938	224	90	17	2	n.a	n.a	236
1939	191	67	16	2	n.a	n.a	322
1940	162	55	14	2	8	5	226
1941	158	34	14	2	8	5	107
1942	126	32	14	2	n.a	n.a	87
1943	111	39	3	n.a	n.a	n.a	116
1944	87	56	2	n.a	n.a	n.a	961
1945	313	183	9	6	n.a	n.a	1367
1946	324	90	50	11	36	2	894
1947	497	155	95	56	106	17	1855
1948	585	97	505	459	n.a	n.a	4184
1949	841	179	1293	193	180	20	1811
1950	860	87	546	52	153	16	2826

in expatriate bungalows while contract day laborers or migrants resided in workers' dormitories or mud huts or tents (Seccombe and Lawless 1986). Temporary housing was progressively replaced by permanent buildings and infrastructures (water, electricity, roads). The Ahmadi oil field in Kuwait was paired with a city designed by the Kuwait Oil Company that mostly housed foreign workers, while Kuwaitis resided in Kuwait City. British and American expatriates in Bahrain lived in Awali camp while Bahraini and Iranian low-skilled workers, who were generally contracted on a daily, weekly, or monthly basis, resided in Manama and were bused in daily by BAPCO (Seccombe 1983, 62). In the eastern provinces of Saudi Arabia, field camps around oil wells and pipelines turned into towns (Vitalis 2006). An oil town such as Dhahran or Ras Tannura comprised an "American city" with shops, bungalows, and movie theaters. These were juxtaposed next to dormitories, bunkhouses, and even shanty towns for Saudis and other foreigners. Whereas foreigners could find themselves trapped for months and even years in these enclaves, company buses took the Saudis, usually single young males, back to their hometowns for the vacation periods. While these housing and living conditions spurred fits of social unrest among migrant communities or locals, they did not affect the overall segregated and hierarchical patterns of migration governance. The urban patterns of segregation created by oil firms served as a matrix for postcolonial urbanization. Even though Gulf cities evolved differently among the monarchies, two common features are the fragmentation of urbanism and the segmentation of spaces in a context of public-private generated urban development (Elsheshtawy 2011). Governments and developers have historically colluded to produce a segregated urban planning marked by class, gender, and race segregation, as can be seen in the examples of Kuwait City (Al-Nakib 2016) and Riyadh (Al-Naim 2008; Menoret 2014). These colonial patterns of urban growth eventually came to be perceived as a spearhead of global modernity, which Yasser ElSheshtawy theorized as a form of "*dubaisation.*" Dubai, Singapore, and other Southern "global cities" (see Hirschman, this volume) offer a model of rapid growth, hypermodernity, concentration, and super-diversity (Vertovec 2007) enmeshed within spatial and social segregation and the political alienation of foreigners.

Ruling Hajj: *Imperial Control over the Islamic Pilgrimage*

Alongside oil-led migration that boomed in the 1930s, another type of mobility was a central challenge for both the material and symbolic imperial project: the circulation of Muslim pilgrims to and from Mecca and Medina.[7] Ottoman, Hashemite, European, and Saudi authorities have successively sought to control the Hijaz region in Western Arabia, a site of power and a hub of transnational cultural, economic, and political networks. In the nineteenth century, the development of modern (steam) transportation increased the number of pilgrims and generated migration around the pilgrimage economy and the development of the holy sites.

Increased mobility among pilgrims also led to the emergence of global health concerns. The British Empire—the first "Muslim power" of the nineteenth century—intensified imperial techniques of migration control, in cooperation with other colonial powers concerned with the management of Muslim pilgrims (France, Italy, the Ottoman Empire). The first global health regulations concerning mobility emerged as a result of the need to regulate pilgrims in the wake of the first global cholera pandemic in 1865.[8] Ottoman and European representatives and health officials met in Istanbul in 1866 to craft a "sanitary world order," resulting in pilgrims bearing the stigma of a "risky group" until the mid-twentieth century (Chiffoleau 2015, 161). Strictly enforced practices of control included issuing passports, organizing transportation and housing, instituting health controls, enforcing mandatory vaccination and quarantine measures, as well as training pilgrims in pilgrimage rituals. These forms of organized mobility by the colonial state led to the emergence of identification techniques and bureaucratic control. Since

---

7 Performing *Hajj*—an annually fixed pilgrimage to Mecca during the last month of the Islamic calendar—is one of the five pillars of Islam, and thus a religious obligation for believers. The *Umrah* is a "smaller" and more flexible version of the pilgrimage; it is optional and can be performed any time during the year.

8 In 1865, around 90,000 pilgrims were stricken (one third of them died) in the Hijaz, and the disease spread to Africa, Europe, and North America (Low 2008).

the holy sites were forbidden to non-Muslims, state management was enforced mostly by Muslim brokers and administrators, with minimal involvement from British officials (Slight 2015).

The poorest pilgrims from the "sending regions" of India who stayed on as beggars in the Hijaz were repatriated at the Raj's expense (Slight 2015, chap. 3). During the same period, interimperial cooperation developed to manage flows of pilgrims: convoys mixed Nigerians with subjects from "Afrique Occidentale Française," flows from Singapore combined pilgrims from British Malaya and Dutch-controlled Indonesia (Chantre 2018).

After King Abdelaziz al Saud conquered Hejaz in 1926, and thus the two holy sites of Islam, with the support of Great Britain, he sought to capture the political dividends of the pilgrimage. Claiming to provide a safer and better-organized Hajj for Muslims, he maintained the sanitary and political management designed by the Ottoman, Hashemite, and British authorities who had previously controlled the Hajj. In the 1950s, the Saudi monarchy began to massively invest oil revenues into pilgrimage infrastructures and policies to control pilgrims. The number of pilgrims jumped from around 100,000 in the 1950s to 700,000 in the 1970s (Tagliacozzo and Toorawa 2016, 132). The Saudi regime promoted an official discourse around the ruling family's destiny as "custodian of the two holy mosques" (the title was formally adopted by King Fahd in 1986), using the religious lexicon to build the country's national identity (Ménoret 2003). The management of pilgrims and religious mobility from the Muslim world became even more central to both domestic and international politics after the Islamic revolution in Iran and attempted coup in Mecca in 1979.

Postcolonial Migration Regime and Regional Interdependence: Oil, Migration, and Pan-Arab Politics, 1960s–1990

The postcolonial migration regime from the 1960s to the 1990s was characterized by the combination of the legacy of colonial institutions with the emancipatory dynamics of regional migration interdependence (Hollifield 1992b, 579). In the wake of the second oil boom, a "migration boom" from neighboring Arab countries occurred. Arab immigration was rooted in regional and international politics of independence—the push for regional integration and Arab unity (see also Tsourapas, this volume). As Gulf economies became increasingly dependent upon oil revenues and foreign labor, migration regimes relied upon regional interdependence between the Arab labor-exporting countries and the oil monarchies (Thiollet 2011). After the decolonization of the former British colonies and the emancipation of Saudi Arabia from American colonization by proxy, therefore, migration systems had a dual dependence upon oil revenues and foreign labor.

Figure 3.1 illustrates the strong correlation between oil prices and migration rates from 1973 onward, keeping in mind that the oil sector largely drove the overall growth of other economic sectors (construction, services, etc.).[9] In the late 1950s and the 1960s, labor immigration started increasing in the GCC states with small native populations

---

9   The number of immigrants minus the number of emigrants over a period of four years, divided by the population of the receiving country over that period. It is expressed as average annual net number of migrants per 1,000 population.

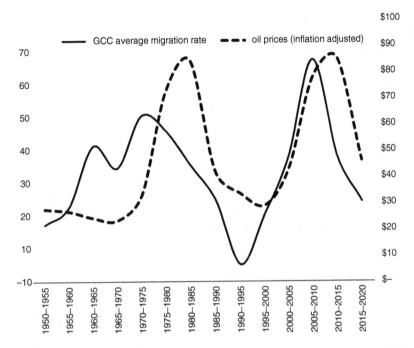

Figure 3.1.   Average migration rate (per 1,000 population) from 1950–2015 for the six GCC countries and oil prices.

(Kuwait, Qatar, the UAE) as oil prices were kept artificially low by British and American oil companies. The 1973 nationalization of oil companies and the creation of OPEC established political control over the oil and gas supply and trading prices by the Gulf states, leading to a sharp price increase. This political emancipation generated the first "oil boom," which was correlated with a sharp increase in migration rates. In the 1970s, foreigners—mainly coming from other Arab countries, India, and Pakistan—comprised 72 percent of the labor force in the Gulf monarchies. In the 1980s, the Middle East had become the largest migrant labor market in history. In 1985, the total workforce in the Gulf was 7.1 million, of which 5.5 million were foreigners (Birks, Seccombe, and Sinclair 1988, 267). The oil price shock of 1986 led to an economic dip and a large outflow of migrants (as well as a sharp drop in overall migration rates). The trough of this trend was reached with the 1991 Gulf War, resulting in hundreds of thousands of migrants departing or being deported from Kuwait and Saudi Arabia. In the late 1990s, economic diversification kicked off in Dubai and in a more limited fashion in Bahrain (Fasano and Iqbal 2003). The demand for foreign labor in the service economy matched that from the oil and gas sectors. This "second migration boom" ended with the 2011 Arab Springs, which led to a downturn in migration rates. The temporal variations in migration rates echo the fluctuations of energy markets and economic dynamics but also register political shocks and dynamics.

In spite of the structural dependence of Gulf states upon oil, migration flows varied in their composition across countries and across time. In the 1970s, some authors claim that 88 percent of immigrants in the Gulf hailed from Arab countries (Choucri 1986, 253).

Importing Arab immigrants was a kind of "migration as diplomacy" (Thiollet 2011) by Gulf governments, who were otherwise minor players in Pan-Arab politics. The circulation of workers from populated Arab countries to labor-demanding oil economies contributed to the dynamics of regional cooperation (Beaugé and Roussillon 1988; Fargues 2000; Thiollet 2017). Arab migration was both a direct consequence and an accelerator of regional integration (see Tsourapas, this volume). It was encouraged by GCC states through formal and informal migration or asylum policies. No formal agreement was ever concluded regarding the numerous Egyptian immigrants in the Gulf, yet Nasser and Sadat promoted emigration for political and economic reasons (Tsourapas 2018b, 59–127). State-facilitated migration processes and private entrepreneurs and migrant networks fed chain migration through recruitment of kin and fellow citizens. Strong ethnic economies emerged for Arab immigrants in semi- and high-skilled jobs, supported by the comparative advantage of a shared language and cultural environment. Fluency in Arabic, for instance, allowed Egyptian and Jordanian-Palestinian teachers and professors to migrate since their degrees were easily recognized by Gulf schools and academia.

Asylum seekers were also included in the overall circulation of Arab workers as "migrants": after 1949 and increasingly so after the Six-Day (1967) and Yom Kippur (1973) Wars, Palestinians were able to enter and settle in most GCC states, although they did not enjoy refugee status under international or regional conventions (like the Casablanca Protocol, signed by the League of Arab States in 1965). Eritrean refugees were granted similar privileges during the Eritrean War of Independence (1962–91), gaining access to residence permits and labor markets in Saudi Arabia based on a royal decree but without formal protection (Thiollet 2011, 110 et seq.).

In the 1980s, however, the composition of immigration flows began to change. The number of Indian and Pakistani immigrants increased. New nationalities also appeared: South Korean contractors in the construction sector and Southeast Asian immigrants in the service sector. Variations in migrant origins are noticeable in Saudi Arabia, and Qatar retained a large proportion of Arab immigrants, notably Yemenis and Egyptians, whereas smaller Gulf countries saw their historical link with former British colonies strengthened by new Asian immigration flows. Overall, Asian immigrants had come to "replace" Arab workers across similar skill categories and sectors (figure 3.2).[10]

This shift to South and then Southeast Asian immigration is usually explained by economic drivers: as oil revenues declined in the 1980s (table 3.3), Asian workers were often said to be "cheaper" (Naufal 2014). Scholars, however, stress the importance of political factors behind the rapid shift in the composition of immigration: Asian migrants were supposedly less likely to integrate and more easily controlled by governments and social actors than Arab nationals (Choucri 1986; Humphrey, Charbit, and Palat 1991). Historian John Chalcraft hypothesizes that in the 1950s and 1960s, migration "was an element in a serious challenge to the rule of beleaguered monarchs" and "formed an important element in oppositional [domestic] assemblages," whereas from the 1970s to the 2000s, it became an "adjunct rather than a challenge to the resurgent power of patrimonial ruling

---

10   Andrej Kapiszewski (2006) documented the "De-Arabization of the Labour Market" in a widely used report, "Arab versus Asian Migrants in the GCC," for the UN Population Division.

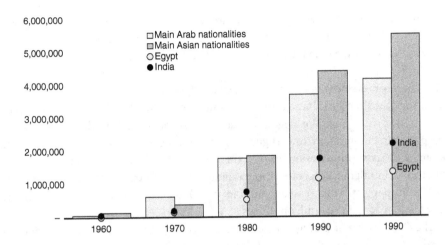

Figure 3.2. Evolution of the composition of immigration to the Gulf by main Arab and Asian nationalities.

Table 3.3. Number and share of immigrants in each GCC country by main groups of origin in 1985.

		Arab	South Asian	Southeast Asian	Other	TOTAL
Bahrain	Stocks	7,600	70,900	10,700	7,700	96,900
	share	8%	73%	11%	8%	100%
Kuwait	Stocks	252,900	242,700	31,200	17,100	543,900
	share	47%	45%	6%	3%	100%
Oman	Stocks	20,900	280,800	4,600	7,800	314,100
	share	7%	89%	2%	3%	100%
Qatar	Stocks	16,400	46,200	4,000	4,100	70,700
	share	23%	65%	6%	6%	100%
Saudi Arabia	Stocks	1,154,200	1,126,300	968,400	273,800	3,522,700
	share	33%	32%	27%	8%	100%
UAE	Stocks	95,500	447,700	25,000	30,300	598,500
	share	16%	75%	4%	5%	100%
TOTAL	Stocks	**1,547,500**	**2,214,600**	**1,043,900**	**340,800**	**5,146,800**
	share	**30%**	**43%**	**20%**	**7%**	**100%**

Source: Birks, Seccombe, and Sinclair 1988, 274.

families" (Chalcraft 2010, 3). In the 1980s, the shift in the origin countries of migrants could also be linked to the imperative of preventing the settlement and integration of foreign workers and their families. Concerns for cultural security as well as regime survival thus drove the selection of immigrants: to preserve monarchical rule, Gulf states came to consider Arab-speaking teachers who had staffed Gulf schools and universities as an army of foreign educators with potentially threatening socialist or antimonarchical ideas. However, rather than a revolutionary shift from Arab to Asian immigration, the changes observed are path-dependent on the colonial migration patterns described earlier.

Migration Regimes since the 1990s: The Quest for Migration Control

From the 1990s onward, immigration continued to grow, albeit irregularly. The early 1990s started with one of the biggest migration crises ever experienced worldwide and a sharp drop in immigration flows (figure 3.1). The 2000s gave way to a "second migration boom," with mass immigration flows in the UAE and Saudi Arabia. As table 3.4 shows, the stock of immigrants increased more rapidly across countries in the early 2000s. The immigrant population increased from 8 to 10 million from 1990 to 2000, jumping to 20 million in 2010 and 25 million in 2015.

The composition of immigrant stocks continued to change across the 1990s and enacted again the former colonial interdependence between South Asia and the Gulf. New migration corridors also emerged with Southeast Asian sending countries. This second migration boom saw Pakistani taxi drivers replace Egyptians and Iraqis, Indian IT specialists coming in large numbers, Filipino rather than Australian nurses, maids from Indonesia rather than Eritrea or Ethiopia, and Chinese companies stepping into the construction sector (United Nations, Department of Economic and Social Affairs 2017b). In the 2000s, the introduction of English as a teaching language alongside Arabic at the secondary and tertiary levels in the UAE, Kuwait, and Qatar led to Indian and Pakistani teachers and professors replacing Arab ones.

Migration diplomacy became geared toward diversifying labor imports in order to reduce the dependence upon sending countries and lower the risk of hosting large, politically active foreign communities. This diversification strategy was only partially effective, eventually leading to a new polarization in the Gulf migration systems: South and Southeast Asia became the main source of immigrants in the region (figures 3.3 and 3.4) and new sectoral dependencies began to emerge for low-skilled and highly skilled jobs. In 2015, Indians were the largest expatriate community in the UAE and Qatar. In the early 2000s, most Indian workers in the Gulf were unskilled or semiskilled workers, but around 20 percent were white-collar and 10 percent were professionals (Ministry of External Affairs, India 2015).

Table 3.4. Immigrant stocks in the GCC.

	Bahrain	Kuwait	Oman	Qatar	Saudi Arabia	UAE	TOTAL
1990	173,212	1,074,391	304,000	309,753	4,998,445	1,306,574	8,166,375
1995	205,979	921,954	539,643	361,673	5,122,702	1,824,118	8,976,069
2000	239,361	1,127,640	623,608	359,697	5,263,387	2,446,675	10,060,368
2005	404,018	1,333,327	666,160	646,026	6,501,819	3,281,036	12,832,386
2010	657,856	1,871,537	816,221	1,456,413	8,429,956	7,316,611	20,548,594
2015	704,137	2,866,136	1,844,978	1,687,640	10,185,945	8,095,126	25,383,962

Source: United Nations, Department of Economic and Social Affairs 2017b.

	Number of Immigrants	Share of Total Immigrant Population (%)
India	8,181,319	32.2
Bangladesh	2,808,582	11.1
Pakistan	2,791,934	11.0
Egypt	2,374,997	9.4
Indonesia	1,789,508	7.0
Philippines	1,507,837	5.9
Yemen	871,375	3.4
Syrian Arab Republic	689,975	2.7
Sri Lanka	654,027	2.6
Nepal	602,692	2.4
Sudan	538,690	2.1
Jordan	463,851	1.8
Afghanistan	376,790	1.5
Myanmar	202,720	0.8
Lebanon	193 020	0.8
Ethiopia	138 123	0.5

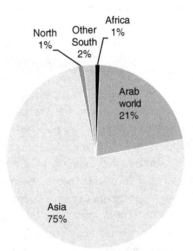

Figure 3.3. Main migrant communities by nationalities and regions of origin in the GCC in 2015.

Source: United Nations, Department of Economic and Social Affairs 2015.

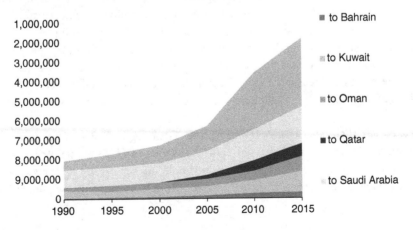

Figure 3.4. Evolution of the number of Indian immigrants to the Gulf countries, 1990–2015.

Source: United Nations, Department of Economic and Social Affairs 2017b.

From the 1990s onward, Gulf governments sought to better control migration flows and foreigners—including Muslim pilgrims. This signaled a "sovereign turn" in Gulf migration governance (Thiollet 2019, 18 et seq.): not only did migration politics become a "hot" issue in times of political crises (1991 and 2011), but Gulf governments also adopted migration and labor market policies that empowered state-led agencies and public bureaucracies at the expense of firms and intermediaries that traditionally operated as brokers of labor migration. States began to exercise stricter control over firms, recruiting agencies, and other market actors.

The 1991 Gulf War sent shockwaves through Gulf governments and Gulf societies, heavily affecting the economies of the monarchies and creating deep insecurity. Migrants frightened by the Iraqi invasion left Kuwait in large numbers. This migrant flight revealed the dependence upon foreign labor in Kuwait and other Gulf states—some sectors of Kuwait's economy became paralyzed by the labor shortage. Secondly, and more structurally, Arab immigrants who were well connected to locals and to larger regional cultural and political networks had come to be seen throughout the 1970s and 1980s as a growing threat to local rulers (Chalcraft 2011; Thiollet 2015).

Governments thus started to openly use various means of coercive and retaliatory policies to heighten control over immigration flows, resorting to the surveillance and occasional repression of foreign residents. If selected deportation had already existed in the 1950s, it became a major instrument of retaliatory diplomacy (Thiollet 2019, 10) in ways that have been studied in other countries around the Mediterranean (Tsourapas 2018a). In 1991, the Kuwaiti government deployed retaliatory policies toward Palestinian migrants because of the Palestinian Liberation Organization's support of Saddam Hussein. Residence permits were canceled or not renewed, state-owned firms laid off Palestinian employees, and Palestinians who had left the country before the invasion were not permitted to return. Yemenis in Saudi Arabia—the main expatriate community in the country, accounting for 27 percent of the labor force in 1990—also faced deportation in retaliation for the tacit support granted to Saddam Hussein by Yemeni president Ali Abdallah Saleh. Approximately one million Yemeni immigrants were sent home after residency procedures were tightened. In 2013, in the wake of the Arab Springs and the democratization movement in Yemen, a large deportation movement once again affected the Yemeni community in Saudi Arabia. Yemenis were the targets of choice (together with Ethiopians) in the "correction" campaigns launched against irregular immigrants—about 600,000 Yemenis were expelled between 2013 and 2014. Yemeni nationals who remained came under acute police surveillance, especially in Jeddah and Yemeni-Saudi border cities. A democratizing and later Houthi-led Yemen posed a serious security threat to Riyadh: the Houthi rebellion in 2013 was supported by Iran, Saudi Arabia's main competitor for regional hegemony in the Middle East. The kingdom started a war on Yemeni soil in 2015 and began targeting the large and long-settled Yemeni diaspora with mass deportations.

The Quest for Migration Control: Managing Gulf-Asian Migration Interdependence
Migration interdependence between Gulf monarchies and Asian sending countries has led to both increased multilateral cooperation and diplomatic tensions. The Abu Dhabi Dialogue, initiated in 2008 to "improve the governance of labour migration in

the Asia-Gulf corridor" through "non-binding regional consultative processes," was organized under the auspices of the International Organization of Migration (IOM) and International Labour Organization (ILO).[11] International NGOs increasingly pressed for legal norms to be adopted on migrant rights (Human Rights Watch 2010, 2014, 2015). Diplomatic struggles between sending and receiving countries became more frequent and were in many cases linked to negotiations on setting up a minimum wage for foreigners in the Gulf. Migrant wage levels are a key variable in determining the amount of remittances sent to countries of origin, many of whom depend heavily on these transfers. In the 2000s, the Gulf rapidly became the largest source of wealth transfer to Asian countries: out of a total of 98 billion USD in remittances, 72 billion USD came from the Gulf (World Bank 2016).[12] Remittances offer a tangible measure of migration interdependence (as shown in the introduction of this volume), and they are central to the bilateral negotiations and arm wrestling between Asian and Gulf governments. Asian sending states are eager to secure emigration channels and remittances but are also concerned about the security of migrants. They started to use "migration bans" against Gulf monarchies to retaliate against migrant abuses and to pressure Gulf governments into improving working conditions and raising wages. In 2011 Indonesia protested the beheading of an Indonesian maid by announcing an emigration ban on female domestic workers to Saudi Arabia. The Saudi government retaliated by banning all labor migration from Indonesia. Similar campaigns were launched by the Philippines against Saudi Arabia in 2012 and Kuwait in 2016. Nepal banned female migration to the Gulf in 2012, and the Indian government forbids the emigration of female workers under thirty years of age. These diplomatic struggles often pit the defense of the civil and labor rights of migrants in the Gulf to wage negotiations by sending countries. In 2016 the murder of a Filipino maid in Kuwait led the Philippines to threaten a ban on the emigration of domestic workers, which was averted only through the Kuwaiti Parliament setting a minimum wage for Filipino maids (State of Kuwait 2016).

The Quest for Migration Control: Leveraging Pilgrims

The quest for migration control in Saudi Arabia and across Muslim countries also included reforms in the management of Hajj and Umrah pilgrimages for both international and domestic migrants.[13] There were around 1.3 million international pilgrims for the Hajj in the late 1990s, a figure rising to 1.8 million in 2019; a further 600,000 "internal pilgrims" were recorded inside Saudi Arabia.[14] Performers of Umrah rose to 11.5 million internal pilgrims in 2018 and 6.7 million foreigners.[15] With over 20 million

---

11 See the official website: http://abudhabidialogue.org.ae/about-abu-dhabi-dialogue

12 Official remittances from the GCC to the Philippines rocketed from almost zero to over 3 billion USD between 1990 and 2011 (Bangko Sentral Ng Pilipinas 2017).

13 See note 7 above.

14 General Authority for Statistics, Saudi Arabia, https://www.stats.gov.sa/en/28

15 General Authority for Statistics for Hajj, https://www.stats.gov.sa/en/28; https://www.stats.gov.sa/sites/default/files/umrah_statistics_bulletin_2018_en.pdf

visitors from within and outside the country, mass circulation implicates both international and internal politics. As migration control progressively became a public concern and settling in Saudi Arabia began to require a preestablished work contract, *Hajj* and *Umrah* became the main entry mechanisms for "overstaying" pilgrims. The historically blurred boundaries among traveler, merchant, and pilgrim have progressively morphed into rigid categories of state-led migration management as official discourse (and *ad hoc* visas) now strictly differentiate between "foreign workers" and Muslim "pilgrims."

In 1987 Saudi Arabia and the Organization of the Islamic Conference (OIC) introduced a quota system to strictly control, by nationality, the annual number of pilgrims.[16] In 2013 quotas were drastically reduced (–20 percent for foreigners, –50 percent for Saudis) under the pretext of the renovation of the holy sites but more pointedly for political concerns (the Arab Springs). The quota system leads to unequal access, granting Muslims from non-Muslim countries more opportunities to perform the pilgrimage than citizens of Muslim countries. Furthermore, quotas vary by nationality, with various African nationals banned over Ebola fears (Sierra Leone, Guinea, and Liberia from 2014 to 2016 and the Democratic Republic of the Congo in 2019). Stricter control over the pilgrimage dovetails with an attempt to more strictly control migration, a process that culminated in labor market and migration reforms that took place in the 2010s.

Illiberal Migration States in the Gulf

Migration governance in the Gulf today is made up of intertwined interventions of states, markets, and social actors, including employers, recruiters, brokers and sponsors, and families and migrants themselves at the domestic and international levels. The role of the state increased significantly in the 1990s, bringing to light a new type of "migration state." This section first discusses the structural features of migration governance in rentier monarchies by introducing the notion of "migration rentiers." It then explores how formal and informal institutions shape segmented labor markets and organize an overarching regime of differential exclusion by managing immigrant lives in segregated environments and exclusionary contexts.

Migration Rentiers: The Gulf Model of Migration Governance

Gulf countries have among the highest ratios of migrants to natives in the world: half of the region's residents are migrants. Despite the abrupt historical variations discussed above, Gulf migration rates have always stayed above 10 percent (except during the 1991 Gulf War), a much higher rate than high-immigrant countries like the United States (between 1 and 6 percent) and Canada (between 2 and 8 percent). This reflects the "demographic imbalance" that scholars and public officials have identified (Al-Shehabi 2014). For labor markets, this "imbalance" created migration dependency (Thiollet 2019) corresponding to the oil dependence of rentier economies. As shown in table 3.5, foreigners account for 40 percent of the overall population in contemporary Bahrain, Oman, and

---

16   A thousand pilgrims annually per one million in population for each Muslim country. For non-Muslim countries more generous and *ad hoc* ratios are negotiated annually.

Table 3.5. Number and proportion of nationals and nonnationals in the Gulf based upon the latest official statistics published by each government (compilation by author).

Country (year, source)	Nationals		Immigrants		Total Population
Bahrain (2017, eGovernment Authority)	677,506	45%	823,610	55%	1,501,116
Qatar (data available from QSA for total population through 2010 census results for total population; for migrant population through Labour Force Survey and ESCWA-UN report on World Migration Stocks for Migrant Population)	243,267	14%	1,456,168	86%	1,699,435
Oman (2013, midyear estimates by NCSI)	2,172,002	56%	1,683,204	44%	3,855,206
Kuwait (2011, Public Authority for Civil Information, PACI)	1,258,254	31%	2,781,191	69%	4,039,445
United Arab Emirates (2010, National Bureau of Statistics)	947,997	11%	7,316,073	89%	8,264,070
Saudi Arabia (2017, Population Characteristics Survey, General Authority for Statistics)	20,408,362	63%	12,143,974	37%	32,552,336
Total GCC	25,707,388	50%	26,204,220	50%	51,911,608

Saudi Arabia; the figure is between 70 and 90 percent for Qatar, Kuwait, and the UAE. Two categories can be formed when combining migration and rentier characteristics: sparsely populated countries that are extremely dependent upon oil and gas revenue (UAE, Qatar, Kuwait) are *extreme* rentier states, while larger societies that are less dependent upon oil and gas revenue (Saudi Arabia, Oman, Bahrain) are *middling* rentier states (Herb 2014).

Migration governance in the Gulf involves various private and public institutions. On the one hand, state policies and public authorities historically delineated a legal context preventing naturalization and integration and, more recently, worked to control the labor market by nationalizing key industries or firms. Since the 1990s, migrants have been held in a state of temporariness by restrictive legal measures and coercive practices like mass deportation. These policies impact livelihoods but do not seem to prevent all foreigners from settling, as several qualitative studies have shown (Thiollet 2010; Thiollet and Assaf 2020; Vora 2013). On the other hand, private actors from the migration industry, local labor markets, and intermediaries shape highly segmented labor markets and enforce intersectional hierarchies between migrants and nationals and between migrant groups themselves. These tactics are not specific to the Gulf; they can be observed in advanced economies like Germany (Constant and Massey 2005) and across the EU (Felbo-Kolding, Leschke, and Spreckelsen 2019) as a key feature of the domestic governance of immigrants. In the Gulf, though, these measures create particularly strong boundaries between both locals and foreigners since they are reinforced by state policies. However, the private-public dichotomy does not fully capture Gulf migration governance, which hybridizes authoritarian state-based monarchical rule with patronage networks channeled both by ethnic kinship (tribes and extended family or *ʿâ'ila*) and by trading families. Ruling elites also maintain their authority thanks to state policies using tax-exemption and welfare policies, combined with ideological and religious control and occasional repression (Al-Naqeeb 1990; Ayubi 1996; Chaudhry 1997; Luciani and Salamé 1988; Ross 2001; Thiollet 2015). Reforms starting in the 1990s have formally "brought the state in" migration governance through policing practices that reinforce discrimination between migrants and nationals and among migrants. These political changes illustrate the workings of *illiberal* migration states, in parallel to *liberal* migration states in Western contexts (Hollifield 2004).

Even if political arrangements and power configurations among tribal elites, ruling dynasties, and important merchant families vary across Gulf countries and have evolved over time, the Gulf states share common traits as migration rentiers, creating a "Gulf model" of migration governance (Thiollet 2017, 22).[17]

The first common feature is the overarching differential or segmented exclusion of migrants.[18] States uphold regimes of exclusionary citizenship with almost no access to naturalization. They also formally and informally discriminate between migrants and nonmigrants in housing regulations and access to social welfare programs and public services. Migrants are "excluded essentials" (Okruhlik 1999): exploited as workers, useful as consumers, but formally excluded from rentier polities.

The second characteristic of the Gulf model is the paradoxical existence of cosmo-politan dynamics within exclusionary contexts. Gulf societies are characterized by super-diversity (Vertovec 2007) due to the significant numbers of migrants shaping the environments and social relations of Gulf cities (Thiollet and Assaf 2020). In the UAE, for instance, public records on residence permits indicate that "a third of the total non-citizen population has lived in the UAE for over ten years" (Lori 2012, 19). In Saudi Arabia, one quarter of the nonresident population was not of "working age," indicating a large number of migrant families in the kingdom (Thiollet 2014). As ethnographers who have studied the daily lives and identities of migrants in the region have noted (Le Renard 2016; Lori 2019; Thiollet and Assaf 2020; Vora 2013; Walsh 2014), there are tensions between exclusion and incorporation, belonging and alienation.

The third feature of the Gulf model is that immigrants are kept "in check," as anthro-pologist Anh Nga Longva (1999) explained, not only by state policies but also by social institutions (like the sponsorship system) that regulate the labor market and also shape the lives, practices, and cultures of the Gulf urban environment. The sponsorship system, or *kafala*, is a central institution of Gulf migration governance. It ties the legal presence of foreigners and their access to the labor market to a local sponsor (in exchange for a fee), establishing a legal bond of dependence, exploitation, protection, and hierarchy within and beyond the labor market. Similar intermediaries in migration governance in other societies across history have been found to create social linkages between foreigners and

---

17   See, for Saudi Arabia, Chaudhry 1997 and Hertog 2011; for Kuwait, Herb 2014.

18   Exclusionary politics targeting immigrants also mesh with multiple vectors of segmentation and exclusion for locals along tribal, ethic, religious, or sectarian and gender identities within countries.

locals but also to foster exploitation (Bosma, van Nederveen Meerkerk, and Sarkar 2013; Harney 1979). The *kafala* system can be described as a way for states to delegate migration control to citizens (Thiollet 2019, 21). Foreign entrepreneurs, themselves sponsored by locals, can also be sponsors (*kafil,* pl. *kufala'*) of fellow countrymen or other foreign nationals. In the 1980s, the *kafala* evolved from being mostly managed and controlled by individual employers to being connected to large recruitment companies; this weakened whatever social solidarities the system generated and opened up the system to mass exploitative practices (Beaugé 1986). The *kafala* works as a rent-seeking behavior (SaadEddin 1982) within oil rentier polities, resulting in what I call "migration rentierism" as nationals and the national economy sustain their livelihoods and wealth by extracting financial resources from migrants. The system is also a means to manifest the political ascendancy of citizens, a numerical minority in most GCC countries, over foreigners.

Human rights activists and scholars have specifically criticized the *kafala* as a mechanism to exploit migrants, a form of quasi-slavery, or as a system extracting a financial rent from the labor of migrant workers. But governments have also criticized the system for weakening state control over immigrants rather than enhancing it; this happens because labor regulation is delegated to social intermediaries (AFP 2016; Khan and Harroff-Tavel 2011). Gulf governments began trying to reform the *kafala* system in the 1990s, but those reforms have had little success after meeting much resistance from within Gulf societies. When Qatar and Bahrain sought to replace the *kafala* with stricter public policing of migration and immigrants, there was strong resistance from citizens and the business sector that benefits financially and socially from a system that maintains foreigners in a position of subaltern dependency (Diop, Johnston, and Le 2015; Lori 2012). The anti-*kafala* coalition brings together strange bedfellows (Tichenor 2008). The system itself results in ambivalent outcomes in highly segmented societies where informal (and formal) processes of inclusion and exclusion have major impacts on migrant rights and lives (Thiollet and Assaf 2020; Vora and Koch 2015).

Labor Market Segmentation

Gulf labor markets are strongly segmented between the public and private sectors, with public policies tending to reinforce the segmentation along the lines of migration rentierism. Rentier states have not only distributed the dividends of oil wealth to citizens through public spending and social benefits but have also used employment policies to buy loyalty from citizens. Even during British colonial rule in the Persian Gulf and American domination by proxy in Saudi Arabia, local rulers sought to secure employment for locals in the nascent oil industry through "nationality clauses" in concession agreements. In the 1990s, nationals were employed in large numbers in the public sector. Putting citizens on the state payroll extended clientelism far beyond royal families and major business allies. These nationalization (*tawteen*) policies shifted the historical labor market segmentation between migrants and nonmigrants across sectors: nationals who were predominantly in the private sector prior to the 1990s started to staff state bureaucracies while foreign workers were progressively banned from obtaining public employment. Migrant workers now mostly work in the private sector, where nationals are underrepresented, if not quasi-absent (see table 3.6). To correct this, governments

Table 3.6.   Share of nationals and nonnationals in the private-sector labor force (%) based upon official statistics published by each government (compilation by author).

Country (year)	Nationals	Nonnationals
Bahrain (2014)	16.2	83.8
Kuwait (2015)	4.1	95.9
Oman (2014)	10.9	89.1
Saudi Arabia (2017)	24.7	75.3
Qatar (2012)	0.7	99.3
United Arab Emirates (2007)	3.7	96.3

have tried to employ more nationals in the public sector through a second round of nationalization policies in the 2000s and 2010s.[19]

States have sought to replace foreign workers in the medium and long run. Starting in 2011 Saudi Arabia launched programs to decrease the number of expatriates in private firms (*Nitaqat*) and provide wage subsidies (*Taqat*) for nationals in private companies. In the Emirates, nationals employed by private companies are entitled by law to the same social security benefits as workers in government firms or offices; they also receive additional benefits through the *Absher* program—an app that allows citizens and residents of Saudi Arabia to access various government services. Gulf governments have also increased taxes on foreign labor by raising the fees for residence permits (*Iqama*) or making changes in work permits or sponsors. Companies that fail to meet the required nationalization of their staff are fined. The policies taken across countries to tackle the nationals-expat wage gap and changing labor market dynamics combine economic incentives with financial and legal constraints. In Saudi Arabia, for instance, the government tops up the salaries of nationals to lower the economic motivation to hire "cheaper" foreign workers. While these policies have not been remarkably successful in integrating locals into the private sector (Hertog 2014), they yield political benefits, having managed, for instance, to dampen the revolutionary fervor among nationals during the Arab Springs (Thiollet 2015).

Beyond formal public regulations, semiformal and informal dynamics driven by private actors and institutions also shape the dynamics of segmentation in Gulf labor markets. As in most labor markets, nationals tend to earn more than foreigners for the same job (Portes and Zhou 1993). In the Gulf, wages also vary for different groups of migrant workers according to nationality. While these inequalities tend to be particularly visible for low-skilled and care workers, they can also be seen in skilled labor. A regional survey shows that "Westerners" earn more than "Arabs," who in turn earn more than "Asians," even in clerical and managerial posts.[20]

---

19   For Bahrain, see Louer 2008.

20   In 2017, a retail bank manager, for instance, earned an average monthly wage of $8,918 if he/she were "Arab," $6,846 if he/she were "Asian," and $10,747 if he/she were "Westerner" (Gulf Business 2017).

The informal labor market plays an important role in migration governance in the Gulf economies. Even if the share of the shadow economy and informal employment seems to be much lower in GCC than other MENA (Middle East/North Africa) countries, informal or semiformal employment is not negligible (Chen and Harvey 2017) and mostly concerns foreign workers.[21] The difficulty lies in estimating a phenomenon that by design is meant to be hidden and for which governments have poor or inaccurate data (de Bel-Air 2017). However, amnesty and deportations campaigns carried in the GCC states since 2010 provide some information on irregular migration and employment. In Saudi Arabia, for instance, a "correction campaign" against irregular immigration in 2013 unveiled, out of a total population of around 10 million foreign residents, around 5 million "irregular situations," including 1 million workers registered as "runaways" by the Ministry of Labor (Thiollet 2015). These numbers highlight the size and economic importance of irregular migration and employment. Irregular employment in the Gulf primarily concerns low-skilled workers, particularly women in domestic service (Fargues and Shah 2017). Rather than "unauthorized entry," irregular migration is mostly about unauthorized residence or work status. Until recent labor market and migration reforms, illicit or semiformal employment was largely tolerated. The unofficial category of "free visas" is a good example of that. Migrant brokers trading work visas bring immigrants into the country and sponsor them but do not employ them, which means that migrants are "free" to find and change jobs, provided that they continue to pay their *kafil* a fee for sponsoring them. Free visas are legally sold by recruitment agencies in both countries of origin and host countries, but as soon as a holder chooses to change jobs he or she may face deportation. The free-visa holder's legal status is a gray zone where arbitrary enforcement, negotiations, and power relations rule. The labor regulations and laws adopted to better control migrant workers that target these informal practices paradoxically "produced" irregularity (Frantz 2018): the rigidity of the *kafala* system created incentives to escape control and enhanced the appeal of the "free-worker." Such practices within the informal or semiformal labor market provide flexibility and lower employment costs for both workers and employers (Dito 2015).

Diversity and Differential Exclusion

Migration governance has historically differentiated between types of migrants based on class (Cohen 1988; Van Hear 2014), creating regimes of differential *inclusion* in Western immigration countries, with skilled and well-off immigrants having more rights than poor and less skilled ones (De Genova 2017; Könönen 2018). In the Gulf exclusionary context, migration governance organizes differential *exclusion* based on class and origin,

---

21   The average size of the shadow economy (as share of the GDP) in the MENA region was around 30 percent in the 1990s (Schneider, Buehn, and Montenegro 2010) and tended to be on the rise in the 2000s and 2010s (Schneider and Medina 2018), but compared to non-GCC economics, the Gulf displays lower undeclared outputs as share of the GDP and much lower labor informality in GCC countries, as proxied by the share of the labor force not contributing to social security: 6.4 percent for the Gulf vs. 67 percent for non-GCC countries (Angel-Urdinola and Tanabe 2012, 2).

creating varied access for Western, Asian, Arab, or African immigrants to labor markets and, in some instances, public services. Since the 1990s, governments have adopted class-based migration policies—in which income determines rights to residence, whether family reunification is allowed, or even access to public services—that seem to lower the impact of migration diplomacy observed in previous historical periods. From around the same time, most GCC countries began to limit the duration of stay for unskilled foreigners while granting long-term residence to the wealthiest, "tiering" residency rights in a way that reinforces social and economic inequalities (Jamal 2015).[22] Kuwait caps family reunion based on income (Government of Kuwait 1992) and the parliament has discussed, since the 1980s, limiting the duration of stay for immigrants (Stanton Russell 1989). The UAE imposes a six-year limit on duration of stay for all migrants while exempting wealthy "expatriates" who own private estates or invest in the Emirates and specific categories of highly skilled professionals and their families, to whom long-term visas and residence rights (5 or 10 years) became accessible in 2019 without *kufala'* (General Directorate of Residency and Foreigners Affairs 2019). Family reunification is only open to wealthy immigrants in the Emirates. In Saudi Arabia a residence cap for unskilled workers led to the introduction of a flat fee on migrant workers' dependents in 2015 and 2017, directly hindering family reunification for low-wage migrants. If most industrialized countries have a form of financial discrimination to residency rights, the Gulf monarchies push that to the extreme by preventing long-term settlement except for the wealthiest. In this way, the process results in "precarious non-citizenship" (Goldring and Landolt 2013).

When it comes to labor rights, a number of international organizations (including the ILO), major NGOs (like Human Rights Watch), and some voices from within GCC countries started in the 2000s to press for greater recognition of the rights of migrant workers and their families (Fakkar 2009). International pressure, coupled with the desire of GCC states to raise their global profile, led to the adoption of a series of labor reforms in the 1990s (Thiollet 2019, 10). These included such measures as limiting maximum working hours, mandatory insurance, capping recruitment fees, and in some places a minimum wage. At the same time, these reforms institutionalized inequality by excluding nearly 3.5 million domestic workers from mainstream labor laws. This legal gap, together with the power given to employers and sponsors of domestic labor, has created an institutional and material basis for exploitation. Delay, nonpayment or underpayment of wages, retention of passports for coercive purposes, and a lack of social insurance and access to health care are frequent occurrences for low-skilled workers (Gardner et al. 2013). These wrongs are rarely redressed by the authorities or the courts (Thiollet 2019, 18). In the construction sector, unskilled workers are housed in remote "labor camps," with no transportation available except for company buses that only go from the dormitory to the work site and back (Bruslé 2012).

---

22   Micro-ethnographies on Sri Lankan maids (Gamburd 1995), construction workers in Qatar (Gardner et al. 2013), Indian middle-class migrants in Dubai (Vora 2013), and British expatriates in the UAE (Walsh 2014) document how social conditions and livelihoods of immigrants may vary.

While the urban environment of Gulf cities is extremely diverse, offering venues and spaces for intergroup encounters, it is also subject to intersectional policing, with gender, ethnic, and class determining access to public spaces (streets, squares, corniche) and leisure spaces such as shopping malls (Thiollet 2010). These formal and informal practices of policing and segregation exerted by recruiters, employers, real estate agents, police, and private security guards put into force a form of illiberal migration governance based on hierarchy, segregation, and discrimination.

If the migration patterns observed in the Gulf appear grounded in extremely specific socioeconomic and political orders of rentier monarchies, this chapter has aimed to show that they are also part of broader trends of migration politics and shape global trends of migration governance.

In recent years, migration governance has been immersed in seemingly contradictory trends across levels and actors: norms diffusion and international advocacy push for labor rights while domestic conditions restrict their implementation; internal politics prompt openness to immigration while migration diplomacy determines the selection of immigrants and enforces the high turnover of foreign workers; domestic policies and everyday practices limit the agency of most immigrants while providing formal rights to some; labor markets and social dynamics at the micro-level challenge state-led migration control. Gulf migration governance invites us to think beyond liberalism and the "liberal paradox" (Hollifield 1992a). In the Gulf, rather than market-driven openness to immigration and political closure vis-à-vis immigrants, government employers and private brokers work together to organize mass immigration in an exclusionary context.

Yet the illiberal practices and policies observed in the Gulf also feature in liberal democracies in Europe and North America: as recent empirical studies show, the gap between business and government preferences (Peters 2015) or between public opinion and migration policy (Morales, Pilet, and Ruedin 2015) has shrunk, leading to converging anti-immigrant policies and practices. The Gulf thus illustrates the relevance of illiberal migration governance. These illiberal "modes of governing" (Gamlen and Marsh 2011, xiii), which include practices that sometimes betray policies on paper, are not regime dependent, as can be seen in such cases as Tunisia and Morocco (Natter 2018), India (see Sadiq, this volume), Japan and Korea (see Chung, this volume) or even recent political developments in Western Europe and North America (see Hollifield, this volume). The coexistence of liberal and illiberal policies and practices, in cases like emigration and diaspora management (Glasius 2018), can be seen in the management of immigration across political regimes. Security concerns increasingly tend to drive migration governance within and between countries (Adamson 2006; Choucri 2002; Rudolph 2003; Weiner 1993). Global migration might be increasingly managed globally on hierarchical grounds that shape the right to move and settle. Skill and class discrimination fuel the global competition for talent, resulting in visa and citizenship policies favoring wealthier migrants (Mau 2010; Shachar and Hirschl 2014). This trend contradicts the liberal convergence hypothesis (Cornelius, Martin, and Hollifield 1994; Hollifield 1992a), which assumes that migration management is progressively underpinned by rights. Large-N comparative policy indexes do not include the Gulf countries (de Haas, Natter, and Vezzoli 2018), but they confirm the (re)structuring of global migration governance through intersectional hierarchies. The place of the Gulf states in the global political dynamics of migration is therefore unambiguous: while outliers, Gulf monarchies offer a magnifying lens to observe illiberal migration governance at work in the rest of the world.

References

Abel, Guy J., and Nikola Sander. 2014. "Quantifying Global International Migration Flows." *Science* 343(6178): 1520.

Adamson, Fiona B. 2006. "Crossing Borders: International Migration and National Security." *International Security* 31(1): 165–99.

AFP. 2016. "Qatar Abolishes 'Kafala' Labor System." *Arab News*. http://www.arabnews.com/node/1023416/middle-east (accessed January 22, 2018).

Al-Naim, Mashary. 2008. "Riyadh: A City of Institutional Architecture." In *The Evolving Arab City: Tradition, Modernity and Urban Development*, edited by Yasser Elsheshtawy, 118–51. London: Routledge.

Al-Nakib, Farah. 2016. *Kuwait Transformed: A History of Oil and Urban Life*. Stanford, CA: Stanford University Press.

Al-Naqeeb, Khaldoun Nassan. 1990. *Society and State in the Gulf and Arab Peninsula*. London: Routledge.

Al-Shehabi, Omar. 2014. *Sukân Al-Kharijî: Mazhahar al Khilal Wa al-Yât al Muhajiha [Population of the Gulf: Manifestations of imbalance and mechanisms to confront it]*. Maktaba Aafaq. Kuwait. http://www.df.ae/forum/view.php?id=40 (accessed September 7, 2018).

———. 2019. "Policing Labour in Empire: The Modern Origins of the Kafala Sponsorship System in the Gulf Arab States." *British Journal of Middle Eastern Studies*. https://doi.org/10.1080/13530194.2019.1580183

Angel-Urdinola, Diego, and Kimie Tanabe. 2012. *Micro-Determinants of Informal Employment in The Middle East and North Africa Region*. Washington, DC: World Bank Group. Working Paper. http://documents1.worldbank.org/curated/en/843621468275089806/pdf/665940NWP00PUB0Box365795B0S PDP01201.pdf

Assaf, Laure. 2017. "Arab Youths of Abu Dhabi: Status Categories, Urban Sociability and the Shaping of Subjectivities in the United Arab Emirates." PhD diss., Paris Ouest Nanterre.

Ayubi, Nazih N. 1996. *Over-Stating the Arab State: Politics and Society in the Middle East*. London: I. B. Tauris.

Bangko Sentral Ng Pilipinas. 2017. "Statistical Information." *Bangko Sentral Ng Pilipinas*. http://www.bsp.gov.ph/statistics/efs_ext3.asp (accessed October 16, 2017).

Beaugé, Gilbert. 1986. "La kafala: Un système de gestion transitoire de la main d'œuvre et du capital dans les pays du Golfe" [The kafala: A system for transitory management of labour force and capital in the Gulf countries]. *Revue Européenne des Migrations Internationales* 2(1): 109–22.

Beaugé, Gilbert, and Alain Roussillon, eds. 1988. *Le Migrant et Son Double: Migration et Unité Arabe*. Paris: Publisud.

Beine, Michel, et al. 2016. "Comparing Immigration Policies: An Overview from the IMPALA Database." *International Migration Review* 50(4): 827–63.

de Bel-Air, Françoise. 2017. "Irregular Migration in the Gulf States: What Data Reveal and What They Conceal." In *Skilful Survivals: Irregular Migration to the Gulf*, edited by Philippe Fargues and Nasra M Shah. Gulf Labour Markets and Migration Programme and Gulf Research Center (GRC), 33–56. http://gulfmigration.org/media/pubs/book/GLMM%20-%20IM%20Volume%20-%20Complete.pdf

Betts, Alexander, and Gil Loescher, eds. 2011. *Refugees in International Relations*. Oxford: Oxford University Press.

Birks, J. S., I. J. Seccombe, and C. A. Sinclair. 1988. "Labour Migration in the Arab Gulf States: Patterns, Trends and Prospects." *International Migration* 26(3): 267–86.

Bjerre, Liv, Marc Helbling, Friederike Römer, and Malisa Zobel. 2015. "Conceptualizing and Measuring Immigration Policies: A Comparative Perspective." *International Migration Review* 49(3): 555–600.

Bosma, Ulbe, Elise van Nederveen Meerkerk, and Aditya Sarkar, eds. 2013. *Mediating Labour Worldwide: Labour Intermediation Nineteenth and Twentieth Centuries*, special issue, *International Review of Social History* 20. Cambridge University Press. www.cambridge.org/fr/academic/subjects/history/social-and-population-history/mediating-labour-worldwide-labour-intermediation-nineteenth-and-twentieth-centuries (accessed September 10, 2018).

Brettell, Caroline, and James Hollifield, eds. 2008. *Migration Theory: Talking across Disciplines*, 2nd ed. New York: Routledge.

Bruslé, Tristan. 2012. "What Kind of Place Is This?. Daily Life, Privacy and the Inmate Metaphor in a Nepalese Workers' Labour Camp (Qatar)." *South Asia Multidisciplinary Academic Journal* 6. http://journals.openedition.org/samaj/3446 (accessed September 7, 2018).

Chalcraft, John. 2010. "Monarchy, Migration and Hegemony in the Arabian Peninsula." *Kuwait Programme on Development, Governance and Globalisation in the Gulf States* 12.

———. 2011. "Labour Protest and Hegemony in Egypt and the Arabian Peninsula." In *Social Movements in the Global South Dispossession, Development and Resistance*, edited by Sara C. Motta and Alf Gunvald Nilsen, 35–58. Basingstoke: Palgrave Macmillan.

Chantre, Luc. 2018. *Pèlerinages d'Empire: Une histoire européenne du pèlerinage à La Mecque*. Paris: Éditions de la Sorbonne.

Chaudhry, Kiren Aziz. 1997. *The Price of Wealth: Economies and Institutions in the Middle East*. Ithaca, NY: Cornell University Press.

Chen, Martha, and Jenna Harvey. 2017. *The Informal Economy in Arab Nations: A Comparative Perspective*. https://www.wiego.org/sites/default/files/resources/files/Informal-Economy-Arab-Countries-2017.pdf (accessed September 10, 2018).

Chiffoleau, Sylvia. 2015. *Le Voyage à La Mecque: Un Pélerinage Mondial En Terre d'Islam*. Paris: Belin.

Choucri, Nazli. 1986. "Asians in the Arab World: Labor Migration and Public Policy." *Middle Eastern Studies* 22(2): 252–73.

———. 2002. "Migration and Security: Some Key Linkages." *Journal of International Affairs* 56(1): 97–122.

Cohen, Robin. 1988. *The New Helots: Migrants in the International Division of Labour*. Farnham, Surrey: Gower.

Constant, Amelie, and Douglas S. Massey. 2005. "Labor Market Segmentation and the Earnings of German Guestworkers." *Population Research and Policy Review* 24(5): 489–512.

Cornelius, Wayne A., Philip L. Martin, and James Frank Hollifield, eds. 1994. *Controlling Immigration: A Global Perspective*. Stanford, CA: Stanford University Press.

De Genova, Nicholas, ed. 2017. *The Borders of "Europe": Autonomy of Migration, Tactics of Bordering*. Durham, NC: Duke University Press. https://read.dukeupress.edu/books/book/2363/ (accessed November 21, 2018).

Diop, Abdoulaye, Trevor Johnston, and Kien Trung Le. 2015. "Reform of the Kafâla System: A Survey Experiment from Qatar." *Journal of Arabian Studies* 5(2): 116–37.

Dito, Mohammed. 2015. "Kafala: Foundations of Migrant Exclusion in GCC Labour Markets." In *Transit States, Labour, Migration and Citizenship in the Gulf*, edited by Abdulhadi Khalaf, Omar AlShehabi, and Adam Hanieh, 79–100. London: Pluto Press. www.jstor.org/stable/j.ctt183p1j8.8 (accessed April 27, 2020).

Elsheshtawy, Yasser, ed. 2011. *The Evolving Arab City: Tradition, Modernity and Urban Development*. London: Routledge.

Errichiello, Gennaro. 2012. "Foreign Workforce in the Arab Gulf States (1930–1950): Migration Patterns and Nationality Clause." *International Migration Review* 46(2): 389–413.

Fakkar, Galal. 2009. "Labor Official Wants Laws Eased for Long-Term Expats." *Arab News.* www.arabnews.com/node/326135 (accessed May 7, 2019).

Fargues, Philippe. 2000. *Générations Arabes: L'alchimie Du Nombre.* Paris: Fayard.

Fargues, Philippe, and Françoise de Bel-Air. 2015. "Migration to the Gulf States: The Political Economy of Exceptionalism." In *Global Migration: Old Assumptions, New Dynamics*, edited by Diego Acosta Arcarazo and Anja Wiesbrock, 139–66. Santa Barbara, CA: Praeger.

Fargues, Philippe, and Nasra M Shah, eds. 2017. *Skilful Survivals: Irregular Migration to the Gulf.* Online. Gulf Labour Markets and Migration Programme and Gulf Research Center (GRC). http://gulfmigration.org/media/pubs/book/GLMM%20-%20IM%20Volume%20-%20Complete.pdf (accessed August 30, 2020).

Fasano, Ugo, and Zubair Iqbal. 2003. *GCC Countries: From Oil Dependence to Diversification.* Washington, DC: International Monetary Fund.

Felbo-Kolding, Jonas, Janine Leschke, and Thees F. Spreckelsen. 2019. "A Division of Labour? Labour Market Segmentation by Region of Origin: The Case of Intra-EU Migrants in the UK, Germany and Denmark." *Journal of Ethnic and Migration Studies* 45(15): 2820–43.

Frantz, Elizabeth. 2018. "How New Technologies Can Help—and Hurt—Migrant Workers." Open Society Foundations—Voices, November 7.

Gamburd, Michele Ruth. 1995. "Sri Lanka's 'Army of Housemaids': Control of Remittances and Gender Transformations." *Anthropologica* 37(1): 49.

Gamlen, Alan John, and Katharine Marsh, eds. 2011. *Migration and Global Governance.* Cheltenham: Elgar.

Gardner, Andrew, et al. 2013. "A Portrait of Low-Income Migrants in Contemporary Qatar." *Journal of Arabian Studies* 3(1): 1–17.

General Directorate of Residency and Foreigners Affairs. 2019. "Long-Term Residence Visas in the UAE." *Government.ae.* https://government.ae/en/information-and-services/visa-and-emirates-id/residence-visa/long-term-residence-visas-in-the-uae (accessed May 2, 2019).

Glasius, Marlies. 2018. "What Authoritarianism Is . . . and Is Not." *International Affairs* 54(3): 515–33.

Goldring, Luin, and Patricia Landolt, eds. 2013. *Producing and Negotiating Non-Citizenship: Precarious Legal Status in Canada.* Toronto: University of Toronto Press.

Government of Kuwait. 1992. "Kuwait al-yawm, jaridat rasmiyat al-hukuma dawla, Ministerial Order No. 2 of 1992, Vol. 38, No. 34."

Gulf Business. 2017. *Gulf Business Salary Survey.* UAE: Gulf Business. https://gulfbusiness.com/jobs/salary-survey/ (accessed September 2, 2018).

Haas, Hein, et al. 2019. "International Migration: Trends, Determinants, and Policy Effects." *Population and Development Review* 45(4): 885–922.

de Haas, Hein, Katharina Natter, and Simona Vezzoli. 2018. "Growing Restrictiveness or Changing Selection? The Nature and Evolution of Migration Policies." *International Migration Review* 52(2).

Harney, Robert F. 1979. "Montreal's King of Italian Labour: A Case Study of Padronism." *Labour / Le Travail* 4: 57.

Hassan, Ahmed 'Abdel Khaleq. 1986. *Al-kafala: Dirasa muqarana bayn al-qanun al-madani wa al-fiqh al-islami [The kafala: A comparative study between civil and Islamic law].* Cairo: Dar al-Hada.

Herb, Michael. 2014. *The Wages of Oil: Parliaments and Economic Development in Kuwait and the UAE.* Ithaca, NY: Cornell University Press.

Hertog, Steffen. 2011. *Princes, Brokers, and Bureaucrats: Oil and the State in Saudi Arabia.* Ithaca, NY: Cornell University Press.

———. 2014. *Arab Gulf States: An Assessment of Nationalisation Policies.* Badia Fiesolana, Italy: Gulf Labour Markets and Migration Programme. GLMM Research Paper. http://eprints.lse.ac.uk/57578/

Hollifield, James. 1992a. *Immigrants, Markets, and States: The Political Economy of Postwar Europe.* Cambridge, MA: Harvard University Press.

———. 1992b. "Migration and International Relations: Cooperation and Control in the European Community." *International Migration Review* 26(2): 568.

———. 2004. "The Emerging Migration State." *International Migration Review* 38(3): 885–912.

Human Rights Watch. 2010. "Middle East: End 'Sponsored' Gateway to Human Trafficking." www.hrw.org/ news/2010/06/14/middle-east-end-sponsored-gateway-human-trafficking (accessed May 3, 2019).

———. 2014. *"I Already Bought You": Abuse and Exploitation of Female Migrant Domestic Workers in the United Arab Emirates*. Washington, DC: Human Rights Watch. www.hrw.org/report/2014/10/22/i -already-bought-you/abuse-and-exploitation-female-migrant-domestic-workers-united (accessed May 3, 2019).

———. 2015. "Detained, Beaten, Deported: Saudi Abuses against Migrants during Mass Expulsions." https:// www.hrw.org/report/2015/05/10/detained-beaten-deported/saudi-abuses-against-migrants-during-mass -expulsions (accessed June 13, 2015).

Humphrey, Michael, Yves Charbit, and Madhavan Palat. 1991. "The Changing Role of Asian Labour Migration in the Middle East." *Revue Européenne des Migrations Internationales* 7(1): 45–63.

Jamal, Manal A. 2015. "The 'Tiering' of Citizenship and Residency and the 'Hierarchization' of Migrant Communities: The United Arab Emirates in Historical Context." *International Migration Review* 49(3): 601–32.

Kapiszewski, Andrej. 2006. *Arab versus Asian Migrant Workers in the GCC Countries*. Beirut: United Nations Secretariat.

Khalaf, 'Abd al-Hādī, Omar AlShehabi, and Adam Hanieh, eds. 2014. *Transit States: Labour, Migration and Citizenship in the Gulf*. London: Pluto Press.

Khan, Azfar, and Hélène Harroff-Tavel. 2011. "Reforming the 'Kafala': Challenges and Opportunities in Moving Forward." *Asian and Pacific Migration Journal* 20(3/4): 293–313.

Klotz, Audie. 2012. "South Africa as an Immigration State." *Politikon* 39(2): 189–208.

Könönen, Jukka. 2018. "Differential Inclusion of Non-Citizens in a Universalistic Welfare State." *Citizenship Studies* 22(1): 53–69.

Le Renard, Amélie. 2016. "'Ici, Il y a Les Français Français et Les Français Avec Origines': Reconfigurations Raciales Autour d'expériences de Dubaï." *Tracés* 30: 55–78.

Longuenesse, Elisabeth. 1985. "Les migrants dans la structure sociale des pays du Golfe." In *Migrations et changements sociaux dans l'Orient arabe*, edited by André Bourgey et al., 169–213, Presses de l'Ifpo. http:// books.openedition.org/ifpo/3357 (accessed January 2, 2020).

Longva, Anh Nga. 1999. "Keeping Migrant Workers in Check: The Kafala System in the Gulf." *Middle East Report* 211. https://merip.org/1999/06/keeping-migrant-workers-in-check/

———. 2005. "Neither Autocracy nor Democracy but Ethnocracy: Citizens, Expatriates, and the Socio-Political Regime in Kuwait." In *Monarchies and Nations: Globalisation and Identity in the Arab States of the Gulf*, edited by Paul Dresch and James P. Piscatori, 114–35. London: I.B. Tauris.

Lori, Noora. 2012. *Temporary Workers or Permanent Migrants? The Kafala System and Contestations over Residency in the Arab Gulf States*. Paris: Institut français des relations internationales (Ifri). Policy Papers. https://www.ifri.org/sites/default/files/atoms/files/notecmcnooralori1.pdf

———. 2019. *Offshore Citizens: Permanent Temporary Status in the Gulf*, 1st ed. Cambridge: Cambridge University Press. https://www.cambridge.org/core/product/identifier/9781108632560/type/book (accessed October 18, 2019).

Low, Michael Christopher. 2008. "Empire and the Hajj: Pilgrims, Plagues, and Pan-Islam under British Surveillance, 1865–1908." *International Journal of Middle East Studies* 40(2): 269–90.

Luciani, Giacomo, and Ghassane Salamé, eds. 1988. *The Politics of Arab Integration*. London: Croom Helm.

Mau, Steffen. 2010. "Mobility Citizenship, Inequality, and the Liberal State: The Case of Visa Policies." *International Political Sociology* 4(4): 339–61.

Ménoret, Pascal. 2003. *L'énigme saoudienne: les Saoudiens et le monde, 1744–2003*. Paris: Ed. la Découverte.

——. 2014. *Joyriding in Riyadh: Oil, Urbanism, and Road Revolt.* New York: Cambridge University Press.

Miller, Michael K., and Margaret E. Peters. 2018. "Restraining the Huddled Masses: Migration Policy and Autocratic Survival." *British Journal of Political Science*: 1–31.

Ministry of External Affairs, India. 2015. *Population of Overseas Indians.* New Delhi: Ministry of External Affairs, Government of India. www.mea.gov.in/images/pdf/3-population-overseas-indian.pdf (accessed February 7, 2017).

Mirilovic, Nikola. 2010. "The Politics of Immigration: Dictatorship, Development, and Defense." *Comparative Politics* 42(3): 273–92.

Morales, Laura, Jean-Benoit Pilet, and Didier Ruedin. 2015. "The Gap between Public Preferences and Policies on Immigration: A Comparative Examination of the Effect of Politicisation on Policy Congruence." *Journal of Ethnic and Migration Studies* 41(9): 1495–516.

Natter, Katharina. 2018. "Rethinking Immigration Policy Theory beyond 'Western Liberal Democracies.'" *Comparative Migration Studies* 6(1).

Naufal, George S. 2014. "The Economics of Migration in the Gulf Cooperation Council Countries." In *Handbook of the Economics of International Migration,* edited by Barry R. Chiswick and Paul W. Miller, 1597–640. http://search.ebscohost.com/login.aspx?direct=true&scope=site&db=nlebk&db=nlabk&AN=604665 (accessed April 8, 2019).

Ochonu, Moses E. 2014. *Colonialism by Proxy: Hausa Imperial Agents and Middle Belt Consciousness in Nigeria.* Bloomington: Indiana University Press.

Okruhlik, Gwenn. 1999. "Excluded Essentials: The Politics of Ethnicity, Oil and Citizenship in Saudi Arabia." In *The Global Color Line: Racial and Ethnic Inequality and Struggle from a Global Perspective,* Research in Politics and Society, edited by Pinar Batur-Vanderlippe, 215–36. Greenwich, CT: JAI Press.

Osterhammel, Jürgen, and Patrick Camiller. 2014. *The Transformation of the World: A Global History of the Nineteenth Century.* Princeton, NJ: Princeton University Press.

Peters, Margaret E. 2015. "Open Trade, Closed Borders Immigration in the Era of Globalization." *World Politics* 67(1): 114–54.

Portes, Alejandro, and Min Zhou. 1993. "The New Second Generation: Segmented Assimilation and Its Variants." *Annals of the American Academy of Political and Social Science* 530(1): 74–96.

Rosenblum, Marc R., and Daniel J. Tichenor. 2012. *The Oxford Handbook of the Politics of International Migration.* Oxford: Oxford University Press.

Ross, Michael L. 2001. "Does Oil Hinder Democracy?" *World Politics* 53(3): 325–61.

Rudolph, Christopher. 2003. "Security and the Political Economy of International Migration." *American Political Science Review* 97(4): 603–20.

Ruhs, Martin. 2017. *The Price of Rights: Regulating International Labor Migration.* http://dx.doi.org/10.23943/princeton/9780691132914.001.0001 (accessed January 23, 2019).

SaadEddin, Ibrahim. 1982. "Oil, Migration and the New Arab Social Order." In *Rich and Poor States in the Middle East: Egypt and the New Arab Order,* edited by Malcolm H. Kerr and al-Sayyid Yasin, 17–69. Boulder, CO: Westview Press; Cairo: American University in Cairo Press.

Schneider, Friderich, Andreas Buehn, and Claudio Montenegro. 2010. *Shadow Economies All over the World: New Estimates for 162 Countries from 1999 to 2007.* Working Paper. Washington, DC: World Bank Group. http://documents1.worldbank.org/curated/en/311991468037132740/pdf/WPS5356.pdf

Schneider, Friderich, and Leandro Medina. 2018. *Shadow Economies around the World: What Did We Learn over the Last 20 Years?* Washington, DC: IMF. Working Paper.

Seccombe, Ian J. 1983. "Labour Migration to the Arabian Gulf: Evolution and Characteristics 1920–1950." *Bulletin (British Society for Middle Eastern Studies)* 10(1): 3–20.

Seccombe, Ian J., and Richard Lawless. 1986. "Foreign Worker Dependence in the Gulf, and the International Oil Companies: 1910–50." *International Migration Review* 20(3): 548.

Shachar, Ayelet, and Ran Hirschl. 2014. "On Citizenship, States, and Markets." *Journal of Political Philosophy* 22(2): 231–57.

Shin, Adrian J. 2017. "Tyrants and Migrants: Authoritarian Immigration Policy." *Comparative Political Studies* 50(1): 14–40.

Slight, John. 2015. *The British Empire and the Hajj, 1865–1956.* Cambridge, MA: Harvard University Press.

Stanton Russell, Sharon. 1989. "Politics and Ideology in Migration Policy Formulation: The Case of Kuwait." *International Migration Review* 23(1): 24–47.

Stanton Russell, Sharon, and Muhammad Ali al-Ramadhan. 1994. "Kuwait's Migration Policy since the Gulf Crisis." *International Journal of Middle East Studies* 26(4): 569–87.

State of Kuwait. 2016. *Ministerial Order No. 2302 of 2016: On the Rules and Procedures of Enforcement of the Provisions of Kuwait Law No. 68/2015 Concerning Domestic Workers.* https://www.ilo.org/dyn/natlex/docs/ MONOGRAPH/106450/130598/F-1730342003/Rules%20of%20enforcement%20of%20Law%20No.%20 68%20of%202015%20on%20D.pdf (accessed May 9, 2019).

Tagliacozzo, Eric, and Shawkat M. Toorawa, eds. 2016. *The Hajj: Pilgrimage in Islam.* New York: Cambridge University Press.

Thiollet, Hélène. 2010. "Nationalisme d'Etat et nationalisme ordinaire en Arabie Saoudite: La nation saoudienne et ses immigrés" [State nationalism and banal nationalism in Saudi Arabia: The Saudi nation and its immigrants]. *Raisons politiques* 37(1): 89–101.

———. 2011. "Migration as Diplomacy: Labor Migrants, Refugees, and Arab Regional Politics in the Oil-Rich Countries." *International Labor and Working-Class History* 79(01): 103–21.

———. 2014. "Resilient Residents: Immigration and Migration Policy in Saudi Arabia." Presented at the Middle East Working Group Seminar Series, Florence. https://www.eui.eu/events/detail?eventid=101329 (accessed August 25, 2020).

———. 2015. "Migration et (contre)révolution dans le Golfe: Politiques migratoires et politiques de l'emploi en Arabie saoudite" [Migration and (counter)revolution in the Gulf: Migration and labor market policies in Saudi Arabia]. *Revue européenne des migrations internationales* 31(3/4): 121–43.

———. 2017. "Managing Transnational Labour in the Arab Gulf: External and Internal Dynamics of Migration Politics since the 1950s." In *The Transnational Middle East: People, Places, Borders*, International Political Economy of New Regionalisms series, edited by Leïla Vignal, 21–43. London: Routledge.

———. 2019. *Immigrants, Markets, Brokers and States: The Politics of Illiberal Migration Governance in the Arab Gulf.* Amsterdam: International Migration Institute. Working Paper.

Thiollet, Hélène, and Laure Assaf. 2020. "Cosmopolitanism in Exclusionary Contexts." *Population, Space and Place*: e2358.

Tichenor, Daniel J. 2008. "Strange Bedfellows: The Politics and Pathologies of Immigration Reform." *Labor: Studies in Working-Class History of the Americas* 5(2): 39–60.

Tsourapas, Gerasimos. 2018a. "Labor Migrants as Political Leverage: Migration Interdependence and Coercion in the Mediterranean." *International Studies Quarterly* 62(2): 383–95.

———. 2018b. *The Politics of Migration in Modern Egypt: Strategies for Regime Survival in Autocracies*, 1st ed. Cambridge: Cambridge University Press. https://www.cambridge.org/core/product/identifier/ 9781108630313/type/book (accessed February 18, 2019).

United Nations, Department of Economic and Social Affairs, Population Division. 2015. *World Population Prospects: The 2015 Revision, DVD Edition.* New York: United Nations Department of Economic and Social Affairs.

———. 2017a. *International Migrant Stock: The 2017 Revision.* New York: United Nations, Department of Economic and Social Affairs, Population Division. Dataset.

———. 2017b. *International Migration Report 2017.* New York: United Nations, Department of Economic and Social Affairs. http://www.un.org/en/development/desa/population/migration/publications/migrationre port/docs/MigrationReport2017.pdf (accessed January 21, 2018).

Van Hear, Nicholas. 2014. "Reconsidering Migration and Class." *International Migration Review* 48(1 Suppl): 100–121.

Vertovec, Steven. 2007. "Super-Diversity and Its Implications." *Ethnic and Racial Studies* 30(6): 1024–54.

Vitalis, Robert. 2006. *America's Kingdom: Mythmaking on the Saudi Oil Frontier.* Stanford, CA: Stanford University Press.

Vora, Neha. 2013. *Impossible Citizens: Dubai's Indian Diaspora.* Durham, NC: Duke University Press.

Vora, Neha, and Natalie Koch. 2015. "Everyday Inclusions: Rethinking Ethnocracy, Kafala, and Belonging in the Arabian Peninsula." *Studies in Ethnicity and Nationalism* 15(3): 540–52.

Walsh, Katie. 2014. "Placing Transnational Migrants through Comparative Research: British Migrant Belonging in Five GCC Cities—Placing Transnational Migrants through Comparative Research." *Population, Space and Place* 20(1): 1–17.

Weiner, Myron. 1986. "Labour Migration as Incipient Diaspora." In *Modern Diasporas in International Politics,* edited by Gabriel Sheffer, 43–74. London: Croom Helm.

———, ed. 1993. *International Migration and Security.* Boulder, CO: Westview Press.

World Bank. 2011. "Global Bilateral Migration Database." *World Bank.* https://datacatalog.worldbank.org/dataset/global-bilateral-migration-database (accessed April 9, 2019).

World Bank. 2016. *Migration and Remittances Factbook 2016.* Washington, DC: World Bank.

4 THE ILLIBERAL PARADOX AND THE POLITICS OF MIGRATION IN THE MIDDLE EAST

Gerasimos Tsourapas

THE MIDDLE EAST HAS BEEN at the forefront of global migration politics—Libya and the oil-producing states in the Persian Gulf have constituted key countries of destination for millions of migrants for over half a century while Egypt, Lebanon, and Morocco remain key countries of origin, with large diaspora communities across the world. At the same time, Southern and Eastern Mediterranean countries have become important transit states for migrant and refugee flows out of the Middle East in recent decades, most recently in the context of the Syrian Civil War and the ensuing refugee crisis. Yet the importance of the Middle East states in shaping contemporary migration flows contrasts with the lack of attention paid to these processes by scholars of international relations and comparative politics. The long tradition of excellent work on cross-border mobility in the Middle East within sociology (Ibrahim 1982), history (Chalcraft 2008; Robson 2017), anthropology (Sayigh 1979), demography (Fargues 2013), as well as economics (Birks and Sinclair 1982; Serageldin and World Bank 1983), has yet to be mirrored in work in political science, which remains dominated by a comparatively small number of single- and small-N case studies. A few notable exceptions aside (Halliday 1977; Choucri 1988; Brand 2006; Thiollet 2011; Norman 2020), the Middle East remains a complex yet underexplored region for scholars of international migration politics.

Taking these observations into account, this chapter serves a twin purpose. First, it introduces the reader to the history and politics of migration into, out of, and across the contemporary Middle East; in that sense, I aim to offer a critical overview of cross-border mobility that complements this volume's parallel chapters on Turkey (Adamson) and the Persian Gulf (Thiollet). The chapter's first part examines the historical evolution of migrants and refugees in the Middle East via a number of stages: initially, colonial and imperial exigencies shaped much of mobility throughout most of the region that constitutes the Middle East, leaving lingering legacies that continue to affect policy-making today. The rise of the modern nation-state in the post–World War I period of decolonization led to the emergence of *migration states* in the Middle East (Adamson and Tsourapas 2020; Sadiq and Tsourapas 2021; see generally Hollifield 2004), which governed population mobility through *colonial* and *postcolonial* migration governance regimes, marked by periods of high- and low-skilled migrant recruitment by host states within and outside the region.

Having established the broad framework of cross-border mobility patterns across the region, the chapter's second part demonstrates how a closer examination of Middle East migratory processes and distinct migration corridors sheds light on existing debates within the field. It adopts an interdisciplinary perspective that puts the works of Albert O. Hirschman (1978) and James F. Hollifield (2004) in conversation with each other, as well as with research on the international politics of autocratic rule. I identify, to paraphrase Hollifield, the emergence of an *illiberal paradox* across most Middle Eastern states' migration policy-making—namely, the contrast between the socioeconomic desire to allow mass emigration and the urge to maintain control over political dissent (Tsourapas 2019, 2020; cf. Natter 2018 for the concept's use in Middle East immigration politics). In other words, the socioeconomic benefits of allowing citizens' "exit" contrasted with the political risks of enabling their "voice" abroad. I draw on a range of case studies from across North Africa and the Middle East in order to detail how governments' attempts to resolve this illiberal paradox have arguably shaped the politics of migration in the Middle East across two levels. First, at the state level, I identify the emergence of *transnational authoritarianism,* namely any effort to prevent acts of political dissent against an authoritarian state by targeting one or more existing or potential members of its emigrant or diaspora communities. Second, at the regional and international levels, I examine the manipulation of *migration interdependence* (Hollifield 2004; Tsourapas 2018; Hollifield and Foley, this volume) via coercion, as interstate rivalry encompasses the abuse, or expulsion, of migrant workers. Overall, through both sections of the chapter, I aim to demonstrate the empirical richness as well as the analytic utility of the Middle East as a crucial region of study for the politics of global migration.

The Evolution of the Migration State in the Middle East

For the purposes of this analysis, I approach the Middle East and North Africa as encompassing the Arab world—thus, Egypt and North Africa, as well as the broader Levant region—and Israel. I do not examine Turkey and the countries of the Persian Gulf, which are discussed elsewhere in this volume. Broadly, the evolution of the Middle East migration system occurs over four time periods. The *colonial* period, encompassing the era of the Ottoman Empire and the colonial Mandate period that ended, roughly, in the years following the end of World War II, is characterized by a rather free circulation of movement within this broad region, as well as long-distance emigration to the Americas, Europe, and sub-Saharan Africa. It is also marked by waves of immigration into the region from Europe. The *postcolonial* period, from the late 1940s until the late 1960s, coincides with the rise of Arab nationalism, as cross-border population mobility is driven mainly by political rather than economic factors. The *oil boom* period, from the late 1960s until the early 1980s, is dominated by economically driven cross-border migratory flows, although national and regional politics continue to play an important role. Finally, the period of *de-Arabization*, from the 1980s to today, is characterized by an influx of Asian and sub-Saharan migrants and the rise of irregular migration, as well as increasing cooperation between Arab and European states. It is also shaped by exogenous shocks, such as the impact of COVID-19 on both labor and forced migration across the entire region.

A Middle East Migration and the Colonial Period

The history of the Middle East has always been associated with mobility. For historian Ibn Khaldun, the very creation of the Arab world was due to the movement of the Banu Hilal tribes from the Arabian Peninsula into Egypt and, subsequently, across North Africa during the eleventh century. Their victories over the Berber populations brought the Arabic language and the Islamic faith to the Maghreb and continued a long process of migration in the region that had existed ever since the introduction of Islam in seventh-century Mecca. Despite some restrictions put in place by the Ottoman Empire, merchants, nomads, clerks, and others would not hesitate to traverse the vast area of the Middle East (Hourani 2013). Modest population movements across the Muslim world persisted, notably in the historic region of the *bilād al-shām* (Syria, Lebanon, Palestine, and Jordan), in the Sinai Peninsula, in Cyrenaica, as well as in parts of the Arabian Peninsula (the Hejaz, Yemen, and Oman). This was particularly true with regard to the processes of the *Hajj*, the annual pilgrimage to Mecca that all adult Muslims must perform at least once in their lifetime. Caravans of tens of thousands of pilgrims would set out across the Middle East to Mecca along well-established routes, the *darb al-Hajj*. Many pilgrims never returned to their homelands, instead establishing their new homes across these routes.

Beyond religion, education was another reason for temporary, or permanent, migration. The *al-Azhar* University in Cairo, established in 970, has welcomed students of the Qur'an and Islamic law ever since. The founding of *Dar al-Ulum* in Cairo, a Training College for Teachers of Arabic, and a separate Teachers' Training College in 1886 substantially increased the number of students into Egypt (Matthews and Akrawi 1949; Tsourapas 2016). At the same time, Egyptian scholars and professionals traversed the region, primarily as teachers of Arabic, which earned Egypt the affectionate nickname *al-Shaqiqa al-Kubrá*, or the Big Sister of the Arab world. Egyptians were recruited to work in Kuwait's first two public schools, *al-Mubārakiyya and al-Aḥmadiyya*, from the mid-1930s onward and in Iraqi schools from 1936 onward. In fact, in the pre-1956 period, secondary school students across the Arab world would receive the *Tawjīhiyya*, the Egyptian Secondary School Certificate, upon graduation (Misnad 1985). Administrators and legal scholars were also sent abroad: one notable example is 'Abd al-Razzāq al-Sanhūrī, who had drafted the Egyptian Civil Code. Al-Sanhūrī traveled to Baghdad to found the city's School of Law in the mid-1930s, and drafted the Iraqi Civil Code in 1943 (Saleh 1979).

Meanwhile, the Levant (also referred to as the *Mashreq*, or the historical region of Syria now encompassing Lebanon, Jordan, Syria, Israel, Iraq, and Palestine) witnessed two particular types of mobility. One was the rise of emigration out of Mount Lebanon and Syria in the mid-nineteenth century, due to communal strife as well as deteriorating local economic conditions (Khater 2001). Waves of emigration from Lebanon continued throughout the twentieth century, particularly in the context of the Lebanese Civil War, creating a thriving Lebanese diaspora across the Americas and sub-Saharan Africa

(Pearlman 2013). Palestine witnessed successive waves of Jewish immigration, or *aliyot*, mainly out of the Russian Empire. Jews sought shelter from the waves of antisemitism in Europe and the frequent pogroms, but also to establish themselves in the Land of Israel. Although the Middle East would eventually come under the control of multiple European powers—the French in the Levant and the Maghreb; the British in Egypt and the Gulf; the Italians in Libya—broad patterns of colonial management of mobility emerged, namely an emphasis on security, policing, and population control.

Middle East Migration and the Postcolonial Period

A number of factors contributed to the rise of Arab nationalism in the Middle East in the interwar period, including the collapse of the Ottoman Empire, the failure to create a unified Arab state at the end of World War I, as well as the strengthening of colonial rule—either directly, in North Africa, or indirectly in terms of League of Nations Mandates in the Levant and Iraq. The continuing immigration of European Jews into the *Eretz Israel*, as per Zionist expectations, also triggered Arab nationalism that culminated in the 1948 Arab-Israeli War. Migration flows in this period are characterized by two monumental events: the Arab-Israeli conflict, particularly the 1948 and 1967 wars, and the rise to power of Arab nationalist forces—most prominently encapsulated in the figure of Egyptian president Gamal Abdel Nasser (1954–70).

The Arab-Israeli conflict has historically resulted in the largest migration movements among Arab populations, both directly and indirectly. In terms of its direct effects, Palestinian emigration to the West grew in light of their continuing struggle with the British authority over the influx of Jews who increasingly abandoned Europe in the aftermath of World War I. But it was the 1948 war and the creation of the Israeli state that resulted in the *Nakba*, or catastrophe, for the Arabs, as over 700,000 Palestinian Arabs fled violence, or were expelled from their homes. The United Nations Relief and Works Agency for Palestine Refugees in the Near East (UNRWA) was created in 1949 to provide relief to refugees in Jordan, Lebanon, Syria, the Gaza Strip, and the West Bank. It became even more important once the Six-Day War in 1967 created an additional 300,000 Palestinian refugees. The dire economic and political situation in the West Bank and the Gaza Strip contributed to continuing outflows of Palestinians, primarily across the Arab world.

Indirectly, Zionist and, since 1948, Israeli policies provided the impetus for Arab states to demonstrate their solidarity with the Palestinians through organized expulsions of their Jewish populations. As with other parts of the global South, the emergence of nationalizing migration states in the Middle East led to the use of forced expulsions to create ethno-religious homogeneity (Adamson and Tsourapas 2020). The Jewish exodus from Arab states was a continuing, violent process of "unmixing" populations that had coexisted for centuries. In North Africa, Jews faced organized persecution following 1948, which led to their exodus either to Israel or to European countries, notably France. Their population in Libya, Morocco, Tunisia, and Algeria diminished from hundreds of thousands in each state to a few hundred by the end of the twentieth century. Similarly, Nasser's ascent to power in Egypt and, in particular, the aftermath of the 1956 Suez Crisis led to organized expulsions of Egyptian Jews. In some cases, Israel was instrumental in organizing these movements, as in the 1950–51 exodus of Iraqi Jews *via Operation Ezra and Nehemiah*, or in the 1949–50 *Operation Magic Carpet* in Yemen. Through these two operations, approximately 120,000 Iraqi Jews and 49,000 Yemenite Jews were brought into Israel.

The forceful removal of European populations who had been living in the Middle East, particularly across North Africa and Egypt, was another key aspect of regional migration during the postcolonial era. Not unlike the 1922 Greek-Turkish population exchange that formed part of the creation of the Republic of Turkey, Arab nation-states encouraged—sometimes passively, sometimes more violently—the exodus of their European communities. The 1969 ousting of King Idris by Colonel Gaddafi in Libya instigated a process of expulsions for both Libya's Jewish and Italian communities, numbering some 37,000 and 20,000 citizens, respectively. Italians, in particular, were ordered to leave the country by October 7, 1970—a day that the regime would annually commemorate as the *Day of Revenge*. Most residents of French Algeria with European ancestry, some 800,000 *pied-noirs*, were evacuated in France after the country's 1962 independence. A similar fate awaited the Greek community of Egypt, which amounted to over 25,000 by the time of Nasser's ascent to power, but of whom roughly 7,000 remained by 1966. Italian Egyptians and Syrians also fled the country in this period.

The era of Arab nationalism also saw the emigration of thousands of political dissidents—from *ancien regime* royalists or communists to members of the Muslim Brotherhood. In Egypt, despite regime repression, hundreds of Muslim Brothers managed to flee to Saudi Arabia in this period (Kandil 2015, 32), Kuwait, Bahrain, or elsewhere—Yusuf al-Qaradawi, for instance, relocated to Qatar; 'Abd al-Latif Mikki fled to Syria (Kandil 2015, 65). Others, such as Sa'id Ramadan, 'Abd al-Hakim 'Abidin, Sa'd al-Din al-Walili, Muhammad Najub Juwayfil, and Kamil Isma'il, were accused of "treason to the [Egyptian] nation," stripped of their nationality while they were in Syria, and forbidden from returning to Egypt (Mitchell 1969, 141). In the Gulf, Palestinian migrants as well as high-skilled, leftists Egyptians were able to organize frequent protests and demonstrations.

But the political nature of cross-border migration in the Middle East during this period is best articulated in two broader conflicts, one involving the rivalry between conservative and revolutionary republics in the Arab world, or the *Arab Cold War*, and the rivalry between Egyptian and Israeli high-skilled professionals dispatched across sub-Saharan Africa. In this process of intra-Arab antagonism, the Egyptian regime was able to employ regional migration as an instrument of soft power partly given the massive developmental needs that the Arab world faced at the time. In particular, Egypt's secondment program (*niẓām al-i'āra li-l-khārij*) gradually became a main component of the Nasserite propaganda machine across the Arab world, together with a variety of other elements, from radio broadcasts of the *ṣawt al-'arab* (*Voice of the Arabs*), to the distribution of Egyptian newspapers abroad, as the literature has already identified, within the context of the "Arab Cold War" (James 2006; Kerr 1978). Nasser himself, in fact, made the connection between political influence and education by calling the *Voice of the Arabs* "an open university" that provided "education in national consciousness" (quoted in Abou-El-Fadl 2015, 232). A British report on Sudan details how "Egypt's cultural leadership in the Arab world is unrivalled and her present Government exploits it to the full in pursuit of political aims. Egyptian teachers are sent to the Sudan; Sudanese teachers are trained in Egypt" (British Foreign Office, TNA—FO 407/237, 1957).

In Africa, Egyptians were pitted against Israelis, as both countries aimed to sway the newly independent African states to their favor. According to the New York Times, "the Egyptians [made] themselves heard everywhere in Africa and play[ed] the part of self-chosen leaders" (March 1, 1956). Indeed, as Muhammad Hasanayn Haykal, a close advisor of Nasser, declared that same year: "Egypt must send selected missions of experts in science, religion, politics, economics, commerce and social services to aid the African peoples, to support them, to collaborate with them and light the path before them." Again, the foreign policy aspect is prominent, for two reasons: Egypt believed it stood to gain potential support at the United Nations from the newly independent African nations (Cremeans 1963), and perhaps more importantly, it aimed to battle the involvement of Israel in the continent. In 1965, Nasser wrote:

> The struggle of the Asian and African peoples is not waged in isolation from the struggle of the Arab nation. In addition to the responsibilities of the development of the African continent following its liberation call for gigantic efforts so that imperialism should not infiltrate and return to it under the pressure of underdevelopment or behind a deceptive mask, such as the Israeli mask, which imperialism tries actively to make use of in Africa. (Nasser 1966, 12)

Middle East Migration and the Oil Boom Period

By the late 1960s, a number of important events would contribute to the end of the postcolonial period in the politics of migration in the Middle East, including the Arabs' defeat in the Six-Day War with Israel in 1967, the death of Nasser in 1970, as well as the increasing concentration of wealth in the oil-producing states of the Gulf (as well as in Libya). The gap between oil producers and nonproducers in the Middle East widened even further following the 1973 Arab-Israeli War, in which an embargo on oil exports led to the quadrupling of oil prices. As wealth soared in Libya and the Gulf, labor migration across the Middle East assumed a new form, dominated by economic rather than political forces, as hundreds of thousands of Egyptians, Yemenis, and Jordanians pursued employment abroad (Seccombe 1985). At the same time, high-skilled Palestinians provided human capital for the entire region. The small numbers of migrants working on fishing and pearling in the Gulf gave way to thousands of workers in Bahrain, Kuwait, Qatar, Oman, Saudi Arabia, and the United Arab Emirates. These had numbered around 800,000 before the 1973 War; by 1974, they had reached roughly 4 million (table 4.1).

This is not to imply that all of these workers were employed in the oil industry; in fact, most of them worked in sectors that experienced a boost because of oil revenues, such as construction, services, or education. With the centrality of the Gulf as a work destination of young Muslims remaining undiminished to this day, migration has dramatically altered the population makeup of oil-producing countries: indicatively, only 9 percent of the United Arab Emirates' population is currently native born. Similarly, a number of smaller labor migration flows occurred elsewhere in the region, including cyclical labor migration of Syrian unskilled workers into Lebanon, as well as Sudanese workers

Table 4.1. Migration interdependence in the Middle East.

Country of Origin	Year	Professional and Technical (A-1)		Other Professional (A-2)		Subprofessional and Technical (B-1)		Other Subprofessional (B-2)		Semiskilled Office and Manual (C-1)		Semiskilled and Manual (C-2)		Unskilled (D)		Total	
		Number	Percent	Number	Percent	Number	Percent	Number	Percent	Number	Percent	Number	Percent	Number	Percent	Number	Percent
Egypt	1975	8,900	2.5%	27,200	7.7%	8,400	2.4%	19,300	5.5%	34,400	9.7%	63,500	18.0%	191,600	54.2%	353,300	100%
	1985	30,900	4.3%	73,200	10.3%	25,600	3.6%	58,700	8.2%	96,100	13.5%	86,600	12.2%	340,400	47.9%	711,500	100%
Jordan	1975	11,100	8.0%	26,800	19.3%	12,900	9.3%	16,500	11.9%	21,900	15.7%	8,900	6.4%	40,900	29.4%	139,000	100%
	1985	26,300	10.2%	52,400	20.3%	29,000	11.3%	41,900	16.3%	38,600	15.0%	20,900	8.1%	48,300	18.8%	257,400	100%
Lebanon	1975	4,400	15.4%	5,100	17.9%	2,900	10.2%	5,600	19.6%	5,700	20.0%	2,600	9.1%	2,200	7.8%	28,500	100%
	1985	13,900	19.8%	12,700	18.1%	9,600	13.6%	17,500	24.9%	10,000	14.2%	4,000	5.7%	2,600	3.7%	70,300	100%
Oman	1975	200	0.6%	200	0.6%	200	0.6%	600	1.9%	3,500	11.3%	7,100	23.0%	19,100	62.0%	30,900	100%
	1985	400	0.9%	400	0.9%	300	0.6%	900	2.0%	5,800	12.6%	17,600	38.3%	20,500	44.7%	45,900	100%
Sudan	1975	2,600	10.0%	3,100	11.9%	1,800	6.9%	3,300	12.7%	2,800	10.8%	4,200	16.1%	8,200	31.6%	26,000	100%
	1985	7,400	8.4%	10,100	11.5%	5,100	5.8%	10,600	12.0%	14,200	16.1%	21,800	24.8%	18,800	21.4%	88,000	100%
Syria	1975	2,200	5.8%	6,800	17.9%	2,000	5.3%	4,900	12.9%	6,900	18.2%	6,100	16.1%	9,100	23.8%	38,000	100%
	1985	7,000	7.3%	20,300	21.1%	6,300	6.6%	12,400	12.9%	13,400	13.9%	18,200	18.9%	18,400	19.3%	96,000	100%
Y.A.R.	1975	100	-	600	0.2%	200	0.1%	800	0.2%	28,100	8.6%	73,800	22.5%	224,800	68.4%	328,400	100%
	1985	300	-	1,500	0.4%	500	0.1%	2,000	0.5%	34,500	8.6%	96,400	24.0%	265,600	66.4%	400,800	100%
P.D.R.Y.	1975	400	0.9%	500	1.1%	400	0.9%	1,000	2.2%	27,000	58.7%	10,000	21.8%	6,600	14.4%	45,900	100%
	1985	1,200	1.4%	1,100	1.3%	900	1.1%	2,300	2.7%	36,700	43.4%	35,500	42.0%	6,800	8.1%	84,500	100%

Source: Serageldin and World Bank 1983, 93.

into Egypt. A significant migration corridor emerged between North Africa and Europe: taking advantage of the post-WWII economic reconstruction processes in Western Europe, thousands of Tunisians, Moroccans, and Algerians settled permanently in France, Belgium, and neighboring states, creating large diaspora communities.[1]

This is not to say that state politics retreated from migration management in the region; yet such politics were pursued according to national interest rather than anything else. North African states developed established institutions for monitoring the activities of their diasporas in Europe, the *amicales* (Brand 2006). Gaddafi's Libya repeatedly linked its immigration policy to its Arab foreign policy priorities, not hesitating to evict or mistreat Egyptian, Tunisian, or Palestinian immigrants in order to force respective political elites into specific policy shifts. Intra-Arab relations have equally been affected by the Palestinian exodus, with the events of Black September in 1970 that saw the expulsion of the Palestine Liberation Front from Jordan, and the Lebanese Civil War (1975–90) being two striking examples. Mirroring the Turkish state's Turkification policies toward its Kurdish minority, the Iraqi state engaged in forced internal migration processes of Yazidis and Kurds in northern Iraq—as part of broader Arabization campaigns—aiming to shift regional demographics in favor of Iraqi Arabs. A large number of Egyptian Christian Copts, which account for over 10 percent of the country's population, emigrated to the West from the early 1970s onward in response, at least partly, to the gradual domination of Islam in the public sphere. Middle East state policies would frequently include a sectarian dimension—Shi'a Muslim populations have frequently been the subject of forced removals in Iraq, Yemen, and elsewhere.

Middle East Migration and the De-Arabization Period

Finally, a long period of de-Arabization has characterized regional migration politics since the early 1980s, marked by an influx of Asian and sub-Saharan migrants and the rise of irregular migration, as well as increasing cooperation between Arab and European states. This is evident in shifting immigration policies across the Gulf states (see Sadiq and Thiollet, *this volume*), whose elites across the Gulf states are traditionally worried about the political effects of immigration within their states. As the Qatari minister of labor Abd al-Rahman al-Dirham stated:

> The question of foreign labor is of great concern. Our social customs are threatened by foreigners. The problem is not just in Qatar but also in other Gulf countries. We prefer it if we can get suitable people from Arab countries who can live in the Gulf area without changing it. (*Middle East Economic Digest [MEED]*, August 1982, 40)

Not surprisingly, the rise of PLO militant activism in the 1970s gradually resulted in the expulsion of Palestinian laborers. "Statistics show," Haddad argued, "that both Saudi Arabia and Kuwait reduced the recruitment of Palestinian laborers" after 1970, opting instead to employ "large numbers" of Egyptians who would not "function as a fifth column and eventually endanger the host countries" (Haddad 1987, 248). This led to the

---

1   This process had already begun in the 1960s, similar to Turkish emigration into Europe (see Adamson, this volume).

emergence of a new migration corridor in the region: since the late 1970s and, in particular, the 1979 takeover of the Grand Mosque in Mecca and the Iranian Revolution, workers from Southeast Asia have gradually replaced Arab labor as the most populous migrant group in the oil-exporting countries of the Gulf (Kapiszewski 2006; see also Sadiq, this volume). This was the result of both a continuous, large migratory wave out of Pakistan and Bangladesh, and the political decision to expel large numbers of Arab workers, particularly in the aftermath of the 1990–91 Gulf War. Believing that the Palestinian and Yemeni political leadership supported the Iraqi invasion of Kuwait, the Gulf states expelled roughly 800,000 Yemeni workers, while the vast majority of Palestinian migrants were also forced to leave Kuwait, where they had sought shelter in the aftermath of the 1948 and 1967 wars (Tsourapas 2015; Van Hear 1998). The regional instability of the early 1990s also led to the return of more than 700,000 Egyptians and roughly 200,000 Jordanians.

A similar process of de-Arabization occurred in Libya, where Gaddafi attracted an increasing number of sub-Saharan African immigrants into the country. From the early 1990s onward, Gaddafi became less interested in Arab unity and instead sought to spearhead closer ties among African states under pan-Africanism. This included the signing of a 1990 integration charter with Sudan and a 1994 agreement with Chad, as well as the 1998 creation of the Community of Sahel-Saharan States (CENSAD), which contained numerous objectives regarding the free movement of people. Gradually, Gaddafi used Libya's position as a host state for African labor to further his diplomatic openings toward African states (Tsourapas 2017; Charbit, this volume). While immigration had distinct economic advantages for the Libyan economy at the time, "the regime sought a leadership role in the international arena to counter its increasing isolation from Arab countries and the West" (Paoletti 2010, 86).

The oil-producing states' shift in their immigration policies away from the recruitment of Arab laborers produced two important results in the regional politics of migration. First, this created the impetus for the irregular migration of Arabs and sub-Saharan Africans through the Mediterranean into Europe. This phenomenon reached considerable proportions in the aftermath of the 2011 "Arab Spring" events. Second, this created the need for the involvement of non–Middle East states in the management of regional migration, namely the EU and EU member-states. Over the past few years, a number of Middle East states have taken advantage of their position as migrant-sending or migrant-transit states in order to sign "Mobility Partnerships" with the EU, such as Jordan, Morocco, and Tunisia (Collyer 2012), or to negotiate *ad hoc* agreements, such as the 2016 EU-Turkey deal (see Adamson, *this volume*). This has led to a renewed emphasis on the securitization of mobility in the region, compounded by a number of external shocks: the emergence of COVID-19 in 2020, for instance, has amplified efforts at migration controls, as states seek to minimize the spread of the virus via national lockdowns of varying degrees of intensity. At the same time, COVID-19 has led to mass waves of repatriation of migrant populations from oil-producing Arab countries (see Sadiq, *this volume*), a process whose long-term repercussions remain to be seen.

The Illiberal Paradox in Middle Eastern Migration Politics

The chapter's first section identified the various opportunities presented to Middle East states by the rise of international migration—from complementing nation-building strategies in the postcolonial period and attaining their developmental goals via labor emigration to European or oil-producing Arab states, to, more recently, drawing on their geopolitical position as refugee host states for economic aid from Western states and international organizations. In fact, scholars have identified how cross-border mobility might serve to strengthen authoritarian rule in the Middle East (Ahmed 2012; Tsourapas 2019). Yet the complexity of migrant and refugee flows arguably poses specific challenges to political elites across the Middle East as well. In the chapter's second part, I analyze Middle East migration through a political science lens that focuses on a twin challenge to authoritarian rule: the rise of diasporic activism and political mobilization outside the territorial limits of the sending state, and the manipulation of migration interdependence in coercive contexts of interstate rivalry. Both of these processes are linked to Middle East states attempts to resolve the *illiberal paradox*, as will be explained below.

James F. Hollifield (2004), examining immigration policy-making in Western Europe and North America, identified the existence of a "liberal paradox." On the one hand, states wish to encourage the free flow of immigrant labor for economic purposes; on the other hand, they seek to maintain immigration restrictions for political and security reasons. Contemporary migration states remain trapped in their need to balance economic and political exigencies: "[I]n order to maintain a competitive advantage, governments must keep their economies and societies open to trade, investment, and migration. But unlike goods, capital, and services, the movement of people involves greater political risks" (Hollifield 2004, 886–87). Notwithstanding its contribution to the literature politics of migration, the liberal paradox thesis focuses on policy-making across liberal democratic destination countries of the global North (Adamson and Tsourapas 2019b). Do countries of origin across the global South—in this case, Middle East autocracies—face a similar dilemma between maximizing economic gains and minimizing political and security risks from mass emigration? I argue for the existence of an *illiberal paradox* across authoritarian migration states, in which the trade-offs are different, but states continue making strategic choices with regard to regime durability: on the one hand, autocracies seek to control their borders and restrict emigration because of domestic political and security reasons—citizens' right to travel abroad comes into conflict with autocracies' wish to maintain order and eliminate dissent; on the other hand, autocracies wish to encourage emigration under an economic rationale that relies on free cross-border mobility to increase migrant remittances, lower unemployment, and address the pressures of overpopulation.

How do autocracies attempt to escape the illiberal paradox? For much of their history, authoritarian regimes tended to prioritize politics over economics by securitizing emigration at the border: the freedom to travel abroad was a privilege, rather than a right, for citizens of mercantilist regimes or, more recently, communist regimes. This securitization assumed a number of forms, from the creation of "blacklists" of political dissenters banned from traveling abroad to the denaturalization of nationals who emigrated without authorization—measures prevalent in much of the "Second" and "Third" Worlds (Messina 1994). Although autocracies continue to prioritize border controls today, mass migration has become more prevalent due to the rise of economic interdependence, technological advances, or more broadly, processes of globalization; at the same time, forced migration flows continue to rise across the world. Numerous autocracies—such as Turkey and Mexico—already had bilateral migration agreements with global North states for much of the twentieth century. Since the 1970s, a number of authoritarian regimes—including China and Egypt—espoused mass emigration while another such wave of liberalization occurred in the aftermath of the collapse of the Soviet Union. Arguably, the Democratic People's Republic of Korea is the only remaining authoritarian regime today that adheres to an isolationist policy that forbids emigration.

Although the shift toward mass emigration offers autocracies considerable material benefits, it does not automatically resolve the illiberal paradox. In fact, Albert Hirschman (1970, 1978) has identified the mutually exclusive processes of *exit* versus *voice*. In the context of migration politics, citizens who are dissatisfied with an existing polity can either protest against it—i.e., exercise voice—or emigrate—i.e., engage in exit (cf. Dowding et al. 2000). In recent years, work on transnationalism and diaspora mobilization demonstrates that Hirschman's binary is not clear-cut. Migrants are able to exercise their voice against authoritarian rule back home, as research on transnational advocacy networks and human rights issues also demonstrates (cf. Keck and Sikkink 2014). How do autocracies respond to the political and security risks generated by émigrés' voice? One possibility would be for them to return to the mercantilist and communist tradition of restricting mass emigration, but that would produce severe economic and political drawbacks in an era of global interconnectedness. In fact, recent trends suggest that autocracies are attempting to bypass the illiberal paradox altogether: they seek to reap the material benefits of free movement while ensuring that migrant and diaspora groups pose little political or security threat to their survival. The next section details the emergence of *transnational authoritarianism* and delineates the main types of transnational authoritarian practices that illustrate its workings.

The Rise of Transnational Authoritarianism

Governments' attempts to resolve the contradictions of the illiberal paradox have resulted in the development of a range of policies of *transnational authoritarianism*. This has distinct repercussions for Middle East states' practices toward their migrant and diaspora communities. First, autocracies extend a range of strategies of *transnational repression* toward their citizens abroad. Syrian authorities have systematically monitored the activities of expatriates abroad, including recording street demonstrations and other protests, as well as monitoring mobile phones and internet usage abroad (Amnesty International 2011). Other regimes also rely on their embassy and consular networks: in Egypt, where exiles have fled in a number of waves over the last seventy years (Dunne and Hamzawy 2019), the military regime employs its staff abroad for spying on the activities of its diaspora communities (cf. Aswany 2008). Beyond allegations of specific embassies reporting back to Cairo on citizens (Ahram Online 2016), embassy delegates and diplomats have frequently attended lectures, events, and exhibitions on Egypt—even academic conferences—in order to gather intelligence on speakers and attendees (Ramadan 2016). Libya has engaged in enforced disappearances of regime dissenters abroad (Tsourapas 2020), while Turkey frequently resorts to the coerced return of people suspected to be part of the Gülen movement (Öztürk and Taş 2020). Gulf countries often choose to threaten or punish their family members back home. When Mohammed al-Fazari, an Omani human rights defender and blogger, defied a travel ban and sought asylum in the United Kingdom, authorities targeted his family: in 2015, his brother was detained for three weeks without charge while, in 2017, al-Farazi's family was barred from traveling abroad (Human Rights Watch 2017). Taken to an extreme, transnational repression engages in lethal retribution against migrant or diaspora members abroad—as in the case of Iraq under Saddam Hussein (Sciolino 1991, 92) or, more recently, the assassination of Saudi journalist Jamal Khashoggi.

Beyond violence, Middle East autocracies also develop strategies of *transnational legitimation* that aim to reward patriotic behavior or to criticize dissent abroad. In the case of Morocco and Tunisia, the state fostered a number of events across European locations with high concentrations of expatriates—these included celebrations of national festivals, parties and cultural activities, performances of folk groups from the home country, but also Arabic classes (Brand 2006). Citizens abroad were incorporated into the sending state's legitimation strategies. This is a broader phenomenon—a Syrian in Sweden, for instance, explains, "I had lots of Arab friends, Egyptians and Palestinians for instance; but I avoided Syrians. There was no way of knowing whether they would report to the embassy . . . perhaps as many as every second Syrian abroad work as informers for the regime" (Jörum 2015). At the opposite end of the spectrum, as Shain writes, "the home regime may impair exiles' operational activities and undermine their claim to political legitimacy by branding them as disloyal and in effect no longer citizens" (Shain 2005, 147). The Egyptian regime aims to stigmatize activists abroad: Mohamed Ali has been called a drug addict, a traitor, a womanizer, and member of the Muslim Brotherhood, beyond being formally stripped of his Egyptian nationality; Ali claims that the regime has invited him to visit the Egyptian embassy in Madrid: "I am scared of someone being paid to murder me" (Wintour 2019). Moroccan expatriates who abstained from social activities organized by the state-sponsored *Fédération des Amicales des Marocains* either expressed fear about returning home, or encountered a number of difficulties by border officials in their attempts to do so (Brand 2002, 9).

Beyond repression and legitimation strategies, autocracies have also developed *transnational co-optation* to respond to the illiberal paradox. For years, the Egyptian regime would reward select groups of its diaspora community in the United States with complimentary annual trips to the homeland, where expatriates would meet with high-ranking political elites, while specific positions at Egyptian universities would be earmarked for high-skilled return migrants (Tsourapas 2015). Alaa Al Aswany's acclaimed novel *Chicago* (Aswany 2008) focuses on the life of an Egyptian émigré in the United States who hopes to become a prominent figure when he returns to Egypt, and so he works as a government spy. Loyal Tunisian expatriates would be praised by the homeland: in fact, the Tunisian minister of the interior advised Tunisians in France that "your role is to preserve this outstanding image of *Tunisiens résidents à l'étranger* and to fight with us against these intruders who are generally as useless at home as they are abroad" (Brand 2006, 112). At the same time, autocratic regimes may decide to discriminate against specific individuals abroad, refuse them access to specific economic rewards, or label them as untrustworthy—in other words, to blacklist them. In the United Arab Emirates, relatives of political dissidents have faced restrictions on their access to any employment opportunities or higher education: "Whenever the family tried to dig deeper to understand why the government was denying access to a service or holding an application pending indefinitely," one Emirati dissident abroad reported, "they would be told, verbally only, that the obstruction was happening at the state security level" (Human Rights Watch 2019). In 2016, an official at the Egyptian embassy in Berlin threatened to cancel researcher Taqadum al-Khatib's doctoral scholarship if he did not surrender his passport and grant access to his personal Facebook account (US Embassy in Egypt 2017).

Finally, transnational authoritarianism also involves *cooperation with a variety of nonstate actors*. Iraq, for instance, has relied on the cooperation of loyal student union members abroad to identify anti-Ba'ath student activists (Makiya and al-Halīl 1998, 62). A number of IOs have cooperated with authoritarian states and have implicated themselves in the workings of transnational authoritarianism. For one, the Gulf Cooperation Council (which includes Bahrain, Kuwait, Oman, Qatar, Saudi Arabia, and the United Arab Emirates) has been a key instrument for the diffusion of repressive measures, as oil-rich Arab monarchies have aimed to tackle the perceived transnational threat of the Muslim Brotherhood (Darwich 2017). Post-coup attempt, Turkey has sought 60,000 red notices against citizens abroad—more than four times the total number of notices issued by Interpol in 2016 (Lemon 2019). Persian Gulf countries, including Qatar, Saudi Arabia, and the United Arab Emirates, are among those that have purchased Pegasus, the Israeli-made software that allows its operator to record phone calls and intercept text messages, including those made or sent on nominally encrypted apps (Groll 2016). The cooperation with multinational corporations is critical: Omar Abdulaziz, who was granted political asylum in Canada, created a critical Twitter hashtag about a member of the Saudi royal family, Turki al-Sheikh, #StopalSheikFromWastingTheNationsMoney. "It had 6,000 tweets in less than 15 minutes," Abdulaziz said. "But then suddenly it was deleted from trends, like it was nothing"—Twitter never revealed why (Maza 2017).

Manipulating Migration Interdependence

Beyond affecting citizen-state relations, the rise of cross-border mobility into, out of, and across the Middle East has also affected interstate relations. The rise of complex forms of migration interdependence, namely the reciprocal political economy effects created by cross-border mobility in both sending and host states, has enabled the use of migrants as political leverage (Tsourapas 2018). The Middle East, which features both major migrant sending states (Egypt, Lebanon, Morocco, Yemen), as well as important migrant host states (Saudi Arabia, United Arab Emirates, Kuwait), allows us to study the effects of migration interdependence in detail. Given the high rates of migration interdependence (figure 4.1), how does this affect the international relations of the Middle East? In particular, are those states that demonstrate high migration interdependence more likely to be coerced by other states and, if so, how?

In previous work, I identify how a host state may leverage its position for coercive purposes against a sending state in one of two ways: by reducing a sending state's migration interdependence through restriction, or by severing it completely through displacement. Restriction refers to host-state policies of curbing migrant remittances, strengthening

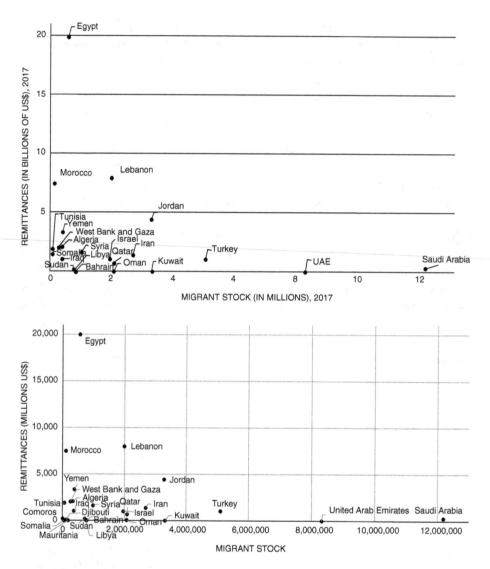

Figure 4.1.   Migrant workers in key Arab host states, 1975 and 1985 (in thousands).
Source: Calculations by author based on World Bank Data.

immigration flows, or both, while displacement refers to host-state strategies of deportation. I also build on the international relations literature on interdependence and, in
particular, on key terms from the literature on interdependence, namely ***vulnerability***.
For Keohane and Nye, "the vulnerability dimension of interdependence rests on the
relative availability and costliness of the alternatives that various actors face" and "can
be measured only by the costliness of making effective adjustments to a changed environment over a period of time" (Keohane and Nye 1977). In the context of migration
interdependence, sending states' vulnerability is established by their inability to make
effective adjustments with regard to the political economy costs incurred by the change

Table 4.2. Sending-state compliance to host-state coercive strategies.

		Sending-State Vulnerability Interdependence	
		No	Yes
Type of Host-State Strategy	Restriction	Compliance unlikely	Compliance somewhat likely
	Displacement	Compliance unlikely	Compliance very likely

in the policy framework through a host-state strategy of restriction or displacement. Arguably, we would expect displacement to be more effective in securing a sending state's compliance (see table 4.2).

How would the manipulation of migration interdependence work in practice, particularly in terms of highly interdependent migration states such as Egypt? In the aftermath of the 2011 Arab Uprisings, the country was vulnerable to migration interdependence: while Egypt had received diverse forms of aid from oil-producing Arab states, particularly Saudi Arabia, under Anwar Sadat and Hosni Mubarak, it was particularly isolated during the rule of the Egyptian Muslim Brotherhood (2012–13). As a result, it was highly unlikely that any displaced Egyptian workers would be re-dispatched to other oil-producing Arab states that had supported Egypt economically before the rise of the Muslim Brotherhood. In fact, not only were Arab oil-producing states unwilling to support Mohamed Morsi by absorbing any costs, but Saudi Arabia, Kuwait, and the United Arab Emirates—the three main host states in 2012—were themselves engaging in a strategy of restriction against Egypt, by arresting Egyptian labor migrants with suspected ties to the Muslim Brotherhood. At the same time, the deteriorating condition of the Egyptian economy implied that the state was unable to absorb the burden of host states' displacement strategies. In November 2012, a few weeks before the Jordanian crisis, Morsi had turned to the International Monetary Fund (IMF) for a $4.8 billion loan in order to help Egypt stay afloat. But Egypt's inability to meet the IMF's loan requirements delayed the signing of the agreement until after Morsi was ousted from power.

Egyptian vulnerability to migration interdependence was adroitly exploited by two weaker neighboring host states: Libya and Jordan had understood that, in the aftermath of the "Arab Spring," Egypt was particularly susceptible, or vulnerable, to migration interdependence. It relied on a steady outflow of emigrants in order to continue reducing its high unemployment figures and increase the inflow of economic remittances. In this context, the presence of migrants within their borders was a potent "weapon of the weak" that less powerful states—the small Kingdom of Jordan and even war-torn Libya—were able to use to their advantage. The manipulation of migration interdependence in the Middle East contributes to conflictual relations—against the expectations of theorists expecting cross-border mobility to lead to interstate cooperation. Egypt was coerced by two considerably weaker neighboring states—Libya and Jordan—into shifting two sets of policies: Jordan forced the Egyptian government to increase its exports of natural gas to the kingdom, while Libya forced it to extradite a number of Gaddafi-era elites. The two new policies were clearly against Egypt's national interests, and the policy shifts occurred only after the two weaker states started deporting Egyptian migrants.

Does this argument travel beyond the cases discussed in this chapter? Labor migration typically features as an element of statecraft and power politics across the global South; for instance, Afghan authorities have not hesitated to manipulate migration interdependence in their bilateral relations with Pakistan since mid-2016. In an effort to force Pakistan to reverse its decision to unilaterally close the Chaman border crossing, weaker Afghanistan recently adopted a law that requires passports, rather than mere identity cards, and frequently deports Pakistani labor migrants. In response, in March 2017, Pakistan relented as its prime minister decided to open the crossing as "a gesture of goodwill." Bilateral disputes between Egypt and Sudan, including the contested border of the Halayeb Triangle, led Khartoum to bar entry to Egyptian men aged between sixteen and fifty without visas in 2017—as part of an ongoing bilateral conflict. At the same time, forced migration may also institute an element of statecraft: a range of Arab states have sought to leverage their position as transit or host states of refugees in order to extract economic concessions from Western states (Greenhill 2010). The growing reticence of European and North American states to receive refugee populations has allowed Middle East states to attempt to manipulate their position as refugee host states in order to continue receiving international aid. In the context of the Syrian Civil War, for instance, Jordan, Lebanon, and Turkey have adopted *refugee rent-seeking* strategies that seek to attract external economic support in order to continue hosting refugee populations within their borders (Tsourapas 2019). A closer look at the politics of migration in the Middle East hints at the growing trend of refugee commodification in Africa, Asia, Latin America, and the broader global South.

An analysis of migration patterns across the Middle East demonstrates both the historical evolution and contemporary complexity of cross-border mobility flows. This chapter introduced the reader to the history and politics of migration into, out of, and across the contemporary Middle East. Serving as a complementary chapter to the discussion of migration politics in Turkey and the Persian Gulf, it aimed to provide a holistic, interdisciplinary introduction to labor and forced migration flows in the region. These were marked, first, by colonial and imperial exigencies that bequeathed lingering legacies that continue to affect policy-making today. The rise of the modern nation-state in the post–World War I period of decolonization led to the emergence of the *migration state* in the Middle East, which governed population mobility through *colonial* and *postcolonial* migration governance regimes and was marked by periods of high- and low-migrant recruitment by host states within and outside the region. In the chapter's second part, a more analytical discussion examined the politics of international migration in the Middle East via the prism of the *illiberal paradox*. As states attempted to resolve the tensions inherent in the management of migration within authoritarian contexts, they developed a range of *transnational authoritarian practices*, while also engaged in the manipulation of *migration interdependence* for political and economic gain.

Overall, through both sections of the chapters, I demonstrated both the empirical richness as well as the analytic utility of the Middle East as a crucial region of study for the politics of migration. As became evident from this brief discussion into regional migration politics, the intricacies of state-led processes of migration management can enhance our understanding of existing theories and concepts—including patterns of migration interdependence and the working of migration states as outlined across this volume. At the same time, however, a focus on the Middle East allows us to identify the extent to which our conceptualization of migration continues to be centered on Western experiences and expectations: the illiberal paradox thesis, for instance, arguably allows for a shift in the scholarly discussion on the politics of cross-border mobility toward the global South, while offering a more nuanced understanding of migration states' policy-making outside the European and North American contexts. In this aspect, the chapter seeks to complement this volume's overall aim of understanding international migration within a truly global context.

References

Abou-El-Fadl, Reem. 2015. "Neutralism Made Positive: Egyptian Anti-Colonialism on the Road to Bandung." *British Journal of Middle Eastern Studies* 42(2): 219–40.

Adamson, Fiona B., and Gerasimos Tsourapas. 2020. "The Migration State in the Global South: Nationalizing, Developmental, and Neoliberal Models of Migration Management." *International Migration Review* 54(3). https://doi.org/10.1177/0197918319879057

Ahmed, Faisal Z. 2012. "The Perils of Unearned Foreign Income: Aid, Remittances, and Government Survival." *American Political Science Review* 106(1): 146–65.

Ahram Online. 2016. "Egypt Embassy in Berlin Denies Sending Reports on Activists to Cairo." February 1, 2016. http://english.ahram.org.eg/NewsContent/1/64/186501/Egypt/Politics-/Egypt-embassy-in-Berlin-denies-sending-reports-on-.aspx

Amnesty International. 2011. "Syria: The Long Reach of the Mukhabaraat: Violence and Harassment against Syrians Abroad and Their Relatives Back Home." https://www.amnesty.org/en/documents/MDE24/057/2011/en/

Aswany, Alaa al. 2008. *Chicago*. London: Fourth Estate.

Birks, J. S., and C. A. Sinclair. 1982. "Employment and Development in Six Poor Arab States: Syria, Jordan, Sudan, South Yemen, Egypt, and North Yemen." *International Journal of Middle East Studies* 14(1): 35–51.

Brand, Laurie A. 2002. "States and Their Expatriates: Explaining the Development of Tunisian and Moroccan Emigration-Related Institutions." Working Paper no. 52. La Jolla: University of California, San Diego.

British Foreign Office and Foreign and Commonwealth Office Records from 1782. "1957." London: The National Archives.

———. 2006. *Citizens Abroad: Emigration and the State in the Middle East and North Africa*. Cambridge: Cambridge University Press.

Chalcraft, John. 2008. *The Invisible Cage: Syrian Migrant Workers in Lebanon*. Stanford, CA: Stanford University Press.

Choucri, Nazli. 1988. "Migration in the Middle East: Old Economics or New Politics?" *Journal of Arab Affairs* 7(1).

Collyer, Michael. 2012. "Migrants as Strategic Actors in the European Union's Global Approach to Migration and Mobility." *Global Networks: A Journal of Transnational Affairs* 12(September): 505–24.

Cremeans, Charles Davis. 1963. *The Arabs and the World: Nasser's Arab Nationalist Policy*. New York: Praeger.

Darwich, May. 2017. "Creating the Enemy, Constructing the Threat: The Diffusion of Repression against the Muslim Brotherhood in the Middle East." *Democratization* 7(2): 1289–306.

Dowding, Keith, Peter John, Thanos Mergoupis, and Mark Vugt. 2000. "Exit, Voice and Loyalty: Analytic and Empirical Developments." *European Journal of Political Research* 37(4): 469–95.

Dunne, Michelle, and Amr Hamzawy. 2019. "Egypt's Political Exiles Going Anywhere but Home." Washington, DC: Carnegie Endowment for International Peace. https://carnegieendowment.org/2019/03/29/egypt-s-political-exiles-going-anywhere-but-home-pub-78728

Fargues, Philippe. 2013. "International Migration and the Nation State in Arab Countries." *Middle East Law and Governance* 5(1/2): 5–35.

Greenhill, Kelly. 2010. *Weapons of Mass Migration*. Ithaca, NY: Cornell University Press.

Groll, Elias. 2016. "The UAE Spends Big on Israeli Spyware to Listen In on a Dissident." *Foreign Policy* (blog). https://foreignpolicy.com/2016/08/25/the-uae-spends-big-on-israeli-spyware-to-listen-in-on-a-dissident/

Haddad, Yvonne. 1987. Islamic Values in the United States: A Comparative Study. New York: Oxford University Press.

Halliday, Fred. 1977. "Migration and the Labour Force in the Oil Producing States of the Middle East." *Development and Change* 8(3): 263–91.

Hirschman, Albert O. 1978. "Exit, Voice, and the State." *World Politics* 31(1): 90–107.

Hollifield, James F. 2004. "The Emerging Migration State." *International Migration Review* 38(3): 885–912.

Hourani, Albert Habib. 2013. *A History of the Arab Peoples*. London: Faber & Faber.

Human Rights Watch. 2017. "Oman: Activist's Family Barred from Traveling Abroad." www.hrw.org/news/2017/02/14/oman-activists-family-barred-traveling-abroad

———. 2019. "UAE: Unrelenting Harassment of Dissidents' Families." www.hrw.org/news/2019/12/22/uae-unrelenting-harassment-dissidents-families

Ibrahim, Saad Eddin. 1982. *The New Arab Social Order: A Study of the Social Impact of Oil Wealth*. Westview's Special Studies on the Middle East. Boulder, CO: Westview.

James, Laura M. 2006. *Nasser at War: Arab Images of the Enemy*. Basingstoke: Palgrave Macmillan.

Jörum, Emma Lundgren. 2015. "Repression across Borders: Homeland Response to Anti-Regime Mobilization among Syrians in Sweden." *Diaspora Studies* 8(2): 104–19. https://doi.org/10.1080/09739572.2015.1029711

Kandil, Hazem. 2015. *Inside the Brotherhood*. Cambridge: Polity Press.

Kapiszewski, Andrej. 2006. *Arab versus Asian Migrant Workers in the GCC Countries*. Beirut: United Nations Secretariat.

Keck, Margaret E., and Kathryn Sikkink. 2014. *Activists beyond Borders: Advocacy Networks in International Politics*. Ithaca, NY: Cornell University Press.

Keohane, Robert O., and Joseph S. Nye, Jr. 1977. *Power and Interdependence*. London: Pearson.

Kerr, Malcolm H. 1978. *The Arab Cold War: Gamal ʿabd Al-Nasir and His Rivals, 1958–1970*, 3rd ed. London: Oxford University Press.

Khater, Akram Fouad. 2001. *Inventing Home: Emigration, Gender, and the Middle Class in Lebanon, 1870–1920*. Berkeley: University of California Press.

Lemon, Edward. 2019. "Weaponizing Interpol." *Journal of Democracy* 30(2): 15–29.

Makiya, Kanan, and Samīr al-Halīl. 1998. *Republic of Fear: The Politics of Modern Iraq*. Los Angeles: University of California Press.

Matthews, Roderic D., and Matta Akrawi. 1949. *Education in Arab Countries of the Near East: Egypt, Iraq, Palestine, Transjordan, Syria, Lebanon*. Washington, DC: American Council on Education.

Maza, Christina. 2017. "Saudi Arabia's Government Might Be Getting Help from Social Media Giants to Shut Down Dissent." December 22. www.newsweek.com/saudi-arabia-crack-down-social-media-dissent-754257

Messina, Claire. 1994. "From Migrants to Refugees: Russian, Soviet and Post-Soviet Migration." *International Journal of Refugee Law* 6(4): 620–35.

Misnad, Sheikha. 1985. *The Development of Modern Education in the Gulf*. London: Ithaca Press.

Mitchell, Richard P. 1969. *The Society of the Muslim Brothers*. London: Oxford University Press.

Nasser, Gamal Abdel. 1966. *On Africa*. Cairo: Ministry of National Guidance, Information Administration.

Natter, Katharina. 2018. "Rethinking Immigration Policy beyond Western Liberal Democracies." *Comparative Migration Studies* 6(4): 1–21.

Norman, Kelsey. 2020. *Reluctant Reception: Refugees, Migration, and Governance in the Middle East and North Africa*. New York: Cambridge University Press.

Öztürk, Ahmet Erdi, and Hakkı Taş. 2020. "The Repertoire of Extraterritorial Repression: Diasporas and Home States." *Migration Letters* 17(1): 59–69. https://doi.org/10.33182/ml.v17i1.853

Paoletti, Emmanuela. 2010. *The Migration of Power and North-South Inequalities: The Case of Italy and Libya*. London: Palgrave Macmillan.

Pearlman, Wendy. 2013. "Emigration and Power—A Study of Sects in Lebanon, 1860–2010." *Politics & Society* 41(1): 103–33.

Ramadan, Nada. 2016. "Egypt's Embassy in Berlin: Part of Sisi's Oppressive Apparatus?" *Al-Araby*, February 2. www.alaraby.co.uk/english/indepth/2016/2/2/egypts-embassy-in-berlin-part-of-sisis-oppressive-apparatus

Robson, Laura. 2017. *States of Separation: Transfer, Partition, and the Making of the Modern Middle East*. Berkeley: University of California Press.

Sadiq, Kamal, and Gerasimos Tsourapas. 2021. "The Postcolonial Migration State." *European Journal of International Relations* (April 10): 1–29. https://doi.org/10.1177%2F13540661211000114

Saleh, Saniyah 'Abd al-Wahhab. 1979. "Attitudinal and Social Structural Aspects of the Brain Drain: The Egyptian Case." *Cairo Papers in Social Science* 5(2).

Sayigh, Rosemary. 1979. *The Palestinians—From Peasants to Revolutionaries*. London: Zed Books.

Sciolino, Elaine. 1991. *The Outlaw State: Saddam Hussein's Quest for Power and the Gulf Crisis*. New York: Wiley.

Seccombe, Ian J. 1985. "International Labor Migration in the Middle East: A Review of Literature and Research, 1974–84." *International Migration Review* 19(2): 335–52.

Serageldin, Ismail, and World Bank, eds. 1983. *Manpower and International Labor Migration in the Middle East and North Africa*. New York: Published for the World Bank by Oxford University Press.

Shain, Yossi. 2005. *The Frontier of Loyalty: Political Exiles in the Age of the Nation-State*. Ann Arbor: University of Michigan Press.

Thiollet, Hélène. 2011. "Migration as Diplomacy: Labor Migrants, Refugees, and Arab Regional Politics in the Oil-Rich Countries." *International Labor and Working-Class History* 79(1): 103–21.

Tsourapas, Gerasimos. 2015. "Why Do States Develop Multi-Tier Emigrant Policies? Evidence from Egypt." *Journal of Ethnic and Migration Studies* 41(13): 2192–214.

———. 2016. "Nasser's Educators and Agitators across al-Watan al-'Arabi: Tracing the Foreign Policy Importance of Egyptian Regional Migration, 1952–1967." *British Journal of Middle Eastern Studies* 43(3): 324–41.

———. 2017. "Migration Diplomacy in the Global South: Cooperation, Coercion, and Issue Linkage in Gaddafi's Libya." *Third World Quarterly* 38(10): 2367–85.

———. 2018. "Labor Migrants as Political Leverage: Migration Interdependence and Coercion in the Mediterranean." *International Studies Quarterly* 62(2): 383–95.

———. 2019. *The Politics of Migration in Modern Egypt: Strategies for Regime Survival in Autocracies*. Cambridge: Cambridge University Press.

———. 2020. "The Long Arm of the Arab State." *Ethnic and Racial Studies* 43(2): 351–70.

US Embassy in Egypt. 2017. "Country Reports on Human Rights Practices for 2017—Egypt." https://eg.usembassy.gov/egypt-2017-human-rights-report/

Van Hear, Nicholas. 1998. *New Diasporas*. London: Routledge

Wintour, Patrick. 2019. "Mohamed Ali: Egyptian Exile Who Sparked Protests in Shock at Mass Arrests." *The Guardian*, October 23, 2019, sec. World News. https://www.theguardian.com/world/2019/oct/23/mohamed-ali-egyptian-exile-in-shock-over-street-protest-arrests

5 MIGRATION AND DEVELOPMENT IN NORTH AND WEST AFRICA

Yves Charbit

The EU and the African States Parties to the Cotonou Partnership Agreements

AS A MAJOR INTERNATIONAL actor the European Union, which could not ignore the issue of underdevelopment, created the equivalent of a ministry of cooperation, formerly Europaid, now the Development and Cooperation Department (DEVCO), which is distinct from its Ministry of Foreign Affairs. The EU signed the so-called Cotonou Partnership Agreements (henceforth CPA), which involve 77 developing countries, out of which 10 are in the Pacific region, 16 in the Caribbean, and 46 in Africa. According to Article 13 of the CPA, "strategies aiming at reducing poverty, improving living and working conditions, creating employment and developing training contribute in the long run to normalising migratory flows." This causal relationship proved unrealistic, as migration flows did not diminish where development took place.

In view of the pending 2020 renewal of the Cotonou Partnership Agreements, in 2015 the EU organized a broad public consultation. It was preceded by the setting up of seven thematic clusters, including one on demographic developments. I thus co-organized with DEVCO staff a panel of fifteen experts: four from EU departments, four representatives of member states of the EU, and seven academics and members of civil society. DEVCO had raised the following questions: "Is the future partnership the right framework to address migration issues? If so, is the partnership more fit to address certain specific migratory issues, while others can be more effectively addressed within other frameworks (bilateral or regional)?" The underlying criticism, shared by the whole panel, was that the CPA was largely a construct covering deep differences between the three regions and the seventy-seven states. Throughout the following pages I shall, however, open the discussion to other contexts beyond the EU-Africa corridor because of a major political factor—EU global development policy *vis-à-vis* underdeveloped countries. This is why the first part of this chapter presents the demographic dynamics of the Pacific, Caribbean, and African states, which are parties to the CPA.[1] I shall focus on the EU and the African states, but allude to the Pacific and Caribbean ones when useful.

---

1 Unless otherwise mentioned, most of data are drawn from Charbit 2015. However, when relevant I updated the figures of some of the tables I had produced in 2015 using the PRB database.

Since detailed accounts of migration flows in the EU-Africa corridor are available in textbooks and scientific journals[2] and in reports from major international organizations such as OIM, UNDP, OECD, UNHDR, UNDSEA, and the World Bank, this chapter focuses on a fundamental question—Do labor migrations contribute to development in Africa?—while keeping in mind that such a wide-ranging issue is impossible to fully cover within the limits of this chapter and that the answer is far from simple. First, the other components of demographic dynamics (age structures, fertility, mortality, marriage patterns, etc.) can both enhance and hinder development. Second, international migration, one of the components of demographic dynamics, are partly driven by the other ones (a married man will be less mobile than a bachelor, poor health is a factor of refusal of entry in countries of immigration, and so on). Viewed from the sending developing countries, international migration plays the role of an adjustment variable as they are the simplest and most immediate response implemented by populations faced with chronic poverty and even more so when they are hit by a crisis, whether political, economic (Charbit and Petit 2011), or climatic. However, as we shall see, international mobility is not that easy to achieve. How can research disentangle the impacts of migrations on development from those of the other demographic components?

To clarify the problem, I first examine the consequences of three major demographic characteristics among those mentioned above on several issues of development. By the same token I discuss how the situation can also induce migrations as responses to the development problems encountered. Thus, I talk about the demographic context as a driver of migrations. Second, do migrations and one of their major corollaries, the transfers of migrants to their home countries, contribute to the development of the latter, at both national and local levels? It will be shown that adopting a sociological perspective provides a better understanding of the complexity of the issue than that allowed by a purely economic approach, even if, as is known, remittances sent by migrants working abroad are a major component of macro-financial flows, often more important than Official Development Assistance (ODA) and Foreign Direct Investment (FDI). Third, I shall discuss the extent to which migrations and transfers really enhance human and economic development in the EU-Africa corridor. More often than not, I do not separate the two, since transfers and migrations are intertwined; for instance, transfers are a form of savings to prepare for return to the home country, even before retirement age. I conclude on the implications for development policies.

The EU and Africa: Past and Present
International Migrations in Historical Perspective

History allows for an understanding of the causes behind the interest now expressed in the development of African countries, most of which were forged from the former colonies of the major European powers. Even before the colonization of Africa began, the continent was subject to major movements of populations due to wars, territorial expansions, and slave trading in former empires such as that of Mandé, which covered present-day Mali, Burkina Faso, Senegal, Gambia, Guinea, Guinea-Bissau, Mauritania,

---

2   Both Castles, de Haas, and Miller 2014 and Flahaux and de Haas 2016 are particularly useful.

and a large part of the Ivory Coast, and which reached its apogee during the thirteenth and fourteenth centuries. The slaves were used to ensure economic production, but they were also the object of thriving traffic, since it has been estimated that between the seventh century and the 1920s seventeen million men and women were sold in the framework of the so-called intracontinental (through the Saharan desert) and oriental (from the East coast of Africa) slave trades (Austen 1987; Pétré-Grenouilleau 2004). At the beginning of the fifteenth century the Europeans instigated the intercontinental trade. At least twelve million people were forcefully transported from Africa to the New World, of which a third went to the Caribbean islands, with the rest mainly destined for Brazil and what was to become the United States (Curtin 1969; Lovejoy 1982), giving rise to a profitable trading triangle. Boats set sail from, for example, London, Bristol, and Liverpool, and Bordeaux, Nantes, and Le Havre, to the African coasts (those of present-day Senegal, Benin, Ghana, Guinea Conakry, and Angola), with goods manufactured in Europe (metal objects, arms, alcohols, textiles). They returned with cargoes of captives sold in exchange. The captives were then sold as slaves and worked on plantations where they produced sugar, tobacco, coffee, and cotton. These products were finally shipped to Europe to complete the third side to the triangle.

In the nineteenth century Great Britain, France, Portugal, Belgium, and Germany forged their colonial empires. The Berlin Treaty of 1885, which brought the parties together at the initiative of Bismarck, the German chancellor, organized the division of Africa among the major powers. New countries were created throughout the continent and they remained until the wave of independencies granted in the 1960s. The borders were often artificial, and for the most part ignored ethnic realities. Thus the Wolof were divided between Senegal and Gambia and the Makonde split between Tanzania and Mozambique (Coquery-Vidrovitch 2010), since according to the rationale of nineteenth-century international relations, it was of paramount importance to maintain a balance among the European powers, and "territorial compensations" were attributed if necessary.

Colonization marked a decisive turning point in emigration, since mobility became almost totally intra-African. Two factors were involved: on the one hand, slavery was banned in the British colonies of the Caribbean in 1834; in the French colonies in 1848, on the other hand, pressure was exerted by the colonial authorities and private businesses in Africa as they considered that they should also be entitled to draw on this pool of labor. The colonial powers displaced the populations as a function of their need to exploit the resources of the African continent (gold, diamonds, different minerals, wood, single crop farming, especially coffee and cacao). In 1925, labor in the French colonies was subject to obligatory work contracts, obliging the populations to either work on plantations or build roads (Barou 2000; Coquery-Vidrovitch 2000). The Mossis of the Upper-Volta, now Burkina Faso, worked on cocoa and coffee plantations in the Ivory Coast (Cordell, Gregory, and Piché 1996). In the Belgian Congo, the private property of King Leopold II, the populations were displaced from the lower Congo and the east of the country to the rich veins of mineral ore of upper Katanga and the diamond mines of Kassai. Sometimes the colonial powers worked together; for example, at the end of the nineteenth century the Belgian Congo started recruiting skilled workers from the French colony in Senegal. African labor was also used to build roads to facilitate trade and supply the populations of cities, just as in the Europe of the Industrial Revolution, but also to

while the growth of the two other groups (Caribbean and Pacific) is slower (table 5.1). As for GNP per capita, the gap between the EU and CPA countries of Africa and the Pacific is quite wide, though narrower in the case of the Caribbean states. A simple comparison of these two indicators (total population and GNP per capita) suggests that current employment and income opportunities in the EU are a factor of attractiveness for potential migrants from CPA countries, especially those of Africa and the Pacific, without even mentioning other factors, notably health and education, as will be shown in the third part of this chapter.

Table 5.2 compares other fundamental demographic indicators. It also gives a hint of future prospects (2050). Growth will be even slower in the EU than now (0.04% as opposed to 0.1% in 2015). The EU displays the demographic characteristics of matured countries: an aged population, low fertility, high life expectancy, and a heavy burden on the active population: four adults only are available to support one old-aged person, as opposed to nine adults in Africa and the Caribbean. Because of its higher fertility, the population of Africa is the youngest (41.4% below 15) and due to high infant mortality and poverty, life expectancy is lower than in the two other CPA groups of countries (58 as opposed to 68 and 72 years).

Structures by Age and Aging

The population of EU countries is increasing very slightly and has entered into an aging process. Combined with demographic stagnation (due to low fertility), the very high

Table 5.1.   Population and GNP per capita in 2016.

Region	Population (thousands)	Population Growth Rate (%)	GNP per Capita in 2020 US$
EU	506,859	0.1	34,131
African CPA	891,782	2.5	3,505
Caribbean CPA	28,403	1.3	12,218
Pacific CPA	10,370	1.1	4,673

Source: Calculations by author based on PRB data, 2017.

Table 5.2.   Demographic indicators in 2016.

Region	Population Growth 2050/2014	Average Annual Growth 2014–50	% <15yrs	% >65yrs	Number of Children	Life Expectancy at Birth	Old-Age Support Ratio
EU	x 0.99	0.04%	15.8%	17.3%	1.53	79.2	4
Caribbean	x 1.2	1%	26.8%	7.1%	2.2	72.1	9
Africa	x 2.14	2.5%	41.4%	3.4%	4.84	58.1	9
Pacific	x 1.45	0.02%	35.6%	4.1%	3.86	68.0	6

Source: Calculations by author based on PRB data, 2017.

life expectancy in the EU will induce accelerated population aging. The old-age support ratio will fall by half from now until 2050 (from four to two persons of working age per pensioner). In Germany, in the early 1990s there were almost three people of working age for every person over the age of sixty. Calculations indicate that within the next decade the ratio will already be less than one to two. There is no doubt that the elderly population will in the future represent an expanding sector of consumption (geriatric and hospital care, aid for the isolated elderly and those in old people's homes, leisure). Last, labor force participation is a major worry with regard to the surging youth population, but it is rendered complicated especially in Africa where the informal economy is poorly documented.

In debates on development, an important argument currently put forward is that of the "demographic dividend." When children become young adults, their status changes from that of consumer to that of producer and the so-called "dependency ratio" between "active" and "inactive" members of the population, which was unfavorable (too many consumers dependent on producers), then becomes economically favorable. This is a reasonable assumption provided that fertility has decreased and that the new generations are less numerous than those preceding them; otherwise no rebalancing will occur. The existence of a demographic dividend therefore supposes that the base of the pyramid has narrowed. South Korea is a good example of this: between 1960, the year when fertility started to decline, and 2010, by which time the fall in fertility was very marked while aging increased at the summit of the pyramid. The contrast between Nigeria and Burkina Faso is striking (figure 5.1).

Reaping the demographic dividend, however, is not that simple. In order to fully exploit this dual advantage (more active generations and fewer dependent ones), the country must have foreseen demographic changes and made the investments required in health and education. It must, on the employment front, have implemented an economic development strategy to provide jobs for the reserve of labor ready to enter into the labor market. If this labor force lacks general education and professional qualifications, this flow of young persons of working age will for the most part exacerbate unemployment and place pressure on the labor market, without actually generating wealth. It will also stimulate individuals to migrate. The "quality" of the population is therefore essential (Africa Union 2013a/b/c/d; Bloom, Canning, and Sevilla 2003; Bloom et al. 2007).

Mortality and Health

As mentioned before, life expectancy varies widely between the EU and the three CPA groups of countries, the Caribbean being the closest to the EU (table 5.2 above). In the latter, because of chronic diseases (cancer, cardiovascular diseases, and diabetes) illness does not imply a high risk of dying. Improvements in health conditions and therapeutic advances can delay death without curing patients. In the CPA countries, infectious and parasitic diseases are deadly and continue to negatively affect development. Sub-Saharan Africa is lagging behind the two other groups of CPA countries, low life expectancy being associated with the high vulnerability of children and women, especially due to maternal mortality (Gaimard 2013). However, as was clear when the HIV-2 epidemics severely hit Africa, poor health and morbidity do not stimulate migrations, except in

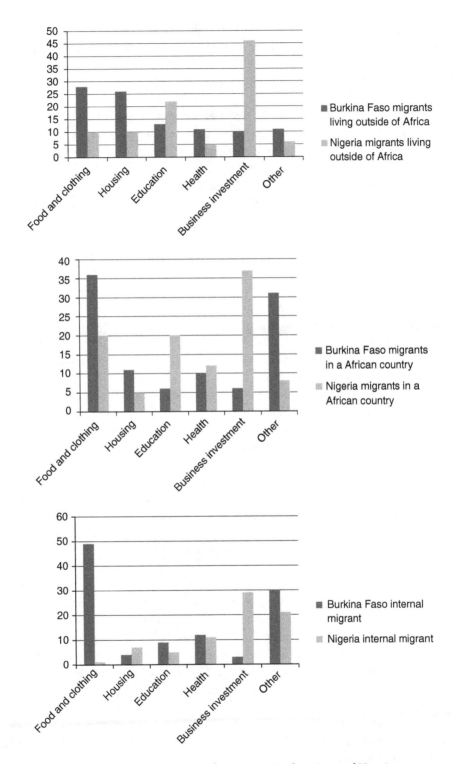

Figure 5.1. Types of expenses for families of migrants in Burkina Faso and Nigeria.

very exceptional instances, when international agreements have been signed to organize the sending of people to Europe to receive highly specialized treatments they cannot get in their own countries.

Fertility

In the EU, only France and Ireland (2.0 children per woman) are just below replacement level (2.1). Elsewhere (Germany, 1.4; Poland, 1.2; Italy, 1.4; Spain, 1.3) low fertility will induce an actual decline of population. For instance, Germany is expected to decline to around 70–74 million people by midcentury, down from over 82 million today. By contrast, demographic growth is rapid in Africa, due to high fertility, a fact not observed in the Caribbean and Pacific islands (table 5.2 above). This induces a growth rate that is too high with regard to the current rates of economic growth, hence making it necessary to constantly increase expenses on health, education, etc. However, in North Africa and at the southern end of the continent the demographic transition is well under way. Fertility in the north and the south of the continent (Morocco, Tunisia, Algeria, Egypt, as well as South Africa, Lesotho, Namibia, Zimbabwe), is much lower than in the western, central, and eastern regions. It follows that one cannot consider Africa as a demographically homogeneous zone. The contrast with other continents is even sharper. In the thirty-five years from 1970–2005, fertility has fallen slightly in Mali (–8.4%), Angola (–6.4%), and Liberia (–0.1%), while it has remained the same (0%) in the Congo, Burundi, Uganda, and Sierra Leone. The contrast with the decreases observed in China (–65%), Korea (–71%), Kuwait (–65%), Thailand (–61%), and Mexico (–64%) is striking. Despite the millions of dollars invested over several years in family planning programs, the results obtained in many of the countries of these regions are modest at best. I shall conclude on the policy implications of this major failure (Charbit 2015).

Remittance and Development

In a recent meeting of the Global Forum on Remittances, Investment and Development that kicked off in Kuala Lumpur on May 8, 2018, the United Nations Secretary-General's Special Representative on International Migration stated: "Migrants are needed in virtually all job markets; they bring skills and they help economies flourish. Although migrants represent just slightly over 3 per cent of the global population, they contributed 9 per cent of global GDP in 2015." It was estimated that of the 258 million people living abroad, over 200 million sent money home. The Asia Pacific region was quoted: the remittances totaled US$256 billion in 2017, amounting to ten times the net official development assistance going to the region (Global Forum on Remittances, Investment and Development 2018). In low- to middle-income countries, remittances (US$529 billion) are more important in volume than ODA and FDI (World Bank 2019), but do transfers of migrants to sending countries really contribute to their development?

Official and Undocumented Remittances

According to a World Bank study, a 10 percent increase in the share of remittances in a country's GDP leads to a 1.2 percent decline in poverty (as quoted in Adams and Page 2003). The question at the end of the previous section, however, is difficult to answer.

First, experts disagree on the negative or positive consequences, whether at the level of national accounting, economic analysis, or social effects (table 5.3).

Second, the oft-heard criticism about the limited contribution of remittances to *economic* development (it is claimed that they are wasted on sumptuary expenses) ignores their contribution to *social* development (education, health, empowerment of women, etc.). In Morocco, according to a survey by CERED, half of the households declared they used them to meet health, education, and everyday expenses (CERED 1996, 212). In Muslim West African countries, the money sent by overseas migrants has been crucial to constructing mosques and organizing social systems of solidarity.

Third, official transfers are only part of the reality; two other components should not be neglected, even if they can only give rise to estimations: "suitcase commerce" and cash transfers via informal channels (*Havala, Fei ch'ien, Chop*). Estimations vary considerably: worldwide, from US$100–300 billion flows through unofficial channels every year. Experts explain the success of informal transfer systems by their advantages, which are almost perfectly symmetrical to the disadvantages of official systems (Adams and Page 2003). They can be summed up in four words: accessibility, efficiency, speed, trust (table 5.4, based on Charbit 2007). Besides their low cost of transactions, they also permit avoiding taxes, eluding government controls, and also possible profits from more favorable foreign exchange rates on the black market.

Let us briefly comment on the last line on the right-hand side of the table. September 11 reinforced the suspicion that informal transfers were suspected of funding terrorist activities and a Report of the US Senate Committee on Banking, Housing and Urban Affairs was issued on November 14, 2001, titled *Hawala and Underground Terrorist*

Table 5.3.   In thousands of persons by age group.

Negative Consequences	Positive Consequences
<ul><li>Importation of foreign products / fragile balance of payments</li><li>Inflationist effects (inelasticity of the supply of goods in contrast with financial flows)</li><li>Aggravation of differences between cities/ countryside</li><li>Nonproductive, sumptuary costs</li></ul>	<ul><li>Inflow of currency (often acute shortage)</li><li>Jobs induced in country by purchasing power</li><li>Reduction of insecurity and poverty</li><li>Micro-coverage of basic needs</li></ul>

Source: Charbit 2015.

Table 5.4.   Negative and positive impacts on the societies of origin of migrants.

Official Systems	Informal Systems
<ul><li>No access to the banking system in rural areas</li><li>Slowness of classical financial institutions</li><li>Absence of trust and maximal formal guarantees</li><li>Impersonal relations</li><li>Costs linked to banking bureaucracy</li><li>Risk of controls on movements of funds by national financial institutions</li></ul>	<ul><li>System of home delivery</li><li>Speed of transactions</li><li>Trust and total absence of written documents</li><li>Social and family control of brokers (colleagues take care of debts)</li><li>Low fixed costs</li><li>Total discretion and invisibility of operations (mafia and terrorist risks)</li></ul>

Financing Mechanisms. But transfers existed long before today's terrorist attacks, as early as the *Fei ch'ien* ("flying money"), which dates back to the Tang dynasty (618–907). More recently, the "Havala" system has been widely used by migrants working in Gulf states to transfer money to their families (India, Bangladesh, etc.). These systems are a very flexible and safe device for reducing the intrinsic risks of carrying money. More generally, they are a very efficient "banking system of the poor," as informal remittances do what official remittances cannot do, to enable a great number of people to send small sums of money at a moderate cost.

For all these reasons, the macro and micro levels must be dealt with separately.

Macro Analysis

Can macro data help to answer the central question of the contribution of remittances to development? I collected three sets of data for 160 countries worldwide (including developed ones):

(1) absolute numbers: remittances received by the country of origin of the worker (billions US$);

(2) ratio of remittances to gross domestic product;

(3) ratio of remittances to the population of the country, i.e., transfers per capita.

Table 5.5 is confined to countries receiving more than US$13 billion.

Absolute value of transfers. African countries lag far behind the other countries. Only Nigeria and Egypt are among the nine countries receiving more than US$13 billion. India and China are far ahead of the other countries because of the large number of migrants from these countries abroad and because of their diasporas. Bangladesh, the Philippines, Egypt, and Pakistan are involved in the corridor with the Gulf states (the Philippines being also involved in the Southeast Asia corridor), while the relationship between Mexico and the United States is well known.

Table 5.5. Three indicators of transfers (2017).

Rank	Country	(109 US)	Rank	Country	% of GDP	Rank	Country	Remittances per Head (US$)
1	India	68,968	1	Tonga	33.7	1	Tonga	1,460
2	China	63,860	2	Kyrgyzstan	32.8	2	Jamaica	870
3	Philippines	32,808	3	Haiti	26.1	3	El Salvador	789
4	Mexico	30,600	4	Nepal	25.5	4	Samoa	715
5	Nigeria	21,917	5	Comoros	18.4	5	Jordan	455
6	Pakistan	19,306	6	Liberia	17.4	6	Armenia	513
7	Egypt	18,325	7	Samoa	16.7	7	Bosnia-Herzegovina	574
8	Bangladesh	15,388	8	Jamaica	16.5	8	Dominican Republic	579
9	Vietnam	13,000	9	Lesotho	14.2	9	Honduras	486

Sources: Calculations by author based on PRB 2018 (population), World Bank 2018 (remittances), IMF 2018 (GDP).

Transfers as percentage of gross domestic product. What can be observed is very different in this regard: three African countries (Comoros, Liberia, Lesotho) appear among the nine leading countries (Tonga, Kyrgyzstan, Haiti). All of these countries are very poor continental ones (Nepal, Kyrgyzstan, Lesotho), or small islands where migration is often the only source of income (Samoa, Tonga, Comoros, Haiti) or countries with a long history of migration (Jamaica and Liberia, for example).

Amounts transferred per capita. This indicator is closest to living conditions and thus to the social stakes of development. It signals the economic dependence of households in relation to transfers. Again they are poor countries, continental or islands, some with a small population (Armenia, Bosnia-Herzegovina); most are currently sending important flows of migrants or have for long constituted diasporas (Samoa, Tonga, Jordan, Dominican Republic, El Salvador, Honduras, Jamaica).

How can the last two development (remittances as a percentage of GDP and remittances per capita) indicators be explained? The comparison between India and Togo is striking (table 5.6). Their populations receive almost the same amount per head (a difference of less than 3 US dollars), a result totally independent of the three macro data, their GDPs, the size of their populations, and the total amount of remittances received.

Clearly, remittances per capita are a debatable indicator because they correspond to a series of widely different contextual factors coalescing in a conundrum that makes it impossible to identify any clear pattern of transfers at the macro level. Three such factors are mentioned here:

- If migrants receive low incomes because they work in countries where the average wage for labor is low (for example, in the mining sector in South Africa in comparison to the wages paid in France in the building sector), they will transfer less money;
- If the migrants cannot spend anything in certain countries (in particular the Gulf States), they are obliged to save and thus will transfer more money; and
- If the country of origin to which these transfers are sent has a small population with considerable migratory flows (the small Pacific islands) then, on the contrary, the transfers per capita will be very high.

Let us nevertheless assume that macro data make sense, whatever the uncertainties at the micro level may be. Table 5.7 provides an element of response to the central question of the contribution of transfers to development. I have calculated the correlation between the transfers per capita and the GDP per capita for nearly all the countries for which the World Bank provided remittance data in 2015 (160), then for 116 developing ones (Africa, Asia, Latin America) and lastly for a subsample of 42 sub-Saharan and North African ones (table 5.7).

Table 5.6. Comparison between India and Togo.

	GDP Billion US$	Total Population (Millions)	Total Remittances (Billion US$)	Rem/Capita (US$)
India	6,490	1,352	68,968	51.1
Togo	1,370	7,8	402	53.8

Table 5.7. Correlation between transfers per capita and GDP per capita.

Countries	Correlation (r2)
160 developing and developed countries	+ 0.33
116 developing countries	+ 0.61
42 African countries including North Africa	+ 0.51

Source: Calculations by author based on World Bank and IMF 2018 (GDP).

The correlation coefficient (r2) shows that their contribution to households' resources is positive but moderate. For obvious reasons the coefficient is weaker (+0.33) when all countries are included in the computation, as French or North American households rely very little on remittances. But note that this is not true of East European states. For instance, Polish and Ukrainian workers, who play an active economic role in the UK, Germany, and France, send money home. Conversely, the correlation is stronger for the 116 Asian, African, and Latin American states (+0.61). What about the 42 African countries? Public opinion in Europe views Africa as poverty-stricken, with low records in terms of the Human Development Indicator. African households are assumed to heavily depend on remittances, from which the argument follows that migration is vital to households, a typical example being an oft-quoted article. In Kayes, a region of Mali with strong emigration, transfers can "fully support more than three people above the poverty threshold for one year" (Azam and Gubert 2002, 220).

And yet the correlation is weaker (+0.51) for the African subsample. As was mentioned about the data in tables 5.1 and 5.2, one of the explanatory factors is the large number of small islands in other corridors (the Caribbean, Southeast Asia, and the Pacific) that have long traditions of emigration flows and receive substantial remittances. The only comparable islands in Africa are Cape Verde and the Comoros, whereas Réunion, the Seychelles, and Mauritius do not follow the same pattern.

To conclude with regard to the moderate correlation between remittances and development, this result is quite *predictable* and rather *desirable* from the standpoint of development. It is a predictable result because the migrants abroad represent only a small fraction of the active population and thus of the potential to create wealth; thus, transfers play a marginal role in GDP. It is a desirable result from the development perspective, since a stronger correlation would imply that migration is a major contributory factor of GDP, which would indicate strong dependence on countries requiring migrant workers and therefore an additional cause of the weakness of the country of origin. Finally, this result leads to two remarks. First, the global macroeconomic observation does not exclude that shortages of labor relating to emigration are *locally* very acute and, reciprocally, that transfers considerably contribute to local development (the case of certain villages in the Senegal river valley). Second, the judgment made on the contribution of transfers to development varies according to whether one privileges the macroeconomic or the microeconomic dimension: families or villages get rich but what about the country? Let us turn to a sociological analysis of the local dynamics of remittances. As was mentioned above, migrations are taken into consideration only as the background that casts light on the rationale of remittances.

Economic and Social Consequences of Remittances and Migration

Remittances at the Micro Level

It is commonly held that remittances and migrations contribute to reducing the poverty of households in the countries of origin. In Africa, the impact on poverty is confirmed by a survey covering thirty-three countries. According to the UN Conference on Trade and Development (UNCTAD), an increase of 10 percent of the remittances leads to a 3.9 percent reduction in the incidence of poverty.

In urban habitats, the example of the housing characteristics is classical. Migrants have contributed to modernizing the urban habitat, their houses far more often equipped with all the items of modern comfort than those of nonimmigrants. Such was the case of Portugal in the 1950s and 1960s before entering the EU, when it was a sending country (Tapinos and Garson 1981 on Portugal and Tunisia; Charbit et al. 1997 on Portugal) and of North Africa, also a major sending region. From the 1980s similar evidence was gathered about rural habitats in North Africa. However, the impacts on farming are contradictory: either shunning direct implication in, or abandoning, the land, which is left fallow; or, conversely, the modernization and mechanization of farming methods (Lazaar 1987; Toepfer 1986; Bencherifa 1996 ; Russel et al. 1990 cited by Hermelé 1997). Migrinter found "mixed results" for returns to a region of Algeria, the Grande Kabylie (1986: 155). One of the reasons lies in the choices made by migrants when they return home. They tend to prefer towns where opportunities for business are much greater than in the villages, not to mention the desire to reconstitute the way of life they had in Europe (leisure, access to health and education amenities). In Turkey, for example, of the 403 migrants who returned between 1979 and 1982, only 60 percent resettled and, above all, only 39 percent of investments were spent for this purpose. What is more, such investments are quickly reassigned to urban property (Toepfer 1986).

But whereas there is consensus on the contribution of remittances to the reduction of poverty, their contribution to reducing social inequalities is more debatable, because migration requires preexisting resources that only more well-off families can use to send a migrant abroad. Thus remittances may actually worsen social inequalities. The positive influence on children's level of schooling as well as on their school performances is largely recognized. Compared to those of households without migrants, children are less often enrolled in the labor market at young ages, and get extracurricular school teaching support. The positive effects of remittances on health are also recognized. More money being allocated to health expenses and to improving housing conditions reduces health risk factors in the household, not to mention the money invested at the village level to set up and improve community public health facilities.

The distribution of remittances by type of expense varies according to their geographical origin, but there is no clear pattern. In the five African countries, internal migrants and those working in another African country contribute mainly to covering primary needs (food and clothing). Those working elsewhere (Europe and the US) often invest more money in housing, business, and education, all of which require larger amounts of money, which corresponds to the macro characteristics of remittances. This broad statement must be qualified. Money sent by migrants is used differently, whatever their place of residence abroad, whereas the degree of national poverty does make a difference, as evidenced by the graphs comparing Burkina Faso and Nigeria (table 5.8 and figure 5.1).

Table 5.8.   Type of expense and geographical origin of remittances in Burkina Faso and Nigeria.

Type of Expense	Migrants from Burkina Faso Working			Migrants from Nigeria Working		
	Outside of Africa	In Another African Country	In Burkina Faso*	Outside of Africa	In Another African Country	In Nigeria**
Food and clothing	28.5*	35.6	49.4	10.1	20.1	1
Housing	26	11.1	3.8	10.5	4.9	7.1
Education	12.4	5.9	9.4	22.1	19.6	4.5
Health	11.3	10,1	12.5	5.1	12	10.6
Business investment	10.4	6.5	3.5	46.5	36.7	29.3
Other	11.4	30.5	21.4	5.7	6.7	47.5

* Figures represent percentage of total remittances spent on each item.
** Remittances sent by internal migrants.
NOTE: The numbers in this table represent percentages of total remittances spent on each item/category.
Sources: Based on Plazza and Navaprette 2011; World Bank Migration Project 2011.

Consequences for wives left behind and who are in charge of their households have long been documented. Indeed, more and more migrating women now look for jobs and are no longer "co-migrants." Nevertheless, in the case of the African countries, male migrants still overwhelmingly outnumber women. In Lesotho, 40 percent of households obtain their main income from transfers from emigrants gone to work in mines in South Africa; miners' land migration is expressed by an exceptionally high rate of women heads of households: 40 percent of households are run by women. It has been argued that women benefit from additional incomes and are better able to control the household expenses. Their implication in the community organization is also greater and their empowerment increases. There are also fewer gender inequalities within families. But other works emphasize the negative consequence of the husband's absence on family cohesion. Also, remittances reduce the need to mobilize the female labor force and women undergo pressure to give up being active. In Morocco, the female labor force has been reduced by approximately 10 percent.

Theorizing Remittances: Individual Migrants, Families, Local Societies
Beyond the mass of somewhat conflicting data, a few existing theories help to unveil the rationales underlying behaviors. As often occurs in sociology, a guiding thread is that analyses must not be confined to the individual migrant as an autonomous actor solely obeying his own economic rationality. He interacts with his family, while his own family not only uses migration in its relationship with other families living nearby but also relies on its network abroad.[3]

The Relative Deprivation Theory
If comparison with other individuals in the same reference group leads to a feeling of *relative deprivation*, the propensity to migrate will be greater, and the aim of the migrant

---

3   Dia 2014 provides a fine analysis of family strategies in north Senegal.

will be that the expected rewards of migration reduce this perceived inequality. In this respect, the return can be analyzed as the moment when the individual has gathered enough objective and subjective items that it signals success, causing the peer group to reassess their position when the individual returns home. The amount of transfers and the repatriation of objects deemed "sumptuary" therefore fulfills a socioeconomic function loaded with meaning. Orthodox economists tend to dismiss these so-called sumptuary or ostentatious behaviors by arguing that they are simple "effects of demonstration" (Fellat 1996, 330), or by stigmatizing them as behaviors that do not correspond to the economic rationality of development. The problem is rather that researchers tend to opt for a specific and single rationality by excluding any other logic. From this angle, social investments (in education, health, community religious centers) can be considered as a contribution to social prestige within the village community, the family, and even as a strategy by certain ethnic groups. Such is the case of the Diakanke migrants of maritime Guinea (Petit 2017) and the Kayes in Mali (Manchuelle cited by Azam and Gubert 2002, 207). Therefore, financial transfers can be analyzed as a factor reducing socioeconomic inequalities whether in the case of a poor family that has succeeded in its strategy to diversify its resources through emigration or, on the contrary, through exacerbating inequalities in the village in the case of an already comfortable family that has opted for emigration. Financial transfers have another consequence: that of bringing the traditional establishment into question, and the takeover of political power by returned migrants. Such was the case in Portugal when it was an emigration country (Charbit et al. 1997).

Why Do Migrants Send Money Home?

At the micro-sociological level, remittances are a concrete and symbolic link between the individual migrant and his family and/or ethnic group. Almost always, families and kinship have covered the cost of migration, and family networks in the EU have facilitated the migrant's search for a job, accommodation, etc. Indeed, the emigrant is repaying a debt, which induces appalling exploitation in backroom sweatshops comparable to that of the nineteenth-century proletariat of the Industrial Revolution in Europe. But the emigrant also sends money to reassert his belonging to his reference group, and to gain access to the matrimonial market in view of his future return.

International emigration (this reasoning is also valid for the rural exodus) is often criticized due to the effect of selection: since it is the young active population that leaves, the place of departure loses its workforce and its already scarce productive skills. However, the individual actor, i.e., the migrant, is not the sole entity that must be taken into account. In developing countries, since the family has a far greater influence on the behaviors of individuals than in industrialized countries, both the decision to migrate and that to return home should be analyzed as the result of interactions between the migrant and his family, especially if the family is large and structured by vertical authority. This is why behaviors have been conceptualized in terms of reciprocal interdependence and the "crucial meso-level" has been cited (Faist 2000). If we consider the entire economic unit represented by the family and the migrant, who collaborate in the short and long terms, the economic benefit is assured for the family, since the cash transfers help to diversify the household's resources. A rural family that wants to change from self-subsistence to a capitalist-type operation is faced by a lack of credit, with the impossibility of borrowing to either purchase land or equip itself with farm machinery. This is precisely the role that will be played by remittances and is emphasized by the surveys available on the uses to which these transfers are put and which mention the purchase of land in rural areas. In other words, the family unit, through the benefits expected from sending one or several cash transfers, undertakes to optimize or at least reassign its resources (Stark 1991).

As for the individual migrant, it is impossible to analyze his motivations and the factors attached to his return separately from those at play during the preliminary phase, that of the initial emigration. The migrant benefits from the family's ability to call up social capital: it gathered the financial resources needed to pay for the departure and called on its own family or community networks to receive the migrant on his arrival abroad (accommodation, administrative procedures, presentation and recommendation to potential employers). A survey performed in Botswana in 1978–79 (Stark 1991, 216–54) showed that exchanges and repercussions are staggered in time and that the remittances increase as a function of three variables: the level of education, the size of herds, and the intensity of drought periods. The remittances are invested in educating the young to ensure future resources (though here the relation can be reversed). Since the herds are the main form of inheritance, the migrant is well advised to make known his entitlement to it. Lastly, sending money in times of drought should not be analyzed as a purely altruistic act, but as a means of limiting the risk of inheriting herds decimated by hunger and thirst. The links between the migrant and the family must be sufficiently strong in order for the system to function. Can the hypothesis of a unilateral breach of contract be considered? The risk is far from being a supposition if the migrant implements another strategy (mixed marriage and definitive integration abroad), but the strength of cultural links and those of identity—which cannot be quantified economically—will result in a rationale of return or coming and going. Thus, noncompliance with the family contract may exclude the migrant from the local matrimonial market, and even from the community. The risk of nonreturn is of course higher for a single migrant than for a married one.

Risk Management

For the family and the individual migrant, if one accepts that the characteristic of rural economies is the almost inevitable recurrence of risk (drought, floods, destruction by insects especially locusts), this constant and recurrent risk is replaced by one that diminishes through time. The departure and then return can be analyzed in two phases: a high initial risk, corresponding to funding the departure and the journey; and a later, lower risk, wherein the initial investments and the farming risks for the family in the home country are to be offset by the remittances. To continue with this idea of minimizing risk: assigning the remittances to education expenses also appears to be a medium- and long-term investment. As for the migrant, he also takes a high initial risk following his arrival abroad, with periods of unemployment or periods of work with poor pay or which fails to match his qualifications; then he is subject to a later, lower risk as his living and working conditions improve. These two risks, high then low, are preferred to a constant risk—that of not emigrating.

The latter theory allows reinterpreting empirical observations. It is logical that the investments take place in sectors of low risk, such as trade. In Turkey a survey in 1978–79 on community and employee-run enterprises set up by migrants who had returned showed that shopkeeping, textiles, clothes-making, and construction are the main sectors in which capital is reinvested (De Tapia 1986; Ben Ali 1996). In addition, for migrants from rural localities, purchasing land, as mentioned earlier, is perfectly rational: it increases landed assets (CERED 1996, 216), and provides a surface area large enough to ensure self-sufficiency and develop commercial farming by selling part of the produce. Lastly, building and improving dwellings clearly ensure the occupants that they will at least be housed and that their property will be enhanced, because of inflationary effects on the housing market. However, in Dakar-Pikine, investments by emigrants do not correspond only to speculative logic (Tall 1994). Finally, it is wrong to claim that remittances invested in housing are depleted by sumptuary expenses.

Implications for Migration and Development Policies

It should be recalled that Article 13 of the CPA states that development was expected to reduce migrations, but this is far from proven, as a representative of one of the member states of the panel mentioned above stated:

> I would suggest to take into consideration two lessons that can be drawn from the implementation of article 13 of the Cotonou agreement. 1) The language of article 13 is extremely outdated when it comes to the nexus between migration and development, that it depicts in very simplistic terms: that more development will lead to a "normalization" of migratory pressure. Thinking has evolved a lot on these aspects, also driven by evidence that more development doesn't automatically lead to less migration, but rather the opposite (the so called "migration hump"). There is currently shared understanding of the complexity of this nexus and current EU policy aims at maximizing the positive effects of migration on development and minimizing the negative ones. 2) The provisions on readmission included in article 13 are implemented quite unevenly, and this is a concern for EU Member States that complain about the lack of cooperation of the ACP countries regarding these aspects . . . When it comes to migration, one has to be aware that there can be a risk of conditionality, meaning subordinating development cooperation instruments to achieving internal migration policy objectives. This is quite a thorny issue, on which the EU Member States are quite divided . . . EU Member States should not use development cooperation instruments to try to achieve internal objectives since development cooperation is an autonomous policy with its own objectives (especially so now, with the Lisbon treaty). However, development cooperation can contribute to the achievement of internal objectives. For instance it is legitimate to use development cooperation funds to reinforce the capacity of the relevant authorities of countries of origin to properly reintegrate readmitted migrants, but it is not legitimate to decrease development cooperation for countries that do not cooperate in readmitting people. (DEVCO 2015)

In view of this major issue for the EU's future development policy, policy implications regarding migrations and remittances were discussed. Some of them are summarized here but are related to the demographic context.

Age Structures, Demographic Dividend, Brain Drain

Age structures and aging have already raised tensions in some EU countries with respect to the job market and will induce gender-, age-, qualification- and sector-specific problems. In sub-Saharan Africa, the demographic dividend may well not be reached in the near future. With their high fertility rates, rapid demographic growth will continue, causing low school enrollment rates and thus poorly qualified manpower. As long as these countries are unable to provide jobs for the growing number of those entering the labor market, it is likely that the pressure to emigrate to find jobs in Europe will not diminish. This last remark leads us directly to the issue of the brain drain. The job market in developing countries offers few opportunities for highly educated individuals. However, the psychological dimension must be added to purely economic motivations. The aspirations and perceptions linked to the specific prestige of living in rich countries, which developing countries cannot satisfy, lead the best qualified to leave for the developed countries. According to the neoclassical analysis, the brain drain is the perfectly rational behavior of economic actors who go where the best job opportunities and living conditions exist. But this vision, true at the individual level, is debatable at the macroeconomic level of states. The brain drain has in no way contributed to reducing the disparity between the salaried employees of rich countries and those of poor countries. On the contrary, the departure of qualified migrants has had a social and economic cost for African countries. Whereas the education of these migrants is borne by them, they do not obtain any benefit in terms of development since the competencies acquired by these qualified migrants are used in the service of the countries of immigration. Table 5.9 shows the extent to which human resources are depleted, especially in countries where the average level of education is low. The comparison among India, France, and three other countries highlights this. According to UNDP (2009), more than 65,000 West African students were enrolled in PhD programs in OECD countries. On the one hand, they amounted to 30–40% of all migrants from the countries under consideration, a proportion comparable to that of France (32.3%) but much lower than that of India (51.2%). On the other hand, among students, the percentage residing in one of the OECD countries is much higher than in India or France: 25.7% in Congo, 12.5% in Cameroon, and 9.6% in the Democratic Republic of the Congo versus 3.5% in India and 4.2% in France.

Table 5.9. Distribution of emigrants from selected countries of origin living in the OECD by level of education.

| Country of Origin | Level of Education of Emigrants in the OECD | | | | |
	Primary	Secondary	Higher	Total	Exodus of Graduates (%)
Rep. of Congo	27.1	34.2	34.9	100	25.7
Cameroon	23.3	32.3	41.9	100	12.5
Dem. Rep. Congo	25.0	32.5	35.5	100	9.6
India	25.5	19.5	51.2	100	3.5
France	32	30.7	32.3	100	4.2

Source: UNDP 2009.

The survey thus confirmed that international emigration to pursue higher education is an essential key for individual success, whatever the perspective of a later return to the country of departure.

But the landscape is changing. First, it is striking to observe that, generally, recent generations of migrants are increasingly educated: for migrants leaving developing countries or emerging economies for the OECD countries, the share of university graduates (levels 5 and 6 in the international classification) has increased by 50 percent during the last ten years. According to this report, immigrants living in the OECD zone "are on average more educated than the indigenous population, with nearly a quarter of them having reached a higher level of education, whereas this is the case for only 20% of the persons born in the country" (OECD 2008; Docquier and Marfouk 2006). Second, this genuine capture of human capital has evolved due to the complexity of the trajectories of qualified migrants. Research converges to conclude that the migration of this category of worker does not necessarily have a negative impact in the medium term on the African countries of emigration (see Petit 2012 for an in-depth analysis). Second, French-speaking students of the Central African and West African CPA countries (Gabon, Cameroon, Rwanda, Congo, RDC, Burundi, and Ivory Coast) increasingly turn to South Africa. This can be explained by a series of economic and political factors: the degradation of the public higher education systems in these regions; the drastic reduction of international and public aid given in CPA African countries to students to study abroad; the immigration policy of South Africa that favors education with an emphasis placed on "quality migration."

Differences in health patterns also impact migration flows. Migration controls of recent epidemics (HIV/AIDS, Ebola) recall the quarantine and preventive measures of past centuries. Beyond this public health issue, migration flows from Africa have greatly helped to match demand with supply for health in the EU. Several EU countries have long suffered from a shortage of doctors and nursing personnel. Confronted by this shortage, the recruitment of foreign professionals has represented the most effective short-term solution, and without decades of hiring poorly paid African, Indian, and West Indian nurses and doctors, the functioning of hospitals in Europe would have been greatly handicapped. For growing ambulatory needs, other niches exist and lessons can be drawn from choices made by some countries such as the Philippines to promote market-oriented training for paramedics and nurses. In Africa, the strong family relationships and networks, imbued with the value of intergenerational solidarity and the respect paid to elders, provide an excellent cultural background for training people, especially women, to benefit from the rapidly expanding labor market in the so-called care economy. As populations in the EU countries become increasingly older, it is foreseeable that they will be in sore need of a labor force with such qualifications. Among qualified migrants, medical professionals have given rise to questions as much in the receiving countries of the EU, and more generally of the OECD, as in the countries of departure (Goldin, Cameron, and Balarajan 2011).

Seen from the developing countries, this recruitment policy is now identified as a danger for the health systems of PCA countries, especially in the context of the HIV/AIDS epidemic in Malawi and South Africa, for example. According to WHO, in 2000 the emigration of doctors and nursing personnel born in Africa and working in the OECD zone was responsible for 12 percent of the total shortage of medical professionals in the region. The rates of expatriation of doctors are higher than 50 percent in the island countries of the Caribbean and the Pacific, as well as in Africa (Mozambique, Angola, Sierra Leone, Tanzania, and Liberia). Several French-speaking African countries also have high rates of expatriation, exceeding 40 percent.

High African Fertility

Third, the rapid demographic growth in Africa is due to high fertility rates. Population growth is excessive with regard to current economic growth rates, leading to constantly increasing expenses for health and education, housing, food production, etc.[4] This is why development policies focus on specific components of population programs aimed at *directly* reducing fertility, like contraception or increasing age at marriage. These policies will indeed reduce incentives to migrate, but only when the girls born in the new generations will reach reproductive age, i.e., roughly over the span of a generation, twenty to twenty-five years later, when these less numerous daughters will replace their mothers. Needless to say, this will happen far too late to reduce *current* pressure to migrate, and of course migration flows have not and will never be sufficient to absorb large increases in population, precisely because of political barriers to immigration. The same objection can be raised regarding indirect factors like education and the empowerment of women, even if the education of women is strategic for the future. Reducing poverty has more immediate results in curbing migration flows, as our theory of change and response strongly suggests (Charbit and Petit 2011; Petit 2017); in other words, development policies are far more crucial when integrating migration issues than pure population policies.

Remittances, Microfinance, and Diasporas

As has been argued, informal channels are preferred because they permit avoiding taxes, escaping government controls, and also possibly benefiting from more favorable foreign

---

4   According to the World Bank (April 1, 2017), "Growth in Sub-Saharan Africa slowed markedly in 2016 to 1.5%, and is projected to recover moderately in 2017 this year to 2.6%. Growth will continue to strengthen in 2018, helped by improvements in commodity prices and domestic conditions. However, the recovery remains fragile with most of the uplift coming from Africa's three largest economies—Angola, Nigeria and South Africa—as they rebound from a sharp slowdown in 2016. . . . Following a decline of 1.1% in 2016, per capita gross domestic product (GDP) will be unchanged in 2017. In Angola, Nigeria, and South Africa, the weak uptick in growth implies that their GDP in per capita terms will continue to contract over the forecast horizon. With high persistent poverty rates, the region is faced with the urgent need to regain the momentum on growth in Sub-Saharan Africa and to make this growth more inclusive. This will require deep reforms to improve institutions for private sector growth, develop local capital markets, enhance efficiency of utilities, improve the quantity and quality of public infrastructure, and strengthen domestic resource mobilization, so as to facilitate structural transformation."

exchange rates on the black market. Policies have been implemented to substitute formal circuits for informal circuits. That would provide African governments with additional means to channel these resources according to their development programs. However, the distinction between these two categories of flows is likely to become blurred due to new technologies. Thus, according to a recent survey of the Bill Gates Foundation, in eleven African countries, electronic payments already account for 17 percent of the remittances, the remainder circulating by bank transfers and by cash. NTICs (New Technologies of Information and Communication) have provided a new perspective for reframing the dynamics of remittances. The first studies devoted to the e-transfer of remittances through mobile phones have shown that migrants tend to change the allocation of the money. Some studies mention that 70 percent of the remittances carried out by e-transfer are devoted to saving money with an aim toward a later return.

Reducing the costs of the transfers should be an objective, because the resulting losses are very high for the poorest countries. In Africa they are 50 percent higher than the global average, and amount to 12 percent of the total transfer (World Bank, 2014, as quoted in DEVCO 2015). At the global level, these costs rise to approximately US$40 billion per annum with very strong national disparities. Indeed, Africa records the highest costs, amounting to approximately 12 percent of the total amount transferred, approximately 50 percent above the world average. In addition, these costs are falling more slowly than in other regions. Also to be taken into account is that the costs of the transfers within the inter-Africa framework are even higher. And they are particularly high between the countries of southern Africa, which receive poor migrants from countries with very low incomes. The member states of the G20 were committed to implementing an "action plan for the development of remittances" intended to reduce the cost of the transfers by 5 percentage points. If it succeeds, this program would make it possible to save approximately US$16 billion every year for the benefit of less developed countries.

The potential for remittances to contribute to local development through microfinance could be further exploited. Cooperation with migrant and civil society associations should be encouraged. This system of granting microcredit has spread very quickly over the last few years in nearly 90 countries, and more than 100 million people among the poorest populations are currently using it. Many microfinance programs in rural regions are sustained by regular payments from migrants. They give access to credit to households that otherwise probably would not have any access to the commercial banking system. Remittances also facilitate the development of saving plans and of insurance programs, which, by reducing risks of insolvency, reinforce the capacity of populations to invest.

Remittances from diasporas should not be forgotten, and CPA-EU collaboration should aim at increasing their already important role in development. Collaboration between the EU and overseas diasporas could contribute to reinforcing the efficiency of remittances, the Africa-EU Chamber of Commerce being a promising initiative. Also, the new African Institute for Remittances (AIR), led by the African Union with the support of the World Bank and the European Commission, aims at building the capacity of the member states of the African Union and remittance senders and recipients to develop and implement concrete strategies and operational instruments to use remittances as development tools for poverty reduction. To support the mobilization of savings in the diasporas, "bonds for migrants" have been created in order to channel remittances. It is hoped that in the long term these bonds will be converted into productive investments in the countries of origin.

Beyond these technical aspects, well-balanced judgment on remittances and development is obliged to speak out against world inequalities and situations of domination. The poorest developing countries receive only a relatively small part of the total volume of remittances, which are far outweighed by transfers in the opposite direction, such as profits transferred by international firms to tax havens and outflows due to transfer pricing, not to mention the vast amounts of money associated with corruption. In view of these flows the contribution of remittances to development is a meager compensation.

References

Adams, R. H., and J. Page. 2003. *International Migration, Remittances and Poverty in Developing Countries.* World Bank Policy Research Working Paper no. 3179, Poverty Reduction Group, Washington, DC.

Africa Union Factsheets:

2013a. "Initiating the Demographic Dividend by Achieving a Fertility Decline."

2013b. "Toward a Demographic Dividend: Invest in Health and Education."

2013c. "Africa and the Challenge of Realizing the Demographic Dividend."

2013d. "Creating Jobs: Challenge for a Demographic Dividend."

Austen, R. 1987. *African Economic History: Internal Development and External Dependency.* London: J. Curry.

Azam, J.-P., and F. Gubert. 2002. "Ceux de Kayes: L'effet des transferts des émigrés maliens sur leur famille d'origine." In *Commissariat général au Plan: Immigration, marché du travail, intégration,* 203–30. Paris: La documentation Française.

Barou, J. 2000. "Migrations et travaux forcés en Afrique subsaharienne à l'époque coloniale." *Hommes et migrations* 1286/1287: 51–61.

Ben Ali, D. 1996. "L'impact des transferts des résidents marocains à l'étranger (R.M.E.) sur l'investissement productif." In *Migration internationale,* CERED, Maroc, 345–62.

Bencherifa, A. 1996. "L'impact de la migration internationale sur le monde rural marocain." In *Migration internationale,* CERED, Maroc, 403–30.

Beauchemin C., and D. Lessault. 2009. "Ni invasion, ni exode: Regards statistiques sur les migrations d'Afrique subsaharienne." *Revue Européenne des Migrations Internationales* 25(1): 163–94.

Bloom, D. E., D. Canning, and J. Sevilla. 2003. *The Demographic Dividend: A New Perspective on the Economic Consequences of Population Change.* Santa Monica CA: RAND.

Bloom, D. E., et al. 2007. *Fertility, Female Labor Force Participation, and the Demographic Dividend.* National Bureau of Economic Research Working Paper no. 13583.

Brou, K., and Y. Charbit. 1994. "La politique migratoire de la Côte d'Ivoire." *Revue Européenne des Migrations Internationales* 10(3): 33–59.

Castles, S., H. de Haas, and M. Miller. 2014. *The Age of Migration,* 5th ed. Basingstoke: Palgrave Macmillan.

CERED. 1996. *Migration internationale: Actes du séminaire sur les migrations internationales.* Série études, Rabat, Maroc.

Charbit, Y. 2007. "Transferts, retours et développement: Données, concepts et problématiques." in *Les migrations internationales de retour dans la perspective des pays du sud,* edited by Véronique Petit, 44–75. Paris: Centre Population de Développement.

———. 2015. "Demographic Developments, Scoping Paper." In DEVCO, *Renewal of the ACP-EU Partnership Agreement: Roundtable Report, Cluster 7, "Demographic Developments,"* April, pp. 25–44.

Charbit, Y., and C. Bertrand. 1985. *Familles, Migrations dans le Bassin Mediterraneen.* Paris: PUF.

Charbit, Y., M-A. Hily, M. Poinard, and V. Petit. 1997. *Le va-et-vient identitaire: Migrants portugais et villages d'origine*. Paris: INED/PUF.

Charbit, Y., and V. Petit. 2011. "Toward a Comprehensive Demography: Rethinking the Research Agenda on Change and Response." *Population and Development Review* 37(2): 219–39.

Coquery-Vidrovitch, C. 2000. "L'économie coloniale des anciennes zones françaises, belges et portugaises (1914–1935)." In *Histoire générale de l'Afrique VII: L'Afrique sous domination coloniale, 1880–1935*, 381–411. Paris: UNESCO.

———. 2010. "Les migrations internationales en Afrique de l'Ouest: Une dynamique de régionalisation renouvelée." *Hommes et migrations* 1286/1287: 48–61.

Cordell, D., J. Gregory, and V. Piché. 1996. *Hoe and Wage*. Boulder, CO: Westview.

Curtin, P. 1969. *The Atlantic Slave Trade: A Census*. Madison: University of Wisconsin Press.

De Tapia, S. 1986. "La création d'entreprises populaires les migrants en Turquie." *Revue Européenne des Migrations Internationales* 2(12): 59–75.

Dia, H. 2014. "La capitalisation de la rente migratoire par les familles senegalaises." In *Questions de Migrations et de Sante en Afrique sub-Saharienne: Recherches Interdisciplinaires en France et au Japon*, edited by Y. Charbit and T. Mishima, 125–48. Paris: L'Harmattan.

Docquier, F., and A. Marfouk. 2006. "International Migration by Educational Attainment, 1990–2000." In *International Migration, Remittances and the Brain Drain*, edited by C. Özden and M. Schiff, 151–99. Washington, DC: World Bank.

Faist, T. 2000. "The Crucial Meso-Level." In *The Volume and Dynamics of International Migration and Transnational Social Spaces*, 187–217. Oxford: Oxford University Press.

Fellat, F.M. 1996. "Transferts et politiques d'incitation aux investissements des émigrés (Maroc)." In *Migration internationale, actes du CERED, Maroc*, 305–26.

Flahaux, M. L., and H. de Haas. 2016. "African Migration: Trends, Patterns, Drivers." *Comparative Migration Studies* 4, no. 1.

Gaimard, M. 2013. *Population and Health in Developing Countries*. Dordrecht: Springer.

Goldin, I., G. Cameron, and M. Balarajan. 2011. *Exceptional People: How Migration Shaped Our World and Will Define Our Future*. Princeton, NJ: Princeton University Press.

Global Forum on Remittances, Investment and Development. 2018. *Remittances: An Untapped Engine for Sustainable Development*. Kuala Lumpur, May 8, UN Department of Economic and Social Affairs.

Hermelé, K. 1997. "The Discourse on Migration and Development." In *International Migration, Immobility and Development: Multidisciplinary Perspectives*, edited by T. Hammar et al., 133–48. Oxford: Berg.

IMF (International Monetary Fund). 2018. *World Economic Outlook Database*. April.

Khabbanji, L. 2011. *Politiques migratoires en Afrique de l'Ouest: Burkina Faso et Côte d'Ivoire*. Paris: Karthala.

Lazaar, M. 1987. "Conséquences de l'émigration dans les montagnes du Rif marocain." *Revue Européenne des Migrations Internationales* 3(1/2): 97–114.

Lovejoy, P. E. 1982. "The Atlantic Slave Trade: A Synthesis." *Journal of African History* 6(4): 445–501.

MIGRINTER. 1986. "Les Maghrébins de la Régie Renault: Solidarités communautaires et implications au Maghreb." *Revue Européenne des Migrations Internationales* 2(1): 137–62.

Mishima, T. 2014. "Anthropologie des Migrations Internationales des Soninkee: formation et Transmission de la Richesse." In *Questions de Migrations et de Sante en Afrique sub-Saharienne: Recherches Interdisciplinaires en France et au Japon*, edited by Y. Charbit and T. Mishima, 99–123. Paris: L'Harmattan.

OECD (Organisation for Economic Cooperation and Development). 2008. *Les personnels de santé dans les pays de l'OCDE: Comment répondre à la crise imminente?*

OIM. 2017. *Measuring Global Migration Potential, 2010–2015*. Issue no. 9, May.

Petit, V. 2012. "Migrants qualifiés et mondialisation: Une étape vers le développement." In *Population, mondialisation et développement: Quelles dynamiques?*, edited by L. Cambrézy and V. Petit, 89–107. Paris: La documentation Française.

———. 2017. *Change and Response: From Theory to Fieldwork.* Dordrecht: Springer.

Pétré-Grenouilleau, O. 2004. *Les traites négrières.* Paris: Gallimard.

Plazza, S., M. Navarrete, and D. Ratah. 2011. *Migration and Remittances Household Surveys in Sub-Saharan Africa: Methodological Aspects and Main Findings.* Working paper of the World Bank Migration Project, March 31.

Population Reference Bureau. 2018. *Database* (online).

Robin, N. 2013. "Recompositions spatiales et mutations économiques." In *OCDE Peuplement, marché er sécurité alimentaire,* 68–74. Paris: OCDE.

Russel, S. S., K. Jacobsen, and W. D. Stanley. 1990. *International Migration and Development in Sub-Saharan Africa.* World Bank Discussion Paper no. 160. Washington, DC: World Bank.

Stark, O. 1991. *The Migration of Labour.* Basel: Blackwell.

Tall, M.S. 1994. "Les investissements immobiliers à Dakar des émigrants sénégalais." *Revue Européenne des Migrations Internationales* 10(3): 137–51.

Tapinos, G., and J. P. Garson. 1981. *L'argent des immigres: Revenus, epargne et dransferts de huit nationalites immigreees en France.* Paris: INED/PUF.

Toepfer, H. 1986. "Réinsertion et comportement régional des émigrés en Turquie." *Revue Européenne des Migrations Internationales* 2(1): 77–93.

Tsourapas, G. 2018. "Labor Migrants as Political Leverage: Migration Interdependence and Coercion in the Mediterranean." *International Studies Quarterly* 62(2): 383–95.

United Nations, Department of Economic and Social Affairs, Population Division. 2015. *Trends in International Migrant Stock: The 2015 Revision.* United Nations database, POP/DB/MIG/Stock/Rev.2015.

United Nations Development Program. 2009. *Rapport sur le développement humain, 2009, Lever les barrières: Mobilité et développement humains.*

UNHCR. 2016. *Global Report for 2016.*

UNDESA. 2015. *International Migration Report.* New York: United Nations.

World Bank. 2016. *Migration and Remittances: Recent Development and Outlook.*

———. 2017. Migration and Remittances Data: Annual Remittances Data (updated August 2017).

———. 2019. Migration and Remittances: Recent Developments and Outlook. Migration and Development Brief 31. Washington, DC: World Bank

PART 3

ASIA AND THE "DEVELOPMENTAL" MIGRATION STATE

6 THE DEVELOPMENTAL MIGRATION STATE IN EAST ASIA

Erin Aeran Chung

The East Asian Paradox

ALTHOUGH THE MAJORITY of English-language scholarship on immigration focuses on flows from the global South to the global North, or from East to West, intraregional and South–South migration is the dominant form of international migration in the contemporary world. According to the United Nations Migration Report, over 40 percent of the 244 million international migrants in 2015 were born in Asia and three of the five largest overseas populations originated from Asia.[1] Since intraregional migration *within* Asia far outnumbers interregional migration *from* Asia, however, Asia hosts almost as many international migrants as does Europe. The number of *internal* migrants throughout countries in the global South, moreover, is roughly three times that of international migrants at an estimated 740 million in 2015, compared to 232 million international migrants (International Organization for Migration 2015). China's internal migrants alone are almost double the total number of international migrants worldwide.[2]

This chapter extends Hollifield's (2004) migration state framework to Northeast Asia (hereafter "East Asia"), highlighting its generalizability as a frame of analysis and its limits. I focus on East Asian democracies, which, for the purposes of this chapter, refer to the countries of Japan, South Korea (hereafter "Korea"), and Taiwan. Similar to countries in Western Europe, Japan, Korea, and Taiwan confronted labor shortages at different stages of their industrial development. But rather than open their borders to migrant

---

1 India had the largest overseas population at 16 million, followed by Mexico (12 million), the Russian Federation (11 million), China (10 million), and Bangladesh (7 million). See https://www .un.org/en/development/desa/population/migration/publications/migrationreport/docs/Migra tionReport2015_Highlights.pdf.

2 In addition to China, the most internally mobile countries in the world today are South Africa, Chile, Mexico, Costa Rica, Brazil, Ecuador, Ghana, India, Indonesia, Malaysia, the Philippines, and Vietnam, according to the International Organization for Migration. See International Organization for Migration 2015.

workers as their European counterparts did from the mid-1960s and 1970s, the three East Asian countries tapped domestic sources of underutilized labor, such as rural workers and women, to meet labor demands until the 1980s. Following three decades of rapid economic growth—during which the GDP growth rate in all three countries reached an average of 10 percent or more (Japan in the 1960s, Korea in the mid-1960s to mid-1970s, and Taiwan in the 1970s)—domestic sources of labor were largely depleted as each country faced more labor shortages from the mid-to-late 1980s. Each country, moreover, has been facing an imminent demographic crisis with rapidly aging populations and fertility rates plummeting below the population replacement level of 2.1 children per woman since 1975 in Japan and since 1984 in Korea and Taiwan (Jones 2007; Jones and Gubhaju 2009; Haub 2011). Taiwan proceeded to establish a limited guest-worker program in the late 1980s, becoming the first East Asian country to do so, and passed the Employment Services Act in 1991 modeled after Singapore's system (see Hirschman, this volume). Japan and Korea, however, continued to keep their borders closed to unskilled foreign labor (until 2004 in Korea and 2019 in Japan), opting instead for piecemeal solutions that would temporarily meet domestic demands for labor.

Despite restrictive policies, immigration to East Asia has grown exponentially over the past few decades. In Japan, the foreign population more than doubled from 850,000 in 1985 to over 2.1 million in 2015, with the largest numbers coming from China, the Korean peninsula, Brazil, the Philippines, and Peru (see figure 6.1). Korea's foreign population has grown more than sevenfold in less than two decades, from approximately 210,000 in 2000 to almost 1.9 million in 2015, with the largest numbers coming from China, Vietnam, and the Philippines (see figure 6.2). And Taiwan's foreign population jumped from less than a little over 250,000 in 1995 to over 637,000 in 2015, with the

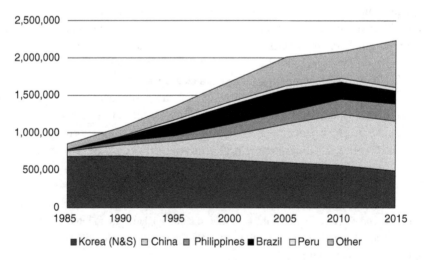

Figure 6.1. Foreign residents in Japan by nationality, 1985–2015.

* The "other" category includes nationals of more than 200 countries in every continent. Among the largest numbers of foreign residents in this category are nationals of Vietnam, the United States, Bangladesh, Nepal, India, Thailand, Indonesia, the United Kingdom, Canada, and Australia.

Sources: Japan Ministry of Justice; Japan Statistical Yearbook

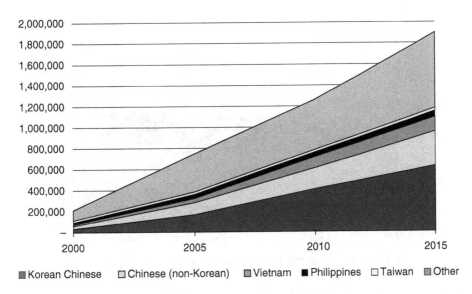

Figure 6.2. Foreign residents in Korea by nationality, 2000–2015.

* The "other" category includes nationals of more than 200 countries in every continent. Among the largest numbers of foreign residents in this category are nationals of Thailand, the United States, Indonesia, Mongolia, Myanmar, Japan, Uzbekistan, Sri Lanka, Cambodia, Pakistan, Canada, Bangladesh, and India.

Sources: Korea Immigration Service; Korean Statistical Information Service

largest numbers coming from Indonesia, Vietnam, the Philippines, and Thailand (see figure 6.3), plus over 62,000 Chinese nationals from mainland China, Hong Kong, and Macao. Compared to their North American, European, and Australian counterparts, however, foreign residents continue to make up a relatively small percentage of the total population in all three countries at approximately 2–4 percent, which is well below the levels necessary to alleviate each country's labor shortages and demographic deficits.

Why have East Asian democracies resisted large-scale importation of foreign labor despite labor shortages and an impending demographic crisis? The dominant comparative scholarship on immigration and citizenship has tended to focus on cultural determinants, especially claims of ethnocultural homogeneity, to explain the East Asian paradox. According to this account, East Asian countries represent exclusionary or "ethnic" citizenship and immigration regimes that privilege descent over liberal norms and apply ascriptive criteria in determining entry and membership rights (Castles and Miller 2009; Vink 2017). Despite their development as liberal democracies—Japan as a mature democracy since the early postwar period and Korea and Taiwan as consolidated democracies since their democratic transitions in the late 1980s and late 1990s, respectively—political elites in the three countries have prioritized social stability over liberal democratic principles in justifying their closed immigration policies. And, in Korea and Japan, ideologies of cultural and racial homogeneity are associated with each country's economic, political, and social development while diversity continues to be associated with social instability (Lie 2001; Shin 2006). Likewise, international norms and pressure have had an uneven, indeterminate impact on East Asian democracies.

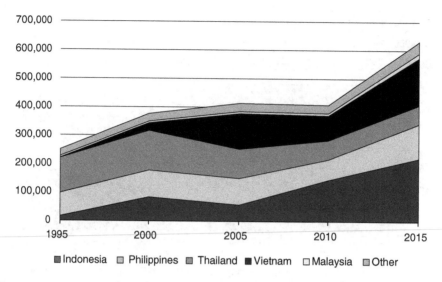

Figure 6.3. Foreign residents in Taiwan by nationality, 1995–2015.

* The "other" category includes nationals of more than 90 countries in every continent. Among the largest numbers of foreign residents in this category include nationals of South Korea, India, Canada, United Kingdom, Myanmar, France, and Singapore.

Source: Taiwan Ministry of the Interior.

Especially in the area of refugee policies, Korea, Japan, and Taiwan have remained immune to international pressure, continuing to hold among the worst records in the industrialized world for accepting refugees (Chung 2010a).

Hollifield and Sharpe (2017) argue that Japan and other countries that have long had closed immigration policies are developing into migration states as they slowly open their borders to meet labor demands and recognize the need to integrate immigrant populations to maintain social stability while addressing cultural and security concerns associated with open borders and growing diversity. To be sure, contemporary immigration policies in the three East Asian democracies resemble those of Europe in the 1960s and 1970s when neither the public nor the government recognized migrant workers as potential citizens or permanent settlers. And there are signs of change: all three countries have finally opened their borders, however slightly, to foreign labor with the development of formal guest-worker programs. Are East Asian democracies simply "latecomers" to immigration that will eventually follow the trajectories of other former reluctant countries of immigration?

Rather than rely on culturalist explanations based on assumptions about a "homogenous society" or the "laggard" narrative that overlooks much of Japan, Korea, and Taiwan's migration histories, I argue that the emergence of what I call a "developmental migration state" in East Asia is consistent with each country's developmental trajectory that is rooted in political economy rather than in cultural traditions. As non-Western countries with among the largest economies in the world that send *and* host substantial migrant populations, East Asian countries do not fit easily into binary categories such as global South/North, developing/developed societies, and countries of emigration/

immigration. Neither do they adhere to the liberal/illiberal migration regime framework. Despite their categorization as liberal democracies, Japan, Korea, and Taiwan have been on a migration trajectory characterized by partially open borders and discrete institutionalized rights for specific subcategories of migrants. They have thus become the exception to the liberal convergence thesis as they have maintained exclusionary immigration policies and low levels of immigration despite high levels of political economic development.

The following section discusses the historical antecedent of the developmental migration state, that is, the trajectory of late development that led to the formation of a developmental state and developmental citizenship in East Asia. Next, I trace the emergence of the developmental migration state in Japan, Korea, and Taiwan, focusing on their migration histories, policies, and adaptative institutions. Finally, I identify the distinguishing characteristics of the developmental migration state and consider comparative implications for our understanding of "negative cases" of immigration.

Developmental Citizenship

In my book *Immigrant Incorporation in East Asian Democracies* (Chung 2020), I argue that contemporary immigration policies and immigrant incorporation models in East Asia emerged from patterns of mobilization and exclusion in each country's path to democracy as "late developers," defined as countries that began to grow from agricultural to industrial economies either just before or during the twentieth century at what are now considered to be rapid rates (Amsden 1989, 140). Japan, Korea, and Taiwan each embarked on a path of rapid economic development from the late nineteenth century (in the case of Japan) to the late twentieth century that transformed them into the third (formerly second), eleventh, and twenty-first largest economies in the world, respectively. Their political development as democracies, however, lagged far behind their economic development, with far-reaching consequences for their citizenship regimes.

Despite Japan's history as a mature democracy, with its roots in the short-lived Taisho period (1912–26), postwar Japan's political system stands out among the world's democracies for its one-party domination by the Liberal Democratic Party (LDP) since 1955 with only two short interruptions: approximately eleven months from 1993 to 1994 and a three-year period following a landslide victory by the opposition, Democratic Party of Japan (DPJ), in the 2009 lower-house elections. Korea and Taiwan's transitions to democracy, by contrast, came much later, following the declaration of President Roh Tae Woo's eight-point program of democratic reforms in 1987 in Korea and Taiwan's first direct presidential elections in 1996, both of which came after their respective "economic miracles" *and* decades of often brutal authoritarian rule.

Although authoritarian (or "soft" authoritarian in the case of postwar Japan until the 1980s) rule did not go unchallenged, all three countries established "developmental" political systems that prioritized economic growth above all else. According to H. Chang (1999, 192), the archetypical developmental state is one that can "create and regulate the economic and political relationships which can support sustained industrialization" and "which takes the goals of long-term growth and structural change seriously, 'politically' manages the economy to ease the conflict inevitable during the process of such change,

and engages in institutional adaptation and innovation in order to achieve those goals."
Two features are central to understanding the social contract of the developmental state:
(1) the state's strategic, goal-oriented approach to the economy (Johnson 1982; Gao 1997)
and (2) the concept of developmentalism, referring to "an ideology or worldview that accords industrialization a higher priority than other societal goals and gives the state the
leading role in promoting it" (Schneider 1999, 283). In other words, *economic* development was the source of *political* legitimacy.

   While each state resorted to violent repression at different levels of intensity and duration throughout their rapid industrialization, political elites of developmental states
nevertheless required the voluntary cooperation of the populace in order to amass
enough human capital to carry out the herculean task of "catching up," as Gerschenkron's
(1962) seminal work on European late developers described. Rather than incorporate
subordinate classes into a community of citizens through the extension of citizenship
rights according to the trajectory that Marshall (1950) describes in his account of British
political development from the eighteenth to early twentieth centuries, late developers
relied on a more nationalistic vision of citizenship that mobilized the citizenry around
the intertwined goals of economic development and national security.

   The institution of citizenship in East Asia is thus a relatively recent state construction
aimed at mobilizing the citizenry around the goals of modernization and rapid industrialization (Chung 2020). If we apply Hollifield's (this volume) "four-sided" game of migration governance—whereby states balance concerns about markets, national security,
social stability or "culture," and rights in managing the challenges of immigration—to
citizenship, we can make the case that East Asian states prioritized security, markets, and
social stability (or "culture") over rights. At the same time, it would be a mistake to assume that East Asian late developers faced trade-offs between four *discrete* priorities. On
the contrary, each state mobilized the population around a common "culture" in which
national security, economic development, and a common, largely homogenous, cultural
identity were intertwined within a narrative of nationhood.

   Rather than a deeply rooted understanding of nationhood predating each state or a
culturally determined ethos emanating from Confucian civilization, the developmental
states in East Asia gained popular support through economic outcomes amidst widely
perceived external threats. In prewar Japan, economic development went hand in hand
with revolutionary nationalism born out of imperialism and, later, war as embodied by
the Meiji slogan of *fukoku kyōhei* ("rich nation, strong army"). Johnson (1982) argues
that this form of economic nationalism remained powerful in postwar Japan, characterizing the Japanese economy as one that was "mobilized for war but never demobilized
during peacetime" (Johnson 1999, 41). In South Korea, the Park Chung Hee administration (in its second administration from 1972 to 1979) recast Japan's developmental model
as a matter of *national survival* that required a massive buildup of heavy industries not
only to strengthen Korea's competitiveness in the global market but also to augment
its national defense industry and end the country's reliance on the United States (Woo
1991). It was also an anticommunist project whereby the state enlisted its citizens to report suspicious activities among neighbors, colleagues, friends, and family, including
acts that could be construed as supporting North Korea, challenging the authoritarian

regime, or fomenting labor unrest (Shin 2006). In Taiwan, the Kuomintang (KMT) like-wise linked economic growth with anticommunism and "unity on the island," justifying the regime's hold on power with national security concerns centered on the imminent threat of invasion by the Chinese mainland (Copper 2009).

This type of "developmental citizenship" (K.-S. Chang 2007, 2012), which required citizens to give up, rather than make claims to, institutionalized rights for national de-velopment, provided an expedient shortcut to mobilizing the population to pursue rapid economic growth while putting other priorities, most notably democracy, on hold (Woo-Cumings 1994, 413–14). It also created hierarchies among citizens and, eventually, among noncitizens. Citizenship for those who were central to national developmental goals—namely, economic elites and, especially, big businesses—offered generous protections while, for the vast majority, it represented a bundle of liabilities that exposed them to the coercive and exclusionary power of the state (Woo-Cumings 1999; Kochenov 2019). Citizenship rights were above all secondary to economic and national-security concerns.

Migration Governance in East Asian Democracies

Is authoritarianism (or "soft" authoritarianism) to blame for the slow liberalization of East Asia's immigration policies? The Japanese, Korean, and Taiwanese developmental states were not unique among late developers; after all, *dirigisme* was central to the devel-opment strategies of Europe's late developers, most notably France and Germany. Should we then expect liberal reforms to accompany democratization and democratic deepen-ing in East Asia in parallel to the way that the "rights revolution" in Western democracies set the foundation for liberal immigration reforms?

If we applied a teleological framework to understanding migration governance based on democratic development, then we should expect that Japan, as a mature democracy, would have liberalized its immigration policies well before Korea or Taiwan, both rela-tively young democracies. Instead, Japan maintained closed borders to unskilled im-migration well after Taiwan and Korea opened theirs. While Korea enacted sweeping immigration reforms not long after its democratic transition, they have led to a widening gap in institutionalized rights *between* migrants and the institutionalization of nonciti-zen hierarchies. And Taiwan's democratic transition and deepening has been accompa-nied by the *restriction* of rights and privileges for select categories of migrants.

The "laggards" narrative assumes that immigration is a new phenomenon in East Asia. While their recent encounter began in the late 1980s and early 1990s, Japan, Korea, and Taiwan had been migration states of sorts well before then. The following sections discuss each country's development as a migration state.

Japan: From a Multiethnic Empire to a Nonmigration State

As a former imperial power that received its largest inflows of migrants into the metro-pole *before* 1945, Japan grappled with the challenges of immigrant incorporation well before its European counterparts encountered large-scale immigration in the postwar era. More than two million Korean and Formosan (Taiwanese) colonial subjects had migrated to the Japanese metropole by the end of the Pacific War; although approxi-mately two-thirds of this population repatriated to the Korean peninsula and Taiwan in the early postwar period, as many as 700,000 remained in Japan even after they were stripped of their Japanese nationality in 1952. Despite the considerable growth of the immigrant community since the late 1980s, colonial-era migrants and their descendants continue to constitute one of the largest foreign populations in Japan (see North and South Koreans in figure 6.1). In addition, over two million emigrants from the Japanese archipelago settled in the Americas and in Japan's former colonies in Asia by the 1960s.

Japan's migration state thus has its roots in prewar Japan's vast empire stretching from Korea and Formosa to Manchuria and the southern Sakhalin Island to the Pacific Islands, eventually expanding into Southeast Asia with the establishment of the so-called Co-Prosperity Sphere (see Myers and Peattie 1984). Japan's colonization of neighboring countries, in particular, facilitated migration from the colonies to the metropole as well as the forced conscription of soldiers and laborers. Although prewar Japan's imperial migration state (see Klotz, this volume) did not face the same trade-offs as liberal migration states, it nevertheless extended limited rights to colonial subjects residing in the metropole on the premise that they constituted part of the multiethnic Japanese empire. Among these rights included suffrage for male subjects from 1925, who consequently held greater political rights than disenfranchised native Japanese women until the postwar period. Colonial subjects were also classified—forcibly—as Japanese nationals both within and outside of the empire regardless of their place of settlement or birth (J. Kim 2014).

In contrast, postwar Japan's migration state prioritized national security and "culture"—newly imagined as ethnically homogenous in the context of decolonization and democratic reconstruction during the American Occupation (1945–52)—over markets and rights. Almost overnight, former colonial subjects lost their Japanese nationality and were reclassified as aliens. No longer sources of much-needed cheap labor and military manpower in Japan's empire, the mostly Korean and Formosan populations that remained in Japan became the subjects of an intensive repatriation campaign overseen by Occupation and Japanese officials. Japanese officials were especially quick to point to this population's subversive potential as hostile former colonial subjects, many of whom created alliances with the Japan Communist Party (see Dower 1999). The shrunken postimperial state thus sought to expel former colonial subjects from the Japanese archipelago both for security reasons and concerns about social stability as Japan reinvented itself as a democratic, culturally homogenous nation.

Another central feature of postwar Japan's migration state was the enactment of strict immigration and border controls that were modeled after the 1924 US Johnson-Reed Immigration Act, which set specific quotas based on country of origin. These controls not only aimed to curb *new* immigration into Japan but *return* migration by former colonial subjects. Korean return migrants, in particular, became postwar Japan's first "illegal" immigrants who, upon encountering politically and socially volatile conditions in the Korean peninsula following their repatriation, attempted to return to a newly fortified Japanese nation-state with closed borders (Morris-Suzuki 2010). As early as 1947, Japanese and American Occupation authorities used the same shipping facilities to return voluntary repatriates and deport unauthorized migrants from the Korean peninsula (Wagner 1951; Chung 2010a).

Postwar Japan's "democratic revolution" during the American Occupation further revised the hierarchy of citizens and noncitizens in two ways. First, Occupation authorities instituted sweeping reforms in almost all areas of social life, including land reforms, a new democratic constitution (drafted in just six days), female enfranchisement and guarantees of gender equality (at least on paper), and labor legislation modeled after Roosevelt's New Deal programs that guaranteed labor rights and protections (see Cohen 1987). Second, alienage—rather than gender or class—became the basis for legal exclusion. As early as December 1945, the Diet (Japan's parliament) revised the Election Law to exclude those with family registries (*koseki*) outside of Japan proper from the vote and, in 1947, passed the Alien Registration Law that required such individuals to register with local authorities as aliens (Chung 2010a). Because the family registry documents descend over several generations, rather than birthplace, these laws specifically targeted former colonial subjects and their descendants, the vast majority of whom were Koreans (see Chung et al. 2020). In 1950, the Diet passed the Nationality Act, modeled after that of Germany and perpetuating the principle of patrilineal *jus sanguinis* from the 1899 Meiji law. Finally, in 1952, Japan became the only former imperial power to unilaterally strip its former colonial subjects of their metropolitan nationalities with the conclusion of the San Francisco Peace Treaty between Japan and the Allied powers. Whereas former colonial subjects elsewhere could choose to keep or renounce their metropolitan nationalities, Koreans and Chinese who remained in Japan proper were given a single narrow path for recovery: petition for naturalization (Chung 2010a). Only a small minority chose this option and even fewer succeeded because of high rejection rates. Between 1952 and 1955, there were fewer than 10,000 naturalizations in Japan (Y. D. Kim 1990).

Naturalization rates have remained low since the early postwar period, not exceeding one percent of the total foreign population since 1952. And Japan's restrictive immigration policies remained largely unchanged until the 1990s. Yet, by the early 1980s, Japan's prewar and postwar migration state had produced one of the most generous systems for extending institutionalized rights and social welfare benefits to its foreign residents.

This unexpected development is a product of an unintended consequence of Japan's abrupt transition from a multiethnic empire with porous borders to a homogenous nation-state with tightly controlled borders and strict descent-based citizenship policies: the formation of multiple generations of foreign residents (extending to six generations in 2020) with roots in colonial-era migration. While the first- and second-generations of the largely Korean resident population in Japan were excluded from social welfare benefits and faced routine discrimination in housing, employment, and education as foreigners until the late 1970s, they gained a wide array of institutionalized rights—on par with those extended to Japanese citizens in the areas of social welfare, civil rights protections, and even some public-sector jobs—by the early 1980s following a series of local and national campaigns in what I describe elsewhere as a "noncitizen civil rights movement" (Chung 2010a). Unlike the first generation of Korean leaders in Japan who mobilized the population around homeland politics, the second generation focused their political movements on their positions as permanent members of their local communities deserving of equal rights. By the late 1980s, Korean resident (known as *Zainichi* Koreans) activists were focused on a nationwide movement to gain local voting rights for foreign residents, having already succeeded in repealing the fingerprinting require-ment for foreign residents and instituting "ethnic" or "multicultural" education in public school curricula in some localities (Chung 2010b). Because the vast majority of foreign residents in Japan at this time consisted of permanently settled *Zainichi* Koreans, most of whom were native born, the noncitizen civil rights movement centered on claims to citizenship rights for this minority community of nonnational "local citizens" rather than on immigration reform.

Meanwhile, Japan had become an increasingly attractive destination for migrant workers with the expansion of the "bubble economy" (1986–91) that was accompanied by the rise of the Japanese yen. Although Japan's borders remained closed to unskilled labor, private brokers and intermediaries in Japan and various sending countries never-theless promoted their migration to Japan, which led to a rapidly growing unauthorized migrant worker population that reached a peak of 300,000 in 1993 (OECD/SOPEMI 2007). The 1990 revision to the Immigration Control and Refugee Recognition Act marked the first major reforms to postwar Japan's immigration policies. In an attempt to quell unauthorized migration while meeting labor demands and maintaining closed borders to labor migrants, the 1990 revision reorganized and expanded visa categories from eighteen to twenty-seven among which included two legal loopholes that formed the foundation for a *de facto* guest-worker program.

First, the long-term resident (*teijūsha*) visa created for ethnic Japanese immigrants (often referred to as *Nikkei*) up until the third generation came with unrestricted entry and employment rights as well as long-term residency rights. While its stated purpose is to encourage coethnics to visit their relatives in Japan, learn Japanese, and explore their cultural heritage, the creation of this visa resulted in the recruitment of a relatively ample pool of unskilled workers largely from Brazil and Peru for small- and medium-sized enterprises (SMEs) in the construction and manufacturing sectors (Tsuda 2003; Chung 2019c; Tian 2019). Only four other visa categories—special permanent resident (created for colonial-era migrants and their descendants), permanent resident, spouse or child of a Japanese national, and spouse or child of a permanent resident—allow for unrestricted economic activities (Chung 2014). Only a year after the creation of this visa, the Brazil-ian population (the vast majority of whom were *Nikkei*) became the third-largest foreign population in Japan, following Koreans and Chinese (see figure 6.1).

Second, the 1990 revision introduced the industrial trainee program that ostensibly offered "interns" and "trainees" from other Asian countries (mostly from China, South Korea, and Southeast Asia) skills-training in public and private organizations in Japan. Their visa, which was good for a single year and renewable for a maximum of three years contingent on a valid employment contract, made their permanent settlement in Japan virtually impossible, reflecting efforts to address concerns that foreign workers from Asian countries would seek to settle in Japan much like Turkish and Yugoslav guest workers had done in Germany (Chung and Tian 2018; Chung 2019c). Because "trainees" were not recognized officially as "workers," their wages and working conditions were unregulated and they were unprotected by labor laws, which made them vulnerable to industrial accidents, unpaid wages, and employer abuse especially in the manufacturing and construction industries in which they were concentrated (Seol 2000; Chung 2010b).

Both legal loopholes had unintended consequences. While the establishment of the long-term resident visa had the intended effect of recruiting unskilled workers to meet demands in labor-starved industries, it also created unforeseen problems. Proponents of the visa assumed that *Nikkei* immigrants would be "invisible" guest workers: as ethnic Japanese, their presence in Japanese society would go unnoticed while their contribution to the labor market would mitigate the need to open the country's borders to foreign labor. Instead, *Nikkei* immigrants faced many of the same challenges of adaptation as other non-Japanese immigrants and, rather than quietly assimilating into Japanese society, became among the most "visible" immigrants in Japan. Their perceived destabilizing influence on social stability became especially pronounced following the 2007–8 global financial crisis during which companies in Japan's automobile, machinery, and information technology industries implemented mass layoffs of contract workers, affecting a disproportionate share of *Nikkei* migrant workers. By 2009, the unemployment rate among Brazilian and Peruvian workers in Japan reached 40 percent (McCabe et al. 2009; Chung 2020). And, unlike their "trainee" counterparts, *Nikkei* migrant workers could remain in Japan despite the termination of their employment contracts and, based on the generous provisions of their long-term residency visa, were eligible for social welfare benefits, including unemployment assistance. In response, Japan implemented a "pay-to-go" program in 2009 modeled after return-migration policies in Europe that provided *Nikkei* Brazilians and Peruvians a one-time payment of 300,000 yen (approximately US$3,000 at the time), plus 200,000 yen for each dependent, for their voluntary repatriation with the specific contingency that they would be ineligible for a long-term visa for at least three years (Sharpe 2014; Chung 2019c).

The industrial trainee program, meanwhile, proved to be an efficient system for meeting labor demands in labor-starved small and medium-sized enterprises, especially in rural areas. Unlike *Nikkei* workers, the ethnically diverse industrial trainees became the "invisible" foreign labor force that policy-makers envisioned for their ethnically Japanese counterparts due to their short-term visas, geographical placement in rural (and often remote) areas, and employment restrictions. Early complaints about labor abuses, including lawsuits that resulted in landmark court decisions affirming labor protections and rights for trainees from 1993, were met not with immigration reform but incremental adjustments to a system that conservative and liberal policy-makers alike have deemed exploitative (Chung 2010b). These include the establishment of the Technical Intern and Training Program (TITP) in 1993 that made trainees eligible for a three-year "designated activities" visa; a 2009 revision to the TITP that gave employers the option of recruiting technical interns directly, thereby bypassing the previous requirement to hire industrial trainees first; and a 2016 revision that strengthened labor protections for both groups and extended the maximum residency period to five years (Chung 2019c; Tian 2019). The 2018 bill that established a formal guest-worker program—marking the first time in postwar Japan's history that the country's borders have been officially opened to migrant workers—does not signify the liberalization of Japan's migration regime. On the contrary, former prime minister Shinzo Abe made clear that this bill—to recruit up to 345,000 guest workers in the agriculture, construction, shipbuilding, hospitality, and nursing sectors over a five-year period—was neither equivalent to a full-fledged immigration policy nor meant to replace the industrial trainee program (Chung and Tian 2018). It is thus meant to complement the industrial trainee program, which has continued to expand, and can be characterized as a continuation of incremental adjustments to an illiberal status quo.

Korea: Multiple Migrants, Differentiated Rights

Japan's occupation of Korea at the turn of the twentieth century (1910–45) set in motion mass emigration from the Korean peninsula not only to the Japanese archipelago but also to Manchuria, maritime Russia, and the Americas (J. Kim 2016). Combined with high rates of emigration following the founding of the Republic of Korea in 1948 that included thousands of students, nurses, and migrant workers to Japan, Germany, Australia, the Middle East, and North America from the 1960s to 1980s, the Korean diaspora, which totaled some 7.5 million in 2019, continues to outnumber immigrants to South Korea. Korea has also been host to descendants of Chinese migrants who began to settle in port cities from the late nineteenth century, after Joseon Korea and Qing China signed a trade agreement in 1882 to authorize Chinese merchants to own and lease land in Korea (C. Lee 2002; Choi 2008; S. Lee 2016). This population of approximately 36,000 Taiwanese nationals now spans five generations. And South Korea continues to receive migrants from North Korea, whose numbers have multiplied from fewer than ten annually during the Cold War to an average of sixty between 1994 to 1998 and a high of over 2,900 in 2009 (see J.-e. Lee 2015). South Korea's Ministry of Unification estimates that over 30,000 individuals settled in South Korea from the North between 1948 and 2017.[3] Since South Korea officially regards North Korea as part of its territory, North Koreans are recognized as South Korean nationals, not as immigrants.

Large-scale immigration to Korea, however, is a relatively recent phenomenon. Like Japan, Korea became an attractive migration destination from the late 1980s, when per capita GDP grew from approximately US$100 in 1965 to over US$5,700 in 1989 (and almost US$32,000 in 2019; see World Bank 2020). And, parallel to Japan, SMEs in the manufacturing, production, and service industries recruited migrant workers informally until Korea adopted the Industrial and Technical Training System (ITTP) in 1991 and the Industrial Trainee Program in 1993 modeled after Japan's industrial trainee system. The migrant population grew exponentially after South Korea normalized diplomatic relations with mainland China in 1992. Since then, Chinese nationals have constituted the largest population of foreign residents in Korea by far and, within this population, ethnic Koreans from China (hereafter "Korean Chinese") have made up between 50 to 65 percent. Of the more than 2.5 million foreign residents in Korea in 2019, almost 30 percent were Korean Chinese (see figure 6.2).

Unlike Japan, Korea did not initially create a long-term resident visa to recruit co-ethnic migrant workers. While the industrial trainee system allocated the largest quotas for ethnic Koreans, they otherwise had limited legal pathways for entry outside of

---

3 The number of North Korean refugees decreased by half after 2011 due to tightened border controls. See the South Korea Ministry of Unification website: www.unikorea.go.kr.

marriage to a Korean national. In 1999, Korea's National Assembly passed the Overseas Korean Act ("Act on the Immigration and Legal Status of Overseas Koreans") that created an "Overseas Korean" (F-4) visa category similar to Japan's long-term resident visa, which provided eligible coethnic immigrants broad employment opportunities, investment rights, property rights, health insurance, and pensions (Park and Chang 2005). The three-year visa can also be renewed multiple times and allows for a status change to permanent resident after just two years of residence (Chung 2019a). Until 2003, the largest population of coethnic immigrants in Korea—Korean Chinese—were, along with ethnic Koreans from the former Soviet Union, ineligible for the Overseas Korean visa. Because most ethnic Koreans from China and the former Soviet Union consist of colonial-era migrants and their descendants, they did not meet the definition of "overseas Koreans" as Koreans (and their descendants) who had previously held South Korean nationality. The overwhelming majority of Overseas Korean visa holders were consequently Koreans from the United States.

Through a series of public campaigns, demonstrations, and lawsuits, Korean Chinese organizations and their supporters succeeded in pressuring the government to revise the law. In response to a 2001 Constitutional Court ruling in favor of the Korean Chinese plaintiffs,[4] the National Assembly passed a revision in 2004 that would change the definition of "overseas Koreans" to those with documentary evidence of household registration (*hojeok*) in Korea (see Chung, Draudt, and Tian 2020). The creation of the H-2 Working Visit visa specifically for ethnic Koreans from China and the former Soviet Union in 2007 additionally provided relatively generous employment rights for coethnic immigrants who do not qualify for the Overseas Korean visa. In 2019, almost 53 percent of all Korean Chinese residents in Korea held an Overseas Korean visa and 26 percent a Working Visit visa (Korea Immigration Service 2020).

Korea's immigration policies, especially as they pertained to unskilled foreign labor, closely resembled those of postwar Japan until the early 2000s. Like Japan, Korea maintained closed borders to unskilled immigration and met labor demands through an informal guest-worker program, on the one hand, and recruitment of coethnic migrant labor, on the other. In both countries, hundreds of civil society organizations, ranging from labor unions and lawyers associations to religious organizations and citizen groups, provided advocacy and services for migrant workers who confronted exploitative practices from their employers without labor protections and, for those with undocumented status, faced the constant threat of deportation. But whereas Japan responded to the problems associated with both foreign labor schemes through incremental adjustments, Korea opted for sweeping immigration and citizenship policy reforms. As I argue

---

4 In 2001, the Constitutional Court ruled that the Overseas Korean Act did not conform to the principle of equality (Article 11) in the Constitution because it discriminated against emigrants who left Korea prior to the establishment of the Republic of Korea in 1948. See the "*Act on the Immigration and Legal Status of Overseas Koreans* Case" (13–2 KCCR 714, 99Hun-Ma494, November 29, 2001). The proceedings are summarized in the "Decisions of the Korean Constitutional Court (2001)," at www.ccourt.go.kr.

elsewhere (Chung 2020), the timing and content of migrant worker advocacy catalyzed rights-based movements that generated significant rights-based legislation in the span of about a decade.

Whereas Japan's democratic roots can be traced to the short-lived Taisho period and its contemporary democratic institutions to the early postwar period, Korea's democratic transition did not occur until the late 1980s. And, in contrast to Japan's top-down democratization process, Korea's struggle for democracy was largely a bottom-up movement made up of a broad coalition of civil society groups. It was the strategic participation of a few key civil-society organizations from this coalition less than a decade after the country's democratic transition that propelled the migrant workers' movement. Democratization-cum–migrant worker activists provided much-needed political capital to the movement through their connections to other civil society organizations and to the top echelon of the new democratic administrations with whom they had fought for democratic reforms; likewise, the content of migrant claims-making drew on the language of rights from the democratization movement, thereby imbuing the movement with the moral authority of recent struggles. By drawing on the ideas, strategies, and networks of the democratization movement—or what I call *civic legacies* (Chung 2020)—the migrant workers' movement reframed the debate from the dangers that migrants posed for Korean society to the threat that an exploitative industrial trainee system posed for the hard-fought rights of Korean workers (see Lim 2010).

After several years of negotiations between activists, government officials, and industry representatives (especially from the Korean Federation of Small and Medium Businesses), Korea officially opened its borders to unskilled workers for the first time with the implementation of the Employment Permit System (EPS) in 2004 and terminated the industrial trainee system in 2007. Reflecting the demands of the rights-based migrant workers' movement, the EPS guarantees foreign workers protections equal to those of native Korean workers according to the country's labor laws and provides three-year visas that can be renewed for an additional two years.

Immigration policies in Korea further diverged from those of Japan with the rapid growth of another category of immigrants: foreign spouses of Korean nationals popularly referred to as "marriage migrants." Korea's rapid industrialization and urbanization depopulated rural areas by more than half (from 19.1 million in 1970 to 9.8 million in 1995).[5] Among the young people migrating to urban areas to pursue higher education and enter the workforce were women who had traditionally been expected to stay home as caregivers for their children and parents-in-law. This demographic shift generated multiple interrelated problems for rural areas: unmarried, aging farmers were unable to care for their parents; the rapidly growing population of residents in rural areas outpaced the anemic elder-care facilities subsidized by local governments; and the decline in the working-age population strained tax revenues in rural districts. In an effort to address what was popularly called the "bride famine," local government officials and agricultural associations in rural areas launched matchmaking campaigns for unmarried farmers to

---

5   See the World Bank data: https://www.worldbank.org.

recruit "brides" from urban areas within Korea and, following the aforementioned 1992 normalization treaty with mainland China, among ethnic Korean women from China (Freeman 2011). With the rise of commercialized international marriage industries throughout Northeast and Southeast Asia, on the one hand, and the deregulation of the industry within Korea in 1999, on the other, the number of "marriage migrants" in Korea reached over 57,000 by the time that the EPS was established in 2004 and expanded to include migrant women from Southeast Asia and Russia (KIS 2007). At its peak in 2009, international marriages made up over 10 percent of all marriages in Korea (KIS 2010).

Marriage migration is not unique to Korea and, to be sure, (largely female) foreign spouses of native citizens constitute one of the fastest-growing immigrant groups in Korea, Japan, and Taiwan. But Korea stands out for the outsized role that "marriage migrants" play in the country's immigrant incorporation policies, programs, and discourse. Their arrival during a critical period of negotiations between civil society activists and government officials over migrant rights shaped a public narrative around their social integration as vulnerable populations in need of state protection (D. Y. Kim 2017). Similar to the migrant workers' movement, seasoned democracy activists—especially feminist activists from Korea's formidable women's movement—publicized the abuses of the marriage migration industry, comparing marriage brokers to human traffickers, and organized campaigns to address domestic and sexual abuse that migrant women faced at the hands of their husbands and in-laws. While campaigns for migrant workers and migrant women alike used the common language of "human rights" in their appeals for political reform, they did not necessarily link their movements to calls for broader immigration reforms. Whereas the migrant workers' movement focused on regulating migrant labor to ensure labor rights protections (but not necessarily family reunification or permanent settlement rights), the migrant women's movement centered on regulating the marriage broker industry, offering support services, and providing legal protections specifically for "marriage migrants" and their children. And, much like the former, advocacy for migrant women drew on the civic legacies of Korea's women's movement and resonated powerfully with the interests of democratic administrations, especially during the two consecutive progressive administrations of Kim Dae Jung (1998–2002) and Roh Moo Hyun (2003–7). In 2005, the Roh administration charged the Ministry of Gender Equality, newly renamed the Ministry of Gender Equality and Family (MOGEF) accordingly, to lead a wide-ranging campaign to provide governmental support services for migrant women and their families, and, during the following year, announced the "Grand Plan" for their social integration that, by 2008, included a budget of roughly 32,580 trillion Korean won (roughly US$31.64 million) and established more than two hundred "multicultural family centers" throughout the country (D.Y. Kim 2015; Chung 2020).

Korea's migration state is thus distinguished by the centrality of rights alongside markets, security, and culture. But rights have not been allocated universally to immigrants; rather, the Korean migration state allocates rights *differentially* to specific migrant populations according to their respective value to national priorities: (1) diaspora engagement policies that target US Korean American professionals (and, to a lesser extent, Korean residents in Japan); (2) coethnic immigration policies that recruit Korean Chinese migrant workers; (3) incorporation policies for North Korean migrants to assist in their transitions to South Korean citizenship; (4) migrant worker policies for guest workers from China and Southeast Asia; and (5) integration policies for largely female "marriage migrants" from China and Southeast Asia. This targeted approach to migration management is embodied in the seminal 2007 Basic Act on the Treatment of Foreigners in Korea (*Jaehan Oegukin Cheou Gibonbeop*), which represents the Korean government's first overarching framework for immigrant incorporation. This sweeping piece of legislation is most notable for its explicit provision to guarantee the human rights of foreigners in Korea. But equally notable are the specific protections prioritized for targeted migrant populations: preferential entry and employment rights for coethnic migrants, labor protections for migrant workers, and social integration for marriage migrants (Chung 2010b, 2020). Other immigration and citizenship reforms further solidified the Korean migration state's differentiated incorporation of migrants where trade-offs between the demands of the market, national security, culture, and rights are weighed differently according to each migrant population. From 2006 to 2010, the National Assembly passed a series of bills that guaranteed human rights protections for foreign workers, local voting rights for permanent residents (the vast majority of whom are multigenerational *Hwagyo* residents), sweeping social integration programs for marriage migrants, and dual nationality for select categories of foreign residents, including marriage migrants and some "overseas Koreans" but excluding *Hwagyo* residents and migrant workers.

Taiwan: Managing Migration in a Multiethnic Society

Unlike Japan and Korea, Taiwan's political elites have neither proclaimed Taiwan an ethnically homogenous society nor shied away from the idea that Taiwan is a "country of immigration." The majority native Taiwanese and the Hakka, who together make up about 85 percent of the total population, are descendants of immigrants from the Fujian and Guangdong provinces who migrated to present-day Taiwan from the fourteenth to the seventeenth centuries; additionally, the minority mainland Chinese arrived in Taiwan after the island was returned to China in 1945. Only the fourteen-plus indigenous tribes in Taiwan do not have immigrant roots.

The bulk of the island's long immigration history, however, is intricately tied to its colonization under Dutch (1624–62), Spanish (1626–42 in northern Taiwan), Chinese (1662–1895; under Ming loyalists until 1683 followed by Qing rule), and Japanese (1895–1945) rule. Some also refer to the postwar authoritarian era under KMT rule as another era of colonial rule in Taiwan (Jacobs 2008). Not only did the KMT enact intensive Sinicization policies, but it also imposed a travel ban that was not lifted until the late 1970s. Migration management by postcolonial Taiwan is thus a recent development. Like Japan and Korea, emigration from Taiwan to North America, Australia, New Zealand, and other parts of Asia (especially to Southeast Asia and mainland China from the early 1990s) dwarfed immigration into Taiwan until the early 2000s. And, also like Japan and Korea, acute labor shortages following three decades of rapid economic growth could no longer be met by internal sources.

But the Taiwanese migration state prioritized market demands for labor well before Japan and Korea by establishing a formal guest-worker program in 1989, leading to the passage of the Employment Services Act in 1991. This act, modeled after Singapore's guest-worker program, allows employers to recruit foreign labor to work in the construction, manufacturing, and, from 1992, domestic care sectors for up to three years (see Hirschman, this volume).[6] This program was supplemented by the 1992 "Go South" policy that encouraged employers to recruit foreign labor from Southeast Asia, particularly Indonesia, the Philippines, and Vietnam, and relocate their businesses there.

Taiwan's swift response to labor shortages, compared to Japan and Korea's delayed and ad hoc responses, is attributable to two factors. First, Taiwan's SMEs hold considerably more political clout than their counterparts in Japan and Korea. Whereas multiconglomerates (Japan's *keiretsu* and Korea's *chaebol*) played central roles in Japan and Korea's "economic miracles," SMEs were at the heart of Taiwan's growth. Second, employers in Japan, Korea, and Taiwan all recruited migrant labor, formally and informally, from Southeast Asia as each country expanded its diplomatic and economic presence in what was becoming one of the most economically dynamic regions in the world by the 1990s; but Taiwan's interests were driven by economic *and* national security concerns. Unlike Japan and Korea, where immigrants from mainland China came to make up the largest population of foreign residents, Taiwan sought to *curb* cross-Strait migration—as well as economic linkages more broadly—from mainland China. The "Go South" policy, accordingly, aimed to decelerate Taiwan's increasing interdependence on mainland China by pivoting to Southeast Asia.

The "Go South" policy not only diversified the pool of migrant workers but also enlarged the population of "marriage migrants" from Southeast Asia. Although women from mainland China continue to make up the largest group of migrant spouses married to Taiwanese nationals, the proliferation of commercialized international marriage agencies in Northeast and Southeast Asia from the late 1990s multiplied the number of marriage migrants to Taiwan, much like they did in Korea. At its peak, marriages between Taiwanese men and migrant women from mainland China and other countries (mostly in Southeast Asia) made up more than 27 percent of all marriages in 2002 (Wang 2011). Between 1998 and 2000, over half of all cross-border marriages were those that involved migrant women from Southeast Asia and, in 2004, marriages involving Southeast Asian spouses outnumbered those with mainland Chinese spouses.[7] Similar to Korea, growing public concern about human trafficking and sham marriages that accompanied the commercialization of the marriage migration industry pressured the Taiwanese government to crack down on marriage brokers from the late 1990s, and in 2009, the Legislative Yuan passed a bill to prohibit commercial matchmaking altogether (Belanger et al. 2010; Huang 2017, 1115).

---

6   Work permits have since been lengthened to nine years from 2007 but guest workers remain ineligible for permanent residency and Taiwanese citizenship regardless of the length of their stay (Wang 2011, 180).

7   Since migrants from mainland China are not included among the foreign population in Taiwanese government records, marriages involving mainland Chinese spouses are not categorized as "international." I thus refer to all marriages involving migrant spouses from mainland Chinese and other countries as "cross-border marriages." See also Chung 2020 and the National Statistical Bureau, *Family*, 2014, https://eng.stat.gov.tw/public/Attachment/410184419KIDMI9KP.pdf.

In contrast to Korea, however, Taiwan's democratic transition did not have a liberalizing effect on its migration management. Rather than the expansion of migrant labor rights in parallel to democratic reforms for native workers, post-authoritarian Taiwan has increasingly constricted migrant rights and privatized migration management. Following the historic election of Chen Shui-bian, the first opposition candidate, to the presidency in 2000, the DPP enacted a sweeping "localization" (*bentuhua*) campaign that centered on revitalizing native Taiwanese culture through the institution of Hakka language instruction in public schools, textbook revisions that highlighted native Taiwanese culture and history, and the promotion of native Taiwanese languages and cultures in the sphere (Chun 2000). The period between the late 1990s and the mid-2000s was also a critical turning point for the expansion of gender equality and women's rights in Taiwan. In response to pressure from a nationwide women's movement, the Legislative Yuan passed a series of bills addressing sexual assault (1997), domestic violence (1998), and sexual harassment (2005) as well as gender equality in employment (2002) and education (2004) (see Brinton 2001; Yu 2009; Y.-M. Kim and Shirahase 2014; Chung 2020).

Similar to Korea, former political dissidents who had championed the rights of ethnic groups and the working class during the democratization movement came to occupy the top echelon of the DPP administration. But one of the first recommendations made by the Chen administration was the removal of foreign workers from Taiwan's minimum wage requirement in the Labor Standards Act (Cheng 2002). The administration, moreover, privatized the migrant worker industry in Taiwan, delegating to private brokers the tasks of importing, distributing, managing, and, sometimes, deporting migrant workers (Chung 2020). And, in contrast to Korea's migrant workers' movement, labor unions that represent workers in the construction and manufacturing industries—the only industries (aside from the domestic care sector that I discuss below) open to foreign workers—have claimed that migrant workers have depressed wages and taken jobs away from native Taiwanese workers, especially aboriginal workers who have historically been concentrated in those industries (Minns and Tierney 2003).

The expansion of gender equality in Taiwanese society, moreover, has had perverse effects on migrant women's rights. The "Go South" policy opened up opportunities for families to import foreign caregivers in response to the elder-care crisis that could not be addressed by underdeveloped welfare facilities, on the one hand, and a deteriorating traditional patriarchal system that relied on the unpaid labor of women, on the other. Not only did this provide households with a relatively inexpensive caregiving option, but it also came with around-the-clock, live-in care. Whereas domestic caregivers have regulated hours and are protected by labor laws, foreign caregivers are not recognized as workers because they live and work in the private homes of their employers. To be sure, the most vocal opposition to legislation that would regulate foreign caregivers' work has come from NGOs that represent the caregivers' employers: the elderly, disabled, and working women (Chien 2018; Chung 2020).

Taiwan's democratization has also been accompanied by the constriction of rights for female migrant spouses. As the KMT government under President Lee Teng-hui implemented a series of democratic reforms following the end of martial law in 1987, the Lee administration announced the Act Governing Relations between the People of the Taiwan Area and the Mainland Area that would, in effect, separate citizenship status and citizenship rights. Because the KMT claimed that the Taiwanese government represented all of China, Taiwanese citizenship policies included mainland Chinese among Taiwanese nationals. Rather than redefine Taiwanese citizenship to exclude mainland Chinese from an expanding set of citizenship rights (that would eventually include voting rights in direct presidential elections from 1996), the act established that only those with permanent household registration in the "free" or "Taiwan" area of the Republic of China (ROC) are eligible for full citizenship rights (Rigger 2002). It additionally created quotas for mainland Chinese spouses eligible for residency status and extended the waiting time between residency and eligibility for full citizenship rights to eight years specifically for mainland Chinese spouses (see Friedman 2015).[8] Subsequent revisions to the Nationality Act eliminated marital citizenship (2000) and introduced financial requirements (2001) and language and comprehensive knowledge exams (2005) for naturalization applicants (Hsia 2009).[9]

In sum, Taiwan's migration state prioritizes national security alongside culture and market demands with little attention paid to rights. Security concerns pertaining to cross-Strait relations (especially fears of a fifth column of mainland Chinese migrants entering Taiwan) override the potential economic and social gains of expanding cross-Strait migration, on the one hand, and coethnic ties with mainland Chinese, on the other. Meanwhile, the delicate balancing act of the island's multiethnic politics has overridden concerns about democratic accountability, much like in Southeast Asian countries (see Hirschman, this volume). The result has been a parallel system of democratic governance for native Taiwanese citizens (including earlier waves of mainland Chinese migrants) and illiberal migration governance for migrant workers and spouses.

The Emergence of the Developmental Migration State in East Asia

Building on Hollifield's (2004) migration state framework, this chapter has analyzed how East Asian democracies have attempted to grapple with the challenges of immigration in a globalizing world. Despite labor shortages from the 1980s and impending demographic crises in all three countries, Japan, Korea, and Taiwan all have maintained relatively closed migrant labor policies. They are thus often described as negative cases of

---

8 In 2009, President Ma Ying-jeou's KMT administration reduced the waiting time for full citizenship rights to six years.

9 In 2000, Taiwan eliminated gender discrimination for citizenship attribution (as Japan had done in 1985 and Korea in 1997) after a sustained campaign by women's organizations. Until then, female migrant spouses automatically gained Taiwanese citizenship upon their marriage to a Taiwanese national but their male counterparts did not. The 2000 reform abolished marital citizenship altogether and widened the scope of individuals eligible for Taiwanese citizenship, primarily benefitting male migrant spouses and their offspring. Female migrant spouses, however, were henceforth required to undergo the process of naturalization in order to gain Taiwanese citizenship (see Chung 2020).

immigration, or countries whose immigration levels are extremely low relative to their levels of development and their historical, social, and/or cultural linkages with other countries in the region (Bartram 2000; Chung and Hosoki 2018).

The migration state framework brings to light the centrality of migration management as a core function of the state in the contemporary period and helps us to better understand the multiple logics of immigration policy. While all states face similar challenges, their responses to such challenges are dependent on how they weigh concerns about markets, rights, security, and culture—or what Hollifield refers to as a "four-sided game" (Hollifield, this volume). Hollifield (1992) argues that the liberal migration state balances contradictory interests in managing migration flows: the state must ensure social stability and national security while addressing labor market demands for the free flow of trade and labor, all the while bound by liberal democratic principles that discourage overtly discriminatory and exploitative practices. In effect, liberal migration states must balance the demands of markets that push them toward greater openness, security and cultural concerns that push them toward closure, and the logic of rights that circumscribes their policy options.

Rather than convergence toward a singular *liberal* migration state, however, the East Asian cases suggest the emergence of a "developmental migration state" in which the intertwined concerns about social stability, national security, and economic development are embodied in the ideology of "developmentalism" that accords national development a higher priority than any other societal goal. In a system where *economic* development is the source of *political* legitimacy, migrants' access to rights correlates with their utility toward national developmental goals. This is not to suggest that the developmental migration state is a diametric opposite of the liberal migration state or, simply, an "illiberal" migration state; on the contrary, it is the product of a social contract that rests on performance or "development" broadly construed, not liberal democratic principles. And, as the Japan, Korea, and Taiwan cases demonstrate, the migration state in East Asia does not necessarily correspond to regime-type; on the contrary, political liberalization in the three countries has not resulted in the emergence of liberal migration states. And the expansion of institutionalized rights for one subcategory of migrants in a single national context has not made them universal, or even accessible, for others.

The emerging "developmental migration state" in East Asia has three distinguishing characteristics: (1) migration governance by an interventionist state; (2) inconsistent application of descent to migration and citizenship policies; and (3) a social contract that rests on performance, not on democratic rights.

First, the developmental migration state is notable for its highly interventionist approach to managing migration. Just as the developmental state intervenes in the substance of overarching, nationally supported goals for the economy—thus concerning itself with what industries ought to exist and which ones are no longer needed, rather than just the rules of economic competition (Johnson 1982)—the developmental migration state applies a strategic, goal-oriented approach to migration management to determine not only who enters and for what purpose but also in recruiting specific groups of migrants to address overarching goals for the economy and society. In other words, the developmental migration state does not simply respond to the demands of the market by

liberalizing immigration policies or establishing diplomatic treaties to open migration flows; on the contrary, migration policy becomes a tool to relieve the pressures of over-population (through emigration policies), increase foreign exchange earnings (through diaspora engagement policies), accelerate infrastructure development (through migrant labor policies), enhance the international competitiveness of critical industries (through favorable visas for "skilled" workers), mend social welfare fissures (by importing caregivers and nurses), and address demographic deficits (by recruiting marriage migrants and through facilitated naturalization policies).

Second, despite the common characterization of East Asian countries as representing "ethnic" migration and/or citizenship regimes, they stand out more for their limited and inconsistent application of descent in their immigration and citizenship policies such that (1) coethnic immigrants are not necessarily privileged over other immigrants in the areas of naturalization, citizenship acquisition, and citizenship rights and (2) coethnicity is *differentially* determined among diasporic groups based on their countries of origin and/ or diasporic journeys (Chung 2019b). Contrary to assumptions about "ethnic" citizenship and migration regimes, coethnic migrants from mainland China in Taiwan face greater hurdles to acquiring full citizenship rights than do non-Chinese migrants; until 2004, Korea's visa categories differentiated between coethnic migrants themselves based on country of origin, privileging one coethnic group over another; and even Japan has begun to phase out ethnic preferences in immigration to further expand its industrial trainee program.

Finally, migration governance in East Asia reflects not convergence toward a liberal migration state but, rather, migration control by developmental states that have historically prioritized economic development, social stability, and national security over liberalism in trade and politics. Extended to migrants, the social contract rests on performance, not on liberal democratic principles or blood-based membership. The utilitarian view of migrant workers as temporary and "disposable" overlaps with the framework of the "neoliberal migration state" (Adamson and Tsourapas 2019); at the same time, the logic of "developmentalism" links migration governance with the interrelated goals of national security, economic development, and social stability. This logic has been applied to each country's visa regimes that have, in turn, institutionalized migrant hierarchies. Not only do visa categories in East Asia determine a migrant's residency status, eligibility for state-sponsored rights and services, geographic mobility, and prospects for permanent settlement and citizenship acquisition, but they are informed by racial, gendered, and class-based ideas that go well beyond demands in the labor market, as illustrated by different categories of coethnic and marriage migrant visas, for example (Chung 2019a).

The COVID-19 pandemic has stretched the limits of all migration states. Across the globe, the pandemic has exacerbated two broad interrelated patterns. First, political elites and the public alike have scapegoated minority and migrant populations in public discourse and everyday interactions. Reports of anti-Chinese and anti-Asian but also antimigrant attacks throughout the world have highlighted the durability of racist tropes that link Asian migrants, and racialized foreigners more broadly, with disease. Second, we have witnessed the enactment of sweeping immigration restrictions in almost every country in the world, on the one hand, and the corrosion of already fragile safety nets and protections for migrants, refugees, and displaced populations, on the other. This combination has made migrants ever more vulnerable to contracting and dying from the virus as they resort to more desperate measures to reach increasingly narrow points of entry; work and live in overcrowded conditions; and continually weigh the risks of dismissal, detainment, and/or deportation against getting tested for the virus.

Before the outbreak of the pandemic, migrant rights in East Asia were tied to the perceived value of their labor. With economic shutdowns and the rise of racist, xenophobic narratives linking migrants and the coronavirus, Chinese and Southeast Asian migrant workers in Japan, Korea, and Taiwan have been denied entry into public places, subjected to verbal harassment, and have been arbitrarily dismissed from their jobs, underscoring their precarious social and legal positions. In Japan, migrant workers from China whose visas were about to expire faced the prospect of transiting through third countries in order to return to China due to travel bans or risk becoming undocumented. In Korea, the pandemic also underscored the material and social consequences of developmental migration policies that allocate rights differentially to specific migrant populations: only permanent residents and migrant spouses were eligible for the government's emergency subsidy. The COVID-19 pandemic has thus forced all states to rethink their migration management tools, as we are reminded of Max Frisch's famous quote: "We asked for workers; we got people instead."

References

Adamson, Fiona B., and Gerasimos Tsourapas. 2019. "The Migration State in the Global South: Nationalizing, Developmental, and Neoliberal Models of Migration Management." *International Migration Review*. doi: 10.1177/0197918319879057

Amsden, Alice. 1989. *Asia's Next Giant: South Korea and Late Industrialization*. New York: Oxford University Press.

Bartram, David. 2000. "Japan and Labor Migration: Theoretical and Methodological Implications of Negative Cases." *International Migration Review* 34(1): 5–32.

Belanger, Daniele, Hye-Kyung Lee, and Hong-Zen Wang. 2010. "Ethnic Diversity and Statistics in East Asia: 'Foreign Brides' Surveys in Taiwan and South Korea." *Ethnic and Racial Studies* 33(6): 1108–30.

Brinton, Mary C., ed. 2001. *Women's Working Lives in East Asia*. Stanford, CA: Stanford University Press.

Castles, Stephen, and Mark J. Miller. 2009. *The Age of Migration: International Population Movements in the Modern World*, 4th ed. New York: Guilford.

Chang, Ha-Joon. 1999. "The Economic Theory of the Developmental State." In *The Developmental State*, edited by Meredith Woo-Cumings, 182–99. Ithaca, NY: Cornell University Press.

Chang, Kyung-Sup. 2007. "The End of Developmental Citizenship? Restructuring and Social Displacement in Post-Crisis South Korea." *Economic and Political Weekly* 42(50): 67–72.

———. 2012. "Economic Development, Democracy and Citizenship Politics in South Korea: The Predicament of Developmental Citizenship." *Citizenship Studies* 16(1): 29–47. doi: 10.1080/13621025.2012.651401

Cheng, Lucie. 2002. "Transnational Labor, Citizenship, and the Taiwan State." In *East Asian Law: Universal Norms and Local Cultures* edited by Arthur Rosett, Lucie Cheng, and Margaret Woo, 85–105. London: RoutledgeCurzon.

Chien, Yi-Chun. 2018. "The Struggle for Recognition: The Politics of Migrant Care Worker Policies in Taiwan." *Critical Sociology* 44(7/8): 1147–61.

Choi, Sheena. 2008. "Politics, Commerce and Construction of Chinese 'Otherness' in Korea: Open Port Period (1876–1910)." In *At Home in the Chinese Diaspora: Memories, Identities and Belongings*, edited by Kuah-Pearce Khun Eng and Andrew Davidson, 128–54. London: Palgrave Macmillan.

Chun, Allen. 2000. "Democracy as Hegemony, Globalization as Indigenization, or the 'Culture' in Taiwanese National Politics." *Journal of Asian and African Studies* 35(1): 7–28.

Chung, Erin Aeran. 2010a. *Immigration and Citizenship in Japan*. New York: Cambridge University Press.

———. 2010b. "Workers or Residents? Diverging Patterns of Immigrant Incorporation in Korea and Japan." *Pacific Affairs* 83(4): 675–96.

———. 2014. "Japan and South Korea: Immigration Control and Immigrant Incorporation." In *Controlling Immigration: A Global Perspective*, edited by James F. Hollifield, Philip L. Martin, and Pia M. Orrenius, 399–421. Stanford, CA: Stanford University Press.

———. 2019a. "Creating Hierarchies of Noncitizens: Race, Gender, and Visa Categories in South Korea." *Journal of Ethnic & Migration Studies*. https://doi.org/10.1080/1369183X.2018.1561061

———. 2019b. "Ethnic Return Migration and Noncitizen Hierarchies in South Korea and Japan." In *Diasporic Returns to the Ethnic Homeland the Korean Diaspora in Comparative Perspective*, edited by Takeyuki Tsuda and Changzoo Song, 179–97. London: Palgrave Macmillan.

———. 2019c. "Japan's Model of Immigration without Immigrants." *Current History* 118(809): 215–21.

———. 2020. *Immigrant Incorporation in East Asian Democracies*. New York: Cambridge University Press.

Chung, Erin Aeran, Darcie Draudt, and Yunchen Tian. 2020. "Regulating Membership and Movement at the Meso-Level: Citizen-Making and the Household Registration System in East Asia." *Citizenship Studies* 24(1): 76–92. doi: 10.1080/13621025.2019.1700914

Chung, Erin Aeran, and Ralph I. Hosoki. 2018. "Disaggregating Labor Migration Policies to Understand Aggregate Migration Realities: Insights from South Korea and Japan as Negative Cases of Immigration." *Comparative Labor Law and Policy Journal* 39(1): 83–110.

Chung, Erin Aeran, and Yunchen Tian. 2018. "Is Japan Becoming a Country of Immigration?: Why More Foreign Labor Doesn't Imply Liberalization." *Foreign Affairs*, August 3.

Cohen, Theodore. 1987. *Remaking Japan: The American Occupation as New Deal*. New York: Free Press.

Copper, John Franklin. 2009. *Taiwan: Nation-State or Province?* 5th ed. Boulder, CO: Westview Press.

Dower, John. 1999. *Embracing Defeat: Japan in the Wake of World War Two*. New York: W.W. Norton; New Press.

Freeman, Caren. 2011. *Making and Faking Kinship: Marriage and Labor Migration between China and South Korea*. Ithaca, NY: Cornell University Press.

Friedman, Sara L. 2015. *Exceptional States: Chinese Immigrants and Taiwanese Sovereignty*. Berkeley: University of California Press.

Gao, Bai. 1997. *Economic Ideology and Japanese Industrial Policy*. Cambridge: Cambridge University Press.

Gerschenkron, Alexander. 1962. *Economic Backwardness in Historical Perspective*. Cambridge: Belknap Press of Harvard University Press.

Haub, Carl. 2011. *World Population Aging: Clocks Illustrate Growth in Population under Age 5 and over Age 65*. Washington, DC: Population Reference Bureau.

Hollifield, James F. 1992. *Immigrants, Markets, and States: The Political Economy of Postwar Europe*. Cambridge, MA: Harvard University Press.

———. "The Emerging Migration State." *International Migration Review* 38(3): 885–912. doi: 10.1111/j.1747–7379.2004.tb00223.x

Hollifield, James F., and Michael O. Sharpe. 2017. "Japan as an 'Emerging Migration State." *International Relations of the Asia-Pacific* 17(3): 371–400. doi: 10.1093/irap/lcx013

Hsia, Hsiao-Chuan. 2009. "Foreign Brides, Multiple Citizenship and the Immigrant Movement in Taiwan." *Asian and Pacific Migration Journal* 18(1): 17–46.

Huang, Lanying. 2017. "The Trafficking of Women and Girls in Taiwan: Characteristics of Victims, Perpetrators, and Forms of Exploitation." *BMC Women's Health* 17: 104. doi: 10.1186/s12905-017-0463-2

International Organization for Migration. 2015. *World Migration Report 2015*. Geneva: IOM.

Jacobs, J. Bruce. 2008. "Taiwan's Colonial History and Postcolonial Nationalism." In *The "One China" Dilemma*, edited by Peter C. Y. Chow. New York: Palgrave Macmillan.

Johnson, Chalmers. 1982. *Miti and the Japanese Miracle: The Growth of Industrial Policy, 1925–1975*. Stanford, CA: Stanford University Press.

——. 1999. "The Developmental State: Odyssey of a Concept." In *The Developmental State*, edited by Meredith Woo-Cumings, 32–60. Ithaca, NY: Cornell University Press.

Jones, Gavin W. 2007. "Delayed Marriage and Very Low Fertility in Pacific Asia." *Population and Development Review* 33(3): 453–78.

Jones, Gavin W., and Bina Gubhaju. 2009. "Factors Influencing Changes in Mean Age at First Marriage and Proportions Never Marrying in the Low-Ferility Countries of East and Southeast Asia." *Asian Population Studies* 5(3): 237–65.

Kim, Daisy Y. 2015. "Bargaining Citizenship: Women's Organizations, the State, and Marriage Migrants in South Korea." PhD diss., Political Science, Johns Hopkins University.

——. 2017. "Resisting Migrant Precarity: A Critique of Human Rights Advocacy for Marriage Migrants in South Korea." *Critical Asian Studies* 49(1): 1–17. doi: 10.1080/14672715.2016.1246951

Kim, Jaeeun. 2014. "The Colonial State, Migration, and Diasporic Nationhood in Korea." *Comparative Studies in Society and History* 56(1): 34–66. https://doi-org.proxy1.library.jhu.edu/10.1017/S0010417513000613

——. 2016. *Contested Embrace: Transborder Membership Politics in Twentieth-Century Korea*. Stanford, CA: Stanford University Press.

Kim, Yŏng Dal. 1990. *Zainichi Chōsenjin No Kika [The naturalization of Korean residents]*. Tokyo: Akashi Shoten.

Kim, Young-Mi, and Sawako Shirahase. 2014. "Understanding Intra-Regional Variation in Gender Inequality in East Asia: Decomposition of Cross-National Differences in the Gender Earnings Gap." *International Sociology* 29(3): 229–48. doi: 10.1177/0268580913518084

Kochenov, Dimitry. 2019. *Citizenship*. Cambridge, MA: MIT Press.

KIS (Korea Immigration Service), Ministry of Justice. 2007. *K.I.S. Statistics 2006* (2006 Chulipguk Oegukin Tong'gye Yonbo).

——. 2010. *K.I.S. Statistics 2009* (2009 Chulipguk Oegukin Tong'gye Yonbo).

——. 2020. *K.I.S. Statistics 2019* (2019 Chulipguk Oegukin Tong'gye Yonbo).

Lee, Chulwoo. 2002. "'Us' and 'Them' in Korean Law: The Creation, Accommodation, and Exclusion of Outsiders in Korean Law." In *East Asian Law: Universal Norms and Local Cultures*, edited by Arthur Rosett, Lucie Cheng, and Margaret Woo, 105–34. London: RoutledgeCurzon.

Lee, Jung-eun. 2015. "Disciplinary Citizenship in South Korean Ngos' Narratives of Resettlement for North Korean Refugees." *Ethnic and Racial Studies* 38(15): 2688–704.

Lee, Sinwoo. 2016. "Blurring Boundaries: Mixed Residence, Extraterritoriality, and Citizenship in Seoul, 1876–1910." *Journal of Korean Studies* 21(1): 71–100.

Lie, John. 2001. *Multiethnic Japan*. Cambridge, MA: Harvard University Press.

Lim, Timothy C. 2010. "Rethinking Belongingness in Korea: Transnational Migration, 'Migrant Marriages' and the Politics of Multiculturalism." *Pacific Affairs* 83(1): 51–71.

Marshall, T. H. 1950. *Class, Citizenship and Social Development*. Cambridge: Cambridge University Press.

McCabe, Kristen, Serena Yi-Ying Lin, Hiroyuki Tanaka, and Piotr Plewa. 2009. "Pay to Go: Countries Offer Cash to Immigrants Willing to Pack Their Bags." *Migration Information Source*, November 5.

Minns, John, and Robert Tierney. 2003. "The Labour Movement in Taiwan." *Labour History* 85(November): 103–27.

Morris-Suzuki, Tessa. 2010. *Borderline Japan: Frontier Controls, Foreigners and the Nation in the Postwar Era*. New York: Cambridge University Press.

Myers, Ramon H., and Mark R.. Peattie, eds. 1984. *The Japanese Colonial Empire, 1895–1945*. Princeton, NJ: Princeton University Press.

OECD/SOPEMI. 2007. *International Migration Outlook*. Paris: OECD.

Park, Jung-Sun, and Paul Y. Chang. 2005. "Contention in the Construction of a Global Korean Community: The Case of the Overseas Korean Act." *Journal of Korean Studies* 10(1): 1–27.

Rigger, Shelley. 2002. "Nationalism versus Citizenship in the Republic of China on Taiwan." In *Changing Meanings of Citizenship in Modern China*, edited by Merle Goldman and Elizabeth J. Perry, 353–72. Cambridge, MA: Harvard University Press.

Schneider, Ben Ross. 1999. "The Desarrollista State in Brazil and Mexico." In *The Developmental State*, edited by Meredith Woo-Cumings, 276–305. Ithaca, NY: Cornell University Press.

Seol, Dong-Hoon. 2000. "Past and Present of Foreign Workers in Korea 1987–2000." *Asia Solidarity Quarterly* 2(2): 6–31.

Sharpe, Michael O. 2014. *Postcolonial Citizens and Ethnic Migration: The Netherlands and Japan in the Age of Globalization, Palgrave Studies in International Relations*. Houndmills, Basingstoke, Hampshire: Palgrave Macmillan.

Shin, Gi-Wook. 2006. *Ethnic Nationalism in Korea: Genealogy, Politics, and Legacy, Studies of the Walter H. Shorenstein Asia-Pacific Research Center*. Stanford, CA: Stanford University Press.

Tian, Yunchen. 2019. "Workers by Any Other Name: Comparing Co-Ethnics and 'Interns' as Labour Migrants to Japan." *Journal of Ethnic & Migration Studies* 45(9): 1496–514. doi: 10.1080/1369183X.2018.1466696

Tsuda, Takeyuki. 2003. *Strangers in the Ethnic Homeland: Japanese Brazilian Return Migration in Transnational Perspective*. New York: Columbia University Press.

Vink, Maarten P. 2017. "Comparing Citizenship Regimes." In *The Oxford Handbook of Citizenship*, edited by Ayelet Shachar, Rainer Bauböck, Irene Bloemraad, and Maarten Vink, 221–44. Oxford: Oxford University Press.

Wagner, Edward W. 1951. *The Korean Minority in Japan: 1904–1950*. New York: Institute of Pacific Relations.

Wang, Hong-Zen. 2011. "Immigration Trends and Policy Changes in Taiwan." *Asian and Pacific Migration Journal* 20(2): 169–94.

Woo, Jung-en. 1991. *Race to the Swift: State and Finance in Korean Industrialization*. New York: Columbia University Press.

Woo-Cumings, Meredith. 1994. "The 'New Authoritarianism' in East Asia." *Current History* 93(587): 413–16.

———. 1999. "Introduction: Chalmers Johnson and the Politics of Nationalism and Development." In *The Developmental State*, edited by Meredith Woo-Cumings, 1–31. Ithaca, NY: Cornell University Press.

World Bank. 2020. *National Accounts Data*. Washington, DC: World Bank.

Yu, Wei-Hsin. 2009. *Gendered Trajectories: Women, Work, and Social Change in Japan and Taiwan*. Stanford, CA: Stanford University Press.

7   INTERNATIONAL MIGRATION AND DEVELOPMENT IN SOUTHEAST ASIA, 1990–2010

Charles Hirschman

ONE OF MY MOST VIVID impressions as a Peace Corps volunteer living in a Malaysian village in the 1960s was the apparent immobility of the population. Most of the people were born in the village or nearby, and few ventured far from home. People in urban areas were only slightly more mobile. Professionals working for the government—teachers, nurses, and police officers—who were rotated from station to station every few years, were the exception. But they too had held strong attachments to place, particularly their hometowns. Most government officers considered their current location to be a temporary place of work and generally went "home" every holiday, and even for weekends if they could. I interpreted the apparent low levels of geographical mobility, or even the desire for geographic mobility, as a sign of underdevelopment and traditionalism. Influenced by the then prevailing theory of modernization, I reasoned that geographic mobility was a key intervening variable between economic development and cultural modernity. As people moved to cities and from place to place, they were exposed to different ways of life, varied cultures, and new ideas. According to the theory, migration, along with education, would lead to modernity—an openness to change and tolerance of diversity. With few signs of industrialization and urbanization that might lead to increasing geographic and social mobility, development seemed like a distant prospect in Malaysia.

How wrong I was! When I returned to my village in the 1970s, many of my old friends were working in Singapore and their children were attending secondary schools and colleges in towns and cities. Within a few decades, Malaysia and other Southeast Asian nations were experiencing rapid rural to urban migration and even significant flows of international migration. Much of this was regional, but there were also flows to the Middle East, Australia, Europe, and North America. Not only were my 1960s observations not predictive of subsequent change, but in my naiveté I assumed that immobility was a characteristic of Southeast Asia's past. As my study of Southeast Asian history deepened, I learned that long-distance migration was one of the defining features of the region. The relatively calm seas and navigable rivers of the region allowed for an ease of movement and an openness to trade. Long-distance trade to China, India, and

Europe of forest products, minerals, and spices had stimulated the growth of Southeast Asian cities with multicultural populations drawn from near and far (Reid 2015). During the heyday of imperialism from the mid-nineteenth to early twentieth centuries, the colonial economy was sustained by mass migration of labor from poorer regions of Asia, particularly from China and India. Migration almost certainly declined during the middle decades of the twentieth century with the Great Depression, World War II, and a relatively slow pace of economic development in the early postwar decades. My experience in the 1960s was probably at the nadir of long-distance migration in Southeast Asia.

Other factors might also have kept migration at low levels in the decades immediately following World War II. The political developments of the postcolonial period focused on building a national identity in the newly independent countries, not attracting peoples from other countries. The rural development programs of the 1950s and 1960s encouraged higher productivity in agriculture, not migration to urban areas. Most towns and cities were centers of administration and small-scale trade with little growth in jobs that might have attracted migrants. My limited social networks might also have biased my impressions. Most of my Malaysian friends and acquaintances in the 1960s were young adults, and I had limited contact with the elderly long-distance migrants who arrived during the early decades of the twentieth century.

Perhaps because I did not understand the significance of migration in Southeast Asia's past, I was unprepared for the resurgence of migration from and to Southeast Asia that began in the late 1970s (Massey et al. 1998, chap. 6). In this chapter, I hope to atone for my lack of vision with a survey of patterns and trends in international migration to and from Southeast Asia from 1990 to 2010. With eleven states and a population of more than 600 million, Southeast Asia, along with its regional association of ASEAN, has emerged as one of the most economically dynamic regions in the world. An examination of migration reveals the unevenness of development and demography across Southeast Asia as well as the forces of political instability and conflict that pushed and pulled peoples within the region and to other parts of the globe. Then, I offer a critical review of bourgeoning research literature on international migration in Southeast Asia. Finally, I offer an interpretation of the political and policy debates over international migration and development in Southeast Asia.

There are two major areas of destination within the region—Thailand on the mainland and Malaysia/Singapore in the area generally labeled as "maritime" (or island) Southeast Asia. These flows correspond to regional patterns of economic growth and labor demand but also to proximity, demography, and political instability. Migration in Southeast Asia is not entirely self-contained—there are also flows to East, South, and West Asia, and also to Europe, Australia, and North America. The destination areas in Southeast Asia, especially Malaysia and Singapore, are also sources of large-scale emigration. International migration in Southeast Asia is a recognizable part of the global migration system, not only in responding to similar forces, but with some of the same origins and destinations.

The migration flows in this analysis are based on the UN estimates of "stocks" of international migrants by country of origin and destination in 1990, 2000, and 2010

(United Nations 2013). These estimates are primarily based on census data from most counties in the world that report data by country of birth. The data are far from perfect—the methods of data estimation and adjustment carry wide bands of uncertainty and may also be biased by assumptions that recent movements are similar to historical patterns of international migration. In spite of these limitations, the UN estimates provide a much stronger evidentiary base for a field that has too often relied on newspaper accounts and fragmentary counts from government agencies.

Southeast Asia

The geographic label of "Southeast Asia" has only been widely used since the middle of the twentieth century, although the region has been well known since the origins of long-distance trade as the "land below the winds," "further India," and "Southern Seas." Most of the early civilizations in the region were based on trade of spices, forest products, and minerals to China and South Asia. Southeast Asian port cities provided safe harbors where the monsoon trade winds met, and traders were generally welcomed. The European "discovery" of the New World was motivated by the search for spices of the East Indies (islands in the eastern Indonesian archipelago). Linguistic and archeological evidence identifies people from Borneo (part of present-day Malaysia and Indonesia) as the settlers of the island of Madagascar off the coast of East Africa more than a millennium ago (Kumar 2011).

With rugged and often mountainous interiors, much of Southeast Asia was lightly settled until the twentieth century. Trade and political networks were often centered on coastal cities that were linked to inland areas by navigable rivers reaching far into the hinterlands. In some regions, rice-growing plains gave rise to numerous empires and civilizations whose monumental architectural edifices (Angkor, Pagan, Borobudur, My Son) inspire awe among twenty-first-century tourists to the region. In spite of the lack of a single dominant Southeast Asian empire and diverse languages and religions, historians and area specialists find some common cultural threads among peoples in the region, including relatively open social systems that adopt and combine religions, cultural beliefs, languages, and even peoples from distant lands (Reid 2015).

The current political map of Southeast Asia, consisting of eleven states, is largely a product of European imperialism. Precolonial Southeast Asian empires and states were not defined by their borders but by power, which radiated outward from a heartland to agricultural (primarily rice) populations and seaborne trade. The power of early states to control hinterlands waxed and waned with economic conditions, natural catastrophes, and challenges from rival empires. Beginning in the early sixteenth century, European naval powers competed with each other to control Southeast Asian trade in spices and other primary products. The Portuguese came first, soon followed by the Spanish, Dutch, English, French, and eventually even the Americans. The initial aim was to monopolize (and plunder) from trade, but eventually—by the mid-nineteenth century—rival European powers had carved up the entire region into colonies with established boundaries that could be surveyed and color-coded on maps. Only by judicious concessions to the British and French was Siam (later Thailand) able to resist direct colonization by a European power.

The independent Southeast Asia countries that emerged in the decade after World War II largely accepted the colonial boundaries established in the late nineteenth and early twentieth centuries. Burma, now known as Myanmar, is a multiethnic country that shares boundaries with India and Bangladesh on the west, China on the north, and Laos and Thailand on the east. The boundaries of modern Burma were fixed by British as they consolidated their rule in the nineteenth century. The modern states of Laos, Vietnam, and Cambodia, formerly French-colonized Indochina, were assembled by nineteenth-century power politics and twentieth-century revolutions and treaties. If modern state boundaries were based on historical patterns of identity and language, much of southern Vietnam would be part of Cambodia, and northeast Thailand would be part of Laos. If boundaries followed early nineteenth-century political domains, Thailand would encompass much of Cambodia, the northern states of present-day Malaysia, and parts of Burma. By language and religion, much of southern Thailand has closer affinity to the peoples of Malaysia than to central and northern Thailand.

The political divisions of maritime Southeast Asia are even more arbitrary. The modern states of Indonesia and Philippines were only unified as political units following Dutch and Spanish conquest. However, the shared experience of colonial rule created nationalist movements of diverse peoples who saw their destiny as unified countries, largely following colonial boundaries. The common feature of the states that became Malaysia was rule by British colonial officials, enterprise, or viceroys.

There are three "microstates" in maritime Southeast Asia, though the reasons for their micro status vary. Singapore is an island of less than 700 square kilometers at the end of Malaysian peninsula. It was part of British Malaya during the colonial era and became part of independent Malaysia for a short period. In 1963, Singapore become an independent country, though it might be more accurately described as a city-state. Historically, Brunei was an important trading state with a substantial hinterland on the island of Borneo, but its status and size were eroded in the nineteenth century with the expansion of Sarawak, which was then ruled by the "white Rajahs"—an English family that installed itself as quasi-colonial despots. After World War II, Britain assumed colonial rule over Sarawak and Sabah—a large territory on north Borneo that had been previously controlled by a British company. Both Sarawak and Sabah became part of Malaysia in 1963. Brunei initially considered joining Malaysia, with which it shares a common language and culture, but its sultan decided he could better preserve his wealth and absolutist rule as an independent "Middle East–style oil sheikdom." Timor-Leste consists of the eastern half of the island of Timor in the middle of the Indonesian archipelago. East Timor remained a remote Portuguese colony during throughout the Dutch colonial expansion of the East Indies (now Indonesia) and even during the first fifteen years of independent Indonesia. When the Portuguese overseas empire collapsed in 1975, East Timor nationalists declared their national independence, but the fledgling nation was soon taken over by Indonesia. After a bloody civil war, a plebiscite, and transitional rule by the United Nations, Timor-Leste finally became an internationally recognized country in 2002.

With a few exceptions such as the island of Java and the Red River Delta in northern Vietnam, low population density characterized most of the Southeast Asia until the twentieth century. However, rapid population growth over the last century has led to densely settled core regions and large metropolitan cities in most of Southeast Asia. At present, Southeast Asia is more populous than the combined countries of the European Union. Table 7.1 shows demographic and economic indicators for each of the eleven states in the region in 2015. Indonesia is the regional giant with a population of more than 250 million—about 40 percent of the total (it also has about 40 percent of the land mass). With populations of 100 and 90 million respectively, the Philippines and Vietnam are each larger than Germany (which has about 80 million). Thailand is as populous (69 million) as France or the United Kingdom. At the other end of the scale, Brunei has a population of less than .5 million and Timor-Leste has only 1.2 million people. The Singapore city-state has less than 6 million, while Laos has less than 7 million. These smaller countries are dwarfed by the megacities of the region, such as Manila and Jakarta, which each have populations of more than 10 million (Hugo 2012, 137). Bangkok and Ho Chi Minh City are not too far behind.

Although levels and trends vary from country to country, longevity in most of Southeast Asia increased rapidly in the decades following World War II, and fertility began to decline in the 1970s and 1980s. In countries with the most advanced demographic transitions, including Singapore and Thailand, natural increase is close to zero. In countries that still average about three children per family, such as the Philippines and parts of Indonesia, substantial natural increase will continue for many more decades. Population growth is the sum of natural increase and net international migration. In general, natural increase and migration are inversely correlated, which means that immigration partially counterbalances low fertility. The actual demographic processes are more complicated because fertility affects labor supply after a lag of twenty years. Moreover, there are not a fixed number of jobs in any economy—labor supply and demand are affected by age distribution, patterns of retirement and school enrollment, and many other economic and social forces with feedback loops.

Among the nondemographic forces affecting labor demand and immigration, none are more important than economic factors. An overview of the regional economy is presented in table 7.2 with recent World Bank estimates of per-capita GNI (in USD) for the last few decades. The World Bank Atlas Method of computing National Income is intended to allow for international comparisons, net of inflation.

On the mainland, Thailand stands out as a middle-income developing country with a per-capita national income double or triple that of its neighbors. The spread of the market economy has led to robust economic growth in Vietnam, Laos, and Cambodia in recent years, but their incomes are still only about USD 1–2,000 per capita compared to over USD 5,000 in Thailand. Myanmar, with continued civil war and slow economic growth, lags even further behind.

In maritime Southeast Asia, Singapore's and, to a lesser extent, Malaysia's economies are approaching developed country levels, while the Philippines and Indonesia lag far behind. Singapore's per-capita income of USD 52,000 is comparable to the United States, and Malaysia's successful economy (USD 10,000 per capita) is also very impressive. The high figure for Brunei is a bit misleading since its population is so small (less than half a million) and it is almost entirely due to the sale of natural resources—oil and natural gas.

Table 7.1. Population, lifetime immigrants, lifetime emigrants, and net lifetime immigrants (in thousands) of world and island Southeast Asia, 1960–2015.

	Land Area (sq. km.)	Midyear Population Estimates in Millions							Average Annual Growth Rate					
		1960	1970	1980	1990	2000	2010	2015	1960–70	1970–80	1980–90	1990–2000	2000–10	2010–15
Southeast Asia	4,502,290	215.4	279.9	356.3	441.9	522.1	595.8	632.8	2.6	2.4	2.2	1.7	1.3	1.2
Mainland	1,939,240	91.0	115.7	144.4	176.5	204.2	224.9	235.0	2.4	2.2	2.0	1.5	1.0	0.9
Thailand	513,120	27.4	36.9	47.4	56.6	63.0	67.2	68.7	3.0	2.5	1.8	1.1	0.7	0.4
Myanmar	676,590	21.0	26.4	33.4	40.6	46.1	50.2	52.4	2.3	2.3	2.0	1.3	0.8	0.9
Vietnam	331,690	34.7	42.7	53.7	66.0	77.6	86.9	91.7	2.1	2.3	2.1	1.6	1.1	1.1
Cambodia	181,040	5.7	7.0	6.7	9.0	12.2	14.3	15.5	2.0	-0.4	2.9	3.0	1.6	1.6
Lao PDR	236,800	2.1	2.7	3.3	4.3	5.3	6.2	6.7	2.4	1.9	2.7	2.2	1.6	1.3
Island	2,563,050	124.5	164.3	211.9	265.5	318.0	370.9	397.8	2.8	2.5	2.3	1.8	1.5	1.4
Malaysia	330,800	8.2	10.8	13.8	18.0	23.2	28.1	30.7	2.8	2.4	2.7	2.5	1.9	1.8
Singapore	680	1.6	2.1	2.4	3.0	4.0	5.1	5.5	2.3	1.5	2.3	2.8	2.3	1.7
Indonesia	1,910,930	87.8	114.8	147.5	181.4	211.5	242.5	258.2	2.7	2.5	2.1	1.5	1.4	1.2
Philippines	300,000	26.3	35.8	47.4	61.9	78.0	93.7	101.7	3.1	2.8	2.7	2.3	1.8	1.6
Brunei Darussalam	5,770	0.1	0.1	0.2	0.3	0.3	0.4	0.4	4.6	4.0	2.9	2.5	1.5	1.4
Timor-Leste	14,870	0.5	0.6	0.6	0.8	0.9	1.1	1.2	1.9	-0.3	2.5	1.5	2.4	2.2

Source: World Bank 2017, World Development Indicators (accessed September 17, 2017, from http://wdi.worldbank.org/tables).

Table 7.2. Gross national income (GNI) per capita and average annual growth rate (AAGR) of GNI per capita in Southeast Asia, 1970–2015.

	Gross National Income (GNI) per Capita						Average Annual Growth Rate of GNI per Capita				
	1970	1980	1990	2000	2010	2015	1970–80	1980–90	1990–2000	2000–10	2010–15
Mainland											
Thailand	210	710	1,490	1,980	4,580	5,690	12.2	7.4	2.8	8.4	4.3
Myanmar	..	..	..	..	860	1,190	--	--	--	--	6.5
Vietnam	..	..	130	400	1,270	1,990	--	--	11.2	11.6	9.0
Cambodia	..	..	..	300	750	1,070	--	--	--	9.2	7.1
Lao PDR	..	..	190	280	1,000	2,000	--	--	3.9	12.7	13.9
Island											
Malaysia	370	1,790	2,400	3,460	8,240	10,440	15.8	2.9	3.7	8.7	4.7
Singapore	960	4,720	11,450	23,670	44,790	52,740	15.9	8.9	7.3	6.4	3.3
Indonesia	80	470	560	580	2,520	3,440	17.7	1.8	0.4	14.7	6.2
Philippines	220	700	720	1,220	2,730	3,520	11.6	0.3	5.3	8.1	5.1
Brunei Darussalam	..	..	12,460	14,680	33,300	38,520	--	--	1.6	8.2	2.9
Timor-Leste	..	..	..	..	2,890	2,180	--	--	--	--	-5.6

Source: World Bank 2017, *World Development Indicators* (accessed September 17, 2017, from http://wdi.worldbank.org/tables).
Note: The World Bank Atlas Method of computing calculating gross national income per capita is designed to reduce the impact of exchange rates and inflation for international comparisons; see http://go.worldbank.org/IEH2RL06U0.

As we will see, these economic and demographic characteristics are highly correlated with flows of international migration.

New Data on International Migration

In contrast to internal migration, there is a paucity of reliable data on international migration. National censuses and surveys generally capture the universe of internal migrants by place of origin and destination with questions on the place of previous residence (and birth) and duration of residence in their current locality. There are, of course, problems of measurement of internal migration because many people are not able to recall the exact dates of prior migrations, especially if they were temporary. Another problem of recall is that most people report the popular name of the place (city, town, or village) where they once lived, but place names often differ from "official" (administratively defined) locations and boundaries. In addition to these familiar problems of measurement, there are additional barriers to data on international migration. Immigrants are generally included in national surveys and censuses if there is a question on country of birth. But emigrants—those who have left the country—including natives and prior immigrants, are not.

One possible source of data on emigrants from every country is the sum of country-of-birth data of international migrants' countries of destination. However, most researchers do not have the time or resources to assemble data from every country in the world to examine patterns of emigration. But international agencies, in collaboration with national statistical systems, have assembled data on flows of migrants from every country to every other country in the world. The United Nations routinely reports estimates of the "stocks" of all international migrants by country of origin and country of destination (United Nations 2013). The United Nations Global Migration Database is assembled from a number of sources, including national censuses on the foreign born (or citizenship) and counts of refugees from international agencies. These empirical sources are used to estimate "stocks" (foreign-born persons) for 232 countries in the world for 1990, 2000, 2010, and 2013. While the UN estimates may be defective because of errors and omissions in census data and in the assumptions used to create the estimates, the UN Global Migration Database represents a quantum leap in comprehensive knowledge on trends in the international flows of migrants around the world (for independent estimates of global migration, see Abel and Sander 2014; World Bank 2017).

The UN Global Migration Database allows for the measurement of "lifetime international migration" based on a comparison of country of birth and current (at the time of interview) country of residence. Since persons can migrate multiple times and to multiple destinations over their life, lifetime migration data do not reveal the full dynamics of migration nor is it possible to identify the timing of migration or the age of a person at the time of migration. Lifetime immigrants include recently arrived workers, dependents, and refugees, as well as those who immigrated many decades earlier and are now permanent residents or citizens. The estimates also miss international migrants who did not survive until the next census in the country of destination. Another limitation is that it is impossible to distinguish permanent migrants from temporary migrants (those who intend to return home or migrate elsewhere). Some people are classified as international migrants because of changes in political boundaries. For example, the collapse of the Soviet Union made many Russians "international migrants" because they are now living outside of Russia in the newly independent states that were once part of the Soviet Union.

In spite of these limitations, the UN estimates of lifetime migration have become a primary source of data for researchers and policy analysts. In this chapter, I rely on the UN data to measure patterns of international migration within Southeast Asian and also to other world regions.

Lifetime Immigration and Emigration in Southeast Asia

The first three rows of table 7.3 show the UN estimates of lifetime migrants—defined as living in country different from one's county of birth—for the world as a whole and also in developed and developing countries in 1990, 2000, and 2010. The absolute numbers are up sharply from 154 million lifetime international migrants in 1990 to 175 million in 2000, and to 221 million in 2010. As a fraction of the world's population, international migration has risen, but less dramatically, from 2.9 percent in 1990 to 3.2 percent in 2010. There is a dramatic difference between relative flows to developed and developing countries. The developed countries—sometimes referred to as the global "North"—includes Europe, Northern America, Australia, New Zealand, and Japan. International migrants

Table 7.3. Estimates of total population, lifetime immigrants, lifetime emigrants, and net lifetime migrants (in thousands) in the world and in Southeast Asian countries: 1990, 2000, and 2010.

| | Number of Persons (in 000) | | | | | | | | | | | |
| | Population | | | Lifetime Immigrants | | | Lifetime Emigrants | | | Net Lifetime Migrants | | |
	1990	2000	2010	1990	2000	2010	1990	2000	2010	1990	2000	2010
WORLD	5,309,668	6,126,622	6,929,725	154,162	174,516	220,729						
More developed regions	1,144,463	1,188,812	1,233,376	82,307	103,389	129,737						
Less developed regions	4,165,205	4,937,810	5,696,349	71,855	71,127	90,992						
Southeast Asia	445,665	526,179	596,708	3,200	5,274	8,695	7,582	11,670	17,793	-4,381	-6,396	-9,098
Mainland	180,056	208,189	227,407	752	1,580	3,490	3,129	4,709	7,835	-2,378	-3,128	-4,345
Thailand	56,583	62,693	66,692	529	1,258	3,224	356	555	834	173	703	2,390
Myanmar	42,007	47,670	51,733	134	98	101	599	1,113	2,385	-465	-1,015	-2,284
Vietnam	68,210	80,286	88,358	28	57	62	1,307	1,916	2,477	-1,279	-1,860	-2,416
Cambodia	9,009	12,198	14,364	38	146	82	364	468	957	-326	-322	-875
Lao PDR	4,248	5,343	6,261	23	22	21	504	658	1,181	-481	-636	-1,159
Maritime	265,609	317,989	369,301	2,449	3,694	5,205	4,452	6,961	9,958	-2,004	-3,268	-4,753
Malaysia	18,211	23,421	28,120	1,014	1,614	2,358	574	1,106	1,575	441	508	783
Singapore	3,016	3,918	5,079	727	1,352	2,165	172	197	291	556	1,154	1,874
Indonesia	181,437	211,540	241,613	466	292	287	1,337	2,010	2,835	-871	-1,718	-2,548
Philippines	61,947	77,932	93,039	159	323	205	2,329	3,447	5,180	-2,170	-3,124	-4,975
Brunei Darussalam	257	331	393	73	104	180	30	46	47	44	58	133
Timor-Leste	740	847	1,057	9	9	11	12	156	32	-3	-146	-21

Source: UN Population Division 2013. International migrant stock by midyear, destination, and origin: 1990, 2000, 2010, and 2013 (accessed September 6, 2017, from http://www.un.org/en/development/desa/population/migration/data/estimates2/estimatesorigin.shtml).
Notes:

a. Lifetime immigrants include all persons living in a country who were born in a different country.
b. Lifetime emigrants include all persons who are currently living outside their country of birth.
c. Net migration is measured as the difference between lifetime immigrants and

rose from 7 percent of the residents of developed countries in 1990 to over 10.5 percent in 2010. Migration to developing countries—Latin America, Asia, and Africa—is much lower. In 2010, only 1.6 percent of the population in developing countries were born in another country—this figure is basically unchanged from the 1990 figure of 1.7 percent.

The UN data reveal that three-fourths of the lifetime immigrants to the North (developed countries) come from the global "South"—Asia, Africa, and Latin America (United Nations 2016, 1). Although international migration is not entirely a function of economic factors, there is a strong association between levels of development and the direction of flows between countries and regions.

This generalization holds for Southeast Asia in the aggregate, but closer examination of particular countries and time periods reveals considerable variations within the region. We begin with a description of lifetime immigration and emigration for the eleven countries of Southeast Asia, which are sorted into two regions: Mainland (Thailand, Myanmar, Vietnam, Cambodia, and Laos) and Maritime (Malaysia, Singapore, Indonesia, Philippines, Brunei, and Timor-Leste). While the terms "lifetime immigration" and "lifetime emigration" may appear to connote permanency of settlement, they are simply indicators of in- and out-migration based on a comparison of country of birth and country of current residence.

Our interpretation of trends over the three time points is conditioned by the cumulative measure of lifetime migration. Lifetime migrants include those who crossed a national boundary many decades ago as well as those in recent years. Changes in the volume of migration (in and out) from 1990 to 2000 and from 2000 to 2010 reflect recent migration flows, but they are also affected by the mortality of migrants following their migration. For example, some of the older immigrants who arrived during the first half of the twentieth century were still alive in 1990, but their numbers were largely depleted by mortality by 2000 and 2010.

The subregional totals for mainland and maritime Southeast Asia, as well as for Southeast Asia as a whole, in table 7.3 are the simple sums of the component countries. This means that regional migrants are double-counted as emigrants from one country and immigrants to other countries in the region. However, the regional and subregional totals still have a useful interpretation as the collective numbers of persons who are counted as international migrants, regardless of destination or origin.

In addition to the absolute numbers, table 7.3 shows lifetime immigration, lifetime emigration, and net lifetime migration. Net lifetime migration is the number of immigrants minus emigrants. There are also estimates of rates of lifetime immigration, lifetime emigration, and net lifetime migration. Technically, these are not demographic rates (based on a population at risk), but simple ratios of the numbers of migrants relative to the national (resident) population in the same year (1990, 2000, or 2010), expressed as percentages. These figures are intended to convey some sense of the magnitude of migration flows, relative to the population of each country.

Collectively, there are more departures than arrivals in Southeast Asia. The sum of lifetime immigrants rose from 3.2 million in 1990 to 8.7 million in 2010, while the number of emigrants rose from 7.6 million to 17.8 million for the same period. In relative terms, the region had a deficit of 1.5 percent net lifetime migrants in 2010—a figure that was 50 percent higher than 1990. On the mainland, the outflows reflect refugees and labor migration, while almost all the outward movement from maritime Southeast Asia consists of labor migrants. These patterns are even more evident when looking at individual countries.

Three Southeast Asian countries are net gainers from international migration. On the mainland, Thailand is a major receiving country—from a half-million lifetime immigrants in 1990 to over three million in 2010. Thailand also loses population from emigration, over 800,000 in 2010. But the overall balance is positive. Almost 5 percent of Thailand's population was foreign born in 2010, and even after subtracting out emigrants, the net international migration rate was still a positive 3.6 percent. These estimates reflect Thailand's economic dynamism relative to the economic stagnation and political turmoil in neighboring countries.

In maritime Southeast Asia, the magnets for international migration are Malaysia and Singapore. Once part of the same country, Malaysia and Singapore share similar demographic and socioeconomic characteristics. Singapore is a city-state with a population of five million in 2010 (up from three million in 1990). Malaysia is considerably larger at 28 million in 2010, but still a relatively moderate-size country. In spite of their political differences, Malaysia and Singapore have followed similar models of export-orientated open-market development. Rapid economic growth has led to labor shortages, which are particularly acute for domestic service and less skilled labor (in manufacturing, construction, services, and agriculture). Both countries rely heavily on migrant labor. In 2010, over 8 percent of the Malaysian population, and an astounding 43 percent of the Singaporean population, were foreign born. Interestingly, both countries also have high emigration rates of over 5 percent in 2010. The reasons for the departures are discussed in the next section.

With the exception of Brunei, all other countries in Southeast Asia have experienced absolute (and net) population losses from international migration. On the mainland, negative net lifetime migration is significant, both in absolute numbers and especially in relative terms. The Vietnam case is well known—over 1.3 million (almost 2 percent) of Vietnam-born persons were reported living in other countries in 1990. The relative rate of population loss (via international migration) was even larger in Cambodia and Laos at 4 and 12 percent, respectively. The three Indochina countries receive virtually no lifetime immigrants. All three countries experienced considerable refugees outflows in the 1970s and 1980s following the wars that devastated Indochina. In spite of the political stabilization and economic recovery during the 1990s and early 2000s, all three countries continued to experience demographic hemorrhages from emigration. By 2010, almost 3 percent of those born in Vietnam, over 6 percent of those born in Cambodia, and 19 percent of persons born in Laos live outside the country. Myanmar has also experienced a comparable outflow with a net lifetime international migration rate of −4.4 percent in 2010.

In maritime Southeast Asia, the two demographic giants of Indonesia and the Philippines are net exporters of people. In 2010, 2.8 million Indonesians and 5.2 million Filipinos (defined by country of birth) were living abroad—about 1.2 and 5.6 percent in relative terms. Although both countries have experienced political strife, the primary reason for emigration from these countries is the surplus of job seekers relative to economic opportunities at home. Timor-Leste is a special case with a small territory in the middle of the Indonesian archipelago and population of only one million in 2010. However, it fits well with the broader pattern of net population loss from international migration. The loss was particularly acute in 2000 when the political transition (and upheaval) was taking place. Brunei is another special case with a population of less than .4 million in 2010—almost half of which is foreign born. Like Middle Eastern petrostates, Brunei reserves high-status positions for nationals and imports temporary labor for everything else.

Lifetime Immigration to Southeast Asia by Country/Region of Origin

In the abstract, migrants could go anywhere. However, real-world constraints, often summarized as the "friction of distance," means that most migrants follow well-worn paths to nearby destinations and other locations where there are family and friends who can provide information and assistance on finding jobs and housing. In table 7.4, we explore the impact of proximity on lifetime migration to each of the countries in Southeast Asian countries (in 1990, 2000, and 2010). This is another way of asking whether there is a regional migration system. Overall, we find considerable support for the significance of proximity on migration to Southeast Asia and from Southeast Asia, but with some exceptions. Proximity appears to be more important for mainland than maritime Southeast Asia.

The entries in the table 7.4 show the percent of all lifetime immigrants in each country (in each year) that originate from other Southeast Asia countries (collectively and individually) as well as from selected countries/regions from the rest of world. In the next section, we explore the role of proximity on the destinations of emigrants from Southeast Asia. As noted earlier, most countries in Southeast Asia are more notable for their emigration than immigration. It is only Thailand and Malaysia/Singapore that have experienced substantial immigration in recent decades (plus Brunei, but it is a special case with a very small population and specialized economy). In 1990, almost 70 percent of 3.2 million lifetime immigrants to Southeast Asia were in just three countries: Malaysia, Singapore, and Thailand. By 2010, the same three countries had 90 percent of the 8.7 million lifetime immigrants in the region—Thailand alone had 3.2 million lifetime immigrants.

Thailand

Thailand is the regional dominant in terms of immigration. In 1990, 75 percent of lifetime migrants to Thailand were from the neighboring countries of Myanmar (Burma), Laos, and Cambodia. This figure rose to 92 percent in 2010. The volume of lifetime immigrants in Thailand rose sixfold from .53 million to 3.22 million over the same period. Some of these migrants are refugees fleeing political unrest in their home countries, particularly Myanmar—which contributed almost half of all lifetime migrants to Thailand in 2010. These major flows also reflect the more dynamic labor market in Thailand as well as the cultural affinity of peoples across borders in mainland Southeast Asia.

Although most mainland SEA countries have recorded positive economic growth in recent years, the economies of Myanmar, Laos, Cambodia, and Vietnam (as measured

Table 7.4.   Lifetime immigrants, lifetime emigrants, and net lifetime migrants as a percent of population in 1990, 2000, and 2010.

	Percent of the Total Population in YEAR								
	Lifetime Migrants								
	1990	2000	2010						
WORLD	**2.9**	**2.8**	**3.2**						
More developed regions	7.2	8.7	10.5						
Less developed regions	1.7	1.4	1.6						
	Lifetime Immigration			Lifetime Emigration			Net Migration		
	1990	2000	2010	1990	2000	2010	1990	2000	2010
Southeast Asia	**0.7**	**1.0**	**1.5**	**1.7**	**2.2**	**3.0**	**–1.0**	**–1.2**	**–1.5**
Mainland	*0.4*	*0.8*	*1.5*	*1.7*	*2.3*	*3.4*	*–1.3*	*–1.5*	*–1.9*
Thailand	0.9	2.0	4.8	0.6	0.9	1.3	0.3	1.1	3.6
Myanmar	0.3	0.2	0.2	1.4	2.3	4.6	–1.1	–2.1	–4.4
Vietnam	0.0	0.1	0.1	1.9	2.4	2.8	–1.9	–2.3	–2.7
Cambodia	0.4	1.2	0.6	4.0	3.8	6.7	–3.6	–2.6	–6.1
Lao PDR	0.5	0.4	0.3	11.9	12.3	18.9	–11.3	–11.9	–18.5
Maritime	*0.9*	*1.2*	*1.4*	*1.7*	*2.2*	*2.7*	*–0.8*	*–1.0*	*–1.3*
Malaysia	5.6	6.9	8.4	3.1	4.7	5.6	2.4	2.2	2.8
Singapore	24.1	34.5	42.6	5.7	5.0	5.7	18.4	29.5	36.9
Indonesia	0.3	0.1	0.1	0.7	1.0	1.2	–0.5	–0.8	–1.1
Philippines	0.3	0.4	0.2	3.8	4.4	5.6	–3.5	–4.0	–5.3
Brunei Darussalam	28.5	31.5	45.7	11.5	14.0	11.9	17.0	17.5	33.8
Timor-Leste	1.2	1.1	1.0	1.6	18.4	3.0	–0.3	–17.3	–2.0

Source and Notes: See table 7.3.

by GNI per capita) are much poorer than Thailand's. Although there is a shared Buddhist heritage among mainland Southeast Asian countries, the national languages and cultures are distinct. However, there is considerable ethnic heterogeneity in each country with borderlands often populated by ethnic groups with members on both sides on national boundaries. For example, the Isan dialect of Thai that is spoken in northeastern Thailand is closer to Lao than standard Thai.

Myanmar/Burma
There are virtually no lifetime immigrants to Myanmar—about 100,000 in a population of 50 million, about .2 of one percent. The absolute number of lifetime immigrants in Myanmar is less in 2010 than it was in 1990. Alone among SEA countries, Myanmar reports no immigrants from other Southeast Asian countries—they are almost all

from China and India. It seems likely that the most of these migrants to Myanmar are the elderly survivors of migrants who arrived many decades ago. There are virtually no Bangladesh-born persons residing in Myanmar, contrary to the claims of the Myanmar government that the Rohingya are recent arrivals from Bangladesh.

Vietnam/Cambodia/Laos

The modern countries of Vietnam, Cambodia, and Laos—the region once known as Indochina—report very low levels of lifetime immigrants, generally well below one percent of their national populations. There appears to have been a blip with a higher number for Cambodia in 2000—perhaps a residue of the UN administration of the country in 1992–93. There are some unexpected quirks in statistical time series that should be regarded with some skepticism. For example, the UN estimates show that about 11–17 percent of the small number of lifetime immigrants (50–60,000) to Vietnam in 2000 and 2010 were born in Libya. This is possible, but we have not been able to find any academic or journalistic accounts to substantiate the report of Libyans in Vietnam. In 1990, almost all foreign-born persons in Vietnam came from Cambodia. In 2000 and 2010, the numbers from other countries have increased, including Southeast Asia, China, Nepal, Libya, and even from Western countries. The very low level of lifetime migration to Laos has not changed from 1990 to 2010, and almost all are from Vietnam, Thailand, and China.

Malaysia and Singapore

The dynamic economies of Malaysia and Singapore have generated labor demand far in excess of domestic labor supply. Fertility has been below the replacement level in Singapore since the 1970s and fertility is currently approaching the replacement level in Malaysia. In 2010, there were over two million lifetime immigrants reported in both countries. This is about 8 percent of the Malaysian population and over 40 percent of Singapore's. Given that most international migrants are in the working ages, the immigrant share of the labor force is considerably higher—probably well over half in the case of Singapore. The profiles of immigrant origins in Malaysia and Singapore are quite different.

Historically, the foreign-born population in Malaysia consisted of workers from China and India who arrived in the early decades of the twentieth century (and the late nineteenth century). By 1990, these populations had almost disappeared, with only 13 and 3 percent of Malaysia's foreign born from China and India, respectively. By 2010, there were virtually no foreign-born Chinese in Malaysia. The new source of labor comes primarily from Indonesia, and also from the Philippines and Bangladesh. Filipinos are concentrated in Sabah, the Malaysian state on the island of Borneo (Kalimantan), which has historical ties to the islands and peoples of the Philippines and Indonesia. In 2010, Indonesia was still the primary source of labor migration to Malaysia, but there are growing numbers from Myanmar and South Asia (primarily Bangladesh, Nepal, and India). Immigrants provide almost all of the workers in domestic service, and significant shares in agriculture, manufacturing, services, and retail trade in Malaysia (Kaur 2010b).

The labor needs in Singapore are much broader—it needs workers at all skill levels. In 2000 and 2010, about half of immigrants to Singapore are from Malaysia. To put this into perspective, Malaysia had over two million lifetime immigrants, but it had also exported one million Malaysian-born persons to Singapore. The Malaysian diaspora in Singapore is very diverse with some laborers in manufacturing and construction, but also many university graduates and other highly skilled workers to staff the rapidly growing medical, educational, and corporate sectors in Singapore. Singapore also attracts expatriate workers in foreign-owned business from Japan, Korea, and Western countries.

Indonesia and the Philippines

Aside from being island archipelagos, Indonesia and the Philippines share few common historical or cultural similarities. Indonesia is primarily Muslim (though with important Hindu and Christian minorities) and experienced 300 years of Dutch colonial rule. The Philippines fell into the Spanish colonial system, followed by American rule for the first half of the twentieth century. Nominally, Roman Catholic, Filipino cultural traditions reflect the creole mixture of Spanish, American, and Indigenous influences. But relatively slow economic development and higher rates of natural increase have given Indonesia and the Philippines similar profiles of international migration. Both counties have experienced net negative lifetime migration with very low levels of immigration and high levels of emigration. Migration flows of both countries are also less centered on the region than for other Southeast Asian countries.

The absolute levels, and distribution by of country of origin, for Indonesia have varied dramatically over the three time points in table 7.3. In 1990, Indonesia had almost a half million lifetime immigrants, but this figure was only .3 of one percent of the national population (table 7.4). The majority were born in China and represent the residue of the early twentieth-century wave of Chinese immigration. By 2000, the number of foreign-born Chinese immigrants was less than 300,000. Almost half of lifetime immigrants to Indonesia in 2000 were born in the new state of Timor-Leste, which had rebelled against the Indonesian attempted invasion. In 2010, there were even fewer immigrants in Indonesia—only .1 of one percent of the national population. The largest group was from China, followed by a very diverse list of origin countries, including some from the region and also from Western countries.

Although the Philippines has absorbed large waves of international migrants over its history, the presence of immigrants was barely evident in 1990. Migration to the Philippines is largely disconnected from the rest of Southeast Asia. The largest groups are from China and other Asian and Western countries, including the United States.

Brunei and Timor-Leste

Brunei and Timor-Leste are such small countries that small absolute numbers can appear to have a huge impact. In spite of their interesting demographic and migration profiles, we suspect that the estimates of immigration and emigration in Brunei are very susceptible to errors of measurement. The high relative (and increasing) share of Brunei's population that is foreign born seems plausible as does the majority from Malaysia in 1990 and 2000. The figure of 50 percent from Japan in 2010 seems much more questionable. I have not found any corroboration of this sudden shift in migrant origins in the research literature. There is virtually no international migration to Timor-Leste. The population of the new nation has increased from .74 million in 1990 to 1.06 million in 2010, but the foreign born has remained at about one percent of the total.

Lifetime Emigration from Southeast Asia to the Rest of the World

Although Thailand, Malaysia, and Singapore have experienced net immigration from 1990 to 2010, the more common characteristic of the region is net emigration. Even the countries that are net recipients of international migration have high levels of emigration. Due to the limitations of the UN Global Migration Database (migration is measured from country of birthplace to country of current residence), it is not possible to assess return migration. Some international migrants may be the children of migrants who were born in country of destination, but then returned to their parental homeland with their parents. In general, neighboring countries are the primary source of immigrants to Southeast Asia, but tables 7.3 and 7.4 show that emigration is less centered on region. Some emigrants from Southeast Asia are working as laborers and domestic workers in West Asia, and others are part of the highly skilled (the "brain drain") professionals who have emigrated to Europe, North America, and Australia/New Zealand.

Thailand

Emigration from Thailand has more than doubled from 356,000 in 1990 to 843,000 lifetime emigrants in 2010—about 1.3 percent of the national population in 2010. In 2010, a little over one-fourth of Thai emigrants were in Asian countries, about the same number in Europe, and one-third were in North America (primarily the United States). Thai emigrants are distinctive because of the breadth of their destinations.

Myanmar

Out-migration from Myanmar has quadrupled from 1990 to 2010 with over two-thirds of them residing in Thailand in 2010. In numerical terms, more than one million people or 2 percent of the native-born population of Myanmar lives in Thailand. The likely cause of net emigration from Myanmar is political unrest. In addition to Thailand, the other major destination of emigrants from Myanmar is South Asia—Bangladesh and India.

Vietnam

The Vietnam-born diaspora—over 2.5 million in 2010 (almost 3 percent of the national population)—is centered in the United States, where more than half live. Vietnamese émigrés are also numerous in Europe and Australia. Aside from a handful in Malaysia and Cambodia, there are few Vietnamese emigrants in other Asian countries (however, see Huong 2010).

Cambodia and Laos

Following the collapse of the US-supported regimes in Indochina in the 1970s, there was an exodus of refugees from Laos and Cambodia in addition to Vietnam. The refugees were initially held in temporary refugee camps in Southeast Asia (Thailand, Malaysia, Philippines) before being permanently settled in Western countries, primarily in the

United States but also in Australia and Europe. In absolute numbers, the largest flow was from Vietnam, but in relative terms, the exodus was greater from Cambodia and Laos. In 1990, 4 percent of the population born in Cambodia was living overseas, and the comparable figure for Laos was an incredible 12 percent. Because most Cambodians and Lao fled across the eastern border, there were substantial fractions living in Thailand in 1990—20 and 33 percent of Cambodians and Lao, respectively.

Over the next twenty years, the outward flow of Cambodians and Lao has accelerated. In 2010, the ratio of émigrés to the national populations had risen to almost 7 percent for Cambodia and 19 percent for Laos. Most of these emigrants have settled in Thailand, which in 2010 had 64 and 70 percent of the Cambodian and Lao diaspora. Some of these may be refugees, but we suspect that many are labor migrants drawn to the booming Thai economy.

Malaysia and Singapore

In spite of their independent states and political rivalries, Malaysia and Singapore appear to share a common labor market. There are more than one million Malaysian born persons who live in Singapore—comprising one-fifth of the total Singapore population. About one quarter of Singaporean emigrants live in Malaysia. Both Malaysia and Singapore have high emigration ratios—about 5.6 to 5.7 percent in 2010. Beyond their exchanges with each other, emigrants from Singapore and Malaysia go primarily to Australia, Europe, and North America. There are also small flows to South Asia.

Indonesia and Philippines

The Philippines has the largest diasporic population of any country in the region, with over five million native-born Filipinos living abroad in 2010, a little under 6 percent of the national population. About one half of the Filipino-born diaspora lives in the North America, primarily the United States.

In relative terms, few Indonesians emigrate—only a bit more than one percent. But 1.2 percent of 240 million people (Indonesia's population in 2010) means that 2.8 million native-born Indonesians were living outside the country in 2010. About one-third of Filipino and Indonesians emigrants are living in the Middle East (West Asia), primarily in the Persian Gulf petro-states. They work as housekeepers, nannies, drivers, and laborers. As noted earlier, the other major destination for Indonesians is Malaysia. A shared language, religion, and culture makes Indonesia a culturally compatible labor reserve for Malaysia.

Brunei and Timor-Leste

The microstates of Brunei and Timor-Leste generate few emigrants in absolute terms, but about 10 percent of the Brunei-born population lives abroad, primarily in India, Malaysia, and Canada. The change in political boundaries when Timor-Leste become independent in 2002 means that the international migration numbers do not reflect actual population movement. Three percent of the Timor-born population lived outside the country in 2010, with about 60 percent in Indonesia and about a third in Australia.

Comparison of UN Estimates with Recent Published Research on Southeast Asia

As noted earlier, the UN Global Migration estimates are imperfect, reflecting problematic source data in addition to the technical assumptions used to construct consistent estimates across all countries. One major advantage of the UN series, however, is that they are not limited to legal flows. In most cases, the source data are based on census counts of foreign-born persons in each country, regardless of legal status. Of course, it is likely that international migrants were more likely than native-born persons to be missed in national censuses. In addition, some migrants may misreport their country of birth.

One of the standard features of most published articles on international migration to (and from) Southeast Asia are counts (or rates based on national population counts). Because the UN estimates have become available only in 2013, earlier studies have necessarily relied on other data sources, including counts or estimates from various government agencies, NGOs, newspaper accounts, and published (and unpublished) figures reported by other researchers (for example, see Athukorala 2006, 21; Hugo 2005, 2012, 125; Kaur 2010b; Massey et al. 1998, 164). The first question is how these estimates of international migration published literature compare with the UN figures, even allowing for a difference in time periods.

Simply put, the published figures on international migration in the research literature are all over the place. Kaur (2010b, 9) reports 13.5 million migrant workers in the ASEAN region, while the UN estimates the total number of foreign-born persons in Southeast Asia at only 8.7 million in 2010 (also see Hugo 2102, 128). Hugo's (2012, 125) estimate of almost 20 million Southeast Asians working in other Asian countries, based on a variety of newspaper and conference paper sources, is pretty close to the UN estimate of almost 18 million lifetime emigrants from Southeast Asia, but this seems to be the result of counterbalancing errors for individual countries. Most researchers do not compare their estimates of international migration with those reported by other scholars or even discuss the quality or completeness of data. It is often unclear if the data refer to stocks or flows. A recurrent observation is that illegal or clandestine migration may be many times larger than the reported or measured numbers of international migrants.

A few comparisons of Southeast Asian migrants from the research literature with the UN estimates illustrate the problem. In an article published in 2010, Lindquist states, "In 2006 . . . there are believed to be around 4.3 million Indonesian international migrants" (Lindquist 2010, 118). The UN estimates that there were 2.0 million lifetime emigrants from Indonesia in 2000 and 2.8 million in 2010 (see table 7.3). Citing figures from a popular magazine (Wine 2008), Mon (2010, 33) said: "According to a Thai-based labor organization, about 10% of Burma's population of approximately 55 million have migrated, either to seek refuge or to earn a living abroad, with about 2 million of these currently living in Thailand alone." These numbers are considerably at odds with the 2010 UN figures of 2.4 million Burmese emigrants (out of a population of 52 million), of whom 1.6 million live in Thailand (see tables 7.3 and 7.4). The discrepancy would even be greater if the reference periods were the same.

The independent estimates of international migration are not always larger than the UN figures. Citing data from the Thai Office of Foreign Workers Administration,

Paitoonpong and Chalamwong (2012, 4) report that there were 1.3 million foreign migrant workers (legal and illegal) in Thailand. The UN estimate in 2010 is 3.2 million (see table 7.3). The World Bank (2015, 2) estimates there are 1 million undocumented immigrants in Malaysia in addition to 2.1 million registered immigrants. This latter figure is very close the United Nations estimate for 2010.

In a comprehensive analysis of international migration from the Philippines, Tan (2009, 1) reports that there are 8.3 million Filipinos living aboard, while the UN estimates for a later date are only 5.2 million (see table 7.3). The same report has counts of Filipinos in the United States that are much higher than the UN estimates (and the US Census Bureau). Perhaps most questionable is Asis and Piper's (2008, 425) report that the Philippines is the world's largest labor-exporting country and had overtaken Mexico as the world's leading country of emigration; the UN reports that there were 5.2 million Filipinos living abroad in 2010 compared to 13 million Mexicans (United Nations 2013). These figures (and many others) seem to be "out of the blue" with little effort to evaluate their validity or even plausibility.

My objective is not to tout the accuracy of the UN estimates (see our cautionary statements above), but to call attention to a major problem for the field. International migration (and migration in general) is a complex phenomenon, and there are reasonable alternative measures that can be debated. The problem, however, is not just disagreements about particular figures but the casual acceptance of almost any numerical data about international migration by many researchers in the field. Most published articles on international migration in (or from) Southeast Asia do not discuss problems of accuracy or comparability and sometimes cite figures without any attribution.

The Migration Transition

Over the last few decades, many European countries that were once sources of emigration to the New World have become countries of immigration with migrants arriving from the global South and from poorer regions of Europe. For example, there are Poles and other Eastern Europeans in Ireland, Africans in Italy, and Latin Americans in Spain. This finding has been popularized as the "migration transition," highlighting cases where developing countries that once exported surplus labor have experienced net immigration because of economic development, declining fertility, and labor shortages (Skeldon 1992; Asis and Piper 2008, 431).

In many developing countries, the influx of new arrivals comes as a bit of surprise to policy-makers, the public, and even to migration researchers. The idea that the migration transition is a "natural process" of economic development appears to have been accepted by some researchers in the field. However, I find little empirical, or even logical, support for claim of a migration transition. Indeed, one of my findings is that development seems to simultaneously lead to high levels of both immigration and emigration. For example, absolute and relative measures of emigration have increased for Thailand, Malaysia, and Singapore even as the pace of immigration has increased to the same countries.

The relative balance of emigration and immigration appears to be a function of the supply and demand for labor of different types (labor migration, professionals, refugees, etc.) and a broad array of other factors, including political dynamics, social networks among migrants, and the presence of institutions (recruiters and brokers) to manage migration. Behind these factors are movements of international capital and technology, some universities aggressively recruiting international students, and relative shortages of eligible brides in some countries. These forces do not necessarily work in tandem according to a single model of economic development, but often move in fits and starts in response to markets, administrative regulations, and institutional pressures. There is likely to be increased levels of migration of all sorts, domestic and international, in response to economic, demographic, and institutional incentives. Perhaps the volume and direction of these various movements will follow a uniform model of a migration transition, but this seems only one among many possibilities.

The Vulnerability and Exploitation of Migrants

Much of the research literature on migration in Southeast Asia has documented the plight of international migrants, especially of vulnerable peoples who are cheated, abused, and taken advantage of by employers and officials. The list of exploited migrants includes domestic workers in Singapore (Amrith 2010; Devasahayam 2010), Vietnamese working in the sex sector in Cambodia (Nguyen and Gironde 2010), and several groups in Thailand, including Lao children (Huijsmans 2008), Cambodian fishermen (Derks 2010), and Burmese factory workers (Fujita et al. 2010; Kusakabe and Pearson 2010). Women and children are particularly likely to be exploited (Killias 2010; Molland 2012). Refugees fleeing from Vietnam in the 1970s and 1980s were often attacked by modern-day pirates who robbed them and then left them to die at sea. At the present moment, the Rohingya are being driven from their ancestral homeland in Myanmar by armed mobs and militias, often with government sanction. The vivid descriptions of the horrific experiences of migrants and minorities are a valuable counterpoise to the abstract and technocratic social science models that dominate much of the research on internal and international migration. In particular, ethnographic accounts allow readers to sense the pathos and trauma of suffering experienced by many migrants.

These accounts may lead to the conclusion that international migration should be discouraged, if not prevented. This interpretation, however, has to be balanced with the understanding that most international migrants were generally destitute and often abused and exploited before they migrated (Mon 2010; Rigg 2007; Maltoni 2007). Long-distance migration is generally the last response after all other options have exhausted. Material and psychic deprivation are common in many traditional rural communities, and many migrants are motivated to flee oppressive conditions, rapacious landlords, meddling parents and relatives, abusive husbands, and blocked opportunities in their home communities. The exposure of the sufferings of migrants should not blind us to the reality of the horrific conditions that often motivate long-distance migration.

The second point about this genre of research is that close ethnographic description also reveals that many migrants are able to circumvent the structures set up to control them. Brokers, government regulators, and employers often seek to tie migrant workers to their initial place of employment, control their sexuality with mandated contraception, prevent family members from joining them, and force them to return home when their contract is up. But many migrants are often able to work around these controls, especially if their labor is in high demand and if they have social networks of fellow kinsmen. In many reported cases, they simply leave unsatisfactory situations and find a better alternative (for example, "30,000 Indonesian maids in Malaysia run away each year," cited in Lindquist 2010, 116). One study of Lao child migrants in Thailand does not fit the standard image of trafficking because the youthful respondents often initiated their migration and choose their place of employment (Huijsmans 2008). Another study finds that Vietnamese sex workers in Cambodia reported that their lives were much better after migration than before (Nguyen and Gironde 2010). The frame of reference for many migrants is their origin communities, where conditions may have been even worse that the exploitative situations in their places of destination.

None of these findings should diminish concern about the pervasive discrimination and exploitation experienced by migrants, but migrants are often remarkably resourceful in evading the efforts of states and employers to control them. There is also some evidence that the long-term outcomes of migrants, especially of their children, are more positive than their initial positions.

International Migration and Economic Development: Public Policy Controversies

Another major strand of research is focused on policy issues, particularly the economic impact of migration on the destination country. Governments often claim that international migration has adverse effects on economic development, the employment and wages of native-born workers, and sociocultural issues, such as crime, public health, and ethnic composition. These policy debates are not unique to Southeast Asia or to developing countries more generally. The integration of immigrants as well as the economic consequences of immigration are central policy and research issues in the United States and Europe (National Academies of Sciences, Engineering, and Medicine 2015, 2017). Indeed, the policy debates and research on international migration in Southeast Asia are often based on theories and models drawn from Europe and North America.

The policy debate is well summarized by Athukorala (2006) as a clash with employers and pro-growth governments on one side and public opinion and the mass media on the other, each supported by "experts." There is little doubt that rapidly growing economies are experiencing labor shortages in many sectors including agriculture, manufacturing, construction, and many services. It is not uncommon to see agricultural lands in Southeast Asia, especially rice fields, lying idle for want of labor. The fishing industry in Thailand is largely dependent on migrant labor (Derks 2010). Migrant workers constitute 70 percent of the construction sector in Malaysia (Narayanan and Lai 2005). Burmese workers are the mainstay of garment and textile production in Thailand (Kaur 2010b, 15; Kusakabe and Pearson 2010, 14). Almost all maids and domestic workers in Malaysia are from Indonesia. Employers and their allies argue that the availability of foreign labor "contributes to economic dynamism and enables the economy to be flexible when structural adjustment is required" (Athukorala 2006, 18).

In spite of the obvious economic need for foreign labor, public opinion is generally hostile to immigrant workers in most Southeast Asian countries (Hugo 2012, 154–55). Some of the hostility is based on the fear of economic competition—the fear that foreign workers take jobs and lower the wages of native-born workers. This view is also expressed by some economists and other researchers with the argument that the presence of "cheap foreign labor" slows investment in labor-saving technology and economic restructuring.

The opposition to immigrants, however, is much deeper than just economic issues. After acknowledging the vital role of immigrants in the Malaysian economy, one researcher commented: "They (immigrants) often resort to crime when unemployed. By bypassing the health screening system for migrant workers, they could be a source of highly contagious diseases" (Kanapathy 2008, 2; also see Kassim 2014). In Thailand, the deleterious social impacts of migrants from Cambodia, Laos, and Myanmar "include security and crime, contagious diseases, HIV/AIDS, human trafficking, prostitution, child labor, poor labor standards, drug trafficking, illegal logging and timber trafficking, ethnic minorities and the Mekong River ecosystem monitoring, rural or agricultural economy way of life and community, stateless children" (Paitoonpong and Chalamwong 2012, 20). Crime is a serious issue in the rapidly growing cities of Southeast Asia, but aside from selected anecdotal cases, there is little evidence that immigrants are more likely to resort to crime than the native born. Immigrants are often scapegoated as criminals in the United States, but the weight of scientific evidence does not support these claims (National Academies of Sciences, Engineering, and Medicine 2015).

A recent article reported on popular attitudes toward foreigners in Singapore:

> Considerable ambivalence arose among Singaporean citizens about an increasing share of noncitizens in the population. The ambivalence is related not only to increasing numbers of unskilled contract workers, but also to foreign talent, seen to be taking away the jobs of locals, and to the increasing number of permanent residents. The fact that many of these permanent residents (though the government does not reveal how many) are from China might be expected to lead to their wider acceptance by the majority ethnic Chinese Singaporeans, but this does not appear to be the case. High levels of immigration, regardless of origin, have instead been accompanied by social tensions. Singaporeans complain of feeling like strangers in their own country, of crowded subways and buses, rising house prices, heightened competition for school places, and dealing with shop assistants who cannot communicate with them. (Jones 2012, 328)

Governments in Southeast Asia are caught in the middle between economic realities and popular resentments, often expressed by the mass media, about immigrants. Thailand, Malaysia, and especially Singapore have generally allowed foreign workers to enter the country as labor shortages have emerged. In the case of Singapore, the labor needs are not just for more workers but also for professionals in engineering, medicine, universities, and the high-tech sector. In a complex balancing act, governments attempt to "manage" immigration with restrictions on who can enter, how long they can stay, where they can work, and whether they can bring dependents (Kaur 2010b, 13; Kusakabe and Pearson 2010, 23). To paraphrase an old saying in the migration field, countries of destination generally want laborers, not people. (The source is Max Frisch, who quipped, "We wanted workers—instead we got people.")

Perhaps the most egregious case of migration management is Singapore's policies to prevent foreign domestic workers from settling in Singapore (Devasahayam 2010).

In addition to policies forbidding domestic workers from bringing dependents to Singapore, the government requires employers to post security bonds to insure that the worker does not become pregnant while living in Singapore. The Controller of Work Passes requires employers to conduct biannual pregnancy tests and orders immediate expulsion of domestic workers who become pregnant (Devasahayam 2010, 51). Before approving Indonesian women to work as maids in Malaysia, immigration brokers screen them to make sure that they are using birth control (Lindquist 2010, 116).

As a relatively small city-state with an authoritarian government, Singapore is better positioned to manage and regulate immigration than Malaysia and Thailand. In spite of extensive attempts to manage immigration, there is a very large presence of unauthorized immigrants in both countries; employers seeking cheap and exploitable labor often work to circumvent government regulations. In this "gray area," immigrants are reluctant to report abusive treatment, nonpayment of wages, and even extortion by the police.

Estimating the economic benefits and costs of immigration and emigration is a complex and controversial topic, even among academic researchers. There are many different questions of interest, such as the impact on overall economic growth, the impact on employment and wages of different groups of workers, and other aspects of labor markets. Economic theory suggests that increases in labor supply will lead to higher output, but the gains will be unequally realized. In particular, native-born workers who are competing directly with immigrants may suffer wage losses. Workers not directly competing with immigrants (in "complementary" jobs) are likely to benefit from the presence of workers. For example, low-skilled immigrant workers in agriculture and construction may "push up" (not "push out") native-born workers to better positions as supervisors or white-collar workers. An immigrant domestic worker can provide childcare and housekeeping services that allow many native-born women to pursue careers and full-time employment.

Since economic theory is indeterminate about the relative balance of benefits and costs immigration, empirical research is necessary to provide evidence. However, assumptions about how to measure competitive and complementary jobs, technological change, capital investments, and other aspects of dynamic economies can have large effects on the estimation of impact of immigrants on labor markets. Immigrants also have effects on the prices of goods (food, housing) and services, and on government revenues and expenditures. (For an overall review of the underlying theories and a variety of empirical estimates for the US economy, see National Academies of Sciences, Engineering, and Medicine 2017.)

As might be expected, the econometric estimates of the impact of immigration on economies in Southeast Asia vary considerably. Ismail and Yuliyusman (2014) conclude that the skilled and semiskilled foreign labor have a positive and significant impact on the economic growth in Malaysia, but that unskilled foreign labor adversely affects growth. In their study of the construction sector in Malaysia, Narayanan and Lai (2005) find little evidence of job displacement of Malaysian workers because most native-born workers were seeking employment in more remunerative sectors. Narayanan and Lai report that the on-the-job skills acquired by immigrant workers (most arrived unskilled) were lost because most immigrant workers returned home. In a comprehensive study, the World Bank (2015, 2) concluded:

Econometric modelling suggests that immigrant workers . . . raise GDP and create employment for Malaysians . . . Low skilled immigrants fill workforce gaps, reduce production costs and expand output and exports . . . immigration increases employment of Malaysians; for every 10 new migrant workers in a sector in a state, there are 5.2 additional Malaysians employed. Immigrant labor slightly increases the wages of most Malaysians. The increase is largest for Malaysians with at least some secondary education but had a negative impact on the wages of the least-educated Malaysians

The World Bank (2015, 2–3) was very critical of the haphazard and fragmented management of immigration policy with various policies and programs scattered over ten government agencies.

There is greater consensus among economists and policy-makers on the positive impact of highly skilled immigrants to the future of "knowledge-based economies," especially in Singapore (Yahaya and Kaur 2010, 26–28). Singapore and other Southeast Asian countries also lose a disproportionate share of their most highly skilled citizens through emigration, and policy-makers have not been successful in stemming the tide. One study finds that the repressive political environment is the major reason of the emigration among highly skilled citizens (Fetzer and Millan 2015). As noted earlier, there are more than one million Malaysian-born residents in Singapore in 2010 (table 7.3). Although I have not been able to find data on the ethnicity and education Malaysian migrants in Singapore, I suspect that the majority are high-skilled Malaysian Chinese. Given the shared culture and history between the countries, Malaysian Chinese are not generally considered foreigners in Singapore.

Immigration, Citizenship, and Belonging in Southeast Asia

Although international migration appears to be a partial solution to balancing out labor surpluses and shortages in Southeast Asia, there appears to be much less progress in the integration of immigrants. Immigrants (and their children) are not welcomed as permanent members in any country in Southeast Asia. The problem is deeper than just the usual frictions that arise from newcomers with different languages, cultures, and religions. The underlying problem is that citizenship and belonging are highly contentious issues in most Southeast Asian countries, even among the native born. The growing number of foreign workers with no claims of permanent residency, rights to bring family members, and little chance of becoming a citizen are even less likely to be accepted or to identify themselves as locals.

The day following the birth of my daughter in a maternity clinic in the heart of Kuala Lumpur, Malaysia, in 1974, I went to the local police station to register her birth. Although I knew what the answer would be, I asked if my daughter would be eligible to be a citizen of Malaysia. The police officer laughed at my query and asked me if any country in the world would grant citizenship merely on the basis of birth. In Malaysia, the rules about citizenship are highly politicized, and only for a short period after Independence was local birth sufficient to allow non-Malays to become citizens. Even among Malaysian citizens, ethnicity and religion grant privileges for schooling, government employment, and much more. Kamal Sadiq (2009) explains the even more divisive politics of ethnic preferences in the East Malaysian state of Sabah (on the island of Borneo). The second-class citizens of Peninsular Malaysia (Malaysians of Chinese and Indian ancestry) are the third-class citizens in Sabah behind Malays and indigenous Sabahans (mostly non-Muslim Kadazandusans). In spite of being outmaneuvered in the game of ethnic politics, Sabah still controls migration policy in the state, and all Peninsular Malaysians are forced to complete immigration forms on entry into the state.

Although Malaysia is an extreme case, the recognition of the privileges of citizenship, ethnicity, and other markers of indigeneity are common throughout Southeast Asia (Aguilar 2014, chap. 6). These nationalistic sentiments are somewhat surprising because they are of relatively recent origin, largely a product of the "high modernism" era from 1945 to 1980 (Reid 2015, chap. 19; also see Scott 1998 and Reid 2010). The first generation of nationalist leaders believed that modernity required a national identity with a common language, culture, and religion. Moreover, modern nation-states were expected to define rules for citizenship, construct educational systems and a government-controlled mass media to popularize national identity, and police national boundaries to separate us from others. The problem is that these ideas of national uniformity were superimposed on heterogeneous populations that were generally multilingual, followed syncretic religions and traditions, and often held plural identities. Cultures that were formerly open to social mobility for outsiders and encouraged intermarriage have turned inward in an effort to create a unified national identity. In reality, however, programs to create a monolithic national identity are often manipulated to privilege those with the "right" ethnic pedigree.

As international migration has increased in recent decades, the pluralism of Southeast Asia's past has been largely forgotten. Migrants are considered to be permanent outsiders with little chance for citizenship and belonging. These ideas—reinforced with harsh policies that restrict mobility, forbid family reunification among immigrant workers, and even use pregnancy as a reason for expulsion—do little to encourage public tolerance or integration.

The word "migration" is almost always reported in the popular media and even in scientific literature as a problem or a crisis. For example, migrants are assumed to overcrowd cities, clog up labor markets, and increase poverty. The other questionable assumption is that most migration is involuntary—people fleeing natural or man-made catastrophes. The reality, however, is more complex, and many migrants are simply seeking greater economic opportunity. Of course migration can and does create social and economic problems, but migration can also be a solution for many preexisting problems. For example, out-migration generally redistributes workers from places of labor surplus to areas where there is greater demand or more opportunity.

Migration is generally selective of persons who are younger, healthier, more flexible, and more willing to endure hardship in hopes of a better life relative to their prospects in their places of origin. Most research that examines long-term outcomes of migration, including remittances, return migration, and intergenerational mobility, finds positive "long-term" effects on places of origin and destination (Massey et al. 1998, chaps. 8–9; Appleyard 1989).

Along with much of the world, Southeast Asia is currently experiencing increasing levels of migration—both domestic and international. The first step toward understanding an important issue is careful measurement of its dimensions: magnitudes, patterns, and trends. Our analysis in tables 7.2 to 7.4 is a rudimentary description of recent trends in international migration to and from Southeast Asian countries. Basic description can, however, set the stage for more in-depth research. One of the most striking findings of this chapter is that emigration is more pervasive in Southeast Asia than immigration. Even for the countries experiencing high levels of immigration, emigration is also very high. Rapid economic growth appears to be highly correlated with above-average levels of immigration. It also seems that demography, economic stagnation, and political unrest are the primary factors that determine emigration.

These preliminary figures and interpretations are only the beginning. There needs to be more intensive study of the demographic, economic, and social characteristics of immigrants and emigrants, their places of origin and destination, and the short-term and long-term outcomes of migration. One of the most disturbing features of my preliminary survey of the field is the casual use of data by many of the leading scholars in the field. Part of the problem, of course, has been the lack of accurate and reliable data on international migration. But the field is changing with more international agencies collecting, tabulating, and distributing data on flows of international migration. There may be important flaws in these data, but they will only be discovered if researchers begin to take seriously their responsibility to compare data from multiple sources and to evaluate their quality.

In the chapter on Asia and the Pacific in the classic volume *Worlds in Motion*, the late Graeme Hugo lamented that much of the literature on international migration (in Asia) was predominately descriptive and atheoretical (Massey et al. 1998, 170). Hugo was the doyen in the field of migration studies in Southeast Asia, and his many publications have been a basic source of knowledge and inspiration for this study. Big theoretical questions are, however, very difficult to test (or even address) in a field with poor data, conflicting schools and hypotheses, and ideologically charged public policies. Perhaps the best way forward might be to first acknowledge that migration has many possible determinants and consequences that cannot always be summed up into a single conclusion that is labeled "good or bad."

As a relative newcomer to the field, I am impressed with the broad range of research questions and methods used to describe and explain the forces that impel migrants to travel long distances in search of a better life. From my reading on international migration in Southeast Asia, I learned a great deal about the lives of migrants and the complex web of institutions and interests that attempt to support, profit from, and control the work and living conditions of migrants. There are two issues that I found missing from most studies. The first is an historical and comparative perspective focused on long-term outcomes. The second is the understanding that migration is highly responsive to incentives and opportunities that often allow individuals (and countries) to learn from prior experiences. These issues are interrelated.

An historical perspective is necessary because short-term outcomes do not always predict the future. Initially, migrants have few choices and there are generally many more people (and institutions) seeking to control them than to help them. These conditions often give migration research a very pessimistic orientation. Immigrants generally take dead-end jobs, live in impoverished areas, and are subjected to injustices, inequities, and indignities by employers, authorities, and sometimes even by fellow kinsmen. However, because immigrants are generally determined and resourceful, many eventually find their way around these controls and experience some social mobility as a result of their geographical mobility. This is not predetermined nor universal and is often contingent on external conditions. Moreover, immigrants generally have children—often referred to as the second generation. The second generation often inherit the perseverance of their immigrant parents, but they also have an advantage over their parents because they are less encumbered by the lack of familiarity with the host society. And most research shows that second-generation immigrants experience upward social mobility relative to their parents. An understanding of the long term may not lead to optimism about long-distance migration, but it might make it less pessimistic.

The decision to migrate, even if it is joining a mass movement with many others, makes people think of comparisons—among places, jobs, languages, social networks, police and government officials, and much more. Once having made a decision, migrants find it easier to make additional decisions to improve their lot in life. They may decide to return to their place of origin or to migrate to a new locality. Or they might decide to learn new skills or seek out new contacts to find better employment. This orientation does not always lead to success; after all, migrants generally start out in disadvantaged situations with few resources. But it does mean that migrants, and migrant flows in general, are very responsive to opportunities and incentives, especially if information is available.

This point is often lost on policy-makers in destination countries, and even by researchers who are trying to inform policy. In most contexts, public policy is designed to extract labor from migrants without providing them opportunities to integrate into the social, cultural, and political life of their host communities. Although there is considerable research showing that migrants are very responsive to opportunities to become full members of the societies in which they live, this theme is generally missing from most research on contemporary public policy discussions of international migration.

References

Abel, Guy, and Nikola Sander. 2014. "Quantifying Global International Flows." *Science* 343(6178): 1520–22.

Aguilar, Filomeno V. 2014. *Migration Revolution: Philippine Nationhood and Class Relations in a Globalized Age*. Singapore: NUS Press.

Amrith, Megha. 2010. "'They Think We Are Just Caregivers': The Ambivalence of Care in the Lives of Filipino Medical Workers in Singapore." *Asia Pacific Journal of Anthropology* 11(3/4): 410–27.

Appleyard, Reginald T. 1989. "Migration and Development: Myths and Reality." *International Migration Review* 23(3): 486–99.

Asis, Maruja M. B., and Nicola Piper. 2008. "Researching International Labor Migration in Asia." *Sociological Quarterly* 49(3): 423–44.

Athukorala, Prema-chandra. 2006. "International Labor Migration in East Asia: Trends, Patterns and Policy Issues." *Asian-Pacific Economic Literature* 20(1): 18–39.

Derks, Annuska. 2010. "Migrant Labour and the Politics of Immobilisation: Cambodian Fishermen in Thailand." *Asian Journal of Social Science* 38(6): 915–32.

Devasahayam, Theresa W. 2010. "Placement and/or Protection? Singapore's Labour Policies and Practices for Temporary Women Migrant Workers." *Journal of the Asia Pacific Economy* 15(1): 45–58.

Fetzer, Joel S., and Brandon Alexander Millan. 2015. "The Causes of Emigration from Singapore: How Much Is Still Political?" *Critical Asian Studies* 47(3): 462–76.

Fujita, Koichi, Tamaki Endo, Ikuko Okamoto, Yoshihiro Nakanishi, and Miwa Yamada. 2010. *Myanmar Migrant Laborers in Ranong, Thailand,* no. 257. Institute of Developing Economies, Japan External Trade Organization (JETRO).

Hugo, Graeme. 2005. "The International Migration System in Asia." *Asian Population Studies* 1(1): 93–120.

———. 2012. "Changing Patterns of Population Mobility in Southeast Asia." In *Demographic Change in Southeast Asia,* edited by Lindy Williams and Michael Philip Guest, 121–63. Southeast Asia Program Publications, Cornell University, Ithaca, NY.

———. 2016. "Internal and International Migration in East Asia." *Population, Space and Place* 22: 651–68.

Huijsmans, Roy. 2008. "Children Working beyond Their Localities: Lao Children Working in Thailand." *Childhood* 15(3): 331–53.

Huong, Lê Thu. 2010. "A New Portrait of Indentured Labour: Vietnamese Labour Migration to Malaysia." *Asian Journal of Social Science* 38(6): 880–96.

Ismail, Rahmah, and Ferayuliani Yuliyusman. 2014. "Foreign Labour on Malaysian Growth." *Journal of Economic Integration* 29(4): 657–75.

Jones, Gavin W. 2012. "Population Policy in a Prosperous City-State: Dilemmas for Singapore." *Population and Development Review* 38(2): 311–36.

Kanapathy, Vijayakumari. 2008. *Controlling Irregular Migration: The Malaysian Experience.* ILO Asian Regional Programme on Governance of Labour Migration Working Paper no. 14. Bangkok: ILO Regional Office for Asia and the Pacific, Asian Regional Programming on Governance of Labour Migration.

Kassim, Azizah. 2014. "Recent Trends in Transnational Population Inflows into Malaysia: Policy, Issues and Challenges." *Malaysian Journal of Economic Studies* 51(1): 91–128.

Kaur, Amarjit. 2004. *Wage Labour in Southeast Asia since 1840: Globalization, the International Division of Labour and Labour Transformations.* Basingstoke: Palgrave Macmillan.

———. 2010b. "Labor Migration in Southeast Asia: Migration Policies, Labor Exploitation and Regulation." *Journal of the Asia Pacific Economy* 15(1): 6–19.

Killias, Olivia. 2010. "'Illegal' Migration as Resistance: Legality, Morality and Coercion in Indonesian Domestic Worker Migration to Malaysia." *Asian Journal of Social Science* 38(6): 897–914.

Kumar, Ann. 2011. "The Single Most Astonishing Fact of Human Geography: Indonesia's Far West Colony." *Indonesia* 92(October 2011): 59–95.

Kusakabe, Kyoko, and Ruth Pearson. 2010. "Transborder Migration, Social Reproduction and Economic Development: A Case Study of Burmese Women Workers in Thailand." *International Migration* 48(6): 13–43.

Lindquist, Johan. 2010. "Labour Recruitment, Circuits of Capital and Gendered Mobility: Reconceptualizing the Indonesian Migration Industry." *Pacific Affairs* 83(1): 115–32.

Maltoni, Bruno. 2007. "Migration in Cambodia: Internal vs. External Flows." In *8th ARPMIN Conference on Migration, Development and Poverty Reduction,* 25–29.

Massey, Douglas S., Joaquin Arango, Graeme Hugo, Ali Kouaouci, Adela Pellegrino, and J. Edward Taylor. 1998. *Worlds in Motion: Understanding International Migration at the End of the Millennium.* Chap. 6, "Theory and Reality in the Asia-Pacific, 160–95. Oxford: Clarendon Press.

Molland, Sverre. 2012. "Safe Migration, Dilettante Brokers and the Appropriation of Legality: Lao-Thai 'Trafficking' in the Context of Regulating Labour Migration." *Pacific Affairs* 85(1): 117–36.

Mon, Myat. 2010. "Burmese Labour Migration into Thailand: Governance of Migration and Labour Rights." *Journal of the Asia Pacific Economy* 15(1): 33–44.

Narayanan, Suresh, and Yew-Wah Lai. 2005. "The Causes and Consequences of Immigrant Labour in the Construction Sector in Malaysia." *International Migration* 43(5): 31–57.

National Academies of Sciences, Engineering, and Medicine. 2015. *The Integration of Immigrants into American Society*. Washington, DC: National Academies Press. https://doi.org/10.17226/21746

———. 2017. *The Economic and Fiscal Consequences of Immigration*. Washington, DC: National Academies Press. https://doi.org/10.17226/23550

Nguyen, Phi Van Evelyne, and Christophe Gironde. 2010. "Negotiating (In)dependency: Social Journeys of Vietnamese Women to Cambodia." *Asian Journal of Social Science* 38: 933–47.

Paitoonpong, Srawooth, and Yongyuth Chalamwong. 2012. *Managing International Labor Migration in ASEAN: A Case of Thailand*. Bangkok: Thailand Development Research Institute. https://think-asia.org/handle/11540/6420

Reid, Anthony. 2010. *Imperial Alchemy: Nationalism and Political Identity in Southeast Asia*. Cambridge: Cambridge University Press.

———. 2015. *A History of Southeast Asia: Critical Crossroads*. Oxford: Wiley Blackwell.

Rigg, Jonathan. 2007. "Moving Lives: Migration and Livelihoods in the Lao PDR." *Population, Space and Place* 13(3): 163–78.

Sadiq, Kamal. 2009. "When Being Native Is Not Enough: Citizens as Foreigners in Malaysia." *Asian Perspective* 33(1): 5–32.

Scott, James C. 1998. *Seeing Like a State: How Certain Conditions to Improve the Human Condition Have Failed*. New Haven, CT: Yale University Press.

Skeldon, Ron. 1992. "On Migration Transitions in East and Southeast Asia." *Asia and Pacific Migration Journal* 1(2): 220–49.

Tan, Edita. 2009. *Supply Response of Filipino Workers to World Demand*. Makati City, Philippines: International Organization for Migration (Philippines).

United Nations. 2013. *Trends in International Migrant Stock by Destination and Origin* (United Nations database, POP/DB/MIG/Stock/Rev.2013). www.un.org/en/development/desa/population/migration/data/estimates2/estimates15.shtml

———. 2016. *International Migration Report 2015*. ST/ESA/SER.A/384

———. 2019. *International Migrant Stock 2019: Migrants by Destination and Origin*. www.un.org/en/development/desa/population/migration/data/estimates2/estimates19.asp

United Nations, Department of Economic and Social Affairs, Population Division. 2015. *World Population Prospects: The 2015 Revision, Volume I: Comprehensive Tables* (ST/ESA/SER.A/379). New York: United Nations.

Wine, Aung Thet. 2008. "For Greener Pastures." *The Irrawaddy* 16(10). Accessed October 9, 2017. www2.irrawaddy.com/article.php?art_id=14366&page=1

World Bank. 2015. *Malaysia Economic Monitor: Immigrant Labor*. Prepared by Southeast Asia Country Management Unit. Washington, DC: World Bank. Accessed October 9, 2017. http://documents.worldbank.org/curated/en/753511468197095162/pdf/102131-WP-P158456-Box394822B-PUBLIC-final-for-printing.pdf

World Bank. 2017. *Global Bilateral Migration Database*. https://data.worldbank.org/data-catalog/global-bilateral-migration-database

Yahaya, Faizal, and Arunajeet Kaur. 2010. "Competition for Foreign Talent in Southeast Asia." *Journal of the Asia Pacific Economy* 15(1): 20–32.

8   THE INDIAN MIGRATION STATE

Kamal Sadiq

INDIA IS A COUNTRY OF ORIGIN and destination in international migration. Once a colony of the British Empire, India is now the world's seventh-largest economy (with an annual growth rate fluctuating between 5 and 7 percent) and the world's second-largest population (1.3 billion people).[1] Despite strong economic gains, the country is also home to one of the highest child-malnutrition rates in the world, five times more than China and twice that of sub-Saharan Africa.[2] Two Indias emerge: one as an economic powerhouse with a well-educated international workforce, known for its world-class medical, engineering, and information and technology professionals; and another defined by a lack of basic nutrition, sanitation, and shelter for significant swaths of rural and urban citizens. These contradictory positions challenge dominant assumptions within the migration state framework in two ways: first, India is not constrained by the liberal paradox, a widely accepted necessary condition of "classic" migration states, and second, the region's late state formation has led to ad hoc and reactionary migration governance policies.

As a country of emigrants, India largely produces two distinct international emigration corridors.[3] The first is emigration from India to primarily advanced Western democracies in North America and Western Europe. According to Indian government sources, emigrant numbers are highest in the United States (4,460,000), followed by Canada (1,016, 185) and the United Kingdom (1,825,000) (see table 8.1). This group mostly consists of high-skilled labor and is often characterized as a human capital "drain" of Indian

---

1   For IMF data on real GDP growth, see www.imf.org/external/datamapper/NGDP_RPCH@ WEO/OEMDC/ADVEC/WEOWORLDl/IND (accessed October 15, 2017).

2   For World Bank data on malnutrition in India, see http://www.worldbank.org/en/news/fea ture/2013/05/13/helping-india-combat-persistently-high-rates-of-malnutrition (accessed October 15, 2017).

3   A smaller emigrant corridor is emerging between India and Singapore and Malaysia, partly based on historical immigrant settlements in these Southeast Asian states.

Table 8.1. Select population of overseas Indians (2016).

Major Emigration Corridor	Overseas Indians (NRI + PIO)[1]	Percentage of Total Overseas Indians (NRI + PIO)
To Western Democracies		
North America		
United States	4,460,000	14.4
Canada	1,016,185	3.2
Europe		
United Kingdom	1,825,000	5.9
Netherlands	225,000	0.7
Oceania		
Australia	496,000	1.6
New Zealand	200,000	0.6
Total:	8,222,185	26.6
To Gulf Cooperation Council (GCC)		
Saudi Arabia	3,004,585	9.7
UAE	2,803,751	9.0
Kuwait	923,260	2.9
Oman	796,001	2.5
Qatar	600,000	1.9
Bahrain	316,175	1.0
Total:	8,443,772	27.3
Total Overseas Indians	30,843,419	

1 "Non-Resident Indian" (NRI) is an Indian-passport holder living abroad. "Person of Indian Origin" (PIO) is a foreign citizen who at some point held an Indian passport or is Indian by descent but lives outside the Republic of India.
Source: Government of India, Ministry of External Affairs (accessed October 3, 2017, from http://mea.gov.in/images/attach/NRIs-andPIOs_1.pdf). The other remaining 14–15 million Indian emigrants are spread across states in Europe, Asia, and Africa.

talent. A second corridor consists of Indian labor emigration to the Gulf Cooperation Council (GCC) states in the Middle East. Indian policies toward this emigrant group seek to safeguard low-skilled Indian manpower labor from rights abuse and to channel their remittances and investments in lieu of state provisions of welfare. A significant percent of overall remittances to India come from the large number of Indian emigrants in the GCC (see table 8.1). According to the Ministry of Overseas Indian Affairs, the Indian community is the second-largest diaspora in the world, with over 30 million people *outside* India—roughly 2 percent of the Indian population (Government of India, Ministry of Overseas Indians 2009, 41; Vezzoli and Lacroix 2010, 8).

India is often characterized as a net *out*-migration country given a complicated mix of conditions that include its vast informal economy, limited employment benefits, and lack of social security protections (International Labor Organization 2016; United

Nations 2013). However, parallel to this trend is an equally significant number of refugees and immigrants who are entering and/or settling *in* India as "survival migrants," escaping impoverishment and weak institutions in neighboring states (Betts 2013). Since relative economic "pull factors" may not be strong, it is chiefly "push factors" in other regional states such as Bangladesh, Nepal, and Sri Lanka that determine immigration into India. Consequently, this chapter focuses on the much larger, yet less visible immigration flow into India, marking it as a country of destination for survival immigrants from the broader South Asia region.[4] This immigration flow is significant because of its scope and impact on domestic and regional policies. In 2000, it was estimated that India hosted 6.4 million international migrants, and by 2015 the number dropped slightly to 5.2 million, roughly the entire population of Costa Rica (United Nations 2016). As the inflows are small by comparison with outflows, India is far from making the transition from a nation of emigrants to a nation of immigrants. Diaspora management is still of great strategic importance.

All states face dilemmas in migration governance (see introduction, this volume, and Weiner 1995). As this chapter argues, the emergence of an Indian migration state is linked to its development of two simultaneous state goals: (1) maintaining national security interests that secure territorial sovereignty, while (2) realigning (and homogenizing) national identity through a narrow redefinition of citizenship norms. Thus, this chapter engages a *longue duree* view of India's path toward migration management that is attuned to the systemic impact of singular "events" across specific periods of time (Braudel and Wallerstein 2009). Such a view highlights the main distinctions between the classic "liberal" migration state in Western Europe and the emerging migration state in India, because, as this chapter suggests, the Indian migration state did not begin at the moment of national independence from British colonial rule in 1947 but arose much later, out of the exigencies of incomplete state formation in the region beginning in the 1970s. Migration was a central feature of nation-state building following the repeat partitions of the subcontinent. The creation of Bangladesh in 1971 and the protracted Sri Lankan civil war that began in 1983 were important critical junctures in the region that produced responses to immigration flows and significantly impacted India's citizenship and migration policy trajectory. The chapter traces the institutional impact of these flows on India in two ways: first, through the narrowing of Indian citizenship criteria with amendments to the Indian Citizenship Act (the fourth section), and second, through the development of an enhanced and militarized border-security regime (the fifth section). Consequently, since national independence in 1947, Indian immigration policies increasingly attempt to bolster territorial sovereignty while simultaneously redefining (and narrowing) Indian citizenship.

The Indian Migration State

The migration state concept directs us to the major dilemmas facing modern states as they attempt to balance among multiple and conflicting policy needs of enhancing

---

4   For an overview of Indian emigration, see Naujoks 2013.

markets, rights, security, and culture (Hollifield, this volume). This internal four-sided game takes on further complexity in an international arena, where foreign policy and nonstate actors skew the domestic interests of the state. All states are migration states to some extent, so what is distinctive about variation in migration management policies among postcolonial states of the global South?

In the South Asia region precolonial migrations were regulated through British colonial policies (Mongia 2018). After independence, these new nation states had to construct distinct national identities while maintaining newly defined territorial borders. Over time, the Indian migration state developed as a response to the management of immigration and refugee flows. This institutional response has occurred along two domains: first, through legal changes in citizenship and immigration procedures and norms, and second, through the building of a militarized international border to assert territorial sovereignty. Overlapping ethnic, religious, and linguistic ties that straddled once contiguous regions add complexity to sorting national identities while maintaining territorial sovereignty. Both are driven by logics of national security that strategically manipulate cultural politics and rights claims.

Hollifield (this volume) proposes that the Western migration state model evolved from a garrison (security) state to a trading (economic) state, before becoming a migration (rights) state in the post-1945 period. This process is characterized by the development of three features of the modern state: security interests, economic interests, and a concern with rights. The "classic" migration state emerged after 1945 as a response to the imperatives of trade and labor needs of post–World War II Europe. In contrast to Hollifield's model, modern India emerged from decolonization, acquiring migration functions differently and later (post-1971) than its European counterparts (see figure 8.1). India's alternative path to the institutionalized development of migration management is distinguished by three features.

First, India was a subject territory, a semi-state consisting of principalities, kingdoms, and the remnants of the Mughal Empire under British direct and indirect colonial rule until 1947. As a subject territory, India was marked by a dependent and subservient relationship to British imperial interests that forcibly extracted material and human

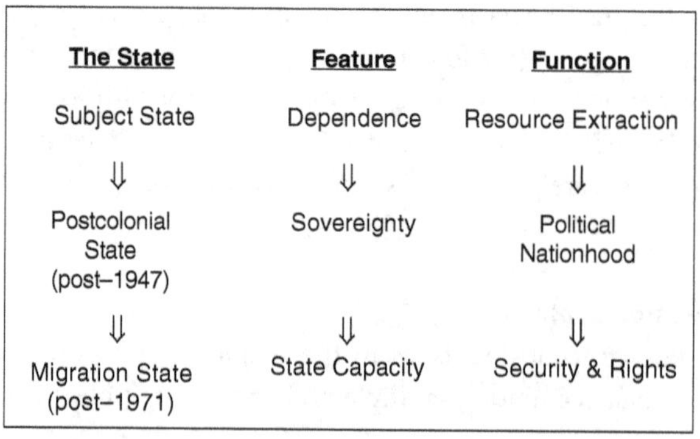

The State	Feature	Function
Subject State	Dependence	Resource Extraction
⇓	⇓	⇓
Postcolonial State (post–1947)	Sovereignty	Political Nationhood
⇓	⇓	⇓
Migration State (post–1971)	State Capacity	Security & Rights

Figure 8.1. Indian "migration state."
Source: Adapted from Hollifield (this volume).

resources from an integrated imperial labor market that connected South and Southeast Asia, the Middle East, and Africa. The British Empire initially relied heavily on slave labor, and later, on the utilization of indentured labor for British plantations. As Sturman (2014, 1441) argues, the system of indenture "was to provide planters with a regular, assured, and cheap labor force similar to what they had had under slavery, thereby alleviating their need to rely upon, or pay market price for, the labor of their former slaves." Historical data suggest that between 1846 and 1940 "4 million Indians traveled to Malaya, more than 8 million to Ceylon, more than 15 million to Burma, and about a million to Africa, other parts of Southeast Asia, and islands throughout that Indian and Pacific oceans" (McKeown 2011, 48). The European garrison and trading state was in fact an imperial state that undermined the rights of native people in British India, forcibly relocated them, and usurped their territorial sovereignty and security (Cooper 2005). The migration of British Indian subjects was managed under the imperatives of empire, either indirectly through the East India Company and its collaborative princely states, or directly from the metropole in London. Colonial migration management ensured labor control of a faraway subjugated population for the economic benefit of the imperial center and its population (Mongia 2018).

Second, neat and clean transitions from one cohering feature of governance to the next rarely occur in postcolonial developing countries because the process of decolonization was fraught with competing visions of a new nation. At independence there were roughly 600 "princely kingdoms" or semi-autonomous regions that comprised one-third of the population and two-fifths of the landmass (Jhala 2019). While the long transition from a subject "semi-state" to a "postcolonial state" sought political and territorial independence from British rule, in the postindependence era the development of a common national identity became essential to nation-building (see figure 8.1). Ideas of membership and belonging transitioned away from an "imperial subjecthood" toward a newly sovereign "postcolonial citizenship" (Sadiq 2017).[5] Overlapping and fluid ethnic, religious, linguistic, and regional identities added to the complexity of asserting a common nationality. Indian leadership embraced a secular and democratic vision, one that could accommodate social plurality and unify its diversity.

In South Asia, the violent territorial and political division of the subcontinent into the independent states of India and Pakistan in 1947 generated restrictive claims to national identities on either sides of a new border. Once a contiguous British territory, at independence a double boundary line was imposed to divide the Indian subcontinent, one separating the Punjab region to the west and another dividing the Bengal region to the east. According to Zamindar this crisis displaced about 20 million individuals (12 million from the region of Punjab alone) who were violently forced to flee to either side of a new border, making it "comparable only to the nearly contemporaneous displacements produced by the Second World War in Europe" (Zamindar 2007, 6). As Adamson (this volume) points out, population exchanges, or the forcible "unmixing" of populations, are

---

5   An initial "proto-citizen" was defined by formal status conferred through a new postcolonial constitution but with little substantive citizenship rights (see Sadiq 2017).

not traditionally viewed as legitimate concerns for migration governance. Yet migration governance in South Asia originates in this violent type of demographic engineering.[6]

The partitioning of the subcontinent resulted in genocidal violence that required ad hoc policy-making to protect and control the flows of refugees arriving at newly formed international borders. The Indian state-in-progress had to reinvent the institutional purpose and form of its institutions by redefining the legal relationship and responsibilities between multiethnic populations—as individuals and ethnic groups—and the secular government and its democratic institutions (Sadiq 2017). In the early period of state formation, newly independent India was in a rush to stabilize its institutions by simultaneously balancing security and economic needs. However, conditions of weak and contradictory stateness meant a cohesive migration function was absent until much later. Thus, India adopted the British legal system in principle and structure as a way to continue long-established mechanisms of governance that were seen as pragmatic and yet coercive toward managing varying castes, religions, and regional-cultural communities. This institutional path dependence marks many postcolonial migration states.

A third element that distinguishes the Indian migration state from the "classic" model is what can be termed a "neighborhood effect" of dense and clandestine coethnic migration flows amid weak institutions. The colonial transfer of power in South Asia was not predicated on the presence of coherent or functioning state and local governing mechanisms. In fact, when colonial powers withdrew from former colonies or dominions, they often left behind local power vacuums that produced internal instability at best or civil war at worst. This resulted in a sequential immigration flow: the migration of coethnic and coreligious refugees or other stateless populations across weak or barely institutionalized borders due to regional turmoil or ethnic conflict, followed by waves of kin-based, economic "survival" migrants fleeing institutional decay in their countries of origin (Betts 2013). This patterned migratory process, while common to many postcolonial and developing countries (Klotz 2013; Klotz, Thiollet, and Tsourapas, this volume), challenges an equally common and paradigmatic focus on a "safe and orderly" migration protocol, such as the recent Global Compact for Migration (2018).

The division of Bangladesh from Pakistan in 1971 and the protracted Sri Lankan civil war that began in 1983 produced a regional security crisis that resulted in the presence of significant refugee and coethnic immigration flows. In responding to the security crisis, India accelerated and strengthened the nationalizing and developmental features of its evolving migration state trajectory (Adamson and Tsourapas 2019; Hollifield and Chung, this volume). In contrast to the post-1945 "liberal" foundations of the European model, India's evolution toward migration management is characterized by moving *from* dependence *to* sovereign independence while coping with ethnicized territorial divisions and mass migrations.[7] Safeguarding territorial and political sovereignty became a

---

6   It must be pointed out that such population exchanges were much more acceptable in the earlier part of the twentieth century and sanctioned by the League of Nations.

7   India is not an "illiberal" state because it is an institutional democracy, with a strong civil and political society (cf. Thiollet, this volume).

critical component of Indian policy—leading to a narrowing of Indian citizenship and the enhancement of a border-security regime.

The Absence of a "Liberal Paradox"

The European "liberal paradox" is defined by the tension between a state's economic openness to foreign migrant labor and the simultaneous push for its political closure. Hollifield (1992 and this volume) identifies the liberal paradox as an essential feature of the migration state. At the center of this paradox is a state that accepts and extends rights to a large, or significant, foreign labor-force that may be ethnically distinct from the host population. The expansion of citizenship rights to distinct foreign nationals, through specific processes of integration or naturalization, often causes social and political contestations between citizens and immigrants in Europe. In such a view, openness to migration becomes a cultural and security "risk" despite its economic advantages. The main dilemma facing these states is how to find an "equilibrium outcome" in the migration policy-making game. Extending the migration state concept to India, we see the logic of migration management develop without the constraints of the "classic" liberal model. It does not apply to India and the South Asia region for three reasons.

First, like many postcolonial states, India's economy does not require or significantly rely on foreign immigrants. Jobless growth in India produces an employment shortage, not a labor shortage. The European liberal paradox (Hollifield 1992) assumes that in order to remain competitive in a globalized world, first-rate talent (such as software engineers) must be recruited from other countries or low-skilled labor with low wages must be imported to maintain or advance profits in sectors that native citizens are unwilling or reluctant to participate in (for example, vineyards in France, dairy or meat-packing in the United States). This economic logic does not apply to countries such as India that have a large domestic pool of *both* high-skilled and low-skilled labor.

Compounding this economic situation are immigrants to India who are often escaping from poverty or persecution in neighboring regional states—it is the "push" from poor neighboring states such as Bangladesh and Nepal that defines such immigration, not the overwhelming "pull" of a developed receiving state. Hence, India is both a *receiving* and *sending* state that often requires divergent institutional state responses. For example, in 2013, India had the largest number of emigrants in the world at 14.2 million; that same year India had a stock of 5.3 million international immigrants (United Nations 2013, 67, 33).

Second, and related to the first, an emphasis on the liberal paradox ignores how a major portion of global migration takes place within the vast developing world. These South–South migrations are regional, and in the case of India remain within the Indian subcontinent as a self-contained "subsystem" with strong links to the Middle East (Thiollet, this volume). They account for the movement of both low-skilled and semi-skilled labor; illegal border crossings; and less visible migration flows, such as state- or university-sponsored students and cultural and technical exchange programs. While emigration out of India is regulated and transcontinental to Western Europe, North America, or the Gulf region, immigration into India is highly regional and often *unregulated*. In 2015, India had the twelfth-largest immigrant population in the world, a drop in rank

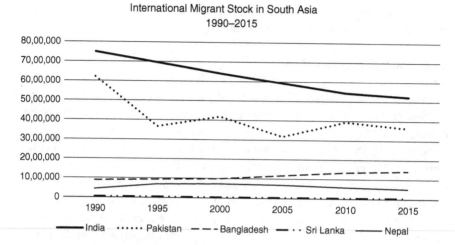

Figure 8.2. International migrant stock in South Asia, 1990–2015.

Source: United Nations, Department of Economic and Social Affairs, Population Division (2017), *Trends in International Migrant Stock: The 2017 Revision* (United Nations database, POP/DB/MIG/Stock/Rev.2017). Data compiled by author. Data used to produce these UN estimates include (i) foreign-born populations and (ii) the number of refugees reported by UNHCR in each country. Data is from midyear estimates.

from 2010 when it had the world's ninth-largest immigrant population (Connor 2017; see also United Nations 2011). Foreign immigrant stocks in the 2001 Indian census (by last place of residence) show that the overwhelming majority of India's immigrants are from neighboring states such as Bangladesh, Nepal, and Sri Lanka (Khadria and Kumar 2015, 66).[8] In the South Asia region, India hosts the largest number of international migrant stock since 1990, although the gap had been noticeably reduced by 2015 (see figure 8.2).

Official estimates of international migrants in India may be significantly lower than actual migration stocks. For example, the 2001 census of India states a figure of 3,084,836 million Bangladeshi immigrants, but such statistics are largely based on self-reporting of legal status or place of birth to official government census takers. For fear of harassment and deportation, both "suspect" minority populations who are genuine citizens and illegal immigrants with questionable legal status do not self-report in official counts. An additional complication with official data within the South Asia region (figure 8.2) is the challenge of separating Partition migration from later waves of regional migrants and refugee flows. Data taken by place of birth, for instance, may include the millions of Pakistani migrants who crossed over Punjab (or Bengal) to settle as Indian citizens in the years after independence. Moreover, unlike European states or rentier states in the Gulf (see Tsourapas and Thiollet, this volume) that have a relatively stable and homogenous citizenry, India is multiethnic with multiple religious, linguistic, caste, and cultural traditions that overlap with immigrant groups from other states within the South Asia region. Political pressure for restricting or expanding immigrant rights take on ethno-religious dimensions in multiethnic, multireligious states, and India is no exception; but unlike

---

8   The census of Nepal 2001 has a figure of 589,050 Nepali emigrants to India. See table 8.2.

Europe and North America until recently, these pressures remained separate from market and industry incentives.

Regional migration within South Asia reflects trends within the broader Asian region. In 2016, Asia was the highest immigrant-originating region in the world, with 77 million migrants of which 48 million remained *within* the region (International Fund for Agricultural Development 2017, 21). Such thick regional migration creates greater interdependence that can also lead to rising tensions between neighboring states. Anti-immigrant sentiments toward Bangladeshi immigrants in India and Indian-origin settlers in the Terai valley in Nepal (the "Madhesis") strain important bilateral relations between India and Bangladesh, and India and Nepal, respectively.

Lastly, and most significant, the liberal paradox and the migration state concept (Hollifield 1992, 2004) assume robust state capacity to govern over and manage migration flows. In order for states to determine who is eligible for what type of rights, they need to be able to identify, enumerate, and distinguish citizens and noncitizens (Sadiq 2009). While high-capacity migration states in Europe, North America, and the Gulf have well-developed and stable citizenship and migration institutions to govern, monitor, and implement policy directives, developing states such as India are characterized by weak and erratic institutional capacity. Cases such as India suggest that there are gradients of institutional strength. State institutions charged with domestic welfare-rights delivery may be disorganized. Border-patrol agents may be corrupt or engage in "networks of complicity"[9] to enable illicit and illegal flows even as military institutions remain strong and well organized (cf. Tichenor, this volume, on the American migration state). Graded institutional capacity reinforces the tension between economic and social rights (for whom and in what scope) and security concerns (over territorial and political closure). A major challenge in India is the selective implementation or uneven development of institutional capabilities. States may choose weak capacity in certain areas by limiting development projects or outright blocking access to development. In many minority-dominant regions, in an effort to keep areas underdeveloped, sections of the state may participate in pilfering resources meant for capacity-building. In some cases, illegal flows are tolerated by states; often, state officials benefit from such illegal emigration or immigration flows. Complete state control over territory is a myth, especially in porous borderlands where state officials may tolerate the informal ("bazaar") economy and its irregular flows, or actively look the other way.[10] For example, smuggled cattle from India, like other lucrative goods across the India-Bangladesh border, can become legal by simply paying a "customs charge" in Bangladesh (Rahman and Bari 2020, 256).

---

9   See Sadiq 2009, chap. 2, "Networks of Complicity."

10   A 2008 Brookings Institution report ranked India sixty-seventh, low in the third quintile, on a weak-state index of developing countries. The report noted that India's "scores are noteworthy for their extreme variability" (Rice and Patrick 2008, 21). The report cited "sectarian violence, terrorism, and human rights abuses" as the country's major challenges, despite robust economic growth (21).

In sum, the "classic" migration state concept (1) relies on the presence of a "liberal paradox," (2) overlooks a more common and much larger South–South regional migration flow, and (3) assumes strong state-capacity to regulate citizenship and migration policy (Hollifield 2004). In this view, India emerges as a variation of the migration state. While India is not constrained by a liberal paradox, it is impacted by thick regional migration flows. It is also subject to partisan party politics that skew rhetoric over immigration and emigration policies in ways that polarize political constituencies and target specific immigrant and minority groups. Indian policy-making responds to these conditions by linking immigration controls and restrictive citizenship norms to national security concerns. In doing so, it attempts to amend colonial legacies of state formation that partitioned the subcontinent and generated significant refugee flows while enhancing border control measures to assert political and territorial sovereignty.

India as a Country of Destination for South Asian Immigrants

Migration management in India developed as a response to three major regional immigration flows. In terms of scale, the first is a smaller and not very contentious migration from the neighboring state of Nepal. Approximately 1–5 million Nepalis work or stay in India; they do not need work permits or visas to travel between the two countries.[11] Article 7 of the 1950 Indo-Nepal Treaty of Peace and Friendship allows Nepalis to immigrate, work, and live in India, but they are restricted from Indian citizenship.[12] Nepal's census data indicates that the overwhelming majority of Nepal's emigrants reside in India (see table 8.2), with 589,050 Nepali emigrants living in India in 2001. However, there has been a steady decline in Nepali emigration. For example, in 1981 approximately 93 percent of all emigrating Nepalis migrated to India; by 2001 that figure had fallen to roughly 77 percent of all emigrating Nepalis (see table 8.2). The decline in emigration to India is attributed to the increasing diversion of Nepali emigration and manpower labor to the Gulf Cooperation Council (GCC) states and to other Southeast Asian states (Kansakar 2003).

A second, larger migration flow into India consists of Sri Lankan refugees, the majority of whom have entered India in various phases between 1983 and 2011 (table 8.3) as an outcome of the decades-long Tamil insurgency led by the Liberation Tigers of Tamil Elam (LTTE).[13] They are primarily Tamil-speaking Hindus, who share ethnic, linguistic, and cultural ties with the Indian state of Tamil Nadu. Under British colonial rule, labor migration between south India and Ceylon (Sri Lanka) was formalized by regimes of indenture and regulated by native *kangani* and *maistry* recruiters, who sent Indian plantation labor across the British Empire. In 1931, it is estimated that 1.5 million ethnic Tamils were

---

11   Daniel Naujoks estimates one million (see Naujoks 2009), while Sunil Raman of the BBC estimates five million (see Raman 2008).

12   For the Treaty of Peace and Friendship between the Government of India and the Government of Nepal, see http://mea.gov.in/bilateral-documents.htm?dtl/6295/Treaty+of+Peace+and +Friendship (accessed July 18, 2018).

13   It will be impossible to assess whether the refugees are from the LTTE or other innocent Tamil civilians displaced by the conflict between the LTTE and the Sri Lankan state.

Table 8.2. Nepali emigrants in India.

Nepal Census	Number of Nepali Emigrants in India	% of Total Nepali Emigrants Abroad
1981	375,196	93.11
1991	587,243	89.21
2001	589,050	77.28

Source: Adapted from V. B. S. Kansakar, "International Migration and Citizenship in Nepal," Population Monograph of Nepal, vol. 2 (Kathmandu: Central Bureau of Statistics, Government of Nepal, 2003), 110–12 (accessed July 19, 2018, from http://cbs.gov.np/image/data/Population/Monograph_vol_1_2).

Table 8.3. Sri Lankan refugees in India.

Period	No. of Refugees
I: 1983–1987	134,053
II: 1989–1991	122,078
III: 1996–2003	22,418
IV: 2006–2011	25,711
Total:	304,260

Source: Government of India, Ministry of Home Affairs, *Annual Report 2011–2012,* 297.
Note: The estimates from *Annual Report 2011–2012,* 297, identify four phases of Sri Lankan refugee flows: July 7, 1983–Decemb er 31, 1987; August 25, 1989–April 30, 1991; July 31, 1996–April 30, 2003; January 12, 2006–November 20, 2011.

enumerated throughout British colonies, with the majority sent to Ceylon and Malaya (Guilmoto 1993). After the British withdrew from the island nation, ethnic, linguistic, and regional tensions led to a bloody and protracted civil war between Tamil-speaking Hindus and Sinhala-speaking Buddhists. Tamils constituted roughly 11 percent of the population and were politically marginalized in the decades after independence (Shastri 1990, 59). Sri Lankan refugees who fled to India were settled in Government of India–sponsored camps in Tamil Nadu (Government of India 2012, 297). These refugees belong to two legal categories: those who are stateless (without Indian or Sri Lankan citizenship) and those who held Sri Lankan citizenship but fled the island nation due to violence.

According to the Indian government, refugee flows from Sri Lanka have occurred in four phases (see table 8.3): 134,053 refugees from 1983–87; 122,078 from 1989–91; 22,418 from 1996–2003; and 25,711 from 2006–11. In March 1995, the Government of India repatriated 99,469 refugees back to Sri Lanka (Government of India 2012, 297). But by 2011 there were still 68,634 Sri Lankan refugees registered in 114 refugees camps in the Indian state of Tamil Nadu and one camp in the Indian state of Orissa, plus 34,108 living outside refugee camps (297). India's long-term policy objective has been the repatriation of all Sri Lankan refugees, even though "no organized repatriation" has occurred since March 1995 (297).

India receives its largest volume of immigrants from its regional neighbor Bangladesh. The India-Bangladesh border is the fifth-longest international border in the world (4,096 km; 2,545 miles) and is notoriously porous and permeable. While a precise figure on the migration *flow* is not systematically available, in 2010 the United Nations estimated India held the "single largest bilateral stock" of international migrants in the global South (United Nations 2012, 3; Khadria and Kumar 2015, 66). This stock consists of nearly 3.2 million Bangladeshis (United Nations 2012, 3). In 2013 the India–Bangladesh migration corridor was ranked third in the world, below the Mexico–US migration corridor (ranked first) and that of the Russian Federation–Ukraine border (ranked second) (World Bank 2016, 5).

Migration across the Bengal borderland is historic. The region was once part of a contiguous territory under British colonial rule. At Indian independence in 1947 a dividing line established a new international border that separated India from "East" Pakistan. A second partition of the subcontinent occurred in 1971, when conflict between East and West Pakistan led to the creation of the independent state of Bangladesh. The conflict produced nearly 10 million Bangladeshi refugees, who left for India between April and December of 1971, making it "the largest single displacement of refugees in the second half of the century" (UNHCR 2003, 59). It is estimated that the Indian state of West Bengal alone received roughly 7.2 million refugees by December 1971 (65). With the help of UNHCR, India established 825 refugee camps across seven states (65). However, not all refugees returned, and over time, kin-based migration across the porous border made immigration into India a key political and security issue. Informal or illegal border crossings by those escaping destitution and poverty characterize this flow—a push factor also common to immigration flows in South East Asia (Hirschman, this volume).

Recent estimates suggests that over the past decade there has been a slight decline in the stock of regional migrants in India (see figure 8.3). The data is unable to distinguish between Partition (1947) refugees from Bangladesh and Pakistan settled in India, and the arrival of more recent "survival" migrants. Given the militarized border between India and Pakistan, it is unlikely that the stock of Pakistani migrants in India are recent arrivals. Similarly, it is difficult to estimate what percentage of the current Bangladeshi migrant stock are intergenerational refugees from the 1971 Bangladesh war of independence.

Partition and irredentism are key determinants in the *sui generis* evolution of the Indian migration state. These historic migrations within the South Asia region continue to impact contemporary immigration into India. While smaller migrations from Nepal and Sri Lanka did not result in significant institutional responses, the volume and character of Bangladeshi immigration continues to shape Indian citizenship policy in profound ways.

The Narrowing of Indian Citizenship

Indian citizenship principles have shifted from a more inclusive *jus soli* norm to a restrictive and discriminatory *jus sanguinis* standard. Initially these legislative amendments were responses to illegal immigration flows that impacted particular regions such as West Bengal, Assam, and Tripura in the northeast of India, but have more recently

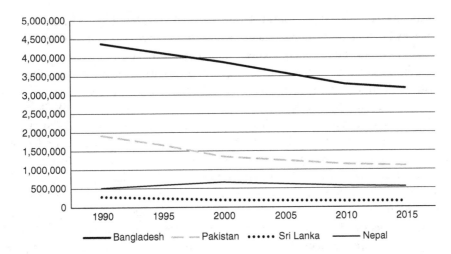

Figure 8.3. Migrant stock in India from select South Asian states, 1990–2015.

Source: United Nations, Department of Economic and Social Affairs, Population Division (2017), *Trends in International Migrant Stock: The 2017 Revision* (United Nations database, POP/DB/MIG/Stock/Rev.2017). Data compiled by author. Data used to produce these UN estimates include (i) foreign-born populations and (ii) the number of refugees reported by UNHCR in each country. Data is from midyear estimates.

risen to the national political stage as a result of polarizing majoritarian identity politics that seeks to homogenize Indian national identity.

Indian citizenship laws were designed around the exigencies of the 1947 partition, which were only codified into law in 1955. As Roy (2010, 31) emphasizes, "citizenship at the commencement of the Republic was riddled with contests . . . embedded in processes of state formation and institutional ordering." Lengthy debates ensued on how to incorporate or exclude Partition refugees and migrants given the massive population exchange. These occurred most notably in India's Constituent Assembly debates, which met for 165 days to debate and draft the 1950 Constitution of India. Scholars note that unlike other constitutions (in Western Europe or North America) that express a "timelessness in their phrasing," India's constitutional language exhibits a "quality of immediacy, of belonging only to the moment of their enactment" (Jayal 2016, 163). Article 5 conferred citizenship based on both *jus soli* principles (to those born in Indian territory) and *jus sanguinis* principles (to those who have one Indian parent). At the moment of independence and on the heels of Partition, coded language distinguished between "refugees" (Hindus and Sikhs who deserved state protection) and "migrants" (whose loyalties were suspect). This was made most evident in Article 6, which was designed to include Hindu and Sikh refugees from Pakistan, while Article 7 restricted Muslims who migrated to Pakistan but later returned to India to make property-right claims or reunite with family. The tension between citizenship rights and territorial and political security is most evident in negotiations over Article 7 of the Indian constitution. Those who advocated restricting return migration from Pakistan did so by highlighting such flows as threats to national security. These important debates during early state formation constructed return migrants (i.e., Muslims) as "saboteurs, spies, and fifth columnists," with their intentions rendered as disloyal (Jayal 2016, 167). This framing of citizenship was plagued by both majoritarian nationalism and security concerns and have since filtered into citizenship amendments by successive Indian governments.

The first legislation to narrow citizenship criteria occurred following the division of the subcontinent in 1971 between Pakistan and Bangladesh. The regional security crisis pushed immigration governance to the top of India's national policy goals. While cross-border migration in the region was historic, the chain migration of kin-based networks led to a rise in migration from Bangladesh in the years after the official end to the conflict. Over time this caused significant demographic imbalances between native communities and those viewed as outsiders (Baruah 1999, 2005; Hazarika 2003).

In 1979, the local Assamese community, a majority Hindu population native to the northeastern Indian state of Assam, began a social and political agitation against Bangladeshi refugees and migrants, largely Muslims, whom they deemed foreign "illegal immigrants."[14] Partisan accusations grew against the central government, claiming that it was not doing enough to curb the immigration flow. In 1983, when it was believed that migrants had found their way onto electoral rolls during a local election, anti-immigrant ethnic and religious tensions resulted in the massacre of over two thousand people in Nellie, Assam (Baruah 1999; Hussain 2000). Prime Minister Rajiv Gandhi negotiated a political settlement to the conflict, the Assam Accord (1985), which resulted in an amendment to the Indian Citizenship Act. It stipulated that (1) migrants who came to India *before* 1966 were classified as genuine citizens, (2) those who came between 1966 and 1971 would be put on a path to citizenship, and (3) those who came *after* 1971 (the year of Bangladesh's independence) would be deemed illegal immigrants subject to deportation to Bangladesh.

Two parallel legal measures determined citizenship eligibility during this period: while the Foreigners Act of 1946 applied to all of India, the Illegal Migrants (Determination by Tribunal) Act, 1983 (IMDT) was separately applied to the Indian state of Assam. Sections 8 and 9 of the 1946 Foreigners Act placed the burden of proving Indian citizenship on those individuals accused of being foreigners. Those who were not able to provide (documentary) proof of citizenship status and nationality were subject to detention and deportation. The 1946 Foreigners Act gives local institutions wide flexibility in identifying and determining citizenship, thus enabling state governments to deport a greater number of suspected illegal immigrants. Legal experts Karnad, Dhawan, and Acharya emphasize that due to "administrative over-zealousness and the communalization of border politics, an unknown number of these are likely to be genuine Indians citizens, passed off as migrants because they are Muslim and too poor to contest the process" (Karnad, Dhawan, and Acharya 2006, 25). The territorial and political security concerns arising from this regional immigration flow trumped concerns over due-process rights.

The 1983 IMDT Act was designed to amend these rights concerns in two ways: by locating due process at the center of citizenship determination, and by placing the burden

---

14   A smaller percentage of local Assamese Muslims are indigenous to Assam.

of proof on the government.[15] Additionally, those suspected to be illegal immigrants were entitled to an appeal process by tribunal. In practice, the rise (and decline) of rights-based politics in India was apparent—rights enhancement came at the expense of efficiency. As Karnad, Dhawan, and Acharya (2006, 25) note, the IMDT Act "observes due process admirably but has only enabled the tribunals in Assam to expel 1,481 illegal migrants (a meagre 0.03% of their estimated total number in the state)." In 2005, the Indian Supreme Court repealed the IMDT Act altogether in a major policy switch, citing inefficiency due to low conviction rates of illegal immigrants. Upholding due-process rights at the expense of an effective identification and deportation regime would no longer be tolerated by the Indian state. This move had far-reaching consequences because the Assam Accord redefined national citizenship criteria and set into motion a dangerous precedent for future changes to the Indian Citizenship Act. With the Assam Accord (1985) regional political pressure transformed national-level citizenship laws.

A second redefinition and narrowing of citizenship eligibility was introduced in 2003. The 2003 amendment to the Citizenship Act modified the provision of citizenship by birth (*jus soli*) contingent on the legal status of *both* parents.[16] Citizenship by birth would not be granted to an individual if one of his/her parents was deemed to be an illegal immigrant at the time of birth. The amendment directly targeted the Muslim Bangladeshi migrant population. Children of mixed-status couples were now ineligible for Indian citizenship. The exclusionary impact of this amendment is significant for Bangladeshi migrant women. Under the Bangladesh Citizenship Order (1972), citizenship by descent passes paternally, only through the father, and so the child of a Bangladeshi illegal immigrant woman and a non-Bangladeshi father is ineligible for Bangladeshi citizenship; in addition, the mother's "illegal" status in India disqualifies her child from Indian citizenship, despite having an Indian father and being born on Indian territory (Karnad, Dhawan, and Acharya 2006, 25). Denied both Indian and Bangladeshi citizenship, a growing population of stateless children in India has emerged (25; also see van Schendel 2002 and Jones 2009). The consolidation of the state's discretionary power in determining citizenship acquisition and loss reveals two exclusionary trends: first, a retreat from citizenship by birth as a right for all residents (*jus soli*), as was established in the initial framing of the Indian constitution; and second, a retreat from civic notions of citizenship that are "indifferent to race, religion, language, ethnicity or social history" (Karnad, Dhawan, and Acharya 2006, 27).

---

15   The IMDT was applicable only to the Indian state of Assam, a border region receiving illegal immigration from Bangladesh.

16   The Citizenship (Amendment) Act 2003, Section 3(c)(iii) reads: "every person born in India on or after the commencement of the Citizenship (Amendment) Act 2003, where—both of his parents are citizens of India or one of whose parents is a citizen of India and the other is not an illegal migrant at the time of his birth, shall be a citizen of India by birth." See Government of India, Citizenship (Amendment) Act, 2003, https://indiankanoon.org/doc/949775/ (accessed November 13, 2017).

The 2003 Amendment to the Citizenship Act has been characterized as a "hinge point" (Roy 2019) to the third (and most controversial) piece of citizenship legislation in India. The National Registry of Citizens (NRC) and the Citizenship Amendment Act (CAA) of 2019, introduced under the Bharatiya Janata Party (BJP)-led government, enables the Indian state to strip citizenship status from those it deems "illegal" even as it extends citizenship on the basis of religion to those outside its territorial sovereignty. The NRC legislation was selectively applied to the Indian state of Assam, to determine the citizenship status of all residents there. However, controversial plans for a national-level "registry of citizens" is set to be in place. In Assam, the exercise was completed on August 31, 2019, with the final list of citizens that excluded 1.9 million residents, many of whom live far below the poverty line and now face an impending deportation and statelessness. Like the Foreigners Act of 1946, the burden of proof fell on individuals to prove nationality. Of those who were excluded from the final registry, many did provide evidentiary documents that were later deemed "insufficient." Families safeguard with their lives layers of yellowing parchment papers that document their ancestral heritage to the region (for example, paperwork indicating their inclusion in the 1951 National Register of Citizens) (Bagchi 2017). Yet, once classified as "doubtful citizens," they now live under a constant threat of detention or deportation. Like the *sans papiers* in France, and the Roma throughout Europe, Indian policy-making is engaging in the selective denationalization of long-standing resident minority populations, many of whom are powerless and too impoverished to contest the legal and bureaucratic process.

While the NRC selectively revokes the citizenship status of long-term populations *within* its territory, the CAA extends citizenship status to those from *outside* its territorial borders. Under the CAA, persecuted minorities who are Hindu, Sikh, Buddhist, Jain, Parsi, or Christian from Afghanistan, Pakistan, and Bangladesh are eligible for expedited citizenship processing, whereas persecuted Muslim minorities such as Ahmadiyyas from Pakistan and Rohingyas from Myanmar are excluded. The implicit political messaging of the CAA is clear and controversial—if citizenship can be granted on the basis of religion, it can also be denied on those grounds. Top legal experts lament, "The CAA, in essence, not only violates the constitutional values of secularism and freedom of religion, but also negates the principle of equal protection and non-discrimination" (Mustafa and Mohammed 2020).

Territorial Sovereignty and Border Security

Indian migration governance can also be traced to the infrastructural development of "militarized" immigration border controls beginning in the early 1960s (Durch 2001). Militarized immigration controls refer to the "cooperation and coordination" among various border security forces (such as the police, paramilitary, and military units), with the goal of preventing and deterring unwanted entry at a territorial border (113). In India, the buildup of such militarized borders is closely connected to the expansion of local and state institutions and the implementation of infrastructure projects, often in response to broader strategic interests and military conflicts.

India shares a border with seven states: Afghanistan, Bangladesh, Bhutan, China, Myanmar, Nepal, and Pakistan. There are few natural barriers between these states, so

Table 8.4. Indian border-management organizations.

Organization	Year Created	War/Conflict	Border Deployment
Border Security Force	1965	Indo-Pakistani War of 1965	Bangladesh and Pakistan
Indo-Tibetan Border Police	1962	Sino-Indian War of 1962	China
Sashastra Seema Bal	1962	Sino-Indian War of 1962	Nepal and Bhutan

Source: Government of India, Ministry of Home Affairs, Annual Report 2016–2017, 34–36. For a history of these organizations see their official websites: (1) Border Security Force: http://bsf.nic.in; (2) Indo–Tibetan Border Police: http://itbpolice.nic.in; (3) Sashastra Seema Bal: http://www.ssb.nic.in.

borders are man-made across very difficult and changing terrain. To govern them, India distinguishes among three types of land borders: the international borderline (IBL), the line of control (LoC), and the line of actual control (LoAC). Each of these borders is governed by a specific border-policing organization (see table 8.4). The Bangladesh and Pakistan border is governed by the Border Security Force (BSF); the security of the Chinese border is entrusted to the Indo-Tibetan Border Police (ITBP); and the borders with Nepal and Bhutan are managed by the Sashastra Seema Bal (formerly the Special Service Bureau; SSB) (Government of India 2017, 34–36).

These border organizations are institutional responses to specific military conflicts in which securing territorial sovereignty and cross-border migration and traffic was essential to their mandates. For example, the Sino-Indian War of 1962 saw the establishment of the Indo-Tibetan Border Police (ITBP) as well as the Special Service Bureau (now Sashastra Seema Bal). The Indo-Pakistani War of 1965 saw the creation of the Border Security Force (BSF), which was deployed at the international border with Pakistan and after 1971 with Bangladesh.

Redoubling its effort to seal its international borders from illegal immigration flows, in 2004 the Indian Ministry of Home Affairs created a Department of Border Management to oversee the implementation of security and surveillance upgrades in border areas, mandated by a Border Area Development Programme (BADP).[17] This project had a 2016/17 budgetary allocation of 99,000 lakh rupees (about 152 million USD) (Government of India 2017, 45).[18] The cornerstone of this infrastructure project is the construction of a border fence sealing the India-Bangladesh border. In 2017, according to the Ministry of Home Affairs, out of a 3,326 km sanctioned length, 2,731 km of fencing had already been completed. This was complemented by the construction of 3,596 km of border patrol roads (out of a sanctioned length of 4,223 km), along with the completion of 2,398 km of flood lighting (roughly 500 km shy of its total sanctioned length) (Government of India 2017, 35–38).

Despite such impressive border construction, border fences rarely are effective in keeping out illegal immigrants. And sections of the India-Bangladesh border are nearly

---

17   Significantly, the Border Area Development Programme (BADP) was introduced following the Citizenship (Amendment) Act of 2003 that restricted Indian citizenship by birth to the legal status of *both* parents.

18   This is based on a conversion of 1 USD to 65 Indian rupees on November 8, 2017.

impossible to fence—especially in the area along the Brahmaputra River, which changes course every year due to monsoon rain. The role of smugglers and traffickers, and the bribery and corruption of border security forces, adds an additional layer of complication in preventing such illegal flows. Across the India-Bangladesh border cattle smuggling alone is estimated to be worth over $500 million (USD) annually (Bhattacharjee 2013).

Yet, despite border fences not being completely effective in stopping illegal flows, they appeal to a nationalizing sentiment for their symbolic value. Border fences and walls may physically separate territory, but they communicate broader divisions between privileged insiders and unwanted outsiders (Jones 2012, 2016). It is not uncommon for state representatives to selectively characterize illegal immigrants and refugees as threats to national security. As Ilgit and Klotz (2014) remind us, a "securitization" of immigration involves state leaders advancing strategic anti-immigrant sentiment among citizen populations. In India such "securitization" is most recently emphasized through religious preference for Hindus, on the one hand, and guarding against threats to territorial sovereignty by Muslims, on the other.

The migration state concept—defined by the tensions and potential strategic gains among market, rights, security, and culture (Hollifield 2004)—offers a prime example of how state policy governs, and is governed by, multiple and conflicting institutional goals. However, once applied outside Western Europe and North America, variations of the concept disrupt the widely accepted construction of the "liberal paradox." While India is often characterized as a major labor-exporting country, this chapter has surveyed the emergence of an Indian migration state as a major receiver of immigration in the South Asia region. It has highlighted two features of India's response to regional immigration flows: the narrowing of citizenship criteria and the enhancement of border security. Amid gradients of institutional strength, India's postcolonial history, geography, and social and ethnic complexity suggest that migration governance underscores national security imperatives that simultaneously seek to redefine national identity and citizenship norms. In this regard, recent policies in India have dramatically shifted course by increasingly favoring both re-territorialized and exclusionary norms, which radically move away from the more inclusive principles of birthright citizenship to the restrictive principles of a blood-based standard with religious preference. Historically, populist leaders have positioned national security interests in a way that advances ethnic majoritarian sentiment, and India is no longer an exception. The recent global pandemic caused by COVID-19 is unlikely to alter such exclusionary trends. In fact, across the globe, the unique nature of the crisis imparts states with greater control over individual movement. As such, it is revealing the partisan character of Indian policy, favoring urban areas over rural ones, while actively targeting specific minority and foreign travelers as sources of contagion.

References

Adamson, B. Fiona, and Gerasimos Tsourapas. 2019. "The Migration State in the Global South: Nationalizing, Developmental and Neoliberal Models of Migration Management." *International Migration Review* (October): 1–30.

Bagchi, Suvojit. 2017. "The Spectre of Eviction That Haunts Assam's Bengali Muslims." *The Hindu,* March 27. Accessed November 13, 2017. www.thehindu.com/society/brittle-bits-of-paper/article17639521.ece

Baruah, Sanjib. 1999. *India against Itself: Assam and the Politics of Nationality.* Philadelphia: University of Pennsylvania Press, 1999.

———. 2005. *Durable Disorder: Understanding the Politics of Northeast India.* New Delhi: Oxford University Press.

Betts, Alexander. 2013. *Survival Migration: Failed Governance and the Crisis of Displacement.* Ithaca, NY: Cornell University Press.

Bharatiya Janata Party (BJP). 2012. "Shri Ravi Shankar Prasad on UID & National Security." Press release, January 21. Accessed November 13, 2017. www.bjp.org/en/media-resources/press-releases/press-chief-spokesperson-a-mp-shri-ravi-shankar-prasad-on-uid-a-national-security

Bhattacharjee, Joyeeta. 2013. *India-Bangladesh Border Management: The Challenge of Cattle Smuggling.* Observer Research Foundation Special Report, issue 1 (July).

Braudel, Fernand, and Immanuel Wallerstein. 2009. "Commemorating the *Longue Durée*." *Review (Fernand Braudel Center)* 32(2): 171–203.

Cooper, Frederick. 2005. *Colonialism in Question: Theory, Knowledge, History.* Berkeley: University of California Press.

Durch, William J. 2001. "Keepers of the Gates: National Militaries in an Age of International Population Movement." In *Demography and National Security,* edited by Myron Weiner and Sharon Stanton Russell, 110–53. Oxford: Berghahn Books.

Government of India. 2009. *Annual Report 2008–2009.* Ministry of Overseas Indians. New Delhi: Ministry of Overseas Indian Affairs.

———. 2012. *Annual Report 2011–2012.* Ministry of Home Affairs. New Delhi: Government of India.

———. 2017. *Annual Report 2016–2017.* Ministry of Home Affairs. New Delhi: Government of India.

Greanleaf, Graham. 2010. "India's National ID System: Danger Grows in Privacy Vacuum." *Computer Law and Security Review* 26: 479–91.

Guilmoto, Christophe Z. 1993. "The Tamil Migration Cycle, 1830–1950." *Economic and Political Weekly* 28(no. 3/4): 111–20.

Hazarika, Sanjoy. 2003. *Rites of Passage: Border Crossings, Imagines Homelands, India's East and Bangladesh.* Delhi: Penguin Books.

Hollifield, James F. 1992. *Immigrants, Markets and States: The Political Economy of Postwar Europe.* Cambridge, MA: Harvard University Press.

———. 2004. "The Emerging Migration State." *International Migration Review* 38(3): 885–912.

Hussain, Monirul. 2000. "State, Identity Movements and Internal Displacement in the North-East." *Economic and Political Weekly,* December 16.

Ilgit, Asli, and Audie Klotz. 2014. "How Far Does 'Societal Security' Travel? Securitization in South African Immigration Policies." *Security Dialogue* 45(2): 137–55.

International Fund for Agricultural Development (IFAD). 2017. "Sending Money Home: Contributing to the SDG's, One Family at a Time." Rome: IFAD. Accessed August 9, 2018. www.ifad.org/web/knowledge/publication/asset/39407416

International Labour Organization. 2016. *India Labor Market Update.* ILO Country Office for India (July). Accessed November 13, 2017. www.ilo.org/wcmsp5/groups/public/---asia/---ro-bangkok/---sro-new_delhi/documents/publication/wcms_496510.pdf

Jayal, Niraja. 2016. "Chapter 10: Citizenship." In *The Oxford Handbook of the Indian Constitution,* edited by Sujit Choudhry, Madhav Khosla, and Pratap Bhanu Mehta, 163–79. New Delhi: Oxford University Press.

Jhala, A. D. 2019. "The Indian Princely States and Their Rulers." In *The Oxford Research Encyclopedia of Asian History.* Oxford: Oxford University Press.

Jones, Reece. 2009. "Sovereignty and Statelessness in the Border Enclaves of India and Bangladesh." *Political Geography* 28(6): 373–81.

_____. 2012. *Border Walls: Security and the War on Terror in the United States, India, and Israel*. London: Zed Books.

_____. 2016. *Violent Borders: Refugees and the Right to Move*. London: Versobooks.

Kansakar, V. B. S. 2003. "International Migration and Citizenship in Nepal." In *Population Monograph of Nepal, Volume 2*. Kathmandu, Nepal: Central Bureau of Statistics, Government of Nepal.

Kapur, Devesh. 2001. "Diasporas and Technology Transfers." *Journal of Human Development* 2(2): 265–86.

Karnad, Raghu Amay, Rajeev Dhavan, and Bhairav Acharaya. 2006. *Protecting the Forgotten and Excluded: Statelessness in South Asia*. New Delhi: Public Interest Legal Support and Research Centre.

Khadria, Binood, and Perveen Kumar. 2015. "Immigrants and Immigration in India." *Economic and Political Weekly* 50(8).

Klotz, Audie. 2013. *Migration and National Identity in South Africa*. New York: Cambridge University Press.

McKeown, Adam. 2011. "A World Made Many: Integration and Segregation in Global Migration, 1840–1940." In *Connecting Seas and Connected Ocean Rims*, Studies in Global Social History, edited by Donna Gabaccía and Dirk Hoerder 42–64. Leiden: Brill.

Mongia, Radhika. 2018. *Indian Migration and Empire: A Colonial Genealogy of the Modern State*. Durham, NC: Duke University Press.

Mustafa, Faizan, and Aymen Mohammed. 2020. "The Great Indian Citizenship Mess." *The Hindu*, January 21. Accessed May 12, 2020. www.thehindu.com/opinion/op-ed/the-great-indian-citizenship-mess/article30609610.ece

Naujoks, Daniel. 2009. *Emigration, Immigration and Diaspora Relations in India*. Washington, DC: Migration Policy Institute. www.migrationpolicy.org/article/emigration-immigration-and-diaspora-relations-india

———. 2013. *Migration, Citizenship and Development: Diasporic Membership Policies and Overseas Indians in the United States*. Delhi: Oxford University Press.

Phillip, Connor. 2017. "India a Top Source and Destination for World Migrants." Pew Research Center, March 3. Accessed November 13, 2017. www.pewresearch.org/fact-tank/2017/03/03/india-is-a-top-source-and-destination-for-worlds-migrants/

Rahman, Mustafizer, and Estiaque Bari. 2020. "Informality in Bangladesh's Agricultural Trade with SAARC: Addressing the Emerging Concerns." In *Trade and Regional Integration in South Asia: A Tribute to Saman Kelegama*, edited by Selim Raihan and Prabir De, 249–66. Singapore: Springer.

Raman, Sunil. 2008. "Nepal Maoists Seek New Order with India." *BBC News*, September 15. Accessed August 7, 2018. http://news.bbc.co.uk/go/pr/fr/-/2/hi/south_asia/7616316.stm

Rice, Susan E., and Stewart Patrick. 2008. *Index of State Weakness in the Developing World*. Washington, DC: Brookings Institution.

Roy, Anupama. 2019. "The Citizenship (Amendment Bill), 2016 and the Aporia of Citizenship." *Economic and Political Weekly* 54(49).

Sadiq, Kamal. 2009. *Paper Citizens: How Illegal Immigrants Acquire Citizenship in Developing Countries*. New York: Oxford University Press.

———. 2017. "Postcolonial Citizenship." In *The Oxford Handbook of Citizenship*, edited by Ayelet Shachar, Rainer Baubock, Irene Bloemraad, and Maarten Vink, 178–99. New York: Oxford University Press.

Shastri, Amita. 1990. "The Material Basis for Separatism: The Tamil Eelam Movement in Sri Lanka." *Journal of Asian Studies* 49(1): 56–77.

Sturman, Rachel. 2014. "Indian Indentured Labor and the History of International Rights Regimes." *American Historical Review* 119(5): 1439–65.

UNHCR. 2003. Statistical Yearbook. New York: United Nations.

United Nations. 2011. *International Migration Report 2009: A Global Assessment*. Department of Economic and Social Affairs, Population Division. New York: UN Publications. Accessed November 13, 2017. www.un.org/esa/population/publications/migration/WorldMigrationReport2009.pdf

———. 2012. *Migrants by Origin and Destination: The Role of South-South Migration* (June). Department of Economic and Social Affairs, Population Division. New York: UN Publications. Accessed August 9, 2018. https://esa.un.org/unmigration/documents/PF_South-South_migration_2013.pdf

———. 2013. *International Migration Policies: Government Views and Priorities.* Department of Economic and Social Affairs. New York: UN Publications. Accessed July 27, 2018. www.un.org/en/development/desa/population/publications/policy/international-migration-policies-report-2013.shtml

———. 2016. *International Migration Report 2015: Highlights.* Department of Economic and Social Affairs, Population Division (ST/ESA/SER.A/375).

Van Schendel, Willem. 2002. "Stateless in South Asia; The Making of the India-Bangladesh Enclaves." *Journal of Asian Studies* 61(1): 115–47.

Vezzoli, Simona, and Thomas Lacroix. 2010. *Building Bonds for Migration and Development: Diaspora Engagement Policies of Ghana, India and Serbia.* Research Report, International Migration Institute, Gesellschaft fur Technische Zusammenarbeit (GTZ).

Weiner, Myron. 1995. *The Global Migration Crisis: Challenge to States and to Human Rights.* New York: HarperCollins.

World Bank. 2016. *Migration and Remittances Factbook 2016*, 3rd ed. Washington, DC: World Bank. Accessed August 9, 2018. https://siteresources.worldbank.org/INTPROSPECTS/Resources/334934-1199807908806/4549025-1450455807487/Factbookpart1.pdf

Zamindar, Vazira Fazila-Yacoobali. 2007. *The Long Partition and the Making of Modern South Asia: Refugees, Boundaries and Histories. New York:* Columbia University Press.

PART 4

THE AMERICAS, THE "LIBERAL" AND SETTLER MIGRATION STATES

9 THE DEVELOPMENT OF THE US MIGRATION STATE

Nativism, Liberalism, and Durable Structures of Exclusion

Daniel Tichenor

THE UNITED STATES HAS BEEN a nation forged by immigration since the earliest days of the republic, yet one that was slow to develop a centralized *migration state*. Americans long have woven immigration narratives and iconography into their collective cultural identity; indeed the idea that the US is "a nation of immigrants" has been popular at least since then-senator John F. Kennedy penned a book of that title sixty years ago.[1] Yet the resonance of Donald Trump's rabid attacks on Mexican immigrants and Muslim refugees during the 2016 presidential campaign also captures the persistent allure of ethnic, racial, and religious hierarchies to many voters.[2] The staying power of anti-immigrant nativism in US politics sometimes has been obscured by policy reforms from 1965 to 1990 that expanded immigration opportunities and noncitizen rights. As this chapter explains, however, beginning in the late nineteenth century the US national state developed a will and capacity for race-based marginalization, repression, and exclusion of immigrants that has never disappeared. Still, policy changes won by nativists in the first half of the twentieth century also did not go unchallenged by organized economic interests or immigrant-rights activists, requiring these restrictive-minded reformers to cut bargains *even at that time* to secure major legal innovation. The same challenges faced pro-immigration reformers from the Cold War onward, as they compromised with restrictionists over ethnic and security concerns. As this chapter underscores, xenophobic nativism and exclusionary capacities of the US state have proven as durable over time as liberal demands for immigrant labor and cosmopolitan devotion to universal human rights.

---

1   John F. Kennedy, *A Nation of Immigrants* (New York: Harper and Row, 1964).

2   Donald Trump, "Donald J. Trump Statement on Preventing Muslim Immigration," press release, December 7, 2015; Julie Hirschfield Davis and Michael Shear, *Border Wars: Inside Trump's Assault on Immigration* (New York: Simon and Schuster, 2019); Julia Young, "Making America 1920 Again?: Nativism and US Immigration, Past and Present," *Journal of Migration and Human Security* 5, no. 1 (2017): 217–35.

Reflecting on the "migration state" and its "liberal paradoxes"[3] in American political development, this chapter aligns with immigration research by social scientists who assess longitudinal patterns and transformations that can only be revealed by employing broad temporal horizons and historical methods.[4] Drawing upon extensive archival research, my analysis focuses on two key developments that have shaped US immigration politics and policy over time. The first is that as much as the American carceral state or national security state,[5] the US government's capacities to exclude, repress, and remove immigrants have grown significantly during the past century and often have fueled the subjugation of particular immigrant groups. Indeed, the *American migration state* that emerged slowly in the nineteenth century demonstrated significant capacities to control and limit immigration—*when* it was especially motivated. This capacity was on display from the savage winnowing of the Chinese population on the Pacific Coast in the late nineteenth century[6] to the "deportation delirium" targeting mostly European political radicals during the First Red Scare.[7]

The muscles of the migration state also appeared with the rise of a visa and consular examination process that established remote control of the inspection process in the 1910s and 1920s, and stringently limited overseas immigration from overseas for decades. At the same time, demand for cheap, "returnable" migrant labor often kept the nation's borders porous, spurred a large-scale guest-worker program, and allowed for refugee admissions when it served grand strategy during the Cold War. Its capacity to launch mass deportations targeting Mexicans, and impacting Mexican Americans, also was evident in so-called "repatriations" in the 1930s, and again during the dragnet raids of "Operation Wetback" in 1954—racial profiling on a massive scale—that

---

3   James Hollifield, *Immigrants, Markets, and States* (Cambridge, MA: Harvard University Press, 1992); James Hollifield, "The Emerging Migration State," *International Migration Review* 38, no. 3 (2004).

4   Daniel Tichenor, *Dividing Lines: The Politics of Immigration Control in America* (Princeton, NJ: Princeton University Press, 2002); Anna Law, *The Immigration Battle in the Courts* (New York: Cambridge University Press, 2010); Aristide Zolberg, *A Nation by Design* (Cambridge, MA: Harvard University Press, 2008); Cybelle Fox, *Three Worlds of Relief* (New York: Oxford University Press, 2012); Janice Fine and Daniel Tichenor, "A Movement Wrestling: American Labor's Enduring Struggle with Immigration 1866–2007," *Studies in American Political Development* 23, no. 2 (2009) 218–48.

5   Marie Gottschalk, *The Prison and the Gallows* (New York: Cambridge University Press, 2006); Amy Lerman and Vesla Weaver, *Arresting Citizenship* (Chicago: University of Chicago Press, 2014); Michelle Alexander, *The New Jim Crow* (New York: New Press, 2012); Douglas Stuart, *Creating the National Security State* (Princeton, NJ: Princeton University Press, 2012); Karen Greenberg, ed., *Reimagining the National Security State* (New York: Cambridge University Press, 2019).

6   Jean Pfaelzer, *Driven Out: The Forgotten War against Chinese Americans* (Berkeley: University of California Press, 2007).

7   Louis Post, *The Deportations Delirium of Nineteen-Twenty: A Personal Narrative of an Historic Official Experience* (Chicago: C. H. Kerr, 1923).

triggered an exodus of Mexican immigrants, both documented and undocumented.[8] Over time, the casting of Latino immigrants, especially the undocumented, as a threat to the nation fueled the militarization of the US southern border and a mass detention system.

A second important development highlighted in the pages that follow is the frequency with which rival and incongruous elements are woven into US immigration reform and policy implementation over time due to competing ideological commitments and interests. As we shall see, this represents a distinctive incarnation of *the liberal paradox* pitting economic demands for openness against legal and political pressures for closure.[9] As I have previously noted,[10] these tensions have produced durable conflicts between cosmopolitans versus economic protectionists on the left, and between pro-business expansionists versus cultural protectionists and border hawks on the right. Major legal and policy innovation is always arduous in an American political system replete with structural veto-points, but these deep conflicts between and within US parties over immigrant admissions and rights long have made comprehensive reform in this policy realm especially daunting. For generations, campaigns for immigration reform regularly have followed a torturous path of false starts, prolonged negotiation, and frustrating stalemate. In the past, when lightning has struck for enactment of significant policy innovations, passage has hinged upon the formation of "strange bedfellow" alliances that are unstable and that demand difficult compromises addressing rival goals and interests.[11] This means that even some of the most restrictive immigration laws in American history have included bargains that create openings for international migration, and that expansive reforms have featured restrictive elements. In the pages that follow, we will explore these dynamics in major policy breakthroughs from the National Origins Quota laws of 1924 and 1928 to the Immigration and Nationality Act (INA) of 1965 to the Immigration Reform and Control Act (IRCA) of 1986.

An American Migration State Emerges: European Recruitment and Chinese Exclusion

From a comparative perspective, the United States often has been described as slow to develop centralized government functions and powers associated with a strong national state. Consistent with this view, the US federal government did not develop either policies or administrative capacities for regulating immigrant admissions and rights for nearly

---

8   Abraham Hoffman, *Unwanted Mexican Americans in the Great Depression* (Tucson: University of Arizona Press, 1974).

9   Hollifield, *Immigrants, Markets, and States*.

10   Daniel Tichenor, *Dividing Lines*; Tichenor, "Strange Bedfellows: The Politics and Pathologies of Immigration Reform," *Labor: Studies in Working-Class History* 5 (Summer 2008): 39–50; Tichenor, "Compromise and Contradiction: Reassessing the Immigration and Nationality Act of 1965," *Labor: Studies in Working-Class History* (2016).

11   Daniel Tichenor, "Strange Bedfellows: The Politics and Pathologies of Immigration Reform," *Labor* 5, no. 2 (Summer 2008): 39–60.

a century after its founding.[12] Indeed, to the chagrin of anti-Catholic nativist groups like the Anti-Masons, Know-Nothings, and the American Protective Association, the federal government for most of the nineteenth century alternated between maintaining a *laissez-faire* approach toward the record numbers of European immigrants streaming into the country or actively recruiting them. Along with welcoming robust European admissions, the US granted white male arrivals swift access to most of the same civil and political rights as citizens. These expansive *de facto* policies rested upon two pillars: the allure of immigrant workers and the perceived clout of new immigrant voters and kindred ethnics. From the 1820s until the start of the Civil War, roughly five million European immigrants settled in the young republic. During the 1820s, immigration accounted for only 4 percent of the steady increase in American population; by the 1850s, immigration accounted for nearly one-third of national population growth. During this period, the federal government remained all but silent on European immigration. Congress passed legislation that required the counting of new arrivals after 1819 to maintain uniform statistics, and it mandated minimum living standards for vessels carrying immigrant passengers to the country. Otherwise, the federal government left control of immigration largely in the hands of the states until the late nineteenth century. In practice, this meant that the tasks of regulating immigration devolved to key maritime states and authorities in their port cities.[13]

Consequently, the modest structures governing immigrant traffic in antebellum America were the creation and ongoing responsibility of a few coastal states, such as New York, Maryland, Massachusetts, Pennsylvania, Louisiana, and South Carolina. State immigration laws authorized exclusion of European immigrants with criminal records, contagious illnesses, and other qualities deemed undesirable, but few were turned away. Maritime states also charged shipmasters small head taxes on their immigrant passengers to cover various expenses such as the care of indigent and sick arrivals. In short, with few exceptions, US legislative and bureaucratic control over immigration for most of the nineteenth century devolved to states and locales on the front lines of receiving newcomers.[14]

This is not to say, however, that the federal government was a silent partner in the development of an American migration state during its first century. In fact, national officials typically focused their energies on using their authority and resources *to recruit* rather than filter European immigrants who they saw as essential for spurring US economic and territorial expansion. During the Civil War, for instance, the administration of Abraham Lincoln and Republicans in Congress saw mass European immigration as

---

12   John Higham, *Strangers in the Land: Patterns of American Nativism, 1860–192* (New Brunswick, NJ: Rutgers University Books, 1955); Maldwyn Allen Jones, *American Immigration* (Chicago: University of Chicago Press, 1980).

13   *Ibid.*; Tichenor, *Dividing Lines*.

14   William S. Bernard, "A History of US Immigration," in *Immigration: Dimensions of Ethnicity*, ed. Stephen Thernstrom, 83–92 (Cambridge, MA: Harvard University Press, 1982); E. P. Hutchinson, *Legislative History of American Immigration Policy* (Philadelphia: University of Pennsylvania Press, 1993), 11–92.

critical to replenishing the nation's labor force and to settling its frontier. The Homestead Act of 1862 offered 160 acres of land free to citizens *and noncitizens* who worked it for at least five years. The stated purpose of the legislation was not to encourage European immigration, but Secretary of the Treasury Salmon Chase and Secretary of State William Seward saw it as a means of doing just that. With Lincoln's blessing, Seward instructed US consular officials in Europe to distribute government-published pamphlets hyping the opportunities promised newcomers under the Homestead Act. The US consuls also hired full-time agents to recruit "industrious" European men.[15] In 1864, Lincoln urged Congress to adopt other measures for attracting immigration to redress "a great deficiency of laborers," and lawmakers obliged with legislation that authorized immigrant labor contracts enabling prospective European arrivals to contract their labor for one year in exchange for free transportation to the US. As a congressional committee concluded one year after the law was put into effect, "the advantages which have accrued heretofore from immigration can scarcely be computed."[16]

Inflows from Europe reached record levels in the post–Civil War decades: immigration soared to 2.3 million in the 1860s, 2.8 million in the 1870s, and 5.2 million in the 1880s. The vast majority of these immigrants first arrived in New York, where they were channeled through a central immigration depot, Manhattan's Castle Garden. New York officials perceived special obligations and burdens in their state's role as the nation's primary regulator of immigration. "While New York has to endure nearly all of its evils, the other States reap most of the benefits of immigration," noted Friedrich Kapp, a state commissioner of emigration in the 1870s. "Our State acts in the interest of the whole Union, by efficiently protecting all the immigrants on their arrival, and by preventing the spread of diseases imported by them over the country at large, and this while deriving far less advantage from immigration than the Western States."[17]

As mass European immigration remade American social, economic, and political life in the decades before and after the Civil War, New York and other maritime states stepped forward to screen and care for immigrants at a time when the federal government lacked both the collective will and administrative capacity to do so. This changed in 1875, however, when the Supreme Court ruled that state regulations in this field were an unconstitutional usurpation of exclusive congressional power to regulate foreign commerce: "The laws which govern the right to land passengers in the United States from other countries ought to be the same in New York, Boston, New Orleans, and San Francisco."[18] Congress slowly responded by adopting the Immigration Act of 1882, essentially providing national authorization for state policies that had been struck down by

---

15   Charlotte Erickson, *American Industry and the European Immigrant, 1860–1885* (Cambridge, MA: Harvard University Press, 1957), 8; Ella Lonn, *Foreigners in the Union Army and Navy* (Baton Rouge: Louisiana State University Press, 1952), 420.

16   *Congressional Globe*, 38th Cong., 1st Sess., app., pp. 1–2; Maurice Davie, *World Immigration* (New York: Macmillan, 1936), 82.

17   Friedrich Kapp, *Immigration, and the Commissioners of Emigration of the State of New York* (New York: Nation Press, 1870), 157–58.

18   *Henderson v. Mayor of New York*, 92 U.S. 259 (1875).

the Court. The new legislation borrowed language from state statutes to restrict admission of "any convict, lunatic, idiot, or any person unable to take care of himself or herself without becoming a public charge."[19] Moreover, these federal immigration laws were enforced by agents at ports-of-entry who once were employed by state governments but now were under the authority of new US bureaucracies.[20]

The politics of Chinese exclusion, however, offer a very different portrait of the emergence of the US migration state. As both historians and political scientists note, a "state of courts and parties" dominated American political life during the late nineteenth century.[21] The return of competitive party politics and judicial influence had pernicious implications for African Americans in the post-Reconstruction era. Republican struggles at the polls ultimately led to the removal of federal troops from the South in 1877 and a broader retreat on civil rights in the years that followed. The federal courts fortified these trends by dismantling most constitutional rights secured by African Americans after the Civil War. Yet whereas the assault on African American rights reflected national acquiescence to state and local racial practices, the demand for Chinese exclusion required an ambitious new realm of national control to be established.[22]

Strikingly, Chinese immigration of the late nineteenth century was miniscule compared to its European counterparts (4 percent of all immigration at its zenith), but it inspired one of the most brutal and successful nativist movements in US history. Official and popular racism made Chinese newcomers especially vulnerable; their lack of numbers, political power, or legal protections gave them none of the weapons that enabled Irish Catholics to counterattack nativists. Chinese workers were first recruited to California from the 1850s through the 1870s as cheap contract labor for mining, railroad construction, manufacturing, and farming. They inspired hostility among white workers for allegedly lowering wages and working conditions, while newspapers and magazines portrayed the Chinese as a race of godless opium addicts, prostitutes, and gamblers. Labor leaders in San Francisco organized large Anti-Chinese clubs, and California politicians learned that anti-Chinese speeches and policies translated into votes.[23]

---

19   Hutchinson, *Legislative History of American Immigration Policy*, 79; Anna Law, "Lunatics, Idiots, Paupers, and Negro Seamen: Immigration Federalism and the Early American State," *Studies in American Political Development* 28 (2014): 107–28.

20   Hidetaka Hirota, "The Moment of Transition: State Officials, the Federal Government, and the Formation of American Immigration Policy," *Journal of American Ethnic History* 99 (2013): 1092–108; Sharon Masanz, "The History of the Immigration and Naturalization Service," Select Commission on Immigration and Refugee Policy, Congressional Research Service, Library of Congress, 96th Cong., 2d Sess. (Washington, DC: US Government Printing Office, 1980), 4–9.

21   Morton Keller, *Affairs of State* (Cambridge, MA: Harvard University Press, 1977); Stephen Skowronek, *Building a New American State* (New York: Cambridge University Press, 1982).

22   Tichenor, *Dividing Lines*, 87–113.

23   Alexander Saxton, *The Indispensable Enemy* (Berkeley: University of California Press, 1971); Roger Daniels, *Asian America* (Seattle: University of Washington Press, 1988); Roger Daniels, *Coming to America: A History of Immigration and Ethnicity in American Life* (New York: Harper

Economic distress inflamed the anti-Chinese movement in the years following the Civil War, as the closing of unproductive mines, the completion of the transcontinental railroad, and the arrival of white settlers from the East led to rampant unemployment. Chinese Exclusion Leagues were formed throughout the state that ultimately spread to other Pacific Coast and Mountain states, and they called on state politicians to meet their Sinophobic demands. While California Democrats like Henry Haight pledged to fight "against populating this fair State with a race of Asiatics," Republican incumbents endorsed all forms of "voluntary immigration" and found themselves swept out of Sacramento. Before long, California lawmakers enacted bipartisan anti-Chinese laws designed to severely restrict their immigration and basic civil and economic rights.[24]

One of the most prominent California laws enacted in the early 1870s prohibited Chinese from landing on state soil without a bond unless they could prove their "good character." The measure was challenged in the state's federal circuit court in 1874, where Justice Stephen Field expressed sympathy with the "general feeling" of Californians that "the dissimilarity in physical characteristics, in language, in manners, religion and habits, will always prevent any possible assimilation of them with our people." He nevertheless invalidated state efforts to curb Chinese entry, advising that "recourse must be had to the Federal government, where the whole power over this subject lies."[25]

This judicial limit on state immigration law dramatically altered the strategy of the anti-Chinese movement. During the Reconstruction period, anti-Chinese activists tended to vigorously oppose enhanced responsibilities for the national state, which they associated with Radical Republican designs of extending civil rights protections and circumscribing state and local racial practices. But judicial limitations on state police powers created new imperatives: Chinese exclusion could be achieved only if new federal regulatory controls were established. "Our only hope is in the National Government," declared Aaron Sargent, a California senator and proponent of Chinese restriction.[26]

Shortly after the court struck down state restrictions on immigration in 1874, Western state officials and their congressional delegations called for national limits on Chinese immigration. Because California and its neighbors were crucial battleground states in highly competitive national elections, leaders and members of both parties in Congress eagerly curried favor with anti-Chinese voters of the West. The Immigration Act of 1875 made it illegal to transport Asian immigrants without their voluntary consent (a response to "coolie labor"), and designated prostitutes and those convicted of felonious crimes as excludable classes. In 1879, a California referendum calling for Chinese exclusion won

---

Perennial, 2002); Erika Lee, *At America's Gates: Chinese Americans during the Exclusion Era, 1882–1943* (Chapel Hill: University of North Carolina Press, 2003); Andrew Gyory, *Closing the Gate: Race, Politics, and the Chinese Exclusion Act* (Chapel Hill: University of North Carolina Press, 1998).

24 Elmer Sandmeyer, *The Anti-Chinese Movement in California* (Urbana: University of Illinois Press, 1973), 40–56.

25 *Ibid.*

26 *Congressional Record*, May 1, 1876, p. 2586.

by a lopsided 150,000 to 900 vote. The same year, Congress passed the Fifteen Passenger Law, barring vessels from transporting more than fifteen Chinese passengers at a time.[27]

Fierce party competition in presidential elections of the Gilded Age transformed the anti-Chinese movement into a national political juggernaut. As the *New York Times* queried in 1880, "Which great political party is foolish enough to risk losing the votes of the Pacific States by undertaking to do justice to the Chinese?"[28] Neither, as it turned out. Large bipartisan majorities in Congress suspended Chinese admissions for ten years with passage of the infamous Chinese Exclusion Act of 1882. In 1884, Congress prohibited Chinese entry from US territories like Hawaii and the Philippines. Four years later, Congress barred reentry of longtime Chinese residents of the US when they temporarily left the country unless they could prove that they had a wife, child, *and* US property valued over a thousand dollars. In his signing statement, President Grover Cleveland sounded the death knell for the Burlingame Treaty that welcomed Chinese immigrants years before. The "experiment of blending . . . the Chinese laboring classes with those of the great body of the people of the United States proved . . . in every sense unwise, impolitic, and injurious to both nations."[29] During another presidential election four years later, Congress passed the Geary Act of 1892 that reinforced Chinese exclusion but also targeted the Chinese population residing in the country. Under the new law, Chinese noncitizens were required to prove that their residence was legal by producing a white witness to testify that they resided in the country prior to 1882. In addition, the legislation denied bail to Chinese defendants in *habeas corpus* proceedings, and required all Chinese residents to carry a certificate of residence.[30]

Significantly, congressional committees placed intense pressure on a young immigration bureaucracy to enforce these new laws forcefully. That is, the move to exclude Chinese newcomers quickly impelled the buildup of bureaucratic capacity to keep out or remove these immigrants. A fresh crop of federal immigration officials assumed posts at Angel Island in San Francisco and other major ports to turn away or deport Chinese immigrants, while border agents patrolled California's southern border and Washington's northern border to prevent Chinese entry overland. In addition, the Supreme Court vigorously affirmed the constitutionality of Congress's power to exclude immigrants on the basis of race and national origin in the *Chinese Exclusion Case* of 1889. Three years later, the Court ruled that the plenary power of nations to exclude noncitizens trumped any due process claims of individual immigrants; it also asserted that plenary power extended to "executive officers," who were entrusted by Congress to act as the "sole and exclusive judge" of immigration enforcement.[31]

27 Sandmeyer, *The Anti-Chinese Movement in California*; Daniels, *Coming to America*; Lee, *At America's Gates*.

28 "The Chinese Must Go," *New York Times*, February 26, 1880.

29 Daniels, *Asian America*, 56–57.

30 Hutchinson, *Legislative History of American Immigration Policy*, 104–5.

31 Charles McClain and Laurene Wu McClain, "The Chinese Contribution to the Development of American Law," in *Entry Denied*, ed. Sucheng Chan, 19–23 (Philadelphia: Temple University Press, 1991).

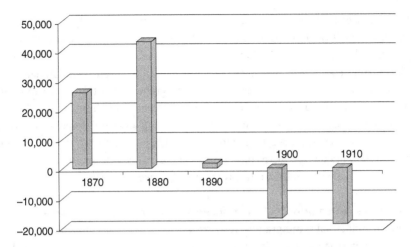

Figure 9.1. Chinese population growth and decline in the United States, 1870–1910.
Source: Census Bureau, *Statistical Abstract* (Washington, DC: US Government Printing Office, 1924).

As a new American migration state emerged via unprecedented legislation, judicial authorization, and federal bureaucratic enforcement, Chinese immigration declined drastically. In the same period, the rabid anti-Chinese movement that consumed most Western US states terrorized Chinese American communities with no protection from local, state, or national officials. During the 1880s, violent attacks against Chinese and Chinese Americans spread from California to many Pacific Northwest and Mountain states. In the 1885 Rock Springs, Wyoming, massacre, twenty-eight Chinese were murdered and every Chinese-owned building, except one, was destroyed. Chinese residents of Tacoma and Seattle suffered looting, arson, and violent riots until few remained. Chinatowns in thirty-one California cities endured riots, arson, and physical expulsions of Chinese. Special anti-Chinese conventions were organized to find ways to "rid the state of the Chinese now here."[32] In short, the Sinophobic movement now sought to complement immigration barriers with vigorous efforts to thin the country's Chinese population. This combination of strict enforcement of exclusionary laws by a new migration state and brutal Western violence ultimately had the desired chilling effect on the Chinese population in the United States (see figure 9.1). After a renewal of Chinese exclusion in 1902, Congress subsequently made exclusion permanent.

During the nineteenth century, the American migration state vigorously recruited able-bodied European newcomers to fuel US industrial and territorial expansion while lethargically assuming centralized control of filtering their arrival at major port cities. Yet as we have seen, the same US migration state demonstrated an early capacity to bare its teeth to advance notions of racial hegemony at the heart of American national identity and power relations in these years. Tellingly, Chinese exclusion activists at the grassroots actively promoted greater power and capacity for the national state in service

32 Anti-Chinese Memorial of the Anti-Chinese Convention of California, March 10, 1886; Daniels, *Asian America*, 60–66; Robert Wynne, "Reaction to the Chinese in the Pacific Northwest and British Columbia," PhD diss., University of Washington, 1964.

of their policy goals. "The strong nations of the earth are now, as they always have been, the most thoroughly homogenous nations, that is to say, the most nearly of one race, language, and manners," the California Anti-Chinese Convention told Congress. "All political history shows homogeneity to be a vast power in a State, and that heterogeneity is a corresponding source of weakness."[33] The significance of this emergent national migration state for European immigration would become clear after the turn of the century. Indeed, the construction of a more elaborate set of legal and bureaucratic barriers to mass immigration from southern and eastern Europe in the early twentieth century would require notable legislative compromises and a major shift in inspection processes overseas. It is to the rise of this restrictive regime that we now turn.

"Restrictions with a Bribe": Closing the Ports and Opening the Borders

The most influential immigration restrictionists of the early twentieth century—including nativist lawmakers Henry Cabot Lodge and Albert Johnson and the Immigration Restriction League's Joseph Lee and James Patten—advanced a nativist policy agenda that they associated with a grand strategy to restore a certain brand of economic, social, and political order to a country enduring wrenching change.[34] From the 1890s until the onset of World War I, nativist reformers of the US immigration restriction movement were stymied by a potent coalition of pro-immigration ethnic and business groups. Wartime national security jitters helped changed their political fortunes, leading to enactment of the Immigration Act of 1917. The new law made all alien admissions contingent upon payment of an eight-dollar head tax and passage of a literacy test. The new requirements slowed the flow of Mexican workers across the southern border, although many simply crossed without inspection or official authorization. When World War I began, the supply of Mexican laborers was more dramatically dampened when rumors that they would be drafted into the US armed forces spurred a mass exodus.[35]

Against this backdrop, southwestern growers, ranchers, miners, railroad companies, and supportive lawmakers pressured the Labor Department—then responsible for the Immigration Bureau and domestic enforcement—to facilitate the importation of thousands of Mexican workers. Bowing to this intense lobbying on the grounds that the war had produced labor shortages, Labor Secretary William Wilson invoked a special clause of the 1917 law (the ninth proviso of section 3) that enabled him to "issue rules and prescribe conditions . . . to control and regulate the admission and return of otherwise inadmissible aliens applying for temporary admission."[36] Wilson ordered that the literacy test, head taxes, and contract labor restrictions be waived for Mexicans; he also led publicity efforts to assure potential guestworkers that they would not be conscripted into the armed forces. Although Mexican contract labor was justified as an emergency wartime measure, an array of southwestern employers of low-wage labor joined with

33   Anti-Chinese Memorial of the Anti-Chinese Convention of California, March 10, 1886.

34   Higham, *Strangers in the Land;* Tichenor, *Dividing Lines*, chap. 5.

35   Mark Reisler, *By the Sweat of Their Brow* (Westport, CT: Greenwood Press, 1976), 24–32.

36   Ibid., 27.

their congressional representatives in demanding extensions of the program after war-time hostilities ceased in 1918. The Labor Department again acceded to this lobbying pressure, as it did in subsequent years. Between 1917 and 1921, roughly 75,000 Mexicans worked as contract laborers in the United States under Wilson's waiver plan, along with an indeterminate number of undocumented workers.[37]

The literacy test proved quite ineffective at limiting southern and eastern European immigration. The policy solution of the immigration restriction movement and its con-gressional allies was to establish an explicitly discriminatory national origins quota sys-tem and an Asiatic Barred Zone. Immigration policy could best serve national interests, they argued, by explicitly invoking the racist ideas of eugenics, when officials recognized "natural inborn hereditary mental and moral differences" and developed systems for se-lecting new residents with the same discernment as a "man who breeds pedigreed plants and animals."[38] The immigration barriers envisioned by restrictionists were formidable and they reflected a vision of nationhood rooted in illiberal notions of ethnic, racial, and religious hierarchy. However, the issue of Mexican migratory labor threatened the im-migration restriction movement in the 1920s. The diverse nativist coalition that emerged from the Progressive Era was united in its hostility toward Asian and southern and east-ern European immigration. But Mexican labor flows were another matter. The northern Immigration Restriction League, the American Federation of Labor (AFL), patriotic societies, and a number of northern lawmakers favored stringent limits on Latin and South American immigration. By contrast, southern and western lawmakers and groups supporting national origins quotas for overseas immigration also extolled the virtues of a cheap and flexible Mexican labor force. Representative John Nance Garner (D-TX) ex-plained that "the prices that [Mexicans] charge are much less than the same labor would be from either the negro or the white man."[39] He assured his House colleagues that Mexi-can laborers were by definition temporary, powerless, and easily expelled. Agricultural interests explained that they did "not want to see the condition arise again when white men who are reared and educated in our schools have got to bend their backs and skin their fingers." The Great Western Sugar Company told Congress that "you have to give us a class of labor that will do . . . back-breaking work, and we have the brains and ability to supervise and handle the business part of it."[40]

With the uneasy 1920s coalition of northern nativists, organized labor, and south-ern and western nativists deeply divided over Mexican labor, the controversy seemed to place the national origins quota system begun in 1921 in jeopardy. Indeed, immi-gration defenders attempted to exploit these fractures within the nativist coalition dur-ing legislative debates of 1924. Representatives Fiorello La Guardia (D-NY) and Adolph

---

37   Tichenor, *Dividing Lines*, 168–70.

38   Oscar Handlin, *Immigration as a Factor in American History* (New York: Prentice Hall, 1963), 152; Prescott Hall, "Immigration Restriction and World Eugenics," *Journal of Heredity* 10, no. 3 (March 1919): 125–27.

39   Reisler, *By the Sweat of Their Brow*, 40.

40   Ibid., 175.

Sabath (D-IL) offered an amendment that placed strict quotas on Western Hemisphere countries. Their hope was to kill the 1924 quota legislation by sundering the disparate restrictionist camp. Faced with stalemate or defeat, the immigration restriction coalition called for a compromise on the divisive Mexican labor question. As one closed-border advocate declared, "I want the Mexicans kept out, but I do not want this bill killed by men who want these and all others admitted in unrestricted numbers."[41]

The Immigration Act of 1924 ultimately erected formidable barriers to southern and eastern Europeans and reinforced Asian exclusion, but was decidedly permissive on Canadian and Mexican admissions. Aliens with ten years' continuous residence in a Western Hemisphere country could enter the US as nonquota immigrants. "Restrictions of immigration and setting up of un-American racial tests has been enacted through a fusion of northern Republicans from urban districts with southern Democrats, *with a bribe tossed to the latter by keeping Mexico open*," observed one pro-immigration lobbyist.[42] As nativist reformers prepared new quota legislation in 1928, they agreed to treat Mexican inflows as a distinctive issue. "These two kinds of restriction are quite separate and independent," New York restrictionist Demarest Lloyd declared in reference to overseas versus Western Hemisphere migration: "We all agree that unity of restrictionists is desirable."[43] Recalling the potential split in 1924, the Immigration Restriction League (IRL) also urged coalitional comity on "the National Origins-Mexican Quota situation."[44] It even expressed sympathy for the dilemma faced by southwestern nativists. "Although the West has become racially conscious and wants to be a white civilization, it also wants to develop and to develop rapidly. For this it needs unskilled labor of a mobile type, like the Mexicans, for it cannot get white labor to do its unskilled work."[45] The 1928 law codified this compromise, reaffirming a bifurcated system that imposed draconian restrictions on European and Asian immigration while remaining open and flexible toward labor inflows from Mexico and other Western Hemisphere countries.

The passage of the Quota Acts in the 1920s initiated an annual ceiling for legal immigrant admissions at 153,714—a sharp decrease from the record annual average of roughly 700,000 immigrants during the first two decades of the twentieth century. By design, more than 80 percent of these immigration slots were reserved for northern and western Europeans. Although this quota system established a formidable legal foundation for restricting overseas immigration, nativist worried about an administrative structure that enforced draconian limits on southern and eastern European arrivals. Their answer was to build new immigration controls administered by the State Department's Consular and

---

41   Ibid., 201.

42   Max Kohler, Undated Notes, Max Kohler Papers, American Jewish Historical Society, Brandeis University, Waltham, MA, Box 5, Folder "Immigration Notes" (emphasis in original).

43   Demarest Lloyd to Joseph Lee, May 17, 1928, Joseph Lee Papers, Massachusetts Historical Society, Boston, Massachusetts.

44   Robert Ward to Joseph Lee, May 17, 1928, Lee Papers.

45   Immigration Restriction League, Executive Committee Bulletin no. 12, June 1, 1928, Immigration Restriction League Papers, Houghton Library, Harvard University, Cambridge, MA.

Visa Bureaus, which relocated the examination of would-be immigrants to consular officers in source countries. This bureaucratic innovation made stateside inspection stations
like Ellis Island obsolete since overseas immigration was now regulated by a visa system
and consular officials that established what Aristide Zolberg aptly called "remote border
control."[46] Immigration restriction became even more severe during the Great Depression. President Herbert Hoover issued an executive order in 1930 calling for "strict enforcement" of section 3 of the Immigration Act of 1917, barring aliens deemed "likely to
become a public charge"—often called the LPC clause. "[T]here is serious unemployment among all wage earners in this country," Washington instructed consular officers
overseas. "The result is that any alien wage earner without special means of support
coming to the US during the present period of depression is, therefore, likely to become
a public charge."[47] Most working-class aliens were deemed inadmissible, and Hoover
boasted in 1932 that tougher enforcement of the LPC clause had resulted in a 94 percent
underissue of available quota slots; immigration that year plummeted to 36,000.

The onset of the Great Depression also changed public perceptions of Mexican labor immigration considerably. AFL president William Green captured the mood when
he asserted that years of unfettered Mexican immigration displaced American workers.
"There are at least 2,000,000 Mexicans in the United States . . . and all wage earners
should be warned of this calamitous condition," Green declared.[48] Green's numbers in
fact were inflated, as those of Mexican origin in the country were roughly 1.3 million.
The Depression was hard on Mexican immigrants, who not only faced the job and food
shortages that confronted all working-class Americans but also received either a fraction of the government assistance provided Anglo-Americans or were denied assistance
altogether. In 1929, President Herbert Hoover authorized an Immigration Bureau crack-
down on undocumented Mexican aliens that became a mass deportation and removal
campaign that affected more than the undocumented. Targeting states with large Latino
populations, such as California, Texas, Colorado, Illinois, and Michigan, it affected citizens and legal permanent residents as well as unauthorized entrants. Those who were
deported or removed lost all of their personal property in the United States, including
homes, cars, and small businesses.[49]

Federal, state, and local officials also initiated a so-called "Repatriation Program" for
other Mexican immigrants. Mexican farmworkers and other immigrants legally residing in the US were offered free train tickets to Mexico. While some voluntarily accepted
the free transportation, others were coerced into returning to Mexico. According to

---

46   Aristide Zolberg, "Managing a World on the Move," *Population and Development Review* 32
(2006): 222–53.

47   J. P. Cotton, Acting Secretary of State, to Diplomatic and Consular Officers, September 15,
1930, Diplomatic Serial no. 992, Max Kohler Papers, Box 3, Folder "Department of State," American Jewish Historical Society, Waltham, MA.

48   William Green to All Organized Labor in Washington, AFL President Statement, August 21,
1930.

49   Tichenor, *Dividing Lines*, chap. 6.

Abraham Hoffman, in addition to the mass deportation campaign, "the actual move-ment of thousands of Mexican nationals was not due solely to federal motivations but was the result of a web of factors spun by acute unemployment, the threat of deportation, [and] the urging of welfare officials."[50] This Mexican removal campaign was accompa-nied by tough enforcement at the US-Mexican border where nearly all working-class immigrants were refused entry under the LPC clause. "We have passed in practically one year from a wide open Mexican border to a practically closed Mexican border." As a later presidential commission on migratory labor noted, "whereas in the twenties we absorbed a Mexican population of about a million, in the thirties we disgorged almost a half million people of Mexican origin."[51]

At the start of World War II, southwestern growers and other business interests, joined by their legislative champions, complained to executive branch officials that war-induced labor shortages necessitated a new Mexican temporary worker program. In re-sponse, an interagency committee was formed to facilitate the importation of Mexican guestworkers. In 1942, the State Department negotiated a special agreement with Mexico establishing the Bracero Program that Congress swiftly approved. Under the bilateral agreement, the US pledged that wages, living conditions, workplace safety, and medical services would be comparable to those of native workers. In turn, the Mexican govern-ment was to supervise the recruitment and contracting of *braceros*.[52] Once the Bracero Program began, neither employers nor federal administrators saw that the negotiated protections of Mexican laborers were honored. Mexican braceros routinely received much lower wages than native workers and endured substandard living and working conditions.

Contrary to the bilateral agreement, the Immigration and Naturalization Service (INS) permitted growers and other employers to directly recruit braceros at the border. If they resisted direct employer recruitment, one INS official recalled, "a good many mem-bers of Congress would be on the Service's neck."[53] The INS generally avoided search and deportation procedures against undocumented workers during harvest seasons because "it could likely result in a loss of crops." One Texas farm group explained enforcement norms to Senator Thomas Connally (D-TX) this way:

> For a number of years, citizens of Mexico entered the United States both legally and ille-gally, engaging in agricultural work. . . . While from time to time they have been picked up

50   Abraham Hoffman, *Unwanted Mexican Americans in the Great Depression: Repatriation Pres-sures, 1929–1939* (Tucson: University of Arizona Press, 1974).

51   *Ibid.;* Francisco Balderrama and Raymond Rodríguez, *Decade of Betrayal: Mexican Repatria-tion in the 1930s* (Albuquerque: University of New Mexico Press, 1995).

52   Arthur Altmeyer, Executive Director of the War Manpower Commission, to Claude Wickard, Secretary of Agriculture, Memo on Proposed Agreement for the Importation of Mexican Workers, July 29, 1942, Box 35, Folder 26 on Mexican Labor, AFL-CIO Department of Legislation Papers, George Meany Archives.

53   Kitty Calavita, *Inside the State: The Bracero Program, Immigration, and the INS* (New York: Routledge, 1992), 32–35.

by the Border Patrol, there has been a tendency on the part of the Border Patrol to concentrate their efforts on deporting only those who were bad . . . This arrangement, although it didn't have the stamp of legislative approval, has worked out very nicely for our farmers down here.[54]

At the same time, the Bracero Program endured for almost two decades after the war ended. Guarded by a "cozy triangle" of agribusinesses, southern and western congressional "committee barons," and a lax immigration bureaucracy, roughly 4.2 million Mexican workers were imported under the Bracero Program from 1942 to 1964. Unauthorized flows across the southern border also continued apace.

Mae Ngai's *Impossible Subjects* argues that the 1924 Johnson-Reed Act's sweeping restrictions "produced the illegal alien" as "an 'impossible subject,' a person who cannot be and a problem that cannot be solved."[55] This section provides evidence that neither undocumented immigrants—nor any other immigrant for that matter—represented an insoluble "problem" for the American migration state before the late twentieth century. From the Gilded Age to the Cold War, the move to restrict immigration quickly impelled the buildup of legal authority bureaucratic capacity to sort immigrants into different categories of belonging and "otherness." This section provides a glimpse into how this US migration state could act with blunt and ruthless effectiveness, while permitting the flow of migrant labor to appease powerful economic interests. The lurking power of the US migration state meant that undocumented immigrants and other unwanted noncitizens were "problems" that *could be* solved when officials and organized interests were sufficiently motivated.

Confronting the Liberal Paradox: Compromise and the Immigration and Nationality Act of 1965

In the decade that followed World War II, Presidents Harry Truman and Dwight Eisenhower were aggressive in challenging draconian immigration policies they saw as damaging to US geopolitical interests. Both administrations enjoyed some success in winning temporary refugee relief for European "displaced persons" and Hungarian insurgents, either taking independent executive action or gaining passage of modest refugee relief laws.[56] However, neither president was able to secure significant changes in federal immigration policies that explicitly favored northern and western Europeans. In fact, congressional defenders of immigration restriction gained passage of the McCarran-Walter Act of 1952 (over a Truman veto) that fortified the exclusionary national origins quota system begun in 1924 and established new bars based on ideology and sexual

---

54   Quoted in Calavita, *Inside the State*, 35.

55   Mae Ngai, *Impossible Subjects: Illegal Aliens and the Making of Modern America* (Princeton, NJ: Princeton University Press, 2004).

56   Harry S Truman, "State of the Union Address to Congress," January 6, 1947, *Public Papers of the Presidents of the United States: Harry S Truman* (Washington, DC: US Government Printing Office, 1953), 10; Gil Loescher and John Scanlan, *Calculated Kindness: Refugees and America's Half-Open Door, 1945 to Present* (New York: Free Press, 1986), 17–62.

preference.[57] "In no other realm of our national life," Truman lamented during his battle with congressional restrictionists, "are we so hampered and stultified by the dead hand of the past, as we are in this field of immigration."[58] Eisenhower fared no better during his two terms, lecturing Congress during his final year in office about the need to liberalize federal immigration laws.[59]

Perhaps no president was more closely identified with the cause of liberal immigration reform than John F. Kennedy. During his Senate tenure, Kennedy joined with pro-immigration colleagues like Philip Hart (D-MI) and Kenneth Keating (R-NY) in proposing unsuccessful bills to replace the McCarran-Walter Act.[60] His 1960 victory invigorated pro-immigration reformers. Despite their high expectations, however, Kennedy got nowhere on plans to alter US immigration law due to potent opposition from conservative Democrats like Senator James Eastland (D-MS) and Representative Frances Walter (D-PA), who controlled the immigration subcommittees of both houses. It was not until 1963, after Walter's death, that JFK proposed legislation to dismantle national origins quotas with a new preference system giving top priority to immigrant job skills and education.[61] The White House soon discovered that Walter's successor as chair of the House immigration subcommittee, Michael Feighan (D-OH), strongly opposed the administration's blueprints for reform.[62]

Some immigration scholars have argued that the nation's grief over Kennedy's assassination combined with Johnson's prowess as a legislative leader "meant the end of the quota system and its replacement by a preference system was virtually inevitable."[63] But few Washington insiders shared this conviction in the first stages of the Johnson administration.[64] Although LBJ famously insisted "there was not time to rest" in pursuit

57   Robert Divine, *American Immigration Policy, 1924–1954* (New York: Da Capo Press, 1972), 177–91; David Reimers, *Still the Golden Door: The Third World Comes to America* (New York: Columbia University Press, 1992), 54–56.

58   *Public Papers of the Presidents of the United States: Harry S Truman* (Washington, DC: US Government Printing Office, 1953), 443–44.

59   *Public Papers of the Presidents of the United States: Dwight D. Eisenhower* (Washington, DC: US Government Printing Office, 1961), 308–10.

60   John F. Kennedy to Lyndon B. Johnson, June 29, 1955, Senate Files, Pre-Presidential Papers of John F. Kennedy, John F. Kennedy Library, Boston, MA; author's interview with Meyer Feldman, December, 1994, Washington, DC.

61   Edward Kennedy, "The Immigration Act of 1965," *Annals of the American Academy of Political and Social Science* 367 (September 1966): 137–38.

62   Abba Schwartz to Theodore Sorenson, November 6, 1963, Theodore Sorenson Papers, Legislative Files, Folder "Legislation 1963, May 21–November 13, 1963," John F. Kennedy Library; Schwartz, *The Open Society*, 116.

63   See, for example, Michael LeMay, *From Open Door to Dutch Door* (New York: Praeger, 1987), 111.

64   Lawrence O'Brien Oral History Interview, September 18, 1985; Paul Douglas Oral History Interview, November 1, 1974, LBJ Library; author's interview with Meyer Feldman; author's interview with Jack Valenti, December 1994; Schwartz, *The Open Society*, 116–21.

of his Great Society agenda, it was unclear early on whether he wanted immigration reform to figure prominently on that agenda.[65] In fact, he was all too familiar with the legislative headaches that immigration reform posed by the time he became president, having been whipsawed by rivals on the issue for years in the Senate. Reporters noted that, as Senate majority leader in 1955, Johnson "exploded with invective" when pressed about holdups on progressive immigration reform.[66] He was well aware of the challenges of leading Senate Democrats who were deeply divided between conservatives opposed to any opening of the gates and liberals committed to dismantling national origins quotas.

When the Ohio Democrat Michael Feighan became chair of the House immigration subcommittee in 1963, he presented a political headache for Johnson and congressional Democratic leaders in their quest for major immigration reform. Backed by a bipartisan majority of subcommittee members, Feighan introduced his own bill, a substitute for the Johnson proposal, in August of 1964.[67] As his staffers put it, the substitute bill was designed "to avoid charges of inaction by the Subcommittee" which "would have opened the door to ramming through the Administration bill."[68] Feighan's bill promised to "preserve the national origins quota formula," to give a preference to immigrants with family ties under the quotas, to maintain exclusions for ideology and sexual preference, and to guarantee that "the principle of the Asia-Pacific Triangle remains as is."[69] Whereas the Johnson administration worked its magic to neutralize a normally obstreperous James Eastland, deft resistance mounted by Feighan and his nativist allies ensured that no action would be taken on the Kennedy-Johnson bill until after the 1964 election.

The Johnson team began its renewed 1965 push for the Immigration and Nationality Act (INA) in the House, where seventy-seven-year-old Emanuel Celler, the longtime champion of immigration reform, introduced the administration's bill as H.R. 2580. Yet an important barrier stood in the way. Celler, as chair of the House Judiciary Committee, was locked in an epic feud with Feighan, who still chaired the committee's Subcommittee on Immigration and Nationality. Celler initially sought to have Feighan removed from the subcommittee, but he soon discovered that the subcommittee majority sided with their defiant chair. As Kentucky Democrat Frank Chelf explained, "I have been on this subcommittee now some eighteen years. I have always been a rather strong believer

---

65   William Leuchtenberg, *In the Shadow of FDR* (Ithaca, NY: Cornell University Press, 1985), 132; Lyndon Johnson, *The Vantage Point* (New York: Holt, Rinehart, and Winston, 1971), 161.

66   Robert Dallek, *Lone Star Rising* (New York: Oxford University Press,1992), 485.

67   John P. Leacacos, "Feighan Argues Merits of His Immigration Bill," *Cleveland Plain Dealer*, August 13, 1964; John P. Leacacos, "Feighan Upsets Administration," *Cleveland Plain Dealer*, August 12, 1964, Press clippings file, Michael Feighan Papers, Seely Mudd Manuscript Library, Princeton University, Box 5.

68   "Points to Be Covered in Brief" memo, August 13, 1964, Feighan Papers, Box 5, Folder "Immigration."

69   "Highlights of Proposed Congressional Action," staff memorandum, no date, Feighan Papers, Box 5.

in the national-origins theory."[70] When Celler scolded Feighan publicly for perpetuating policies that unfairly discriminated against would-be immigrants and kept out desperate refugees, Feighan retorted, "How about giving the welfare of the American people first priority for a change?"[71] For two months, Feighan dominated hearings on H.R. 2580, peppering administration officials with questions about a new merit-based preference system and its potential impact on the number and diversity of newcomers. According to Johnson's chief liaison to Congress, Lawrence O'Brien, "he had his own views and he was going to be disruptive procedurally to accomplish his objectives." O'Brien added that "there's nothing worse than to have a subcommittee chairman . . . get his nose out of joint."[72]

Frustrated by Feighan's roadblocks, LBJ and House Democratic leaders successfully maneuvered in the spring of 1965 to expand the immigration subcommittee to add Johnson loyalists like Jack Brooks (D-TX) as crucial swing votes. Despite this tactical blow, Feighan privately told anti-immigrant lobbyists that he enjoyed enough bipartisan backing to seriously limit radical policy change. "There is no need for you to be worried about developments because there is no possibility of the opposition here opening 'pandora's box'" and dramatically expanding immigration opportunities, he reassured anxious nativists.[73] Yet Feighan also understood that Johnson and reformers now had enough political momentum to overcome delaying tactics. It was time, he concluded, for supporters of the national origins quota system and McCarran-Walter restrictions to try to influence inevitable legislation. "My greatest concern is that the people who advocate the 'sitting duck' approach to national issues will open the 'box.'"[74] Reporters noted at the time that new political realities—"the pro-administration majorities and a genuine Presidential push"—persuaded opponents of reform that their best strategy was to shape a compromise plan.

In the end, Feighan and his allies agreed to abolish national origins quotas and the so-called Asiatic Barred Zone in exchange for a significant alteration in the administration's proposed preference system for immigrant admissions. The Kennedy-Johnson blueprints for reform consistently envisioned replacing national origins quotas with high-skilled immigration. "At present, [the national origins system] prevents talented people from applying for visas to enter the United States," Kennedy observed in 1963. "It often deprives us of immigrants who would be helpful to our economy and our culture." Legal preferences, he argued, "should be liberalized so that highly trained or

---

70   Paul Duke and Stanley Meisler, "Immigration: Quotas vs. Quality," *The Reporter* 32, no. 1 (January 14, 1965), 30–32.

71   "Celler—Calling for Hold-Up," staff memorandum, September 22, 1964, Feighan Papers, Box 5.

72   O'Brien Oral History Interview, LBJ Library.

73   Jean Kerbs to Michael Feighan, Western Union telegram, no date; and Feighan to Kerbs, letter, no date, Feighan Papers, Box 5, Folder "Immigration."

74   Jean Kerbs to Michael Feighan, Western Union telegram, no date; and Feighan to Kerbs, letter, no date, Feighan Papers, Box 5, Folder "Immigration."

skilled persons may obtain a preference without requiring that they secure employment here before emigrating."[75] Immigrant merit and skills were to trump discriminatory restrictions based on race, ethnicity, religion, or nationality. In May 1965, however, Feighan proposed a compromise with the White House that profoundly altered these plans to make family reunification, rather than occupational skills and education, the centerpiece of a new preference system for immigrant admissions. Feighan was convinced (incorrectly, as he later discovered) that reserving most visas for immigrants with family ties to US citizens and legal permanent residents would decidedly favor European applicants and thus maintain the nation's ethnic and racial makeup.[76] Feighan and other House opponents of the Hart-Celler bill agreed to dismantle the national origins quota system and the so-called Asiatic Barred Zone. However, in exchange Johnson would have to sacrifice the administration's emphasis on individual merit. Convinced that family-based immigration was far preferable to discriminatory national origins quotas, the White House eventually acceded to Feighan's demand to make immigrant skills, education, and professional occupations far less important than family ties.[77]

The administration bill's new legal preference system established four preference categories for family reunification, which were to receive nearly three-quarters of total annual visas. Spouses, minor children, and parents of US citizens over the age of twenty-one were granted admission without visa limits. Two preferences were established for economic goals, including a preference not to exceed 10 percent of the annual visas for "qualified immigrants who are members of the professions, or who because of their exceptional ability in the sciences or the arts will substantially benefit prospectively the national economy, cultural interests, or welfare of the United States." The revised bill left a quarter of annual visas for economic-based admissions and refugee relief.[78] This revised preference system was well received by conservative Democrats in the Senate, most of whom opposed Johnson's original immigration proposal.

The compromise plan's emphasis on family-based immigration even reassured Senator Strom Thurmond of South Carolina, who switched to the Republican Party in 1964 and vigorously opposed a new merit-based admissions process that he believed would trigger seismic shifts in the volume and composition of US immigration. "The preference which would be established by this proposal are based," Thurmond told colleagues and constituents, "on sound reasoning and meritorious considerations, not entirely dissimilar in effect from those which underlie the national origins quotas of existing law."[79] In other words, as the Japanese American Citizens League and other Asian groups

---

75 *Congressional Record*, July 23, 1963, pp. 13132–33.

76 Carl Bon Tempo, *Americans at the Gate: The United States and Refugees during the Cold War* (Princeton, NJ: Princeton University Press, 2008), 92–94.

77 Reimers, *Still the Golden Door*, 69–74.

78 William S. Stern, "H.R. 2580: The Immigration and Nationality Amendments of 1965—A Case Study," PhD diss., New York University, 1974.

79 *Congressional Record*, September 17, 1965, p. 24237.

protested, the new system was designed to perpetuate racial biases codified in federal immigration law for generations:

> Inasmuch as the total Asian population of the United States is only about one half of 1 percent of the total American population, this means that there are very few of Asia-Pacific origin in this country who are entitled to provide the specific preference priorities to family members and close relatives residing abroad. . . . Thus, it would seem that, although the immigration bill eliminated race as a matter of principle, in actual operation immigration will still be controlled by the now discredited national origins system and the general pattern of immigration which exists today will continue for many years yet to come.[80]

Along with the legal preference system, the "non-quota status" of Mexican immigration in particular and Latin American admissions in general were a prominent concern for restrictionists in both houses of Congress during the legislative wrangling of 1965. In the House, Feighan pointed out that no numerical limitations were placed on Western Hemisphere immigration in the 1920s because the numbers were so small; in 1965, he warned colleagues that Latin American entries "has shown a steady increase each year" and that demographic research indicated that the Latin American population was sure to grow "from some 69 millions to some 600 millions."[81] In negotiations with Feighan and other House stalwarts, however, Johnson was unwilling to budge on this issue. The notion of cap on Western Hemisphere immigration was adamantly denounced by Secretary of State Dean Rusk and other foreign policy advisers, who argued that taking such a step would be a huge setback to relations with Central and South American countries. Indeed, Rusk warned the president that such a measure would alienate Latin American nations already outraged by Johnson's decision to send US troops into the Dominican Republic on April 28, 1965. "We will vex and dumbfound our Latin American friends," Rusk told key White House advisers, "who will now be sure we are in final retreat from Pan Americanism."[82]

The administration's stand on Western Hemisphere immigration came under withering attack in the Senate, however. In particular, southern Democrats led by Sam Ervin, Jr. (NC) threatened to block action on S. 500 in the Senate immigration subcommittee unless concessions were made. Public opinion also presented a challenge for liberal immigration reformers. Consistent with other surveys, a June 1965 Gallup poll found that only 7 percent of respondents favored increasing immigration opportunities, while 72 percent preferred decreased or unchanged immigration levels.[83] Facing a major logjam and

---

80　Reimers, *Still the Golden Door*, 73; *Congressional Record*, September 20, 1965, p. 24503; Robert Goldfarb, "Occupational Preferences in US Immigration Law," in *The Gateway: Issues in American Immigration*, ed. Barry Chiswick, 412–48 (Washington, DC: American Enterprise Institute).

81　Michael Feighan, "Highlights of the Immigration Issue," January 18, 1965, copy on file with the author.

82　Irving Bernstein, *Guns or Butter: The Presidency of Lyndon Johnson* (New York: Oxford University Press, 1996), 256.

83　Carl Bon Tempo, *Americans at the Gate: The United States and Refugees during the Cold War* (Princeton, NJ: Princeton University Press, 2008), 92–94.

eager to convince the public that his reform plan was not "a revolutionary bill," Johnson and pro-immigration lawmakers compromised with Ervin and his restriction-minded colleagues on an annual ceiling for Western Hemisphere immigration. As O'Brien explained, "Listen, we're not going to walk away from this because we didn't get a whole loaf. We'll take half a loaf or three-quarters of a loaf."[84]

Buoyed by compromises on the admissions preference system and a new ceiling on Western Hemisphere immigration, the Immigration and Nationality Act of 1965 passed both houses with large bipartisan majorities. The new immigration system provided 170,000 visas for immigrants originating in the Eastern Hemisphere (no country was to be allotted more than 20,000 visas), and 120,000 visas for Western Hemisphere immigrants (no per-country limits). Spouses, minor children, and parents of American citizens were exempted from these numerical ceilings. All other persons from the Eastern Hemisphere were placed on waiting lists under seven preferences: four preference categories and 74 percent of visas were reserved for family reunification, two preference categories and 20 percent for needed professionals and unskilled workers, and one preference category and 6 percent of visas for refugees.[85] It is revealing that in the end, Johnson's success in winning passage of the Immigration and Nationality Act depended significantly upon painful compromises, including cross-cutting reform packages that both expanded and restricted immigration opportunities in new ways.

The Long and Winding Road: Strange Bedfellows and the Immigration Reform and Control Act of 1986

After the 1960 election, the American Federation of Labor-Congress of Industrial Organizations (AFL-CIO) lobbied hard for the Bracero Program's termination. The Kennedy administration and Democratic leadership in Congress lent their support to the effort. Yet growers and other business interests exerted considerable pressure of their own on members of Congress. The American Farm Bureau Federation, the National Cotton Council, the United Fresh Fruit and Vegetable Association, the National Beet Growers, ranchers, and other business interests rallied to save the Bracero Program. In 1961, these pressure groups won a two-year extension of the program but failed to win reauthorization in 1963 despite vigorous lobbying. Sweeping immigration reform in 1965 dismantled national origins quota in favor of a new preference system that emphasized family-based immigration, but it also placed a 120,000 annual ceiling on Western Hemisphere visas.[86] Reformers did not anticipate that this new ceiling and the end of the Bracero Program would swell unauthorized Mexican inflows.

The issue of illegal immigration inspired more media attention, public concern, and remedial proposals by policy-makers than did any other migratory issue of the 1970s. The dramatic rise in apprehensions and deportations of unauthorized migrants was

---

84 O'Brien Oral History Interview, LBJ Library; Tichenor, *Dividing Lines*, 215.

85 Lyndon Johnson, "Remarks on the Immigration Law," *Congressional Quarterly* (October 1965), 2063–64.

86 Author's interview with Rep. Henry B. Gonzalez, March, 1996; Calavita, *Inside the State*, 163–69.

unmistakable and troubling to decision-makers. Strikingly, it was liberal Democrats who led the assault on illegal immigration. At Senate hearings on the problem in 1969, Senator Walter Mondale (D-MN) warned that if the federal government did not "stop that hemorrhaging . . . along the Texas border and along the California border," labor protections and antipoverty programs would be compromised.[87] A year earlier, Cesar Chavez and his Farm Workers Association (FWA) desperately urged Senator Robert Kennedy (D-NY) to pressure INS officials "to remove Wetbacks . . . who are being recruited to break our strike."[88] In 1971, Representative Peter Rodino (D-NJ), chair of the House Judiciary Committee's Subcommittee on Immigration, led pro-labor liberals in the pursuit of employer sanctions legislation to resolve the perceived illegal immigration crisis.[89] Rodino's employer sanctions legislation initially passed the House in 1972 but languished in the Senate where Eastland refused to allow the Judiciary Committee he chaired to take action.[90] When Rodino reintroduced his bill a year later, new resistance emerged in the House from fellow Democrats who warned that the measure would lead to job discrimination against Latinos, Asians, and anyone who looked or sounded foreign.[91]

Amidst the legislative impasse, President Gerald Ford established a Domestic Council Committee on Illegal Immigration, which urged in 1976 that the administration "aggressively pursue legislation [imposing] penalties for employers who knowingly hire aliens not authorized to work."[92] Its report observed that little reliable, "quantified" evidence existed regarding the size of the unauthorized population or its impact on American society. But in explaining why illegal immigration must be discouraged, it appealed to values beyond traditional economic and cultural anxieties. Indeed, it placed special emphasis on the rule of law and equal rights: "People who are underground . . . cannot be protected from abuse on the job or from landlords, discrimination, disease, or crime; they may avoid education for children, and they are unable or reluctant to assert political or legal rights."[93] This was not the familiar assault on undocumented immigration who take American jobs, consume public benefits, and promote crime and disease. Unauthorized immigration's dangers lay not only with its disregard for the rule of law, its fiscal burdens, or its economic impact on poor citizens, but also with its propensity to create "a substantial underclass" anathema to post-1960s notions of nondiscrimination

---

87 Reimers, *Still the Golden Door*, 202.

88 Cesar Chavez to Robert F. Kennedy, Western Union telegram, August 11, 1968, Robert F. Kennedy Papers, Container #71, Senate Legislative Subject Files, John F. Kennedy Presidential Library.

89 Andrew Biemiller to Peter Rodino, September 8, 1972; Biemiller to Rodino, March 23, 1973; Rodino to Biemiller, May 15, 1973, Papers of the Legislation Department of the AFL-CIO, Box 71, Folder 28, George Meany Archives.

90 See, for example, *New York Times*, December 31, 1974.

91 *Congressional Record*, September 12, 1972, pp. 30164, 30182–83; National Council of La Raza documents made available to the author by the national office of the NCLR.

92 Preliminary Report of the Domestic Council Committee on Illegal Immigration, December, 1976, p. 241.

93 Ibid., 212–14.

and equal rights. The report also cautioned against a vigorous internal enforcement campaigns that targeted the unauthorized population for removal. "Mass deportation is both inhumane and impractical," the Domestic Council concluded. Ford's INS director, Leonard Chapman, reiterated this view when he warned Congress that mass deportation campaigns might require "police state" tactics "abhorrent to the American conscience."[94] It remained silent, however, on how policy-makers should deal with the large number of undocumented aliens residing in the country.

In 1977, the Carter White House wasted little time in proposing a comprehensive plan for addressing illegal immigration. The reform package included: stiff civil and criminal penalties on those who engaged in a "pattern or practice" of hiring undocumented aliens; use of the Social Security card as an identification document for verifying employee eligibility; enhanced Border Patrol forces at the Mexican border; and an amnesty program that would confer legal resident alien status on all aliens living in the country before 1970.[95] The White House proposal galvanized opposition from growers and other free market expansionists as unfair to employers, from the National Council of La Raza, the Mexican-American Legal Defense and Education Fund (MALDEF), and various cosmopolitans as detrimental to civil rights, and from law-and-order conservatives and classic restrictionists as rewarding law-breakers with amnesty.[96] With immigration reform mired in conflict, a bipartisan Select Commission on Immigration and Refugee Policy (SCIRP) was formed for the purpose of studying the controversial illegal immigration problem and all other facets of US immigration and refugee policy and issuing recommendations for future reform.

The SCIRP completed a sweeping final report in 1981 that portrayed "lawful immigration" as "a positive force in American life," serving the national interest in terms of economic growth and productivity, reuniting families, and advancing key foreign policy imperatives.[97] But it also concluded that illegal immigration was an urgent problem that needed to be controlled before legal immigration could be expanded. The SCIRP noted that unauthorized entries created a vulnerable shadow population that had few incentives to report crimes, health problems, or exploitation by employers.[98] It also asserted that unrestrained illegal immigration encouraged a perilous disregard for the rule of law: "illegality erodes confidence in the law generally, and immigration law specifically."[99]

---

94 "Illegal Aliens," Hearings before the Subcommittee on Immigration, Citizenship, and International Law of the Committee on the Judiciary, February 4, 26, 1975, House of Representatives, 94th Cong., 1st Sess., pp. 34–35.

95 White House Statement, August 4, 1977, Patricia Roberts Harris Papers.

96 "Memorandum to Interested Parties from the Mexican-American Legal Defense and Education Fund: Statement of Position Regarding the Administration's Undocumented Alien Legislation Proposal," November 11, 1977, Papers of the Leadership Conference on Civil Rights, Container 23, Folder "Issues: Alien Civil Rights."

97 Transcript of SCIRP meeting, May 7, 1980, p. 34, Record Group 240, Box 26, National Archives.

98 Lawrence Fuchs, American Kaleidoscope (Hanover, NH: University Press of New England, 1990), 252.

99 Transcript of SCIRP meeting, p. 34.

To address the problem, the SCIRP endorsed the familiar scheme of enhanced Border Patrol resources and employer sanctions. But it also underscored the notion that the efficacy of sanctions hinged upon faithful enforcement and the development of a tamper-resistant national identification card as the linchpin of a security and universal system of employee eligibility. All sixteen commissioners also agreed on a generous legalization program for undocumented aliens already residing in the country.[100]

Two young lawmakers—Senator Alan Simpson (R-WY), who served on the SCIRP, and Representative Romano Mazzoli, a moderate Kentucky Democrat with ties to the SCIRP chair Father Theodore Hesburgh—took the lead in pressing for immigration reform. Early in 1982, the pair introduced omnibus legislation on illegal and legal immigration. The measure met fierce resistance from a broad coalition of business interests (the US Chamber of Commerce, National Association of Manufacturers, agribusinesses, the Business Roundtable), ethnic and civil rights groups such as NCLR and MALDEF, the ACLU, religious lobbies, and a new immigrant rights organization, the National Immigration Forum. Left-Right opposition to the Simpson-Mazzoli initiative was reflected in the resistance of both the Reagan administration, which saw employer sanctions and national identification cards working at cross-purposes with its regulatory relief agenda, and House Democrats led by the Hispanic Caucus, which raised familiar concerns about discriminatory impacts of sanctions and other provisions. Gridlock was overcome only after three more years of wrangling, and the resulting Immigration Reform and Control Act of 1986 (IRCA) depended upon a compromise package of watered-down employer sanctions provisions, legalization for undocumented aliens living in the country since 1982, and a new Seasonal Agricultural Worker program to appease grower interests.

The measure proved highly successful in granting legal status to nearly three million undocumented aliens, but employer sanctions proved to be a "toothless tiger." This was largely by design: In the absence of a reliable identification system for verifying employee eligibility that the SCIRP described as a linchpin for effective enforcement, the employer sanctions provisions lacked teeth. By the late 1980s, it was clear to national policymakers that the IRCA had done virtually nothing to discourage illegal immigration. But legislators were eager to shift their attention to the politically painless task of expanding legal immigration. The Immigration Act of 1990 unified cosmopolitans and free market expansionists behind a 40 percent increase in annual visa allocations that benefited both family-based and employment-based immigration.[101] The "grand bargains" of the 1980s, like their forbears, left key dilemmas posed by unauthorized immigration for future Congresses to resolve.

Soon after passage of the IRCA, an underground industry of fraudulent documents flourished in both Mexico and the US, enabling unauthorized migrants to obtain work with ease. But if the legislative design of employer sanctions discouraged their efficacy, the Reagan administration was less than zealous in their enforcement. The INS tended to enforce employer sanctions with considerable forbearance toward offenders. Alan

---

100   *New York Times,* August 24, 1981.

101   The arduous path to the Simpson-Mazzoli legislation in 1986 is discussed in depth in Tichenor, *Dividing Lines,* chap. 9.

Nelson, the INS commissioner under Reagan, was urged to pursue a policy of "least employer resistance" by stressing business education over penalties.[102] The IRCA authorized a 70 percent increase in the INS budget, with an annual $100 million targeted for employer sanctions enforcement. Tellingly, $34 million was spent on enforcing sanctions in fiscal year 1987, $59 million in fiscal year 1988, and below $30 million annually in ensuing years.[103]

From his perch on the Senate immigration subcommittee, Senator Simpson pressed the Reagan and Bush administrations to take a harder line on employer sanctions. Yet despite his clout as Republican minority whip, Simpson made little headway during either Republican presidency. "Even when we direct the Administration to do such things as 'study' the employer sanctions verification system and develop a more secure system, if necessary, we get no action," he lamented.[104] Few of Simpson's congressional colleagues shared his disquietude over the inefficacy or uneven enforcement of employer sanctions. In fact, the most vigorous oversight of sanctions focused on whether they should be repealed because they unfavorably burdened small businesses (led by Orrin Hatch) or because they engendered increased job discrimination against legal aliens or citizens who look or sound foreign (led by Edward Kennedy). Few conservative politicians of the 1980s, most of whom embraced "regulatory relief" and free markets, or their liberal counterparts, dedicated to universal rights and inclusion, worried about the efficacy of employer sanctions.

Although many Americans have made pro-immigration narratives central to US nationhood, race-based nativism has proven to be a persistent feature of national politics and policy over time. As we have seen, starting in the Gilded Age, the US national state developed a will and capacity to systematically exclude, marginalize, and remove immigrants on the basis of race and ethnicity. That is, xenophobic nativism and exclusionary capacities of the US state have proven as durable over time as liberal demands for immigrant labor and cosmopolitan devotion to universal human rights.

Focusing on long-term historical patterns and transformations, this chapter has trained a spotlight on two key developments related to *the migration state* and *the liberal paradox* in the US over time. The first is that as much as "the carceral state" and "the national security state," the US government's capacities to restrict the entry and rights of immigrants have grown significantly for more than a century. Indeed, the *American migration state* that emerged slowly in the nineteenth century eventually demonstrated significant capacities to control and limit immigration when pressed into service from Chinese exclusion to "Operation Wetback." Through the rise of a visa and consular

---

102   Author's anonymous interviews with Reagan administration officials, 1996; see also US Commission on Immigration Reform, *US Immigration Policy: Restoring Credibility* (Washington, DC: US Government Printing Office, 1994), 95.

103   Ibid.

104   Alan Simpson to Lawrence Fuchs, January 24, 1991, Correspondence Files of Lawrence Fuchs, made available to the author by Fuchs.

examination process, it also established remote control of the inspection process to stringently limited overseas immigration. At the same time, demand for cheap, "returnable"
migrant labor often kept the nation's borders porous, spurred a large-scale guest-worker
program, and allowed for refugee admissions when it served geopolitical interests during the Cold War. Nevertheless, along with an unprecedented militarization of the US
southern border during the past quarter-century, the American migration state in recent
years has deported record levels of immigrants and annually confined approximately
400,000 people awaiting deportation or asylum in detention centers.

A second key development underscored in this chapter is that *the liberal paradox*
pitting economic demands for openness against legal and political pressures for closure
yielded rival and incongruous elements that have become woven into US immigration
reform and policy implementation over time. Durable conflicts between cosmopolitans
versus economic protectionists on the left, and between pro-business expansionists versus cultural protectionists and border hawks on the right, have made comprehensive
immigration reform maddeningly elusive. They also typically have made major policy
innovation contingent upon building fleeting "strange bedfellow" alliances that are unstable and that demand difficult compromises addressing rival goals and interests. This
has meant that even some of the most restrictive immigration laws in American history
have included bargains that create openings for international migration, and that expansive reforms have featured restrictive elements. As this essay has chronicled and table 9.1
captures, these cross-cutting dynamics have shaped major policy breakthroughs, from
the National Origins Quota laws of 1924 and 1928 to the Immigration and Nationality Act (INA, or Hart-Celler Act) of 1965 to the Immigration Reform and Control Act
(IRCA) of 1986.

The enduring power of nativist and restrictionist traditions in American politics
and policy are unmistakable not only in the draconian actions advanced by the Trump
administration in its first three years (such as a targeted refugee ban, ending DACA,
family separation and child detention, and income-based assaults on legal immigration
and naturalization) but also in the swift and sweeping changes it initiated in response
to the COVID-19 pandemic. Early on, the Trump White House suspended refugee resettlement and invoked a 1944 public health law to bypass established protocols to block
entry of people seeking asylum at national borders, and later issued a more sweeping
regulation barring asylees in response to the coronavirus. These actions are consistent
with the administration's resistance to providing relief to refugees and asylees, having
already decreased the annual cap from 110,000 in the last year of the Obama administration to 18,000 in 2020. Trump officials also halted green cards for most of those seeking to legally immigrate to the United States, and then denied visas to tens of thousands
of temporary workers. Trump's Department of Homeland Security announced that it
would deport all foreign students attending universities only offering online courses
for safe distancing, only to change course a few days later under intense criticism from
higher-education leaders. The Trump administration also has streamlined the deportation process during the pandemic, threatened sanctions on countries that do not accept deported migrants, and rebuffed calls to release immigrant families from detention
centers where COVID-19 infection rates exploded. All told, the coronavirus pandemic
enabled Trump officials to impose significant new restrictions on immigrants, refugees,

Table 9.1. Immigration reform and its implementation: Restrictions and openings.

	Restrictions	Openings
National Origins Quota Laws of 1924 and 1928	National origins quota system	Unrestricted Western Hemisphere immigration
	Asiatic Barred Zone	Mexican labor ecruitment
	Strong, exclusionary overseas inspection system	Weak, underfunded system of border control
Hart-Celler Act of 1965	Imposed new limits on Western Hemisphere immigration	Dismantled national origins quota system
		Raised the legal immigration ceiling
	Family reunification visas expected to benefit primarily European immigrants and to keep Asian immigration lower	Established New Legal Preference System (with most visas reserved for family reunification, and skills second)
Immigration Reform and Control Act of 1986	Strengthened Border Patrol; enhanced the militarization of the U.S.-Mexico border	Amnesty Program
		SAW (Special Agricultural Worker) and RAW (Replenishment Agricultural Worker) Programs
	Employer sanctions	
	Frank antidiscrimination amendment unenforced	Employer sanctions was a toothless tiger in design and implementation
		Frank amendment: Legalization program for most undocumented immigrants

Source: Census Bureau, Statistical Abstract (Washington, DC: US Government Printing Office, 1924).

asylum seekers, and foreign workers, many of which they failed to launch before the public health crisis.[105]

The US migration state, both in its historical development and its contemporary character, is as much defined by nativist traditions of ethnic, racial, and religious bias as by more inclusive and cosmopolitan traditions. This conclusion, underscored by evidence throughout this chapter, raises important questions for scholars who have asserted that Western industrial democracies in the Cold War era made a definitive "turn from an ethnoracial to a universalistic immigration policy."[106] "A liberal norm of racial nondiscrimination . . . accounts for the turn to universalistic policies in the United States," Christian Joppke notes. "This was a general turn, not specific to the United States but

---

105 Candice Norwood, "Trump Restricts Immigration amid the Pandemic," *National Public Radio,* July 28, 2020; Catherine Shoichet and Priscilla Alvarez, "How Trump Is Using the Pandemic to Crack Down on Immigration," *CNN,* July 14, 2020; Leila Seidman, "How Trump's Coronavirus Orders Affect Visas and Green Cards," *Los Angeles Times,* July 23, 2020; Alisa Reznick, "'You Can Either Be a Survivor or Die': COVID-19 Cases Surge in ICE Detention," *National Public Radio,* July 1, 2020.

106 Christian Joppke, *Selecting by Origin* (Cambridge, MA: Harvard University Press, 2005), 91. See also Fuchs, *American Kaleidoscope;* Matthew Frey Jacobsen, *Whiteness of a Different Color: European Immigrants and the Alchemy of Race* (Cambridge, MA: Harvard University Press, 1999).

commanded by the exigencies of liberal stateness as such."[107] However, given the propensity of competing camps—and *rival state actors*—in American politics to employ different liberal arguments to advance or oppose various policy goals, it is unclear how *liberal stateness* in fact *commands* particular policy outcomes. The resilience of race-based nativism and the sustained marginalization of key immigrant groups in the US underscore what Ira Katznelson calls "liberalism's crooked circle" or what Rogers Smith described as the "relative reversibility" of racial justice reforms securing in the 1960s.[108] Indeed, as we have seen, the American migration state that developed from the late nineteenth century through the Cold War was torn between demands for tractable labor and the exclusion and subjugation of particular immigrant groups. The immigration policy regime that emerged reflects a contrasting set of restrictions and openings, the product of political fissures that continue to polarize the American polity.

107   Joppke, *Selecting by Origin*, 91.
108   Ira Katznelson, *Liberalism's Crooked Circle* (Princeton, NJ: Princeton University Press, 1996);
Rogers Smith, *Civic Ideals* (New Haven, CT: Yale University Press, 1997).

10 WHO BELONGS?

Politics of Immigration, Nativism, and Illiberal Democracy in Postwar America

Neil Foley

MANY AMERICANS TODAY LIVE with a sense of cognitive dissonance about who they are as a nation. The United States, unlike most European nations, claims to be a nation of immigrants, yet it also tries to keep out the many immigrants, refugees, and asylum seekers it deems undesirable. It welcomes immigrants when their labor is needed and turns them away when it is not. But this bipolar economic view of immigration over the last century fails to account for the interlaced politics of citizenship, immigrant exclusion, and unremitting nativism that lies at the very heart of American national identity, which is the subject of this chapter. Culture and demography, more than economic and political developments, best explain the rapid growth of reactionary nationalist parties in Europe and xenophobic nativists in the US in the twenty-first century.

It is important to understand that "nativism" (a term rarely used in Europe) has a particular purchase in the history of the US. The *Oxford English Dictionary* defines nativism as "the attitude, practice or policy of protecting the interests of the native-born . . . against those of immigrants." This definition aptly describes the xenophobia (and racism) of nationalist and far-right parties in Europe opposed to nonnative migrants from non-European countries. But this definition is only partially accurate in the case of the United States, where native-born descendants of migrants from Europe have historically excluded from citizenship native-born Blacks (enslaved or free), Asians, Caribbean islanders, Latin Americans, and of course Native peoples of North America. Moreover, the majority of enslaved Americans, Native Americans, and Mexicans residing in the territory ceded to the US after the US-Mexico War in 1848 were not immigrants. Northern Mexico (the US Southwest) was their homeland. Nativism in the US is thus more than simply an "attitude" toward immigrants to protect the rights of the native born. As historian John Higham adroitly pointed out, nativism embodies an "intense opposition to an *internal minority* on the ground of its foreignness (i.e. un-American) connections," such as Irish Catholics. As with attitudes toward Islam in the West today, Anglo Protestants viewed Catholicism as an alien faith with no place in American civilization, a conviction that gave rise to the American Party ("Know-Nothings") in the 1850s and resulted in the moniker "nativist," shorthand for Anglo-American nationalists.[1] Predominantly white and Protestant, nativists embraced an ideology of European-descent superiority that predated the nation's founding by over a century, rendering all nonwhite, non-Christian peoples quintessentially un-American and culturally foreign.[2]

Nativism also does not simply ebb and flow throughout US history, like various ethno-nationalist awakenings, nor does it occur in cycles like immigration restriction politics and laws, such as the 1798 Alien and Sedition Acts, the "Know-Nothings" of 1850s, Chinese Exclusion in the 1880s, the race-based National Origins Quota Act of 1924, and more recently, President Donald Trump's immigration and refugee restriction policies, including the "Muslim ban" that restricted travel to the US from immigrants from Muslim-majority nations. Rather, nativism has been part of the nation's DNA from the start, its source code, which operates as a necessary mechanism for policing the boundaries of who belongs and who does not. Even as the nation has become less Protestant and "Anglo-Saxon" over the last century and more multicultural than ever in the post–World War II era, many Americans want to ensure that the United States remains a nation of predominantly European-descent whites.[3]

The rise of nativism in the US is primarily a response to unprecedented demographic changes in the last fifty years as a result of immigration (and declining white birth rates), causing many white Americans to fear the loss of "their" country.[4] Already less than

---

1   John Higham, *Strangers in the Land: Patterns of American Nativism* (1955; repr. New Brunswick, NJ: Rutgers University Press, 2008), 4 (quote); emphasis added.

2   The literature on the pervasiveness of white supremacist ideas among the nation's founders is extensive, but see Ibram I. Kendi, *Stamped from the Beginning: The Definitive History of Racist Ideas in America* (New York: Nations Books, 2016); Robert G. Parkinson, *The Common Cause: Creating Race and Nation in the American Revolution* (Chapel Hill: University of North Carolina Press, 2016); Nicolas Guyatt, *Bind Us Apart: How Enlightened Americans Invented Racial Segregation* (New York: Basic Books, 2016); Nell Irvin Painter, *The History of White People* (New York: W.W. Norton, 2010).

3   See, for example, David Neiwert, *Alt-America: The Rise of the Radical Right in the Age of Trump* (London: Verso, 2017); Kathleen Belew, *Bring the War Home: The White Power Movement and Paramilitary America* (Cambridge, MA: Harvard University Press, 2018). On the rise of ethno-nationalism in Europe, see Sasha Polakow-Suransky, *Go Back to Where You Came From: The Backlash against Immigration and the Fate of Western Democracy* (New York: Nation Books, 2017); Gabriella Lazaridis, Giovanna Campani, and Annie Benveniste, eds., *The Rise of the Far Right in Europe: Populist Shifts and "Othering"* (London: Palgrave Macmillan; 2016); Elizabeth Fekete, *Europe's Fault Lines: Racism and the Rise of the Right* (London: Verso, 2018).

4   The literature on immigration is vast, but see Aristide R. Zolberg, *A Nation by Design: Immigration Policy in the Fashioning of America* (New York: Russell Sage Foundation, 2008); Daniel J. Tichenor, *The Politics of Immigration Control in America* (Princeton, NJ: Princeton University Press, 2002); Susan F. Martin, *A Nation of Immigrants* (Cambridge: Cambridge University Press, 2011). Rogers Smith and Desmond King suggest that Donald Trump's bigoted campaign rhetoric and racial policies represent a "vision of white protectionism" rather than "white nationalism."

half of children in the US under age fifteen are white. For President Trump's supporters, "making America great again" had less to do with restoring America's prestige abroad than making "America first" nationalism central to American national identity. Since the 1990s the media has made most Americans acutely aware that ethno-racial minorities will outnumber whites by midcentury, if not before, when Latinos, Blacks, and Asians will form the majority of the US population. They already outnumber whites in San Diego, San Francisco, Los Angeles, and San Jose in California; Washington DC, New York City, Miami, Houston, Memphis, and Las Vegas. And they are the majority in four states—California, Texas, New Mexico, and Hawai'i, as well as the District of Columbia. Immigration, and more recently declining white birth rates, have been the driving force behind the demographic changes of the last fifty years, especially immigration from Mexico and more recently Central America, the Caribbean, Asia, and Africa, as well as the growing number of refugees and asylum seekers from Africa, the Middle East, and South Asia. This demographic conquest over the last half century began in the decades after the enactment of the Immigration and Nationality Act of 1965 (also known as the Hart-Celler Act). At the time Latinos constituted only 4 percent of the total population, or less than one-third the population of African Americans. Today they are over 18 percent of the population, having overtaken African Americans in 2003 as the nation's largest minority group, and now outnumber Blacks in seven of the ten largest cities in the United States—New York, Los Angeles, Houston, San Diego, Phoenix, Dallas, and San Antonio.[5]

The rapid increase in immigration from Mexico, both legal and illegal, raised concerns that immigrants "take our jobs" and will, by their sheer numbers, change America to be more like them than they like us. Almost thirty years ago *Time* magazine ran a cover story, "America's Changing Colors," in which it asked, "What will the US be like when whites are no longer the majority?" During those years it seemed a stretch for many Americans to think that white people would one day be a minority—"strangers in their own land."[6] But the priority given to family reunification visas of the 1965 immigration act over the last half century has resulted in changes to more than America's colors. As *Time* noted, "Long before that day arrives, the presumption that the 'typical' US citizen is someone who traces his or her descent in a direct line to Europe will be part of the past." That time has already come, particularly among the younger generation, by far the

---

I fail to see the distinction. Smith and King, "White Protectionism in America," *Perspectives on Politics* 19, no. 2 (2021): 460–78.

5   "Hispanics Now Largest Minority, Census Shows, *New York Times*, January 22, 2003, www .nytimes.com/2003/01/22/us/hispanics-now-largest-minority-census-shows.html (accessed February 15, 2018); William H. Frey, "The US Will Become 'Minority White' in 2045, Census Projects: Youthful Minorities Are the Engine of Future Growth, *Brookings*, www.brookings.edu/blog/ the-avenue/2018/03/14/the-us-will-become-minority-white-in-2045-census-projects/ (accessed May 13, 2018).

6   Arlie Russell Hochschild, *Strangers in Their Own Land: Anger and Mourning on the American Right* (New York: New Press, 2016).

most diverse generation in the history of the nation, the majority of whom trace their ancestry to Africa, Asia, and Latin America. As *Time* presciently put it, "The 'browning of America' will alter everything, from politics and education to industry, values and culture . . . and it is irreversibly the America to come."[7]

This looming demographic reality ("demographobia"?) explains much, but not all, of the anti-immigrant animus of many Americans today whose economic and cultural anxieties President Trump sought to soothe in his 2016 campaign promise to "make America great again" and build a wall on the border to keep Mexicans out. But in order to fully understand how nativism operates in the US today in ways different from the past, we cannot regard former president Trump's sordid suggestion to end immigration from "shithole" African countries, El Salvador, and Haiti as simply evidence of yet another "cycle" of anti-immigrant rhetoric and nativist politics, another eruption of white nationalism as in past eras. A century before the nation's founding, British colonizers and slaveholders conceived of the New World as rightfully theirs—an "English Israel," in the words of the New England Puritan minister Cotton Mather—and set about establishing the institutional and political foundations for the newly independent United States. Native peoples lived for centuries on this "virgin land," but they had to be cleared from the area, like the forests, before European settler colonists could farm the land and reap the economic and political rewards of being independent, white yeoman farmers.[8]

Thomas Jefferson, the political and ideological guardian of the yeomanry, described Native peoples in the Declaration of Independence as "merciless Indian savages." The author of the radical idea that "all men are created equal" also enslaved over six hundred human beings over the course of his life, including Sally Hemings, twenty-eight years his junior, with whom he sired six children. Until his dying breath Jefferson steadfastly held to his belief that "blacks . . . are inferior to the whites in the endowments of body and mind."[9] The newly forged nation, founded on the "self-evident truth" that all men are created equal, and "endowed by their Creator with certain unalienable rights . . . [of] life, liberty, and the pursuit of happiness," was never intended to include Indians, Africans, or Asians—anyone, in short, who was not "white."[10] While it may seem to many as an overstatement that ignores the complex issues surrounding the nation's founding, it is

---

7   "Beyond the Melting Pot," *Time*, April 9, 1990, 15:28.

8   Cotton Mather quoted in Kendi, *Stamped from the Beginning*, 52. See also Henry Nash Smith, *Virgin Land: The American West as Symbol and Myth* (Cambridge, MA: Harvard University Press, 2007, reprint).

9   Thomas Jefferson, *Notes on the State of Virginia* (1794), Query XIV, 209, Evans Early American Imprint Collection, https://quod.lib.umich.edu/e/evans/N20681.0001.001?rgn=main;view=fulltext. See also Kendi, *Stamped from the Beginning*, especially chaps. 7–12; Gerald Horne, *The Counter-Revolution of 1776: Slave Resistance and the Origins of the United States of America* (New York: NYU Press, 2016, reprint)

10   The British established similar settler colonial polities in Australia, Canada, and South Africa. See, for example, Klotz and Triadafilopoulos/Taylor, this volume, on the development of migration systems in South Africa and Canada, respectively.

nevertheless an unassailable fact that white men founded the US as a republic based on the assumption of white cultural and racial superiority over non-European peoples of the world, the consequences of which are still being felt today.[11]

Origins of White Nativism and the Naturalization Act of 1790

The origins of white nativism go back centuries before the nation's founding to religious conflict and imperial rivalries in Europe, where ideas of whiteness gradually took shape in the fifteen and sixteenth centuries when Europeans carried throughout the Atlantic and Indian Ocean worlds their notions of white Christian superiority over denizens of Africa, the Middle and Far East, and later the New World. It is therefore unsurprising that the first order of business of the first session of the First Congress of the United States was to pass a law that explicitly restricted citizenship to "any Alien being a *free white person*" and "a man of good moral character."[12] The Naturalization Act of 1790 was intended to encourage immigration from Europe and offered those immigrants (regardless of religious affiliation) a "path to citizenship" after fulfilling a residence requirement and other qualifications. Most women were excluded from citizenship, as were indentured servants, enslaved persons, free Blacks, Native Americans, and later Asians.

While this law may seem obviously racist, it probably did not seem that way to the Founding Fathers and members of Congress who believed that only free, white people were capable of understanding and upholding the principles and obligations of republican self-rule. The ineligibility of native-born American Indians, Blacks, and all non-European denizens and immigrants to become naturalized citizens curtailed many of their rights, including the right to vote in most states, and rendered them permanent second-class citizens based solely on their racial status. African Americans of course won their citizenship rights shortly after the Civil War and the passage of the Reconstruction amendments. Native Americans were finally granted citizenship in 1924, but the Supreme Court ruled in the early 1920s that South Asian Indians and Japanese immigrants were ineligible for citizenship under the 1790 law.[13] During World War II, over 200,000 Japanese residents and Japanese Americans were interned because it was widely believed that all Japanese could never become, by virtue of their race, loyal, bona fide Americans. Japanese Americans would remain, like other Asian Americans, "forever foreign."[14]

---

11   As of this writing, massive Black Lives Matter protests have taken place around the world over the murder of yet another unarmed Black man, Floyd George, on May 25, 2020, by the Minneapolis police during an arrest.

12   The full text of the Naturalization Act can be found here: http://www.indiana.edu/%7Ekdhist/ H105-documents-web/week08/naturalization1790.html; emphasis added.

13   The best study of the racial basis of naturalization law is Ian Haney Lopez, *White by Law: The Legal Construction of Race* (New York: NYU Press, 2006, reprint).

14   In the United States many Asians cope with the stereotype of being "model minorities" and "honorary whites"—always honorary, never "real" Americans. See Ellen D. Wu, *The Color of Success: Asian Americans and the Origins of the Model Minority* (Princeton, NJ: Princeton University

The importance of the Naturalization Act to the formation of an American national identity cannot be underestimated. It explains, in part, how Europeans of German, French, Dutch, and British origin began to think of themselves collectively as "white persons" in contradistinction to Africans, Indians, and Asians; and it had profound consequences for all immigrants and noncitizens who desired to become citizens from 1790 to 1952, when the racial qualification for naturalized citizenship was finally repealed. For example, the law said nothing about Mexicans, or Syrians, South-Asian Indians, Filipinos, and other dark-skinned immigrants who sought to become citizens. They often had to have their claim to white racial status adjudicated in the courts. Particularly confusing were cases that involved mixed-race applicants. Was a person who was half white and half Indian a white person? The district court of Oregon ruled in *In re Camille* (1880) that "half-breed Indians" were not considered white persons: "Indians have never, ethnologically, been considered white persons . . . From the first our naturalization laws only applied to the people who had settled the country, the European or white race."[15] Even Indians who renounced their tribal affiliations and adopted the ways of the White Man were ruled ineligible for citizenship. In the Supreme Court case *Elk v. Wilkins* (1880), John Elk stressed that he had voluntarily separated himself from his tribe and had "taken up his residence among the white citizens of a state." But the Supreme Court was not persuaded that association with whites made Indians into white people. Instead, it ruled that Indians were citizens of "alien nations . . . within the territorial limits of the United States," which made John Elk a "legal alien" in his native land and barred by law from US citizenship.[16]

Impact of Naturalization Law on Immigration from Mexico

The Naturalization Act also played a key role in the immigration restriction laws of 1917, 1921, and especially the 1924 National Origins Quota Act, which favored "Nordic" European immigrants over "swarthy" Slavic peoples, east European Jews, and immigrants from southern and southeastern Europe (mainly Italy, Greece, Albania, Bulgaria, and other countries of the Balkan Peninsula), who were regarded as racially inferior and too different to assimilate into Anglo-Saxon Protestant culture. The law also barred all immigration from the so-called "Asiatic Barred Zone," from Afghanistan to China and the Pacific islands, including Japan, on the grounds that only those eligible to become

---

Press, 2014); Erika Lee, *The Making of Asian America: A History* (New York: Simon & Schuster, 2015); Mai M. Ngai, *Impossible Subjects: Illegal Aliens and the Making of Modern America* (Princeton, NJ: Princeton University Press, 2004). On limiting the mobility of Asians and Africans in Southern Africa, see Klotz, this volume.

15   *In re Camille*, 6 F. 256 (District Court, Oregon 1880); Martha Menchaca, "Chicano Indianism: A Historical Account of Racial Repression in the United States," *American Ethnologist* 20 (August 1993): 583–603.

16   *Elk v. Wilkins*, 112 U.S. 94 (1884). In 1924 Congress passed the Indian Citizenship Act conferring citizenship on all Native Americans in the U.S. Act of June 2, 1924, Public Law 68–175, 43 Stat. 253, ch. 233, p. 253.

naturalized citizens ("free white persons") would be allowed entry into the United States. In this sense the naturalization law presaged the eugenics movement of the late nineteenth and early twentieth centuries that influenced the Dillingham Commission (1907–11) to recommend reduced immigration from eastern and southern Europe, as well as popular thinking on the perils of interracial marriage, the necessity of sterilization laws, and the credible collapse of white civilization worldwide. Eugenicists had lost confidence in the social Darwinist notion of "survival of the fittest"—what worried them was survival of the unfit.[17] A century earlier the authors of the Naturalization Act also believed in the necessity of excluding the "unfit"—nonwhites—as a menace to republican self-government.

The impact of the naturalization law was also felt beyond the borders of the US at a critical moment in pre–World War II diplomatic relations, when the "whites only" citizenship provision threatened to undermine relations with Mexico. It began with a routine naturalization case in 1935 involving a Mexican immigrant, Timoteo Andrade, who took out papers to become a citizen. A legal resident of Buffalo, New York, Andrade was denied citizenship on the grounds that he was not white. The judge, John Knight, cited a recent case on California's Alien Land Laws, *Morrison v. California* (1934), in which the judge reflected on the racial nature of Mexicans: "There is a strain of Indian blood in many of the inhabitants of Mexico as well as in the peoples of Central and South America. Whether persons of such descent may be naturalized in the United States is still an unsettled question."[18] Knight decided to settle the question and denied Andrade's application for citizenship. His ruling, the judge soon learned, threatened US relations with Mexico precisely at a moment in American history—just prior to the outbreak of World War II—when the President Roosevelt sought to be "good neighbors" with Mexico and all of Latin America by promising an end to US military intervention and welcoming the development of strong trade and cultural ties, particularly with Mexico.[19]

---

17   Lothrop Stoddard, *The Rising Tide of Color and the Threat against White World Supremacy* (New York: Charles Scribner's Sons, 1920); Madison Grant, *The Passing of the Great Race, Or the Racial Basis of European History* (New York: Charles Scribner's Sons, 1915). See also Daniel Okrent, *The Guarded Gate Bigotry, Eugenics, and the Law That Kept Two Generations of Jews, Italians, and Other European Immigrants Out of* America (New York: Scribner, 2019). On the Dillingham Commission, see Katherine Benton-Cohen, *Inventing the Immigration Problem: The Dillingham Commission and Its Legacy* (Cambridge, MA: Harvard University Press, 2018).

18   "Opinion of District Judge Knight, Dec. 11, 1935, Petition No. 2272-P-24049, in the matter of Timoteo Andrade to be admitted a Citizen of the United States of America," United States District Court, Western District of New York, Andrade Files/US; and *Morrison v. California*, 29 U.S. 82 (1934). For a detailed analysis of the Andrade naturalization case, see Neil Foley, *Mexicans in the Making of America* (Cambridge, MA: Harvard University Press, 2014), 52–60, from which this section is adapted.

19   See Edward O. Guerrant, *Roosevelt's Good Neighbor Policy* (Albuquerque: University of New Mexico Press, 1950); Bryce Wood, *The Making of the Good Neighbor Policy* (New York: Columbia University Press, 1962); Luis G. Zorrilla, *Historia de las Relaciones entre Mexico y los Estados*

Judge Knight's ruling took the Mexican and US governments by surprise. The Mexican consul general of New York, Enrique Elizondo, learned of the ruling from articles in the *Buffalo Courier-Express* and *the New York Times*.[20] He quickly sent a copy of the ruling to the Mexican ambassador, Francisco Castillo Nájera, and the foreign minister of Mexico, Eduardo Hay, asking them how best to "fight this insult to the nation."[21] Shocked at the implication of the ruling, Elizondo reminded the ambassador: "Only [free white] persons eligible for naturalization can be admitted as immigrants to the US [according to the 1924 Johnson-Reed Act]. If Mexicans are denied the right to become American citizens, practically the entire population [of Mexico] will be denied the right to immigrate to this country, which would place us in a similar status as that of Asian countries."[22]

Knight's ruling, if allowed to stand, troubled the US Department of State. Not a single Mexican immigrant had ever been denied citizenship on account of racial status.[23] State Department officials nonetheless understood that Knight was merely following the letter of the naturalization law, since Andrade's declaration that he was "half Indian" automatically rendered him ineligible for citizenship. An appeal would likely fail to reverse Knight's ruling, which would provoke a frosty response from the Mexican government and virtually all other Latin American nations whose indigenous populations were quite numerous. Rather than risk losing on appeal, Undersecretary of State Summer Welles recommended that the State Department attempt to have Knight's ruling delayed until a strategy could be devised to have it reconsidered. Ambassador Castillo Nájera agreed, since in order to win on appeal, he acknowledged, "we would have to prove that persons of 'Indian blood' were of the 'white race,' which obviously would not succeed."[24]

Unidos de América, 1800–1958 (Mexico, 1977); Cesar Sepúlveda, *Las Relaciones Diplomáticos entre México y los Estados Unidos en el Siglo XX* (Monterrey, 1953).

20   "Indian Blood Bars Mexicans as Citizens," *New York Times*, December 12, 1935, clipping in III-2335-2, Expediente 2, Archivo Histórico de la Secretaría de Relaciones Exteriores (hereafter cited as Andrade Files/MX); *Buffalo Courier-Express*, December 12, 1935, clipping attached to letter from Enrique L. Elizondo to Secretario de Relaciones Exteriores, December 12, 1935, Andrade Files/MX.

21   Enrique L. Elizondo to Embajador de México, December 13, 1935; and Enrique L. Elizondo to Secretario de Relaciones Exteriores, January 2, 1936, III-2335-2, Andrade Files/MX.

22   Enrique L. Elizondo to Secretario de Relaciones Exteriores, December 12, 1935, III-2335-2, Andrade Files/MX.

23   In 1897 an attempt was made to deny citizenship to Ricardo Rodríguez of San Antonio on the grounds that he was an "Indian Mexican," but the court ruled that the Treaty of Guadalupe Hidalgo with Mexico trumped the naturalization law for all Mexicans. *In re: Rodríguez*, 81 F. 345 (W.D. Tex. 1897); Martha Menchaca, *Naturalizing Mexican Immigrants: A Texas History* (Austin: University of Texas Press, 2011), 122–25.

24   Francisco Castillo Nájera to Secretario de Relaciones Exteriores, December 18, 1935, III-2335-2, Andrade Files/MX; Enrique L. Elizondo to Secretario de Relaciones Exteriores, January 3,

After much consultation with the State Department and his own foreign minister, Castillo Nájera hired a preeminent immigration attorney, Frederick T. Devlin, who successfully petitioned Judge Knight to reopen the Andrade case based on "new evidence" of Andrade's true ancestry. Devlin sought to prove that Andrade was actually of "Spanish blood" by introducing testimony from Andrade's mother, Maria Bera Andrade. Devlin asked: "What does Mexican blood mean to you?" To which she responded: "To me, Mexican blood is the blood of the people living in Mexico." Devlin tried another tactic. He wanted to know how she could be sure that her ancestry was free of Indian blood. "Mexican blood" might mean part Indian, she confessed, but added: "I have heard that we were a mixture of Spanish and Mexican. I never heard that we were mixed with Indian blood." How, Devlin wanted to know, did Maria Bera Andrade distinguish a "Mexican" from "a pure-blooded Indian from the back country." She and her town folk in Jalisco knew exactly who the Indians were by what villages they lived in, the native languages they spoke, and other cultural markers, such as dress, traditions, food, and so forth. In her district, she told Devlin, "when the Indians come from the neighboring towns, the people say, 'Here come the little Indians.' They never say, 'Here come the little Mexicans.'"[25] Case closed. Timoteo Andrade is not one of the little Indians. Judge Knight reversed his ruling, and the Mexican Foreign Ministry and US State Department could congratulate themselves for having erased that part of Andrade's ancestry that made him, and by implication all Mexicans, ineligible not only for naturalized citizenship but also for the right to immigrate to the United States.

Knight's ruling was a hollow victory as far as the Mexican chargé d'affaires, Luis Quintanilla, was concerned, since the naturalization law remained in force that would deny citizenship to Mexican immigrants of Indian ancestry—the very race, he wrote, that "formed the basis of our nationality." Mexicans, he warned, could be barred from immigrating, like the Japanese and Chinese.[26] Quintanilla was right, of course, and a State Department promptly informed Ambassador Castillo Nájera that the American government could order, "discreetly and confidentially," that naturalization inspectors not question whether Mexicans desiring citizenship were Indian or not, and simply continue to recognize their right to naturalization.[27] In other words, Mexicans were to be treated, for the purposes of naturalization, *as if* they were white. Not everyone agreed. Eugenicist author Glenn Hoover, writing in *Foreign Affairs*, argued that the population of Mexico consisted primarily of Indians "with but a veneer of European culture" and should be ineligible for citizenship. "It seems that there is a tacit understanding among all departments of the federal government," he complained, "that anyone born south of the Río Grande is a white person." If "interbreeding" between Indian Mexicans and Nordic

---

1935, III-2335-2, Andrade Files/MX; Manuel J. Sierra to Enrique L. Elizondo, January 14, 1936, III-2335-2, Andrade Files/MX.

25   Ibid.

26   Luis Quintanilla to Eduardo Hay, June 17, 1936, III-2335-2, Andrade Files/MX.

27   Francisco Castillo Nájera to Secretario de Relaciones Exteriores, December 24, 1935, III-2335-2, Andrade Files/MX.

whites could not be prevented, Hoover lamented, "his descendants will be our descendants, and the 'Gringo' [pejorative for "Anglo"] and 'Greaser' [pejorative for "Mexican"] will be one."[28]

The US shared a long, complicated history with Mexico, as well as a long, porous border, crossed and recrossed by millions of Mexican migrants since 1848. For the United States to have denied citizenship to Mexican immigrants and legal residents would have sabotaged President Roosevelt's Good Neighbor Policy with Mexico and other Latin American nations, especially at a time when the United States was concerned by the extreme to which race-based laws, like the naturalization law and sterilization laws of the 1920s, had become models for Hitler and the National Socialist Party in creating their own grim program of "racial hygiene."[29] For many, but certainly not all, the idea of limiting citizenship to "free white persons" was not compatible with democratic ideals, as they had come to be understood since 1790, particularly where Indians in the US were concerned. With the passage of the Indian Citizenship Act of 1924, American Indians were naturalized en masse in an effort to assimilate them into mainstream white culture. In effect, the act superseded the "white only" provision of the Naturalization Act. Why then would "Indian Mexicans" be any less eligible for citizenship than their American Indian kin in the US? As one Texas journalist observed of the Andrade case, "the law's position that an Indian is not fit to be an American is an absurdity itself."[30] Given the overwhelming preponderance of Mexicans of indigenous ancestry, and the size of the Mexican-origin population in the United States, it would not be entirely mistaken to suggest, as one anthropologist has, that mixed-race Indian Mexicans in the US comprise the single-largest tribe of North American Indians.[31]

Nativism in an Era of US-Mexico Cooperation: The Bracero Program

The period between 1924 and 1965 saw relatively little immigration to the United States with the exception of migrant Mexicans working mostly in the border states of California, Arizona, and Texas. The Great Depression curtailed most immigration, including cross-border migration, but led to mass deportation of Mexicans, some of them US citizens, in the border states because jobs were scarce and emergency relief programs were intended for citizens, not immigrants. But between 1942 and 1964, Mexico provided much of the agricultural labor in the United States—five million guest workers, called

---

28   Glenn E. Hoover, "Our Mexican Immigrants," *Foreign Affairs* 8 (October 1929–July 1930): 4.

29   James Q. Whitman, *Hitler's American Model: The United States and the Making of Nazi Race Law* (Princeton, NJ: Princeton University Press, 2017); Stefan Kühl, *The Nazi Connection: Eugenics, American Racism, and German National Socialism* (Princeton, NJ: Princeton University Press, 2002).

30   "Mexicans Barred?" *Dallas Journal*, n.d., clipping in Serie III-2335-2, Andrade Files/US. He also suggested that Andrade could have claimed that being half Spanish was the same as being half African, since "the Moorish infiltration onto Spain would reasonably be represented by this time in the blood of practically all the families of Spain."

31   Jack D. Forbes, *Aztecas del Norte: The Chicanos of Aztlán* (Greenwich, CT: Fawcett, 1973), 13.

braceros.[32] Begun as a bilateral emergency war program between Mexico and the United States in 1942, and continued until 1964, the Bracero Program provided temporary Mexican contract laborers to work in agriculture to offset the loss of US workers to the armed services and defense industries. Those unable or unwilling to sign six-month temporary work contracts under the Bracero Program crossed the border illegally as "wetbacks" or *mojados* (literally, "wet people"), a pejorative designation used by growers in the Southwest for Mexican laborers generally, regardless of legal status. The historical truth is that the United States had relied heavily on Mexican labor in the border states since the late nineteenth century, decades before immigration laws were enacted to restrict immigration from Europe or require a head tax and literacy test for immigrants from Mexico and other countries of the Western Hemisphere. In fact, both the US and Mexican governments regarded the entry of Mexicans into the United States until World War I mainly as cross-border "labor migrants" rather than immigrants.[33]

The partnership between Mexico and the United States forged during World War II to supply the United States with temporary laborers survived numerous disagreements in its twenty-two-year history, mainly over the poor treatment of braceros in the US, who were segregated in separate schools, denied entrance into shops and cafés, and in many ways treated much like African Americans in the South. There was not much Mexico could do to change the way white Americans treated its citizens abroad, but it could cancel the Bracero Program if the United States failed to honor and enforce the provisions of the agreement, which is exactly what Mexican president Miguel Alemán did in 1948 when the Immigration and Naturalization Service went "rogue."

The revised bracero agreement of 1948 could not guarantee employer compliance with contracts, or prevent their hiring "wetback" labor. Nevertheless, both governments signed an agreement requiring employers of braceros to sign an oath not to employ undocumented workers and to provide all hospital and medical costs for occupational accidents and illnesses suffered or incurred by Mexican agricultural workers.[34] The worst that could happen to employers who violated the terms was to have their contracts canceled. No fines were levied against employers of undocumented workers, and those whose contracts were canceled, especially employers in the four border states, generally

---

32   Estimates vary from 4.5 to 6 million. An important scholar of the Bracero Program puts the number at 5 million. Kitty Calavita, *Inside the State: The Bracero Program, Immigration, and the I.N.S* (1992; repr., New Orleans: Quid Pro Quo Books, 2010), 1.

33   Manuel García y Griego, "The Importation of Mexican Contract Laborers to the United States, 1942–1964: Antecedents, Operation, and Legacy," in *The Border That Joins: Mexican Migrants and US Responsibility*, ed. Peter G. Brown and Henry Shue (Totowa, NJ: Rowman and Littlefield, 1983), 55; Calavita, *Inside the State*.

34   "Agreement Not to Employ Illegal Workers," Anexo "B," and "Occupational Diseases and Accidents," Anexo "C," Centro de Contratación de Trabajadores Ilegales en Harlingen, Texas, n.d., legajo 1453–5, Embajada de México en Estados Unidos de América (AEMEUA) del Archivo Histórico "Genaro Estrada," Secretaria e Relaciones Exteriores, Mexico City (hereafter cited as AEMEUA).

had little difficulty hiring undocumented migrants willing to work for wages below those guaranteed under the Bracero Program.[35]

Tensions brewed between the State Department and the Mexican government over the latter's refusal to allow braceros to be recruited from its northern state of Chihuahua, bordering on New Mexico and Texas. Mexico worried that the congestion of unemployed braceros in the north would overwhelm the limited resources of border cities, like Nuevo Laredo and Ciudad Juárez, to care for them. The State Department argued that if these workers were not formally recruited at the border, it would be "impossible to prevent their entry as wetbacks" who would receive only one-third the wages of legally recruited braceros.[36] Meanwhile, thousands of Mexicans headed for the border at Ciudad Juárez because they had lost hope of receiving contracts at recruitment centers located away from the border in the northern cities of Monterrey (Nuevo León) and Guaymas (Sonora)—with no recruitment center at all in the northern state of Chihuahua, which bordered west Texas and New Mexico.[37]

In an unprecedented move that took the US and Mexican governments by surprise, the Immigration and Naturalization Service opened the border at El Paso on October 13, 1948, in direct violation of the bilateral agreement, to thousands of Mexican workers and turned them over to American growers desperate for labor. Over four thousand dashed across the border in two days where they were put under "technical arrest" and then "paroled" to the Texas Employment Commission to be transported to cotton fields in west Texas and New Mexico. The unilateral opening of the border by the INS made headlines in both countries.[38] Grover Wilmoth, district INS director, claimed that he received instructions from Washington to "use his own judgment" in meeting the "critical and urgent need for farm laborers." Wilmoth denied that by opening the border he allowed Mexicans to enter the United States illegally; rather, he said, "we endeavored to

---

35   "Boletín Informativo Publicado por el Comisionado de Inmigración y Naturalización y Director Federal del Servicios de Empleos," n.d., attached to letter from Gustavo Padrés, Jr., Cónsul Comisionado de San Antonio, to Secretario de Relaciones Exteriores, April 5, 1951, legajo 1452–6, AEMEUA.

36   Paul J. Reveley, Department of State, to Rafael de la Colina, Charge d'Affaires ad interim of Mexico, September 3, 1948; Rafael Nieto, Consejero, to Secretario de Relaciones Exteriores, September 4, 1948, legajo 1452–8, AEMEUA.

37   "Informe Concentrado de los Sucesos Registrados en Esta Frontera, Relacionado con Nuestros Braceros," Raúl Mitchel, Cónsul General de México (El Paso), October 19, 1948; Jay C. Stilley, "Special Bulletin," October 26, 1948, legajo 1453–1, AEMEUA.

38   "Flagrante Contradicción del Convenio Entre México y E. U.," *Excelsior*, October 17, 1948; "Es una Esclavitud Voluntaria Para los Mexicanos, *Excelsior*, October 19, 1948; clipping, "Fué un Acto Desesperado de EE. UU. la Admisión de Braceros," n.p., October 21, 1948; "US Abandons Move to Keep Mexicans Out," *New York Times*, October 17, 1948; "México Rompió Ayer el Pacto con E. U. Relativo a los Braceros," *Excelsior*, October 19, 1948, in legajo 1453–1, AEMEUA.

take into custody all Mexican farm laborers who effected illegal entry." In other words, he opened the border so that Mexican laborers could be "taken into custody" and delivered to growers, instead of deporting them immediately to Mexico, as the bilateral agreement required.[39]

Infuriated by the flagrant violation of the agreement, the consul general of El Paso, Raul Michel, fired off a letter to Wilmoth demanding to know why he had given the order to let Mexicans into the United States in absolute violation of the Bracero Program. He demanded that Wilmoth "rectify or ratify, whichever the case may be, the absolute refusal of cooperation given to this Consulate by your [Immigration] Service."[40] Within days President Miguel Alemán canceled the renewed 1948 Bracero Agreement and ordered the Mexican Army to the border to prevent Mexicans from leaving the country illegally.[41] The Mexican chargé d'affaires, Rafael de la Colina, delivered a formal protest, described as a "stemwinder" by US diplomats, informing the State Department that the Mexican government had terminated the agreement as a direct consequence of the INS "permitting and, in fact, facilitating the illegal entry of Mexican farm workers into Texas." Paul Daniels, head of the Division of American Republics at the State Department, apologized for the "serious instance of non-compliance" and issued an order to the INS that all Mexicans who had been allowed to enter illegally be promptly returned to Ciudad Juárez.[42] The Mexican chargé d'affaires suggested that the US government punish the INS officials responsible for the action in order for both governments to "find a quick and satisfactory solution to this disagreeable matter."[43]

Border tensions and incidents tried the patience of government officials on both sides of the border throughout the duration of the Bracero Program. The INS, US Employment Service, and the State Department often blamed Mexico for the "wetback problem"

---

39 "Immigration Head Denies 'Pressure,'" *El Paso Times*, October 21, 1948, legajo 1453–1, AEMEUA.

40 Raul Michel, Consul General of Mexico, to George C. Wilmoth, US Immigration Service, October 16, 1948, legajo 1453–1, AEMEUA.

41 Alfonso Anaya, Presidente, Asociación Mexicana de Periodistas, October 20, 1948, exp. 546.6/1–32, caja 594, Alemán Papers, AGN. The Mexican Constitution of 1857 (in effect until 1917) established freedom of exit (and travel within the country). The 1917 Constitution, however, restricted exit to ensure that migrating workers crossed into the US with signed contracts. David Fitzgerald, *A Nation of Emigrants: How Mexico Manages Its Migration* (Berkeley: University of California Press, 2009), 40–41.

42 Paul Daniels, Department of State, to Rafael de la Colina, Chargé d'Affaires ad interim, October 22, 1948, attached to letter from Rafael de Colina to Secretario de Relaciones Exteriores, October 22, 1948, legajo 1452–8, AEMEUA.

43 Rafael de la Colina, Encargado de Negocios ad interim, to Secretario de Relaciones Exteriores, October 18, 1948; State Department Note no. 4946, October 18, 1948, attached to letter from Rafael de la Colina, ibid., legajo 1452–8, AEMEUA; and LULAC Resolution No. 2, June 12, 1949, attached to letter from Jacob I. Rodriguez to President Miguel Aleman, June 29, 1949, exp. 546.6/1–32, caja 594, Alemán Papers.

for not increasing its border force in an effort to prevent workers from leaving Mexico. Mexican officials, on the other hand, believed that the problem of illegal entry was mainly the responsibility of the United States, since it had failed to impose sanctions on employers of undocumented workers. Those employers formed a powerful farm bloc in American politics, with support on Capitol Hill, and few politicians wanted to risk arousing the wrath of American farmers. Rather than confront the problem at its source—the employer—the US concentrated its efforts instead on cat-and-mouse apprehensions and deportations, often of the same "mojados." Border Patrol agents sometimes joked that "deportees beat them back into the US."[44] The joke was often not far from the truth. After a raid on his farm, a carrot farmer in southern California loaned his own trucks to the INS to help border patrolmen transport 310 of his 345-man carrot harvesting crew to the border for deportation to Mexicali. "The sooner they get to Mexicali," the field foreman reasoned, "the sooner they can re-cross the border and start back to work."[45]

Two years later a New York Times headline proclaimed "Mexicans Convert Border into Sieve," and an immigration official characterized the mass movement of Mexicans across the border as "perhaps the greatest peacetime invasion ever complacently suffered by any country under open, flagrant, contemptuous violation of its laws."[46] In 1953 the Border Patrol apprehended a record number of one million Mexicans entering the country illegally. The equivalent of 10 percent of the population of Mexico had crossed the border into the US since the end of World War II, according to one immigration official, who candidly admitted that "there is nothing to stop the whole nation moving into the United States if it wants to."[47]

In response, President Eisenhower announced the decision to launch "Operation Wetback" to round up and deport half a million undocumented migrants, which Attorney General Herbert Brownell called "the greatest anti-alien drive in the history of the Southwest."[48] Once again the US government was torn in two directions. While the

---

44 "Mexicans Convert Border into Sieve," New York Times, March 27, 1950, legajo 1453-1, AEMEUA.

45 "Thousands of Mexicans Illegally Cross US Border Each Month," Los Angeles Times, May 2, 1950; Mae M. Ngai, Impossible Subjects: Illegal Aliens and the Making of Modern America (Princeton, NJ: Princeton University Press, 2005), 147–52.

46 "Mexicans Convert Border into Sieve," New York Times, March 27, 1950, legajo 1453-1; "Protección a Nuestros 'Espaldas Mojadas,'" Excelsior, October 16, 1951; "Los 'Espadas Mojadas' Invaden Varias Industrias de Edos. Unidos," Excelsior, November 19, 1951, legajo 1454-3, AEMEUA.

47 "Mexican Border-Jumpers Set Two-a-Minute Mark in April," New York Times, May 10, 1953, in letter from Rafael Nieto, Mexican Embassy, to Luis Padilla Nervo, Secretario de Relaciones Exteriores, May 11, 1953, legajo 1454-3, AEMEUA. On the Bracero Program, see Ernesto Galarza, Merchants of Labor: The Mexican Bracero Story, An Account of the Managed Mirgration of Mexican Farm Workers in California, 1942–1960 (Charlotte, CA: McNally and Loftin, 1964); and Calavita, Inside the State.

48 "The 'Wetback' Influx," New York Times, April 17, 1953; "Brownell Tours 'Wetback' Border," New York Times, April 16, 1953; "Government Maps War on Wetbacks," Los Angeles Times, June 10, 1954.

Korean War made it necessary to increase agricultural production, which could only be achieved with the assistance of Mexican laborers, Congress came under increasing pressure from American citizens to do something about "the invasion of the wetbacks." Emanuel Celler, chairman of the House Judiciary Committee, became alarmed when he learned that immigration authorities had arrested 579,000 Mexicans for illegally entering the US in 1950. His committee worked out an amendment to the immigration law making "it a crime to harbor and employ illegal immigrants."[49] The legislation, passed in 1952, made it a crime to *harbor* deportable aliens, but the Texas congressional delegation inserted the so-called "Texas Proviso" explicitly exempting employers from any penalties for *employing* undocumented workers.[50] Only those "harboring" undocumented workers faced penalties, such as coyotes and other human traffickers, whose very livelihood depended on their ignoring national and international laws.

Mexican Americans in the postwar era, many who were the descendants of bracero workers, unauthorized immigrants, and resident Mexican nationals, increasingly demanded their full citizenship rights in a country that for over a century regarded them as "foreigners" and "wetbacks" insufficiently European and "white" to be considered authentic Americans, forgetting that Mexicans had longer and stronger ties to North America than did the late-arriving British colonists and Anglo settlers. Nativist Anglo Americans nonetheless believed that Mexicans came from the wrong side of the border that divided mostly white North America from Mexico and its dark-skinned progeny of indigenous origin. But as Chicano activists of the 1960s reminded Anglo Americans, alluding to the US-Mexican War that resulted in the loss of half of Mexico's territory: "We didn't cross the border, the border crossed us."

Demographic Change and the Immigration and Nationality Act of 1965

More than fifty years ago, the Immigration and Nationality Act was signed into law by President Lyndon B. Johnson at the foot of the Statue of Liberty. As noted earlier, this law abolished the national origins quota system enacted in 1924 in an era when eugenic racial science was widely accepted and immigration policy was based on race and ethnicity. In 1963 President John F. Kennedy urged the Congress to repeal the discriminatory 1924 law, suggesting the damage it did to the image of the US in a globalizing world: "It neither satisfies a national need nor accomplishes an international purpose. In an age of interdependence among nations, such a system is an anachronism for it discriminates among applicants for admission into the United States on the basis of the accident of birth."[51] As numerous historians and immigration scholars have noted,

---

49 "Wetback Inquiry Gets Instructions," *New York Times*, April 12, 1951; Respuesta de Carl W. Strom, Cónsul General de los Estados Unidos, al Discurso Inaugural del Dr. Guerra en la Conferencia sobre Trabajadores Migratorios, July 16, 1951, exp. 671/14501, caja 1062, Alemán Papers.

50 See García y Griego, "Importation of Mexican Contract Laborers," 63.

51 John F. Kennedy, *Public Papers of the Presidents of the United States* (Washington, DC: US Government Printing Office, 1964), 594–97, quoted in "The Legacy of the 1965 Immigration Act: Three Decades of Mass Immigration," September 1, 1995, https://cis.org/Report/Legacy-1965-Immigration-Act.

large-scale immigration was not the objective of the 1965 law but rather its unintended consequence. President Johnson said when he signed the bill: "The bill that we sign to-day is not a revolutionary bill. It does not affect the lives of millions. It will not reshape the structure of our daily lives, or really add importantly to either our wealth or our power." And Senator Ted Kennedy, one of the bill's sponsors, asserted, "It will not upset the ethnic mix of our society."[52] Their pronouncements turned out to be highly mistaken.

The 1965 law replaced race-based quotas with a preference system based on im-migrants' family relationships with US citizens or legal permanent residents (and to a lesser degree their skills), believing it would better preserve the country's pre-dominantly Anglo-Saxon, European base. Family reunification thereafter became the cornerstone of US immigration policy. Despite the law's visa quotas (120,000 visas for Western Hemisphere immigrants and 170,000 for immigrants from the Eastern Hemisphere), the number of new lawful permanent residents rose from slightly un-der 300,000 in 1965 to an average of about 1 million each year until the mid-2000s. A decade after the law's passage immigration from Europe, which had been steadily declining, was eclipsed by immigration from Latin America (mostly Mexico), Asia (at first from Vietnam), and decolonized countries of Africa. By the end of the first decade of the twenty-first century, almost 90 percent of all immigrants came from non-European countries. According to the Pew Research Center Hispanic Trends Project, the foreign-born population had risen from 9.6 million in 1965 to a record high of 45 million in 2015. The largest share of today's immigrant population is from Mexico (about 11.6 million), and together with India, the Philippines, China, Vietnam, El Salvador, Cuba, South Korea, the Dominican Republic, and Guatemala, these ten countries account for nearly 60 percent of the current immigrant population (see fig-ures 10.1 and 10.2).[53]

No one could have predicted how the Immigration and Nationality Act would radi-cally alter the racial and ethnic makeup of the United States. When the law was passed, whites of European descent comprised 84 percent of the US population and Blacks 10 percent, while Hispanics accounted for 4 percent and Asians for less than 1 percent. A lit-tle over fifty years later, 62 percent of the US population is white, 18 percent is Hispanic, and 6 percent is Asian. By 2065, according to Pew Research Center projections, just 46 percent of the US population will be white, the Hispanic share will rise to 24, Asians will comprise 14 percent—and the country will be home to 78 million foreign born.[54] This is "irreversibly the America to come" that *Time* presaged in 1990 and that prompted Leonel Castillo, the former commissioner of the INS, to suggest that the Statue of Liberty was

52   Daniel J. Tichenor, *Dividing Lines: The Politics of Immigration Control in America* (Prince-ton, NJ: Princeton University Press, 2002), 211–18; "Fifty Years On, the 1965 Immigration and Nationality Act Continues to Reshape the United States," *Migration Policy Institute*, Octo-ber 15, 2015, www.migrationpolicy.org/article/fifty-years-1965-immigration-and-nationality-act -continues-reshape-united-states.

53   Ibid., "Fifty Years On."

54   Ibid., "Fifty Years On."

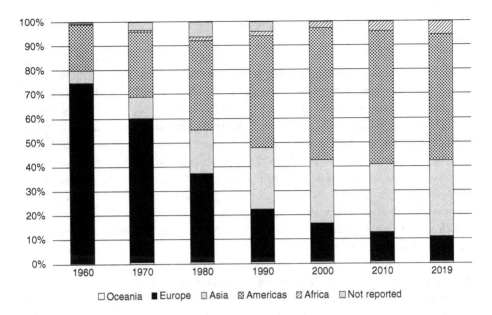

Figure 10.1. US immigrant population by world region of birth, 1960–2019.

Source: Originally published on the Migration Policy Institute's Migration Data Hub, https://www.migrationpolicy .org/programs/data-hub/charts/regions-immigrant-birth-1960-present. Reprinted with permission.

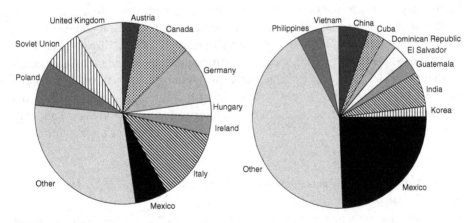

Figure 10.2. Top-ten largest US immigrant groups, 1960 and 2019.

Source: Originally published on the Migration Policy Institute's Migration Data Hub, https://www.migrationpolicy. org/programs/data-hub/charts/largest-immigrant-groups-over-time. Reprinted with permission.

Note: The figure for China includes Hong Kong.

"facing the wrong way" and "should be turned around" to face Asia and Latin America, not Europe.[55]

The 1965 act also inadvertently laid the foundation for the steep rise in illegal immigration since the 1970s. When Congress terminated the Bracero Program in 1964, many former bracero workers continued crossing the US-Mexico border, this time illegally as "wetbacks." But tens of thousands stayed, settled down, and raised families in towns and cities across America, proving the truth of the saying that there's nothing more permanent than temporary workers. The end of the Bracero Program, combined with the 1965 immigration law's cap of 120,000 from all countries of the Western Hemisphere, fueled the rise of illegal immigration from Mexico, since the demand for Mexican labor greatly exceeded the hemispheric cap. In short, by ignoring the historical need for Mexican labor in the United States for over a century, the law, in effect, *created* illegal immigration, which soon became the lightning rod for nativist backlash politics and rhetoric after 1980 and continuing to the present.

Fixing the Hole in the Wall: Immigration Reform in the 1980s

The national news media dubbed the 1980s the "Decade of the Hispanic," recognizing Latinos' rapid population growth and potential influence in American mainstream life, economically, culturally, and politically.[56] While the Latino population had not made exceptional economic, educational, or political headway in the 1980s, politicians and businesses nevertheless read the demographic writing on the wall: Latinos were the fastest-growing population and were predicted to outnumber African Americans by the turn of the century, if not sooner, and hasten the "tipping point" in the twenty-first century when whites would no longer be a majority of the population. In anticipation of these changes, in 1980 the Census Bureau added "Hispanic" as an ethnic category (to avoid creating a new racial classification). In the past when the census counted Latinos as "white," it was often difficult to distinguish Hispanics from "non-Hispanic whites."[57]

Although there was growing recognition throughout the 1970s that illegal immigration from Mexico needed to be addressed in Washington, it was hardly a priority for President Jimmy Carter, whose hapless administration was in its final death throes after two years of double-digit inflation, high unemployment, and the year-long crippling hostage crisis in Iran at the decade's end. Nevertheless, during his administration

---

55   Mercedes Olivera, "Immigration Rocketing, Former INS Chief Says," *Dallas Morning News*, February 28, 1980.

56   According to one journalist, the phrase was first used in 1978 to refer to Hispanic appointees in the Carter administration: "The blacks had the decade of the '60s; women had the '70s. The '80s will be the decade for Hispanics." Frank del Olmo, "Latino 'Decade' Moves into the '90s"; *Los Angeles Times*, December 4, 1989.

57   Today many Hispanics identify as racially white, although they often view themselves as culturally different from European or "Anglo" whites. On the choices ethnic Mexicans are forced to make as a consequence of making *latinidad* an ethnicity, see Julie A. Dowling, *Mexican Americans and the Question of Race* (Austin: University of Texas Press, 2014).

Congress created the Select Commission on Immigration and Refugee Policy (SCIRP) to review the nation's immigration and refugee laws and make recommendations to Congress. SCIRP executive director Lawrence Fuchs and commission chair, University of Notre Dame president Theodore Hesburgh, were committed to examining immigration without the eugenic assumptions about racial hierarchies that informed previous immigration commissions, most notably the Progressive-era Dillingham Commission, which over fifty years earlier concluded that immigration from southern and eastern Europe posed a serious threat to the nation's cultural homogeneity. The fundamental conclusion of the SCIRP report was that immigration in general continued to be beneficial to the nation, but that rising levels of illegal immigration were creating a shadow population of residents living outside the law. "We think the front door to America . . . should be opened a bit wider," Hesburgh said, "and the back door, the illegal one, closed."[58]

The national print media featured articles with headlines such as "Los Angeles Swells with Aliens," and interviews with Border Patrol and nativist INS officials who warned that the "brown horde" had grown rapidly in the last decade and that Los Angeles was already "infested" with Mexicans.[59] The engine driving the rapid growth of the Hispanic population in the 1980s was immigration from Mexico, both legal and illegal, and when Cuban president Fidel Castro allowed 125,000 "marielitos" (refugees, including 2,000 prisoners and mental patients) to immigrate to the United States in 1980, Congress began to take seriously the need for comprehensive immigration reform as well as its refugee policy. In 1980 President Jimmy Carter signed the Refugee Act, which created a uniform resettlement program and more than tripled the limit for refugees from 17,400 to 50,000. In all, the foreign-born population increased from 9.6 million in 1970 to 14.1 million in 1980 (including over 400,000 refugees from Vietnam and Cambodia) and to 19.8 million in 1990, an increase of over 100 percent in two decades, and accounting for one-third of America's population growth. In the same two decades the percentage of the Hispanic population almost doubled: from 4.7 percent in 1970 to 9 percent in 1990, partly as a result of native Hispanic births, but mainly as a result of legal and illegal immigration from Mexico.[60]

---

58   "Notre Dame's President Offers Solutions on Aliens," *New York Times*, August 24, 1981 (Hesburgh's quote); Jimmy Carter, "Communication to Congress," quoted in David Gutiérrez, *Walls and Mirrors: Mexican Americans, Mexican Immigrants, and the Politics of Ethnicity* (Berkeley: University of California Press, 1995), 200; Tichenor, *Dividing Lines*, 250. See also Foley, *Mexicans in the Making of America*, chap. 7, from which this section is adapted.

59   Howard Swindle, "Los Angeles Swells with Aliens," *Dallas Morning News*, May 31, 1980; Peter H. Schuck, *Citizens, Strangers, and In-Betweens: Essays on Immigration and Citizenship* (Boulder, CO: Westview Press, 1998), 12; William A. V. Clark, "Residential Patterns: Avoidance, Assimilation, and Succession," in *Ethnic Los Angeles*, ed. Roger Waldinger and Mehdi Bozorgmehr (New York: Russell Sage, 1996), 115.

60   Campbell J. Gibson and Emily Lennon, *Historical Census Statistics on the Foreign-born Population of the United States: 1850–1990* (Washington, DC: US Bureau of the Census, 1999), www.census.gov/population/www/documentation/twps0029/twps0029.html.

After SCIRP issued its final report on the question of immigration reform, the Reagan administration's interagency Task Force on Immigration and Refugee Policy submitted its carrot-and-stick recommendations that included penalties against employers who knowingly hired illegal aliens; legal status ("amnesty") for undocumented immigrants; and a pilot program to allow 50,000 Mexican "guest workers" each year for two years—in effect, a renewal of the Bracero Program begun in World War II and ended in 1964.[61] The bipartisan Simpson-Mazolli Bill was introduced in the Senate in 1982, where many Republicans and Democrats opposed either employer sanctions or amnesty for distinct ideological reasons, although in general both parties remained enthusiastic about legal immigration as beneficial to America's prosperity. The Reagan administration remained committed to the bill's amnesty provision for undocumented immigrants and defied House Republicans who insisted that "illegal aliens" should be punished, not rewarded, for breaking the law. In a televised debate with Democratic presidential nominee Walter Mondale in 1984, Reagan said: "I believe in the idea of amnesty for those who have put down roots and lived here, even though sometime [sic] back they may have entered illegally."[62] Like other conservative advocates of the free market unfettered by immigration restrictions and government regulation, Reagan parted ways with those calling for reduction in legal immigration but joined with others who supported "earned citizenship"—amnesty—for those here illegally.

After years of congressional wrangling over the details of amnesty, employer sanctions, and limited guest-worker program, President Reagan signed the Immigration Reform and Control Act (IRCA) into law in November 1986. IRCA marked the first time in our nation's history that a law made it illegal for employers to hire undocumented workers. These workers could be arrested and deported, of course, but neither they nor their employers faced penalties under labor and employment laws.[63] The problem, as it soon became clear, was that the employer sanctions provision of the bill had failed almost entirely to accomplish its twin goals: to deter illegal immigration and to protect US workers.[64] Designed to curtail illegal immigration, IRCA succeeded mainly in making

---

61   On the politics of immigration reform in the 1980s, see Tichenor, *Dividing Lines*, 242–88. On the conflict within the Reagan White House over the recommendations of the task force, including how to deal with "illegal aliens," see Thomas R. Maddux, "Ronald Reagan and the Task Force on Immigration, 1981," *Pacific Historical Review* 74 (May 2005): 195–236. For a comprehensive overview of the four-year legislative history of the Immigration Reform and Control Act, see Nancy Humel Montwieler, *The Immigration Reform Law of 1986* (Washington, DC: Bureau of National Affairs, 1987).

62   "Text of the Second Reagan-Mondale Debate," *Washington Post*, October 22, 1984.

63   Calavita, *Inside the State*, 71–75; Luis Plascencia, *Disenchanting Citizenship: Mexican Migrants and the Boundaries of Belonging* (New Brunswick, NJ: Rutgers University Press, 2012), 10; Michael C. LeMay, *Anatomy of a Public Policy: The Reform of Contemporary American Immigration Law* (Westport, CT: Praeger, 1994), 10.

64   See, for example, Jay Matthews, "Upsurge in Illegal Aliens Is Reported: Word Gets Home That Work Is Easy to Find despite New Law," *Washington Post*, July 9, 1987; Patrick McDonnell, "Border Arrests of Illegal Aliens Up 2 Months in Row," *Los Angeles Times*, March 2, 1988; "Illegal Aliens: Still Coming," *Economist*, no. 7799 (February 1993), 26.

immigration policy more liberal, and more expansive, especially for guest workers and the millions who qualified for amnesty.

But by the 1990s the number of unauthorized immigrants was reaching historic proportions, over 60 percent of them from Mexico. As the United States, Mexico, and Canada sought closer integration of their markets for capital, commodities, and goods—a borderless North American economy—the United States was simultaneously barricading—militarizing—the border. "This sort of schizophrenia toward Mexico is nothing new," some immigration scholars have noted. "Throughout the twentieth century the United States regularly encouraged or welcomed the entry of Mexican workers while publicly pretending not to do so."[65] From the time of Mexico's entry into the General Agreement on Tariffs and Trade (GATT) in 1986 and its membership in the trinational North American Free Trade Agreement (NAFTA) in 1994, the US-Mexico border would remain closed to the free movement of migrating workers, while capital flows and goods would pass through the border in both directions with little hindrance.

Citizens in the border states came increasingly to resent Mexicans coming to the United States to take advantage of liberal welfare policies. They deeply resented the Supreme Court ruling in *Plyler v. Doe* (1982) that prevented Texas from denying public education to the undocumented school-age children. They believed that many undocumented immigrants served as drug couriers for the Mexican cartels, spreading their poison to the nation's youth. And they resented undocumented Mexican mothers who crossed the border to "drop anchor babies." The media fanned the flames of nativist xenophobia with stories on gang warfare, crime, blighted neighborhoods, identity theft, and the "secret" agenda of immigrants to reconquer the Southwest for Mexico. The opening salvo in the backlash decade of the 1990s began, to no one's surprise, in California, where the majority of undocumented Mexican immigrants resided, and where the Republican Party hoped to capitalize on the state's—and the nation's—growing hostility to immigration in general, and Mexican "illegal aliens" in particular.

Backlash of the Native Born from 1990s to the Present

The Immigration and Naturalization Service estimated that almost half of the undocumented immigrant population in the United States resided in California in the 1990s. The state's population surged nearly 26 percent in the 1980s, adding about six million new residents fueled by the booming aerospace and other industries that made the Golden State a magnet for both citizen and immigrant job seekers, as well as ground zero for mounting xenophobia toward "alien immigrants" who Anglos feared were changing California—and America—into something foreign, strange, and "third world."[66] If the federal government was unwilling or unable to deter unauthorized entry from Mexico and other countries, the states would pass laws to make life harder for undocumented

---

65   Douglas S. Massey, Jorge Durand, and Nolan J. Malone, *Beyond Smoke and Mirrors: Mexican Immigration in an Era of Economic Integration* (New York: Russell Sage Foundation, 2003), 84.

66   Hans P. Johnson, *Undocumented Immigration to California: 1980–1993* (San Francisco: Public Policy Institute of California, 1996): 1–132; Rebecca Trounson, "California's Population Growth to Slow in Coming Decades," *Los Angeles Times*, April 25, 2012.

immigrants and their children. In less than a decade the nation went from granting amnesty to three million undocumented immigrants during the "Decade of the Hispanic"
to the backlash 1990s and post-9/11 era when states, fueled by popular fears and uncertainty, passed harsh laws against unsanctioned immigrants, like California's Proposition
187 to deny unauthorized immigrants state welfare, education, and medical services;
Arizona's SB 1070, which allows police officers to arrest unauthorized immigrants under
the state's trespassing law; and at the federal level, an attempt by the House of Representatives to pass a law in 2005 (the Sensenbrenner immigration bill H.R. 4437) that would
make unlawful presence in the US a felony offense.

In the years preceding the ballot initiative, Proposition 187 ("Save Our State"), in 1994,
California had led the country in efforts to establish English as the official language of
the nation. "English First" and "US English" advocates, like former California senator
S. I. Hayakawa and Texas representative James Horn, worried that the "dangerous spread
of 'bilingualism' in our society" threatened to divide the nation into different linguistic
camps, much like francophone Quebec in Canada.[67] The ascendancy of English globally as the language of technology and finance has grown steadily since World War II,
as has the influence of the English-language media—from Hollywood movies to music
videos—on youth cultures of the world. A Rand Corporation survey in 1985 found that
more than 95 percent of US-born, second-generation Latinos were proficient in English,
and that over half of all third-generation Latinos spoke no Spanish at all. "The plain fact
is that making English the official language of the United States," wrote one linguist, "is
about as urgently called for as making hotdogs the official food at baseball games."[68]
Nevertheless, Proposition 63, the referendum making English California's official language, passed with a lopsided 73 percent of the vote.[69]

Within a few years, Arizona, Colorado, and Florida also voted to designate English
as their official language and to restrict the use of other tongues in official government
business. Opponents called the movement for "English only" thinly veiled nativism—
linguistic bigotry—aimed primarily at the large population of Mexican immigrants in
the Southwest and Cubans in Florida, where Miami had already become a bilingual city.[70]
John Tanton, founder of the Federation for American Immigration Reform (FAIR), an

---

67   Quoted in Geoffrey Pullum, "Here Come the Linguistic Fascists," *Natural Language & Linguistic Theory* 5, no. 4 (December 1987): 606.

68   Geoffrey Pullum, *The Great Eskimo Vocabulary Hoax and Other Irreverent Essays on the Study
of Language* (Chicago: University of Chicago Press, 1991), 118.

69   "California Makes English Official Language of State," *Toronto Star,* November 5, 1986; Marcia
Chambers, "California Braces for Change with English as Official Language," *New York Times,* November 26, 1986. This section is adapted from Foley, *Mexicans and the Making of America,* chap. 8.

70   Six other states declared English their official language: Georgia, Illinois, Indiana, Kentucky,
Nebraska, and Virginia. John R. Emshwiller, "California Voters Expected to Make English the
State's Official Language," *Wall Street Journal,* October 31, 1986. One of the earliest signs of language nativism occurred in south Florida when Dade County voters rescinded a resolution that
declared the county to be officially bilingual. Olmo, "Se Habla Inglés."

immigration restriction organization, railed against the "non-economic" consequences of the "Latino onslaught" and that hyper-reproductive Mexican immigrants would have disastrous consequences for America's future: "Can homo contraceptivus compete with homo progenitiva if borders aren't controlled? . . . Perhaps this is the first instance in which those with their pants up are going to get caught by those with their pants down."[71] Unless the United States could stop or reverse the browning of America, Tanton asked rhetorically, will the "present majority [whites] peacefully hand over its political power to a group that is simply more fertile?"[72]

While many saw California's Proposition 63 as an expression of linguistic chauvinism and nativist animus against the 1.6 million undocumented immigrants residing in the state, a majority of Californians had more practical concerns about taxes, the dire budget deficit, an overgrown social welfare system, jobs, crime, and border security, and they blamed undocumented immigrants for economic problems afflicting the state. The failure of IRCA in 1986 to staunch the flow of unsanctioned migrants from Mexico led California and four other states—Texas, Arizona, Florida, and New Jersey—to sue the federal government to recover billions of dollars expended on unauthorized immigrants who, they argued, were the federal government's responsibility. Pete Wilson, a two-term Republican senator elected as governor of California in 1990, lent his support to Proposition 187 and made it the centerpiece of his reelection campaign, blaming "illegal aliens" for costing the state an estimated $3 billion annually in public services and bankrupting the state. The initiative, if passed, would bar undocumented immigrants from receiving welfare, education, nonemergency medical care, and other services paid for by the state—and require teachers and health care workers to report suspected "illegal aliens" to immigration authorities.[73]

Many Californians who supported the initiative felt that the future of the state was at stake. One proponent of 187 believed that a cultural showdown between Anglos and Latinos was inevitable: "They've never merged into the culture . . . it's kind of an island of English-speaking people surrounded by . . . lots of Mexicans." Another supporter, an advertising executive, feared the power of the Latino vote as the Mexican American population continued to grow: "Hispanics could take over . . . They are going to do it legislatively. And there are already radical forces within the Latino community that promote that." Another proponent believed Latinos were a favored minority and that the

71   For a full text of the memo, see "'Witan Memo' III," *Southern Poverty Law Center,* October 10, 1986, www.splcenter.org/get-informed/intelligence-report/browse-all-issues/2002/summer/the-puppeteer/witan-memo-iii.

72   Zita Arocha, "Chavez Quits US English Organization: Ex-Reagan Aide Objected to Memo," *Washington Post,* October 20, 1988; Justin Akers Chacón and Mike Davis, *No One Is Illegal: Fighting Racism and State Violence on the US-Mexico Border* (Chicago: Haymarket Books, 2006), 245–46.

73   Robin Dale Jacobson, *The New Nativism: Proposition 187 and the Debate over Immigration* (Minneapolis: University of Minnesota Press, 2008); Jeffrey R. Margolis, "Closing the Doors to the Land of Opportunity: The Constitutional Controversy Surrounding Proposition 187," *University of Miami Inter-American Law Review* 26 (Winter 1994): 363–401.

federal government had turned a "blind eye" to immigration from Mexico: "I've often wondered how we would have reacted if China were on our border instead of Mexico . . . Yes, I think it would be much different. We'd have tanks and everything at our border."[74] The proposition passed handily, with 59 percent of the voters approving the measure, although district judge Mariana Pfaelzer granted an injunction blocking 187 on the ground that it was in conflict with federal immigration authority.

In Mexico, politicians and the press roundly condemned the California initiative as racist and xenophobic, as did many leaders of Latin American countries who argued that such legislation, if acted upon, would severely damage US relations with Latin America. Upon his arrival at the first Summit of the Americas, convened in Miami in 1994 and attended by representatives from thirty-four nations of North, Central, and South America to discuss the formation of trade blocs and open markets, Guatemalan president Ramiro de León Carpio attacked Proposition 187 as "a flagrant and massive violation of human rights, especially to children." El Salvadoran president Armando Calderon Sol said it was "inconceivable in the United States that a state could vote for something which violates . . . international children's rights."[75] Mexican president Carlos Salinas de Gortari declared that the vote "tramples and ignores" the basic human rights of migrant workers in California. Of the undocumented residents of California who would be denied educational and medical services, Salinas asked: "What will happen to the children? Will they return to Mexico? Wash windshields in California? Sell newspapers on the streets or beg?" In Mexico City two thousand Mexican citizens marched to the US embassy under the banner of the Convención Nacional Democrática (National Democratic Convention) to protest California's ballot initiative and denounce "Wilson culeeeeero" (asshole Wilson); they also called President Salinas's response to 187 "tibia y tardía" (too little too late). After 187 was passed, some vandalized the McDonald's in Mexico City's Zona Rosa tourist district, and in San Diego, Mexican consul general Ramón Xilotl warned that progress toward implementing the North American Free Trade Agreement (NAFTA) could be jeopardized if California's "sentimiento antimexicano" spread to the rest of the United States.[76]

The militarization of the border began in earnest during President Bill Clinton's administration in 1994, the same year as California's Proposition 187, when Attorney General Janet Reno announced "Operation Gatekeeper." Modeled after a similar program—Operation Blockade (renamed "Hold the Line")—along the Texas-Mexico border at El Paso, Operation Gatekeeper added a thousand immigration agents, new surveillance

---

74   Quotes from Jacobson, *New Nativism*, 31, 34, 43.

75   "Latin American Leaders Attack California's New Proposition 187," *Star Tribune*, December 10, 1994.

76   Ugo Pipitone, "187: la Limpieza Étnica del Vecino," November 1, 1994, *Diario de Juárez*, December 2, 1994; Juan José Hinojosa, "187: La Raíz del Problema," *Proceso*, November 14, 1994; Emilio Pradilla Cobos, "Neoliberalismo, TLC [NAFTA], y Xenofobia en EU," November 3, 1994, November 5, 1994; and Elena Gallegos y Emilio Lomas, "Reitera México su Rechazo a la Propuesta 187," *La Jornada*, November 10, 1994.

tactics, and two parallel fences and lighting to the stretch of border between urban Ti-juana, Mexico's third-largest city, and San Diego, the eighth-largest city in the United States.[77] Other operations were launched at key border points: Operation Safeguard in Arizona (1996) and Operation Rio Grande in Brownsville, Texas (1997). In the first year of Operation Gatekeeper Border Patrol agents apprehended almost a half million un-sanctioned immigrants, surpassing apprehensions in other heavily traveled corridors of illegal entry at Tucson, Arizona, and El Paso, Texas. By 2000 nearly seventeen hundred migrants had died along the US-Mexico border, the majority of them in the deserts of Sonora and Arizona, the so-called "Devil's Highway," or drowned in the Rio Grande.[78] As one journalist put it, "there is an unlucky man in the Sonoran Desert today who will die for a chance to pluck dead chickens in Georgia or change diapers in a rest home in Nevada."[79]

Mexico's entry into NAFTA in 1994 was supposed to create enough jobs that would reduce the need for the increasingly hazardous "safety valve" of Mexicans risking their lives to find good-paying jobs in the United States. But the results were mixed. The surge in direct foreign investment in Mexico led to an increase of 500,000 jobs in manufac-turing from 1994 to 2002, but the agricultural sector, where almost a fifth of Mexicans worked, lost 1.3 million jobs. Corn, the crop upon which the pre-Hispanic Mayan civili-zation was built over eight centuries ago and to which 60 percent of Mexico's farmland was devoted, could be grown more cheaply on heavily subsidized agribusiness farms in the United States.[80] As Mexico's protective tariffs were lowered each year during a fifteen-year transition period, imports of US corn increased by 400 percent. Displaced corn farmers in the rural reaches of southern Mexico—Yucatan, Veracruz, Oaxaca—were forced to join migrant streams from central and northern Mexico to the United States to earn a living wage. Mexico's assistant agriculture secretary, José Luis Solis, ad-mitted that NAFTA "would have a significant effect of massive unemployment in the

---

77   Joseph Nevins, *Operation Gatekeeper: The Rise of the "Illegal Alien" and the Making of the U.S.-Mexico Border New York: Routledge, 2002),* 61–94; Bill Ong Hing, *Defining America through Im-migration Policy* (Philadelphia: Temple University Press, 2004), 184–205; "La Operación Guardían, tan Nociva como la Propuesta 187," *La Jornada,* November 6, 1994.

78   Wayne Cornelius, "Death at the Border: Efficacy and Unintended Consequences of US Im-migration Control Policy," *Population and Development Review* 27, no. 4 (December 2001): 661–85; Wendy Brown, *Walled States, Waning Sovereignty* (New York: Zone Books, 2010), 110 (quote); Hing, *Defining America,* 189; B. Drummond Ayres, Jr., "Stepped-up Border Staff Cuts Illegal Crossings," *Austin American-Statesman,* December 13, 1994; Elise Ackerman, "Finally, an Effective Fence," *US News and World Report,* October 19, 1998. For a narrative account of fourteen Mexi-cans, the "Yuma 14," abandoned by their "coyote" and left to die in the Arizona desert, see Luis Alberto Urrea, *The Devil's Highway: A True Story* (Boston: Little, Brown, 2004).

79   Richard Rodriguez, "The 'Great Wall of America' and the Threat from Within," *Los Angeles Times,* September 5, 2010.

80   "The US state of Iowa produced twice as much corn as all of Mexico in the early 1990s, and at half the price." See Martin, this volume.

Mexican countryside," but that cheap corn would benefit the majority of Mexicans since 75 percent of the population was urban.[81] A decade after its ratification, according to a Carnegie Endowment report, "NAFTA has not helped the Mexican economy keep pace with the growing demand for jobs." With the number of visas allotted for Mexican workers grossly inadequate to meet demand, unsanctioned migration continued to increase after NAFTA, as did apprehensions along the border, which increased from 700,000 in 1994 to more than 1.3 million by 2001. During the same period the number of undocumented immigrants increased from 3.5 million to 9.3 million, despite Operation Gatekeeper and INS raids.[82] NAFTA, in short, resulted in the free flow of capital and goods across the border at the same time that the United States was building border fences to keep Mexicans out—a borderless economy and a barricaded border—that, according to Mexico's former president, Carlos Salinas, was supposed to empower a richer, more prosperous Mexico "to export goods, not people."[83]

In 1996 Congress passed the Illegal Immigration Reform and Immigrant Responsibility Act (IIRIRA), a landmark immigration reform law that included some of the toughest provisions ever enacted against unauthorized immigrants: it doubled the number of Border Patrol agents to ten thousand over a period of five years, authorized the construction of a fourteen-mile fence on the border stretching eastward from the Pacific Ocean, enacted harsh penalties for smuggling, and streamlined procedures for expediting deportation without appeal to the courts. IIRIRA also sought to remove the lure of welfare benefits and public services for undocumented immigrants, but it went a step further by limiting benefits for legal immigrants, who would be ineligible for social services for their first five years in the country, and their sponsors would have to sign an affidavit of financial support for the first five years.[84]

The election of George W. Bush in 2000 continued the pattern of formulating immigration reform and greater integration with Mexico under NAFTA at the same time that the administration presided over the massive buildup of border security and enforcement begun almost a decade earlier. Bush announced his interest in reviving a guest-worker program with Mexico, similar to the Bracero Program that ended in 1964, that

81   Susan Ferriss, "Mexican Farmers Charge NAFTA Wrecking Corn Trade: Free Trade Erodes Traditional Base of Rural Economy," *Edmonton Journal,* September 7, 2003.

82   Demetrios G. Papademetriou, John J. Audley, Sandra Polaski, and Scott Vaughan, *NAFTA's Promise and Reality: Lessons from Mexico for the Hemisphere* (Washington, DC: Carnegie Endowment for International Peace, 2004), 6, 48; Norman Caufield, *NAFTA and Labor in North America* (Urbana: University of Illinois Press, 2010), 103–6; Belinda Coote, *NAFTA: Poverty and Free Trade in Mexico* (Oxford: Oxfam, 1995), 21–22; Mike Davis, "The Great Wall of Capital," in *Against the Wall: Israel's Barrier to Peace,* ed. Michael Sorkin (New York: New Press, 2005), 90–97.

83   Elisabeth Malkin, "Nafta's Promise, Unfulfilled," *New York Times,* March 23, 2009.

84   US Congress, *Illegal Immigration Reform and Immigrant Responsibility Act of 1996, Conference Report,* 104th Cong., 2nd Sess. (Washington, DC: US Government Printing Office, 1996); Austin T. Fragomen, Jr., "The Illegal Immigration Reform and Immigrant Responsibility Act of 1996: An Overview," *International Migration Review* 31 (Summer 1997): 438–60.

would give legal status to laborers from Mexico to work in the United States on temporary work contracts. Mexican president Vicente Fox also supported the idea of a guest-worker program that included amnesty for the millions of undocumented migrants already in the US.[85] But talks about immigration reform came to a complete standstill after the terrorist attacks on September 11, 2001, as the administration's War on Terror reframed immigration reform as a national security issue.

Before 9/11, immigration restrictionists worried mainly about the effects of an impoverished global South on the American economy and culture: immigrants taking American jobs and the mushrooming cost of providing social, medical, and educational services to undocumented immigrants. Others worried about the ominous cultural and linguistic consequences of the "browning of America." After 9/11, Americans were principally preoccupied with their safety and security: immigrants, legal and illegal, became suspected "fifth columnists" for terrorist organizations like al-Qaeda and more recently ISIS. Immigrants don't just "take our jobs"—they take our lives. America would never be safe until the federal government sealed the US-Mexico border from surreptitious entry by dangerous terrorist aliens. To make the border more secure from illegal immigrants, drug smugglers, and foreign terrorists, the House Homeland Security chairman Peter King urged DHS to deploy more unmanned aerial vehicles—drones—along the border because, he said, "We need to treat the border as a quasi-war zone."[86] By conflating illegal immigration with terrorism, border enforcement merged with the War on Terror and the War on Drugs to create, as one critic put it, "what can only be described as a permanent state of low-intensity warfare along the US-Mexican border."[87]

In Congress supporters of immigration reform, led by Republican senator John McCain and Democratic senator Ted Kennedy, introduced legislation to create a guest-worker program and offer a "path to citizenship" for undocumented immigrants. House Judiciary Committee chairman Jim Sensenbrenner fiercely opposed the bipartisan bill because it did not include provisions to secure the border against illegal immigration. He proposed his own bill, H.R. 4437, the "Border Protection, Anti-Terrorism and Illegal Immigration Control Act," which called for the construction of a seven-hundred-mile reinforced fence along the border, and included two provisions that were so shockingly punitive that millions of Americans took to the streets to protest: the bill made "illegal presence" in the United States an "aggravated felony" instead of a civil offense—in other words, unauthorized immigrants could be subject to sentencing guidelines similar to

---

85   For an analysis of Bush's proposed reform of the agricultural worker program, see Camille J. Bosworth, "Guest Worker Policy: A Critical Analysis of President Bush's Proposed Reform," *Hastings Law Review* 56 (May 2005): 1095–120; Dan Eggen and Helen Dewar, "Bush Weighing Plan for Mexican Guest Workers," *Washington Post,* July 25, 2001.

86   George Cahlink, "New Homeland Security Chairman Sees Larger Role for UAVs in Border Security," *Defense Daily,* October 14, 2005.

87   Davis, "The Great Wall of Capital," 93.

those for murder, rape, and sexual abuse of a minor. The bill would also subject any person found guilty of assisting an undocumented immigrant to a prison sentence of up to five years. It included no guest-worker or legalization provisions. Nonetheless, the Sensenbrenner Bill, the most draconian anti-immigrant legislation ever seriously proposed, easily passed in the Republican-dominated House, 239 to 182, with the majority of members voting along party lines (92 percent of Republicans in favor and 82 percent of Democrats opposed).[88]

In response to the bill, 3.5 million immigrants and native-born Americans organized peaceful marches in 120 cities from March to May 1, 2006, including Los Angeles, Chicago, New York, San Antonio, Houston, Dallas, Phoenix, San Francisco, Detroit, and Atlanta. Many carried signs, reading "We Are America," and "Hoy Marchamos, Mañana Votamos" (Today We March, Tomorrow We Vote).[89] Senator Kennedy, addressing 200,000 people at a rally in Washington, DC, told those gathered: "I look across this historic gathering and I see the future of America. You are what this debate is about. It is about good people who come to America to work, to raise their families, to contribute to their communities, and to reach for the American dream. This debate goes to the heart of who we are as Americans. It will determine who can earn the privilege of citizenship. It will determine our strength in separating those who would harm us from those who contribute to our values."[90] Despite pleas across the nation for a kinder and gentler immigration policy, raids and deportations authorized by the Department of Homeland Security (DHS) continued unabated. The president of the National Council of La Raza, Janet Murguía, declared at its annual convention in 2008, "Our nation's immigration laws need to be enforced. But what is happening today with these raids is an assault on civil rights, common decency and basic human dignity."[91]

With the House and Senate divided over immigration reform, both parties managed to agree on a bill that both houses could support: the construction of a reinforced fence

---

88   Rachel L. Swarns, "Tough Border Security Bill Nears Passage in the House," New York Times, December 14, 2005. For an overview of the bill and the protest marches that followed its passage in the House, see Leo R. Chavez, The Latino Threat: Constructing Immigrants, Citizens, and the Nation (Stanford, CA: Stanford University Press, 2008), 152–76.

89   Table 8.1: "Selected Immigrant Rights Marches, Spring 2006," 36, in Xóchitl Bada, Jonathan Fox, and Andrew Selee, Invisible No More: Mexican Migrant Civil Participation in the United States (Washington, DC: Woodrow Wilson International Center for Scholars, 2006); "Churches Take Immigration Reform Fight into the Streets," National Catholic Reporter, March 31, 2006; Adrian D. Pantoja and Cecilia Menjívar, "The Spring Marches of 2006: Latinos, Immigration, and Political Mobilization in the 21st Century," American Behavioral Scientist 52, no. 4 (December 2008): 499–506.

90   "Senator Kennedy Rallies for Immigration Reform," April 10, 2006, www.tedkennedy.org/ownwords/event/immigration_rally.

91   Quoted in Roberto Suro, "Out of the Shadows, into the Light," in Rallying for Immigrant Rights: The Fight for Inclusion in 21st Century America, ed. Kim Voss and Irene Bloemraad (Berkeley: University of California Press, 2011), 255.

along the border. A week before the midterm elections in 2006, President Bush reluctantly signed the Secure Fence Act authorizing the construction of a seven-hundred-mile border fence at a cost of $3 million per mile. Mexican president Fox was even less pleased than Bush and issued a statement, signed by nearly every Central and South American member state of the Organization of American States, calling the "secure fence" legislation a unilateral measure that "goes against the spirit of understanding . . . between neighboring countries" and that undermines "cooperation in the hemisphere."[92] After signing the act, President Bush hoped that Congress might pass the Development, Relief and Education for Alien Minors (DREAM) Act, which would grant legal residence to any undocumented minor brought to the United States as a child, provided they attended college or served in the military. The DREAM Act had already failed to pass three times as separate bills or attachments to omnibus bills between 2003 and 2005. Adversaries of the act, calling it the Nightmare Act, warned that passage would lead to even more immigration under family reunification provisions, and that amnesty—even for children brought to the United States illegally through no fault of their own—would offer continued incentive to Mexican migrants to enter the United States unlawfully.[93]

Drug smuggling had always been a concern of those advocating stricter border enforcement and the construction of a fence, but it was only part of a larger complex of fears and anxieties that affected those living in the border states, as well as many Americans in cities across the country where "minorities" outnumbered whites. In 2004, two years before construction of the seven-hundred-mile border fence began, a loose network of mostly white men calling themselves the "Minutemen," including founders Jim Gilchrist (Minuteman Project) and Chris Simcox (Civil Homeland Defense), converged on the border to defend the sovereignty of the nation against the Brown Peril, doing what they claimed the government had failed to do, namely, enforce immigration laws at the US-Mexico border.[94] Armed with lawn chairs, binoculars, and in some instances, weapons, many Minutemen expressed the nativist concern that "illegal aliens" were not simply ignoring immigration laws, damaging property, transporting drugs, and taking jobs from US citizens, they were also changing America in ways they did not like—and they aimed "to take America back."

Minutemen saw themselves as patriots committed to protecting America from legions of "illegal aliens," the "enemy within," and the advance guard of an invading army. A sociologist who spent years on the border conducting interviews in Minutemen camps narrates a conversation with "Earl," a veteran of the first Gulf War and gunstore owner in his mid-forties, who explains, "What's happening is nothing less than invasion. . . . We have already lost California. I walk around parts of Los Angeles and no one speaks

---

92   Michael A. Fletcher and Jonathan Weisman, "Bush Signs Bill Authorizing 700-Mile Fence for Border," *Washington Post*, October 27, 2006.

93   On the DREAMer immigrant youth movement, see Walter J. Nicholls, *The DREAMers: How the Undocumented Youth Movement Transformed the Immigrant Rights Debate* (Stanford, CA: Stanford University, 2013).

94   See website for Minuteman Project, minutemanproject.com/jim-gilchrist.

English, all the signs are in Spanish. I feel like a complete outsider in my own country." Their goal, the interviewer tells us, "is deceptively simple: to prevent the collapse of America."[95] When Simcox launched his Civil Homeland Defense volunteer border militia, the white supremacist blog Stormfront, calling itself a "White Nationalist Community," enthusiastically supported his nativist effort "to stop the Mexican invasion" and praised the border militia as "Aryan warriors" who "seek nothing less than an end to the Browning of America."[96] The Minutemen were mostly older, white, retired, and often divorced working-class men who felt they had been left behind by America's rapidly changing economy and made to feel increasingly powerless and unimportant, strangers in their own land.[97]

In spring 2010 the Arizona senate passed one of the most controversial anti-illegal immigrations bills on record: SB 1070, "Support Our Law Enforcement and Safe Neighborhoods Act." The bill institutionalized racial profiling by requiring that police check the legal status of those they have a "reasonable suspicion" of being in the country illegally during "any lawful stop, detention or arrest" in the enforcement of local or state laws. In effect, Arizona would become the first state to demand that immigrants—or anyone who "looked like" one—carry documents demonstrating that they are in the country legally.[98] In just three decades, from 1980 to 2010, the Latino population increased 180 percent, while the white population declined from 72 percent to 58 percent, and the white school-age population dropped to 43 percent, compared to 83 percent of the seniors. Like California and Texas, Arizona was on the fast track to becoming a majority-minority state. Eight other states took steps toward passing similar legislation: Florida, Kentucky, Mississippi, Missouri, Oklahoma, North Carolina, Tennessee, and Virginia. In the first half of 2013, according to the National Council of State Legislatures, forty-three states and the District of Columbia passed a total of 377 laws and resolutions related to immigration, an 83 percent increase from the 206 laws and resolutions enacted in the first half of 2012.[99]

Nativism Redux and the Decline of Liberal Democracy
President Trump embodied the worst fears of nativists determined to save America from becoming more multicultural than it already is. In the first three years he lowered the

95   Harel Shapira, *Waiting for José: The Minutemen's Pursuit of America* (Princeton, NJ: Princeton University Press, 2013), 2.

96   Quoted in Roxanne Lynn Doty, *The Law into Their Own Hands: Immigration and the Politics of Exceptionalism* (Tucson: University of Arizona Press, 2009), 59–60.

97   Ibid., 121.

98   For a summary of the bill's main provisions, see Mara Knaub, "SB 1070: What It Says," *Tribune Business News*, May 30, 2010. For a complete text of the bill, see www.azleg.gov/legtext/49leg/2r/bills/sb1070s.pdf. On nativist and antifederal government politics leading to the passage of SB 1070, see Jeff Biggers, *State Out of the Union: Arizona and the Final Showdown over the American Dream* (New York: Nation Books, 2012).

99   National Council of State Legislatures, *Immigrant Policy Project*, September 6, 2013, www.ncsl.org/issues-research/immig/immgration-report-august-2013.aspx; "Anti-Illegal Immigration Laws in States," *New York Times*, April 22, 2012.

ceiling for refugee resettlement to record lows, restricted travel to the US from Muslim-majority nations, and promised to end the Deferred Action for Childhood Arrivals (DACA) program unless Congress appropriated billions of dollars to build a wall on the US-Mexico border. In January 2018 the Department of Homeland Security terminated the Temporary Protective Status (TPS) program for 200,000 Salvadorians who had been living in the US for over a decade. Trump also dismantled the Central American Minors (CAM) program that permitted refugee children ("unaccompanied alien minors") from the Northern Triangle states (Honduras, El Salvador, and Guatemala) to join their legally present parents in the United States. And in 2018 he introduced a "zero-tolerance" policy calling for the prosecution of all individuals who illegally enter the United States, resulting in the separation of parents from their children when they enter the country together.

The rapid succession of nativist, anti-immigrant policies should come as no surprise. In his announcement to seek the Republican nomination for president on June 16, 2015 Trump characterized immigrants from Mexico as "rapists" and a threat to the nation's security, reflecting the views of many Americans in his political base—mostly white, non-college-educated voters—but also the majority of college-educated white women and men.[100] What Trump managed to do in a very short time was to zero in on the need for America to seal itself off from Europe's refugee crisis by accepting even fewer refugees, and at the same time terminate the Temporary Protection Status for Central Americans already in the US, some for decades, who faced deportation. These and other policies can be viewed in the context of anti-immigrant backlash politics that began in earnest in the 1990s, but also owed to the fateful role of Cold War US foreign policy in the case of Northern Triangle and other countries. ("We are here because you were there").[101]

A democracy that guarantees the constitutional rights of all its citizens (equal protection of the laws), but abridges them for noncitizens and nonwhite citizens on spurious

---

100   "Revised Executive Order Bans Travelers from Six Muslim-Majority Countries from Getting New Visas," March 6, 2017, www.washingtonpost.com/world/national-security/new-executive-order-bans-travelers-from-six-muslim-majority-countries-applying-for-visas/2017/03/06/3012a42a-0277-11e7-ad5b-d22680e18d10_story.html?utm_term=.a62a9b853879; "Trump Moves to End DACA and Calls on Congress to Act," September 5, 2017, www.nytimes.com/2017/09/05/us/politics/trump-daca-dreamers-immigration.html; "Trump Administration Says That Nearly 200,000 Salvadorans Must Leave," January 8, 2018, www.nytimes.com/2018/01/08/us/salvadorans-tps-end.html; "Trump Administration Ends Obama-Era Protection Program for Central American Minors," August 16, 2017, www.washingtonpost.com/politics/trump-administration-ends-obama-era-protection-program-for-central-american-minors/2017/08/16/8101507e-82b6-11e7-ab27-1a21a8e006ab_story.html?utm_term=.66c8395965fe

101   See, for example, Stephen G. Rabe, *Killing Zone: The United States Wages Cold War in Latin America* (New York: Oxford University Press, 2015); Greg Grandin, *The Last Colonial Massacre: Latin America in the Cold War* (Chicago: University of Chicago Press, 2011); Rebecca Gordon, "The Current Migrant Crisis Was Created by US Foreign Policy, Not Trump," *The Nation*, August 16, 2019, https://www.thenation.com/article/archive/central-america-migrant-crisis-foreign-policy-trump/ (accessed May 20, 2020).

legal and constitutional grounds (e.g., slavery, Alien and Sedition Acts, Jim Crow laws, lynchings, race-based migration laws, Japanese internment, mass incarceration of African Americans and Latinos, state and federal laws against LGBTQ marriage, voter suppression, anti-immigrant and anti-Muslim policies, and ongoing police murders of unarmed Black men and women), is certifiably illiberal (although considerably less so than Russia, Turkey, Hungary, Poland, Venezuela, Nicaragua, and Pakistan). As many political theorists have pointed out, beginning with Alexis de Tocqueville over 150 years ago, rule by the majority can easily lead to the "tyranny of the majority," which explains how slavery and later Jim Crow laws endured for over two centuries until the civil rights acts of the 1960s. Or how raced-based citizenship and immigration laws endured for over 150 years, from the Naturalization Act of 1790 to the Immigration and Nationality Act of 1965. The cherished belief in the virtues and liberal values embodied in the Declaration of Independence and the Constitution—the hallmark of American national identity—is challenged by the blunt facts of history.

A similar argument can be made for many European democracies that have enacted liberal immigration and refugee policies since World War II, only to reverse course in this century in response to the growing political pressure of ethno-nationalist parties, such as Alternative für Deutschland, Front National (now National Rally) in France, Freedom Party in Netherlands, U.K. Independence Party, Danish Peoples Party, and the League in Italy. In the Netherlands, Denmark, and Germany, for example, many third- and higher-generation Africans, Muslims, and Turks are rarely accepted as truly Dutch, Danish, or German because their race, religion, and culture mark them as lesser citizens. Rapidly changing demographics due to migration and low fertility rates of whites have fueled fears that "Europe is committing suicide," as British journalist Douglas Murray put it in the first sentence of his book *The Strange Death of Europe: Immigration, Identity, Islam* (2017). Murray's bleak prophecy recapitulates French author Jean Raspail's nativist warnings against the barbarians at the gate in his bestselling 1973 novel, *The Camp of the Saints*, which depicts in apocalyptic terms how mass immigration destroys France and Western civilization. More recently, the French author Renaud Camus published *Le Grand Remplacement* (The Great Replacement) in 2011, warning that French culture and civilization was in imminent danger of being subverted by Muslims.

Like their counterparts in Europe, nativist authors in the US have published dozens of books in the last two decades that make similar arguments, with titles like *Alien Nation*; *The Death of the West*; *State of Emergency*; *Disuniting of America*; *In Mortal Danger*; *Barbarians*; and *Adios America!* As the former chairman of the House Immigration Reform Caucus, nativist representative Tom Tancredo declared that undocumented migrants had a "death grip" on the nation and warned, "We are committing cultural suicide. . . . The barbarians at the gate will only need to give us a slight push, and the emaciated body of Western civilization will collapse in a heap."[102] Like Tancredo, nativists believe that immigrants from Mexico and other countries of Central and South America and the Caribbean have no place in Western civilization.

---

102   Quoted in Tony Horwitz, "Immigration—and the Curse of the Black Legend," *New York Times*, July 9, 2006.

White nationalists summon a vision of a bygone America when whites were 85 percent of the population, as they were in 1960; and Blacks, Asians, and Latinos together constituted only 15 percent of the total population. They and their nativist predecessors, going back to Benjamin Franklin and Thomas Jefferson, among other Founding Fathers and presidents, believed deeply that America was a country founded by and for "free white persons" and must forever remain so. But the US was never a country of only white persons, beginning with Native peoples and African Americans, enslaved and free—up to the present moment when immigrants from Latin America, Asia, and Africa, documented and undocumented, proclaim "We are America," as they did during the protests against the Sensenbrenner bill in 2006 (to make unlawful presence in the US a felony offense). Like millions of immigrants before them, they came mainly to find jobs, to escape oppression, to reinvent themselves, and to raise their children in a land where the rule of law prevailed. That much has not changed for the majority of immigrants. But for over ten million undocumented immigrants, living in the shadows of America can be a frightening experience. They never know the day or the hour when ICE (Immigration and Customs Enforcement) will appear at their homes or workplace with orders to deport them from the America they consider home to their countries of origin.

The threat of deportation has been most frightening for foreign-born children (DREAMers) who, through no fault of their own, were brought to this country illegally by their undocumented immigrant parents and have been living in fear of being deported to countries they have not lived in since they were infants. According to one study, two out of three were younger than ten when they came, and three out of four were born in Mexico.[103] Many learned that they were not US citizens only when they were older and could not provide Social Security numbers for job applications or driver's licenses, or take advantage of scholarship offers to college.[104] The Obama administration took a small step in 2012 to provide relief to DREAMers by implementing the Deferred Action for Childhood Arrivals (DACA) program, which enabled DREAMers to apply for a two-year deferral of deportation and made them eligible for federal work permits and driver's licenses.[105] In 2017 President Trump's attorney general, Jeff Sessions, announced that the administration was rescinding DACA in a six-month phaseout.[106]

---

103   William Perez and Daniel G. Solorzano, *We Are Americans: Undocumented Students Pursing the American Dream* (Sterling, VA: Stylus, 2009), xxv. See also Hillary S. Kosnac et al., eds., *One Step In and One Step Out: The Lived Experience of Immigrant Participants in the Deferred Action for Childhood Arrivals (DACA) Program* (University of California, San Diego: Center for Comparative Immigration Studies, 2015).

104   Quoted in Marie Friedman Marquardt et al., *Living "Illegal": The Human Face of Unauthorized Immigration* (New York: New Press, 2013), 250.

105   On DREAMers and the contemporary politics of immigration see Tom K. Wong, *The Politics of Immigration: Partisanship, Demographic Change, and American National Identity* (New York: Oxford University Press, 2016).

106   "Trump Administration Rescinds DACA, Fueling Renewed Push in Congress and the Courts to Protect DREAMers," *Migration Policy Institute*, September 15, 2017, www .migrationpolicy.org/article/trump-administration-rescinds-daca-fueling-renewed-push

The Russian novelist Fyodor Dostoyevsky allegedly said that "the degree of civilization in a society can be judged by entering its prisons." It can also be judged by the degree to which a society extends, or fails to extend, humane treatment to refugees and immigrants. Beginning in 2018, when tens of thousands of refugees fled the violence and economic hardships of Guatemala, Honduras, and El Salvador to seek asylum in the US, Trump ordered the Department of Homeland Security to refuse them entry, expedite deportation procedures, and most controversially, separate children from their mothers at the border as a way to deter future migrants. In 2020 Trump used the public health emergency of the COVID-19 pandemic to close the labor market to immigrants despite the roles many played in providing essential services, such as health care, agriculture, transportation, and "critical manufacturing," which includes everyone along the food supply chain, from immigrant meatpackers to grocery store workers, line cooks, and delivery drivers. Trump invoked the Defense Production Act, having declined to use it to boost production of respirators and coronavirus test kits, to declare meat a "scarce and critical material essential to the national defense."[107] Workers in meatpacking plants were forced back to work without safety precautions, despite the high rate of infections in meat plants.[108] Infection rate were highest, according to the *New Yok Times* COVID-19 database, in food processing and correctional facilities—"39 of the 40 largest known virus clusters" in the US.[109] As one journalist put it, "The question is not whose work is essential, but for *whom* it is essential."[110] With COVID-19 deaths approaching the 100,000 threshold in May 2020, the highest number of any country, Trump issued a proclamation closing the US border for sixty days under the guise of containing the

-congress-and-courts-protect-dreamers (accessed May 11, 2020). On June 18, 2020, the Supreme Court ruled that the Trump administration could not end the DACA policy protecting 700,000 DREAMers from deportation. "Trump Can't Immediately End DACA, Supreme Court Rules," *New York Times*, June 18, 2020, www.nytimes.com/2020/06/18/us/trump-daca-supreme-court .html?action=click&module=Top%20Stories&pgtype=Homepage (accessed June 18, 2020).

107   "President Trump Issues Executive Order Invoking Defense Production Act for Meat and Poultry Processors," *Lexology*, April 29, 2020, www.lexology.com/library/detail.aspx?g=8b56e613 -8e13-4327-bf51-08d68a52ada6 (accessed May13, 2020).

108   *Advisory Memorandum on Identification of Essential Critical Infrastructure during COVID-19 Response*, US Department of Homeland Security, March 28, 2020, https://www.cisa.gov/sites/ default/files/publications/Version_3.0_CISA_Guidance_on_Essential_Critical_Infrastructure _Workers_1.pdf (accessed May 9, 2020); "Trump Declares Meat Supply 'Critical,' Aiming to Reopen Plants," *New York Times*, April 28, 2020, www.nytimes.com/2020/04/28/business/economy/ coronavirus-trump-meat-food-supply.html (accessed May 7, 2020); "Trump Deems Farmworkers 'Essential' but Not Safety Rules for Them," *Politico*, www.politico.com/news/2020/05/12/trump -farmworkers-essential-coronavirus-safety-250142 (accessed May 8, 2020).

109   "Coronavirus Live Updates: The Outbreak Is Worsening Globally, the W.H.O. Warns," *New York Times*, May 8, 2020, www.nytimes.com/2020/06/08/world/coronavirus-live-updates .html?action=click&module=Top%20Stories&pgtype=Homepage (accessed May 8, 2020).

110   John Patrick Leary, "Es-sen-tial: Adjective," *The New Republic* (June 2020), 9.

"invisible enemy."[111] Trump came to power scapegoating immigrants and refugees, and he continued to double down on them in the wake of the worst pandemic since 1918.

A century after the passage of the Immigration and Nationality Act of 1924 that imposed restrictions based on national origin and barred immigration from Asia on the grounds that only "free, white persons" eligible for naturalized citizenship could be admitted, the US witnessed the resurgence of xenophobic populist politics, beginning with Proposition 187 in California in 1994 to deny social, medical, and educational services to undocumented immigrants, mostly from Mexico; the backlash against Muslims in the aftermath of 9–11; and the Great Recession (2007–9). The election of Donald Trump in 2016 captured and capitalized on nativist fears with the promise of restoring America to its former greatness when there were far fewer immigrants from Latin America, Asia, and Africa. But there is no turning back the demographic clock to a greater, whiter America, no "back to the future" tribal immigration politics of the 1920s.[112] Even with immigration at historic lows, with more Mexicans returning to Mexico than entering the US, white Americans are on target to comprise less than 50 percent of the population in a little over two decades. Declining birth rates, not immigration, are the main drivers of demographic change in the twenty-first century.[113] As the population ages, demand for young immigrant workers will increase, although Mexico's aging population and low birth rate (about the same as the US) rule out the possibility of its ever again providing a limitless reservoir of labor as it did in the 1990s. What the future holds for the 10.5 million undocumented immigrants who continue to live in fear of deportation, and thousands of refugees denied entry and deported to their home countries, is an open question.

The slow but steady reversal of rights since World War II does not augur well for the future of liberal democracy in the United States or other democracies that have embraced reactionary nationalist policies. As the third decade of the twenty-first century dawns, US and European democracies are at a crossroads. Antiracist movements have held protests in hundreds of cities around the world in the wake of George Floyd's murder and ongoing racism in Western countries. The Black Lives Matter movement in the US, organized in 2013 after the acquittal of George Zimmerman, Trayvon Martin's murderer, continues to demand deep-seated economic and cultural change, as well as an end to militarized policing of communities of color. Reactionary white nationalists, fearing

---

111 "Trump's Covid-19 Immigration Proclamation May Be Legal, But It's Still an Abuse of Power," *Just Security*, www.justsecurity.org/69952/trumps-Covid-19-immigration-proclamation-may-be-legal-but-its-still-an-abuse-of-power/ (accessed May 7,2020).

112 James F. Hollifield, "The Migration Challenge," *Governance in an Emerging New World* (Spring series, Issue 619), May 6, 2019, www.hoover.org/research/migration-challenge (accessed June 13, 2020).

113 Canada, in contrast, continues to have a liberal immigration policy. See Triadafilopoulos/ Taylor, this volume.

the demographic decline of the white population, cling to a vision of the future in which they prevail over the majority nonwhite population that is ineluctably and, as *Time* presaged decades ago, "irreversibly the America to come." To what degree America's nonwhite majority in the second half of the century will influence immigration policy from Asia, Latin America, and Africa—not to mention domestic and foreign policy—is a question that hinges in large part on America's willingness to reinvent itself as a global nation of immigrants and a refuge for those seeking escape from violence and extreme poverty.

11 CANADA

The Quintessential Migration State?

Phil Triadafilopoulos and Zack Taylor

HAS CANADA SOLVED the liberal paradox? In contrast to other liberal democracies, the politics of immigration in Canada has been relatively subdued. Bucking the trend toward greater restrictiveness, Canadian governments have steadily increased annual immigration levels. Cross-party political consensus in support of an expansive immigration policy has endured economic slowdowns in the early 1980s and 1990s, the recessions of 2001–2 and 2009–10, and the global pandemic of 2020. The consensus on immigration extends to widespread support for Canada's policy of official multiculturalism and its liberal citizenship regime. Unlike the United States, Canada's close ally and neighbor, populist anti-immigrant politics in Canada remain marginal.[1] The dismal showing of the People's Party of Canada in the 2019 federal election demonstrated this point vividly.

Canada's distinctiveness in the areas of immigration and multiculturalism has been attributed to its isolated geography and progressive immigration and multiculturalism policies. While we agree that geography and policy are important, we argue that political and institutional factors must also be taken into consideration. Specifically, we emphasize the interaction of three distinctive features of the Canadian case: the relative concentration of immigrants and associated cultural communities and institutions within large metropolitan areas, Canada's relatively liberal citizenship policy, and its Single Member Plurality (SMP) electoral system. The confluence of these factors has magnified the electoral importance of new Canadian voters, heightening competition among parties for the support of new Canadians, and thereby limiting anti-immigration politics. This has resulted in a robust cross-party political consensus on the basic features of Canada's immigration policy.

We begin with a brief overview of the development of the Canadian migration state, from Canada's founding in 1867 to its centennial in 1967. This one-hundred-year period witnessed Canada's transformation from a country that carefully sifted immigrants according to racial criteria in the name of building a "white man's country" to adopting a universal admissions system that granted preference according to prospective

---

1 With the partial exception of the province of Quebec, which we discuss below.

immigrants' human capital. The decade following the introduction of the "points system" in 1967 witnessed rapid changes in sources of immigration, the introduction of official multiculturalism in 1971, the entrenchment of Canada's universal admissions system in the Immigration Act of 1976, and the liberalization of citizenship policy with the passage of the Citizenship Act of 1977. While important changes to immigration policy have been introduced since then, the foundations of the regime that was consolidated in the 1970s remain in place even as the 1976 act has given way to the Immigration and Refugee Protection Act (IRPA) of 2001.

After considering the idiosyncratic features of the Canadian model, specifically its expansionary trajectory and support among the general public, we survey explanations highlighting the importance of geography and policy and then develop our claim regarding the interaction of settlement patterns, citizenship policy, and Canada's electoral system. We conclude by arguing that the portability of the Canadian model of immigration and multiculturalism is limited. While other countries may borrow from Canada with respect to policy, given the contingent factors shaping the politics of immigration in Canada, policy-makers in other states cannot expect to enjoy the leeway granted to Canadian governments. That being said, the liberalization of citizenship policy across most liberal-democratic states and growing share of voters with a migration background suggest that changing political considerations may lead political actors in other countries to reconsider how they approach the politics of immigration. Germany stands out as a case in point.[2] Although Angela Merkel famously rejected multiculturalism in 2010, she has also spearheaded Germany's development of liberal immigration policy and "welcome culture." The German case demonstrates that electoral considerations can help steer policy in a more liberal direction, even where geography and previous policy legacies are not as advantageous as in Canada.

Toward a Liberal Migration State: From White Canada to the Points System

The challenge of reconciling immigration's economic benefits and the imperatives of nation-building is long-standing. Canada, along with Australia, the United States, and other countries, pursued this balancing act quite differently in the years before and after World War II. The liberal migration state theorized by James Hollifield is very much a post–World War II phenomenon. Prior to this, immigrant-receiving countries used racially discriminatory policies to sift immigration in a manner that complemented their nation-building prerogatives. As David FitzGerald and David Cook-Martin have pointed out, these policies were not antithetical to the democratic norms of the day.[3]

---

2   Triadafilos Triadafilopoulos, "Germany's Post-2015 Immigration Dilemmas," *Current History* 118, no. 806 (2019): 108–13; Florian Trauner and Jocelyn Turton, "'Welcome Culture': The Emergence and Transformation of a Public Debate on Migration," *Österreichische Zeitschrift für Politikwissenschaft* 46, no. 1 (2017): 33–42; Karen Schönwälder and Triadafilos Triadafilopoulos, "The New Differentialism: Responses to Immigrant Diversity in Germany," *German Politics* 25, no. 3 (2016): 366–80.

3   David FitzGerald and David Cook-Martin, *Culling the Masses: The Democratic Origins of Racist Immigration Policy in the Americas* (Cambridge MA: Harvard University Press, 2014).

On the contrary, democracy and prevailing understandings of liberalism were perfectly compatible with racially discriminatory exclusions.

This is clear in the Canadian case. Although immigration has been an important part of Canada's political development since Confederation in 1867, up until the late 1960s discriminatory policies ensured that only those deemed suitable from a racial point of view were admitted. In practical terms, this meant that entry into Canada was limited to white Europeans, preferably from the British Isles and other parts of Western Europe. Nonwhite immigrants were considered poor material for the task of nation-building and were subject to exclusionary laws and administrative practices. Canada's first prime minister, Sir John A. Macdonald, vividly expressed the thinking underlying these policies in a statement on immigration policy made in 1885:

> [All] natural history, all ethnology shows that while the crosses of the Aryan races are successful—while the mixture of all those races which are known or believed to spring from common origins is more or less successful—they will amalgamate. If you look around the world you will see that the Aryan races will not wholesomely amalgamate with the Africans or the Asiatics. It is not desired that they should come; that we should have a mongrel race; that the Aryan character of the future of British America should be destroyed by a cross or crosses of that kind. . . . Let us encourage all the races which are cognate races, which cross and amalgamate naturally, and we shall see that such amalgamation will produce, as a result, a race equal if not superior to the two races which mingle. But the cross of [Aryan and non-Aryan] races, like the cross of the dog and the fox, is not successful; it cannot be, it never will be.[4]

Macdonald's views on immigration and integration were broadly shared among political elites and the public and informed immigration policy-making through the nineteenth and twentieth centuries. Immigration policy was designed with an eye to maintaining Canada's status as a "white man's country."[5] An explicit hierarchy of "races" also distinguished ranks of European immigrants; while immigrants from the British Isles and northwestern Europe were actively recruited, those from southern and eastern Europe were greeted with far less enthusiasm and subjected to assimilatory pressures based on the principle of "Anglo conformity."[6]

---

4   Cited in Daiva Stasiulis and Yasmeen Abu-Laban, "Unequal Relations and the Struggle for Equality: Race and Ethnicity in Canadian Politics," in *Canadian Politics in the 21st Century*, 6th ed., ed. Michael Whittington and Michael Williams (Toronto: Thompson-Nelson, 2004), 377. Also see Paul Gordon Lauren, *Power and Prejudice: The Politics and Diplomacy of Racial Discrimination*, 2nd ed. (Boulder, CO: Westview Press, 1996), 41.

5   Triadafilos Triadafilopoulos, "Building Walls, Bounding Nations: Migration and Exclusion in Canada and Germany, 1870–1939," *Journal of Historical Sociology* 17, no. 4 (2004): 385–427; Marilyn Lake and Henry Reynolds, *Drawing the Global Colour Line: White Men's Countries and the International Challenge of Racial Equality* (Cambridge: Cambridge University Press, 2008), 6.

6   Raymond Breton, "From Ethnic to Civic Nationalism: English Canada and Quebec," *Ethnic and Racial Studies* 11, no. 1 (1988): 88–89; Joseph Levitt, "Race and Nation in Canadian Anglophone Historiography," *Canadian Review of Studies on Nationalism* 8 (1981): 1–16; David Nock,

Immigration preferences reflected the prevailing "scientific racism" of the late nineteenth and early twentieth centuries. Scientific racism informed a global-level cultural code "founded largely on phenotypical distinctions within which the peoples of advanced industrial societies, northwest European whites, were the elect; this moral status . . . legitimized political domination and economic exploitation of the less worthy."[7] This code influenced immigration and citizenship policy-making, providing ideas that shaped judgments on the suitability of racialized groups. The ubiquity of racial classifications and the linking of race with national identity generated a noteworthy similarity of immigration restrictions and controls across settler countries. Immigration policies were designed with an eye to protecting societies deemed "vulnerable to contamination from immigration and 'hybridization' [from] those who would pass along their deficiencies."[8] Liberalism's comfortable coexistence with social Darwinism, scientific racism, and xenophobia during this period of policy innovation ensured that the equality it propounded was reserved for members of the "civilized peoples."[9]

Prohibitions on political rights and de facto barriers to naturalization for "unsuitable races" also marked the Canadian state's evolving membership regime. As Andrea Geiger has pointed out, "The denial of the franchise to naturalized citizens of Asian ancestry was the keystone of the racial hierarchy established by British Columbia during the late nineteenth and early twentieth centuries."[10] The harmonization of naturalization across the British Dominions, which culminated in the New Naturalization Act of 1914, tightened naturalization requirements and granted the secretary of state absolute discretion in the granting of citizenship along with the power to revoke the citizenship of naturalized immigrants.[11]

"Patriotism and Patriarchs: Anglican Archbishops and Canadianization," *Canadian Ethnic Studies* 14 (1982): 85–100.

7   Aristide R. Zolberg, "Dilemmas at the Gate: The Politics of Immigration in Advanced Industrial Societies," unpublished paper presented at the 1982 meeting of the American Political Science Association.

8   Kay J. Anderson, "The Idea of Chinatown: The Power of Place and Institutional Practice in the Making of a Racial Category," in *Immigration in Canada: Historical Perspectives*, ed. Gerald Tulchinsky (Toronto: Copp Clark Longman, 1994), 230; W. S. Wallace, "The Canadian Immigration Policy," *Canadian Magazine* 30 (1907–8): 358.

9   Triadafilos Triadafilopoulos, *Becoming Multicultural: Immigration and the Politics of Membership in Canada and Germany* (Vancouver: UBC Press, 2012), 23.

10   Andrea Geiger, *Subverting Exclusion: Transpacific Encounters with Race, Caste, and Borders, 1885–1928* (New Haven, CT: Yale University Press, 2011), 144.

11   H. F. Angus, "The Legal Status in British Columbia of Residents of Oriental Race and Their Descendants," *Canadian Bar Review* 9, no. 1 (1931): 10. Requirements for naturalization included: five years' residence or five years of service to the Crown; an intention to continue to reside in Canada or serve the Crown; good character; knowledge of English or French. Reasons for rejection were not required and appeal was impossible.

Canada's discriminatory immigration policies began to be challenged after the Second World War as a consequence of the discrediting of scientific racism, the emergence of human rights, and the acceleration of the decolonization movement.[12] Like racial segregation and other forms of exclusion, discriminatory immigration policies were targeted by reformers, including aggrieved domestic constituencies, foreign governments, and international organizations. Pressure from the Committee for the Repeal of the Chinese Immigration Act moved the government to strike the act in 1947.[13] The repeal of discriminatory naturalization regulations soon followed, lifting bars to citizenship for Chinese immigrants and other groups that had long faced discrimination in this area.[14] Similarly, efforts to counter charges of discrimination against nationals from Canada's Commonwealth partners in South Asia led to the establishment of a quota system allowing for limited migration from India, Pakistan, and Ceylon.[15]

The unraveling of Canada's postwar immigration regime was driven by an interplay of domestic and international forces. Decolonization had transformed power relations globally, placing racial discrimination at the top of the agendas of the Commonwealth and the United Nations (UN). As Canada's ability to play an independent role in world affairs as a "middle power" depended on the preservation and functioning of both organizations, it could not avoid weighing in on questions concerning racial justice. However, progressive positions taken on issues such as South African apartheid left Canada vulnerable to charges of hypocrisy with regard to its immigration policy. Domestic critics, such as the Canadian Council of Churches, the Canadian Jewish Congress, the Negro Citizenship Association, and the Canadian Congress of Labour, highlighted the discrepancy between the government's liberal rhetoric and the reality of ongoing discrimination against "Asiatics," "Negroes," and individuals of

---

12   Triadafilopoulos, *Becoming Multicultural,* chap. 3. Also see George M. Fredrickson, *Racism: A Short History* (Princeton, NJ: Princeton University Press, 2002), 127–32; Lauren, *Power and Prejudice,* 146–53; FitzGerald and Cook-Martin, *Culling the Masses,* 173; Debra Thompson, "Race, the Canadian Census, and Interactive Political Development," *Studies in American Political Development* 34 (April 2020): 65.

13   Ninette Kelley and Michael Trebilcock, *The Making of the Mosaic: A History of Canadian Immigration Policy* (Toronto: University of Toronto Press, 1998), 321–22.

14   Carol Lee, "The Road to Enfranchisement: Chinese and Japanese in British Columbia," *B.C. Studies* 30 (1976): 44–76; F. J. McEvoy, "'A Symbol of Racial Discrimination': The Chinese Immigration Act and Canada's Relation with China, 1942–1947," *Canadian Ethnic Studies* 14, no. 3 (1982): 24–42; Patricia E. Roy, *The Triumph of Citizenship: The Japanese and Chinese in Canada, 1941–67* (Vancouver: University of British Columbia Press, 2011).

15   Canada, House of Commons, Special Committee on Estimates, *Minutes of Proceedings and Evidence,* no. 11, March 14, 1955, p. 301. According to the terms of the quotas, 150 Indians, 100 Pakistanis, and 50 Ceylonese were to be granted access to Canada on a yearly basis. In addition, Canadian citizens could sponsor their wives, husbands, unmarried children under 21, fathers over 65, and mothers over 60.

"mixed-race." These and other advocacy groups, along with governments in the Caribbean and elsewhere, challenged Canada's commitment to antidiscrimination, civil rights, and liberal democratic principles by exposing its maintenance of discriminatory immigration policies and administrative practices. Virtually all of these appeals included arguments pertaining to Canada's obligation to live up to its commitment to international human rights and the elimination of discrimination based on race, color, or creed.[16]

The pressure mounted by domestic and international critics proved to be irresistible and Canadian officials were eventually compelled to reconsider Canada's immigration policies.[17] In 1962, the Canadian government announced that it would no longer refer to race in its admissions decisions.[18] This move was strengthened in 1967, with the introduction of the so-called "points system" and the expansion of immigration offices in regions outside of Europe and the United States.[19]

The points system established a standard set of measures for weighing applicants' qualifications. Prospective immigrants received a score based on their age, education, training, occupational skill in demand, knowledge of English or French, relatives in Canada, arranged employment, and employment opportunities in area of destination. A personal assessment by an immigration officer was added to the tally. Applicants meeting the threshold set by the government (initially fifty assessment points) would be admitted as independent immigrants and would enjoy the right to sponsor dependents as well as "nominated relatives." The points system made human capital the principal criterion for determining the suitability of immigrants, universalizing immigrant admissions.

Immigration flows to Canada shifted markedly in the late 1960s and early 1970s as a result of these changes. Whereas Europeans accounted for approximately 80 percent of total immigration up until 1967, by 1974 this figure had fallen to under 40 percent. Conversely, non-European immigration increased significantly. Total flows from India stood at 2,233 persons in 1966; by 1974 this figure had climbed to 12,868. Similar increases where registered for immigration from the Caribbean, Asia, and other previously restricted source regions. By 1974, Hong Kong, Jamaica, India, the Philippines, and Trinidad stood among Canada's top-ten immigration source countries.[20]

The changes to immigration policy introduced in 1967 were entrenched in statute through the passage of the Immigration Act of 1976. The act enunciated the fundamental objectives of Canadian immigration policy:

---

16   For details, see Triadafilopoulos, *Becoming Multicultural*, chaps. 3 and 4.

17   Ibid.; FitzGerald and Cook-Martin, *Culling the Masses*, 173–83.

18   Langevin Côté, "Immigration Rule Change Starts Feb. 1," *The Globe and Mail*, January 20, 1962; "The Opening Door," *The Globe and Mail*, January 22, 1962.

19   Freda Hawkins, *Canada and Immigration: Public Policy and Public Concern*, 2nd ed. (Kingston: McGill-Queen's University Press, 1988), 162.

20   *Green Paper on Immigration and Population, Vol. 1, Immigration Policy Perspectives* (Ottawa: Department of Manpower and Immigration, 1974), 84.

1. Promotion of economic, social, demographic, and cultural goals
2. Endorsement of family reunification
3. Fulfillment of Canada's international obligations under the United Nations Convention and 1967 Protocol relating to refugees
4. Nondiscrimination in immigration policy[21]

The government of Pierre Elliott Trudeau also passed a significantly liberalized Citizenship Act in 1977, which reduced the residency requirement from five to three years and provided for a "wholly permissive stance on the issue of multiple nationality."[22]

The passage of the Immigration Act of 1976 was preceded by a period of economic malaise and growing discontent tied to changes in immigration policy—Canada experienced a wave of anti-immigration sentiment, as previously excluded groups settled in Canada's urban centers. Officials expressed concern that public discontent might threaten the future of immigration policy. The 1974 Green Paper on immigration and population captured this pessimistic mood and advanced policy options that included a call for "explicit targets for the number of visas to be issued annually on a global, regional and possibly post-by-post [i.e., country-by-country] basis." Such a policy could "enable the immigration program to be deliberately related to national demographic/population growth policies as these are developed."

Given the mounting concerns over the consequences of the changes to immigration policy introduced in 1967, the liberal character of the 1976 act was puzzling; one would have expected a greater restrictiveness. In his attempt to make sense of this puzzle, political scientist John Wood noted that members of Parliament serving on a committee undertaking public consultations "were impressed by the publicity-catching and vote-mobilizing ability of minority ethnic organizations," which "represented the largest proportion . . . of all organizations that appeared before [their committee]."[23] Competitive electoral districts in metropolitan areas contained a high proportion of "ethnic" voters whose support was essential for victory. In the course of drafting the 1976 act, at least four Liberal cabinet ministers and several other members of the Liberal caucus warned that a policy of tighter controls "could do damage to a party that was already in difficulty."[24] The Liberal Party's electoral success "depended on minority ethnic support."[25] According to Wood, both the 1976 Immigration Act and the 1977 Citizenship Act were part of a more general strategy on the part of the Liberal Party to harness the support of new ethnic voters. The reduction of

---

21   As outlined in Section 3, Part 1, of the act. See Valerie Knowles, *Strangers at Our Gates*, 169.

22   Donald Galloway, "The Dilemmas of Canadian Citizenship Law," in *From Migrants to Citizens: Membership in a Changing World*, ed. T. Alexander Aleinikoff and Douglas Klusmeyer (Washington, DC: Carnegie Endowment for International Peace, 2000), 99; Irene Bloemraad, *Becoming a Citizen: Incorporating Immigrants and Refugees in the United States and Canada* (Berkeley: University of California Press, 2006), 49–50.

23   Wood, "East Indians and Canada's New Immigration Policy," 558.

24   Ibid., 559.

25   Ibid., 559.

the residency requirement in the new Citizenship Act would allow immigrants who arrived in the early 1970s "to become citizens—and grateful voters—in time for the coming general election."[26] Like their Liberal counterparts, Conservative Party MPs in competitive urban constituencies had good reason to reject policies that might alienate a significant proportion of their electorate. They continued to compete with the Liberals for the votes of "new urban-ethnic Canadians" and could ill afford to alienate these swing voters.[27]

Wood's explanation of the distinctive political dynamics driving immigration policy-making in the mid-1970s provides a useful means of understanding the general features of Canada's immigration policy regime. As elaborated below, the Canadian regime is marked by a strong cross-party political consensus on the necessity of immigration and acceptance of multiculturalism. Our focus on the interplay of settlement patterns, citizenship policy, and the effects of Canada's SMP electoral system builds on Wood's pioneering work.

Attributes of the Canadian Model: Expansionary Immigration Policies and Positive Public Opinion

The liberal character of Canadian immigration policy has endured regardless of the partisan orientation of governments. In 1989, Conservative prime minister Brian Mulroney severed the long-standing link between annual immigration flows and prevailing economic conditions by committing Canada to maintaining an expansive immigration policy regardless of fluctuations in the unemployment rate. From the mid-1990s onward, Canada admitted an average of 250,000 immigrants per year. Under Prime Minister Stephen Harper's Conservative Party, annual immigration levels reached 257,900, 259,000, and 260,400 in 2012, 2013, and 2014 respectively.[28] Since forming government in 2015, Prime Minister Justin Trudeau's Liberal government has expanded Canada's immigration program. Annual admissions increased from 271,845 in 2015 to 296,346 in 2016, before dipping to 286,479 in 2017. Targets for 2019, 2020, and 2021 were set at 330,000, 340,000, and 350,000[29] and revised upward in October 2020—in the midst of Canada's "second wave" of COVID-19 infections—to 401,000 in 2021, 411,000 in 2022,

---

26 Ibid., 559.

27 John C. Courtney, "Campaign Strategy and Electoral Victory: The Progressive Conservatives and the 1979 Election," in *Canada at the Polls, 1979 and 1980: A Study of the General Elections*, ed. Howard R. Penniman (Washington, DC: American Enterprise Institute for Public Policy Research, 1981), 139. Also see Thirstan Falconer, "Building an Ethnic Coalition? The Liberal Party of Canada, Ethnocultural Communities and the 1962 and 1963 Federal Elections in Metro Toronto," *American Review of Canadian Studies* 48, no. 3 (2018): 281–96.

28 Laurent Martel and Carol D'Aoust, "Permanent and Temporary Immigration to Canada from 2012 to 2014," Statistics Canada: Catalogue No. 91–209-X, 2016.

29 Immigration, Refugees and Citizenship Canada, *2018 Annual Report to Parliament on Immigration*, Catalogue no. Ci1E-PDF (2018), 12.

and 421,000 in 2023.[30] These significant increases in annual admissions levels have been supported by all of Canada's major political parties.

Canada's foreign-born population grew from 17.4 percent in 1996 to 21.9 percent in 2016. By comparison, as of 2018 the foreign-born population in the United States stood at 13.6 percent and 16 percent in Germany.[31] As noted above, the diversity of countries of origin of immigrants has dramatically increased over the past half century. In 2016, 48.1 percent of Canada's foreign-born population was born in Asia, while 27.7 percent was born in Europe. And whereas African-born immigrants made up 1.7 percent of the foreign-born population in the 1971, they counted for 8.5 percent in 2016.[32] The top-ten source countries in 2017 were India, the Philippines, the People's Republic of China, Syria, the United States, Pakistan, France, Nigeria, the United Kingdom, and Iraq.[33]

The diversification of immigration has transformed Canada's demographic complexion. Canada's "visible minority" population—that part of the population that is defined as neither white nor Indigenous (as per the Employment Equity Act, 1981)—was 22.3 percent in 2016. While the population of the country as a whole increased by 21.7 percent between 1996 and 2016, the visible-minority population more than doubled in absolute terms, from 3.2 million to 7.3 million. As a majority of immigrants who have arrived over the past twenty-five years have come from non-European countries, 65 percent of the foreign-born population was nonwhite in 2016, up from 44 percent in 1996.[34] Canada's demographic transformation will continue. According to Statistics Canada forecasts, the foreign-born could rise to as much as 30 percent, and the visible minority to as much as 35.9 percent, by the year 2036.

Canada's religious landscape has also been transformed by immigration. While Christianity remains Canada's largest religion, counting 22.1 million adherents, or 67.3 percent of the total population, "the number of Canadians who belong to other religions—including Islam, Hinduism, Sikhism, Buddhism, Judaism and Eastern Orthodox Christianity" has been growing rapidly.[35] Islam is the fastest-growing religion in Canada, with over 1 million adherents, constituting 3.2 of Canada's population. The share

30   Immigration, Refugees and Citizenship Canada, "Government of Canada Announces Plan to Support Economic Recovery through Immigration," October 30, 2020, www.canada.ca/en/immigration-refugees-citizenship/news/2020/10/government-of-canada-announces-plan-to-support-economic-recovery-through-immigration.html.

31   Jynnah Radford, "Key Findings about U.S. Immigrants," Pew Research Center, 2019, www.pewresearch.org/fact-tank/2019/06/17/key-findings-about-u-s-immigrants/.

32   Statistics Canada, *Immigration and Ethnocultural Diversity: Key Results from the 2016 Census*, October 25, 2017, www150.statcan.gc.ca/n1/en/daily-quotidien/171025/dq171025b-eng.pdf.

33   Immigration, Refugees and Citizenship Canada, *2018 Annual Report to Parliament on Immigration*, Catalogue no. CilE-PDF (2018), 28.

34   Calculated from Statistics Canada's 1996 and 2016 Public-Use Microdata Files. All computations, use, and interpretation of these data are entirely those of the author.

35   Pew Research Center, *Canada's Changing Religious Landscape*, June 27, 2013, www.pewforum.org/2013/06/27/canadas-changing-religious-landscape/.

of individuals reporting they had no religious affiliation has also increased, reaching 7.8 million, or 23.9 percent of the population in 2011.[36]

Public opinion has become more supportive of mass immigration over time. In 2019, 34 percent of Canadians believed that immigration levels were too high, down from 61 percent in 1977. Some 80 percent of Canadians believe that the economic impact of immigration is positive.[37] The Pew Research Center's 2018 Global Attitudes Survey asked respondents in eighteen countries whether immigrants constituted a burden on their country or made it stronger. Canadians expressed the most positive views on this point, with 68 percent stating that immigrants made Canada stronger and only 27 percent claiming that immigrants constituted a burden.[38]

Canadians' views on multiculturalism have been similarly positive. Stuart Soroka and Sarah Roberton note that "there is broad support for multiculturalism and immigration, and that support has not decreased in recent years; indeed, it may even have increased slightly."[39] Most polls taken since the publication of Soroka and Roberton's report in 2010 suggest steady support for multiculturalism. For example, a survey by the Environics Institute for Survey Research noted the percentage of Canadians who consider multi-culturalism to be a very important element of Canadian identity had increased from 37 percent in 1997 to 54 percent in 2015.[40]

How Canadians understand multiculturalism is open to question. The same Environ-ics poll in which 54 percent of Canadians held multiculturalism to be a very important element of Canadian identity also reported that 50 percent believed too many immi-grants were not adopting Canadian values.[41] A 2015 survey revealed that 75 percent of

---

36   Statistics Canada, *Immigration and Ethnocultural Diversity in Canada: National Household Survey, 2011*, Catalogue no. 99-010-X2011001 (2013).

37   Environics Institute for Survey Research, *Focus Canada—Fall 2019: Canadian Public Opin-ion about Immigration and Refugees*, November 5, 2019, www.environicsinstitute.org/docs/default -source/project-documents/focus-canada-fall-2019—-immigration-refugees/focus-canada-fall -2019-survey-on-immigration-and-refugees—-final-report.pdf?sfvrsn=56c2af3c_2.

38   Ana Gonzalez-Barrera and Phillip Connor, "Around the World More Say Immigrants Are a Strength than a Burden," PEW Research Center, May 14, 2019, www.pewresearch.org/ global/2019/03/14/around-the-world-more-say-immigrants-are-a-strength-than-a-burden/.

39   Stuart Soroka and Sarah Roberton, *A Literature Review of Public Opinion Research on Cana-dian Attitudes towards Multiculturalism and Immigration, 2006–2009*, Citizenship and Immigra-tion Canada, Catalogue no. Ci4–74/2011E-PDF (2010), 41.

40   Environics Institute for Survey Research, *Focus Canada—Spring 2015: Canadian Public Opin-ion about Immigration and Multiculturalism*, June 30, 2015, www.environicsinstitute.org/docs/ default-source/project-documents/focus-canada-2015-survey-on-immigration-and-multicultur alism/final-report.pdf?sfvrsn=71f7c79e_2.

41   "[T]he proportion of Canadians who [do not think immigrants adopt Canadian values] has actually declined from 72 per cent in 1993. Such concern is now at the lowest level in the 25 years over which this survey questions has been put to Canadians." Michael Adams and Keith Neuman, "Canadian Exceptionalism in Attitudes toward Immigration," *Policy Options*, April 2,

Canadians believed that "ethnic groups should blend into Canadian society." Canadians' opinions on Islam and Muslims also diverge from what one would expect given their support for multiculturalism. An Angus Reid poll released in April 2017 revealed that only 33 percent of Canadians had a "generally favorable opinion" of Islam (as compared to 68 percent for Christianity).[42] The same poll showed that a majority of Canadians opposed wearing the niqab and burka in public. Among respondents 55 and older, 81 percent opposed wearing the burka in public.

Antipathy to religious accommodation is especially pronounced in Quebec, where Premier François Legault's Coalition Avenir Quebec (CAQ) successfully campaigned on a platform that included promises to reduce annual immigration levels, introduce a "values test" for immigrants, and ban the wearing of religious symbols by public servants.[43] The CAQ has overseen the implementation of these promises since taking office, enjoying the continuing support of a majority of Quebecers.

During the lead-up to the October 2019 federal election, some commentators claimed that Canada's cross-party political consensus on immigration and multiculturalism was vulnerable.[44] An influential survey by the polling firm EKOS pointed to an intensification of "ideological and partisan polarization" around issues of immigration and predicted the imminent "reshaping of the political landscape in Canada."[45] A steep increase in the number of asylum seekers crossing the Canada-US border irregularly in 2017 and 2018 fed into this growing sense of pessimism. To top things off, Maxime Bernier, a former Conservative cabinet minister and unsuccessful leadership candidate, founded the People's Party of Canada (PPC).

Echoing populist politicians in other countries, Bernier likened Canada's immigration program to "a very dangerous type of social engineering" that would "bring increasing cultural balkanization, distrust, social conflict, and potentially violence."[46] The PPC's platform included calls to reduce total immigration levels to between 100,000 and 150,000 immigrants per year, "eliminate all funding to promote multiculturalism" and

2018, https://policyoptions.irpp.org/magazines/april-2018/canadian-exceptionalism-attitudes-toward-immigration/.

42   David Korzinski, "Religious Trends: Led by Quebec, Number of Canadians Holding Favourable Views of Various Religions Increases," Angus Reid Institute, April 3, 2017, http://angusreid.org/religious-trends-2017/.

43   René Bruemmer, "Quebec Election, the Day After: Here's What the CAQ Promises to Do during the 39-Day Election Campaign," Montreal Gazette, October 2, 2018.

44   Stuart Thomson, "'I Don't Think Canada Will Be the Great Exception' to Populist Disruption, Expert Says," National Post, July 19, 2019.

45   EKOS, "Increased Polarization on Attitudes to Immigration Reshaping the Political Landscape in Canada," April 15, 2019, www.ekospolitics.com/index.php/2019/04/increased-polarization-on-attitudes-to-immigration-reshaping-the-political-landscape-in-canada/.

46   Maxime Bernier, "Speech—The People's Party of Canada Position on Immigration and Multiculturalism," July 24, 2019, www.peoplespartyofcanada.ca/speech_the_people_s_party_of_canada_position_on_immigration_and_multiculturalism.

repeal the Multiculturalism Act, reduce the number of refugees and other noneconomic immigrants, and only select immigrants that shared "basic Canadian values."[47]

Despite significant media coverage, the PPC performed dismally, capturing only 1.6 percent of the popular vote and no seats in the House of Commons. Justin Trudeau's unabashedly pro-immigration Liberal Party won a renewed mandate, albeit in a minority parliament. Despite receiving a slightly higher share of the national popular vote than the Liberals, the Conservative Party's leader remained the second-place party in Parliament because it ran up vote surpluses in rural Western Canadian districts. The Conservative Party's leader, Andrew Scheer, resigned in the face of mounting criticism of his campaign. Some of Scheer's critics argued that the party required a leader who could more effectively compete against the Liberals in the immigrant-heavy suburbs and mid-sized cities ringing Toronto (the so-called "905" region, referring to the telephone area code).[48]

The 2019 campaign demonstrated the durability of the Canadian approach to immigration policy. None of the major parties politicized immigration or multiculturalism and the PPC failed miserably. The populist winds reshaping politics in other liberal democracies scarcely left a trace in Canada. The resilience of pro-immigration politics in Canada begs for an explanation. After reviewing arguments that emphasize the effects of geography and public policy, we develop our argument regarding the interplay of immigrant settlement patterns, citizenship policy, and Canada's SMP electoral system. We contend that Canadian political parties have maintained their support for mass immigration and official multiculturalism because it is in their political interests to do so.

Explaining Exceptionalism

Geographic Isolation, Selective Immigration, and Multiculturalism

The outcry over a relatively modest increase in irregular land border crossing in 2017–18 makes clear that Canadians expect their governments to retain firm control over migration. Geography has helped Canadian governments meet this demand and this, in turn, has generated support for mass immigration. According to Jeffrey Reitz, Canada's geographic isolation "from all countries other than the US has limited illegal immigration and has made legal immigration more attractive. This factor has been important in sustaining the political perception of Canadian immigration as being controlled in the national interest."[49]

---

47   Bernier, "Speech"; Justin Ling, "How Maxime Bernier Lost His Seat: Canada's Nationalist People's Party Has Run a Familiar Populist Playbook—and Ended Up a Joke," *Foreign Policy*, October 20, 2019, https://foreignpolicy.com/2019/10/20/canada-maxime-bernier-populism-peoples-party/.

48   Ken Boessenkool, "How the Harper Model Worked, and Why It's Now Broken," *CBC News*, January 30, 2020, www.cbc.ca/news/canada/calgary/conservative-party-harper-model-election-ken-boessenkool-1.5444639.

49   Jeffrey Reitz, "The Distinctiveness of Canadian Immigration Experience," *Patterns of Prejudice* 46, no. 5 (2012): 531; Irene Bloemraad, *Understanding "Canadian Exceptionalism" in Immigration and Pluralism Policy* (Washington, DC: Migration Policy Institute, 2012), 4–6.

Canadian governments have acted quickly when control over Canada's borders appears has been challenged. Responses often include the introduction of new regulations that enhance their powers to regulate migration.[50] The Trudeau government included several measures aimed at reducing the flow of irregular asylum seekers in a 2019 omnibus budget bill.[51] Nevertheless, arguments highlighting the importance of geography rightly note that Canada's relative isolation has kept overall numbers of irregular migrants low. This has granted Canadian governments the luxury of not having to deal with the kinds of large, unplanned, and politically charged movements of migrants that have roiled politics in other countries.

Explanations of Canadian exceptionalism have also highlighted the success of Canadian policies on immigration, settlement, and integration. Reitz notes that Canada's preference for highly skilled immigrants, and the employment of a selection system designed to find them, has helped policy-makers attract "large numbers of immigrants [who] have minimum qualifications for survival in a modern economy." [52] This, in turn, has helped governments make the case that immigration contributes positively to the Canadian economy. Daniel Hiebert similarly notes that

> framing immigration in economic terms and presenting it as a solution to the nation's problems has led to a mutually reinforcing set of outcomes: Canadians expect immigration to be coordinated with economic need and, as a result, they have typically supported immigration mainly when it is aligned with economic concerns.[53]

The claim that successful policies generate support for immigration has a circular quality: Canada selects immigrants likely to succeed; their success grants credence to claims that immigration has a positive economic impact "with minimal social costs or impact on expenditures required to maintain the welfare state."[54] Given the success of immigrants' children and grandchildren, Canada's immigration policy is a gift that keeps on giving, producing positive, self-reinforcing multigenerational outcomes.[55]

Scholars have also suggested that multiculturalism policy has shaped Canada's distinctive immigration politics. Multiculturalism policy is entrenched in Section 27 of the Canadian Charter of Rights and Freedoms and the Multiculturalism Act, 1988. According to Irene

---

50   Triadafilopoulos, *Becoming Multicultural*, 106.

51   Teresa Wright, "Refugee Advocates 'Shocked and Dismayed' over Asylum Changes in Ottawa's Budget Bill," *The Globe and Mail*, April 9, 2019.

52   Reitz, "The Distinctiveness of Canadian Immigration Experience," 525.

53   Daniel Hiebert, *What Is So Special about Canada? Understanding the Resilience of Immigration and Multiculturalism* (Washington, DC: Migration Policy Institute 2016), 5.

54   Jeffrey Reitz, "Economic Opportunity, Multiculturalism, and the Roots of Popular Support for High Immigration in Canada," in *Anti-Immigrant Sentiments, Actions, and Policies: The North American Region and the European Union / Sentimientos, acciones y políticas antiinmigrantes: América del Norte y la Unión Europea*, ed. Monica Verea (Mexico City: Universidad Nacional Autonoma de Mexico, Centro de Investigaciones sobre America del Norte, 2012), 300.

55   Reitz, "Economic Opportunity, Multiculturalism," 300–301.

Bloemraad, this acknowledgment of Canada's status as an officially multicultural country has enhanced multiculturalism policy's symbolic resonance, encouraging the development of a national identity "that embraces immigration, diversity, and tolerance" and appeals to "old" and "new" Canadians alike.[56] In the words of Keith Banting and Will Kymlicka:

> [T]he fact that Canada has officially defined itself as a multicultural nation means that immigrants are a constituent part of the nation that citizens feel pride in; multiculturalism serves as a link for native-born citizens from national identity to solidarity with immigrants. Conversely, multiculturalism provides a link by which immigrants come to identify with, and feel pride in, Canada. From their different starting points, there is convergence on high levels of pride and identification with a multicultural conception of Canadian nationhood. . . . [I]n the absence of multiculturalism, these links are more difficult to establish, and national identity is more likely to lead to intolerance and xenophobia.[57]

Taken together, explanations that highlight the consequences of policy point to the fortuitous interaction of a selective immigration policy that admits immigrants with the skills and talent needed to be economically successful and a multiculturalism policy that encourages a shared national identity characterized by openness and toleration. According to Augie Fleras, this "mutually reciprocating effect" has moved Canada along the path to becoming an "immigration society."[58]

We agree that geographic isolation and public policy has played an important role in building public support for mass immigration in Canada. Admissions policies have succeeded in attracting large numbers of hard-working, highly qualified immigrants with decidedly middle-class aspirations. Multiculturalism policy has fostered a particular ethos that generates support for immigration and diversity (albeit within limits). Nevertheless, policy-oriented explanations neglect the interplay of another set of important, contingent factors, namely, settlement patterns, citizenship rules, and Canada's SMP electoral system.

Settlement Patterns, Citizenship Regime, and Electoral Rules
Settlement Patterns

Canada's 338 parliamentary seats are distributed according to a complex procedure that seeks to balance "representation by population with regional imperatives of a federal House of Commons."[59] Despite shortcomings in the operationalization of the principle of representation by population, its effects are in our estimation extremely important.

---

56   Bloemraad, *Understanding "Canadian Exceptionalism,"* 8.

57   Keith Banting and Will Kymlicka, "Canadian Multiculturalism: Global Anxieties and Local Debates," *British Journal of Canadian Studies* 23, no. 1 (2010): 60–61.

58   Augie Fleras, "Canadian Exceptionalism: From a Society of Immigrants to an Immigration Society," in *Immigration, Racial and Ethnic Studies in 150 Years of Canada*, ed. Shibao Guo and Lloyd Wong (Leiden: Brill Sense, 2018), 301.

59   Michael Pal and Sujit Choudhry, "Is Every Ballot Equal? Visible-Minority Vote Dilution in Canada," *IRPP Choices* 13, no. 1 (2007): 12, https://irpp.org/wp-content/uploads/assets/research/strengthening-canadian-democracy/is-every-ballot-equal/vol13no1.pdf.

Table 11.1. Parliamentary representation of metropolitan areas and provinces, 1987–2013 Representation Orders.

	RO 1987	RO 1996	RO 2003	RO 2013
Ontario	33.6%	34.2%	34.4%	35.8%
Greater Toronto and Hamilton Area	13.2%	15.3%	16.6%	18.0%
British Columbia	10.8%	11.3%	11.7%	12.4%
Vancouver and the Lower Mainland	4.4%	5.3%	5.5%	6.8%
Québec	25.4%	24.9%	24.4%	23.1%
Greater Montréal	10.5%	10.3%	10.7%	10.7%
Three largest urban regions combined	28.1%	30.9%	32.8%	35.5%
Total number of electoral districts	295	301	308	338

Note: Districts are assigned to a Census Metropolitan Area if 75 percent of their population was located within the CMA.

Table 11.1 compares the parliamentary representation of Canada's three largest metropolitan areas—the Greater Toronto and Hamilton Area (GTHA), comprising the Toronto, Hamilton, and Oshawa Census Metropolitan Areas (CMAs); British Columbia's Lower Mainland region, comprising the Vancouver and Abbotsford CMAs; and Greater Montréal—and their provinces over the past four seat redistributions, each of which is referred to as a "representation order" in Canadian law. Each metropolitan area's share of parliamentary representation has increased over time. Even Greater Montréal's parliamentary representation is increasing despite the province of Québec's decreasing over time. After the 2013 redistribution, about 35.5 percent of Canada's federal electoral districts are located in these three urban regions.

It is precisely in these three regions where most immigrants have settled over the past half-century, spawning large, multigenerational communities that feature dense ecologies of secular and faith-based institutions and own-language media outlets. Ontario, British Columbia, and Québec collectively account for 71.1 percent of Canada's foreign-born population. Much of that population is concentrated in and around Toronto, Vancouver, and Montréal. As shown in table 11.2, the three largest metropolitan areas account for 35.5 percent of parliamentary seats and 38.1 percent of the national population, but 64.3 percent of immigrants and 68.9 percent of visible minorities. Particular groups are even more concentrated: about three-quarters of Chinese and South Asian Canadians live in the top three urban regions. Moreover, two-thirds of Canada's half-million Hindus, 37 percent of Sikhs, and 43 percent of Muslims live in the GTHA, and 40 percent of Sikhs live in Greater Vancouver.

Immigrant populations and associated cultural communities are further concentrated *within* these regions. First- and second-generation immigrants together make up 78 percent of the City of Toronto's population and 70 percent of the City of Vancouver's population. The visible minority population in the City of Toronto exceeds 50 percent, while that of Markham, a suburban city of 342,970 just north of Toronto, is 78 percent,

Table 11.2. The metropolitan concentration of immigrants, 2016.

Region	Electoral Districts (RO 2013) Seats	cum%	Total Population %	cum%	Foreign-born %	cum%	Visible Minorities All %	cum%	South Asian %	cum%	Chinese %	cum%	Black %	cum%
GTHA	61	18.0	19.8		38.9		41.7		52.9		41.2		40.6	
Montréal	36	28.7	11.1	30.9	12.2	51.1	11.6	53.3	4.4	57.3	5.6	46.8	22.0	62.6
Lower Mainland	23	35.5	7.2	38.1	13.2	64.3	15.6	68.9	16.1	73.4	29.7	76.5	2.6	65.2
Other Metro – W	40	47.3	12.6	50.7	14.0	78.3	15.2	84.1	14.9	88.3	12.7	89.2	12.9	78.1
Other Metro – On	31	56.5	10.0	60.7	8.9	87.2	7.7	91.8	5.9	94.2	5.9	95.1	10.0	88.1
Other Metro – Qc	11	59.8	3.2	63.9	1.1	88.3	1.0	92.8	0.1	94.3	0.3	95.4	2.6	90.7
Atlantic Metros	9	62.4	2.2	66.1	0.8	89.1	0.9	93.7	0.5	94.8	0.7	96.1	1.7	92.4
Nonmetro – W + N	44	75.4	12.1	78.2	5.7	94.8	3.8	97.5	3.8	98.6	2.3	98.4	2.8	95.2
Nonmetro – On	29	84.0	8.4	86.6	3.3	98.1	1.2	98.7	1.0	99.6	0.7	99.1	1.7	96.9
Nonmetro – Qc	31	93.2	9.0	95.6	1.2	99.3	0.8	99.5	0.1	99.7	0.4	99.5	2.0	98.9
Nonmetro – Atl	23	100.0	4.4	100.0	0.7	100.0	0.5	100.0	0.2	100.0	0.4	100.0	1.0	100.0

Table 11.3. Percentage of federal electoral districts by percentage foreign-born by province, 1996–2013 Representation Orders.

	BC			Prairies			Ontario		
	RO 1996	RO 2003	RO 2013	RO 1996	RO 2003	RO 2013	RO 1996	RO 2003	RO 2013
0–20% foreign born	50	44	36	78	75	56	48	45	37
20–40% foreign born	32	31	31	22	25	39	28	28	31
> 40% foreign born	18	25	33	–	–	5	24	26	31
Total	100	100	100	100	100	100	100	100	100

	Québec			Atlantic			North		
	RO 1996	RO 2003	RO 2013	RO 1996	RO 2003	RO 2013	RO 1996	RO 2003	RO 2013
0–20% foreign born	81	76	71	100	100	100	100	100	100
20–40% foreign born	16	16	18	–	–	–	–	–	–
> 40% foreign born	3	8	12	–	–	–	–	–	–
Total	100	100	100	100	100	100	100	100	100

Note: Numbers are percentages that sum vertically. Census year for RO 1996 is 1996; RO 2003 is 2006; and RO 2013 is 2016. Foreign-born does not include nonpermanent residents.

up from 72.3 percent in 2011.[60] Other Greater Toronto suburbs, including Brampton, have seen similar increases in their share of visible minority residents. In British Columbia, five cities in Greater Vancouver have visible minority populations of over 50 percent, including Richmond (76.3 percent), Burnaby (63.6 percent), and Surrey (58.5 percent).[61]

Table 11.3 illustrates growth in high-immigrant districts over seventeen years as immigration has continued and new seats have been created in high-growth urban areas. Most high-immigrant districts—those with greater than 40 percent foreign-born population—are located in British Columbia and Ontario (and especially in the GTHA and Greater Vancouver). At the 2016 census, immigrants comprised more than 40 percent of the population in 31 percent of districts in Ontario, 33 percent in British Columbia, and 12 percent in Québec. If we include electoral districts with at least 20 percent immigrant population, the threshold is met by 62 percent of districts in Ontario, 64 percent in British Columbia, 30 percent in Québec, and 44 percent in the Prairie provinces. This point is given added force when we take into consideration visible minorities—which include not only recent waves of immigrants but also their Canadian-born relatives.

---

60   Julia Whalen, "Census 2016: More Than Half of Torontonians Identify as Visible Minorities," *CBC News*, October 25, 2017, www.cbc.ca/news/canada/toronto/census-visible-minorities-1.4371018.

61   Tara Carman, "Visible Minorities Now the Majority in 5 B.C. Cities." *CBC News*, October 27, 2017, www.cbc.ca/news/canada/british-columbia/visible-minorities-now-the-majority-in-5-b-c-cities-1.4375858.

In his analysis of the 2016 census, Andrew Griffith identifies forty-one federal districts nationwide in which more than half of residents are visible minority. Of these, twenty-four have visible minority populations of between 50 and 70 percent. All seventeen with a visible minority population of 70 percent or more are located in the Toronto (thirteen) and Vancouver (four) metropolitan areas.[62]

The relative concentration of groups can be interpreted in two ways. On the one hand, immigrants make up a substantial proportion of the population in a substantial number of federal seats—too many, we would argue, to ignore.[63] At the same time, immigrants and visible minority groups are neatly concentrated in only a few metropolitan areas, facilitating access to them during campaigns. As table 11.2 suggests, this is especially true when we consider groups such as South Asians: 50 percent of South Asians live in 8 percent of districts; 75 percent live in only 20 percent of districts.

The spatial concentration of immigrants aids voter recruitment by parties. The concentration of immigrants sharing a common language and cultural origins facilitates the formation of community-oriented institutions such as social clubs, self-help organizations, religious organizations, and media outlets.[64] Stephen White suggests that social networks generated by immigrant settlement patterns provide political parties with opportunities to exercise "interpersonal influence" (by cultivating relationships with the leadership of community-oriented institutions) to favorably influence voters' political opinions.[65]

An Efficient Citizenship Regime

None of this would matter if immigrants lacked the vote. Canada's highly efficient citizenship regime has helped transform immigrants' latent political potential into real power. The rate at which immigrants acquire Canadian citizenship through naturalization is high. In 2006, the naturalization rate for immigrants with three or more years of legal residency was 85 percent; the rate for immigrants with five or more years was 88.3 percent, eight percentage points higher than the rate in 1986.[66] In 2011, of the 6,042,200

---

62   Andrew Griffith, "What the Census Tells Us about Citizenship," *Policy Options*, March 20, 2018, https://policyoptions.irpp.org/magazines/march-2018/what-the-census-tells-us-about-citizenship/.

63   Also see Jerome H. Black and Bruce M. Hicks, "Electoral Politics and Immigration in Canada: How Does Immigration Matter?" *Journal of International Migration and Integration* 9, no. 3 (2008): 248; Sean Speer and Jamil Jivani, "The Urban/Rural Divide and a More Inclusive Canada," *Policy Options*, June 5, 2017, https://policyoptions.irpp.org/magazines/june-2017/the-urbanrural-divide-and-a-more-inclusive-canada/.

64   Miriam Lapp, "Incorporating Groups into Rational Choice Explanations of Turnout: An Empirical Test," *Public Choice* 98, no. 1/2 (1999): 171–85.

65   Steven White, "Canadian Ethnocultural Diversity and Federal Party Support: The Dynamics of Liberal Partisanship in Immigrant Communities," *PS: Political Science & Politics* 50, no. 3 (2017): 710–11.

66   Li Xu and Pamela Golah, *Citizenship Acquisition in Canada: An Overview Based on Census 1986 to 2006* (Ottawa: Citizenship and Immigration Canada, 2015), ii.

foreign-born people in Canada eligible to acquire citizenship, 5,175,100, or 85.6 percent, reported that they had done so.[67] More impressively, the 2011 National household Survey also found that of Canada's total population, "78.3% were Canadian citizens by birth, another 15.8% were Canadian by naturalization and the rest, 6.0%, did not have Canadian citizenship."[68] Ontario "had the largest eligible immigrant population and the highest proportion of immigrants who had obtained citizenship (87.0%)." Quebec and British Columbia's proportions of eligible immigrants who had obtained citizenship stood at 85.1 and 84.3 percent respectively.[69] Canada's naturalization rate is consistently higher than that of Australia (74 percent in 2011) and the United States (43.7 percent in 2010). Canada's high naturalization rate is based on its relatively liberal citizenship policy. In order to qualify for citizenship, an immigrant must

- be a permanent resident
- have lived in Canada for three out of the last five years
- have filed taxes (if necessary)
- pass a test on rights, responsibilities, and knowledge of Canada
- prove their language skills
- swear an oath of allegiance to the Queen
- pay a fee of $530

Prime Minister Stephen Harper's Conservative government aimed to make citizenship harder to obtain by raising the "citizenship fee" from $100 to $530, setting a higher standard of language competency, toughening the written test, and increasing the residency requirement from three out of four years to four out of six years. Although these reforms succeeded in driving down the naturalization rate among some groups, it is still in the range of 85 percent.[70] Moreover, since replacing Harper's Conservative Party government in 2015, Justin Trudeau's Liberals have reversed several of these changes, shortening the residency requirement and promising to waive the citizenship fee altogether.[71] We should therefore expect that any decline in Canada's naturalization rate will be temporary.

Electoral System
Canadian political scientists have long known that Canada's SMP electoral system rewards regionally concentrated support and penalizes diffuse support, especially when is spread evenly across the country.[72] Given the regional concentration of immigrant

---

67   Statistics Canada, *Obtaining Canadian Citizenship, National Household Survey (NHS) 2011,* Catalogue no. 99–010-X2011003, 3.

68   Ibid., 3.

69   Ibid., 4.

70   Griffith, "What the Census Tells Us about Citizenship."

71   Mann Almhidi, "Federal Government Commits to Waiving Citizenship Application Fees," *The Globe and Mail,* December 24, 2019.

72   Alan Cairns, "The Electoral System and the Party System in Canada, 1921–1965," *Canadian Journal of Political Science* 1, no. 1 (1968): 55–80.

and visible minority populations in Canada, the electoral system increases the potential payoff for targeting immigrant-dense electoral districts.[73] As SMP systems reward the first-place parties with all the spoils (making a second-place finish largely inconsequential), even small swings in the vote preferences of regionally concentrated groups may translate into a relatively large swing in the seats count of competing parties.[74] In short, parties may reap a high electoral return on investment by concentrating recruitment efforts on particular immigrant groups.

Through the 1990s and early 2000s, districts with high concentrations of immigrant and visible minority voters consistently supported the Liberal Party of Canada.[75] The Liberals under Prime Minister Jean Chrétien leveraged this support to win majority governments, taking advantage of vote splitting on the right between the Progressive Conservative Party and Reform Party/Canadian Alliance. After the merger of the Progressive Conservatives and Canadian Alliance in 2004, and in light of difficulties in building a strong base of support in Québec,[76] the Conservatives focused their efforts on competing for the votes of immigrants and visible minority groups, particularly in the Greater Toronto Hamilton Area and the Greater Vancouver region. Stephen Harper's former adviser, Tom Flanagan, noted that the "emerging conservative coalition" would be based on a combination of traditional Tory voters, western populists and "ethnic voters, new Canadians, mostly in Ontario."[77] The Conservative "ethnic outreach" strategy included symbolic gestures that "signaled to multicultural communities that the Conservatives cared about their issues."[78]

---

73   Daniel Westlake, "Multiculturalism, Political Parties, and the Conflicting Pressures of Ethnic Minorities and Far-Right Parties," *Party Politics* 24, no. 4 (2018): 423.

74   Drew Linzer, "The Relationship between Seats and Votes in Multiparty Systems," *Political Analysis* 20, no. 3 (2012): 400–416; Ronald Rogowski and Mark Andreas Kayser, "Majoritarian Electoral Systems and Consumer Power: Price-Level Evidence from the OECD Countries," *American Journal of Political Science* 46, no. 3 (2002): 526–39.

75   Antoine Bilodeau and Mebs Kanji, "The Immigrant Voter, 1965–2004: The Emergence of a New Liberal Partisan?" in *Voting Behaviour in Canada*, ed. Cameron D. Anderson and Laura B. Stephenson (Vancouver: UBC Press, 2010), 65–84; André Blais, "Accounting for the Electoral Success of the Liberal Party in Canada," *Canadian Journal of Political Science* 38, no. 4 (2005), 821–40; Allison Harell, "Revisiting the 'Ethnic Vote': Liberal Allegiance and Vote Choice among Racialized Minorities," in *Parties, Elections, and the Future of Canadian Politics*, ed. Amanda Bittner and Royce Koop (Vancouver: UBC Press, 2013), 40–160; White, "Canadian Ethnocultural Diversity and Federal Party Support."

76   Joshua Gordon, Sanjay Jeram, and Clifton van der Linden, "The Two Solitudes of Canadian Nativism: Explaining the Absence of a Competitive Anti-Immigration Party in Canada," *Nations and Nationalism* 26, no. 4 (2020): 902–22; Tom Flanagan, "The Emerging Conservative Coalition," *Policy Options*, June 1, 2011, https://policyoptions.irpp.org/magazines/the-winner/the-emerging -conservative-coalition/, 105–6.

77   Ibid., 106.

78   Ibid., 106.

Table 11.4. Safe and unsafe seats by region, 2004–2011 (2003 Representation Order).

Region	Safe Seats					Unsafe Seats	Total
	CPC	Liberal	NDP	BQ	Total		
Nonmetropolitan	51	10	4	3	68	61	129
GTHA	4	8	2	0	14	36	50
Lower Mainland BC	5	2	3	0	10	7	17
Greater Montréal	0	6	0	0	6	27	33
Other Western CMAs	22	1	1	0	24	11	35
Other Ontario CMAs	5	4	3	0	12	14	26
Other Québec CMAs	0	0	0	0	0	10	10
Atlantic CMAs	0	1	2	0	3	5	8
Total	87	32	15	3	137	171	308

Note: Seats are assigned to a CMA if more than 75 percent of their population is located within that CMA. A seat is considered "safe" if a party won it in all four elections held between 2004 and 2011.

Beyond that it was mainly the patient effort of establishing contact—visits by Harper and other leading Conservatives, notably Jason Kenney, to ethnic events; recruiting multicultural candidates and political organizers; printing political materials in languages other than English and French.[79]

According to Flanagan, the Conservatives' ethnic outreach strategy helped the party win "a treasure trove of seats" in the 2011 federal election. "It was this batch of new seats in Ontario, mainly in the GTA, that gave the Tories their majority in 2011."[80] Flanagan has a point: of the 28 seats the Conservatives gained from the Liberals between 2004 and 2011, 18 had an immigrant population of over 40 percent, of which 10 were majority immigrant.

As highlighted in table 11.4, the vast majority of Conservative safe seats during the 2000s were located in nonmetropolitan areas and in western cities, not including Greater Vancouver. Indeed, they consistently held 51 of 68 nonmetropolitan seats, and 22 of 24 seats in Calgary, Edmonton, Regina, Saskatoon, Winnipeg, and other Western CMAs.[81] The Liberal pool of safe seats was smaller and more diffuse. In seeking to grow their seat count, both parties had an incentive to shift resources into the metropolitan area with the largest pool of unsafe seats whose geographically proximate residents were potentially open to their appeals, namely, the GTHA.

The Liberals won back most of the high-immigrant seats gained by the Conservatives in 2011 in Greater Toronto and Vancouver in the 2015 federal election. They benefitted from Stephen Harper's unpopularity and a strategic blunder on the part of Conservative

---

79 Ibid., 106.

80 Ibid., 106.

81 In this analysis, a seat is considered "safe" if a party won it in all four elections held between 2004 and 2011, which were held under the 2003 representation order.

strategists. The Conservative sought to maintain their appeal to new Canadian voters while also capitalizing on latent anti-Muslim public opinion through a pledge to ban full face veils during citizenship ceremonies, the introduction of a "tip line" through which Canadians could report "barbaric cultural practices," and a promise to strip citizenship from dual citizens accused of terrorism.[82] Although the Conservatives' strategy granted them a brief advantage during the campaign, it ultimately "backfired as many voters were repelled by what they perceived as gratuitous anti-immigrant proposals."[83]

To sum up, Canada's major political parties recognize the importance of competing in districts with high concentrations of immigrants and visible minority voters. They do so out of self-interest: the seat-rich metropolitan regions centered on Toronto and Vancouver are where the greatest electoral payoffs are and where many of Canada's ethnocultural communities and associated institutions are concentrated. They are also where the county's population growth, fueled by immigration, is occurring.

Attracting the votes of immigrants and their communities into a party's electoral coalition is therefore the difference between winning and losing national elections. This logic of electoral competition dampens the political mobilization of anti-immigrant rhetoric and generates broad support for the fundamental features of Canada's immigration policy, including relatively high levels of annual admissions and the maintenance of a policy of official multiculturalism. As the Conservatives' experience in 2015 and the People's Party's 2019 debacle make clear, an anti-immigrant populist strategy is risky. Whether there are ways of making such a strategy work remains an open question. What is clear is that, for the most part, parties in Canada will avoid alienating immigrant and visible minority voters, whom they believe are key to their success.[84]

Canadian immigration policy is founded on a durable cross-party political consensus. This consensus has enabled Canadian governments to maintain high levels of

---

82   Stephanie Levitz, "Conservatives Get Blasted by Member for Driving Away Muslims," *Global News*, May 27, 2016, https://globalnews.ca/news/2726855/conservatives-get-blasted-by-member-for-driving-away-muslims/; Ken MacQueen, "Who Gets to Be a Canadian?" *Maclean's*, October 7, 2015, www.macleans.ca/politics/ottawa/who-gets-to-be-canadian/2015.

83   Will Kymlicka, "The Precarious Resilience of Multiculturalism in Canada," *American Review of Canadian Studies* (forthcoming). Also see Christopher Dornan, "The Long Goodbye: The Contours of the Election," in *The Canadian Federal Election of 2015*, ed. Jon H. Pammett and Christopher Dornan (Toronto: Dundern Press, 2016), 20; Adam Radwanski, "Tories' Culture War Appears to Have Defined Campaign," *The Globe and Mail*, October 7, 2015; Harold D. Clarke, Timothy B. Gravelle, Thomas J. Scotto, Marianne C. Stewart, and Jason Reifler, "Like Father, Like Son: Justin Trudeau and Valence Voting in Canada's 2015 Federal Election," *PS: Political Science & Politics* 50, no. 3 (2017): 704.

84   Randy Besco and Erin Tolley, "Does Everyone Cheer? The Politics of Immigration and Multiculturalism in Canada," in *Federalism and the Welfare State in Multicultural World*, ed. Elizabeth Goodyear-Grant, Richard Johnston, Will Kymlicka, and John Myles (Montréal: McGill-Queen's University Press, 2018), 291–318.

immigration across time, and even increase annual admissions despite profound economic and, today, pandemic-related challenges. The public's support for mass immigration has increased over time and populism, while present, has not played a significant role in shaping immigration policies. As such, it is reasonable to claim that Canada has enjoyed some success with respect to its management of the liberal paradox.

We have shown that Canada's immigration policy regime developed in response to shifts in norms concerning racial discrimination after the Second World War. Admissions policies that had aimed at maintaining Canada's status as a "white man's country" gave way to selection criteria aimed at recruiting well-educated and highly skilled individuals regardless of their ethnicity and race. The result was the incremental pluralization of Canada's demographic profile to the point where in the 2000s most immigrants are nonwhite and from the global South. This important change was not unique to Canada. Other liberal-democratic countries also liberalized their immigration and citizenship policies and have been similarly transformed by immigration. What is distinctive about the Canadian case is the lack of political backlash generated by this profound transformation. Again, it is the consensual nature of Canadian politics that is noteworthy.

Most accounts of Canadian exceptionalism emphasize Canada's relative geographic isolation, which inhibits unwanted migration flows. Extant accounts also emphasize the importance of policies, especially as regards Canada's success in recruiting well-educated and highly skilled immigrants who are able to integrate successfully and pass on their work ethic and aspirations to their children. Successful immigrants, in this telling, beget not only successful children but also support among the public for immigration. Policy-oriented explanations also point to the symbolic importance of Canada's official multiculturalism policy and its role in shaping a shared national identity founded on distinctive public ethos. While Canadians may not be sure as to the precise aims of multiculturalism policy, they support it nonetheless and see it as an important element in Canada's prevailing national identity.

We acknowledge the importance of geography and policy but add an additional explanation based on the interplay of immigrant settlement patterns, an efficient citizenship regime, and Canada's SMP electoral system. As we have pointed out, the political logic generated by the interaction of these factors has created incentives for all of Canada's major political parties to compete for the support of new Canadian voters. It stands to reason that anti-immigration rhetoric and a rejection of multiculturalism are not helpful in this regard. Unlike most other countries, then, a pro-immigration approach serves as the baseline in Canadian party politics at the federal level. Parties that have deviated from this baseline have failed and these failures, in turn, have underscored the need to avoid antagonizing new Canadian voters.

As we pointed out, this is not a new phenomenon. The conjunction of factors cited by John Wood as key to making sense of the puzzling passage of a liberalized Immigration Act in 1976 have only intensified in the succeeding years. The proportion of the Canadian population made up of immigrants and their children has increased markedly and will continue to do so given Canada's immigration targets. It is highly likely that the concentrated metropolitan geography of immigrant settlement will also persist. Given Canada's nonpartisan legislative reapportionment process, more immigrant-dense electoral districts will be created in the GTHA and the Lower Mainland of British Columbia.

To win national elections, Canadian political parties will have no choice but to continue to appeal to immigrant populations.

The importance of contingent elements making up the Canadian model of immigration and integration raises questions about its portability. Geography is indeed key to making some sense of a country's destiny—states can work to improve their neighborhoods through diplomacy and foreign aid but cannot move. Similarly, the interplay of settlement patterns, citizenship policies, and electoral systems is highly contingent and therefore not replicable. In this sense, all countries are to some degree exceptional and the ability to borrow from or mimic others is circumscribed.

Nevertheless, we do see other countries learning from Canada. This is perhaps clearest with respect to the adoption of selective immigration policies that target the well educated and highly skilled (in some cases through the adoption of modified points systems).[85] With respect to integration, the rejection of multiculturalism in many liberal-democratic states has obscured the degree to which integration and diversity policies have become widely adopted.[86] Germany stands out as an important case in point. The success of the populist and anti-immigrant *Alternativ für Deutschland* (AfD) party has led many to overlook the wholesale transformation of immigration, citizenship, and integration policies under center-right Christian Democratic Union–led governments headed by Chancellor Angela Merkel. Germany has introduced an aggressive immigration policy whose cornerstone is the recruitment of skilled immigrants.[87] The aim of developing a "welcome society" has been key in this regard, as German policymakers have acknowledged that skilled immigrants have choices and will not opt for countries in which they are stigmatized and disadvantaged with respect to their legal status and symbolic standing.[88] Merkel has also overseen the liberalization of Germany's citizenship policy (removing remaining obstacles to birthright citizenship for children of immigrants with legal resident status),[89] invested significant resources to assist state and local governments meet their responsibilities with respect to settlement and integration (especially in the wake of the 2015 refugee crisis and acceptance of over one million asylum seekers and refugees),[90] and supported the aim of "integrating Islam" into Germany's elaborate system of church-state relations (through the work of the Deutsche

---

85   Triadafilos Triadafilopoulos, ed., *Wanted and Welcome? Highly Skilled Immigration Policies in Comparative Perspective* (New York: Springer 2012).

86   Keith Banting, "Transatlantic Convergence? The Archaeology of Immigrant Integration in Canada and Europe," *International Journal* 69, no. 1 (2014): 66–84.

87   Holger Kolb, "When Extremes Converge," *Comparative Migration Studies* 2, no. 1 (2014): 57–75.

88   Trauner and Turton, "'Welcome Culture.'"

89   Joyce Marie Mushaben, *Becoming Madam Chancellor: Angela Merkel and the Berlin Republic* (New York: Cambridge University Press, 2017), 270–71.

90   Diana zu Hohenlohe, *Dealing with the Refugee Crisis: The Recent Asylum Law Reforms in Germany—From Asylum Procedure Acceleration to Fostering Integration*, Max Planck Institute for Comparative Public Law & International Law (MPIL), Research Paper 2017–06 (2017).

Islam Konferenz).[91] While these endeavors do not spring from a common source, commentators have noted that many in the CDU have recognized that their party needs to adapt itself to a society increasingly marked by growing diversity, particularly in urban centers.[92]

This last point suggests that we should be more attentive to how immigration is changing the political landscape of liberal-democratic states. In this sense, we can draw on the Canadian case to inform comparative research that tries to better understand how the interplay of settlement patterns (and related systems of electoral districting), citizenship policies, and electoral systems interact to influence the strategies of political parties with regards to immigration and integration policy-making. While the Canadian case may remain exceptional, it may nevertheless point toward a cross-national trend that the rise of populism, and attendant academic attention, has concealed.

---

91 Elisabeth Musch, "Consultation Structures in German Immigrant Integration Politics: The National Integration Summit and the German Islam Conference," *German Politics* 21, no. 1 (2012): 73–90.

92 Oliver Schmidtke, "Between Populist Rhetoric and Pragmatic Policymaking: The Normalization of Migration as an Electoral Issue in German Politics," *Acta Politica* 50, no. 4 (2015): 391–92.

12 MIGRATION AND ECONOMIC DEVELOPMENT

North American Experience

Philip L. Martin

MIGRATION CAN GENERATE TRIPLE wins, for migrants who move and achieve higher incomes as well as for receiving countries that get jobs filled and sending countries that receive remittances from returnees and development assistance from diasporas. The most identifiable winners are migrants who benefit from higher wages and new skills acquired abroad; their remittances increase family income at home and often improve education and healthcare outcomes for children in migrant families (World Bank 2005; Adams 2006). Countries that admit migrants increase employment and generate multiplier effects, as when the availability of migrants creates or preserves jobs for local workers. Migrant-sending countries that receive remittances and the return of more skilled workers can experience faster economic growth.

The greatest gains from voluntary migration involve low-skilled workers. The reason is simple: the gaps in wages and opportunities between countries are largest for low-skilled workers. One study found that the average wage gains of low-skilled workers who move to the United States, even after adjusting for the fact that living costs are higher in the US, were four to ten times. For example, low-skilled workers who earned an average of $400 a month in Mexico earned $1,600 a month in the US, and some of those earning $200 a month in Vietnam earned $2,000 a month in the US (Clemens, Montenegro, and Pritchett 2009).

The fact that migrants can increase their incomes by up to ten times after crossing national borders provides a powerful incentive to move, especially since the $4,500 average per capita income in the 170 poorer countries in 2015 was only a tenth of the $42,000 average in the thirty richer countries (World Bank 2017). Several economists have estimated that world GDP, $78 trillion in 2015, could double if large numbers of low-skill migrants moved from poorer to richer countries and found jobs, increasing their incomes by five or ten times.[1]

---

1 *The Economist* (July 13, 2017) summarized the argument for mass migration doubling world GDP, which rests on the assumption that migrants would not increase unemployment nor change

Richer countries that prevent such migration leave "trillion dollar bills" on the sidewalk, according to Clemens (2011). Other analysts note that billions of people would have to move and find jobs without displacing natives for world GDP to rise with more migration as projected. Furthermore, if migrants introduce into destination countries the attitudes and cultures that keep their countries or origin poor, there could be a net *decrease* in global GDP instead of an increase, a reminder that mass migration may bring unanticipated changes (Borjas 2016).

A series of reports, including the report of the Global Commission on International Migration in 2004 and the UNDP's *Human Development Report 2009*, highlighted the benefits of economically motivated migration to low-skilled migrants and their developing countries of origin. These reports called on richer countries to open more doors to low-skilled workers from poorer countries in order to allow more of the world's workers to earn higher wages, send home remittances, and return with new skills and ideas that speed up development. The flow of remittances to developing countries surpassed Official Development Assistance in the mid-1990s and, at over $429 billion in 2016, remittances were three times ODA flows (World Bank 2016).

Economic development is usually defined as a sustained increase in a country's per capita income. Income is not the only measure of development, but growth in per capita income is the most widely used indicator to compare the level of development across countries. The UNDP's Human Development Index adds other indicators, such as life expectancy, infant mortality, and education levels, and has a similar ranking of countries.[2] The UN's 2030 Sustainable Development Goals defined sustainable development as the type that meets the needs of current residents without diminishing the ability of future residents to satisfy their needs.[3]

Regardless of how development is defined, more development should slow the large-scale emigration of low-skilled workers in search of economic opportunity. When economic opportunities are similar across countries, relatively few low-skilled workers migrate despite freedom of movement, as within the European Union, raising the question of how currently richer countries can help to speed up development in poorer countries.

There are three major ways in which richer countries could help poorer countries economically: trade, migration, and aid. The trade approach reflects a straightforward application of economic theory: if richer countries open their borders to more goods from developing countries, goods rather than people will cross national borders. The migration approach opens border gates to immigrants or migrant workers and assumes that remittances and returns will speed development in migrant areas of origin. Finally,

---

the institutions that led to growth in rich countries after their arrival and settlement. The article dismisses worries about more crime, wage depression, crowding, and changing culture, but argues politics could remain unaffected by restricting the right of newcomers to vote. www.economist .com/news/world-if/21724907-yes-it-would-be-disruptive-potential-gains-are-so-vast-objectors -could-be-bribed.

2   http://hdr.undp.org/en/content/human-development-index-hdi.

3   www.un.org/sustainabledevelopment/sustainable-development-goals/.

aid involves money flowing from richer to poorer countries to speed development that creates opportunities at home.

North American Migration

Canada and the United States have 5 percent of the world's people and a quarter of the world's migrants. Canada has one of the world's highest rates of immigration, aiming to increase its population by almost 1 percent a year with mostly Asian immigrants. The US has 20 percent of the world's migrants, including a quarter who are unauthorized.

Canada aims to increase its population of 37 million by 300,000 or almost 1 percent a year via immigration to settle a vast country and offset low fertility. Immigration to Canada peaked between 1895 and 1913, when 2.5 million immigrants arrived, including 400,000 arrivals in the peak year of 1913, when Canada had 7.6 million residents, so that immigration increased Canada's population by over 5 percent in one year. The US had 1.2 million immigrants in 1913, adding 1.2 percent to its population of 97 million.

Canada opened its doors to Asian immigrants in 1962, and introduced a point system in 1967 to give immigrant visas to young people with more education who spoke English or French. Today, persons who achieve at least 67 of 100 possible points may receive an immigrant visa. Of the 300,000 immigrants anticipated or targeted for admission in 2017, 172,000 or 57 percent were expected to be admitted because one member of the family achieved at least 67 points or was nominated for an immigrant visa by provincial governments.[4] Another 84,000 immigrants were sponsored by relatives in Canada, and 44,000 were resettled refugees and recognized asylum seekers.

About 40 percent of immigrants to Canada are from the Philippines (51,000 in 2015), India (40,000), and China (20,000), followed by 10,000 to 11,000 each from Iran, Pakistan, and Syria. Most immigrants settle in metro Toronto, Vancouver, and Montreal, the three cities with a third of Canadians. Except for the US, which sent 7,500 immigrants to Canada in 2015, no Western Hemisphere country is among the top ten among sources of immigrants to Canada.

The Western Hemisphere plays a far larger role in Canada's temporary worker admissions. Some 177,000 foreign workers arrived under the International Mobility Program (IMP) in 2015 and 73,000 under the Temporary Foreign Worker Program (TFWP), a total of 250,000, slightly fewer than the 270,000 immigrants admitted. An additional 126,000 foreign students who can work part-time while they study were admitted in 2015.

The leading countries of origin for IMP workers in 2015 were the US, with 28,000 temporary workers admitted, India, 21,000, France, 18,000, and China, 15,000. Brazil and Mexico, each with 2,500 admissions, were the only Latin American countries in the IMP's top twenty. This was different for the TFWP, where Mexico with 23,000 admissions

---

4   About 72,000 or 42 percent of economic migrants arrive via the point selection system, 51,000 or 30 percent are provincial nominees, 29,000 or 17 percent are skilled workers selected by the Quebec government, and 18,000 earned immigrant visas by acting as caregivers in Canadian homes for several years (www.cicnews.com/2016/10/immigration-plan-2017-canada-increased -immigrants-through-economic-family-sponsorship-programs-108621.html).

accounted for almost a third of the total. Jamaica, 8,500, and Guatemala, 6,000, were also prominent suppliers of often low-skilled guest workers.

The United States has 20 percent of the world's international migrants and perhaps half of the unauthorized foreigners in industrial countries. There were 43 million foreign-born US residents in 2014, and they were almost a seventh of the 320 million Americans. Half were Hispanic, including 28 percent who were born in Mexico and 5 percent each born in China, India, and the Philippines (Brown and Stepler 2016).

A quarter of US migrants, some 11 million, are unauthorized, and their fate has been debated for more than a decade. The number of unauthorized foreigners rose rapidly in the late 1990s and again after recovery from the 2000–1 recession, peaking at over 12 million in 2007 before declining during and after the 2008–9 recession to 11 million (Passel and Cohn 2016a). About 55 percent of unauthorized foreigners are Mexicans.

The 160 million–strong US labor force included 27 million foreign-born workers in 2016, including eight million who were not unauthorized to work in the US (Passel and Cohn 2016b). The number of unauthorized foreigners fell 9 percent since its peak in 2007, while the number of unauthorized workers fell 4 percent, suggesting that mostly nonworkers left the US during and after the 2008–9 recession.

For its first century, the US welcomed Europeans to settle the country, followed by a period of qualitative restrictions beginning in the 1880s that barred the entry of Chinese, communists, and others. During the 1920s, the US added quantitative restrictions or quotas, and today US immigration law is second in complexity only to tax law.

Most US immigrants today are from Latin America. Immigrants differ from US-born residents in the best predictor of earnings, years of education. US-born adults, when ranked by their years of schooling, form a diamond shape, with a wide bulge in the middle for the 60 percent of native adults who are high school graduates but lack college degrees. Immigrants have more of an hourglass shape, since Asians are more likely than US-born adults to have more than a college degree and Latin Americans more likely to have less than a ninth-grade education (Martin and Midgley 2010).

Congress has been debating what to do about unauthorized migration for the past decade. The policy spectrum is framed by restrictionists who want more fences and agents on the Mexico-US border and tougher controls inside the US to prevent unauthorized foreigners from getting jobs, and admissionists who want a path to immigrant status and eventual US citizenship for most unauthorized foreigners. The House in 2005 enacted an enforcement-only bill to deal with unauthorized migration, while the Senate in 2006 and 2013 enacted comprehensive bills that included more enforcement and legalization of the unauthorized.

Immigration burst into the headlines in June 2015 when Donald Trump announced his bid for the Republican presidential nomination by accusing illegal Mexican migrants of bringing drugs and crime to the US. Trump was elected president in November 2016 on an America First platform, with promises that included a wall on the Mexico-US border and the removal of most unauthorized foreigners.

President Trump issued three executive orders during his first week in office in January 2017, setting in motion plans to build a wall on the Mexico-US border, increase deportations, and punish sanctuary cities that refuse to cooperate with the Department of

Homeland Security (DHS) to detect unauthorized foreigners and reduce refugee admissions. The border memo envisions a $21 billion wall and the addition of 5,000 Border Patrol agents to the current 21,000. The interior enforcement memo laid out plans to double the number of Immigration and Customs Enforcement (ICE) agents from 10,000 to 20,000 and to prioritize the detection and removal of unauthorized foreigners convicted of US crimes while making almost all unauthorized foreigners subject to deportation (Martin 2017).

The refugee executive order banned the entry of nationals of seven countries: Syria, Iran, Iraq, Somalia, Sudan, Libya, and Yemen, and reduced refugee admissions to 50,000 a year. Parts of this executive order were blocked by federal courts, prompting modified versions in March 2017 that the US Supreme Court permitted to be implemented (*Rural Migration News* 2017).

Trade and Migration

The factor-price equalization theorem suggests that freer trade can be a substitute for migration. Fewer low-wage workers should move from poorer to richer countries if the goods such workers produce can be traded more freely. With freer trade, economies grow faster as capital and labor is reallocated to where it is most productive, there are economies of scale in production as firms produce for larger markets, and competition between foreign and domestic firms lowers prices for consumers in all participating countries.

Comparative advantage assumes that countries export commodities that require intensive use of their relatively cheaper factor, so that capital-intensive richer countries export capital-intensive goods and labor-intensive countries export labor-intensive goods. In North America, comparative advantage suggests that the US should export airplanes to Mexico and import fruits and vegetables from Mexico. Over time, wages and the cost of capital in the US and Mexico should converge, reducing incentives to migrate, so that freer trade is a substitute for migration (Samuelson, 1948).

In the US, the executive branch's Office of the US Trade Representative (USTR) takes the lead in negotiating trade agreements. Under the Trade Promotion Authority granted by Congress to the president, the USTR negotiates Free Trade Agreements (FTAs) and presents them to Congress for an up or down vote within ninety days; in other words, Congress may not amend FTAs.

NAFTA and USMCA

The North American Free Trade Agreement was the first reciprocal and rules-based trade agreement between an industrial and a developing country. Canada and the US signed a Free-Trade Agreement in 1989 with little fanfare in the US, and Mexican president Carlos Salinas in 1990 proposed a similar FTA with the US to lock recent Mexican economic policy changes into an international agreement and thus reassure foreign investors. The major opposition to NAFTA arose in the US, where presidential candidate Ross Perot in 1992 predicted that there would be a "giant sucking sound" as US jobs moved to Mexico. Unions led by the AFL-CIO made the defeat of NAFTA their primary goal in 1993.

NAFTA was narrowly approved by the US Congress in 1993 and went into effect January 1, 1994. The purpose of NAFTA was to increase trade and investment between Canada, Mexico, and the US, and a hoped-for side effect was less unauthorized Mexico-US migration. NAFTA accomplished its trade and investment goals, helping to forge integrated supply chains between Canada, Mexico, and the US, especially in the auto industry, but encouraged more Mexico-US migration, a migration hump.

NAFTA has never had majority support in US opinion polls. Candidate Trump in summer 2016 called NAFTA the "worst trade deal ever negotiated by the US government," and threatened to withdraw, but as president authorized a re-negotiation. Americans may be warming to NAFTA. From a low of 38 percent who agreed that NAFTA was overall good for the US in 2005, 48 percent agreed that NAFTA was overall good in 2017, and only 6 percent had no opinion.

The clearest success of NAFTA is the auto industry (Bennett and Sharpe 2014). NAFTA allows cars with at least 62.5 percent North American content to be traded freely between Canada, Mexico, and the US, encouraging many of the world's major auto producers to build assembly plants in Mexico and creating 800,000 jobs in auto assembly and parts factories by 2020. Over forty auto firms assemble cars in Mexico including Nissan, the largest Mexican producer and the seller of a quarter of cars bought in Mexico. Almost four million cars and light trucks were produced in Mexico in 2019, and Mexico is projected to make over five million vehicles by 2025.

Mexican auto and auto parts plants pay employees more than Mexico's minimum wage of $4 a day in 2017, often $2 an hour or $1,200 a month plus overtime and benefits that range from free meals to transportation and bonuses.[5] Most Mexican auto plants are unionized under so-called protection agreements that involve union leaders signing contracts before new plants are built, which means that newly hired workers work under contracts they had no role in negotiating.[6]

Freer trade speeded up changes in all three countries, including the movement of labor out of agriculture in Mexico and de-industrialization in Canada and the US. Workers displaced from factory jobs in Canada and the US did not move to Mexico, but especially youth in the already poor rural Mexican families dependent on producing corn that could be imported at lower cost from the US soon realized that they could get ahead only with both geographic and occupational mobility, by getting out of rural Mexico and small-scale farming.

---

5   Christina Rogers and Dudley Althaus, "Mexico's Auto-Production Boom Is Driving Up Labor Costs," *Wall Street Journal*, August 15, 2016, www.wsj.com/articles/mexicos-auto-production -boom-is-driving-up-labor-costs-1471201920.

6   Most Mexican auto workers belong to unions affiliated with the Confederacion de Trabajadores de Mexico (CTM), the largest union federation whose affiliates have four million members. CTM unions often sign so-called protection contracts with new plants before they are built, so that all newly hired workers are union members and their dues are deducted from their wages. By pre-signing with one union, other unions cannot try to organize workers at a pre-signed plant.

The US state of Iowa produced twice as much corn as all of Mexico in the early 1990s, and at half the price. Rural Mexican youth were often unable to get jobs in the auto and other factories that were created in response to NAFTA, since they lacked secondary school diplomas and lived far away from where auto factories and parts plants were being built. The result was a Mexico-US migration hump from rural Mexico that peaked in 2000 (Martin 1993). An average of over 3,000 Mexicans a day were apprehended just inside the US during the late 1990s, when the Mexican labor force increased by a million a year but only 350,000 formal sector jobs a year were created. The US, by contrast, was adding over 10,000 jobs a day or 2.5 million jobs a year, and many farm, construction, and service employers were eager to hire rural Mexicans with relatively little education.

The Mexican government and many researchers urged the US government to expand and create new guest-worker programs so that Mexican workers leaving agriculture could enter the US legally. President Clinton strongly opposed new and expanded guest-worker programs, saying: "When these programs were tried in the past, many temporary guest workers stayed permanently and illegally in this country. Hundreds of thousands of immigrants now residing in the US first came as temporary workers, and their presence became a magnet for other illegal immigration."[7] In other words, Clinton rejected the notion that large-scale Mexico-US migration was inevitable and feared that admitting some Mexicans as guest workers would increase rather than decrease illegal migration.

During the 1990s, illegal Mexico-US migration surged, peaking in 2000 when over 1.8 million Mexicans were apprehended just inside US borders, an average of over 4,000 a day. Mexico-US migration slowed during the 2000–1 recession, but surged again during the US economic boom of 2002–7, when Mexican-born workers were very prominent in home-building and many service sectors. By 2007, over 10 percent of the 120 million people born in Mexico were living in the US, and 60 percent of the estimated 12 million unauthorized foreigners in the US were Mexicans (Passel and Cohn 2016b). Over 8 million unauthorized foreigners were in the US labor force, making one in twenty US workers unauthorized.

The 2008–9 recession slowed Mexico-US migration, as the US unemployment rate topped 10 percent and federal and state enforcement efforts made it more difficult for unauthorized foreigners to enter the US and find jobs. Mexico-US migration began falling, so that the upsurge in Mexico-US migration between 1990 and 2010 appears as a hump, first rising with the changes wrought by NAFTA before falling below the level that would have occurred if there had not been NAFTA. As Mexico-US migration continues to fall, the figure also illustrates the migration avoided by freer trade.

The migration hump was not anticipated by politicians who suggested that freer trade would smoothly reduce Mexico-US migration. Mexican president Carlos Salinas predicted in 1990 that freer trade would create enough new jobs in Mexico to absorb those who were displaced by NAFTA in rural Mexico. He said the US faced a choice of "accepting Mexican tomatoes or Mexican migrants who will harvest them in the United States,"

---

7   Quoted at http://migration.ucdavis.edu/mn/more.php?id=1769.

suggesting that corn farmers would become tomato farmers and export their tomatoes to the US. Few corn farmers had the capital or marketing connections to grow tomatoes for the US market, but existing Mexican tomato farmers were able to increase their exports, so that Mexican tomato exports and Mexico-US migration increased together (Martin 2005).

The NAFTA experience shows that industrial countries can succeed in "attacking the root causes" of unwanted migration with freer trade, but with a migration hump that persists for a decade or more. There are many reasons for migration humps, but the simplest is that freer trade can displace workers quickly, while time is normally required to invest in factories or other businesses that create jobs in the poorer countries. If workers made worse off by freer trade have connections to jobs abroad, they may cross national borders, leading to a migration hump.

There are other reasons why trade and migration can rise together, as when countries do not share the same technologies. If tractors plow cornfields in the United States and oxen pull plows in Mexico, trade theory assumes that the reason for this difference is that Mexico has lower wages, not that tractors are unavailable in Mexico—that is, differences in labor and capital intensities are due solely to differences in factor endowments. In reality, rural Mexicans may not have access to tractors or credit to buy them, and some Mexicans may migrate to the US to get the money to buy tractors, the "missing markets" argument for migration. Similarly, if the better infrastructure of the US makes Mexican workers more productive in the US than in Mexico, migration may increase alongside trade as US producers expand, as occurred with the US shoe industry in the 1990s, which employed experienced Mexican workers who were more productive in the US (Taylor and Martin 2001).

The closer economic integration symbolized by NAFTA raised the aspirations of Mexicans faster than economic development could fulfill them, prompting more Mexico-US migration. There was much talk of a new era in Mexico in 1994, with many predicting that Mexico would become a Tiger Economy akin to fast-growing Asian economies, with employment rising in factories created by foreign investors. However, there was a sharp devaluation of the Mexican peso in winter 1994 that made employment in the US more attractive, and Mexicans streamed north. Before the devaluation, Mexicans used foreign savings that poured into the country in anticipation of a NAFTA boom to purchase imported consumer goods rather than invest in infrastructure. When foreigners stopped investing, the economy collapsed (*Migration News* 1995).

The Mexico-US migration hump lasted about fifteen years, from the early 1990s until the 2008–9 recession. Between 1995 and 2000, a net 2.3 million Mexicans moved to the US, while between 2009 and 2014, the Mexican-born population in the US fell by 140,000 (Gonzalez-Barrera 2015).

Mexico-US migration is poised to remain on a downward trajectory due to slower labor force growth in Mexico and better education systems in rural areas that prepare Mexican youth for jobs in Mexico. Meanwhile, the US has made it more difficult to cross the Mexico-US border illegally and work. This combination of decreasing push factors in Mexico, tougher and more costly illegal border crossings, and more difficulty finding work in the US promises less illegal Mexico-US migration in the future. However, legal guest-worker migration from Mexico to the US (and Canada) is rising, with over 250,000 H-2A and H-2B visas issued each year to Mexicans to fill seasonal US jobs (GAO 2015).

NAFTA has twenty-two chapters, and chapter 16, "Temporary Entry for Business Purposes,"[8] aims to facilitate the entry of Canadian and Mexican business visitors, traders and investors, intra-company transferees, and specified professionals:

- business visitors are those who are primarily paid in their country of residence,
- a treaty trader or investor is an executive or supervisor moving to the country to engage in trade or manage an investment,
- an intra-company transferee is a manager or worker with specialized knowledge moving to a branch of a multinational to provide services, and
- NAFTA professionals are persons with at least a first university degree in seventy-plus occupations who have a job offer from an employer in the NAFTA country they are seeking to enter.[9]

The US is the major destination for NAFTA-related business visitors (Martin 2011). The first three groups of NAFTA-related migrants enter the US with visas that existed before NAFTA went into effect. For example, business visitors use B-1 visas to enter the US, treaty traders and investors use E-1 and E-2 visas, and intra-company transferees use L-1 and L-2 visas.

NAFTA created a new TN (trade-NAFTA) visa for the fourth group, NAFTA professionals. US employers may offer jobs to Canadians and Mexicans who have college degrees and are coming to the US to fill jobs that require college degrees, and Canadian and Mexican employers may make similar job offers to Americans. There has never been a quota on the number of TN visas available for Canadians, but there was a 5,500 a year quota on TN visas available to Mexicans between 1994 and 2004.

There are separate procedures for issuing TN visas to Canadians and Mexicans. Canadian professionals can receive three-year TN visas at US ports of entry by showing a qualifying job offer from a US employer and providing proof of their bachelor's degree and Canadian citizenship. Mexicans, by contrast, must obtain TN visas at US consulates in Mexico.

US employers seeking TN visas for Mexicans must file the same Labor Condition Attestations (LCAs) that are filed by employers seeking H-1B workers. The Mexicans designated in approved LCAs take their qualifying US job offer and proof of their bachelor's degree to a US consulate in Mexico to receive renewable three-year TN visas (extended from one to three years since 2008). Unlike H-1B visas, the TN visa does not allow dual intent to work and immigrate, that is, TN visa applicants must show that they intend to return to Canada or Mexico.

---

8   The text of chapter 16 is available at http://tcc.export.gov/Trade_Agreements/Exporters _Guides/List_All_Guides/NAFTA_chapter16_guide.asp.

9   The list of professionals covered by NAFTA Appendix 1603.D.1 is at http://canada.usembassy .gov/business/doing-business-in-america/professions-covered-by-nafta.html.

The number of Canadian professionals entering the US with NAFTA-TN visas almost quadrupled between 1995 and 2000, but fell after the IT bubble burst in 2000 to less than 60,000 a year in 2003 and 2005. Many of the Canadians moving to the US during the late 1990s were nurses, prompting criticism and new US testing requirements that sharply limited the influx (Gabriel 2008).

Admissions of Canadian TN visa holders have risen to almost 70,000 a year recently, but are still below the almost 90,000 a year level of 2000. The number of Mexican entries rose even faster, but from a very low base, doubling between 2006 and 2008 to almost 20,000 a year. Admissions of spouses and dependents, who receive TD visas and do not obtain a derivative right to work because of their relationship to a TN visa holder, have fluctuated between 12,000 and 22,000 a year over the past decade.

The NAFTA experience shows that a liberal free-mobility provision can be included in a free-trade agreement between an industrial and developing country if entries are limited to those with at least college degrees in specified occupations. There is little controversy about the entry and employment of Canadian and Mexican TN visa holders in the US, although especially Canadians complain because dependents of TN visa holders do not automatically receive the right to work in the US. The movement of Americans to Canada and Mexico with TN visas has been limited, but the oil shale boom in Alberta contributed to the movement of about 35,000 American workers a year to Canada.[10]

The United States-Mexico-Canada Agreement (USMCA) that replaced NAFTA in 2020 included several provisions aimed at returning auto jobs to the US. The North American content requirement was raised from 62.5 to 75 percent, and 40 to 45 percent of auto components must be made by workers earning at least $16 an hour to trade freely throughout North America. The USMCA also includes protections for digital services, such as a prohibition of tariffs on digital products and protections for electronic intellectual property. Mexico enacted legislation that gives workers the right to elect union leaders in direct elections with secret ballots.[11] Given Trump's threats, most business leaders were relieved that the USMCA made few substantive changes to NAFTA outside the auto sector.

CAFTA-DR
The Dominican Republic–Central America–United States Free Trade Agreement (CAFTA-DR), which went into effect in 2006, lowers trade and investment barriers between the US and Costa Rica, the Dominican Republic, El Salvador, Guatemala, Honduras, and Nicaragua.[12] Most imports from these countries entered the US without tariffs

---

10   Ricardo Lopez, "Canada Looks to Lure Energy Workers from the U.S.," *Los Angeles Times*, November 12, 2012, www.latimes.com/business/la-fi-canada-recruit-20121111,0,6209802.story.

11   Under the 2019 labor law, unions must win the support of at least 30 percent of the workers in a workplace to be recognized as their bargaining representative, and the Labor Ministry is to review the 500,000 contracts signed under the old system when there were no elections.

12   CAFTA-DR was strongly opposed by US unions, and was approved by the House on the 217–215 vote on July 28, 2005.

before 2006 due to the Caribbean Basin Initiative, but it was hoped that the CAFTA-DR FTA would increase investment in participating countries by strengthening protections for foreign investors.

The effects of the CAFTA-DR FTA are similar to the effects of NAFTA. Trade and investment between CAFTA-DR member countries and the US has increased: two-way trade was $60 billion in 2014, up 70 percent from $35 billion in 2005. US exports to CAFTA-DR countries in 2014 were $31 billion, and US imports from CAFTA-DR countries were $28 billion, giving the US a slight trade surplus.

US investments in the CAFTA-DR countries increased, especially to build factories to assemble computers and electronics and in services such as insurance and telecoms. CAFTA-DR exports of fruit and coffee to the US increased, as did US exports of grains and meat to CAFTA-DR countries. Trade and investment patterns between the US and CAFTA-DR member countries evolved similarly to those between Mexico and the US, but with an emphasis on lower-value goods; the CAFTA-DR countries do not have a relatively high-wage auto industry.

The CAFTA-DR countries traditionally had a large agricultural sector that included indigenous people who tended their own small plots and worked seasonally on estates, a persisting legacy of colonial times. There has been significant out-migration from rural areas as education spreads, aspirations rise, and diasporas in the US make rural residents aware of opportunities elsewhere. The traditional export crops of bananas, coffee, and sugar are being produced with ever-fewer workers, prompting out-migration from agriculture, including to factories in urban areas and to Mexico and the US.

CAFTA-DR includes protections for workers. The US provides technical assistance and requires CAFTA-DR countries to enforce their labor laws or face fines of up to $15 million per failure-to-enforce.[13] One reason US unions opposed the CAFTA-DR FTA is that governments in these countries allegedly fail to protect local workers: only two of 200 textile factories in Guatemala had collective bargaining agreements in 2005.

Unions complain that CAFTA-DR remedies for labor law violations are inadequate, and point to a case filed in 2008 that resulted in a decision 2017 that the Guatemalan government did not effectively enforce its labor laws.[14] The US government successfully proved that the Guatemalan government was not enforcing its labor laws, but could not prove that persisting labor violations affected Guatemala-US trade by giving Guatemala-based firms unfair trade advantages, so there was no remedy. Unions complain that the difficulty of proving that a country's failure to enforce its labor laws "in a manner affecting trade" winds up yielding hollow remedies for workers.

Puebla and Caravans

The Mexico-US migration hump of the 1990s led to a US backlash exemplified by Proposition 187 in California in 1994 and the enactment of new federal laws against

---

13   https://ustr.gov/about-us/policy-offices/press-office/fact-sheets/2011/may/cafta-dr-labor -capacity-building.

14   https://aflcio.org/2017/6/26/us-trade-policy-fails-workers.

unauthorized foreigners in the US in 1996.[15] In response, the Mexican government proposed the Puebla Process or Regional Conference on Migration (RCM) to deal jointly with migration issues.[16]

The first meeting of the RCM was held in Puebla, Mexico, in March 1996 and led to the Binational Study of Mexico-US Migration, which involved Mexican and US researchers estimating the number of Mexican-born persons in the US, their characteristics, factors sustaining the flow, impacts in both countries, and policy options. The Binational Study was the first migration study funded jointly by both governments, and succeeded in showing that extreme assertions about "20 million Mexicans" in the US were wrong. The study highlighted the responsibility of both governments for policies that facilitated unauthorized Mexico-US migration (US Commission on Immigration Reform 1997).

The Binational Study estimated that there were seven million Mexican-born US residents in 1996, equivalent to 8 percent of Mexico's population. Mexicans traditionally did not become naturalized US citizens—only 500,000 or 7 percent of Mexican-born residents had become naturalized US citizens by 1995—but Proposition 187 and changes to Mexican laws on dual nationality prompted almost 250,000 Mexicans to naturalize in 1996. The Binational Study acknowledged that the US and Mexican governments facilitated the recruitment of Mexican workers in the 1940s and 1950s, setting in motion migration networks that continued to encourage especially rural Mexicans to move north for opportunity (*Migration News* 1997).

The Binational Study emphasized that migration was far more important to Mexico than the US. In 1996, the five million Mexican-born workers employed in the US were equivalent to a sixth of all Mexicans with paid employment. About 15 million Mexicans had formal jobs covered by social security in Mexico in 1996 (IMSS), so the five million Mexicans employed in the US were equivalent to a third of Mexicans with formal sector jobs. Most Mexican migrants came from 109 of Mexico's 2,400 *municipos* in nine of Mexico's thirty-one states. There was an inevitable tension between US efforts to reduce illegal migration and Mexican efforts to protect its citizens in the US.

Mexican and US officials have continued to meet periodically to discuss binational migration issues, including in July 2017 when Presidents Peña Nieto and Trump "agreed to explore new mechanisms for Mexican agricultural workers to work in the US." Trump has several times assured US farmers in that they would have "plenty of access" to foreign workers, and the Trump Vineyard Estates in Virginia hires Mexican guest workers via the H-2A program.[17] The H-2A program allows an unlimited number of guest workers to

---

15   Proposition 187 would have barred unauthorized children from K–12 schools and tightened restrictions on the access of unauthorized foreigners to health and other state-funded services. Most of its provisions were declared unconstitutional and not implemented (https://migration.ucdavis.edu/mn/more.php?id=492).

16   www.rcmvs.org.

17   Trump Vineyard Estates requested certification to hire 29 H-2A workers in 2017. Trump's Mar-a-Lago resort and Jupiter golf course in Florida were certified to employ 77 H-2B workers in 2017. CNN reported that Trump companies employed at least 1,256 H-2A and H-2B workers,

be hired by US farmers who are certified to employ them (Martin 2014). Certification, in turn, requires farmers first to try to recruit US workers, and then if failing in the attempt, to provide free and approved housing for guest workers, and to pay a super minimum wage to H-2A workers known as the Adverse Effect Wage Rate.

The RCM organizes annual discussions among eleven countries: Belize, Canada, Costa Rica, El Salvador, Guatemala, Honduras, Mexico, Nicaragua, Panama, Dominican Republic, and the United States. The two major objectives of the RCM are to provide a forum for "frank and honest discussion on regional migration issues" and to "protect the human rights of migrants ... [and] strengthen the links between migration and development." RCM discussions are grouped into three major categories:

1. Migration management, including countering smuggling and trafficking
2. Human rights, including dealing with child migrants and the return of deported migrants
3. Migration and development, including remittances and guest workers

The lead agencies in the RCM are Foreign Affairs ministries, with many countries also sending representatives from their interior ministries. RCM decisions and declarations are made by consensus, and many deal with reducing the smuggling and trafficking of persons. Since 2001, a technical secretariat advises member countries on migration issues with an annual budget of less than $300,000, half provided by the US and a quarter by Canada.

A major accomplishment of the RCM has been the ability of Central American leaders to press the US government to offer Temporary Protected Status to their citizens in the US when natural disasters strike countries of origin. Hurricane Mitch killed 10,000 people in Honduras and Nicaragua in late October 1998, left three million people homeless, and severely damaged both countries' economies, prompting Honduran president Carlos Flores Facusse to warn that a new wave of migrants will go "walking, swimming and running up north" unless the US provided assistance.

In response, the Clinton administration suspended deportations to Guatemala, Honduras, El Salvador, and Nicaragua and offered Temporary Protected Status (TPS) to nationals of these countries who were in the US that permitted them to work as an "humanitarian effort to help the four governments cope with the devastation caused by Hurricane Mitch."[18] A Gallup survey done for the US Information Agency estimated that 600,000 adults in Honduras, Nicaragua, Guatemala, and El Salvador might try to migrate to the US in the summer of 1999, and that 292,000 had already left home for the US, including 106,000 Hondurans, 3.5 percent of that country's adults. According to

---

most from Romania and South Africa, between 2000 and 2015 (https://migration.ucdavis.edu/rmn/more.php?id=2044).

18 After touring the devastation, First Lady Hillary Rodham Clinton said: "There is a double-edged problem here for those countries, with the immigrants. One is that they cannot accommodate people at this time. They've literally nowhere for people to live or be put. They also would collapse completely, in some cases, without the funds coming in from the people who are working and sending remittances." Quoted in https://migration.ucdavis.edu/mn/more.php?id=3451.

the poll, most Central Americans who were preparing to try to enter the United States believed they would be allowed to stay even without proper documents because of the TPS granted to those in the US when Hurricane Mitch struck.[19]

El Salvador suffered earthquakes in January–February 2001, prompting President Francisco Flores to ask the US to provide TPS to the estimated 335,000 Salvadorans in the US illegally at the time. There were about a million El Salvadorans in the US and six million in El Salvador in 2001. As with Hurricane Mitch, discussions of appropriate migration responses to natural disasters in the RCM paved the way for Central American leaders to request, and for the US government to provide, TPS to generate remittances that assist in rebuilding.

Some 325,000 foreigners from thirteen countries had Temporary Protected Status in the US in January 2017. TPS, created in 1990, can be granted when a natural or other disaster strikes the country of origin of foreigners who are in the US at the time. TPS enables these foreigners to live and work legally in the US under the assumption that their remittances will help to rebuild their countries of origin. In summer 2017, the largest group of TPS recipients was from El Salvador, 195,000 or 60 percent of all TPS residents, followed by 57,000 or 18 percent Hondurans and 50,000 or 15 percent Haitians.

The RCM has had success in helping unauthorized foreigners from Latin American countries in the US when natural disaster strikes their countries of origin to obtain TPS. The RCM has had less success in widening channels for regular migration or promoting migration and development.

The RCM was not successful dealing with caravans of Central Americans who set out for the US to seek asylum on the basis of gang and domestic violence at home. Six caravans of Central Americans crossed Mexico en route to the US in 2018 and 2019, including families with children and solo children under eighteen. Caravans often form in Honduras and add Guatemalans and Salvadorans as they travel north. Caravans attract donations of food and transportation while transiting Mexico, and help to protect migrants from gangs.

Once in the US, Central Americans who pass a credible fear test are allowed to apply for asylum. There is a backlog of over a million immigration cases, and children under eighteen can be detained for a maximum of twenty days, so most Central American asylum seekers are released for the several years required until their cases come before immigration judges.[20] While waiting, adults can receive work permits and children can attend US schools.

President Trump criticized this catch-and-release policy for encouraging parents to enter the US illegally with children in order to be released into the US. To discourage family asylum seekers, a family separation policy in May–June 2018 separated children from their parents and encouraged the parents to return to their countries of origin. Family separation was roundly criticized and soon stopped.

---

19   https://migration.ucdavis.edu/mn/more.php?id=1798.

20   The 1997 Flores settlement, modified in 2001, limits the detention of unauthorized children to twenty days, and requires that children be held in licensed child-care facilities.

Other policies proved more effective, especially US pressure on the Mexican government to prevent the entry and travel through Mexico of Central Americans headed to the US to apply for asylum. The US threatened to block the US border to Mexican goods unless the Mexican government stopped the caravans, which it did. The US began to return asylum seekers who had applied for asylum in the US to Mexico to wait for their hearings before US immigration judges, so that 60,000 mostly Central Americans were returned under the Migration Protection Protocols or "Remain in Mexico" program.

Finally, the US signed Asylum Cooperation Agreements with Central American countries that required Hondurans and Salvadorans who passed through Guatemala to apply there. Those who nonetheless arrive in the US are returned to Guatemala.

COVID-19 and Migration

The arrival of the COVID-19 virus in the US in February–March 2020 led to stay-at-home orders for US residents and the closure of US borders to nonessential travelers, including unauthorized foreigners and asylum seekers. Apprehensions of foreigners just inside the Mexico-US border fell to less than 40,000 a month in January–February 2020. In March 2020, President Trump directed that apprehended foreigners be returned to Mexico within two hours of their interception to "keep the infection and those carrying the infection from entering our country."

Emergencies such as COVID-19 increase the power of the executive relative to other branches of government. President Trump in April 2020 issued a "Proclamation Suspending Entry of Immigrants Who Present Risk to the U.S. Labor Market During the Economic Recovery Following the Covid-19 Outbreak" that bars some legal immigration to the US for sixty days. The US admits 1.1 million immigrants a year, but most are already inside the US and adjust their status to immigrant after being sponsored by US relatives or employers. Trump's proclamation deals with some foreigners outside the US who are waiting for immigrant visas, and will have relatively little effect on legal immigration unless it is renewed.

President Trump is sending mixed migration messages with his COVID-19 actions. On the one hand, the security or garrison state is evident in Trump's closure of US borders to nonessential travel, the quick return of apprehended foreigners, and the temporary ban on some legal immigration. However, the trading or economic state is evident in the decision to consider several hundred thousand temporary foreign workers to be essential despite 30 million unemployed US workers after six weeks of stay-at-home orders. Trump's version of the migration state uses elements of security and economics to adjust migration flows.

North America is something of an outlier in regional migration systems, with Canada and the US anticipating large numbers of settler migrants. The NAFTA-USMCA and CAFTA-DR represent the US approach to unwanted migration—substitute trade and investment that speeds up economic growth in a bid to reduce unauthorized and asylum seeking migration. There are few migration provisions in these free-trade agreements, but the arguments made in favor of them included the hope that more trade in goods would be a substitute for the migration of people.

The NAFTA experience demonstrates that this economic theory is correct in the long run, so that trade has become a substitute for large-scale Mexico-US migration. However, the first fifteen years of NAFTA were marked by one of the largest migration movements in history, with the stock of Mexicans in the US rising from 3 million in 1990 to 12 million in 2007. This migration hump had ramifications, including the bolstering of support for Trump's election in 2016.

The Mexico-US migration hump reflected a combination of freer trade, rapid Mexican labor force growth, and slow job creation in Mexico. Rural Mexicans followed well-established networks to the US, where employers who had been hiring Mexicans for decades expanded. Rural Mexicans were leaving for the US before NAFTA, but the free-trade agreement speeded up changes in Mexico, compressing a process that may have stretched over several decades into fifteen years. The USMCA is unlikely to restart large-scale Mexico-US migration.

The CAFTA-DR countries are at a different stage of development. Especially the Northern Triangle countries of El Salvador, Guatemala, and Honduras appear to be on the upside of the migration hump, with more people seeking to emigrate. The US developed Central American diasporas during the 1980s, and family unification and TPS swelled the number of Guatemalans, Hondurans, and Salvadorans since. Slow economic growth, widespread inequality, persisting violence, and a paucity of local opportunities promise continued emigration pressures.

The US approach to unwanted migration centers on enforcement as a short-term strategy and freer trade as a long-term strategy. This US approach appears to have "worked" with NAFTA and Mexico, but may be contributing to a migration hump in Central America. The COVID-19 emergency in 2020 increased the power of President Trump to deal with migration, which Trump did by closing the border to nonessential travelers but not goods, and defining guest workers to be essential travelers.

References

Adams, Richard. 2006. "International Remittances and the Household: Analysis and Review of Global Evidence." *Journal of African Economies* (Centre for the Study of African Economies) 15(2): 396–425.

Bennett, Douglas C., and Kenneth E. Sharpe. 2014. *Transnational Corporations versus the State: The Political Economy of the Mexican Auto Industry*. Princeton, NJ: Princeton University Press.

Binational Study of Mexico-US Migration. 1997. *Migration between Mexico and the United States*. Washington, DC/Mexico City: Commission on Immigration Reform. http://migration.ucdavis.edu/mn/cir/binational/toc.html

Borjas, George. 2016. *We Wanted Workers: Unraveling the Immigration Narrative*. New York: W.W. Norton.

Brown, Anna and Renee Stepler. 2016. "Statistical Portrait of the Foreign-Born Population in the United States, 2014." Pew Research Center, Hispanic Trends. www.pewhispanic.org/2016/04/19/statistical-portrait-of-the-foreign-born-population-in-the-united-states/

Clemens, Michael. 2011. *Economics and Emigration: Trillion-Dollar Bills on the Sidewalk?* Center for Global Development Working Paper no. 264. https://papers.ssrn.com/sol3/papers.cfm?abstract_id=1912544

Clemens, Michael, Claudio Montenegro, and Lant Pritchett. 2009. *The Place Premium: Wage Differences for Identical Workers across the US Border*. HKS Faculty Research Working Paper Series RWP09–004,

John F. Kennedy School of Government, Harvard University. https://dash.harvard.edu/bitstream/han-dle/1/4412631/Clemens%20Place%20Premium.pdf

Gabriel, Christina. 2008. "A Healthy Trade? NAFTA, Labor Mobility and Canadian Nurses." In *Governing International Labour Migration: Current Issues, Challenges and Dilemmas*, ed. Christina Gabriel and Hélène Pellerin, 112–30 (London: Routledge/RIPE Studies in Global Political Economy).

GAO (Government Accountability Office). 2015. *H-2A and H-2B Visa Programs: Increased Protections Needed for Foreign Worker.* March 6. www.gao.gov/products/GAO-15-154

Global Commission on International Migration. 2005. *Migration in an Interconnected World: New Directions for Action.* Geneva: IOM. www.iom.int/cms/en/sites/iom/home/what-we-do/migration-policy-and-research/migration-policy-1/global-commission-on-internation.html

Gonzalez-Barrera, Ana. 2015. *More Mexicans Leaving Than Coming to the U.S.* Pew Research Center, Hispanic Trends. www.pewhispanic.org/2015/11/19/more-mexicans-leaving-than-coming-to-the-u-s/

Martin, Philip L. 1993. *Trade and Migration: NAFTA and Agriculture.* Washington, DC: Institute for International Economics.

Martin, Philip L. 2005. Chapter 8 "Mexico-US Migration." Chap. 8 in *NAFTA Revisited: Achievements and Challenges*, ed. Gary Hubauer and Jeffrey Schott, 438–65. Washington, DC: Institute for International Economics.

Martin, Philip L. 2006. *GATS, Migration, and Labor Standards.* IILS Discussion Paper 165/2006. www.ilo.org/public/english/bureau/inst/publications/discussion/dp16506.pdf

Martin, Philip L. 2011. "Mexico-US Migration, NAFTA and CAFTA, and US Immigration Policy." In *Migration, Nation States, and International Cooperation*, ed. Randall Hansen, Jobst Koehler, and Jeanette Money, 75–86. New York: Routledge.

Martin, Philip L. 2014. "The H-2A Program; Evolution, Impacts, and Outlook." Chap. 2 of *(Mis)managing Migration: Guestworkers' Experiences with North American Labor Market*, ed. David Griffith, 33–62. Santa Fe, NM: SAR Press.

Martin, Philip L. 2020. "President Trump and Migration after 100 Days." *Migration Letters* 17(1), special issue, "Diaspora Politics." www.tplondon.com/journal/index.php/ml/article/view/902

Martin, Philip, and Elizabeth Midgley. 2010. *Immigration in America 2010.* Population Bulletin Update, June 30. www.prb.org/wp-content/uploads/2006/12/Population-bulletin-immigration-update2010.pdf

Migration News. 1995. "Devaluation and Mexico to US Migration." Vol. 4, no. 2 (March). https://migration.ucdavis.edu/mn/more.php?id=553

Migration News. 1997. "Binational Study." Vol. 4, no. 9 (October). https://migration.ucdavis.edu/mn/more.php?id=1329

Passel, Jeffrey, and D'Vera Cohn. 2016a. "Overall Number of U.S. Unauthorized Immigrants Holds Steady since 2009." Pew Research Center, Hispanic Trends. www.pewhispanic.org/2016/09/20/overall-number-of-u-s-unauthorized-immigrants-holds-steady-since-2009/

Passel, Jeffrey, and D'Vera Cohn. 2016b. "Size of U.S. Unauthorized Immigrant Workforce Stable after the Great Recession." Pew Research Center, Hispanic Trends. www.pewhispanic.org/2016/11/03/size-of-u-s-unauthorized-immigrant-workforce-stable-after-the-great-recession/

Rural Migration News. 2017. "Trump: Immigration." Vol. 23, no. 3 (July). https://migration.ucdavis.edu/rmn/more.php?id=2061

Samuelson, Paul. 1948. "International Trade and the Equalization of Factor Prices." *Economic Journal* 58(230): 163–84.

Taylor, J. Edward, and Philip L. Martin. 2001. "Human Capital: Migration and Rural Population Change." In *Handbook of Agricultural Economics, Volume I*, ed. Bruce Gardener and Gordon Rausser, 457–511. Amsterdam: Elsevier Science.

UNDP (United Nations Development Programme). 2009. *Overcoming Barriers: Human Mobility and Development.* Human Development Report. http://hdr.undp.org/en/content/human-development-report-2009

US Commission on Immigration Reform. 1997. *Binational Study on Migration: Executive Summary.* Washington, DC: US Commission on Immigration Reform.

World Bank. 2005. *Global Economic Prospects: The Economic Implications of Remittances and Migration.* www.worldbank.org/prospects/gep2006

World Bank. 2016. *Trends in Remittances, 2016: A New Normal of Slow Growth.* http://blogs.worldbank.org/peoplemove/trends-remittances-2016-new-normal-slow-growth%20

World Bank. 2017. *World Development Indicators.* http://data.worldbank.org/products/wdi

13 INTERNATIONAL MIGRATION AND REFUGEE MOVEMENTS IN LATIN AMERICA

Miryam Hazán

International Migration and Refugee Movements in the Americas

FROM A HISTORICAL PERSPECTIVE, international migration has played a very important role in the nation-making process of many Latin America countries, shaping their demographic, economic, and political characteristics. During the late nineteen and the beginning of the twentieth centuries, countries in the region, including Argentina, Venezuela, Brazil, Chile, Mexico, Guatemala, and Costa Rica, to name a few, competed with the United States to bring onto their shores the white European settlers who were emigrating in large numbers to the Americas. Their goal was to build more "civilized," whiter-looking societies since this was perceived as a necessary step to ensure their economic modernization (FitzGerald and Cook-Martin 2014; Yankelevich 2020). Thus, from the 1870s to the 1930s the region as a whole became the second-largest global recipient of immigrants after the United States (Acosta 2018, 4).

Not all countries, however, were equally successful in this competition. Mexico and Central American countries, for example, were able to attract very few Europeans compared with Argentina, Brazil, and Uruguay (FitzGerald and Cook-Martin 2014). Others attracted significant numbers of immigrants but not predominantly from southern or northern Europe as expected. This was the case of Peru, which received a large number of Asians, and of Chile, which attracted a mixture of Europeans and Middle Easterners as well as newcomers from other countries within the region (Acosta 2018).

By the 1940s, immigration had waned in most countries, with the notable exception of Venezuela, which did not receive as many immigrants as in previous decades but, exceptionally in the region, became an important destination from the 1950s onward as it developed its oil industry (Acosta 2018). Following the US example, and despite the waning number of newcomers, Latin American countries, including those that had not received large numbers of immigrants, adopted restrictive policies against foreigners

Dr. Miryam Hazán is an employee of the Inter-American Commission on Human Rights and the Organization of American States, and the perspectives presented in this chapter do not necessarily represent the views of the General Secretariat of the OAS, the OAS, or the IACHR as institutions. They reflect her personal views.

based on ethnic, racial, political, and moral grounds as part of their nation-bulding projects (FitzGerald and Cook-Martin 2014; Acosta 2018; Yankelevich 2020). This took place
in a context in which they also pursued nationalistic, inward-looking economic policies
such as import-substitution industrialization.

Restrictions became stiffer during the 1970s as Latin America became a proxy battleground of the Cold War conflict between the United States and the Soviet Union, and
the notion of national security took hold in the highly nationalistic political discourses
that prevailed in the region at the time, especially in countries where right-wing military
dictatorships controlled the government. In this context, immigrants were portrayed
primarily as enemies, while the main concern in the immigration arena was to curtail
the arrival of so-called "communists" or any person who appeared to be one, which, in
practice, included any person who showed a concern for social justice (see the discussion of national security in the introduction to this volume).

Overall, however, immigration was not a major national concern in most countries
of the region and thus it did not appear prominently in the political debate. By the 1980s,
for instance, and until the first decade of the twenty-first century, the most evident international migration trend in Latin America was South–North migration, primarily to the
United States, which was the result of a combination of push and pull factors in countries
of origin and destination (Massey et al. 1994; Massey et al. 1993). Push factors included
wage differences between countries of origin and destination; lack of effective social protection systems; and market failures, which exposed people to hardship in difficult times
and encouraged emigration especially in contexts in which there were already established
migratory networks. In the late twentieth century and the first decade of the twenty-first,
migratory flows further accelerated due to massive dislocations and displacements that
resulted from economic liberalization and free-trade policies implemented in countries
of origin, which produced a migration hump (Martin 2006; Martin, this volume). Pull
factors encompassed major economic and demographic transformations in destination
countries toward service-oriented and knowledge-based economies and aging populations, which in turn created conditions that attracted new labor migration.

The most important emigration country in the region was Mexico, which became
the largest source of immigration to the United States in its history. El Salvador, Honduras, and Guatemala also became a major source of immigration to the US, a trend
that started in the late 1970s when they confronted major political conflicts, and which
continued after these conflicts ended, primarily for economic reasons.

During the 1980s, 1990s, and the beginning of this century, Latin America also registered the emergence and consolidation of subregional migratory systems or corridors.
These systems presented migratory dynamics that resembled South–North migration
trends between Mexico, Central America, and the US. Some of these systems include
the one that exists today between Nicaragua and Costa Rica; and the north of Panama to
Costa Rica; Guatemala to Mexico; Guatemala, El Salvador, and Honduras to Belize; Paraguay and Peru to Argentina; and Peru to Chile, among others. While some of these subsystems had their origins in historical migratory dynamics that already existed between
countries of origin and destination, these dynamics consolidated during the 1990s and
the early 2000s in the context of the economic reforms and demographic transformations that increase economic interdependence between source and destination countries.

Today, virtually all countries in Latin America are affected by at least one facet of international migration, which includes emigration, immigration, transit, and return. Many of them present most of these facets simultaneously. In this way, international migration is reshaping again the demographic, economic, social, and cultural characteristics of these countries as well as their notions of political community (see Gomes, this volume). This time around, however, the predominant migratory flows are not from Europe, the Middle East, and Asia. Instead, they originate within the region and move in different directions including from South to North, as the United States remains an important destination country, and from North to South, as return migration, especially to Mexico and the north of Central America, has become increasingly relevant; and intraregionally between existing migration subsystems such as the ones mentioned above. In addition, the region has also registered migration from the Caribbean countries, primarily from Haiti, and from overseas, including from Africa and Asia, that tends to flow north toward the United States and even Canada.

In 2019, there were 11.7 million international immigrants in Latin America and the Caribbean, up from 6.6 million in 2000 (UNDESA 2019). While the number of international migrants as a share of the total population of the region is only 1.8 percent, a very low number compared to other regions of the world, for some countries the percentage of immigrants as a share of the total population is much larger, above 4 percent such as in the cases of Costa Rica, Panama, Argentina, and Chile. Furthermore, the region is also the source of a large number of immigrants who have settled in North America in recent decades. Of the 58.6 million immigrants in that region, 26.6 million originate from Latin America and the Caribbean, which means that many countries of the Americas are predominantly source countries with all the consequences that this implies for their economic, social, and political development. For instance, migration from the region to the United States constitutes the second-largest migration corridor in the world after Europe to Europe regional migration, which is equivalent to 41.9 million people (UNDESA 2019).

At the same time, Latin America has recently become the source of large numbers of forcibly displaced populations across international borders, estimated at around six million people, whether or not they are classified as asylum seekers or refugees, considering that many of them do not meet the criteria of the 1951 Refugee Convention and its 1967 Protocol. This is one reason why it is common to refer to them as "mixed reasons" migrants.[1] This includes those who have left Venezuela and north Central American

---

1   It is interesting to note that many displaced populations in the region do meet the criteria of the extended definition of refugee of the Cartagena Declaration on Refugees adopted in Cartagena de Indias, Colombia, on November 22, 1984. This definition not only includes people who have a well-founded fear of being persecuted because of their race, religion, nationality, membership in a particular social group, or political opinion, but also "people who have fled their countries because their lives, security or freedom have been threatened because of widespread violence, a foreign aggression, internal conflicts, a massive violation of human rights and any other circumstance that has gravely perturbed the public order." See UNHCR, *Cartagena Declaration on Refugees*, available at www.unhcr.org/en-us/about-us/background/45dc19084/cartagena-declaration-refugees

countries such as Guatemala, Honduras, and El Salvador for other countries within the region, the US, and overseas. In addition, since April 2018 Nicaragua has also become a source of forcibly displaced populations, primarily to Costa Rica.[2] The reasons for displacement in the region include political repression, widespread violence committed either by gangs, organized crime, and/or state actors, gender and sexual-based violence, economic deprivation, food insecurity related to economic mismanagement, limited access to health services and medicines, the effects of climate change, and natural catastrophes, among others.

While these populations have not received the protection they most likely deserve, countries of the region have generally offered a more welcoming environment than the one experienced by refugees in other parts of the world, even in some cases going so far as adapting their legal frameworks to facilitate refugee/migrant reception. In that regard, Latin America also displays some of the greatest potential for setting a path toward a global migration governance framework where the protection of populations that flee threatening or difficult situations becomes possible. This is an ongoing process, and it may change as a consequence of the COVID-19 pandemic, the measures that governments have adopted to contain it, and the economic crises that have unfolded as a result that may bring about the reemergence of discrimination and xenophobia; but the process remains one worth observing and studying, as the region presents different realities and lessons that have been missed frequently in the international dialogue.

In this chapter, I present a general overview of international migration and refugee dynamics in Latin America and analyze some future trends and realities looking ahead several years. As part of the overview I identify the main drivers of population movements, as well as some of the impacts that migration is having on countries of origin, transit, and destination, with a particular emphasis on Mexico, one of the most affected countries in the region by different international human mobility dynamics today. I also look at the most significant challenges and opportunities with respect to migration and international displacement in the region. I lay out future population movements based on demographic, economic, social, and political trends; present some aspects of regional human mobility governance; identify some regional developments, which may have an impact at a global scale; and, finally, lay out some approaches that can be promising

---

-adopted-colloquium-international-protection.html. However, while the majority of countries have incorporated the declaration into their normative frameworks, only in the cases of Mexico and Brazil has it really been applied to displaced populations, primarily from Venezuela and on a very small scale.

2   An estimated 5.5 million Venezuelans had left their country as of October 5, 2020 (IOM 2020). Of those, only a few have been recognized as refugees (a total of 143,402 by October 5, 2020) or as asylum seekers (a total of 806,416 by October 5, 2020). Others have benefited from special permits offered to them by some countries of the region (2.4 million by October 2020) and the rest are irregular (an estimated 2,056,919 by October 5, 2020). The number of displaced populations also includes around 470,000 people from north of Central America who are asylum seekers and refugees worldwide, as well as 102,000 asylum seekers from Nicaragua worldwide that left their country of origin since April 2018 because of the political conflict there (UNHCR 2020).

for making international migration and the movement of refugees and other displaced populations a win-win-win game for those countries that are trying to cope in the most effective ways possible with some of the challenges generated by the international human mobility dynamics of the twenty-first century.

Emigration and Its Consequences in South–North Migration

For the past four decades, the most characteristic feature of international migration in Latin America has been South–North emigration, primarily from Mexico, which, along with El Salvador, Honduras, and Guatemala, has been the biggest source of migratory flows to the United States in its history. Today, 11.2 million foreign-born Mexicans live in the US along with 936,000 Guatemalans, 1.4 million Salvadorans, and 665,000 Hondurans (Radford 2019).

Even while their numbers have decreased more recently (Passel and Cohn 2019), Mexicans still constitute the largest immigrant group to the United States, a notable development that has transformed the economy, society, and politics of the US by changing the ethnic and demographic composition of different communities large and small across its territory. Furthermore, this migration, along with that from the north of Central America, has also served to reignite already existent nativist sentiments that have polarized the polity and opened up the political doors to new illiberal political manifestations and policies (see Tichenor and Foley, this volume).

Migration from Mexico, El Salvador, Honduras, and Guatemala has been driven primarily by low-skilled labor migrants for whom there are few legal avenues into the US. As a result, Mexicans, along with Salvadorans, Hondurans, and Guatemalans, constitute the largest majority of the unauthorized population in the US, which by 2017 was 10.5 million (Passel and Cohn 2019). Furthermore, while the original reasons for migration from these countries have varied, since many Guatemalans and Salvadorans originally came to the US as a result of the civil wars that took place in their countries in recent decades, they have converged, thus converting international migration from Mexico and the north of Central America to the US into the largest migratory system of the Western Hemisphere with common characteristics (see Martin, this volume).

The most frequent reasons for migration within this system have been primarily economic, and are related to the dislocations and displacements produced by the policies of economic modernization that Mexico and then El Salvador, Honduras, and Guatemala implemented in the last few decades, which focused on opening their economies and strengthening the exporting sector through economic integration with the US. Theoretically, high emigration levels were supposed to wane as new jobs were generated as a result of these reforms and demographic pressures that resulted from high population growth rates diminished (Martin 2006).

This may arguably have been the case of Mexico, since net migration flows from this country are now down to zero and even negative.[3] However, today, apart from family

---

3   In the context of the COVID-19 pandemic, Mexico has experienced a major economic downturn, which has been aggravated by recessionary economic policies adopted by the government.

reunification, which has also been a major reason for migration, within the Central America–Mexico–US corridor, the motives for emigration, especially from El Salvador, Honduras, and Guatemala, are becoming more mixed, such as the high levels of violence in the region, the uprooting of people due to the effects of climate change, and the devastation of natural disasters. The impact of such events makes it hard to predict when the economies of these countries may generate enough opportunities for flows to slow. In the meantime, those who leave for these relatively new reasons follow the irregular paths of economic migrants since they typically fall into the cracks of international protection systems as they do not qualify for them, a situation that has arguably generated a crisis in the North and Central American region with no apparent end in sight.

The significant levels of irregularity, which has been a common factor among migration from Mexico and the north of Central America, means that almost half or above half of all first-generation immigrants from these places live in the United States with an unauthorized status (Cohn, Passel, and González-Barrera 2017). This has created a number of challenges for both countries of destination and of origin that are unique to the Central America–Mexico–US migratory system, and represent some of the most complex international migration challenges not only in Latin America but in the world, with potentially large negative effects on or the migrants, their families, and the development of their communities of origin and destination.

In the United States, the large levels of irregularity among first-generation Mexicans, Guatemalan, Salvadorans, and Hondurans have turned these immigrant populations into the most vulnerable groups in the country. As a result, they are prone to be poorer than any other immigrant, ethnic, or racial group (irregularity is, among other things, a predictor for poverty); and to be more often the victims of crime and of abuse and exploitation by employers. However, one of the most consequential effects of their irregularity has been long-term separation from their families, which on many occasions has resulted in long-term emotional consequences for themselves and their family members.

Family separations and breakdowns are the result of the fact that immigrants have settled for longer periods of time in their country of destination than they would have done otherwise because of higher levels of US immigration control at the border (Duran and Massey 2004), as well as the presence of organized crime in northern Mexico, which has increased the risks and costs associated with traveling back and forth to their countries of origin.

Because many of these immigrants left their spouses or partners and children behind, and their chances of reunifying with them are very slim due to their immigration status, many immigrants have spent many years without seeing other family members (Hazán 2016). This makes it hard for them to maintain and reproduce bonds of affection with loved ones, a situation that may cause stress and depression to all those affected, and a sense of abandonment in the specific case of their children leading to emotional and

---

As a result, some specialists have speculated that there will be a new wave of Mexican migration (O'Neil 2020). Even if this were to happen, however, it is unlikely that it will show the same volumes of the Mexican migration waves of recent years.

developmental consequences. One 2015 study based on ninety-three interviews with immigrants in the US from El Salvador, Honduras, and Guatemala found that those who have left children behind had been separated from them eight years on average (Hazán 2016). Because of this, many migrants have attempted to bring their children to the US, even if that has meant exposing them to a long and dangerous trip by land through Mexico and, depending on where they originated, other countries.

Long-term family separations are thus tied to the rising numbers of unaccompanied minors traveling to the United States from Mexico and now more prominently from Central America (Hinojosa and Wynn 2014), a dynamic that has been accentuated by the increasing levels of violence in the region, which may have compelled more immigrant parents to bring their children to the US. This situation, along with the emigration of women with children and other family members (e.g., fathers with their children, adult siblings with younger siblings), has contributed to the sense of crisis today in the South–North migratory movement from Central America. It was amply exploited throughout the tenure of the Trump administration, especially concerning the so-called "caravans," composed of people who emigrate together in large numbers as a safer alternative to using a guide or *coyote* to facilitate their migratory process.

A second factor behind family separations and ruptures has been the large numbers of deportations from the United States to Mexico and Central America, which reached more than 3.8 million people from 2008 through 2019 according to data from the US government.[4] Many of the deportees had established families in the US and had American-born children from whom they have been forced to separate. As a result, many American-born children of immigrants are growing up in the US without at least one of their parents. They often have been forced to relocate to their parents' country of origin, both traumatic and disruptive changes that most likely will have serious impacts on their emotional and developmental well-being, and thus possibly compromising their potential to become contributing members of the host societies. The recent policies adopted by the US administration of separating parents from their children immediately upon crossing the border in order to prosecute the parents, and of long-term detention of irregular migrants without regard for their family situation and links to their communities, along with further restrictive measures adopted in 2020 using the COVID-19 pandemic as a justification, will only aggravate situations like this.

In coming years, the effects of irregular migration on family structures and on the emotional well-being of children of migrants, regardless of the place they were born (country of origin or destination), will be one of the biggest challenges to be addressed with respect to the impact of international migration on the developmental process of the Latin American region. A political change in the US may diminish these effects, especially if current policies that produce family separation are halted and a comprehensive immigration reform that facilitates regularization and family reunification is

---

4   Data from Immigration and Customs Enforcement available at www.ice.gov/removal-statistics /2016 up to 2016; www.ice.gov/removal-statistics/2017#wcm-survey-target-id for 2017; and www .ice.gov/features/ERO-2019 for 2018 and 2019.

implemented in its place. However, even if present policies change, it will be a long-term process to overcome all the negative effects that these policies are having on migrants and their families with clear impacts on the development of communities of origin and destination. Decisive efforts and investments on the part of national governments and international donors, as well as consistent cooperation among all affected countries, will be needed in order to overcome the social and economic costs associated with irregular migration under increasing levels of immigration control. Promising policies to address the impacts of migration in places of origin so that migration can still be a win-win-win game include the design of social programs and policies that target specifically vulnerable populations:

1. **Support for *minors*** *who are forced to be separated for long periods of time from at least one of their parents as a result of international migration, and who require emotional and psychological support to overcome their sense of loss.* There is some evidence that children of migrants in Central America are more vulnerable than other youth given the long-term absence of their parents and current levels of violence, manifested in a higher propensity to join or be victimized by gangs and organized criminal organizations, early pregnancy and parenthood, early dropout from school, and higher levels of consumption of drugs and alcohol (see Portes and Rumbaut 1993 on segmented assimilation).

2. **Support for the *partner/spouse of migrants*** *who are left alone and who would benefit from programs that allow them to make a living by cultivating their entrepreneurial skills,* especially if they are unable to receive remittances because their partner/spouse has settled with someone else or has suffered some harm.

3. **Programs for *young people*,** *particularly those who grew up without their parents and need to learn how to make a living,* especially after they stopped receiving remittances on a regular basis from their parents. This is a common occurrence as migrants age or suffer a health or legal problem that makes them unable to provide for their family back home.

4. **Support for the extended family of migrants,** *especially seniors who have been left in charge of taking care of the children of migrants, or who lack the right support to deal with health and poverty problems associated with old age,* especially in the absence of effective social protection systems, and who do not have family members to support them because they all emigrated.

5. **Support for the Dreamers, those** *US minors who have been uprooted from their country of birth because of the forced return of their parents.* Even though they may be living with their parents after deportation, they still suffer from the dislocation. In addition, this applies to young people who may not have been born in the US but were taken there by their parents and grew up there and may soon face deportation because of their immigration status to a country they may not know anymore—the so-called Dreamers.

6. **Programs for migrants and return migrants** *who have confronted major emotional stress because of their separation and/or breakdowns of their families and require interventions to learn skills to address their particular situations.*

Measures to address the needs of these populations should be combined with long-term programs that can contribute to the reduction of current migration levels from north Central American countries by generating sustainable economic opportunities in places of origin. These should be initiatives that strengthen the institutional capacity of local governments to generate economic growth and to prevent and respond to adverse social and environmental situations.

While demographic dynamics might contribute to the reduction of migration rates from north of Central America, in the mid-to-long term as the working age population stops growing, this still may take one or two decades depending on the country. In this region, El Salvador will be the first country whose current fertility levels and dependency ratios will converge with those of more developed countries such as the United States, Canada, and more recently Mexico, to be followed by Honduras and then by around 2040 by Guatemala (Giorguli-Saucedo, García-Guerrero, and Masferrer 2016). Nonetheless, other factors, if not properly addressed, such as violence and environmental degradation, may continue to be sources of international displacement from this region not only to the US but to neighboring countries as well. For instance, temperature increases as a result of climate change, which will result in more droughts and food insecurity in Central America and Mexico, are projected to be important factors that will drive migration to the US for at least the next three decades (Lustgarten 2020).

Mexico from Country of Emigration to Country of Transit, Return, and Destination
The high levels of emigration to the United States that Mexico experienced for many decades have transformed the latter country in a significant way. For instance, within the Latin American region, Mexico is one of the countries that has been the most impacted by international migration dynamics, first as a country of emigration and then as a country of transit and return, and more recently, of destination for new immigrants and refugees. For these reasons it is one of the most interesting examples of a contemporary "migration state," comparable to Turkey, which presents similar characteristics (see Adamson, this volume). Both countries have a long history of emigration to a country of the global North with important political and economic consequences for them (Germany and Western Europe in the case of Turkey and the US in the case of Mexico). Both countries have a strong diaspora community that compelled the state to find ways to manage their relationship with them to contain potential political opposition and to participate in developmental projects. In addition, they have a strategic geographic location, which has turned them into important places of transit of mixed migration flows (migrants and forcibly displaced populations) from third countries. This situation has created for them a continuous tension with the destination countries of the transit populations (the European Union in the case of Turkey and the US in the case of Mexico; see Adamson and Geddes, this volume) as well as complex internal dilemmas. These states have to wrestle with the obligation to protect the rights of migrant populations, in the Mexican case constitutionally mandated since 2011, and the pressure to act as buffer states, which implies militarizing their borders and increased human rights violations within their territories.

Mexico as a Country of Emigration

For most of the twentieth century and during the first decade of the current one, Mexico experienced large levels of emigration to the United States to the point that it can be properly characterized as a nation of emigrants (FitzGerald 2019; Hazán 2014). A great proportion of this emigration was circular. That is, migrants went back and forth primarily through the Emergency Farm Labor Program, better known as the *Bracero Program*, a guest-worker program that lasted from 1942 to 1964, but also through backdoor channels. In both cases, Mexican migrants rarely settled permanently in the US.

This circular characteristic of Mexican migration led the US government to respond differently to Mexican migration than to migration from other parts of the world. For example, when US authorities introduced restrictions to migration from other parts of the world (e.g., literacy tests), such restrictions on Mexicans were waived, and when the doors were closed to worldwide immigration in 1924, Mexicans were still allowed to come in (see Tichenor, this volume). This response did not show any specific generosity toward Mexican migrants, but instead they were allowed in because they were considered to be endowed with a "homing pigeon instinct" that drove them to return (Zolberg 1999). During the *bracero* years, 4.6 million contracts were signed, with many individuals returning several times on different contracts (Bracero History Archive 2020). It is estimated that around two million Mexicans entered the United States through this program (Callard 2009), while another significant number entered through irregular channels.

During the 1980s, Mexican migration became more permanent, especially after the implementation of the 1986 Immigration Reform and Control Act, which facilitated the regularization of 2.7 million immigrants through two different programs: the Legally Authorized Worker (LAW) program for undocumented immigrants who had resided five years or more in the US; and the Special Agricultural Workers (SAW) program for those who had worked in agriculture during the past six months before the program was enacted. Around 70 percent of those taking advantage of the LAW program and 81 percent of the SAW program were Mexicans (Donato, Durand, and Massey 1992). This program, along with the family reunification procedures that were established in the 1965 Hart-Celler Act, facilitated the gradual settlement of a larger number of Mexicans in the US. This process was intensified due to changes in their condition in the US labor market from temporary to more permanent jobs and to changes in immigration law and further immigration enforcement, which increased the incentives for settlement rather than traveling back and forth (Duran and Massey 2004).

The large levels of emigration to the US that Mexico experienced for decades, both temporary and permanent, reshaped the demographic and social landscape of many places and regions of origin, which were transformed by the remittances sent by emigrants in the US. However, these communities also lost valuable segments of their working-age population, part of Mexico's demographic bonus. In this regard, many places in Mexico saw levels of poverty diminish thanks to emigration. At the same time they confronted high levels of population loss, a situation that today is compromising future economic development.

For its part, the Mexican state reacted in different ways to the emigration phenomena. From the 1940s until the 1980s, governments implicitly recognized that they could not prevent emigration, even though the exploitation of Mexican workers in the US was considered as an offense to national pride, especially in the context of nationalistic political regimes. For instance, as the Mexican population started to grow after a big population loss because of the Mexican Revolution, emigration started to be seen and used as a safety valve to contain social unrest and political conflict at home. For this reason, after negotiating a second guest-worker program with the US during World War II as part of the *Bracero* Program, the Mexican government at the time promoted the recruitment of laborers from Mexico's central plateau, a densely populated region with limited job opportunities (Corwin 1978), from which then a great proportion of the Mexican immigrant population in the US originated. During this period, the only explicit policy the Mexican government pursued was to protect the rights of Mexican workers in the United States, including those who came through the *Bracero* Program and thus arrived through the backdoors.

In the 1990s, after the numbers of Mexicans living in the US increased, and the Mexican expatriate community had become more politically active, showing a clear support for the Mexican opposition, the government transformed its policy of no policy to a policy of engagement with its diaspora. An important step in this regard included the creation of the Program for Mexican Communities abroad in 1991 within the Ministry of Foreign Relations,[5] which, among other things, led Mexican consular offices to become more proactive in supporting the different Mexican communities in many American cities and in engaging with them. The Mexican government also, for the first time, pursued a proactive policy to engage the Mexican-American community in the US as a way of establishing a positive and long-term relationship with them to advance Mexico's strategic interests vis-à-vis the US.

In 1994, Proposition 187 was approved in California, where a large number of Mexicans lived. This proposition prohibited undocumented immigrants from using non-emergency health care, public education, and other services, establishing a state-run citizenship screening system. Although it was eventually declared unconstitutional by the US district court and never really implemented, the approval of this ballot measure convinced the Mexican government that the best way to support the Mexican community in the US was to facilitate the naturalization process of first-generation Mexicans who could qualify for citizenship so that they could better advocate for their rights. As a result, in 1996 the Mexican Congress passed a bill that changed Mexico's nationality law, allowing dual citizenship. This decision was crucial in empowering the Mexican community in the US, since naturalization rates among Mexican immigrants were very low compared to other immigrant communities, one reason being that Mexicans did not want to lose their Mexican citizenship.

Mexico's decision to change its nationality law also represented a substantial transformation of the idea of the political community for this country, from one inward looking and suspicious of outsiders' influence toward a more inclusive one. It implied a complete change of perceptions about emigrants from one that considered them as traitors in the

---

5   The support of Mexican expatriates for Cuahutémoc Cárdenas during the presidential elections of 1988 convinced the Partido Revolucionario Institucional (PRI) government of Carlos Salinas de Gortari of the need to redefine and control the relationship with the Mexican diaspora.

national imaginary—they were pejoratively called *pochos* (*pocho* refers to rotten or dis-colored fruit)—to one that considered them as people who could keep their allegiance to Mexico and contribute to its development. Eventually, they would even be called "he-roes" by Mexican president Vicente Fox.

In practice this change of perception was very much aligned with economic and po-litical changes that were taking place in Mexico. Mexico moved from a closed econ-omy under import substitution industrialization to one of the most open in the world, through the policies of economic deregulation and integration with the US consistently pursued by Mexican governments starting in the mid-1980s. And Mexico shifted from authoritarian rule to a more pluralistic and democratic regime.

Over the ensuing years after the creation of the Program for Communities Abroad, and the recognition of dual citizenship, the Mexican government adopted a number of policies that aimed at strengthening its relationship with the Mexican diaspora. These included the creation of the Institute for Mexicans Abroad, and the institutionalization of a program that aimed at mobilizing collective remittances that migrants were already sending to their places of origin, known as the 3x1 program. Through this program ev-ery dollar that Mexicans sent for social infrastructure and productive projects in their communities of origin would be matched by the federal, state, and local governments. In 2005, legislation was approved to grant Mexicans abroad the right to vote, and in subsequent years they were granted some form of political representation in states such as Zacatecas, Michoacán, and Chiapas, through the election of members of Congress to their legislatures representing their immigrant communities living abroad.

These and other policies pursued by the Mexican government expanded the spaces of civic engagement and political representation of Mexican expatriates in Mexico. Some analysts saw this as an effort by the Mexican state to control the politics of Mexicans abroad and to turn them into a motor of development at the same moment that the state was relinquishing its responsibility to deliver social goods to many sectors of the popula-tion while pursuing neoliberal economic policies (Smith and Bakker 2008). It is worth noticing that throughout this period of engagement, the Mexican government also be-came more proactive in addressing the needs of the Mexican communities abroad, espe-cially through its consular network, at a time when the US was increasing its policies of immigration control and targeting the undocumented community, a large proportion of whom were of Mexican origin.

Recent political changes in Mexico, however, especially the arrival of a new adminis-tration in 2018 with more inward-looking nationalistic policies, may change the level of engagement of the Mexican state toward the Mexican expatriate community compared with previous governments. This is reflected not only in the fact that the overall budget for the consular offices has been dramatically cut—Mexico's diplomatic offices suffered a 75 percent budget reduction—but also to the fact that the 3x1 program, highly valued by Mexican immigrant organizations, was eliminated without much consultation. Further-more, and perhaps more symbolically, the new Andrés Manuel López Obrador (AMLO) administration, far from advocating for the interests of Mexicans in the United States at a time when they became the target of the anti-immigrant policies of the US under the Trump administration, chose to collaborate with that administration even when as

Trump demonized Mexican immigrants as "rapists" and "killers." Notoriously, during a state visit to Washington, DC, on July 8, 2020, Mexican president López Obrador declared to the astonishment of many observers that President Trump had "changed his attitude" and that he treated Mexicans "with kindness and respect" (Guerrero 2020). In sharp contrast, during that visit he declined to meet with leaders of the Mexican expatriate community even though many of them had traveled to Washington, DC, from all over the US, braving the COVID-19 pandemic, to greet him.

Mexico as a Country of Return

As the realities produced by decades of high emigration levels have become more apparent, Mexico is also experiencing an uneasy transition from a country of emigration to a country of return, transit, and destination. The Mexican census reported that between 2005 and 2010, 1.39 million people moved from the United States to Mexico, twice the number of people who moved between 1995 and 2005, a figure that includes returning migrants and their family members. Similarly, the National Survey of Demographic Dynamics (ENADID) reported that between 2009 and 2014, a million expatriate Mexicans and their family members moved from the US to Mexico (González-Barrera 2015). The evidence that has emerged from Mexican national surveys is complemented by the evidence from the US, which shows a decline in the size of the Mexican foreign-born population (Passel and Cohn 2019)

The main reason for return has been family reunification—61 percent have expressed that as their main reason for return (González-Barrera 2015; Hazán 2014). This is not surprising considering that many family members were left behind, either small children or aging parents, with whom the emigrants might have wanted to reunify. In this regard, it is worth noting that the majority of those who returned were still irregular in the United States according to evidence from surveys performed with return migrants in Mexico (Hazán 2014). As mentioned above, their immigration status probably made it hard for them to travel back and forth, and so when there was a need to attend to their family members left behind, they chose to go back to their places of origin. Among the return population, there are also people who came back to Mexico to reunify with family members who had been deported from the US, and were barred from returning (Hazán 2014).

Because of the large number of èmigrès who are returning to Mexico, either as a result of a deportation or on their own volition, Mexico confronts today the complex test of successfully reintegrating this population into its economy and society, while providing them with adequate services, especially to those who were forced to return as a result of a deportation.[6]

Returnees have the potential of contributing to the development of local communities and to their country of origin. The return population includes people who have increased their human capital levels at a faster pace than if they would have remained

---

[6] Deportees constituted 14 percent of the total return population by 2015 (González-Barrera 2015), although this number might have increased as a result of growing numbers of deportations and diminishing numbers of recidivism in recent years.

in their country of origin, especially those who were in their host country for a longer time. These returnees could also be new sources of entrepreneurship and investment. However, to tap into their potential contributions there is the need to implement adequate programs that facilitate their reintegration into the labor market and that provide resources (including capital) and know-how to those who want to open new businesses. This would turn their migration experience into a win-win-win situation as they already contributed to their host country, and through the appropriate use of their entrepreneurial skills, they would be able to make new contributions to their places of origin beyond the remittances they might have already sent.

In line with this thinking, from 2014 to 2018, the Mexican government implemented a program to facilitate the reintegration of this population, "We Are Mexicans" (*Somos Mexicanos*). This program was consistent with Mexico's new constitutional and legal obligations after the country changed its Constitution in 2011, granting preeminence to the international and inter-American systems of human rights over national law. The Mexican government also passed a new migration law that same year, which superseded the migratory provisions of the general population law that until then had governed Mexico's responses to its migratory realities (Morales Vega 2012). The new constitutional provisions included in Article One argued that "every person that enters, transits, leaves or returns to the Mexican territory enjoys all the human rights acknowledged in the Constitution."[7] The law mandated that the Mexican state have a comprehensive migratory policy framework that addressed and protected the rights of migrants in all facets of migration, including return migration. With regard to this last aspect, the new immigration law stated that the Mexican state should facilitate not only the return process but also the social reinsertion of returning Mexicans and their families in their communities of origin through inter-institutional programs, one of them being the *Somos Mexicanos* program.[8]

This program, however, seems not to have been continued by the new administration of President López Obrador, which, for instance, did not list the attention to returnees as one of its priorities in the Strategic Plan of the National Institute for Migration, the institution in charge of implementing Mexico's migratory policy as stated in the new law, set up for its tenure.[9] The new administration also did not devote any new resources to the program, and so far the government only assists returnees in their process of repatriation primarily by facilitating return to their communities of origin.[10]

---

7   See Gobierno de México, *Estrategia somos Mexicanos,* www.gob.mx/inm/acciones-y -programas/estrategia-somos-mexicanos

8   See Cámara de Diputados del Consejo de la Unión, *Ley de Migración,* Última Reforma DOF 21-04-2016, Secretaría General de Servicios Parlamentarios.

9   See Instituto Nacional de Migración, *Plan Estratégico del Instituto Nacional de Migración 2019–2024,* www.gob.mx/inm/acciones-y-programas/plan-estrategico-del-instituto-nacional-de -migracion-2019-2024-24336. Information also collected through a July 7, 2020 interview with a Mexican official who had worked with the return population for years.

10   Information collected through a July 7, 2020 interview with a Mexican official who had worked with the return population for years.

A major issue of concern with regard to the return population is the need to provide adequate services to the children of returnees, a large number of whom are American born. It is estimated that 600,000 American-born children are living in Mexico, which in practice constitutes the largest immigrant group to Mexico (Jarvis 2019), even while these children are also entitled to Mexican citizenship, thanks to Mexico's dual citizenship laws adopted in 1996. The process to register and obtain it, unfortunately, has been arduous for many of them, among other things due to the lack of access to a birth certificate in the United States or other documentation, a situation that affects their access to educational and social services (Giorguli and Bautista León 2018). Apart from this issue, which awaits a solution, additional issues of concern include the significant barriers that returnees and their family members face with respect to access to social rights such as education, health, housing, and the labor market, which impedes their successful socioeconomic integration into Mexico's society. Many questions remain. Would they integrate effectively into the Mexican society, contributing to Mexico's development, or would they become part of an underclass? With respect to their American-born children, would they adapt and integrate into their communities of reception in Mexico or would they be disillusioned and exercise their right of return to the US and join the American underclass, having been unable to acquire the right skills to compete in the American economy? With the passage of time, these questions are becoming more urgent not only for Mexico but also for the US. Answers to these questions will become increasingly relevant for the future of both countries as these children come of age.

Mexico as a Country of Transit and Destination

Mexico also confronts the challenge of protecting the foreign populations that transit through its territory on their way to the United States. For many years, large numbers of Central Americans, primarily from El Salvador, Honduras, and Guatemala, circulated through Mexico, even while irregular migration was a criminal and punishable offense according to the General Law of Population of 1974, which was Mexico's normative framework that guided its immigration policy at the time (Morales Sanchez 2008). The criminalization of migration, along with the increasing levels of violence in Mexico, led to important violations of the human rights of transit migrants by criminal gangs and state actors that prey on the migrants. Many migrants perished making the journey, while the Mexican government pursued a policy of higher or lower levels of detaining migrants in different parts of the country, depending on domestic dynamics but also on the level of pressure from the US. The pressure became more prominent, especially after Mexico joined the North American Free Trade Agreement (NAFTA). For instance, since the implementation of NAFTA, Mexican authorities collaborated in a more proactive way with American officials in controlling Central American migration along the US border and at strategic points in Mexico along railroads and freeways and in airports.[11]

---

11   Author's interview with Ernesto Rodriguez, former director of the *Unidad de Política Migratoria* (Unity of Migratory Policy), the institution in charge of Mexican statistics on migration on November 22, 2019. Some of the programs implemented by the Mexican government that reflected

The legal contradiction of criminalizing migration in Mexico, while pursuing a policy aimed at protecting Mexican emigrants in the US, along with the major criticisms the country confronted as a result in the international arena, led the Mexican government to change the General Law of Population in 2008 to decriminalize irregular migration. However, human rights violations continued on a constant basis while Mexican immigration authorities were accused of corruption and human rights abuses by national and international civil society organizations (Morales Vega 2012).

In 2010, a major event placed Mexico in an even more difficult situation in the international and national arenas. On August 24 of that year, the bodies of seventy-two undocumented migrants were found by the Mexican military at a ranch in the village of Huizachal in the municipality of San Fernando, Tamaulipas. These migrants were shot in the back of the head and then piled together. The majority of them were from Central America and some from South America. The military learned of the incident after an Ecuadorean migrant who survived the massacre by faking his death made his way out of the ranch and arrived at a military checkpoint where he asked for help.

The massacre caused a major international outcry from different countries including the United States, Ecuador, El Salvador, Honduras, Guatemala, Venezuela, Brazil, and from the international community including the United Nations, the Organization of American States, Amnesty International, and from civil society organizations within the country. As the pressure mounted, and in a context in which there were increasing violations of human rights in Mexico as a result of the government's fight against the drug cartels, in 2011, just a year later, the Mexican Congress approved the constitutional change to grant preeminence to the international and inter-American law of human rights over national law, enacting at the same time the new migration law.

This new law represented a major change in Mexico's understanding of migration from a normative and policy perspective and in the way migrants were treated. It established that the human rights of all migrants, regardless of their nationality, place of origin, age, gender, ethnic or racial background, and legal status should be respected and protected. It also called for an integral approach in Mexico's migration policy, one that guarantees the protection of vulnerable populations including minors, women, indigenous people, adolescents, and seniors, as well as those who have been the victims of a crime, and for the facilitation of the international mobility of persons, guaranteeing order and security. It also aimed at strengthening the fight against organized crime, especially against the trafficking and kidnapping of migrants, and of human trafficking in all its modalities. The law also acknowledged international migration as a structural phenomenon that required shared responsibility solutions among source and destination countries and the collaboration of national and international institutions.

---

this collaboration was the Plan Frontera Sur of 2001 (Southern Border Plan) and the Agreement for the Creation of the High-Level Group for Border Security with Guatemala. While both programs were created with the argument that they had the goal of protecting the human rights of migrants in practice, their main effect was to militarize Mexico's southern border and provide more security to that region (González-Arias 2019).

In accordance with the international legal standards that the country had embraced through the reform of Article One of the Constitution, the new migratory law granted equal rights to nationals and foreigners, especially in relation to the observance of individual guarantees, and required the state to exercise due process in the expelling of foreigners, a step previously performed at the discretion of the executive with no legal limitation. Taking into consideration Mexico's long experience as an emigration country, the law also established that the state has to pursue a consistent migratory policy, which means that it has to respect, at all times, the rights of migrants just as the Mexican state demands respect of the rights of its nationals in other countries of the world. This perspective should be applied to all instances of the migratory process, including admission, transit, permanence, deportation, and the assisted return of foreigners within its territory.

In this regard, the law not only reaffirmed the relevance of decriminalizing irregular migration but actually required the Mexican state to protect human rights as the key principle of the law. As a result, the National Institute of Migration, an autonomous institution within the Ministry of Interior, originally created in 1993, whose functions in managing and regulating migration were finally strictly defined, was expected to train and certify its personnel to pursue the principles of "legality, objectivity, efficiency, professionalism, honesty and the respect of human rights."[12] In addition, the Ministry of Interior could pursue collaborative agreements to protect and defend migrants with other dependencies and entities of the federal government, state governments, and civil society organizations, which could be related to the functions of control, verification, and regulation of migration.

In practice, however, detentions could be carried out only by immigration authorities. They were authorized to request documents, unless they requested the help of other agencies through specific agreements, and this had to be done without authorities entering into any discriminatory or arbitrary practice. Any migrant detained was also entitled to appeal to a migratory administrative procedure that should strictly abide by the law, and in which the migrant could choose a person who represented him or her and could also count on consular assistance. In addition, the migrant had to be provided with clear information about his or her processual rights (Morales Vega 2012). With this new law, along with a new Law for Refugees, Complementary Protection, and Political Asylum also approved in 2011,[13] the Mexican state moved effectively from a primarily immigration control approach toward international human mobility and ultimately toward a primarily rights-based approach (see Hollifield, Martin, and Orrenius 2014; introduction, this volume). In practice, however, the capacity of the Mexican state to protect immigrants was still very limited in the same way, as it was not even able to protect its own citizens, as reflected in the growing numbers of homicides and other violent crimes in

---

12   Article 22 of the Migratory Act, May 25, 2011, Senado de la República, LXI Legislatura.

13   Cámara de Diputados del H, Congreso de la Union, *Ley sobre Refugiados, Protección Complementaria y Asilo Político [Law about refugees, complementary protection, and political asylum]*. Published in the *Diario Oficial de la Federación*, January 27, 2011.

Mexico. Yet a direct effect of the law seemed to have been a reduction in the number of detentions of Central Americans in the country in the ensuing years, as the role of immigration officials evolved from deterring to protecting migrants (Rodríguez Chaves 2016).

According to Ernesto Rodriguez, former director of the Unit for Migratory Policy, the number of Central American migrants detained in Mexico diminished notably starting in 2006 as a result of the economic crisis in the United States, which had the effect of reducing the overall levels of migration from Mexico and Central America to the US. Then when flows were increasing again in 2012, detentions remained low in Mexico, most likely as a result of the implementation of the new law (see figure 13.1). This situation meant that more Central American migrants were arriving and being detained in the US. From this perspective, the migratory crisis in the US in 2014 was due to a record number of unaccompanied minors and women and children in family units arriving at the US border. The crisis can be explained by the fact that the size of the flows from Central America increased overall, but also by the fact that Mexico was not controlling them as effectively as it did in previous years. According to Rodriguez, Mexico stopped close to 60 percent of the flows, because Mexican priorities had changed with the new law.

Evidently, the falling rates of detention did not pass unnoticed by U.S authorities, especially as the rates of Central American migration increased. For that reason, one of the strategies of the US government in containing the migratory crisis it confronted was to put pressure on Mexico to stop the flows that transited through its territory. The Mexican response was the implementation of the *Programa Frontera Sur* (Southern Border Program) in 2014, through which Mexico gradually went back to strictly enforcing migration by shutting down transit lines along its southern border. Mexico's intervention was clearly helpful in reducing the flows to the US, reflected in the fact that the number of detentions in the US of Central American migrants in 2015 decreased while the number of detentions in Mexico increased (see figure 13.1).[14]

In this respect, Mexico's approach to international human mobility became dual and fraught with contradictions. On the one hand, the country went back to controlling migration in a stricter way in practice and became a buffer state for the US since most Central Americans had no intention of staying in Mexico. On the other hand, Mexico pursued a rights-based approach, trying to improve, without much success, the human rights conditions of migrants transiting through Mexico. Detention centers also became the focus of policy based on the country's new normative imperatives.[15] President Enrique Peña Nieto implemented the Southern Border Program, and he was widely criticized for yielding to US pressure and for the perpetuation of human rights violations

---

14   Mexico was particularly effective at containing, for the US, the flows of Central American unaccompanied minors, because in contrast to the US, it did not have a specific law that protected them such as the William Wilberforce Trafficking Victims Protection Reauthorization Act.

15   According to Ernesto Rodriguez, Mexico did return to its previous role of controlling migration more strictly, but it also played a more significant role in improving conditions for migrants, and assumed a more leading role in defending a rights-based approach when dealing with international migration realities. Author's interview with Ernesto Rodriguez, November 22, 2019.

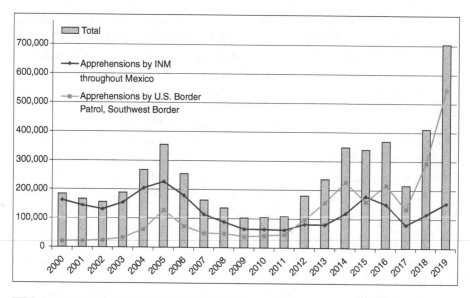

Year	Apprehensions by INM throughout Mexico	Apprehensions by U.S. Border Patrol, Southwest Border	Total
2018	117,141	293,545	410,686
2019	155,302	548,046	703,348

Figure 13.1. Apprehensions of undocumented Central American migrants by the Mexican INM and the US Border Patrol Southwest Border, by calendar year 2000–2019.

Source: Compiled by Ernesto Rodriguez Chávez based on SEGOB, UPM, INM de México: Boletín de Estadísticas Migratorias, and US Border Patrol Southwest Border: Alien Apprehensions by Citizenship Calendar Year (unpublished data 2000–15 and estimated data 2016–19).

Note: The same person may have been apprehended and counted more than once in a year.

against migrants (in a context in which overall violence in Mexico continued unabated). One could argue that their perspective had changed after the new normative approach the country had embraced, reflected in the fact that in the international arena Mexico took a leading role in securing a global agreement for a safe and orderly process of migration. The Mexican president gave a powerful speech on September 9, 2016, before the convention of the first United Nations Summit for Refugees and Migrants (Castillo 2016). Mexico along with Switzerland became one of the host countries for negotiations related to the Global Compact for Safe, Orderly and Regular Migration, which was finally signed by 164 countries on December 10, 2018.

This dual approach to international human mobility, even with all its inherent contradictions (Castillo 2016), became increasingly untenable once Donald Trump arrived in power in the United States in 2016 with a very nativist agenda for immigration, one that especially targeted Mexico for its apparent lack of cooperation with its northern neighbor in controlling immigration at its southern border. Mexico, he argued, had to pay for a wall along the southern border since the lack of border control was Mexico's responsibility. One of the tactics that the US president chose to pursue was blackmailing Mexico with the threat of imposing new trade tariffs on Mexico while at the same time placing the continuation of NAFTA into question.

Mexico was able to resist US pressure for a while, but the situation became harder when a new form of Central American migration emerged, the so-called "caravans." The first of these caravans were organized in 2017 and early 2018 by *Pueblo sin Fronteras,* an organization founded in 2009 in Dallas, Texas, with an aim to protect the human rights in the US. The NGO expanded its work south of the border, to protect migrants along the migrants on their way to the US. This move was inspired in great part by the killing of the seventy-two Central American migrants in San Fernando, Tamaulipas.[16] Numbering sometimes thousands of people, the caravans, which primarily originated in Honduras, were made up of migrants who traveled together in large groups as a way for allowing safer passage for all of them and they were joined by other migrants along the way in El Salvador and Guatemala as they made their way through Mexico to the US. For their part, people who joined the caravans argued that they were fleeing persecution, poverty, and violence in their home countries and seeking asylum in the US (BBC News 2018), even while some migrants admitted that they were sponsored by or politically manipulated by pro-migrant organizations (Lee 2019).

By late 2018, the political attention to the caravans created a chaotic situation, which presented Mexico with unique challenges in managing its response to the new wave of migrants. In particular, a caravan organized in early October 2018, which was not supported by *Pueblos sin Fronteras* but summoned via a fake *Facebook* post, which impersonated a well-known left-wing Honduran politician, Bartolo Fuentes, reached seven thousand people (Bensinger and Zabludovsky 2018). This all occurred within the context of the US midterm elections, and the caravan's formation was politically manipulated by the Trump administration in an effort to influence the outcome of the US congressional elections. In this context, the US president sent the American military to the border as a symbolic move, while pressure mounted on Mexico to act and stop it (Ryan 2018). For Mexico, the US move posed a unique challenge. As mentioned above, up until then, Mexico had been collaborating with the US government in containing the flows though the Southern Border Program. However, the large number of people who joined this caravan, and the attention it drew from the press and from human rights activists, made it very hard for the Mexican government to stop it through the operations it had launched in different spots along its southern border and in the migrant routes. In a crisis mode, the Mexican government's response could not be anything but confusing. First, it threatened to stop the migrants by force to appease the American president, but fearing a humanitarian crisis it allowed the migrants to stay in southern Mexico through a last-minute plan dubbed *Estás en tu Casa* ("*You Are at Home*"; Gobierno de México 2018).

---

16   For information about the organization of the first caravans organized in early 2017 and 2018, see the Pueblo Sin Fronteras website at www.pueblosinfronteras.org (last accessed October 31, 2020).

Through this program, the Mexican government offered migrants one-year temporary work permits, but only in the states of Oaxaca and Chiapas where they were expected to remain. The Central Americans, however, did not intend to stay in Mexico, much less confined to only the two states as the Mexican government offered. In the end, the only option for the government was to accompany them and to guarantee that the caravans moved in a safe and orderly way, very much in accordance with the Mexican law. In this context Mexican authorities faced much scrutiny by civil society organizations, which had been empowered to support the government by protecting the migrants under the aegis of the 2011 migratory law.

Having widely criticized the Mexican government for its policies at the southern border, which according to him violated human rights, the new Mexican president Andrés Manuel López Obrador was elected in Mexico with the promise of addressing the root causes of migration from Mexico and Central America, and of protecting the human rights of Central American migrants transiting through Mexico. Failing to grasp the complexity of the situation that Mexico faced vis-à-vis the US with a strongly anti-immigrant president, one of the first things the López Obrador administration offered was the issuing of one-year humanitarian visas to Central Americans so that they could work all over Mexico. This policy was interpreted by both Mexican and American observers as a problem, because most likely Central Americans did not want to stay in Mexico as was evident in the *You Are at Home* policy proposed by the previous administration. It still would have the effect of encouraging them to migrate to the US in larger numbers since they now had a safe passage through Mexico, a situation that would make the management of the flows very difficult for Mexico and the US (González-Arias 2019). An increase of the flows during 2018 and early 2019, after Mexico had issued 15,000 of those visas by February of that last year, increased the pressure from the US government to stop the flows (González-Arias 2019).

Having lost its capacity to control the flows in the context of the new policies, and after major threats from the Trump administration to raise tariffs against Mexico by up to 25 percent by October of that year unless Mexico could prove that it had substantially reduced the flows, the Mexican government ended up signing an agreement with the US (Navarro 2019). This agreement in practice put an end to the rights-based approach toward international migration that the country had adopted after the 2008 reform to the law to decriminalize migration, and through its 2011 constitutional and legal reforms.

Through this agreement, Mexico accepted to register all migrants who entered through its southern border, granting asylum to those who requested it, and to deploy 6,000 members of the newly created National Guard to all the territory but especially to its southern border to help Mexican migratory authorities to control the flows.[17] Mexico also accepted the expansion of the US program known as Migration Protection Protocols

---

17   The 2011 Migratory Law only allowed the Mexican immigration authorities to detain migrants. But the law allowed for the Interior Ministry to request the collaboration of other authorities in protecting the migrants, and this provision of the law is the one that was used to justify the deployment of the National Guard.

(MPPs), a program that since early 2019 allowed the US authorities to send asylum seekers who entered its territory through Mexico back while they waited for their asylum cases to be processed on the other side of the border. In addition, and in reality in accordance with its own constitutional requirements based on Mexico's international obligations and its own law, Mexico offered to protect the human rights of those who would stay in Mexico as well as granting them access to health, education, and opportunities in the labor market (VOA 2019). In return, the US agreed to expedite the processing of Central Americans asylum applications and to support López Obrador's original agenda on immigration aimed at addressing the root causes of migration although without any indication of how it would do so.

The new agreement succeeded in reducing the levels of irregular migration at the US-Mexico border and those transiting through Mexico. By end of September 2019, Mexico had deployed not 6,000 but 25,000 National Guard troops to assist in migration enforcement. In total, 81,000 migrants had been apprehended and 62,000 returned to their countries of origin. At the same time, Mexico had also taken back 39,000 migrants from the US under MPPs (Soto 2020). This enforcement-only approach by the López Obrador administration came at a great price: it created a humanitarian crisis at both Mexico's southern and northern borders. In the south it resulted in the persecution of migrants and the massive violation of their human rights, including denial of access to due process and to safe and dignified conditions as a result of the overcrowding of Mexico's detention centers known euphemistically in Mexico as "migrant stations" (Ronquillo 2020). Meanwhile, in northern Mexico, Central Americans waited in dire conditions at constant risk to their safety and lives, as they became the target of organized crime along the border.

Furthermore, as migrants became more noticeable, and amid the tensions that the new enforcement policies created in communities of transit in the Mexican southern border and across migrant routes, where conflicts between the native population and newcomers became more common, the levels of intolerance and xenophobia in Mexico toward migrants and refugees showed a marked increase (Pineda 2019).

In addition, Mexico, like Turkey (see Adamson, this volume), became a de facto refugee country, even if not yet at the magnitude experienced in Turkey. According to the Migration Policy Institute, one year after the agreement was signed, the number of asylum requests in Mexico more than doubled from 30,000 people in 2018 to 71,000 in 2019, exposing the limitations of the Mexican refugee system and its inability to protect asylum seekers and refugees. At the same time the government adopted measures to strengthen the Mexican Commission to Assist Refugees (Soto 2020). The humanitarian situation was made worse by the COVID-19 pandemic in 2020. In this context, the Mexican government has not been able to guarantee the health conditions of migrants and asylum seekers awaiting the resolution of their cases in Mexico, and the government cannot provide adequate conditions for those waiting at the Mexican northern border for the processing of their asylum cases in the US.

Mexico as a Country of Destination

In addition to these dynamics, in the coming years Mexico may become an important destination for labor immigrants as its population dynamics acquire similar characteristics to those of Canada and the United States. Mexico is already a recipient country for Guatemalan immigrants who come to work in the agricultural sector (cocoa, coffee, watermelon, papaya, green pepper, and soy), construction and commerce in the southern states of Chiapas, and to a lesser extent Campeche and Quintana Roo. Guatemalan women also work as domestic or household servants in those states. However, the flow of these workers has remained relatively stable and limited to the south of Mexico, and recent attempts by the Mexican government to provide work permits to Central American migrants on their way to the US does not seem to have changed this dynamic. The number of Guatemalans who have come to work in southern Mexico over the past decade is difficult to estimate since many travel back and forth on a daily basis and others only stay temporarily. So far, the Central American immigrant population in Mexico is relatively small, although the numbers may increase given the growing number of asylum seekers and refugees from Guatemala, Honduras, and El Salvador. According to the Mexican census, in 2010 there were 31,888 Guatemalans, 8,864 Salvadorans, and 9,980 Hondurans (Meza González 2015). The new 2020 Mexican census may show a large increase as a result of recent developments, even though it is hard to know how many Central American migrants will actually have settled in Mexico in the long term. As Mexican society ages and the size of its active population diminishes, the demand for Central American workers may expand to other regions and sectors of the Mexican economy. The question is whether they will be willing to come. At this point, wage differentials between Guatemala and Mexico are not sufficiently high to act as an incentive to attract many more workers. Sixty percent of Guatemalan immigrants in the south of Mexico earn only up to one minimum wage, and 25 percent up to two, which means that they can be making as much or only slightly less in Guatemala. For instance, their wages have decreased in recent years as Mexico has tried to regulate migration flows across its southern border. Thus, immigration from Central America will be determined by the extent to which economic conditions in Mexico improve vis-à-vis its southern neighbors, and by the size of the new migratory networks that are created as a result of the recent increases in the number of refugees.

International Displacement, Asylum Seekers, and Refugees in Latin America

Mexico and Central America are only one part of a larger story of migration in Latin America. Apart from a growing number of labor migrants within Latin America (see Gomes, this volume), which the International Labor Organization reports has increased from 3.2 million in 2010 to 4.3 million in 2015 (ILO 2015), Latin America is today the source of substantial population movements of internally and internationally displaced populations. Many of these populations are quite vulnerable and in need of international protection, even while they are not necessarily acknowledged as refugees, since they fall through the cracks of existing legal frameworks for refugees and asylum seekers. The main countries of forced displaced populations are El Salvador, Honduras, and Guatemala in Central America, and Venezuela in the Southern Cone. In addition, Nicaragua has also become a source of forced migration since April 2018 due to increasingly more violent forms of political repression adopted by the government there (AFP 2018).

El Salvador is considered today among the countries in the world with the largest internally displaced population in relation to the size of its total population. According to the International Displacement Monitoring Center, in 2016 the number of people forcibly displaced in Salvador reached 200,000, which is equivalent to 3,600 people displaced per 100,000 inhabitants. During 2019, the number of forced migrants reached new heights. That year alone a total of 454,000 people had been displaced because of conflict and violence and 1,900 people because of disasters (IDMC 2020). This prompted the Salvadoran National Assembly to pass a new law to protect, aid, and offer durable solutions to people internally displaced (United Nations 2020). Guatemala and Honduras have also shown high levels of internal displacement, reaching 257,000 people and 190,000 people respectively in 2016 (IDMC 2017). Displacement has been primarily the result of the violence perpetrated by gangs and organized crime, but also by governmental authorities that in their fight against criminal organizations have adopted repressive policies that have contributed to increased violence as well. Other sources of displacement include drought, with up to 3.5 million people affected in 2016, in what is known as the dry corridor that runs across the territory of Guatemala, Honduras, and El Salvador, and other phenomena related to climate change and environmental disasters (OCHA 2016). The scenario of internal displacement represents a major challenge for the north Central American countries within the next few years, one that will require decisive action on the part of Central American governments with the support of international agencies and donors to provide sustainable solutions to alleviate the root causes. The effects of this displacement are also now apparent in other countries of the region. Those who can leave have been traveling to neighboring countries and especially to the United States, taking advantage of the strong migratory networks that already exist, which in turn has prompted the US and Mexico to adopt a number of measures to stop the growing flows of refugees from Central America as was described above.

In looking ahead, new sources of internal and international displacement within the north Central American region will continue to be related to climate change and social instability unless governments of the region work with international agencies, along with other donors and organizations, to develop effective response systems to prevent and mitigate the effects of droughts, floods, and environmental catastrophes. They also must address the root causes of violence and economic underdevelopment, a situation that will became more daunting because of the economic effects that the pandemic has induced. It is estimated that climate-related internal migration could reach 3.9 million people by 2050 in Mexico, Guatemala, Honduras, and El Salvador if effective measures to prevent the effects of climate change are not adopted (World Bank Group 2018).

Venezuela: New Source of Major International Forced Displacements

Along with the north Central American countries, Venezuela has become within the span of the past five years one of the main sources of forced migration in the world (see Gomes, this volume). In 2015, the number of Venezuelans residing abroad was 697,562. By October 2020, this number had exploded to 5.5 million (IOM 2020). The first cohorts of Venezuelan migration went to the United States, Spain, Italy, and Portugal respectively, traditional countries of destination for Venezuelan migration. Today, however, the majority are settling all around South America, including in Colombia, Peru, Ecuador, Chile, Argentina, and Brazil. These countries are facing the challenge of offering legal protection to this population, as well as access to humanitarian aid, basic public services, and, when possible, access to the labor market.

Until now, countries of the region have responded to the Venezuelan crisis by considering some of them as asylum seekers, but most commonly by offering them some alternative form of legal protection to reside for an extended period within their territories with access to employment and social services. These include temporary residence permits, humanitarian visas, regional visa arrangements including those linked to Mercosur (Southern Common Market), and until recently, UNASUR (Union of South American Nations) and labor migration visas. According to the data portal of the interagency support platform created by the United Nations to address the Venezuelan refugee crisis, by October 2020, 2.4 million Venezuelans have benefited from some form of resident or regular stay permits. In addition, a total of 806,416 had requested asylum and 143,402 had been recognized as refugees (IOM 2020).

Looking five to twenty years out, the current Venezuelan population movement is projected to continue for the next few years, after the current pandemic is over and South American economies recover, unless economic and political conditions change in Venezuela. The crisis will have generated a number of Venezuelan diasporas in the region, which if integrated appropriately in their countries of reception will bring new opportunities for economic growth. Many Venezuelan èmigrès have high levels of education and thus offer the potential of contributing in a significant way to their countries of reception. Even those who do not have very high levels of education tend to be more educated than the average of the population of the country of reception. This situation suggests that if managed appropriately and with the right resources and support on the part of international organizations and donors, their ultimate economic and social integration will be successful, setting an example for the region and the world. The main challenge will be for Venezuela, a country that will take generations to recover the human capital lost as a result of its current crisis.

Nicaragua: A New Source of Displacement?

An additional source of internationally displaced populations is Nicaragua, due to the political crisis and violent government repression that this country has confronted since April 2018. By March 2020, more than 100,000 Nicaraguans had requested asylum primarily in Costa Rica and to a lesser extent in Panama and other countries (United Nations 2020). This has created a major challenge especially for Costa Rica—not only because of the size of the refugee population in proportion to its population (five million people) but also because Costa Rica has not been able to create a special policy to deal with forced migration similar to policies elsewhere in South America for dealing with the Venezuelan refugee crisis. The political environment, in which a right-wing anti-immigrant coalition almost won the presidency in the last presidential election, makes it very hard. As a result, most Nicaraguans have been encouraged to apply for asylum, which has become a de facto permit to discourage irregularity in the country while more permanent solutions become politically viable. The advantage of the asylum process is that while the asylum applications are processed, Nicaraguans can remain legally in the country and gain access to the labor market. Nonetheless, this has overwhelmed the capacity of Costa Rica's asylum system and presents a major challenge for the country to integrate this incoming population, a task that has become even more daunting in the context of the pandemic caused by COVID-19.

In this regard, and up until very recently, other regions of the world were considered more problematic with respect to forced migration. The World Bank, for example, has dedicated a lot of attention to forced migration, covering almost all regions of the world, including Africa, Europe, Central Asia, the Middle East, and North Africa, but not the Americas. Yet it is Latin America—which faces some of the biggest challenges, but with the opportunity to develop comprehensive frameworks that can protect displaced populations—that until now has fallen through the cracks of existing protection frameworks.

A New Era of Immigration in Latin America?

While the outflow of people from Latin America to other parts of the world, especially the United States and Europe, has been more characteristic of the region during recent decades, international migration is transforming many countries. Such is the case of Belize, a country that has received the largest number of immigrants (and refugees) in Latin America as a share of its total population, primarily from Guatemala but also from Honduras and El Salvador, a bit like Lebanon in the Middle East but much more stable (see Tsourapas, this volume). Newcomers are reshaping Belize, changing the ethnic and cultural makeup of the county, from a predominantly creole society to one where mestizos and Spanish speakers more broadly are becoming the dominant group. Immigration in Belize acts largely as a substitute for emigration, and migration is vital for the economic well-being of this small country: 15 percent of its population are immigrants, while 15 percent of Belizeans are residing abroad, primarily in the US (Smith and Castillo 2018).

Apart from the Nicaraguans and Venezuelans who have arrived in recent years due to the political crisis in their countries of origin, Costa Rica, and to a lesser extent Argentina and Panama, are also important receiving countries, with some segments of their economies increasingly dependent on foreign workers, while Brazil and Chile have become new destinations as well (Stefoni 2018). Without the Nicaraguans who work in the citrus industry, and the Ngobe-Buglé indigenous migrants from Panama who work in the coffee and banana industries, Costa Rica's agricultural sector would have been in serious trouble long ago because of its demographic dynamics, including a low fertility rate and rapidly aging population. Other sectors of the Costa Rican economy also would suffer without access to foreign workers, including the construction and services. Professional women in Costa Rica would not have been able to enter the workforce so easily without access to domestic workers from Nicaragua, which is the country of origin of 75 percent of Costa Rica's immigrants. In the most recent census, Nicaraguan migrants represented 9 percent of the Costa Rican population (OIT 2016).

As surprising as it may seem because of its current domestic economic and political instability, until very recently Venezuela was also an important receiving country in

Latin America, considering that by 2010, 4.2 percent of its population were immigrants, primarily from historically war-torn neighboring Colombia (Stefoni 2018). Although many of them are returning today to Colombia—possibly 300,000 have done so—the irregularity of many Colombians still living in Venezuela, including possibly around 80,000, are persons of concern for the United Nations High Commissioner on Refugees (UNHCR), which is one of the reasons why UNHCFR still maintains a presence in the country.[18]

Despite years of economic turbulence, Argentina also became a country of destination in the past two decades, primarily for Bolivians, Peruvians, Ecuadorans, and Paraguayans, but also for Venezuelans fleeing deprivation. Venezuelans now represent one of the most important migratory systems in the Southern Cone (OIT 2016). In 2010 UN estimates suggest that immigrants represented 4.4 percent of the population of Latin America (Stefoni 2018). In 2004, Argentina implemented a landmark immigration law that became a touchstone for the region for the protection of migrants. Argentina took a leadership role in debates on regional mobility for South Americans by proposing the Mercosur Residence Agreement, which is currently in place and has been used to offer protection to Venezuelans who are arriving in some Mercosur member countries (see also Gomes, this volume). However, in 2017 the president issued a decree whereby immigrants who have committed any type of offense, including minor ones, as well as those who had entered clandestinely into the country, could be summarily expelled. Moreover, the decree changed the criteria for expulsion, eliminating the use of family reunification as grounds to oppose an expulsion order (Acosta 2017). These measures reflect a dramatic change of course in policies toward immigrants, which if adopted in other countries of the region could create major problems for the economic and social integration of migrants, thereby creating greater social and political instability in the region.

In all of these new destination countries, the overriding issues are how to address the participation of immigrants in the informal economy, and how to provide access to social protection and to health and educational services for the immigrant population in countries that have limited resources and have struggled to address the needs of their own populations. Most countries of the region have revised their Constitutions, and in some cases passed concrete immigration reforms, as has been the case of Mexico, compelling them to protect the human rights of immigrants and refugees, including their economic, social, and cultural rights.

Thus, international and forced migration presents Latin American with many challenges and opportunities that will determine the demographic, economic, social, and political future of countries throughout the region. How these countries and the region handle the challenges and opportunities will set an example to the rest of the world—one to be followed or to be avoided.

References

Acosta, D. 2017. *Argentina's Restrictive Turn on Migration: Trump's First Imitator in the Americas?* Florence: Robert Schuman Centre for Advanced Studies, European University Intitute.

---

18   Author's conversation with Juan Carlos Murillo, from UNHCR Geneva, specialist on Venezuela, May 3 and 7, 2018.

———. 2018. *The National versus the Foreigner in South America: 200 years of Migration and Citizenship Law.* Cambridge: Cambridge University Press.

AFP. 2018. "Miles de nicaragenses buscan emigrar porla ola de violencia." June 14.

BBC News. 2018. *"Migrant Caravan: What Is It and Why Does It Matter?" November 26.* https://www.bbc .com/news/world-latin-america-45951782

Bensinger, K., and Zabludovsky, K. 2018. *"A Mysterious Imposter Account Was Used on Facebook to Drum Up Support for the Migrant Caravan." BuzzFeedNews*, December 16. Accessed October 31, 2020, from https://www.buzzfeednews.com/article/kenbensinger/a-mysterious-imposter -account-was-used-on-facebook-to-drum

Bracero History Archive. 2020. G.M. Roy Rosenzweig Center for History and New Media. http://braceroar chive.org/about

Callard, A. 2009. "American History Museum Explores the Era of the Bracero." *Smithsonian Magazine*, September 17.

Castillo, A. 2016. *"The Mexican Government's Frontera Sur Program: An Inconsistent Immigration Policy."* Council on Hemispheric Affairs, October 26.

Corwin, A. 1978. "Mexican Policy and Ambivalence toward Labor Emigration to the United States." In *Immigrants—and Immigrants: Perspectives on Mexican Labor Migration to the United States, edited by A. Corwin,* 176–219. Westport, CT: Greenwood Press.

Donato, K., Durand, J., and Massey, D. 1992. "Changing Conditions in the U.S. Labor Market: Of the Immigration Reform and Control Act of 1996." *Population Research and Policy Review* 11(2): 93–115.

Duran, J., and Massey, D., eds. 2004. *Crossing the Border: Research from the Mexican Migration Project.* New York: Russell Sage Foundation.

D'Vera, C., Passel, J., and González-Barrera, A. 2017. *"Rise in U.S Immigrants Form El Salvador, Guatemala and Honduras Outpaces Growth from Elsewhere."* Pew Research Center, December 17. http://www.pewhispanic.org/2017/12/07/ rise-in-u-s-immigrants-from-el-salvador-guatemala-and-honduras-outpaces-growth-from-elsewhere/

FitzGerald, D. 2019. *Refugee beyond Reach: How Rich Democracies Repel Asylum Seekers.* New York: Oxford University Press.

FitzGerald, D., and Cook-Martin, D. 2014. *Culling the Masses: The Democratic Origins of Racist Immigration Policy in the Americas.* Cambridge, MA: Harvard University Press.

Giorguli, S., and Bautista León, A. 2018. *Radiografía de la Migración de Retorno 2015.* Sistema Nacional de Información sobre Migración de Retorno y Derechos Sociales. *Notas para la Integración de los Retornados*, no. 1 (June).

Giorguli-Saucedo, S., García-Guerrero, V., and Masferrer, C. (2016). *A Migration System in the Making.* Center for Demographic, Urban and Environmental Studies. Mexico City: El Colegio de México.

Gobierno de México. 2018. *"El Presidente Enrique Peña Nieto anuncia el Plan 'Estas en tu casa' en apoyo a los migrantes centroamericanos que se encuentran en México."* October 26. ww.gob.mx

González-Arias, A. 2019. "Entre la racionalidad instrumental y lo apropiado." *Foreign Affairs Latinoamérica*, June 13.

González-Barrera, A. 2015, November 19). *"More Mexicans Leaving than Coming to the U.S."* Pew Research Center, November 19. http://www.pewhispanic.org/2015/11/19/ more-mexicans-leaving-than-coming-to-the-u-s/

Guerrero, M. 2020. "Crónica desde el abandono, o de cómo AMLO nos entregó a los migrantes ante Trump." *Nexos*, July 18.

Hazan, M. 2014. *Understanding Return Migration to Mexico: Towards a Comprehensive Policy for the Reintegration of Returning Migrants.* San Diego: Center for Comparative Immigration Studies.

———. 2016. *Diagnóstico y propuestas de acción para atender a los niños y niñas adolescentes migrantes acompañados y no acompañados que transitan en el corredor de centro y norteamérica; así como a los hijos de migrantes en países de origen, tránsito y destino.* Washingon, DC: Banco Interamericano de Desarrollo.

Hinojosa, R., and Wynn, M. 2014. *5 Basic Lessons from "the Crisis" of Central American Migrants: Poverty and Violence Are Root Causes, but U.S. Labor Demand Remains the Key Driver*. North American Integration and Development Center, University of California, Los Angeles.

Hollifield, J. F., Martin, P. L., and and Orrenius, P. M. 2014. *Controlling Immigration: A Global Perspective*. Stanford, CA: Stanford University Press.

IDMC. 2017. *Global Report on Internal Displacement*. Internal Displacement Monitoring Center. http://www.internal-displacement.org/global-report/grid2017/

———. 2020. *El Salvador*. Internal Displacement Monitoring Center. https://www.internal-displacement.org/countries/el-salvador

ILO. 2015. *Global Estimates on Migrant Workers*. December. International Labour Office.

IOM. 2020. *Operational Portal, Refugees and Migrants from Venezuela*. June 5. International Organization for Migration. https://r4v.info/en/situations/platform

Jarvis, B. 2019. "The Deported Americans." *California Sunday Magazine*, January 31. https://story.california sunday.com/deported-americans.

Lee, S. 2019. "Who's Funding the Migrant Caravans?" *World Magazine*, April 15. https://world.wng .org/2019/04/who_s_funding_the_migrant_caravans

Lustgarten, A. 2020. "The Great Climate Migration." *New York Times Magazine*, July 22.

Maldonado Castillo, C. 2016. "The Cartagena Process: 30 Years of Innovation and Solidarity." *Forced Migration Review*, no. 49 (May).

Martin, P. 2006. "The Trade Migration and Development Nexus." In *Migration, Trade and Development*, edited by J. E. Hollifield, 11–34. Dallas: Federal Reserve Bank of Dallas.

Massey, D., Arango, J., Hugo, G., Kouaouci, A., and Taylor, E. 1993. "Theories of International Migration: A Review and an Appraisal." *Population and Development Review* 19(3): 431–66.

Massey, D., Arango, J., Hugo, G., Kouaouci, A., Pellegrino, A., and Taylor, E. 1994. "An Evaluation of International Migration Theory: The North American Case." *Population and Development Review* 20(4): 699–751.

Meza González, L. 2015. "Visitantes y Residentes: Trabajadores Guatemaltecos, Salvadoreños y Hondureños en México." *Canamid, Policy Brief Series, PB#4* (October).

Morales Sanchez, J. 2008. *Despenalización de la migración irregular en México: Análisis y perspectivas de la Ley General de Población de 21 de julio de 2008. Temas de Migración y Derecho*, 105–38. https://archivos .juridicas.unam.mx/www/bjv/libros/6/2993/10.pdf

Morales Vega, L. G. 2012. "Categorías migratorias en México: Análisis a la Ley de Migración." *Anuario Mexicano de Derecho Internacional* 12: 929–58.

Navarro, B. 2019. "*Trump amenaza con aranceles a México en represalia por la inmigración*." *La Vanguardia*, May 31. https://www.lavanguardia.com/internacional/20190531/462576802105/trump-aranceles-mexico-eeuu-inmigracion-muro.html

OCHA. 2016. "El Niño: Overview of Impact, Projected Humanitarian Needs and Response." Office for the Coordination of Humanitarian Affairs, September 21.

OIM. 2018. *Dinámicas Migratorias en Fronteras de países de América del Sur*, vol. 10. Geneva: Fondo de la OIM para el Desarrollo.

OIT. 2016. *La migración laboralen América Latina y el Caribe*. Organización Internacional de las Migraciones, Oficina Regional para América Latina y el Caribe, Lima.

O'Neil, S. K. 2020. "*Mexican Migration Could Be the First Crisis of 2021*." *Bloomberg News*, July 24. https://www.bloomberg.com/opinion/articles/2020-07-22/mexican-migration-could-be-first-crisis-of-2021?sref=hF44HboC

Passel, J., and Cohn, V. 2019. "*Mexicans Decline to Less than Half the U.S. Unauthorized Immigrant Population for the First Time*." Pew Research Center, June 12. https://www.pewresearch.org/fact-tank/2019/06/12/us-unauthorized-immigrant-population-2017/

Pineda, G. 2019. *"Encuesta revela aumento de xenofobia en mexicanos contra migrantes."* CC News, June. https://news.culturacolectiva.com/mexico/encuesta-revela-aumento-de-xenofobia-en -mexicanos-contra-migrantes/

Public Law 96-212, United States Refugee Act of 1980, 96th Cong., March 17. https://www.govinfo.gov/con tent/pkg/STATUTE-94/pdf/STATUTE-94-Pg102.pdf

Radford, J. 2019. *"Key Findings about U.S. Immigrants."* Pew Research Center, June 17. https://www.pewre search.org/fact-tank/2019/06/17/key-findings-about-u-s-immigrants/

Rodríguez Chaves, E. 2016. *Migración Centroamericana en Tránsito Irregular por México: Nuevas Cifras y Tendencias.* Canamid (Central America–North America Dialogue), CIESAS, MacArthur Foundation, Georgetown University.

Ronquillo, V. 2020. *"A un año del acuerdo migratorio de México con EEUU, la crisis humanitaria es más grave."* Inter Press Service, June 20. http://www.ipsnoticias.net/2020/06/ano-del-acuerdo-migratorio -mexico-eeuu-la-crisis-humanitaria-mas-grave/

Ryan, P. 2018. *The US Military Doesn't Have Any Idea What the Thousands of Troops Deployed to the Border Should Do When the Migrants Show Up."* Business Insider, November 14. https://www.businessinsider .com/us-military-is-in-the-dark-about-their-role-as-migrant-caravans-arrive-2018-11

Smith, M. P., and Bakker, M. 2008. *Citizenship across Borders: The Political Transnationalism of El Migrante.* Ithaca, New York: Cornell University Press.

Smith, M., and Castillo, P. Forthcoming. *Thirteen Years-Plus Isn't Time to Integrate.* Belmopan, Belize: IADB.

Soto, A. 2020. *One Year after the U.S-Mexico Agreement, Reshaping Mexico's Migration Policies.* Migration Policy Institute, June. https://www.migrationpolicy.org/sites/default/files/publications/OneYearAfterUS -MexAgreement-EN-FINAL.pdf

Stefoni, C. 2018. *Panoroma de la migración internacional en América del Sur.* Santiago, Chile: CEPAL.

United Nations. 2020. *"New El Salvador Law, A Victory for Forced Displacement Victims: UN Refugee Agency."* January 10. https://news.un.org/en/story/2020/01/1055131

———. 2020. *"Nicaragua: After Two Years Of Crisis, More than 100,000 Have Fled the Country."* March 10. https://news.un.org/en/story/2020/03/1059051

UNDESA. 2019. *Trends in International Migration 2019.* New York: United Nations.

UNHCR. 2018. *Operational Portal, Refugee Situations.* Venezuela Situation, April 26. https://data2.unhcr.org/ en/situations/vensit

———. 2018. *Refugee Portal, Venezuela.* April. https://data2.unhcr.org/en/situations/vensit

———. 2018. *Situational Update, Venezuelan Situation.* February. Geneva, Switzerland.

———. 2020. *Displacement in Central America.* June. https://www.unhcr.org/en-us/displacement-in-central- america.html

USAID. 2018. *Fact Sheet: U.S. Assistance for Venezuelans in Colombia.* May 8. Washington, DC.

VOA. 2019, September 09). *"En qué consiste el acuerdo migratorio entre México y EE.UU.?"* VOANoticias, September 9. https://www.voanoticias.com/inmigracion/en-que-consiste-el-acuerdo-entre-mexico -y-estados-unidos

World Bank Group. 2018. *Groandswell, Preparing for Internal Climate Migration, Policy Note #3.* Washington, DC: World Bank Group.

Yankelevich, P. 2020. *Los Otros: Raza, Normas y Corrupación en la Gestión de la Extranjería en México, 1900-1950.* Madrid: Iberoamericana.

Zolberg, A. 1999. *"Matters of State: Theorizing Immigration Policy."* In *The Handbook of International Migra-tion: The American Experience,* edited by C. Hirschman, P. Kasinitz, and D. Josh. New York: Russell Sage Foundation.

14   THE MIGRATION STATE IN SOUTH AMERICA

Charles P. Gomes

DEMOGRAPHIC OR POPULATION politics has always been an important tool in the socioeconomic development of South America. The aim of this chapter is to trace the recent shifts in the history of migration in the region by presenting the changes in the politics of immigration across South American countries. Consistent with the thesis of this volume, the main argument is that states matter, and no immigration occurs in a political vacuum. The effects of migration policies on shaping the history and identity of the countries of the Western Hemisphere since the colonial period are too relevant to be ignored. Similar to other countries in the Americas, the socioeconomic and political history of South America is strongly associated with the history of immigration and population management. A simple review of recent books tells us that after the decimation of the native population either by colonizers, infectious diseases, or the violent invasion ("conquest") of indigenous territories, several colonial states, especially Brazil and the United States, developed their economy by bringing forced migrants (slaves) from the African continent to work in huge plantations for more than two centuries. After the end of slavery and the traditional period in the late nineteenth century, the newly independent Brazil and the United States strategically replaced slavery with cheap agricultural and urban migrants from Europe in the early twentieth century. This brief history of the Western Hemisphere shows us why the national identity of all countries in the Americas is so strongly associated with migration. Even if almost all official national days in the Americas are celebrated on the day of their independence from the imperial powers, all countries also have holidays associated with the native population, the forced migrants from Africa, or the immigrants from Europe.

Despite the long history of migration in the Americas, after the first half of the twentieth century, South America underwent a paradigm shift in its migration politics. Nationalistic policies became predominant in the region and big countries, like Brazil, launched eugenicist policies to restrict migrants on a racial basis.[1] Argentina created two laws with

---

1   Fabio Koifman, *Imigrante ideal: O Ministério da Justiça e a entrada de estrangeiros no Brasil (1941–1945)* (Rio de Janeiro: Civilização Brasileira, 2012).

clear restrictive intent, one in 1902 and another in 1910 (Ley de Residencia de Extranjeros de 1902, no. 4144; Ley de Defensa Social de 1910, no. 7209).[2] Only after the Second World War did Brazil and Argentina reopen their borders, mainly to refugees. But soon after this period, the nationalistic tone resurfaced in both Argentina and Brazil, pushed by the economic policy of "import substitution industrialization."[3] The goal was to have a strong domestic industrial base where national companies would replace multinational ones. The labor market would give priority to national citizens over foreign workers. Immigration policy in both countries sought to protect the labor market from foreign competition. These protective and nationalistic immigration policies remained in place until the re-democratization period and the beginning of neoliberal economic policies in the mid-1990s. The transition came after significant pressure was applied by leading economic sectors to gain access to more foreign labor. National and multinational companies pushed governments to establish flexible migration policies to manage the growing demand for labor that would come with the "new economic openness." Indeed, ever since South American economies became more open, all states have been engaged in neoliberal reforms that affect population movements in the region. Several international agreements opened borders to free trade in the region and stimulated free markets inside Latin America (the Andean Community, Mercosur, and, most recently, UNASUR). All of these shifts in economic policy were followed by agreements on free movement and free residence of migrants inside the region, leading to an increase in numbers of new migrants, mostly coming from countries in the region.

The opening of markets raises a question that will guide the first part of this chapter: Can we say that South America is on a path to again become a new immigration region, like North America and Europe? And a related question: What kind of migration states will emerge? "Migration states,"[4] as presented by Hollifield (2004; the introduction to this volume), emerge most strongly in the postwar period "where states are constrained by 'embedded liberalism' and rights-based politics" (p. 10). As Hollifield asserts, "From a strategic, economic and demographic standpoint, trade and migration go hand in hand; because the wealth, power and stability of the state is now more than ever dependent on its willingness to risk both trade and migration and international security and stability are dependent on the capacity of states to manage migration. Yet it is extremely difficult, if not impossible, for states to manage or control migration unilaterally or even bilaterally" (p. 10). The tendency to create regional economic regimes, inspired by the European Union, shows a new and better way to manage regional migration flows and consolidate emerging migration states. This chapter will test the "emerging migration state" hypothesis in the following ways: (1) by exploring how political pressures from economic

2   Lucila Nejamkis and Lila García, "Legislación y políticas migratorias en Argentina," in *Políticas y reformas migratorias en América latina: Un estudio comparado*, ed. Natalia Caicedo Camacho (Lima: Universidad del Pacifico, 2020).

3   Werner Baer, "Import Substitution and Industrialization in Latin America: Experiences and Interpretations," *Latin American Research Review* 7, no. 1 (Spring 1972): 95–122.

4   James F. Hollified, "The Emerging Migration State," *International Migration Review* 38 (2004): 885–912.

actors propel governments in South America to adopt more liberal migration policies; (2) by tracing how rights-based politics led by civil society push states to a more open border policy under the protection of the new liberal constitutions in the region; (3) by showing how free trade agreements in the region encouraged freedom of movement and consolidation of labor markets; (4) by looking at how security concerns are pushing new right-wing governments in Latin America to restrict migration in the region; and (5) by showing how the Venezuelan exodus (over 5.5 million to date according to UNHCR and IOM) and ensuing refugee crises can illustrate and help us to test the argument about emerging migration states in South America.

This chapter is structured as follows: (1) a brief overview of migration history in the region and the two main consequences that flow from it—a predominantly intraregional migration and a constant North–South migration mainly from Europe to Latin America; (2) a discussion of the transformation of the two biggest migrant-receiving countries in the region, Brazil and Argentina, the shifts in their migration policies, and the impact of increasing immigration; (3) a review of new policy developments in the region and how they have contributed to the intraregional flow of migrants in Latin America, particularly the project to create a Latin American citizenship led by UNASUR and how this project can succeed or fail in the contemporary political landscape of the region; and (4) a look at how the massive flow of Venezuelan migrants in the region tests the consolidation of "migration states" in South America and illustrates the limits of the regional migration regime.

A Brief Overview of Migration History in the Region

In the last three decades, international migration in Latin America has been driven by intraregional flows, while emigration from the region has declined.[5] Steady economic growth in Latin American countries[6] and migration policies favoring freedom of movement and the granting of residence rights to nationals of South American states[7] are the two main factors explaining this demographic change. According to census data, since 2000, intraregional migration largely surpassed emigration, as shown in figure 14.1.

Immigration to Latin America continues following a pattern of South–South migration, mainly from sub-Saharan Africa, but also North–South migration, from Europe. Since the beginning of the European economic crisis in 2007 and the "lost decade,"[8] data confirm a bigger migration flow from Europe to Latin America than the other way around. Since 2010, new migration corridors developed between Europe and Latin

---

5   www.cepal.org/en/infographics/international-migration-latin-america-and-caribbean; www.migrationpolicy.org/regions/south-america

6   https://web.bndes.gov.br/bib/jspui/bitstream/1408/6242/1/RB%2043%20O%20ciclo%20econ%C3%B4

7   www.ippdh.mercosur.int/publicaciones/migracion-derechos-humanos-y-politica-migratoria/; www.cels.org.ar/web/wp-content/uploads/2020/10/CELS_Migrantes_digital_Final-1.pdf

8   Takeo Hoshi and Anil K. Kashyap, "Will the U.S. and Europe Avoid a Lost Decade? Lessons from Japan's Post-Crisis Experience," *IMF Economic Review* 63, no. 1 (2015): 110–63.

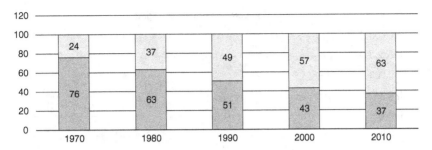

Figure 14.1. Latin America and the Caribbean: Percentage of immigrant populations by regional origin, 1970–2010.
Source: ECLAC (Economic Commission for Latin America and the Caribbean).

America, according to the International Organization for Migration—IOM.[9]Argentina and Brazil are the main receiving countries, while Bolivia, Paraguay, Peru, Colombia, and recently Venezuela are the main sending countries. During the last ten years, the level of immigration in Brazil increased by a factor of ten, reaching 100,000 new migrants settling in the country per year. The country went from issuing 6,000 work permits to foreign migrants at the end of the 1980s, to 60,000 work permits per year in the last decade.[10] In the past five years, the Ministry of Justice in Brazil in partnership with the "OBMigra lab" issued an annual report on the insertion of international migrants and refugees into the Brazilian labor market. Figures 14.2 and 14.3 show the pattern of temporary and long-term international migration, respectively, to Brazil from 2011 until 2015. Temporary migrants came mostly from the global North, while long-term migrants came mostly from neighboring countries in South America and the Caribbean and from European countries. During this period, Brazil registered 7,742,000 new immigrants into the country, as measured by legal immigrant registrations.

Argentina, with even higher numbers than Brazil, saw the flow of international migrants grow in the same proportion, around 250,000 new temporary and permanent international migrants settling per year from 2011 until 2015.[11]

Recent data and research on migration in the region show two new trends that have been ignored by most studies of migration in Latin America:

(1) Rich countries from the Northern Hemisphere have at certain times more national citizens leaving their territory than foreign migrants coming in. Portugal,[12] Spain,[13]

---

9   https://publications.iom.int/system/files/pdf/dinamicas_migratorias_2015.pdf

10   www.comillas.edu/images/OBIMID/relatorio_OBMIGRA_2015_final.pdf

11   www.migraciones.gov.ar/pdf_varios/estadisticas/radicaciones_2011-2015.pdf

12   www.ine.pt/xportal/xmain?xpid=INE&xpgid=ine_destaques&DESTAQUESdest_boui=224712736

13   www.ine.es/prensa/cp_2017_p.pdf

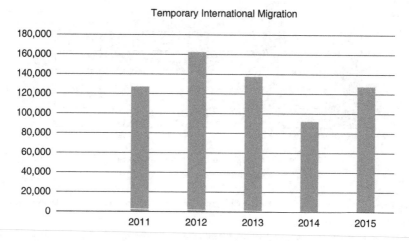

Figure 14.2. Temporary international migration.

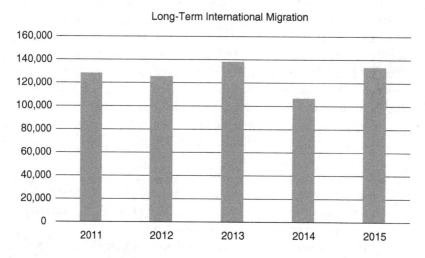

Figure 14.3. Long-term international migration.

and France illustrate the trend of emigration from the Northern to the Southern Hemisphere. Studies from the National Institute of Statistics in France (INSEE) and the equivalent agencies in Portugal (INE) and Spain (INE) show that migration is not a one-way street, from lower-income countries in the South to developed countries in the North.[14] In 2019 total net migration to the EU was 1.5 million, up from roughly half a million in 2006.[15] Not only is the number of emigrants from Europe increasing, but the amount

---

14   www.insee.fr/fr/statistiques/1521331

15   https://ec.europa.eu/info/strategy/priorities-2019-2024/promoting-our-european-way-life/statistics-migration-europe_en

Table 14.1.   Top countries receiving remittances (2005–2018) (current USD billions).

2005		2010		2015		2018	
China	23.63	India	53.48	India	68.91	India	78.61
Mexico	22.74	China	52.46	China	63.94	China	67.41
India	22.13	Mexico	22.08	Philippines	29.80	Mexico	35.66
Nigeria	14.64	Philippines	21.56	Mexico	26.23	Philippines	33.83
France	14.21	France	19.90	France	24.06	Egypt	28.92
Philippines	13.73	Nigeria	19.75	Nigeria	21.16	France	26.43
Belgium	6.89	Germany	12.79	Pakistan	19.31	Nigeria	24.31
Germany	6.87	Egypt	12.45	Egypt	18.33	Pakistan	21.01
Spain	6.66	Bangladesh	10.85	Germany	15.81	Germany	17.36
Poland	6.47	Belgium	10.35	Bangladesh	15.30	Viet Nam	15.93

Source: IOM World Migration Report 2020

of remittances also received by EU countries has risen sharply. Contrary to what the majority of immigration economic development studies contend, remittance does not occur exclusively from rich to poor or developing countries. Well-developed nations from Europe are on the list of top remittance-receiving countries. According to the *IOM World Migration Report*[16] from 2020 (table 14.1), France and Germany together with India, China, Mexico, the Philippines, and Egypt are among the top-ten remittance-receiving countries in the world that enrich their economies with the money sent from their migrant populations abroad.[17]

According to an IOM study as well, Europe receives high remittances from Latin American countries (LAC) that clearly show a win-win immigration economic game between the two regions. Spain, due to its obvious cultural ties, heads the list, as shown in the table from this study (table 14.2).[18]

Spain is among the countries with the highest levels of migration to South America. According to the ECLAC (Economic Commission for Latin America and Caribbean), more than 100,000 Spanish nationals migrated to Latin America between 2006 and 2017.[19] This number does not take account the flow of return migrants and dual nationals estimated to be three times the number of Spanish migrants. Latin America comes just after Europe as the main region to which Spanish citizens migrate. Data from the National Institute of Statistics (Instituto Nacional de Estatistica) in Madrid show how Spain's migratory balance was negative until 2015, and despite becoming positive after 2016, the number of Spaniards leaving the country to settle abroad has remained constant, around 300,000 people annually. According to the INE, in 2019, "the main

---

16 https://publications.iom.int/system/files/pdf/wmr_2020.pdf
17 https://data.worldbank.org/indicator/BX.TRF.PWKR.CD.DT
18 https://publications.iom.int/system/files/pdf/migration_routes_digital.pdf
19 https://repositorio.cepal.org/bitstream/handle/11362/44377/1/S1800785_Perez_es.pdf , p. 21.

Table 14.2.   Principal EU countries receiving remittances from Latin America 2010

Country of Destination	Amount (USD millions)	Percentage of Total of Remittances That Entered
Spain	2,588	56
France	435	9
Portugal	420	9
Italy	338	7
Germany	245	5
Belgium	177	4
Netherlands	114	2
United Kingdom	70	2
Rest of the 19 EU countries	207	4
Total	4,594	100

Source: IOM using data from the World Bank, 2011, Bilateral Remittance Estimates for 2010 using *Migrant Stocks, Host Countries Incomes,* and *Origin Countries Incomes.*

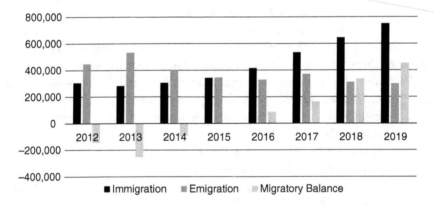

Figure 14.4.   Net migration flows in Spain, 2012–2019.
Source: Instituto Nacional de Estadística–Spain: population figures, June 2020.

nationalities of foreign migrants to Spain were Colombian (with 76,524 arrivals in Spain), Moroccan (72,778) and Venezuelan (57,700)."[20] This is a new international migration subsystem between Europe and Latin America that has received little attention from scholars (figure 14.4).

(2) The biggest flows of migrants today are in the Southern Hemisphere (South–South migration), a fact that receives less attention from politicians and policy-makers than South–North migration.[21] If we count refugees, the level of South–South migration is even bigger, meaning that neighboring countries to conflict zones are the ones

---

20   www.ine.es/en/prensa/cp_e2020_p_en.pdf, p. 6.
21   Fiona Adamson and Gerasimos Tsourapas, "The Migration State in the Middle East: Nationalizing, Developmental and Neoliberal Models of Migration Management," paper prepared for

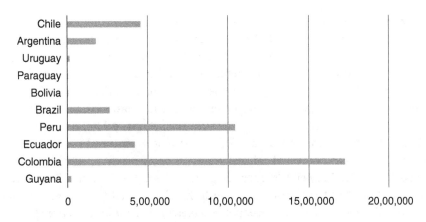

Figure 14.5.   Venezuelan migratory flow.
Source: IOM/UNHCR data from November 2020.

who receive most of the demographic pressure and have to cope with large humanitarian flows, while rich countries in the North insist on keeping asylum seekers far from their borders. The number of Colombians escaping from conflict zones to Ecuador and on a smaller scale to Argentina and Brazil illustrates well the South–South refugee migration pattern. More recently, Colombia, Peru, Ecuador, and Brazil are hosting large numbers of Venezuelans who are fleeing conflict and deprivation. Despite the election of a hard-right government in Brazil following the impeachment of President Dilma in 2016 and the decision of the Ministry of Justice to immediately to deport Venezuelans in December of that year, a national federal court blocked the move and gave legal protection to the migrants. The National Committee on Refugees (CONARE) in Brazil recorded more than 100,000 asylum applications and the National Council of Immigration (CNIg) estimates that more than 150,000 migrants from Venezuela have arrived since 2016.[22] The Venezuelans tend to arrive through the northern border of the country (state of Roraima), escaping from famine, economic deprivation, and political persecution.[23]

Figure 14.5 shows that when people are escaping from violence, famine, and other human rights abuses in Venezuela, they tend to go to neighboring countries. According to data provided by UNHCR and IOM in their common data platform "R4V," more than 5.5 million Venezuelans have already left the country and the huge majority of them are now living in Colombia, Peru, Ecuador, Chile, Brazil, and Argentina.[24]

The war in Syria illustrates, as well, the same situation where bordering states bear the brunt of humanitarian crises and refugee flows. Lebanon, Jordan, and Turkey have ten

presentation at the 11th Annual Meeting of the American Political Science Association (APSA), San Francisco, CA, August 31–September 3, 2017.

22   https://r4v.info/es/situations/platform/location/7509
23   www.nepo.unicamp.br/publicacoes/livros/atlasvenezuela/atlas_venezuela.pdf
24   https://r4v.info/en/situations/platform

times more Syrian refugees than Europe. Despite this fact, EU countries want to force refugee populations to remain in the region in hopes that when the conflict subsides, they can be repatriated quickly. And in exchange for money from the EU, Turkey signed an agreement to take back the Syrian refugees from Europe, to keep them in their territory, control their borders, and prevent their departure (see Adamson and Tsourapas, this volume).[25] Similarly, the US government by executive order banned Venezuelans, suspending visas in a clear attempt to prevent them from seeking refuge outside of Latin America.[26] In October 2017, a federal court judge suspended the ban, asserting that Trump's executive order "plainly discriminates based on nationality" in a way that is opposed to federal law and "the founding principles of this Nation."[27] These conflict situations show the liberal paradox on which this chapter and this volume are based: from one side, governments are under political pressure to close borders; from the other, the same governments are urged to respect the rights of migrants and asylum seekers, as required by liberal constitutions that guarantee the right of migrants to due process and equal protection under the law as well as the international law of "*non refoulement*" of asylum seekers. The Brazilian government's decision to deport Venezuelans, the US decision to ban new migrants from Venezuela, Europe's intent to send asylum seekers back to Turkey—all of these measures are contested in the courts, which play a big role in limiting harsh immigration controls. As Hollifield states: "If an individual migrant is able to establish some claim to residence on the territory of a liberal state, his or her chances of being able to remain and settle will increase. At the same time, developments in international human rights law have helped to solidify the position of individuals vis-à-vis the nation-state, to the point that individuals (and certain groups) have acquired a sort of international legal personality, leading some analysts to speculate that we are entering a post-national world."[28] This is one of the most important assertions of this chapter: liberal constitutions guarantee openness to migration and protection for asylum seekers. The chance for asylum seekers and migrants to remain in the countries of Latin America has improved due to the re-democratization of Latin American countries, the consolidation of liberal democracies, and the incorporation of international legal protections into constitutions throughout the region.

With regional integration in Latin America, migration management has been one of the most important topics on the regional agenda. Starting with the Latin America free trade agreement of the 1960s, then the Andean Community of Nations, followed by Mercosur, ending most recently with the creation of the Union of South American Nations (USAN), the region is on the path to implement a common market and the

---

25   www.consilium.europa.eu/en/press/press-releases/2016/03/18-eu-turkey-statement/

26   www.whitehouse.gov/the-press-office/2017/09/24/enhancing-vetting-capabilities-and processes-detecting-attempted-entry

27   www.washingtonpost.com/world/national-security/federal-judge-blocks-trumps-third -travel-ban/2017/10/17/e73293fc-ae90-11e7-9e58-e6288544af98_story.html

28   James F. Hollifield, "Governing Migration," in *Global Migration: Challenges in the Twenty-First Century*, ed. Kavita Khory (Basingstoke: Palgrave Macmillan, 2012), 198.

right to free movement and residence for nationals of the member states. USAN wants to put into operation a common passport among its members based on the model of the one that already exists among the countries of Mercosur. In the near future, the idea is to develop a real Latin American citizenship where the duties and rights of the nationals of the region will vary according to their country of residence and later, after creating a common legal ground among the member states' constitutions, rights and duties will be interchangeable. The move to regularize the situation of irregular migrants in the region is clear in several multilateral and bilateral agreements among the member states. One of the effective signs of this move is the fact that Mercosur expanded the clause of free movement and residence among its members to include Bolivia in 2009,[29] Peru in 2011,[30] Colombia in 2012,[31] and Ecuador in 2014.[32] The consolidation of these policies implies that the two biggest receiving countries (Argentina and Brazil) and the two biggest sending countries (Bolivia and Colombia) agree on the free movement of their citizens and the elimination of irregular migration that has been, until recently, the rule and not an exception in South America.

Emerging Migration States: Brazil and Argentina

The argument advanced in this section is that demographic change is a function of political choices to define who may enter or leave the national territory, and how to increase or decrease birth rates through different programs of family support. A study of the politics of migration can be viewed from different perspectives: through the new laws on migration, policies of colonization or land occupation, indigenous land demarcation, the scope of protection offered to migrants by law or in national constitutions, international conventions and agreements signed and ratified, and regional political integration (Mercosur, Andean Community, UNASUR). National development policies and population management, as well as legal norms, create and frame immigration policies and drive them to be more liberal or restrictive toward migrants. Indigenous or internal migrations are also covered by all these policies, but this section focuses only on international migration and the measures taken by governments to manage the flow of people across national borders, as well as how liberal or restrictive these policies have been in Brazil and Argentina.

This section of the chapter focuses on the period after re-democratization from the mid-1980s and the implementation of neoliberal policies in almost all the main countries of immigration in the region, but especially in Argentina and Brazil, that push the opening of borders for trade as well as the whole process of privatization for international

---

29   www.migracion.gob.bo/documentos/pdf/acuerdomercosur.pdf

30   Decreto Supremo no. 047–2011-RE, Ratifican la adhesión del Perú al Acuerdo sobre Residencia para Nacionales de los Estados Partes del Mercosur, Bolivia y Chile.

31   www.migracionoea.org/index.php/en/general-index-2015/46-sicremi/publicacion-2014/informeparte-ii-eng/602-colombia.html

32   www.cancilleria.gob.ec/2016/03/02/los-ciudadanos-de-los-estados-parte-de-mercosur-pueden-acceder-a-una-visa-de-residencia-permanente/

capital, thus promoting the insertion of the region in the global economy. Along with
the globalization of the region comes the pressure for a more flexible labor market and
openness to immigration. In this context, Brazil and Argentina launched new migration
policies that resulted in the creation of more liberal immigration laws.

The most important shift in migration management was the commitment of new
democratic governments to reform their immigration policies, and give them the power
to reinforce the liberal spirit of regional economic and political integration in the region.
The following sections of the chapter review the reform of immigration policy in Argentina and Brazil. Although similar, each country took a different path to reform based on
the principle of human rights and the rejection of nationalistic and securitizing principles dating from the military dictatorship. The common principle of the reforms is that
laws governing international flows should not only deal with immigrants but also with
nationals who live in other countries. The two countries broke with old nationalistic and
restrictive policies toward immigrants but also created laws to help their own migrants
outside their national territory.

Brazil

The first move toward a more liberal approach to international migration comes with re-
democratization and the first amnesty program for irregular migrants during the presidency of José Sarney (center-right politician) in 1988.[33] Besides Bolivia, Argentina, Uruguay, Paraguay, and Chile, the three main countries to benefit from the program were,
in order of importance, China, Lebanon, and South Korea. Ten years later, another amnesty program took place during the presidency of Fernando Enrique Cardoso (1997),
rejecting the nationalistic and securitizing immigration law enacted in 1980 during the
dictatorship period. Under the amnesty, Latin American nationals, as in the previous
amnesty, benefited the most, and Bolivians were at the top of the list. The Cardoso government implemented a neoliberal economic agenda, including privatizations, regional
free trade agreements, and more pro-immigration policies. President Cardoso's administration also enacted the Refugee Law of 1997 that expanded the definition of a refugee.
Other than the classic definition from the Geneva Convention, a refugee, according to
the new Brazilian law and following the Cartagena Declaration on Refugees, can also be
a person fleeing a region of "serious and widespread violation of human rights."[34]

Neither President Cardoso nor his successor Lula da Silva succeeded in passing a
new migration law. Despite their attempts, the several migration bills put forward never
succeeded even to become a topic in the agenda of the Brazilian Congress, much less
be approved or rejected by vote among the members of the two chambers, the Senate and the House of Representatives. Therefore, what explains the regularization of
hundreds of thousands of international migrants during the decades following the

---

33   Charles P. Gomes et al., *Migraciones Laborales en Sudamérica: El Mercorsur ampliado* (Gine-
bra: Oficina Internacional del Trabajo, 2004), www.ilo.org/wcmsp5/groups/public/---ed_protect/
---protrav/---migrant/documents/publication/wcms_201702.pdf

34   www.planalto.gov.br/ccivil_03/leis/L9474.htm

re-democratization of the country if Brazil was still under the nationalistic and restrictive migration law from the 1980s? The explanation can be found in the autonomy of
the National Council of Immigration in creating legal solutions capable of regularizing
migrants behind closed doors and in most cases contradicting the restrictive principles
of immigration law from the time of the military dictatorship.

The National Council of Immigration (Conselho Nacional de Imigração—CNIg) is a
deliberative body composed of the council president; one member each from the ministries of Labor, Justice, Foreign Affairs, Agriculture, Health, Industry and Commerce,
Science and Technology; and representatives from the private sector: the National Council of Industry, the National Council of Agriculture, and the main labor unions. The
Council was set up to define the objectives of immigration policy, labor market needs, to
improve the legitimacy of policy, and to close any loop holes. This mandate allowed the
Council to take control of immigration policy and bypass the legislature. Behind closed
doors, this group, composed of bureaucrats and members of the private sector and civil
society, isolated from the public opinion and the legislative debate, delivered a liberal
policy outcome in accordance mainly with the wish of the members of the private sector
(representatives of industry and agriculture companies) and the representatives of civil
society (NGOs who were in favor of migrants' rights).

But in 2017, after almost thirty years of trying to form coalitions between left- and
right-wing parties, consensus was achieved and the new law was presented and passed
both in the Senate and Congress with a huge majority and signed by the president.
Almost all the resolutions and norms created by the National Council of Migration
became articles in the new Migration Law approved on May 24, 2017, by the National
Congress.[35]

In addition to thirty types of work visas, the law expanded humanitarian visas and in
one of its provisions prioritized the regularization of migrants and decriminalization of
irregular migration. The humanitarian visa is supposed to be used for "refugee-like" situations where people are fleeing regions with inhumane living conditions due to natural
disasters or even famine, like in the case of Haiti. More than 100,000 Haitians were regularized under this regulation from the National Council of Immigration since 2012.[36]
The first intention of the government was also to use the humanitarian visa clause of the
migration law to accommodate Venezuelans who were applying for asylum in the country. By the end of 2019, the new secretary of justice who chairs the National Committee for Refugees (CONARE) decided otherwise. In her view, people fleeing because of
inhumane living conditions in their country of origin (lack of food and health care) are
covered under article 1 of the Brazilian Refugee Law, which defines refugees as "people
fleeing from a region of massive violation of human rights."[37] The other important aspect

---

35 www.planalto.gov.br/ccivil_03/_ato2015-2018/2017/lei/L13445.htm

36 https://portaldeimigracao.mj.gov.br/images/publicacoes-obmigra/Executive%20sum
mary%202019.pdf

37 www.justica.gov.br/news/collective-nitf-content-1564080197.57/sei_mj-8757617-estudo-de
-pais-de-origem-venezuela.pdf

of the law is that individuals without means will not need to pay for their visas to come to Brazil, which is different from the other types of work and residence visas.

Another important point is that the new law officially incorporates what was already established by the constitutions of 1988, meaning that all foreign residents should have the same rights as Brazilian nationals, including health care and education as well as social welfare. Under the new law, immigrants can also join labor unions and participate in strikes and protests, a sharp break with the previous law, which was based on the principle of national security whereby foreigners represented a threat, and the creation or even the participation of immigrants in political associations or parties was not permitted and could be grounds for deportation.

Regarding the protection of Brazilian migrants abroad, the Congress approved in 1994 a change in the 1988 Constitution that had restricted national citizenship to people born in the national territory. The change reinforces the dual conception of citizenship both by birth (*jus solis*) and by blood (*jus sanguinis*) for Brazilians born abroad when one of the parents has Brazilian nationality. The new law also facilitates money transfers, eliminating fees for remittances made by Brazilians abroad. The government knows that most remittances sent from young Brazilian migrants are intended to supplement the low pension income received by their parents in Brazil.

The law requires all administrative decisions regarding migrants to be well founded before an individual can be deported or denied naturalization. It makes clear that all administrative decisions can be contested in front of a federal judge in case of a conflict. The new law shows a clear intent to stop discretionary measures taken by the government regarding migrants. Despite these clear provisions, several administrative acts regarding foreigners have been contested in federal courts. The two most important court decisions concern, first, the refusal of entry of Haitians into Brazil and Peru (state of Acre) in 2011, and second, the recent case of the massive deportation of Venezuelans from the Brazil border state of Roraima in 2016. In both cases, public advocates represented the plaintiffs and they succeeded in suspending government decisions that were taken in the name of national security, based on the contention that this migratory influx represented a threat to public order.

Until now, human rights activists and NGOs have been invoking the Constitution in court cases in order to protect the rights of migrants and refugees. Before the full implementation of the new migration law, federal courts created a new jurisprudence with cases concerning the social rights of migrants, such as their rights to participate in political demonstrations and to have access to social security and public education. In most of the cases, migrants have succeeded in their demands and governments were obliged to step back and guarantee these constitutional rights. The judicialization of politics, or politics of rights according to activists, is well established in Brazil and reinforces the liberal paradox where states are eager to close borders in the name of national security and to protect the social contract but are unable to do so because of the pressure of legal activists to protect migrants' constitutional rights.[38] The liberal paradox is

---

38   James Hollifield, Philip L. Martin, and Pia M. Orrenius, eds., *Controlling Immigration: A Global Perspective* (Stanford, CA: Stanford University Press, 2014).

present in Brazil where the market and the politics of rights are strong forces against nationalistic and pro-securitization political groups that insist on the slogan "Brazil for Brazilians."

The extreme-right government that came into power in January 2019 did not present any new project to change the actual liberal migration law of 2017. However, the Minister of Justice Sergio Moro, in June 2019, signed a new regulation (Ordinance 666) to expedite the deportation of migrants consider to be a "danger to the National Security." The first article of Moro's ordinance makes clear the intent to define immigration as a national security problem and to portray migrants as a possible threat to the national interest, similar to the immigration law from the 1980s under the military dictatorship: "This Ordinance regulates the impediment of entry, repatriation, summary deportation, reduction or cancellation of the term of stay of a person dangerous to the security of Brazil . . . . The person who is subject to the deportation measure referred to in this Ordinance will be personally notified to present a defense or to leave the country voluntarily, within up to forty-eight hours, counted from the notification." "Moro's Ordinance 666" (later to become Ordinance 770[39]) violates not only the migration law and its stated objective to decriminalize immigration but also the Brazilian Constitution, which guarantees fundamental rights of due process and equal protection before the law with no distinction between nationals and foreigners. A few weeks after the promulgation of Ordinance 666,[40] the head of the Public Prosecutor's Office (PPO), an agency of the Brazilian judicial system and independent from the government,[41] questioned the constitutionality of the ordinance at the Brazilian Constitutional Court (Supremo Tribunal Federal). According to the head of the PPO, Raquel Dodge, the ordinance represented an assault on "the dignity of all individuals" and ignored the legal protection that the Constitution guarantees to all individuals, foreigners as well as nationals. Despite the challenge by the head of the PPO against the Ministry of Justice, the ordinance is still in place. But according to records, no lawyer or public defender has registered in their files any case of deportation based on the Moro ordinance, which suggests that the ordinance is alive on paper but not in action. The Department of Migration still had not answered the official demand made by one civil society organization as to whether the ordinance has been implemented and, if so, in what circumstances.[42]

Argentina

Historically, Argentina was the first country in Latin America to implement a clearly liberal immigration law. The Avellaneda law dates from 1876 and remained in effect for a little more than a century despite the restrictive measures created against migration

---

39   www.in.gov.br/web/dou/-/portaria-n-770-de-11-de-outubro-de-2019-221565769

40   www.in.gov.br/en/web/dou/-/portaria-n-666-de-25-de-julho-de-2019-207244569

41   To know more about the Public Prosecutor's Office, see Fabio Kerche, "The Brazilian Councils of Justice and Public Prosecutor's Office as Instruments of Accountability," *Revista de Administração Pública* 54, no. 5 (September–October 2020), www.scielo.br/scielo.php?script=sci_arttext&pid=S0034-76122020000501334&lng=en&nrm=iso&tlng=en

42   www.connectas.org/Categoria/pais/brasil/

by the laws of 1902 and 1910.[43] The liberal 1876 law finally was repealed by the military regime in 1981. Besides the explicit intent to bring migrants from Europe to settle in the country (similar to policies of many US states in the nineteenth century; see Foley and Tichenor, this volume), the most important goal of the 1876 law was to establish and guarantee equal rights among Argentineans and foreign citizens. The migration law enacted by the military regime in 1981 is based on the legal and mercantilist doctrine of "national security," protecting the national labor market from foreign competition, expediting deportations and summary expulsions, and granting broad discretionary power to the government in controlling the entry of foreigners.

The period of Raul Affonsin's government (1984–99), the first president elected after the end of the military dictatorship, can be considered a transitional period that did not change the law but made some decisions in favor of increasing immigration. The Affonsin government implemented an amnesty for irregular migrants and took several decisions to facilitate emigration of nationals from bordering countries.[44] During this period, several regional laws were also passed to allow migrants in different cities to vote in municipal and regional elections. These decisions make Argentinean migration policies far more liberal than other countries in South America that still do not grant political rights to foreign residents. The next government (1989–99), under the presidency of Carlos Menem, did not succeed in passing a new migration law but took strong measures to facilitate immigration. The Menem government implemented a new amnesty for irregular migrants and signed several agreements with bordering countries and Peru to facilitate labor migration. The government also granted Argentineans living abroad the right to vote in presidential elections. Beginning in 1993, Argentineans living abroad were allowed to vote in legislative elections and to elect their own representatives to the national Congress.

Much like Brazil, Argentina took over twenty years to repeal the immigration laws based on a national security logic that dated from the period of military rule. Only in December 2005 did the Argentinean Congress and Senate approve a new migration law based on the doctrine of human rights.[45] One provision of this law extended the rights of individuals to migrate, requiring the government to guarantee the rights of migrants: "The right to migrate is essential and inalienable of all people and the Republic of Argentina guarantees this right based on the principles of equality and universality."[46] Migrants also would come to enjoy social rights such as public education and healthcare, the civil rights of due process and equality before the law, the right to counsel, the right to family

43   Nejamkis and García, "Legislación y políticas migratorias en Argentina."

44   Susana Novick, *Politias migratórias en La Argentina: Experiencias del pasado, reformas actuales y expectativas futuras* (Buenos Aires: Consejo Nacional de Investigaciones cinetificas y técnicas, 2010).

45   www.migraciones.gov.ar/pdf_varios/campana_grafica/pdf/Libro_Ley_25.871.pdf

46   Article 4 states: "El derecho a la migración es esencial e inalienable de la persona y la República Argentina lo garantiza sobre la base de los principios de igualdad y universalidad." http://servicios .infoleg.gob.ar/infolegInternet/anexos/90000-94999/92016/texact.htm

reunification, and political rights, including the right to vote in and to stand as a candidate in local elections.

The 2005 law provided for the regularization of undocumented migrants, including those who were stateless and those who had overstayed their visa. The law halted deportation retroactively, empowering migration agencies to use every means to regularize the undocumented foreign population. As with the Brazilian amnesties, Chinese and Latin American migrants made up the majority of the population regularized by the law. The program of regularization took place from 2006 to 2009 and many stateless people from Bolivia, Peru, and Paraguay received their papers. The government regularized over 600,000 people just from these three countries. The national government worked with local authorities to provide better protection for the economic, social, and medical needs of the migrants.

Concerning citizenship, Argentina had since the nineteenth century both *jus solis* and *jus sanguinis* in its nationality law. After the 2005 migration law, the government made some adjustments to accommodate Argentineans living abroad and their families, with special provisions for the children of Argentinean nationals born abroad. Expatriates have five years after the birth of a child to register the child in an Argentinean consulate or embassy. When the child turns eighteen, s/he has up to three years to apply for Argentinean nationality.[47]

The judicialization of immigration politics is a powerful force in Argentina. Civil society organizations and public advocates have used the courts to protect migrants from deportation and summary expulsions. The most important legal battle now is the one concerning President Mauricio Macri's executive order of 2017 (DNU 70/2017—Decreto de Necesidad de Urgencia) barring entry of migrants with criminal records and providing for expedited removal of those individuals who have committed crimes in Argentina.[48] The Center for Legal and Social Studies (CELS) and the Argentine Commission for Refugees and Migrants (CAREF) have challenged the constitutionality of this decree in the courts. In the first instance, federal judge Ernesto Marinelli rejected the challenge. But in March of 2018, the Chamber of Federal Administrative Litigation agreed with the civil society organizations and declared the decree unconstitutional.

The Court ruled that governing by decree (executive order) in this area is unconstitutional. Two of the three judges pointed out that the decree "establishes a series of restrictions on the right to due process that are not consistent with the aims that the law claims to pursue" and that the decree "infringes on the lawmaking function of the legislature and thus violates the constitution"; moreover, the decree pursues remedies that are incompatible with human rights law and the constitution. The government appealed to the Supreme Court of Justice of the Nation (CSJN—Corte Suprema de Justicia de la Nación). Following legal maneuvers, the CSJN asked the general federal prosecutor to analyze the admissibility of the case before the court and the constitutionality of the decree in question. The prosecutor contested both the admissibility of the case and, implicitly, the

---

47   www.acnur.org/fileadmin/Documentos/BDL/2001/0120.pdf?view=1

48   www.migraciones.gov.ar/pdf_varios/residencias/Decreto_70-2017.pdf

constitutionality of the decree by declaring: "I understand that the grievances contained in the appeal are but a mere repetition of statements that fail to overturn the lower court ruling . . . . I therefore think that the extraordinary appeal filed by the government is inadmissible."[49] The Court generally tends to agree and to follow the federal prosecutor's position in most such cases. However, a recent judgment adopted by the Court (the "Barrios Rojas" case[50]), supporting the migratory authorities' decision to deport a woman who had resided in the country for almost twenty years with a family and strong social ties, shows how far the Court will go in following the arguments of the minister of justice (a position which corresponds to that of the US attorney general).

A new left-wing government came to power in Argentina in December 2019, promising to abolish the "Macri Decree," but almost a year after the election, the government has yet to make good on its campaign promise.[51] That said, deportations and summary expulsions have gone down dramatically since the new government came to power.[52] But civil society organizations and public advocates say that there are still many cases outstanding before the courts, seeking to halt deportation and expulsion orders based on the Macri Decree. Indeed, following these measures, civil society organizations expect that soon a derogation of the decree will come, either by a Supreme Court of Justice decision or an "executive order" from the new government.

Mercosur and Beyond

The long process of economic and political integration in Latin America (Mercosur) reached a major turning point in November 2002 when the freedom of mobility in the region became a topic during the Mercosur meeting. The migration agreement signed at that time among the four members of Mercosur (Argentina, Brazil, Uruguay, and Paraguay), along with Bolivia and Chile, established a compromise for a "definitive regularization" of all nationals from the region living in one of the other countries that are parties to the agreement. Soon after, all countries also signed the Brasilia Agreement on free movement, right of residence, and right to work for all nationals belonging to the member states that constitute the "Amplified Mercosur agreement" (Argentina, Brazil, Paraguay, Uruguay, Bolivia, and Chile). In 2012, Peru, Colombia, and Ecuador also joined this agreement. While Colombia ratified the agreement in the same year, Ecuador did so only in 2014. Bolivians are a good example of the success of this Free Movement and Right of Residence Agreement. Over 600,000 Bolivians live in Brazil and over a million live in Argentina. All were regularized by the amnesty programs implemented in

49   www.fiscales.gob.ar/procuracion-general/la-procuracion-opino-que-es-inadmisible-el -recurso-de-la-direccion-nacional-de-migraciones-contra-la-sentencia-que-declaro-la-inconsti tucionalidad-del-dnu-702017/

50   www.saij.gob.ar/descarga-archivo?guid=rstuvwfa-llos-comp-uest-020000132pdf&name =20000132.pdf

51   www.clarin.com/politica/alberto-fernandez-dijo-dnu-mauricio-macri-expulsar-extranjeros -peligroso-confirmo-evalua-derogarlo_0_v-Cbs5ZK.html

52   www.facebook.com/watch/live/?v=2395130734117503&ref=watch_permalink

both countries but mostly they benefited from the Mercosur agreement on regularization and right of residence. Since the ratification of the agreement by Bolivia in 2008, an average of 15,000 Bolivians applied for the Mercosur residence visa to work and live in Brazil according to the most recent data.

In 2012, Venezuela joined Mercosur but did not sign all the protocols and agreements. For example, Venezuela resisted signing the agreements on free movement, and the rights to residence and to work. When the Venezuelan government decided to do so it was too late, and by December 2016, Mercosur member states excluded Venezuela from the bloc due to their "violation of the democratic order." Whereas upholding democratic principles is considered one of the pillars governing Mercosur, recent moves by President Maduro in Venezuela were deemed to be authoritarian and to run counter to the democratic norms of the bloc. Because of the large number of Venezuelan migrants escaping the political and economic crisis of the country, the Brazilian National Council of Immigration made a legal resolution in March 2017 allowing all Venezuelans to apply for a two-year residence permit that grants them the right to work, the benefit of public health care, education, and other social services.

In 2004, Mercosur signed a cooperation agreement with the Andean Community of Nations (Comunidad de los paises Andinos) that comprises Bolivia, Peru, Colombia, Ecuador, and Venezuela. The agreement is on free trade but also reinforces the already existing agreement on free movement and the right of residence of the nationals from the region. These states also signed a letter of intent to accelerate South American political integration by creating a common citizenship for nationals of member states and a single passport. The idea behind this initiative is to deepen not only the economic but also the social and political integration of the region.

With this initiative in mind, the twelve South American countries signed the Constitutive Treaty of the Union for South American Nations—USAN or UNASUR (Union de las Naciones Suramericans). The treaty does not replace Mercosur or the Andean Community of Nations because it is still only an intergovernmental regional organization and not fully institutionalized. But the hope is to launch a common foreign policy, a single free market, and a common citizenship throughout the region. The agenda of the UNASUR initiative is to unify Mercosur and the Andean Community, plus the other countries from the region outside these agreements, Guyana and Suriname. The Union capital is in Quito, and the organization's objective is to be highly active and play an important role in conflict resolution among countries in the region. The Union has made a strong commitment to political integration. However, the Venezuelan political crisis and the coming to power of new right-wing governments in the region has sidelined the UNASUR integration project for the last two years.

Migration governance remains, however, a topic of constant discussion in the annual meeting of Mercosur ministers of interior and justice (what the British and Europeans call justice and home affairs or JHA). Still much depends on which minister and which government is chair of the meeting of ministers. The agenda of the working group is to manage the migrant flows in the region more efficiently and, above all, to facilitate freedom of movement of South American citizens in the region. The ministries and agencies in charge of refugees in each country have their own broader agenda. Following the

Cartagena Declaration in 1984, many countries in Latin America, including the Caribbean, Central America, and Mexico, meet every ten years to consider a common plan of action for managing refugee flows and asylum seeking in the region. The last meeting in Brasilia in 2014 laid out a series of compromises to expand the definition of a refugee based on Cartagena to include individuals fleeing countries where there is a clear violation of human rights. The Brasilia group also outlined a common policy to deal with large refugee flows in the region starting with the Colombians, then to people from Central America, especially the Northern Triangle countries, and now the flood of Venezuelans. This series of migration and refugee laws, agreements, and treaties in Latin America show that the region has strong normative pillars for building a liberal migration and refugee regime that allows for better governance of migration not only from Latin America but also to Latin America from other parts of the world.

The Exodus of Venezuelans: Testing the Limits of Migration Governance in Latin America

In 2018, Venezuela was second only to Syria as to the number of its nationals fleeing the country. According to IOM and UNCHR data, more than 5 million Venezuelans have fled the country as a result of the political, social, and economic crises. Comparable to large migratory flows in other regions of the world (see particularly Thiollet, Tsourapas, and Klotz, this volume), the great majority of Venezuelan migrants and refugees are fleeing to neighboring countries: Colombia (1.72 million), Peru (1.04 million), Ecuador (300,000), Chile (450,000), Brazil (260,000), Argentina (210,000), and on a smaller scale to other countries in Latin America, the Caribbean, and even to North America. As noted above, Venezuela is not fully integrated into the Mercosur protocols on free movement or the UNASUR initiative to create a South American passport, which is yet to be implemented. To some extent, Venezuela's neighbors are free to apply their own migration and refugee policies without any intraregional legal constraints. However, because Venezuela is part of the Mercosur free trade regime, and a party to the UNASUR agreement as well as other economic treaties with neighboring countries, the leeway to impose border controls and to restrict migration is limited by (1) regional economic and political integration regimes already in place; (2) other migration rules, like the agreement on visa-free travel among countries in the region; and (3) the constraints of judicial activism, whereby civil society organizations and public advocacy groups are able to invoke liberal immigration and refugee laws against the governments' desire to restrict the flows of Venezuelan migrants. At the end of the day, countries in the region have respected liberal economic arrangements and rules governing migration, despite some governments' attempts to impose restrictions on the movement of Venezuelan nationals.

Looking at the two largest, emerging migration states in the region, Brazil was the first to be foiled in its attempt to implement a massive deportation of Venezuelans at the beginning of the exodus, which put great pressure on the northern border. In December 2016, the federal police moved to deport around 450 Venezuelans who were living in Boa Vista, the capital of the state of Roraima that shares a border with Venezuela. Before the deportation order, the Venezuelans were held in the federal police facility without access to counsel or civil society organizations. The federal police were acting based on a provision of the old 1980 immigration law that permits summary deportation of foreigners in an irregular status, if their presence is contrary to the national or public interest. A public advocate used several legal instruments to fight the deportation: (1) the principle of habeas corpus prohibits the detention of the Venezuelans; (2) Article 5 of the Brazilian Constitution guarantees fundamental rights to all individuals, not just citizens, including the right to equal treatment and due process of law; (3) Article 22.9 of the American Convention on Human Rights is incorporated into Brazilian law and states that "collective expulsion of Aliens is prohibited"; (4) deportation of the Venezuelans violates the principle of "non refoulement" because many of them were asylum seekers. An injunction suspended the deportation and it was followed by a federal judge decision ruling:

> Even though the deportation agency is an instrument used for the removal of the national territory of those who are in an irregular situation, one cannot lose sight of the fact that the administrative decision approving the deportation violates the due process of law, in view of the fact that the Constitution guarantees equal treatment between Brazilians and foreigners residing in Brazil (art. 5, caput) . . . this postulate, which undoubtedly constitutes one of the pillars of the Democratic Rule of Law, guarantees the individual not only the right to know about issues that may interfere in his/her legal sphere, but also participation, allowing him/her to influence what is decided (substantial due process of law).

This targeted lawsuit by a public defender in Brazil dramatically altered the federal government's response to the Venezuelan exodus. Following the decision handed down by the federal judge in December 2016, the government developed several new administrative rules to regulate and facilitate the access to temporary residence cards for the Venezuelans, and in 2020, the National Committee on Refugees (CONARE) decided to recognize as refugees more than 40,000 Venezuelans, based on the Cartagena principle that defines a refugee as a "person fleeing from a region where human rights are violated on a large scale." Another important aspect of the administrative reforms that is unique to Brazil is the creation of a humanitarian operations center at the border. The so-called "welcome operation" is led by the Brazilian army with the help of several other federal agencies, international organizations like UNHCR, IOM, and UNICEF, and national and international NGOs, which together set up at least thirteen humanitarian shelters able to house, feed, and offer basic assistance to all migrants arriving at the border. Part of the plan is to facilitate the relocation of migrants to other more economically prosperous cities in different states of the federation like Sao Paulo and Rio de Janeiro. More than 44,000 migrants have already been resettled in approximately 400 cities around the country.[53] There are four types of resettlements: (1) employment by a specific company that needs skills offered by the migrants, such as food processing plants that have employed thousands of Venezuelans; (2) shelter to shelter—Venezuelans stay in a new shelter in a host city for three to six months until they find a job; (3) family reunification, when the migrants' family members have sufficient income to host their relatives; and

---

53 www.gov.br/acolhida/historico/

Table 14.3. Trip cost and mode of transportation (in USD), by host country, 2019.

Country	Less than $100	$100–500	$500–1000	More than $1,000	Unknown	Mode of Transportation**
	Share of Respondents* Who Paid					
Argentina	1%	27%	44%	22%	6%	Air (75%)
Brazil	77%	10%	0%	0%	13%	Land (100%)
Chile	1%	34%	44%	19%	2%	Air (81%)
Costa Rica	0%	12%	48%	37%	2%	Air (95%)
Ecuador	22%	71%	5%	1%	1%	
Guyana	20%	79%	1%	0%	0%	Sea (81%)
Paraguay	5%	47%	29%	13%	7%	Land (61%)
Trinidad and Tobago	7%	80%	5%	1%	6%	Sea (88%)
Uruguay	1%	27%	49%	21%	3%	Air (57%)

* No data were collected for the questions on trip cost in Colombia and Peru.
** No data were collected for the question on mode of transportation in Colombia, Ecuador, and Peru.
Source: MPI publication with IOM from DTM, collected between January and December 2019

(4) civil society sponsorship programs, including associations of Brazilian or foreign families that are able to host and receive Venezuelans.

Unlike Brazil, the flow of Venezuelans to Argentina was less problematic. Argentina was among the first countries to recognize that the Mercosur agreement on the right to residence would apply to Venezuelans. Since the beginning of the migration crisis, Argentina decided to respect the right of Venezuelans to enter and reside on its territory. The type of migrants arriving in Argentina is completely different from those arriving in Brazil. Because of the distance traveled, most of the migrants are middle class and they are able to pay for the long flights from Venezuela to Argentina. A study presented by the "Migration Policy Institute" reinforces this point.[54] Table 14.3 shows both the travel costs and mode of transportation of migrants who arrived in Argentina, Brazil, and other countries in the region.

Most of the migrants to Argentina are skilled workers who could more easily find a job. Venezuelan migrants in Argentina and Chile have higher levels of education compared to the ones who migrated to other countries in the region. In Argentina, many of the Venezuelans are working in the oil and gas sector.

Low-skilled migrants are in a more precarious situation socially and economically. Table 14.4 shows the difficulties Venezuelans face when fleeing to different countries in the region. . These data also reflect integration policies in host countries like Brazil, which has an active policy, compared to others like Guyana, which has no plan for receiving the Venezuelans and where civil society organizations are not active in offering shelter, food, and basic healthcare.

---

54   www.migrationpolicy.org/sites/default/files/publications/mpi-iom_venezuelan-profile_english-final.pdf

TABLE 14.4 Main Challenges Respondents Reported Facing on Their Journeys, by Host Country, 2019

Country	Lack of Financial Resources	Access to Food	No Place to Sleep	Lack of Transportation	Lack of Safety	Issues with Migration Documents	Lack of Information	Health	Arrests
Argentina	14%	8%	24%	23%	29%	24%	9%	5%	1%
Brazil	48%	34%	27%	39%	26%	8%	12%	10%	2%
Chile	4%	0%	0%	0%	0%	0%	0%	0%	0%
Colombia	91%	46%	31%	48%	28%	31%	56%	21%	2%
Costa Rica	60%	17%	13%	4%	32%	18%	13%	15%	0%
Ecuador	62%	29%	24%	16%	30%	19%	51%	17%	2%
Guyana	71%	80%	66%	35%	6%	6%	10%	9%	1%
Paraguay	13%	32%	28%	12%	20%	28%	12%	20%	0%
Peru	48%	20%	8%	47%	23%	24%	14%	14%	8%
Trinidad and Tobago	14%	14%	11%	6%	10%	5%	6%	4%	4%
Uruguay	32%	16%	25%	16%	29%	19%	16%	8%	3%

Notes: The sample size for this question was 78 (Argentina), 317 (Brazil), 79 (Chile), 6,811 (Colombia), 175 (Costa Rica), 3,698 (Ecuador), 306 (Guyana), 25 (Paraguay), 2,166 (Trinidad and Tobago), and 140 (Uruguay). Other challenges include deportations, which in no case exceeded 2 percent of a country's sample.
Source: MPI publication with IOM, data collected between January and December 2019

These data also show how the financial condition of the migrants drives the response of governments in the region. Lower-income migrants are more vulnerable, and their need for protection necessitates a humanitarian response that mobilizes not only national governments but also international agencies, organizations and NGOs. The flow of Venezuelans to Argentina never became a humanitarian crisis as was the case in countries bordering Venezuela, such as Colombia, Peru, Brazil, and Ecuador, which faced political pressure to close borders and restrict the entry of migrants from the beginning of the crisis but which also were compelled to compromise and abandon harsh policies because of legal constraints and active judiciaries. Most of these countries now offer Venezuelans temporary residence cards. And in the case of Peru, the government has allowed Venezuelans to apply for asylum.

Emerging migration states in Latin America are trapped in a liberal paradox insofar as they face economic forces that push them toward greater openness, while security concerns and powerful conservative political forces push them toward closure. The management of migration as proposed by the United Nations Global Compact provides a solution to the paradox. The goal to overcome the security dilemma and the securitization of migration promoted by some politicians and the open borders dilemma that arises from economic needs is to have a "safe, orderly and regular migration" into the country as spelled out in the Global Compact. These three characteristics are key factors that reveal whether a country is or is not a "migration state." This is an idealistic position that only an island country very isolated in the ocean would be able to achieve. Nonetheless, "safe, orderly and regular migration" should be the guiding principles that all states pursue to overcome the liberal paradox and to avoid falling into a nationalist, beggar-thy-neighbor policy, which is a no-win situation for all concerned.[55]

By developing free trade agreements alongside freedom of movement and the right to residence, states in South America have paved the way for more legal, orderly, and regular migration. On the one hand, South America is taking an approach similar to that of the EU (see Geddes, this volume), but on the other, it is going beyond the EU model by allowing asylum seekers to move to other to countries in the region (contrary to the European Dublin convention),[56] and coping with the refugee and migration crisis through the creation of good practices reflected by the policies to welcome and receive refugees instead of transferring this population to a third safe country, such as Europe did with Turkey when dealing with the Syrian migration flow to the European continent.

Both Europe and South America learned from their freedom of mobility agreement: freedom to migrate inside the region simultaneously brings "order" to the flows and the legality of this migration gives states greater control allowing them to cooperate and to ensure public "safety." Better regional governance of migration does not eliminate demographic and political pressures, as the Venezuelan crisis attests. Humanitarian and migration crises can destabilize even the best migration states and undermine regional migration regimes (like the 2015–16 crisis in Europe; see Geddes and Adamson, this volume), provoking a populist backlash as happened in the United States and Western Europe, creating economic and social burdens for some countries like Colombia, Peru, Ecuador, and Brazil and less for others like Argentina and Chile.

As this chapter shows, despite populist backlash and right-wing politicians coming to power in the region (right-wing Argentinian president Macri in 2015, extreme-right president Bolsonaro in 2018), the South American migration regime remains strong. It was conceived over two decades ago by a majority of center-right governments in the region. The chapter demonstrates that the South American migration regime is not easily changed by the arrival of conservative governments in the region. The huge flow of Venezuelans to neighboring countries tested the strength of this regime. The positive responses of the countries in the region to welcome this population proves that the norms of freedom of movement in South America are strong enough and that the national judiciaries in the region have been willing to play an essential role in reinforcing such norms against the attempts of conservative governments to close borders.

---

55   https://refugeesmigrants.un.org/sites/default/files/180711_final_draft_0.pdf

56   https://eur-lex.europa.eu/legal-content/EN/TXT/PDF/?uri=CELEX:41997A0819(01)& from=EN

PART 5

EUROPE, TURKEY, AND THE LIBERAL AND "POSTIMPERIAL" MIGRATION STATE

15   MIGRATION GOVERNANCE IN TURKEY

Fiona Adamson

IN 2020, TURKEY HOSTED more refugees than any state in the world, and its location at the intersection of multiple regions and migration routes makes it a key player in regional migration governance. It has captured headlines by taking in more than three million Syrian refugees who have fled the civil war in neighboring Syria. Its geographic position on the border of the European Union means that it has been viewed as central to European efforts to control its borders and reduce migration into Europe—the most visible illustration of this has been the 2015 and 2016 deals struck between the EU and Turkey that involve large aid packages from the EU in exchange for enhanced migration control by Turkey.

Yet Turkey's significance for understanding global migration governance goes beyond its current role in hosting refugees. It is an important case that highlights a number of features of the contemporary "migration state"—especially in the global South (Hollifield 2004; Adamson and Tsourapas 2020). Turkey is simultaneously a country of immigration, emigration, and transit migration. It also has a history of contested nation-building, which shapes aspects of its approach to migration governance. In addition, Turkey is at best an unconsolidated democracy and at worst a country with many features of authoritarianism. All these factors suggest the need to unpack the "migration state" concept and understand how migration management works in contexts beyond liberal democracies in Europe and North America (see also Chung, Thiollet, and Tsourapas, this volume).

As a "postimperial" migration state, Turkey provides a useful example of the complexity of governance issues faced by states vis-à-vis the cross-border mobility of people, and how these relate to other factors such as a country's history, geographic location, domestic politics, security concerns, and foreign relations. Turkey faces numerous challenges related to complex and mixed migration flows, which involve linkages to a range of economic, humanitarian, and security factors. Finally, the case of Turkey also illustrates both the power and limits of state-centric approaches to migration. In Turkey, state policy and interests are central to understanding migration governance—but these are not the only factors. A full picture of migration governance in the region also involves paying attention to the role of nonstate actors, such as civil society groups, non-state armed organizations, and gray economy networks, as well as subnational regions and entities such as cities.

In this chapter, I examine some of the dynamics of migration governance in Turkey, placing the Syrian refugee crisis in its broader historical and geographical context and showing how migration dynamics in Turkey affect—and are affected by—its economic interests, domestic politics, and foreign policy goals. The chapter begins with a discussion of the nature of the "migration state" in Turkey, tracing its emergence from the ruins of one of the world's great empires, and pointing to the importance of migration policy as a component of modern state-building. It moves on to discuss how the development of the migration state in Turkey has been influenced by regional and geopolitical dynamics, including its position at the crossroads of Europe, the Middle East, and Eurasia. It then discusses how migration has interacted with Turkey's economic interests over time, with a particular focus on the history of Turkish labor emigration to Europe, and the subsequent emergence of state diaspora engagement policies. This is followed by a discussion of how the domestic and regional security context relates to issues of migration and mobility, especially with respect to Turkey's Kurdish conflict and the Syrian civil war. The chapter then moves on to discuss two contemporary issues—Turkey's response to the Syrian refugee crisis, and its attempts to use the issue of migration as a tool of diplomacy and a means of projecting state power—before concluding with some thoughts on the strength and limits of the "migration state" concept as applied to Turkey.

The Historical Context: From Empire to Nation-State

The contemporary state of Turkey emerged out of the remnants of one of the great historical empires—the Ottoman Empire, which at the height of its power in the seventeenth century stretched from the area of modern Algeria in the west, to Hungary, the Balkans, and the Black Sea region in the north, to contemporary Egypt, Saudi Arabia, Jordan, Israel/Palestine, Lebanon, Syria, and Iraq in the south and east. The transformation of this central core of the empire into a modern-day republic and nation-state provides the backdrop for understanding the emergence and dynamics of the contemporary "migration state" in Turkey. As both a former imperial power and a relatively new nation-state, Turkey's history of migration has been closely tied to broader postimperial state- and nation-building processes (Cooper 2005; Klotz 2013; Adamson and Tsourapas 2020).

As the political scientist Aristide Zolberg noted, the formation of new states is often accompanied by the generation of large flows of refugees (Zolberg 1983). The transition from the Ottoman Empire to modern Turkey was no different in this respect. The early period of the Turkish state can be characterized as a period of state-formation and nation-building in which state migration policies were utilized to forge a national state from what was left of the old empire. This included state management of policies of forced migration, such as population exchanges, expulsions, and ethnic cleansing. The political transformation from empire to nation-state involved a significant shift in how populations were organized and managed—from a vast multiethnic space characterized by internal mobility and shifting frontier zones to a clearly demarcated territorial state defined by linear borders and a homogenous national identity. As part of this process of nationalization numerous population movements occurred—including large outflows of Armenians and other Christian minorities toward the end of the empire, as well as exchanges of Muslim ("Turkish") and Christian ("Greek") populations at the beginning of the Republican period in the 1920s (Yildirim 2007; Robson 2017, 74; Hirschon 2003; Triadafilopoulos 1998).

This forceable "unmixing" of populations was viewed in many cases "as a legitimate, internationally sanctioned form of state building" by international actors such as the League of Nations at the time (Robson 2017, 74). It resembled other instances of the un-mixing of populations that have occurred in the wake of the collapse of large land-based empires—such as the Austro-Hungarian Empire in Central and Eastern Europe or the Soviet Union at the end of the Cold War (Brubaker 1996). Forced expulsions, population exchanges, and the generation of refugee flows are not usually studied as migration-related policies. Nevertheless, if migration is defined as the movement of people across borders, these constitute significant examples of forms of "migration governance" in the first half of the twentieth century.

Nation-building in Turkey involved processes of "Turkification" or a homogenization of national identity within the new borders of the state, including various non-Turkish areas, such as the largely Kurdish areas in the southeast area of the new country (Yildiz 2001). At the same time, the Turkish state also used immigration policies during its first decades of existence—and beyond—to promote the development of an ethno-religiously defined Turkish identity, encouraging the migration of Muslims from a variety of states in the Balkans (Akgündüz 1998; Içduygu and Sert 2015; Kirişci 2000). This is no differ-ent, of course, from the many other states that have historically used migration policy as a form of nation-building (Zolberg 2006; Triadafilopoulos 2004). From 1934 to 2006 migration to Turkey was governed by Turkey's Law on Settlement, which prioritized "Turkish descent and culture" as a criteria for allowing immigration. Indeed, the re-lationship between migration and "nation-building" in Turkey has continued to be a significant factor in migration governance—even up to the present day. Expulsions of minority populations continued throughout the history of modern Turkey, including Greek populations in the 1950s–60s.[1] Moreover, struggles over national identity have led to widespread internal migration and displacements within Turkey from the 1980s onward in the context of the Turkish state's conflict with the Kurdistan Workers' Party (PKK) in the southeast of the country (Ayata and Yükseker 2005). This concern about national identity also extends to more contemporary debates surrounding the impact of the influx of large numbers of Arab Syrian populations into Turkey since 2011, including in the traditionally Kurdish areas of the southeast. In addition, a new global context in the twenty-first century has brought about new forms of "transnational nation-building" in which Turkey has used policies of engagement with its diaspora to extend and project its national identity into European states and elsewhere. All these dynamics will be dis-cussed in greater detail below.

---

1   Jay Walz, "Turks Expelling Istanbul Greeks: Community's Plight Worsens during the Crisis," *New York Times*, August 9, 1964.

The Geographical Context: Migration Dynamics at a Regional Crossroads

In addition to Turkey's history, Turkey's geographical location is significant for understanding the migration dynamics it faces. Turkey is linked to and part of migration systems in Europe, the Mediterranean, and the broader Middle East as well as the Caucasus and former Soviet Union. During much of its contemporary history, Turkey has been considered a labor-exporting and migration-sending state, although it has always also had migration inflows (Kirişçi 2007). Like many other states in the "global South," however, Turkey can now be considered simultaneously a sending, receiving, and transit state. It "sends" both high-skilled and low-skilled workers to Europe, the Middle East, and elsewhere. It receives low-skilled workers from neighboring countries, especially those in the Balkans, Eastern Europe, and the former Soviet Union. And it is a major transit state for migrants from countries farther afield such as Afghanistan, Pakistan, Bangladesh, and Iran who are trying to get to Europe (İçduygu and Yükseker 2012). These "mixed migration" flows, which include a combination of economic migrants and asylum seekers, as well as both regular and irregular migrants, are typical of many regions of the world and present challenges both to Turkey and, by extension, to Europe, which is often the desired final destination of migrants who pass through Turkey.

Like Mexico vis-à-vis the United States, Turkey is also affected by the policies of its European neighbors to the northwest (see Hazán and Geddes, this volume). The migration and asylum policies of European states, the border-control policies of the European Union, and the external pressures that Europe exercises on Turkey as a candidate country to join the European Union all have significant effects on Turkey's approach to migration and its ability to formulate autonomous migration policy. In addition, however—and as we shall see below in the discussion of the refugee crisis and the 2016 EU-Turkey migration deal—they also provide Turkey with unique forms of leverage and bargaining power in its relations with Europe (Greenhill 2016).

The pressures coming from Europe are multiple and at times contradictory. On the one hand, Turkey has faced pressure from the European Union to liberalize its migration and asylum policies in order to bring it into line with EU asylum laws as part of the overall process of accession, and in the broader context of EU harmonization of its asylum laws (Kirişçi 1996). Following Turkey's acceptance as an official candidate for membership in the European Union it began the process of negotiation and accession, which included the adoption of sets of laws and constitutional amendments to bring it into line with the requirements for EU membership, known as the Acquis Communautaire or the *acquis*. In 2005 Turkey produced a plan to modernize and update its migration and asylum laws to bring them into harmony with EU requirements. This eventually led to the 2013 Law on Foreigners and International Protection (LFIP), which was officially adopted in 2014 and which replaced the earlier Law on Settlement (İçduygu and Üstübici 2014).

At the same time, Turkey has faced equally strong pressure from Europe to control its borders and limit migration flows (see Geddes, this volume). The EU has often treated Turkey as a buffer zone between Europe and migration source countries to the south and east, especially the war-torn states of Syria and Iraq. This has occurred within the overall accession process of strengthening the external borders of the European Union but also within the larger policy of the externalization of EU migration control and its delegation of border control responsibilities to third-party states. These contradictory policies from Europe—e.g., simultaneously encouraging the liberalization and restriction of migration flows—are neither new nor limited to Turkey. The EU has had similarly contradictory policies toward Eastern European states in the 1990s via pre-accession programs such as TACIS, and toward Mediterranean states in the 2000s via the Barcelona process. More recently, the migration control deals struck with Turkey to control its borders can be understood as a larger effort by Europe to manage what it perceives as a "migration crisis" by pushing the border of Europe deeper into Europe's periphery and beyond. This includes enhanced border control and screening measures by states in the Maghreb, the Middle East, and sub-Saharan Africa (Andersson 2014; Charbit, this volume).

The relationship between Turkey and Europe in many ways embodies larger North-South dynamics in terms of pressures for migration control and border enforcement coming from "Northern" states at the same time that pressures for out-migration are increasing from "Southern" states. In Turkey's case, this dynamic is replicated on its own borders, and compounded with the outpouring of refugees from Syria and elsewhere, such as Afghanistan. Again, the similarities with Mexico, which is also facing an increase in migration from the south due to displacement and gang activity in Honduras and elsewhere, are striking (Hazán, this volume).

The "neighborhood effects" on migration flows to Turkey also demonstrate the ways in which geopolitics intersect with migration governance. Refugee flows from conflicts in Iraq, Afghanistan, and to some extent Syria are all in some respects "externalities" of US and NATO policies in the region, which included the invasion and extended counterinsurgency campaign in Iraq 2003–11, as well as a now two-decade-long US-led war in Afghanistan that began in the wake of the September 11, 2001 terrorist attacks by al-Qaeda on New York and Washington, DC.

In a similar vein, large geopolitical changes, such as the end of the Soviet Union in 1991, precipitated new migration flows to Turkey from countries from the former Soviet Union, including Russia, the Caucasus, and Central Asia. Some of this included high-skilled migration, but much of it also included irregular migration, including a significant amount of circular migration from Russia and Eastern European states (Içduygu and Yükseker 2012, 448; Parla 2019). Georgia, which borders Turkey on the northeast, is also a significant source of migration to Turkey. On top of a historically large Georgian diaspora within Turkey (approximately 2.5 million), there have also been several waves of migration from Georgia to Turkey since the early 1990s. Since the establishment of a visa-free regime with Georgia in 2006, there is significant circular migration in the agricultural sectors for seasonal work, as well as the construction industry and domestic service sector (Hosner 2016; Kalça and Ari 2016). Turkey also has large numbers of female domestic workers from a number of other neighboring countries, as well as from countries from farther afield, such as the Philippines.

Migration and Development: From Labor Migration to Diaspora Engagement

The influx of economic migrants from neighboring regions to Turkey, especially since the 1990s, stands in stark contrast with much of modern Turkey's history as an emigration state (Kirişçi 2007). Starting from the 1960s and 1970s, Turkey encouraged the export of labor as part of its overall economic development strategy. Like many other countries in the global South, labor emigration was promoted as a means of reducing unemployment, alleviating the strain on the infrastructure that had resulting from massive internal rural to urban migration, and as a way of increasing foreign exchange reserves through remittances, which kept the value of the Turkish lira artificially high (Martin 1991).

Turkey began to send migrant workers to Germany and other states in Western Europe in the 1960s as part of a managed labor recruitment and "guest-worker" policy, resembling in some ways the US-Mexico Bracero Program policy of the 1940s (see Tichenor, this volume). In contrast with the Bracero Program, which focused on agricultural labor, Turkish migration to Europe was largely tied to industrial manufacturing jobs and organized via recruiting schemes as a means of address postwar Germany's need for additional labor during a period of rapid economic growth. German employers established a recruitment bureau in Istanbul in July 1960 in order to channel workers to firms in West Germany and Germany and Turkey signed a bilateral labor agreement in 1961. The bilateral agreement created an official framework for workers' migration, regulating issues such as migration levels, worker benefits, and the responsibilities of both the sending and receiving countries. It was revised in 1964 and similar agreements were signed with Austria, Belgium, and the Netherlands (1964) followed by agreements with France (1965) and Australia and Sweden (1967) (Akgündüz 1993, 155). Turkey entered into multiple labor agreements in order to fall "back on other countries if one showed signs of saturation and diminished absorption ability" (Bahadir 1979, 105). Indeed, following the 1973 oil embargo that precipitated an economic crisis and a decline in the need for labor migrants in Europe, Turkey signed additional agreements with Libya (1975), Jordan (1982), and Qatar (1986).

These arrangements were a common feature of labor migration during the period—in addition to Turkey, European countries such as Greece, Spain, Portugal, and Italy sent labor migrants to Germany and other European countries, just as former colonies such as Algeria, Tunisia, and Morocco, and India, Pakistan, and Bangladesh during this same period were sources of labor migration to France and Britain respectively (see also Lucassen, this volume). Labor remittances came to play a significant role in Turkey's economy. Official figures for annual workers' remittances ranged from between $1 billion and $2 billion annually between 1973 and 1986. The amount of unofficial transfers is likely to have been substantially higher. Between 1973 and 1975 official labor remittances equaled between 93.7 and 99.8 percent of exports in Turkey (Richards and Waterbury 1990, 390–91). In addition to the desire to ease unemployment and urban migration, and attract remittances, Turkish migration policy at the time was also viewed as a way of ensuring that workers would acquire new skills and training that could be tapped into later upon their return, when they would also bring with them foreign capital (Sayari 1986, 92–93).

The period of managed labor migration from Turkey to Germany and other countries in Western Europe illustrates the significant role that migration played as part of the economic development plans and state governance of Turkey's domestic economy at the time. Until 1973, during the *gastarbeiter* or guest-worker period of migration, over 700,000 Turkish workers migrated to Germany. Originally designed to be a temporary pool of labor, many workers stayed, brought families, and settled in Germany. Following restrictions on labor migration in the 1970s and 1980s, the populations nevertheless actually grew via family reunification policies, the migration of asylum seekers, and irregular migration. As the author Max Frisch famously said, "We asked for workers; we got people instead" (Rist 1979, 95).

This group of workers in Germany and elsewhere—along with high-skilled migrants, political exiles, and others—forms the basis of a considerable population of Turkish (or Kurdish)-origin people in Germany (approximately three million) and Europe (approximately five million), now sometimes referred to as "Euro-Turks" but which also are increasingly seen by the Turkish state as constituting a diaspora to be engaged with (Kaya 2011). Even in the early days of migration, however, Turkey was involved in the everyday lives of its citizens abroad in Europe. Thus, there were numerous forms of migration governance that related to the emigration of workers abroad—including policies that managed their exit and recruitment, the policies directed toward them while abroad, and the policies related to their potential "return" to Turkey (Tsourapas 2020). With regard to the latter, migration between Turkey and Germany over time became more circular and balanced; by 2013 approximately 50,000 Turks from Germany were returning to Turkey every year, and approximately 30,000 per year going to Germany.[2]

The management or courting of populations abroad can be seen as a type of migration governance that is common to labor-sending countries of emigration. Indeed, Turkey's policies toward its citizens abroad resemble the type of governance mechanisms that have been used in Europe by other emigration states in the 1960s and 1970s, such as those of Algeria, Tunisia, and Morocco in France (Brand 2006). From the onset, Turkey treated emigrants to Germany and elsewhere in Europe as temporary labor migrants who would remain citizens of Turkey and eventually return. During this period Turkey was involved in the governance and management of its citizens abroad via the provision of state religious, educational, and consular services in Europe (Østergaard-Nielsen 2003). Turkish citizens living in Germany and elsewhere in Europe registered births, marriages, and deaths with Turkish consulates, and received advice on pensions (Aydin 2014).

Turkey also sent state-funded teachers to teach Turkish lessons in German schools, as well as sending religious leaders or imams to Germany to cater to the growing population. It established the Turkish Islamic Union of the State Office of Religious Affairs (DITIB) in Cologne, Germany, which was organized under Turkey's Ministry of Religious Affairs (Diyanet) and which sent imams and other religious figures to Germany (Aksel 2014, 202). Turkey also for the first time passed a law allowing dual citizenship in Turkey in 1981 and included Turkish citizens abroad within its constitution in 1982, as well as establishing the Higher Coordination Council for Workers, which included the Social Affairs and Economic Affairs Committees that were designed to foster the attachments of citizens abroad to Turkey (Aksel 2014: 203–4).[3]

---

2 Erdem Güneş, "Turkey-Germany Migration Two-Way Street, Figures Show," *Hürriyet Daily News*, March 16, 2013.

3 Article 62 reads: "The Government takes measures to ensure family unity of the Turkish citizens working in foreign countries, to educate their children, to meet their cultural needs and to

Turkey's ongoing engagement with citizens abroad can be seen as a form of state "diaspora management" or "diaspora engagement" policy that has become increasingly common around the world, especially in states in the global South (Adamson 2019; Gamlen 2014; Délano and Gamlen 2014; Ragazzi 2014; Mylonas 2013; Varadarajan 2010). In 2010, a formal Office for the Turks Abroad and Related Communities (YTB) was established in Turkey. The office combined elements of earlier policies that had been aimed at Turkish citizens abroad in Europe as well as Turkish "ethnic kin" in the Balkans or former Soviet Union, in addition to managing international students on government scholarships (Öktem 2014, 13–16). Part of this strategy included leveraging the diaspora as a resource that could be utilized as a tool of state economic and lobbying power in order to increase Turkey's presence and influence in Europe (Aksel 2014, 205).

The case of Turkish emigration to Europe helps demonstrate the complexities of migration governance in countries in the global South. While much of what is considered to be "migration management" in Europe and North America involves immigration policy and border control or, alternatively, policies of integration, naturalization, and citizenship, labor-sending states have an additional layer of migration governance policies that can be conceptualized as the management of emigration and the governance of citizens and diasporas abroad. This adds an additional component to the "migration state" and also points to the ways in which the management of migration can at times lead not just to the governance of flows of people across state borders but also to the transnationalization and de-territorialization of some functions of the state as it adapts to a situation in which increasing numbers of its citizens live beyond its territorial borders (Adamson and Demetriou 2007).

Migration and Security: Transnational Repression, Conflict, and Displacement

Turkey's engagement with its diaspora abroad, however, has not just been a function of its economic interests or its desire to secure economic benefit via labor remittances. There has also been a security dimension to some Turkish state diaspora policies. Like other states, especially illiberal states facing challenges from internal opposition groups, Turkey has engaged in forms of transnational repression vis-à-vis some members of its diaspora (Moss 2016). In other words, it has sought to monitor and police opposition groups that operate in diaspora communities beyond the borders of the state. The Turkish state has for many years engaged in the surveillance and long-distance policing of opposition political activists in Germany, France, and elsewhere. The Kurdistan Workers' Party (PKK), which has been involved in an armed conflict with the Turkish state since 1984, has been the main target of Turkish state activities, although the state has also targeted other leftist organizations, dissident Islamist organizations, and—more recently, since an attempted coup in July 2016—members of a broader Islamic movement linked to Fethullah Gülen—a cleric residing in Pennsylvania of the United States whom President Recep Tayyip Erdoğan has accused of being behind the coup attempt (Adamson 2020).

---

provide social security, to protect their link to the motherland and to facilitate their coming back." See Aksel 2014, 203.

The actions of the Turkish state vis-à-vis organizations in the diaspora associated with the PKK points to the links between migration, governance, and security in the Turkish case, especially as it relates to the decades-long conflict between the Turkish state and the PKK—a separatist group that has fought in the past for independence and more recently for autonomy. The conflict has killed approximately 40,000 and displaced over a million people inside Turkey. In many respects, the conflict is also illustrative of the ways in which the issues of migration, security, and conflict become intertwined in particular contexts.

In the case of the Kurdish conflict in Turkey, there are numerous ways in which security and migration have become linked. First, the conflict created a large pool of internally displaced people within Turkey, as villagers from the southeast of the country were forced to evacuate the region and flee to neighboring cities or urban areas in the western part of the country. This largely took place during the 1990s, although renewed fighting has led to further displacements in recent years. Second, the conflict in the southeastern part of the country, and the domestic political situation in Turkey, led to the emigration of large numbers of political exiles, refugees, and asylum seekers to Europe and elsewhere. Following the military coup in 1980, for example, the government banned a number of political parties, and over 20,000 leftists were arrested around the country, including approximately 3,000 Kurdish activists accused of promoting separatism. During the period, a group of Kurdish intellectuals, activists, and militants had arrived in Western Europe as part of the approximately 60,000 political exiles who, according to Turkish government statistics, fled Turkey for political reasons following the 1980 military coup.[4]

Across all of Western Europe, almost 350,000 Turkish citizens applied for political asylum in various European countries between 1983 and 1994 (Faist 2000, 93). Throughout the period, the number of foreigners seeking admittance to Germany under its asylum policies rose by almost 8,000 percent. Thus, economic push and pull factors were transformed, to some extent, into a new set of political push and pull factors. These built upon earlier migration patterns and flows, as refugees and political asylum seekers from Turkey drew upon the networks that had been forged by previous economic migrants and made their way to Germany, continuing an established pattern of chain migration.[5]

It was members of this group that began to organize a Kurdish nationalist movement in Europe and establish European branches of the PKK's political wing, the ERNK, in a number of European states. In addition, Kurdish activists set out to mobilize and politicize segments of the "Turkish" immigrant communities in Europe, which had been established as a result of the migration patterns that had emerged during the 1960s and 1970s. This period can be viewed as a period in which a distinctively Kurdish diaspora identity and nationalist movement emerged in Europe. Kurdish political exiles from Turkey arguably set up a "diaspora engagement" policy that was managed largely via the PKK and was closely linked to the ongoing military conflict in southeastern Turkey. In 1982, the new constitution of Turkey had strictly prohibited the use of the Kurdish language, Kurdish publications, the establishment of Kurdish political parties, or other

---

4   *Hürriyet*, September 13, 1997.
5   See also Hazán, this volume, for parallels with the United States and Central America.

expressions of Kurdish identity. Expressions of Kurdish ethnicity were criminalized. Europe provided a space in which Kurdish intellectuals and activists could escape the repression of the Turkish state and work to codify and standardize a Kurdish language and culture by drawing on the opportunity structures that were available within Western European states, particularly Germany and Sweden. The 1990s thus saw a period of intense Kurdish activism in Europe in response to the shutting down of the political space in Turkey, which continued until the arrest of the PKK leader Abdullah Öcalan in 1999 and the admittance of Turkey as an official EU candidate in the same year, which stimulated a period of political liberalization related to the EU *acquis* process.

The existence of a politically active diaspora in Europe and elsewhere has impacted on the Kurdish conflict in Turkey in a number of ways. The diaspora in Europe has provided a space for political mobilization, fundraising, and recruitment for the conflict as well as publicizing it to new audiences in Europe (Adamson 2013). Networks in Europe have become linked to the conflict in the southeast of Turkey, which are in turn also linked to cross-border networks in neighboring countries such as Syria and Iraq. Political opposition in the diaspora has been treated as a security issue by the Turkish state, and indeed elements of the conflict have become transnationalized, diffusing aspects of the conflict from Turkey to communities in Europe, where rival groups compete for support from members of the diaspora.

The dynamics of the Kurdish conflict in Turkey have become more complicated following the outbreak of war in neighboring Syria in 2011. Kurdish populations are spread out across the region, inhabiting areas of Turkey, Syria, Iraq, and Iran. There are strong cross-border links in the region, stemming from the Ottoman era and including family and other ties that transcend state borders. The PKK has always operated across national borders: in the 1980s and 1990s the leadership of the PKK was based in Damascus, operated training camps in Lebanon, and had mountain bases in parts of Iraqi Kurdistan. Policies of border liberalization in the 2000s, which allowed free movement between Syria and Turkey, combined with the building of new translocal structures in the Kurdish population, strengthened ties across the borders of Turkey, Syria, and the Kurdish Regional Government (KRG), a region that obtained increasing autonomy following the 2003–11 Iraq war. In Syria, Kurdish groups closely affiliated with the PKK became involved in the Syrian civil war, especially in the fight against the so-called Islamic State (ISIL), and also established an autonomous quasi-state in the region called Rojava (Dal 2017).

The conflict in Syria and its links to the conflict in southeastern Turkey placed pressure on the management of the Turkish-Syrian border. On the one hand, the Turkish state had an interest in limiting the cross-border mobility of both Kurdish and Islamist fighters in the region. Southeastern Turkey became a gateway for foreign fighters entering the conflict in Syria—both for Islamist fighters supporting the Islamic State and anti-Islamist fighters fighting on the side of Kurdish groups. In addition, the spillover of the conflict in Syria included the spread of ISIL activities in Turkey. Between 2013–16 Turkey suffered numerous suicide bombings and terror attacks across the country, many of which were attributed to ISIL-linked groups. During this time there were contradictory pressures coming from the international community with respect to the Turkish-Syrian border. Keeping the border open potentially facilitated the activities of the Islamic State and other armed groups in the region, allowing for ISIL to bring in new recruits and supplies, sell oil and other commodities, and receive medical treatment and other assistance in the border regions of Turkey. Yet closing the border prevented refugees fleeing the conflict from crossing into Turkey. In a sense, the Turkish-Syrian border was an extreme example of the dilemmas faced by states in how to simultaneously facilitate the flows of some border-crossers while limiting the access of others.

Like other parts of the world in recent years, Turkey has tried to manage its border issues by building walls. In 2017 Turkey completed a 700-kilometer wall along most of its 900-kilometer border with Syria at a cost of 400 million USD. The wall includes a "system comprising of sophisticated lighting, sensors and security cameras." A further wall on the Iranian border was started in August 2017 as part of a new Integrated Border Security System. The wall is designed to deter smugglers and disrupt cross-border operations by Kurdish militants, but it also has the effect of separating local villages and families and disrupting long-standing trading routes.[6]

The Refugee Crisis

The conflict in Syria, in addition to affecting the dynamics of Turkey's Kurdish conflict and placing pressure on Turkish border regimes, also led to a massive outflow of refugees and displaced persons throughout the region. In 2018, Turkey hosted the largest number of Syrian refugees in the region (3.6 million registered), followed by Lebanon (2.2 million estimated, 1 million registered) and Jordan (1.2 million estimated, 600,000 registered). It is estimated that in 2018 Turkey hosted approximately 65 percent of all registered Syrian refugees in the region.[7]

While Turkey is a member of the 1951 United Nations Convention Relating to the Status of Refugees (and adopted the Convention's 1967 Protocol), its original instrument of accession limited its application only to refugees coming from Europe.[8] In a strict legal sense, then, Turkey can only accept European asylum seekers as "refugees." Nevertheless, Turkey has allowed the United Nations High Commissioner for Refugees (UNHCR) to operate within its boundaries and conduct Refugee Status Determination with the understanding that those who are given such status will be resettled in a third country. For refugees within its boundaries, Turkey offers temporary protection rather than permanent resettlement. Most Syrians in Turkey have been provided with a temporary protection status under Turkish domestic law. Under the 2014 Law on Foreigners and International Protection (LFIP) non-European refugees can be given a "conditional refugee status, humanitarian residence permit or temporary protection" until they are

---

6   Burak Akinci, "Spotlight: After Syria, Turkey Is Building Second Security Wall along Border with Iran; Iraq May Be Next," *Xinhua Net*, August 12, 2017.

7   UNHCR, "Syria Regional Refugee Response," https://data2.unhcr.org/en/situations/syria (accessed October 20, 2020).

8   UNHCR, "Refugees and Asylum Seekers in Turkey," www.unhcr.org/tr/en/refugees-and -asylum-seekers-in-turkey (accessed October 20, 2020).

processed by the UNHCR. Due to the high volume of refugees in Turkey, such processing can take years.

Syrians as a group, however, have been granted special protection under the Temporary Protection Regulation of 2014. Subsequently, some small numbers have also received work permits or access to Turkish citizenship, although the vast majority exist in a precarious state, often surviving by work in the gray economy, which is widespread in Turkey. There are estimates that over 300,000 Syrian children are engaged in informal work in Turkey, as well as growing reports of forced marriages of Syrian women who have been taken on (illegally) as a second wife.[9] Only 10 percent of Syrian refugees live in Turkish government-run camps, most of which are found close to the Syrian border in southeastern Turkey. The vast majority of Syrians rather live in southeastern cities such as Gaziantep, Urfa, and Kilis or in major urban areas such as Istanbul, Ankara, and Izmir. Indeed, it is estimated that there are more Syrian refugees in Istanbul than in all of Europe.

Turkey has done far more to support Syrian refugees than any country in Europe or North America. The Syrian refugee crisis is also not the first time Turkey has taken in refugees—earlier examples include its role in accepting tens of thousands of Jewish refugees from Europe during World War II, as well as around 20,000 Bosnians and 18,000 Kosovars during the Balkan wars of the 1990s.[10] It also received 200,000 Kurdish refugees fleeing Saddam Hussein in 1991 on a temporary basis. Turkey has spent approximately $8 billion domestically to address the Syrian refugee crisis, including building more than twenty-two camps that are run by the Turkish government via its Disaster and Emergency Management Presidency (AFAD), with some additional support from the United Nations and NGOs. Turkey's approach to the refugee crisis has generally been a unilateral one in which it has carefully guarded its sovereignty. It has preferred to take on the responsibility of hosting refugees rather than delegating responsibilities to the UNHCR or the International Migration for Migration (IOM). It has also been wary of too much external intervention and international scrutiny. For example, it took steps in 2015 to limit academic research on refugees within Turkey by requiring permissions. Nevertheless, despite government restrictions on external actors, there are countless examples of domestic civil society organizations in the country, especially women's groups, stepping in to assist and express solidarity with Syrian refugees.

At the same time, however, the country's Syrian refugee policy has in many ways exacerbated or intersected with a number of already-existing domestic problems and conflicts. Turkish domestic politics have become increasingly polarized in recent years, and opponents of the ruling Justice and Development Party (AKP) accuse the current government of manipulating the refugee issue for political gain. A 2016 push to naturalize Syrians was met with opposition that was xenophobic but also politically motivated—many

9   Ibrahim Doğus, "How Syrians in Turkey Are Coping with a Polarised Political Climate," *New Statesman*, July 15, 2017.

10   One could also include much earlier examples, such as the fleeing of Sephardic Jews from Spain, Portugal, and Italy in the late fifteenth century.

saw Erdoğan as trying to use the Syrian crisis to expand his political base and electoral support by offering citizenship to large numbers of pious Sunni Muslims—a group from which the AKP draws its political support and which would resemble similar strategies of incorporating new migrants as potential voters that have been used by political parties in other parts of the world (Sadiq 2008). The timing of the proposal, which came during the same period that Erdoğan was pushing a controversial referendum to expand his own powers, added to the suspicion. Secularists who oppose Erdoğan's populist use of religion accuse the AKP of using the crisis to further Islamicize the country. Turkish nationalists decry the growing Arabic influence in the country. The numbers of Syrians working in the informal sectors have also undercut wages in many parts of Turkey and increased housing prices, causing local resentment. Widespread discrimination exists, and increasing incidents of local violence against Syrians have occurred. In the Kurdish-dominated areas of southeastern Turkey, there is also concern that the influx of Syrian Arabs is linked to government policies designed to change the ethnic balance in the region, thus undercutting bids for increased Kurdish regional autonomy.[11]

Migration and State Power: Migration and Diplomacy

Turkey's role in managing the Syrian refugee crisis has brought to the fore the ways in which cross-border migration flows affect not just the internal context of states but also their relations with one another (Adamson and Tsourapas 2019). In particular, the role Turkey plays as a host to Syrian refugees and as a major transit state for migrants trying to reach Europe has emerged as a key factor in Turkey-EU relations over the past several years. Europe's interests in preventing the flow of migrants and refugees to the continent have raised the importance of Turkey as a buffer and transit state and in some ways increased Turkey's bargaining power vis-à-vis Europe. This, combined with Erdogan's heated rhetoric toward Europe, has created tensions in the relationship, but also allowed Turkey to use its leverage to extract significant concessions and financial resources from the EU (Greenhill 2016).

In November 2015, Turkey signed a Joint Action Plan with the European Union in which the EU committed to giving Turkey EUR 3 billion to assist with managing the refugee crisis. In return, Turkey committed to using sea patrols and border restrictions to prevent the exit of migrants and refugees to Europe, as well as to crack down on passport forgeries and human trafficking and return those who failed to meet refugee determination criteria to their countries of origin—thus becoming "a 'wall of defense' against the flood of refugees" attempting to reach Europe.[12] The Joint Action Plan was supplemented by the March 2016 EU-Turkey deal, in which Europe agreed to take one registered Syrian refugee in Turkey for every Syrian asylum seeker crossing the Turkish border into Greece who was subsequently returned—the so-called "one-in, one-out" deal. In exchange, Europe committed to speeding up the liberalization of visas for Turkish citizens

---

11   See, e.g., Dogus, "How Syrians in Turkey Are Coping."

12   "Refugee Law and Policy: Turkey," available at www.loc.gov/law/help/refugee-law/turkey .php.

and committed an additional EUR 3 billion in assistance to Turkey—bringing the total assistance package to EUR 6 billion. Since the signing of the deal, Turkish president Erdoğan has continued to capitalize on Europe's dependence on Turkey and has used heated rhetoric to remind Europe of this. Speaking in November 2016, Erdoğan threatened to open the border gates to Europe, arguing that "the West needs Turkey."[13]

The refugee issue is not the only migration-related diplomatic incident that has arisen between Turkey and other states in recent years. In the lead-up to the April 2016 referendum in Turkey, tensions erupted between Germany and the Netherlands, which tried to limit campaign rallies in the Turkish diaspora, and Erdogan, who accused Germany and the Netherlands of being "fascists and Nazis."[14] Since the July 2016 coup attempt, there have also been tensions over Turkish demands to crack down on opposition groups in Europe as well as over its arrest of German citizens in Turkey. In August 2017 Erdoğan appeared to be trying to intervene in German domestic politics by suggesting that Turks living in Germany should not cast a vote for any of the three major political parties— Angela Merkel's Christian Democratic Union (CDU), the center-left Social Democratic Party (SDP), or the Greens—calling them all "enemies of Turkey."[15]

The rhetoric toward Europe also fits with Erdoğan's apparent strategy of using the issue of migration and the existence of a large Turkish diaspora within Europe as a means of exerting Turkish power and influence in the region. This has taken place in a changing geopolitical context that emerged following the attacks of 9/11, the subsequent Global War on Terror and wars in Iraq and Afghanistan, and the emergence of Islam and religion as issues front and center on the world stage. This period has also coincided with the rise of the religiously oriented Justice and Development Party (AKP) in Turkish domestic politics and a growth in religiosity in parts of Turkey's diaspora in Europe. The transformation in identity is reflected in the academic literature on Europe's Turkish population: whereas in 1996 the sociologist Claus Leggewie published a piece titled "How Germany's Turks Became Kurds," by 2009 the sociologist Gökce Yurdakul had produced the book *From Guest Workers into Muslims* (Leggewie 1996; Yurdakul 2009).

Turkey has increasingly turned to "its" diaspora as a potential source of soft power and influence—at the same time as it has more generally been drawing on its imperial past and its identity as a majority Muslim country as a way of projecting a more expansive national identity both at home and abroad (Adamson 2019). In this context, the state has at times positioned itself as the protector of Turks in Europe, arguing that it is standing up for their interests in the face of discrimination and anti-Muslim sentiment, echoing in certain respects some of the rhetoric employed by Israeli prime minister Netanyahu positioning Israel vis-à-vis Europe's Jewish population following such incidents

---

13   Tulay Karadeniz and Nick Tattersall, "Erdoğan Warns Europe That Turkey Could Open Migrant Gates," *Reuters*, November 25, 2016.

14   "Erdoğan Brands Dutch Government 'Nazi Remnants and Fascists,'" *Reuters*, March 11, 2017.

15   Bulent Usta, "Erdoğan Tells Turks in Germany to Vote against Merkel," *Reuters*, August 18, 2017.

as the January 2015 Paris attacks.[16] This use of Islamic identity as a form of soft power has been married with an explicit attempt to leverage the diaspora as a tool of state economic and lobbying power—to make (in the words of a member of the TYB Advisory Committee) "the Turkish diaspora among the most influential diasporas in the world."[17]

Turkish attempts to project an expansionist form of nationalism abroad via its diaspora have ruffled the feathers of some of the states in which the "Turkish diaspora" resides. In Germany Turkish state activities are viewed in some quarters as contradicting Germany's efforts at promoting integration—a view that has not been helped by incidents such as Erdoğan's 2008 speech in Cologne in which he argued that the Turkish state was against the "assimilation" of migrants and that it supported tying (former) nationals and their descendants to Turkey (Mügge 2012, 20). Turkey has also been vocal about religious discrimination and anti-Muslim sentiment in Europe to the extent that it at times promotes itself as the protector of Turkish and/or Muslim communities in Europe—an approach that could be viewed as interventionist and in relation to European states' declared interests in domesticating and institutionalizing Islam in Europe (Laurence 2012).

The use of migration policy as a tool of state power that can lead to diplomatic crises has not been limited to Turkey-EU relations, however. In October 2017, this extended to Turkey's relationship with the United States, in which both countries suspended the issuing of visas to the citizens of its counterpart, effectively shutting down travel and exchange between the two countries. The incident was related to developments in Turkey since the July 2016 coup attempt, and has been viewed as yet another indication of deteriorating relations between Turkey, the United States, and Europe.[18]

Until recently, Turkey was often considered to be a country of emigration due to the large numbers of labor migrants who moved to Europe in the mid-twentieth century. More recently, it has hit the news headlines as host to the largest number of refugees in the world, including over three million Syrians who have fled the violence of the ongoing civil war to the south. In reality, Turkey has always experienced a mix of immigration and emigration and today is best understood as simultaneously being a migration sending, receiving, and transit state. Due to its particular geographical location, Turkey has become a significant player in multiple regional migration systems—as host to refugees from the Middle East; as a recipient of labor migrants from countries of the former Soviet Union; and as a sender of transit and labor migrants to Europe. The latter relationship has been particularly significant as Turkey has attempted to use both its diaspora

---

16　Tovah Lazaroff, "Netanyahu to French, European Jews after Paris Attacks: Israel Is Your Home," *Jerusalem Post,* January 1, 2015, www.jpost.com/Israel-News/Netanyahu-to-European-Jews-after-Paris-attacks-Israel-is-your-home-387309 (accessed June 13, 2015).

17　Cited in Aksel 2014, 205.

18　Kareem Shaheen, "US-Turkey Row Escalates with Tit-for-Tat Travel and Visa Restrictions," *The Guardian,* October 9, 2017.

and its geographical location at the border of Europe as a means of exerting political leverage. This strategy, of course, is only successful in the context of Europe's ongoing interest in securing its borders and maintaining relatively restrictive migration policies.

Turkey is an interesting example of a contemporary "migration state"—as is the case for many other states, the management and governance of migration flows is an increasingly important state function. Yet the ways in which Turkey engages in migration governance are markedly different in many respects from migration states in Europe and North America. Turkey's approach to migration governance cannot be understood without bringing in the broader context of Turkey's history as a postimperial state, and its unique geography which affects how migration dynamics intersect with broader issues of economic development, conflict, and security. Finally, it should be noted that the Turkish state is only one of many actors involved in forms of migration governance in the region. Particularly significant are nonstate actors, including armed organizations and traffickers, but also international organizations and supra-state actors, such as the UNHCR, IOM, and European Union, and substate actors such as regions and—in the case of Syrian refugees—localities and cities. The Turkish case thus shows both the promise and limits of the "migration state" approach for understanding migration governance in the global South.

References

Adamson, Fiona B. 2013. "Mechanisms of Diaspora Mobilization and the Transnationalization of Civil War." In *Transnational Dynamics of Civil War*, edited by Jeffrey Checkel, 63–89. Cambridge: Cambridge University Press.

———. 2019. "Sending States and the Making of Intra-Diasporic Politics: Turkey and Its Diasporas." *International Migration Review* 53(1): 210–36.

———. 2020. "Non-State Authoritarianism and Diaspora Politics." *Global Networks* 20(1): 150–69.

Adamson, Fiona B., and Madeleine Demetriou. 2007. "Remapping the Boundaries of 'State' and 'National Identity': Incorporating Diasporas into IR Theorizing." *European Journal of International Relations* 13(4): 489–526.

Adamson, Fiona B., and Gerasimos Tsourapas. 2019. "Migration Diplomacy in World Politics." *International Studies Perspectives* 20(2): 113–28.

Adamson, Fiona B., and Gerasimos Tsourapas. 2020. "The Migration State in the Global South: Nationalizing, Developmental and Neoliberal Models of Migration Management." *International Migration Review* 54(3): 853–82.

Akgündüz, Ahmet. 1993. "Labour Migration from Turkey to Western Europe (1960–1974): An Analytical Review." *Capital & Class* 17(3): 153–94.

———. 1998. "Migration to and from Turkey, 1783–1960: Types, Numbers and Ethno-religious Dimensions." *Journal of Ethnic and Migration Studies* 24(1): 97–120.

Aksel, Damla B. 2014. "Kins, Distant Workers, Diasporas: Constructing Turkey's Transnational Members Abroad." *Turkish Studies* 15(2): 195–219.

Andersson, Ruben. 2014. *Illegality, Inc.: Clandestine Migration and the Business of Bordering Europe.* Berkeley: University of California Press.

Ayata, Bilgin, and Deniz Yükseker. 2005. "A Belated Awakening: National and International Responses to the Internal Displacement of the Kurds in Turkey." *New Perspectives on Turkey* 32: 5–42.

Aydin, Yasar. 2014. *The New Turkish Diaspora Policy: Its Aims, Their Limits and the Challenges for Associations of People of Turkish Origin and Decision-Makers in Germany.* SWP Research Paper RP/10. Berlin: German Institute for International and Security Affairs.

Bahadir, Sefik Alp. 1979. "Turkey and the Turks in Germany." *Aussenpolitik* 30(1): 100–114.

Brand, Laurie A. 2006. *Citizens Abroad: Emigration and the State in the Middle East and North Africa.* New York: Cambridge University Press.

Brubaker, Rogers. 1996. *Nationalism Reframed: Nationhood and the National Question in the New Europe.* New York: Cambridge University Press.

Cooper, Frederick. 2005. *Colonialism in Question: Theory, Knowledge, History.* Berkeley: University of California Press.

Dal, Emel Parlar. 2017. "Impact of the Transnationalization of the Syrian Civil War on Turkey: Conflict Spillover Cases of Isis and PYD-YPG/PKK." *Cambridge Review of International Affairs* 29(4): 1396–420.

Délano, Alexandra, and Alan Gamlen. 2014. "Comparing and Theorizing State–Diaspora Relations." *Political Geography* 41: 43–53.

Faist, Thomas. 2000. *The Volume and Dynamics of International Migration and Transnational Social Spaces.* Oxford: Oxford University Press.

Gamlen, Alan. 2014. "Diaspora Institutions and Diaspora Governance." *International Migration Review* 48(S1): 180–217.

Greenhill, Kelly M. 2016. "Open Arms behind Barred Doors: Fear, Hypocrisy and Policy Schizophrenia in the European Migration Crisis." *European Law Journal* 22(3): 317–32.

Hirschon, Renée, ed. 2003. *Crossing the Aegean: An Appraisal of the 1923 Compulsory Population Exchange between Greece and Turkey.* Oxford: Berghahn Books.

Hollifield, James F. 2004. "The Emerging Migration State." *International Migration Review* 38(3): 885–912.

Hosner, Roland. 2016. *Estimates for Georgian Migrants in Turkey: Regular and Irregular Migration.* ENIGGMA Working Paper. Vienna: International Center for Migration Policy Development (ICMPD).

İçduygu, Ahmet, and Deniz Sert. 2015. "The Changing Waves of Migration from the Balkans to Turkey: A Historical Account." In *Migration in the Southern Balkans: From Ottoman Territory to Globalized Nation States,* edited by Hans Vermeulen, Martin Baldwin-Edwards, and Riki Van Boeschten. IMISCOE Research Series. Berlin: Springer.

İçduygu, Ahmet, and Aysen Ustübici. 2014. "Negotiating Mobility, Debating Borders: Migration Diplomacy in Turkey-EU Relations." In *New Border and Citizenship Policies,* edited by Helen Schwenken and Sabine Russ-Sattar, 44–59. Berlin: Springer.

İçduygu, Ahmet, and Deniz Yükseker. 2012. "Rethinking Transit Migration in Turkey: Reality and Representation in the Creation of a Migratory Phenomenon." *Population, Space and Place* 18: 441–56.

Kalça, Adem, and Yilmaz Onur Ari. 2016. "Circular Migration between Georgia and Turkey: Is Triple Win a Solution for Illegal Employment?" *Proceedings of the International Conference on Eurasian Economies,* Kaposvár, Hungary.

Kaya, Ayhan. 2011. "Euro-Turks as a Force in EU-Turkey Relations." *South European Identity and Politics* 16(3): 499–512.

Kirişçi, Kemal. 1996. "Is Turkey Lifting the 'Geographical Location'?: The November 1994 Regulation on Asylum in Turkey." *International Journal of Refugee Law* 8(3): 293–318.

———. 2000. "Disaggregating Turkish Citizenship and Immigration Practices." *Middle Eastern Studies* 36(3): 1–22.

———. 2007. "Turkey: A Country of Transition from Emigration to Immigration." *Mediterranean Politics* 12(1): 91–97.

Klotz, Audie. 2013. *Migration and National Identity in South Africa, 1860–2010.* New York: Cambridge University Press.

Laurence, Jonathan. 2012. *The Emancipation of Europe's Muslims: The State's Role in Minority Integration.* Princeton, NJ: Princeton University Press.

Leggewie, Claus. 1996. "How Turks Became Kurds, Not Germans." *Dissent* 43: 79–83.

Martin, Philip L. 1991. *The Unfinished Story: Turkish Labour Migration to Western Europe: With Special Reference to the Federal Republic of Germany.* Geneva: International Labour Organization.

Moss, Dana M. 2016. "Transnational Repression, Diaspora Mobilization, and the Case of the Arab Spring." *Social Problems* 63(4): 480–98.

Mügge, Liza. 2012. "Ideologies of Nationhood in Sending-State Transnationalism: Comparing Surinam and Turkey." *Ethnicities* 13(3): 338–58.

Mylonas, Harris. 2013. *The Politics of Diaspora Management in the Republic of Korea.* Issue Brief no. 81, 1–12. Seoul: Asian Institute for Policy Studies.

Öktem, Kerem. 2014. *Turkey's New Diaspora Policy: The Challenge of Inclusivity, Outreach and Capacity.* Istanbul Policy Center, Stiftung Mercator Initiative. Istanbul: Sabanci University.

Østergaard-Nielsen, Eva. 2003. *Transnational Politics: The Case of Turks and Kurds in Germany.* London: Routledge.

Parla, Ayse. 2019. *Precarious Hope: Migration and the Limits of Belonging in Turkey.* Stanford, CA: Stanford University Press.

Ragazzi, Francesco. 2014. "A Comparative Analysis of Diaspora Policies." *Political Geography* 41: 74–89.

Richards, Alan, and John Waterbury. 1990. *A Political Economy of the Middle East: State, Class, and Economic Development.* Boulder, CO: Westview Press.

Rist, Ray C. 1979. "Migration and Marginality: Guestworkers in Germany and France." *Daedalus* 108(2): 95–108.

Robson, Laura. 2017. *States of Separation: Transfer, Partition, and the Making of the Modern Middle East.* Berkeley: University of California Press.

Sadiq, Kamal. 2008. *Paper Citizens: How Illegal Immigrants Acquire Citizenship in Developing Countries.* New York: Oxford University Press.

Sayari, Sabri. 1986. "Migration Policies of Sending Countries: Perspectives on the Turkish Experience." *Annals of the American Academy of Political and Social Science* 485(1): 87–97.

Triadafilopoulos, Triadafilos. 1998. "The 1923 Greek-Turkish Exchange of Populations and the Reformulation of Greek National Identity." Paper presented at the international conference on *Exchange of Populations between Greece and Turkey: An Assessment of the Consequences of the Treaty of Lausanne Conference.* University of Oxford, September 17–20.

———. 2004. "Building Walls, Bounding Nations: Migration and Exclusion in Canada and Germany, 1870–1939." *Journal of Historical Sociology* 17(4): 385–427.

Tsourapas, Gerasimos. 2020. "Theorizing State-Diaspora Relations in the Middle East: Authoritarian Emigration States in Comparative Perspective." *Mediterranean Politics* 25(2): 135–59.

Varadarajan, Latha. 2010. *The Domestic Abroad: Diasporas in International Relations.* New York: Oxford University Press.

Yildirim, Onur. 2007. *Diplomacy and Displacement: Reconsidering the Turco-Greek Exchange of Populations, 1922–1934.* London: Routledge.

Yildiz, Ahmet. 2001. *Ne Mutlu Türküm Diyebilene: Türk Ulusal Kimliğinin Etno-Seküler Sinirlari, 1919–1938* [Happy is the one who can say I am Turk: The ethno-secular borders of Turkish national identity, 1919–1938]. Istanbul: Iletisim Yayinlari.

Yurdakul, Gokce. 2009. *From Guest Workers into Muslims: The Transformation of Turkish Immigrant Associations in Germany.* Cambridge: Cambridge Scholars.

Zolberg, Aristide. 1983. "The Formation of New States as a Refugee-Generating Process." *Annals of the American Academy of Political and Social Science* 467(1): 24–38.

———. 2006. *A Nation by Design: Immigration Policy in the Fashioning in the United States, 1750—2000.* New York: Harvard University Press and Russell Sage Foundation.

BEYOND THE MIGRATION STATE

Western Europe since World War II

Leo Lucassen

IN THE POSTWAR PERIOD, "migration states" developed in Western Europe, with rights-based immigration policies that constrained the power of the state to manage and control migration.[1] From the 1950s onward and driven by German labor market interests, Western European countries slowly agreed to accept European labor migrants, especially after the Treaty of Rome in 1957.[2] There then developed an extensive semi-continental free migration system within the European Union, but with increasingly hard borders for immigrants from outside it.

In the same period, Western Europe witnessed a considerable amount of immigration from other continents, which came through four different channels.[3] First, there were the so-called "guest workers" from North Africa and Turkey. Second, colonial migrants from Asia, Africa, the Caribbean, and Russia arrived in France, the UK, Portugal, the Netherlands, and Germany.[4] The third channel brought refugees from Africa, the

---

1   James F. Hollifield, "The Emerging Migration State," *International Migration Review* 38, no. 3 (2004), 885–912; see also James F. Hollifield and Michael Orlando Sharpe, "Japan as an 'Emerging Migration State,'" *International Relations of the Asia-Pacific* 17, no. 3 (2017): 371–400.

2   Emmanuel Comte, *The History of the European Migration Regime* (Abingdon: Routledge, 2018). A more elaborate discussion can be found in Leo Lucassen, "The Rise of the European Migration Regime and Its Paradoxes (1945–2020)," *International Review of Social History* 64, no. 3 (2019): 515–31.

3   Eastern Europe also to some extent attracted non-Europeans through various bilateral agreements with Asian, African, and Latin American socialist states. Thus, in the 1980s, there were hundreds of thousands of guest workers from Angola, Mozambique, Vietnam, and Cuba working in the German Democratic Republic and Czechoslovakia. Peter Kivisto and Thomas Faist, *Beyond a Border: The Causes and Consequences of Contemporary Immigration* (Thousand Oaks, CA: Sage, 2010), 68.

4   About two million *"Aussiedler"* from Russia who entered Germany in the 1990s and early 2000s can be defined as a special kind of postcolonial migrant; Ulbe Bosma *et al.*, eds., *Postcolonial*

Middle East, and parts of South and Southeast Asia. Fourth, workers who were more highly skilled came from all other continents. Those developments had already begun after World War I[5] and turned what had been countries of emigration into countries of immigration,[6] reflecting shifting demographic interdependence between different parts of the world, one of the key subjects of this volume. Gradually, the new situation led to increasing pessimism about integration,[7] first in Western Europe but more recently in Eastern Europe too, pessimism that was fueled by neoliberal downscaling of the welfare state and rising ethno-nationalism.[8] As Thomas Piketty has recently argued, that particular shift has been caused by a widening rift between social democratic parties and those who traditionally vote for them, especially since those parties too embraced neoliberalism during the course of the 1980s and 1990s. There followed a recalibration of the political scale in which radical identitarian rights parties, like the Front National (Rassemblement National, or National Rally, since 2018) in France, now combine nativism with an egalitarian discourse in a bid to become attractive to sections of the working class.[9]

The aim of this chapter is to establish how and to what extent migration dynamics in Europe, as well as reactions to immigration, have fundamentally changed since the second half of the twentieth century. I will do so in three steps, the first of which is an evaluation of the postwar changes that buttressed the European "migration state." There will

---

Migrants and Identity Politics: Europe, Russia, Japan and the United States in Comparison (New York: Berghahn, 2012).

5   See, for example, Clifford Rosenberg, *Policing Paris: The Origins of Modern Immigration Control between the Wars* (Ithaca, NY: Cornell University Press, 2006).

6   In the period 1840–1940 some fifty-six million Europeans left the continent; Patrick Manning, *Migration in World History* (London: Routledge, 2012), 151. In the second half of the twentieth century another fourteen million emigrated, most of them for the Americas and Oceania: Leo Lucassen et al., *Cross-cultural Migration in Western Europe 1901–2000: A Preliminary Estimate*, IISH Research Paper no. 52 (Amsterdam: International Institute of Social History, 2014), 29.

7   For this concept, see Leo Lucassen and Jan Lucassen, "The Strange Death of Dutch Tolerance: The Timing and Nature of the Pessimist Turn in the Dutch Migration Debate," *Journal of Modern History* 87, no. 1 (2015): 72–101.

8   Markus Crepaz, *Trust beyond Borders: Immigration, the Welfare State, and Identity in Modern Societies* (Ann Arbor: University of Michigan Press, 2008); Jens Rydgren, "Immigration Sceptics, Xenophobes or Racists? Radical Right-Wing Voting in Six West European Countries," *European Journal of Political Research* 47, no. 6 (2008): 737–65. More journalistic but insightful is Sasha Polakow-Suransky, *Go Back to Where You Came From: The Backlash against Immigration and the Fate of Western Democracy* (London: C. Hurst, 2017).

9   Thomas Piketty, *Capital and Ideology* (Cambridge, MA: Harvard University Press, 2020), 788–89; similar observations have been made for the United States: Arlie Russell Hochschild, *Strangers in Their Own Land: Anger and Mourning on the American Right* (New York: New Press, 2016). See also Michèle Lamont, "Addressing Recognition Gaps: Destigmatization and the Reduction of Inequality," *American Sociological Review* 83, no. 3 (2018): 419–44.

Table 16.1. Number of colonial/postcolonial migrants in western and southern European states (1945–2000).

Country	Year	Number (in millions)	Main Origins
West Germany	2000	5	Russia, Eastern Europe
France	1970	2	Algeria, Vietnam, West Africa
United Kingdom	1970	2	South Asia, West Indies, Eastern Africa
Portugal	1980	0.650	Mozambique, Angola
Netherlands	1980	0.550	Indonesia, Suriname, Antilles
Italy	2000	0.550	Latin America
Spain	2000	0.180	Latin America
Belgium	2000	0.125	Congo
Total		11.055	

Sources: Bosma et al., *Postcolonial Migrants and Identity Politics,* 5; Smith, *Europe's Invisible Migrants,* 32; Klaus J. Bade and Jochen Oltmer, "Germany," in Bade et al., *The Encyclopedia of Migration and Minorities in Europe,* 65–82, at 79.

then follow a brief comparison of the political and popular reactions to immigrants in the last two centuries to enable us to historicize and enrich Hollifield's "migration state" approach with its distinction of "markets," "rights," "security," and "culture."[10] The third step takes us beyond the perspective of statist international relations, which although useful for understanding policies and reactions in receiving countries, create a somewhat myopic view of what migration actually is and how we should qualify its effects both on sending and receiving societies. To escape the highly policy- and media-driven migration discourse, I have introduced the much broader "cross-cultural" perspective, which sheds new light on the relationships between migration and the social, economic, cultural, and political changes that Europe has experienced in the past century.

Migration and the State
One of the most conspicuous changes in Europe's migration patterns is the strong increase in the number of immigrants from Asia and Africa in the second half of the twentieth century, most of whom ended up in cities in Western and Southern Europe (table 16.1). Although those migrants were driven by the well-known household dynamics that have motivated internal European migrants for centuries,[11] the world they had to navigate was very different from that of their nineteenth-century predecessors, for by the later twentieth century they faced cultural barriers, discrimination, and more recently mortal danger—but also one in which ideologies of equality and human rights asserted themselves.

---

10 Hollifield, "The Emerging Migration State."

11 Leslie Page Moch, *Moving Europeans: Migration in Western Europe since 1650* (Bloomington: Indiana University Press, 2003).

After World War II especially, conflicting forces forged new migration patterns in ways that few could have imagined and which affected the timing and composition—the "quality"—of migration. To understand the resulting changes I will concentrate on decolonization, the emergence of the welfare state, and the rise of an international human rights regime (the "humanitarian turn") as three interrelated developments. Let us start with migrations we could describe by saying, "we are here, because you were there."

Decolonization

Since the late fifteenth century, European states, beginning with Portugal, Spain, France, the United Kingdom, and the Netherlands, set up trading strongholds along the coasts of Africa and Asia. Meanwhile, Spain and Portugal colonized South America and the Caribbean in a violent expansion that came at huge cost. The invaders decimated the indigenous Amerindian population, largely owing to the contagious diseases they introduced, and their arrival led to the forced migration of millions of enslaved Africans whom the Spanish and Portuguese transported to the New World to work on plantations, first in the Caribbean and Brazil and then, from the end of the eighteenth century onward, in the US South.[12] During the course of the nineteenth century most of Africa and large parts of South and Southeast Asia, as well as the Middle East, were brought under indirect colonial rule, with the indigenous inhabitants usually defined as subjects, not citizens, without the right to move to the metropole.[13]

This principle began to be eroded with the onslaught of the Great War, when the demand for labor and soldiers was met by hundreds of thousands of colonial migrants, of whom France recruited by far the highest numbers.[14] In 1914, Algerians who had been formally accorded French citizenship since 1848 were granted the freedom to move to the "Hexagone." Large numbers of men, especially men from Kabyle who had long been traditional seasonal migrants within North Africa, now flocked to France, at first with the full intention of returning. The partial easing of limitations on migration for colonial subjects triggered the restrictive dimensions "culture" and "security" of Hollifield's four-dimensional model, which portrays colonial migrants as essentially dangerous and, in spite of their formal status as citizens, as not belonging.[15] However, after the end of World War II, many more Algerians decided to settle permanently. Then, once Algeria had been granted independence in March 1962, immigration to France from Algeria, including that of returning French colonists (the *pieds-noirs*) and colonial soldiers (Harkis),

---

12   Sven Beckert, *Empire of Cotton: A Global History* (New York: Random House, 2014); Damian Pargas, *Slavery and Forced Migration in the Antebellum South* (Cambridge: Cambridge University Press, 2014).

13   With regard to long-term consequences for postwar migration trends, see Ulbe Bosma, *The Making of a Periphery: How Island Southeast Asia Became a Mass Exporter of Labor* (New York: Columbia University Press, 2019).

14   Eric Storm and Ali Al Tuma, eds., *Colonial Soldiers in Europe, 1914–1945: "Aliens in Uniform" in Wartime Societies* (London: Routledge, 2015).

15   Rosenberg, *Policing Paris*.

continued until it was severely curtailed in 1974. Considerable numbers of Maghrebiens, Moroccans, and Tunisians also settled in France, until they totaled 2.5 million at the end of the twentieth century, amounting to 4 percent of the French population. Supplemented by considerable numbers from Francophone West Africa and other parts of the former colonial empire,[16] immigrants—including Europeans—amounted to roughly 10 percent of the population, a figure similar to that seen in neighboring countries.[17]

The United Kingdom experienced large-scale postcolonial immigration from both the Caribbean in the West and India, Pakistan, and later Bangladesh in the East. Somewhat later there was immigration from former African colonies too, such as Nigeria, Kenya, and Uganda. As in France, such migration was the result of a mixture of the demand for labor and the political desire to hold onto the grandeur of the empire. The Commonwealth ideal explains the principle of free migration, and it was only when the former colonizers began to feel that too many of their former colonial subjects were taking the opportunity to settle in Great Britain that the 1962 Commonwealth Immigrants Act was introduced to stem the flow. Citizenship of the United Kingdom and Colonies (CUKC) remained in place, but only citizens who held passports issued under direct British authority were exempt from immigration control. All others from colonies and newly independent nations like India and Pakistan (New Commonwealth countries) required a special permit issued by the Ministry of Labour.[18] The 1950s and 1960s saw latent xenophobic and sometimes outright racist reactions emerge in Britain, especially in working-class neighborhoods, which were stoked and exploited by politicians such as the Conservative MP Enoch Powell, whose "Rivers of Blood" speech in April 1968 became notorious.[19]

The Netherlands experienced two distinct periods of postcolonial immigration. As in France and the United Kingdom, the first, from the Dutch East Indies (Indonesia), coincided with "Les Trente Glorieuses," so that the timing overlapped a booming economic business cycle. However, the opposite was true of the exodus from Suriname of

---

16   Alec G. Hargreaves, *Immigration, "Race" and Ethnicity in Contemporary France* (London: Routledge, 1995); Neil MacMaster, *Colonial Migrants and Racism: Algerians in France, 1900–62* (Houndmills: Macmillan, 1997); Jennifer E. Sessions, *By Sword and Plow: France and the Conquest of Algeria* (Ithaca, NY: Cornell University Press, 2011).

17   Michèle Tribalat, "Une estimation des populations d'origine étrangère en France en 2011," *Espace Populations Sociétés, nos.* 1/2 (2015).

18   Randall Hansen, *Citizenship and Immigration in Post-war Britain: The Institutional Origins of a Multicultural Nation* (Oxford: Oxford University Press, 2000). See also Leo Lucassen, *The Immigrant Threat: The Integration of Old and New Migrants in Western Europe since 1850* (Urbana: University of Illinois Press, 2005), 126.

19   Although ethnic and cultural diversity has become much more accepted in the UK over the years, the discomfort with colonial migrants and their offspring has not disappeared, as became painfully visible with the threats to deport the Caribbean "Windrush generation" by Theresa May's Conservative government in the spring of 2018. See Trevor Harris, eds., *Windrush (1948) and Rivers of Blood (1968): Legacy and Assessment* (London: Routledge, 2019).

some 150,000 descendants of former enslaved African plantation workers and contract workers from India and Java, who left the former Dutch colony immediately before and after its sudden independence from the Netherlands in 1975. From an economic perspective the timing of their settlement was much less favorable, for it came at the start of a protracted period of recession that lasted more than a decade. It too prompted racist reactions.[20] Approximately eleven million migrants from former colonies and colonization regions (Russia) entered Western and Southern Europe during the second half of the twentieth century.

The Welfare State

A different mechanism but with similar effects became visible with the permanent arrival of the families of guest workers in Western European countries in the 1970s and 1980s, which coincided with the beginning of a long recession. Initially the migration of Italian, Spanish, Yugoslavian, Turkish, and Moroccan guest workers, most of them men although with a number of women among them, seemed to follow the well-known pattern of demand for labor in highly industrialized and commercialized areas.[21] As early as the late 1940s employers in Western Europe were confronted with a tight labor market in a number of sectors, such as metals and mining, so together with national authorities they devised schemes to recruit temporary low-skilled "guest workers," first from Southern Europe and somewhat later from North Africa and Turkey. Both receiving and sending regions, as well as the workers themselves, expected temporary working stays, and during the boom years of the 1960s everything pointed in that direction. Migration was highly volatile and characterized by a high degree of circular and return mobility, as workers reacted to the demand for labor.

The situation changed rather suddenly in 1973 with the oil crisis, although in the end the decision by Western European states to end recruiting programs and restrict immigration rather unexpectedly had the opposite effect, because instead of leaving, most guest workers activated embedded rights to residency and family reunification. Others, whose rights were less secure, profited from migration rights advocates and social movements that invoked the principle of equality and often successfully pressured the courts into leniency.[22]

It was only then that migrants and receiving societies realized that they had not only entered new geographical territory, but figuratively the welfare state as well, and that by making financial contributions to society they had generated social rights from the

---

20 Rob Witte, *Racist Violence and the State* (London: Longman, 1996).

21 Eleonore Kofman *et al.*, *Gender and International Migration in Europe: Employment, Welfare and Politics* (London: Routledge, 2000).

22 James F. Hollifield, *Immigrants, Markets, and States: The Political Economy of Postwar Europe* (Cambridge, MA: Harvard University Press, 1992); Saskia Bonjour, "Between Integration Provision and Selection Mechanism: Party Politics, Judicial Constraints, and the Making of French and Dutch Policies of Civic Integration Abroad," *European Journal of Migration and Law* 12, no. 3 (2010): 299–318. See also Bevelander, this volume.

moment they had started work. The same was true for residency rights, which made it difficult to expel them, even when they became unemployed. Finally, guest workers activated the right to family life that had been secured early on, albeit largely unintentionally,[23] and although at first few made use of it, that changed when from 1973 onward it became clear that if they were to leave Western Europe they would find the door closed should they wish to return.

As a result, the decision to stop recruitment and close the borders had precisely the opposite of the desired effect and activated certain of the "embedded" social and legal rights that were typical of postwar European liberal democracies.[24] That led to a considerable chain migration of family members, quadrupling the original guest-worker population, just when the economy was declining and the sectors that employed most of them—mines, textile, and metal industries—were losing their global competitive advantage and by the end of the 1970s were having to close their doors. How dramatic and countercyclical the mass migration of the time was is well illustrated by table 16.2, which shows an almost perfect inverse correlation between the business cycle and Moroccan immigration to the Netherlands in the 1980s.

The unfortunate timing had severe consequences for the ensuing settlement process of migrants workers who had been selected for low skills or none, and of course that of their descendants. They had no choice but to try to settle in the worst parts of large cities, while many lost their jobs, with dim prospects of ever finding work again. Moreover, parts of the indigenous population began to close ranks as a discourse of "unintegrated Muslims" began to dominate. That all manner of social and cultural problems would be the result surprises scarcely anyone. However, instead of diagnosing the failure of multiculturalism, it would be more appropriate to highlight socioeconomic and political dynamics and emphasize how surprisingly many children of immigrants have climbed the social ladder.[25]

The Refugee Regime
The third factor that shaped a migration dynamic different from that of the preceding centuries was the postwar turn to humanitarianism,[26] which stimulated international

---

23   Saskia Bonjour and Marlou Schrover, "Public Debate and Policy-Making on Family Migration in the Netherlands, 1960–1995," *Journal of Ethnic and Migration Studies* 41, no. 9 (2015): 1475–94.

24   For somewhat similar unintended effects in the United States, see Douglas S. Massey and Karen A. Pren, "Unintended Consequences of US Immigration Policy: Explaining the Post-1965 Surge from Latin America," *Population and Development Review* 38, no. 1 (2012): 1–29. See also Tichenor and Hazan, this volume.

25   Maurice Crul *et al.*, eds., *The European Second Generation Compared* (Amsterdam: Amsterdam University Press, 2012); Frank Kalter *et al.*, eds., *Growing Up in Diverse Societies: The Integration of the Children of Immigrants in England, Germany, the Netherlands, and Sweden* (Oxford: Oxford University Press, 2018).

26   Steven L. B. Jensen, *The Making of International Human Rights: The 1960s, Decolonization, and the Reconstruction of Global Values* (Cambridge: Cambridge University Press, 2016).

Table 16.2. Cross-cultural migration rates in Europe (excluding Russia) as a percentage of the average population per half century (1801–2000).

Year	Emigration from Morocco	Immigration to Morocco	Unemployment among Moroccans
1970	600	400	0
1971	3900	700	0
1972	2400	700	1
1973	2800	600	1
1974	3500	600	1
1975	7900	600	2
1976	5700	800	3
1977	5800	700	4
1978	7200	800	5
1979	7700	1000	10
1980	10400	1100	10
1981	8400	1300	20
1982	6500	2100	30
1983	4900	2300	40
1984	4700	2100	41
1985	5700	1500	41
1986	6600	1400	38
1987	7100	1100	35
1988	8200	1300	45
1989	8500	1100	51
1990	9600	1000	42
1991	9100	1100	42
1992	7400	1000	38
1993	6100	1100	35
1994	3500	1100	35
1995	3200	1200	32
1996	4500	1100	25
1997	4900	900	21
1998	5500	700	21
1999	4700	700	18
2000	4500	600	13
2001	5200	600	10
2002	5200	600	14
2003	4900	700	17
2004	3700	800	22
2005	2400	1100	20
2006	2100	1400	17
2007	1700	1500	11
2008	2100	1300	10

Source: Lucassen and Lucassen, *Globalising Migration History,* table 170.

cooperation on the situation of refugees[27] but also saw the rise of new ideas about integration (multiculturalism)[28] and, not least, raised awareness of the ultimately horrific consequences of racism and discrimination. The new approaches worked together to bring about an "ethical revolution" that formed an important counterweight to blatant racism and open discrimination.[29]

In themselves refugee migrations are nothing new. Indeed they are closely linked to the religious wars of the sixteenth and seventeenth centuries that furthered religious homogeneity, although it should be noted that until the twentieth century refugees of religious wars made up only small minorities of international migrants. Things changed with the rise of the nation-state in the nineteenth century, the breakup of multiethnic agglomerations like the Ottoman and Habsburg empires, and the Bolshevik takeover in Russia, which put millions on the move. Awareness grew that some form of supranational arrangement was necessary to deal with refugees, especially those who had become stateless after Lenin revoked the citizenship of almost a million Russian expatriates in 1921. To solve the problem the League of Nations appointed the Norwegian explorer Fridtjof Nansen (1861–1930) as the first High Commissioner for Refugees, and indeed the passport for stateless persons was named after Nansen.[30] In the end, some 450,000 such passports were issued and recognized by fifty-two nations.

No actual right to apply for asylum was realized, however, as became chillingly clear when Nazi Germany's neighbors appeared unwilling to take in Jewish refugees after 1933.[31] Authorities in the Netherlands even decided that all German Jews must be sent back to Nazi Germany, precisely because they were "refugees," leaving German Jews wishing to escape Nazi Germany with no choice but to try to hide their Jewish identity so that they could pass as "normal" German migrants.[32] Although nowadays the Dutch policy might seem bizarre in light of the postwar refugee regime, when fleeing to save one's life became the sine qua non to be accorded refugee status, at the time it raised few

---

27 Megan Bradley, *The International Organization for Migration: Challenges, Commitments, Complexities* (London: Routledge, 2020).

28 Rita Chin, *The Crisis of Multiculturalism in Europe: A History* (Princeton, NJ: Princeton University Press, 2017).

29 Lucassen and Lucassen, "The Strange Death." See also Maartje van der Woude, "Euroskepticism, Nationalism, and the Securitization of Migration in the Netherlands," in *Crimmigrant Nations: Resurgent Nationalism and the Closing of Borders*, ed. Robert Koulish and Maartje van der Woude (New York: Fordham University Press, 2020), 227–48, at 236.

30 Randall Hansen, *Constrained by Its Roots: How the Origins of the Global Asylum System Limit Contemporary Protection* (Washington, DC: MPI, 2017); Matthew Frank and Jessica Reinisch, *Refugees in Europe, 1919–1959: A Forty Years' Crisis?* (London: Bloomsbury, 2017).

31 Paul R. Bartrop, *The Evian Conference of 1938 and the Jewish Refugee Crisis* (Basingstoke: Palgrave Macmillan, 2018).

32 Corrie van Eijl, "Tracing Back 'Illegal Aliens' in the Netherlands, 1850–1940," in *Illegal Migration and Gender in a Global and Historical Perspective*, ed. Marlou Schrover et al. (Amsterdam: Amsterdam University Press, 2008), 39–56.

eyebrows, even within the Dutch Jewish community, where many were afraid that the refugees would jeopardize their fragile integration process and fuel antisemitism.[33]

The contours of a new refugee regime became visible at the end of World War II, when the Allies were confronted with anything from ten to twenty million displaced persons, some of them Germans who had been expelled from Eastern Europe.[34] To repatriate and resettle them, the United States established the United Nations Relief and Rehabilitation Administration (UNRRA), supported by forty-four nations. Many were able to start new lives in Western Europe, the Americas, and Israel, but there were many others whose return to the Soviet zone meant certain death. These initiatives led to the foundation of the UNHCR and the drafting of the Geneva Refugee Convention in 1951, which granted persecuted people in fear for their lives the right to apply for asylum.[35]

Initially, relatively few people sought asylum in Europe and nearly all of them were refugees from the Soviet bloc (Hungary 1956, Czechoslovakia 1968). That changed slowly during the 1970s and 1980s when the number of asylum seekers from Asia and Africa increased sharply due to Cold War conflicts fought on those continents, and to the increasing availability of quick and cheap connections (figure 16.1).[36]

Randall Hansen has argued recently that the refugee regime newly adopted in 1951 was fit only for regular, manageable outflows and was quite unable to deal with sudden mass displacement.[37] The sharp increase in numbers of asylum seekers flocking to Western Europe from the mid-1980s onward to escape repressive regimes in the Middle East and the civil war in Yugoslavia was indeed unexpected, but in the somewhat longer run and in spite of political opposition and relatively high unemployment, receiving states were successful in integrating large numbers. The case of Germany is telling in this respect, as after the reunification in 1990 it received not only a considerable number of asylum seekers from the Balkans and the Middle East but also roughly three million *Aussiedler* from the Soviet Union, descendants of erstwhile German emigrants who had settled in Russia since the seventeenth century (figure 16.2).[38]

Hansen is right, however, that European countries lack a permanent infrastructure to accommodate any sudden influx of refugees, as became clear in 2014 and 2015 when the

---

33   Bob Moore, *Refugees from Nazi Germany in the Netherlands, 1933–1940* (Dordrecht: M. Nijhoff, 1986), 29.

34   Hansen, *Constrained by Its Roots.*

35   Initially this was limited to Europeans (fleeing communism), but in 1967 the treaty acquired global coverage.

36   Aristide Zolberg et al., *Escape from Violence: Conflict and the Refugee Crisis in the Developing World* (Oxford: Oxford University Press, 1989).

37   Randall Hansen, "State Controls: Borders, Refugees, and Citizenship," in *The Oxford Handbook of Refugee and Forced Migration Studies*, ed. Elena Fiddian-Qasmiyeh et al. (Oxford: Oxford University Press, 2014), 253–64.

38   Amanda Klekowski von Koppenfels, "From Germans to Migrants: *Aussiedler* Migration to Germany," in *Diasporic Homecomings: Ethnic Return Migration in Comparative Perspective*, ed. Takeyuki Tsuda, 103–32 (Stanford, CA: Stanford University Press, 2009).

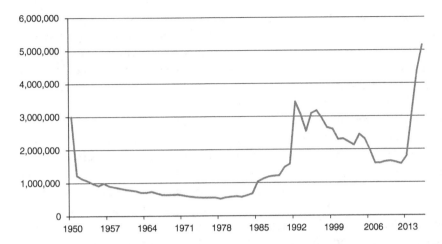

Figure 16.1. Yearly immigration and emigration of Moroccans and the unemployment rate among this group in the Netherlands (1970–2008).

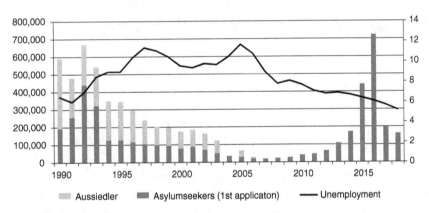

Figure 16.2. Stock of refugee population in Europe 1950–2016 (without *Aussiedler*).
Source: UNHCR, Global Trends, http://www.unhcr.org/3ebf9ba62.html.

number of asylum seekers in Europe rose steeply, largely due to the civil war in Syria. That situation also brought to light an unintended effect of the EU's Dublin Convention of 1990, which was that the southern member states (Greece, Italy, and—to a lesser extent—Spain) were burdened with the reception and sheltering of large numbers of asylum seekers and other migrants.[39] Although German chancellor Angela Merkel has pleaded for a fairer and more cooperative system to distribute refugees throughout EU member states, there is currently no such system in place.

These three exogenous shocks—decolonization, the welfare state, and the refugee regime—have together modified the migration and integration dynamics in European

39 David FitzGerald, *Refuge beyond Reach: How Rich Democracies Repel Asylum Seekers* (Oxford: Oxford University Press, 2019). See also Geddes, this volume.

states and deeply influenced migration policies at both national and European Union levels. Although business cycles and the demand for labor remain important both for migrants and countries of reception,[40] push factors in the countries of origin of colonial migrants and asylum seekers and pull factors in countries of reception, sometimes as unintended effects of policies, did not necessarily coincide with the demand for labor. Moreover, from an economic perspective, that situation played its part in the arrival of a less positive selection of migrants in terms of human capital.[41]

To a certain extent those three shocks were of a passing nature, or "one-offs." The decolonization process, *Aussiedler* included, has largely come to a natural end,[42] whereas most European welfare states have been made "migration proof" by their adoption of limited and multistage entitlement to benefits, depending on premiums paid and length of service. Because of that, although they have the right to migrate and secure jobs elsewhere, migrants from other member states within the European Union are initially excluded from welfare provision and only gradually enter the system, and are always dependent on their contributions. That therefore explains why Eastern European labor migrants who flocked to the United Kingdom have tended to pay more tax than they have received in welfare and use of public services.[43] Not only have social security benefits been "rationed"; due to the freedom of movement of EU migrants, there was no "beat-the-ban" reaction such as that precipitated by the 1962 Commonwealth Immigrants Act or the immigration restrictions in 1974.[44]

Only the refugee regime could be considered a structural change, but there are clear signs that European states are working to dismantle the commitments made in the 1951 and 1967 treaties, if not formally—for, after all, no state has yet withdrawn from the Refugee Convention—then at least in practice. The first sign of that was the introduction of visa and carrier sanctions in the EU during the first half of the 1990s,[45] which made it much more difficult to reach EU territory legally in a normal way, followed by the more recent outsourcing policies have that pushed the borders of the EU further into the Middle East and Africa. By paying countries in Europe's border regions, like Turkey, Libya, and Mali, to stop migrants from leaving, a "persuasion game" has developed.[46] With its Migration Partnership Framework, launched in 2016, the EU follows countries

---

40   Chin, *The Crisis of Multiculturalism.*

41   See also Bevelander, this volume.

42   Although there are protracted effects, as the recent arrival of refugees from Latin America (Venezuela, for example) in Spain shows.

43   Jonathan Wadsworth *et al., Brexit and the Impact of Immigration on the UK* (London: LSE, 2016).

44   Ceri Peach, *West Indian Migration to Britain* (London: Oxford University Press, 1968), 48.

45   Sarah Collinson, "Visa Requirements, Carrier Sanctions, 'Safe Third Countries' and 'Readmission': The Development of an Asylum 'Buffer Zone' in Europe," *Transactions of the Institute of British Geographers* 21, no. 1 (1996): 76–90.

46   Alexander Betts, "The International Politics of Migration," *St. Antony's International Review* 6, no. 2 (2011): 134–50.

like Australia, which reached agreements with Asian countries, including Cambodia, to send back its asylum seekers.[47]

We can conclude that when it comes to people from other continents, the preoccupation of the European migration state has partly shifted from "rights" and "markets" to "security" and "culture," while at the same time creating internal freedom of movement and allowing higher-skilled "third-country nationals" to enter its labor market. This raises the question of the extent to which postwar immigrants are perceived as a greater threat than previously, and how feelings about immigrants might have changed the long-term settlement process.

The Immigrant Threat, Then and Now

The idea that migrants who entered through one of the three postwar channels would be unable to integrate is not new. In fact it is rooted in earlier culturalist and racist conceptions of Jews, Catholics, Africans, and Asians. Notwithstanding the postwar humanitarian turn and the "ethical revolution" in the 1960s, such perceptions did not suddenly vanish after Auschwitz; they have lingered long enough to be thrown into relief once again by the globalization of the Black Lives Matter movement in 2020. After the war, xenophobic racism was reinvigorated with the arrival of colonial migrants. Politicians like Enoch Powell in Great Britain and Jean-Marie Le Pen in France mobilized anti-immigrant sentiments, but were limited in their success by a prevailing antiracist discourse and the positive interpretation of multiculturalism.[48]

As guest workers and their families were seen to be settling permanently, the spirit of this ethical revolution ran out of steam and migrants and their integration became increasingly problematized, especially in primordial cultural terms.[49] An important turning point was the Rushdie Affair (1988–89), when groups of Muslims in Europe took to the streets to demand that a book by Salman Rushdie be banned because they considered it blasphemous.[50] That action came as a shock to many, on both the right and left of the political spectrum, and strengthened the idea that multiculturalism had failed and that migrants from Islamic countries especially harbored all kinds of deeply rooted illiberal convictions. Further buttressed by Huntington's highly influential "Clash of Civilizations" framework, criticism of Islam spilled over into outright hatred and racializing of Muslims.[51] A new atmosphere of Islamophobia thickened after the terrorist attacks

---

47 Nanda Oudejans, "What Is Asylum? More than Protection, Less than Citizenship," *Constellations* 27, no. 3 (2020): 524–39.

48 Chin, *The Crisis of Multiculturalism*.

49 Noam Gidron and Peter Hall, "The Politics of Social Status: Economic and Cultural Roots of the Populist Right," *British Journal of Sociology* 68, no. 1 (2017): 57–84.

50 Lucassen and Lucassen, "The Strange Death." Some authors have labeled this mentality, more negatively, as a new religion, which nourished Islamization; Francesco M. Bongiovanni, *Europe and the End of the Age of Innocence* (New York: Palgrave Macmillan, 2018), 20.

51 Samuel P. Huntington, *The Clash of Civilizations and the Remaking of World Order* (New York: Simon & Schuster, 1996).

on September 11, 2001 in New York and Washington, in 2004 in Madrid, and in 2005 in London, and which culminated in Jihadist onslaughts in Western Europe from 2015 to 2018. The result was that fears of Islam as a threat to both culture and security almost fully converged and became a strong breeding ground for radical-right populist parties.

As a result, current public debates on migration and integration in Western Europe are fraught with misunderstanding, selective perception, and deliberate misrepresentation. Whether they concern the Brexit discussion or the so-called "refugee crisis," their tone is invariably pessimistic or outright apocalyptic. That view is commonplace not only among many politicians and journalists but in certain cases also spread by serious commentators and scholars too, including David Goodhart, Paul Collier, and David Miller.[52] In the words of Jim Hollifield, this is an example of a time when fears about security and culture clearly dominate markets and rights:

> If insecurity is cultural as well as physical, debates about markets and rights can be quickly overwhelmed by symbolic politics that paint immigrant groups as existential threats. Shifting the immigration debate from interests (economic and security) and law (process and policy) to values and culture accentuates ideology and intensifies the symbolic dimension of politics.[53]

It is tempting to interpret this shift as a reaction to changing demographics. Whereas in the first half of the twentieth century the three million immigrants from other continents constituted barely 1 percent of the European population, after World War II their number rose to almost twenty-five million, or 5 percent. They were concentrated in the west and northwest of Europe, and when added to intra-European migrants their numbers meant that approximately 10–12 percent of populations in Western European states were foreign born.[54]

From a historical perspective, however, there is much less new under the sun than these presentist worries assume. Anti-immigrant sentiment and xenophobia have been part and parcel of nation-states from the very beginning and there are striking parallels with previous clashes between immigrants and natives.[55] The Irish who settled in the

---

52   David Goodhart, *The British Dream: Success and Failures of Post-War Immigration* (London: Atlantic, 2013); Paul Collier, *Exodus: Immigration and Multiculturalism in the 21st Century* (London: Allen Lane, 2013); David Miller, *Strangers in Our Midst: The Political Philosophy of Immigration* (Cambridge, MA: Harvard University Press, 2016).

53   James F. Hollifield, "Back to the Future: Trump's Executive Orders on Migration and Refugees," *H-Diplo/ISSF (Diplomatic/International History), Policy Roundtable I-8* (2017): 8–11.

54   Nancy Foner and Leo Lucassen, "Legacies of the Past," in *The Changing Face of World Cities: Young Adult Children of Immigrants in Europe and the United States*, ed. Maurice Crul and John Mollenkopf (New York: Russell Sage, 2012), 26–43.

55   For the United States see Aristide Zolberg, *A Nation by Design: Immigration Policy in the Fashioning of America* (Cambridge, MA, and New York: Harvard University Press and Russell Sage Foundation, 2006), 155–56. For France see Gérard Noiriel, *La tyrannie du national: Le droit d'asile en Europe (1793–1993)* (Paris: Calmann-Lévy, 1991).

United Kingdom in large numbers from the 1840s onward were confronted with wide-spread discrimination, often a mixture of anti-Catholic and ethnic prejudice, which in the 1850s and 1860s led to mob violence in cities like Stockport and Wolverhampton.[56] The American Party (the "Know Nothings") in the 1850s used the same vicious anti-Catholic rhetoric to stigmatize Irish immigrants,[57] and similarities with anti-Muslim sentiment of recent decades are striking.[58] Like Muslims today, Catholic Irish migrants were accused of harboring illiberal and antidemocratic values, repressing women, and aiming to dominate the world, demographically and ideologically, by orders of the Pope in Rome.

Thirty years later in the wake of the xenophobic and antisemitic Boulanger movement ("French jobs for the French"),[59] it was Italian and Belgian labor migrants in France who became the targets of anti-immigrant sentiments.[60] In 1893, at least eight Italian immigrants were hunted down and killed by native workers in the salt mine region of Aigues Mortes, in the Camargue.[61] Anti-Italian sentiment was further aroused by Italian and Russian anarchists, who unleashed a wave of terrorist attacks in Europe and North America, killing among others the American president, the Russian head of state, the French president, the Austrian head of state, and the Spanish prime minister.[62] From the early 1930s in various countries, such as France and the Netherlands, both European and North African migrants were problematized, as were Jewish refugees from Nazi Germany. They were regarded not only as unfair competition for native workers but also as a cultural threat in general.[63] This serves as an important reminder that when comparing attitudes now and then, essentialist and racist ideas about immigrants should be understood in their proper historical context and that in the past, too, cultural differences

---

56   Kyle Hughes and Donald M. MacRaild, *Ribbon Societies in Nineteenth-Century Ireland and Its Diaspora: The Persistence of Tradition* (Liverpool: Liverpool University Press, 2018), 245–46.

57   John Higham, *Strangers in the Land: Patterns of American Nativism, 1860–1925* (1955; repr., New Brunswick, NJ: Rutgers University Press, 2008). See also Tyler Anbinder, *Nativism and Slavery: The Northern Know Nothings and the Politics of the 1850s* (Oxford: Oxford University Press, 1992).

58   Aristide Zolberg and Long L. Woon, "Why Islam Is Like Spanish: Cultural Incorporation in Europe and the United States," *Politics and Society* 27, no. 1 (1999): 5–38.

59   Kevin Passmore, *The Right in France from the Third Republic to Vichy* (Oxford: Oxford University Press, 2013), 49–50, 70, 71.

60   Robert Stuart, *Marxism and National Identity: Socialism, Nationalism, and National Socialism during the French Fin de Siècle* (New York: State University of New York Press, 2006), 58; Gérard Noiriel, *Le creuset français: Histoire de l'immigration, XIXe–XXe siècles* (Paris: Éditions du Seuil, 1988), 258–59.

61   Gérard Noiriel, *Une histoire populaire de la France: De la guerre de Cent Ans à nos jours* (Marseille : Agone, 2018). See also Lucassen, *The Immigrant Threat*, 82.

62   Richard B. Jensen, *The Battle against Anarchist Terrorism: An International History, 1878–1934* (Cambridge: Cambridge University Press, 2004).

63   Rosenberg, *Policing Paris*.

between Europeans were seen as insurmountable, just as they are with Africans, Asians, and Muslims today.[64] Or, as Joel Perlmann and Roger Waldinger so succinctly put it, distorted ideas about migration now and then lead many to be too optimistic about the past and too pessimistic about the present.[65]

Despite the clear historical record, the idea that the "old" migrants were fundamentally different from the "new" ones sticks quite stubbornly. The argument runs as follows: back then they were all Europeans, all Judeo-Christians; they were frugal, entrepreneurial, skilled, and willing to adapt, whereas immigrants today threaten our culture, refuse to integrate, and are primarily drawn by our welfare state. Such juxtapositions not only belie historical facts and carry the risk of damaging the idea of equal citizenship, they are also a recurring phenomenon in the history of immigration.[66] In *Alien Immigrants to England*, published in 1897, for example, the economic historian William Cunningham warned readers against the dangerous and parasitic Jewish migrants from Eastern Europe who were entering Great Britain at the time. Cunningham considered them "incomparable" to the thrifty Walloons and French Huguenots who had found refuge in England in the sixteenth and seventeenth centuries, a comment quite similar to today's alarmist discourses about the postwar immigration of colored people from the colonies and labor migrants from Islamic countries, who would change the game fundamentally.[67]

Another reason why awareness of the striking similarities to past immigrants remains underdeveloped is the dominant idea among politicians and policy-makers that migration is a problem, something to be "solved." NGOs and international organizations like the UNHCR and IOM, whose aim it is to help migrants, seem to think this too, and even migration scholars contribute to this alarmist sentiment, albeit unintentionally. Following the preoccupation of politicians and policy-makers, some suggest that we should identify the root causes or "drivers" of migration and prevent people from leaving the global South in the first place. That perspective treats migration not only as a predicament but also as an anomaly for modern nation-states, and legitimizes the widely held conviction that irregular migrants are to be blocked wherever possible.[68] More recently,

---

64   See also Nancy Foner, *From Ellis Island to JFK: New York's Two Great Waves of Immigration* (New Haven, CT: Yale University Press, 2002); Richard Alba and Victor Nee, *Remaking the American Mainstream: Assimilation and Contemporary Immigration* (Cambridge, MA: Harvard University Press, 2005); Joel Perlmann, *Italians Then, Mexicans Now: Immigrant Origins and Second-Generation Progress, 1890 to 2000* (New York: Russell Sage Foundation, 2005); Klaus J. Bade *et al.*, eds., *Encyclopedia of Migration and Minorities in Europe: From the 17th Century to the Present* (Cambridge: Cambridge University Press, 2011).

65   Joel Perlmann and Roger Waldinger, "Second Generation Decline? Children of Immigrants, Past and Present—A Reconsideration," *International Migration Review* 31, no. 4 (1997): 893–922.

66   Tamar de Waal, "Liberal Democracy and the Judeo-Christian Tradition," *Netherlands Journal of Legal Philosophy* 49, no. 1 (2020): 7–21.

67   William Cunningham, *Alien Immigrants to England* (London and New York: Swan Sonnenschein and Macmillan, 1897).

68   For example, Collier, *Exodus: Immigration and Multiculturalism in the 21st Century.*

climate change and high fertility rates in the Arab world and sub-Saharan Africa have been added to this pool of fears and negative associations.[69]

Considered from a broader historical perspective, however, that framework presents two major problems. First, it contradicts solid evidence from historians, economists, and social scientists which shows convincingly that migration, now as then, does not generally drive down wages nor does it put the locals out of work. In fact it often stimulates economic growth.[70] That is true even when we focus exclusively on those migrants who are widely believed to have negative financial and cultural impacts on receiving societies.[71] Secondly, and more importantly, it perceives migration as an exception to the assumed rule that societies are sedentary. Hence the predilection for connecting meteorological phenomena like tsunamis, earthquakes, and hurricanes—all of them things devoid of human agency—with "emptying" of the world's poorer regions and seeing them as probable initiators of the mass migrations, which are their consequence unless harsh measures and tight migration controls are imposed.[72] It is no coincidence that current discussions on migration often abound with "water speech": streams, flows, waves, tsunamis, dams, and dikes, nor that politicians react by building walls to keep migrants out.[73]

As an antidote to such interpretations, what we know of the history of world migration leaves us not only well placed to compare xenophobia from different time periods but also allows us a much deeper insight into the narrowly political, exceptionalist, and presentist gaze. Since the 1990s historians have been unveiling and studying the systemic function of migration for human societies in a highly interdisciplinary way, looking at migration's key role in wreaking social and cultural change.[74] If we wish to understand the impact of migrants, we need a much broader definition of migration. In the remaining part of this chapter I will therefore explore this less trodden path, which will help us better understand the evolution of the "migration state" in Europe, especially in the postwar period.

---

69   See Charbit, this volume. For balanced and nuanced studies on these issues, see Étienne Piguet *et al.*, eds., *Migration and Climate Change* (New York: UNESCO and Cambridge University Press, 2011); Paul Puschmann and Koen Matthijs, "The Demographic Transition in the Arab World: The Dual Role of Marriage in Family Dynamics and Population Growth," in *Population Change in Europe, the Middle-East and North Africa: Beyond the Demographic Divide*, ed. Koen Matthijs et al., 119–65 (Farnham: Ashgate, 2015); Alex Sager, "Book Review: Strangers in Our Midst: The Political Philosophy of Immigration by David Miller," *LSE Blog Review of Books* (London: LSE, 2016), http://blogs.lse.ac.uk/lsereviewofbooks/2016/09/06/book-review-strangers -in-our-midst-the-political-philosophy-of-immigration-by-david-miller/.

70   Abhijit Banerjee and Esther Duflo, *Good Economics for Hard Times: Better Answers to Our Biggest Problems* (Public Affairs, Juggernaut Books, and Allen Lane, 2019).

71   Lucassen and Lucassen, "The Strange Death."

72   Collier, *Exodus: Immigration and Multiculturalism in the 21st Century*.

73   Reece Jones, *Violent Borders: Refugees and the Right to Move* (New York: Verso, 2016).

74   Manning, *Migration in World History*; Jan Lucassen and Leo Lucassen, 'Theorizing Cross-Cultural Migrations: The Case of Eurasia since 1500," *Social Science History* 41, no. 3 (2017): 445–75.

The Cross Cultural Migration Rate (CCMR) Approach

When analyzing why people move, certainly when we consider the past, state borders have their limits and can produce gross anomalies. Why shine a spotlight on Belgians, say, who cross the French border and settle twenty kilometers up the road, while ignoring the millions of Chinese and Russian citizens who migrate over much longer distances within their own countries and often end up in culturally very different regions? Why neglect temporary migrations over national borders? And why are highly skilled migrants so seldom included in the discussion?

To answer those questions migration scholars need a much broader perspective that will supersede current political and societal obsessions and media depictions. Inspired by world historians like Patrick Manning and profiting from the work of numerous historical demographers, geographers, and historians who take a much broader view of people on the move, we developed the Cross Cultural Migration Rate (CCMR).[75] The Cross Cultural Migration Rate begins with cultural instead of national boundaries, thereby merging internal and international and permanent and temporary migrations in one coherent long-term framework. The basic idea is that to understand the social and cultural impact of migration on human societies we must go beyond a definition of migrants derived from the nation-state. We must be able to examine more broadly how migrants, from different cultural backgrounds beyond the merely national, change both the places where they settle and often those they left. After all, most migration is not simply from A to B but far more circuitous, and in many cases involves repeated return migration even after a number of generations, as well as circular and serial displacements. To reveal the complete picture, the Cross Cultural Migration Rate approach distinguishes among four types of migrants:

1. People moving from rural areas to cities, either within states or coming from abroad (to cities);

2. People who move within rural areas to culturally and ecologically different settings (colonization);

3. People who move temporarily as seasonal workers from peasant areas to far more commercial farming regions; and

4. People who migrate temporarily for longer periods (temporary multi-annual migrants), such as soldiers, sailors, skilled workers, and missionaries.[76]

---

75 Jan Lucassen and Leo Lucassen, "Theorizing Cross-Cultural Migrations: The Case of Eurasia since 1500," *Social Science History* 41, no. 3 (2017): 445–75. Moch, *Moving Europeans;* see also Jan Kok, "The Family Factor in Migration Decisions," in *Migration History in World History: Multidisciplinary Approaches,* ed. Jan Lucassen et al., 213–48 (Leiden: Brill, 2010); Adrian Favell, *Eurostars and Eurocities: Free Movement and Mobility in an Integrating Europe* (Malden, MA: Blackwell, 2008); Nancy Green, *The Other Americans in Paris: Businessmen, Countesses, Wayward Youth, 1880–1941* (Chicago: University of Chicago Press, 2014).

76 Jan Lucassen and Leo Lucassen, "The Mobility Transition Revisited, 1500–1900: What the Case of Europe Can Offer to Global History," *Journal of Global History* 4, no. 3 (2009): 347–77;

Table 16.3. Shifts in the European "migration state" (1945–2020).

	1801–1850	1851–1900	1901–1950	1951–2000
To Cities	7.7	12.3	7.2	5.7
Colonization	0	0	2.6	0
Seasonal	1	2.6	0.8	0.2
Temporary Multiannual	6.7	3.3	25.6	5
Immigration	0	0	0.8	4.8
Emigration	1.6	7.4	7.1	2.9
Total CCMR	**17**	**25.6**	**44.1**	**18.6**

To calculate the total proportion of cross-cultural migrants in the total population in a given period, we must add those who left Europe (emigration) and those from other continents who entered Europe (immigration) (table 16.3).

Presenting the first half of the twentieth century as an all-time high, this approach yields a different view of Europe's migration history since 1800 from the one conveyed in mainstream scholarship. In the 2003 edition of their well-known handbook on international migration, Stephen Castles and Mark Miller wrote that effectively the age of migration began after World War II and reached a peak in the 1980s when international migration expanded in both volume and significance.[77] Even if we accept Castles and Miller's limitation to international migrations, their account suffers from ahistorical bias.[78] Apart from the impact of the two world wars, North America had already experienced very high levels of international migration of Irish, Jews, Italians, and Chinese from 1880–1920, quite similar to those a century later.[79] Like present-day unskilled migrants from abroad, be they Mexicans to the United States, Moroccans to the Netherlands, or Pakistanis to England, earlier migrations excited similar fear and opposition, thus feeding the culture/security nexus of the "migration state." As Banerjee and Duflo succinctly remarked, in those days Ireland and Norway were the "shit-hole" countries that even the very poor left for the United States,[80] while Jews and Catholics aroused

---

idem, eds., *Globalising Migration History: The Eurasian Experience (16th–21st Centuries)* (Leiden: Brill, 2014).

77   Stephen Castles and Mark Miller, *The Age of Migration: International Population Movements in the Modern World*, 3rd ed. (New York: Guildford Press, 2003), 4. This presentist bias has largely been remedied in the sixth (2020) edition, for which Hein de Haas has stepped in as main editor.

78   As already noted by Ewa Morawska, "The Sociology and Historiography of Immigration," in *Immigration Reconsidered: History, Sociology, and Politics*, ed. Virginia Yans-McLaughlin, 187–240 (Oxford: Oxford University Press, 1990).

79   Foner, *From Ellis Island to JFK*; Perlmann, *Italians Then, Mexicans Now*; Lucassen, *The Immigrant Threat*; and Roger Waldinger, "Did Manufacturing Matter? The Experience of Yesterday's Second Generation: A Reassessment," *International Migration Review* 41, no. 1 (2007): 3–39.

80   Banerjee and Duflo, *Good Economics for Hard Times*, 25–26.

similar cultural fears to those that Muslims bring with them today. In that sense the "Clash of Civilizations" is nothing new, but simply runs along fault lines different from those of the not-so-distant past.

Organizational Migrants

War is the main reason why the all-time high figures for migration came in the first rather than the second half of the twentieth century. In addition to the uprooting of millions of civilians as refugees and displaced persons, the two world wars involved tens of millions of young men and women members of the armed forces who were sent to fight in and occupy other countries. A great many of those millions were stationed very far from home, and there are various excellent reasons to regard them—as well as others who moved while working for transnational businesses or as missionaries and diplomats for their organizations—as cross-cultural migrants whose presence had effects on the relationship between migration and social change.

The displacement of so many people wrought fundamental and unexpected social changes, not least because organizational migrants are invested with power and prestige. They not only interact with native populations in various ways but also dramatically change the demographic and cultural composition, something especially true of the soldiers who enforced the relocation of millions of people in Europe during and after the two world wars.[81] Large-scale ethnic cleansing not only relocated but also killed millions, and the most dramatic example of that is of course the genocide of Jewish Europeans, which reduced their number from roughly ten million in 1939 to barely four million in 1945. That experience had dramatic repercussions for the cultural and demographic outlook of Eastern Europe, where until 1940 some 75 percent of Europe's Jews lived but where only a few hundred thousand remained after the war. Poland is by far the most extreme case, for in September 1939 at the outbreak of World War II almost 10 percent of Poland's population was Jewish, about three million people, of whom barely 10 percent survived the war and of whom only some 90,000 were still alive in Poland in 1947.[82] As a result, an entire culture became effectively extinct, and combined with the resettlement of "national minorities" directly after 1945 and emigration to Israel by many survivors, nation-states in Eastern Europe became much more homogeneous than in fact they had ever been. This would cast its shadow forward by creating a social climate deeply unfriendly to migration. Postwar ethno-nationalism in Poland, Hungary, Romania, and Czechoslovakia directed against African and Asian guest workers during the communist era, and more recently against Muslim refugees from the Middle East, is inseparably linked to that process of forced homogenization.[83]

---

81   Christopher Rass, ed., *Militärische Migration vom Altertum bis zur Gegenwart* (Paderborn: Ferdinand Schöningh, 2016).

82   Alex Bein, *The Jewish Question: Biography of a World Problem* (Rutherford: Fairleigh Dickinson University Press, 1990), 25–27.

83   Stephen M. Saideman and R. William Ayres, *For Kin or Country: Xenophobia, Nationalism, and War* (New York: Columbia University Press, 2005); Jan C. Behrends and Patrice G. Poutrus,

A second example of fundamental reshuffling of populations through social engineering with soldiers and police as executors is to be found in Stalin's policy of resettling millions of Russians within the Soviet Union. Again, war not only uprooted millions of soldiers, many of whom had never before been out of their home regions; it was also instrumental in a large-scale process of social engineering whereby a considerable part of the population was either killed or displaced to Central Asia and Kazakhstan, which was culturally and ecologically entirely different terrain.[84]

Soldiers as migrants influenced not only the states for which they fought and those they occupied but also the societies they left behind. An interesting example concerns African American GIs, who helped liberate Europe and subsequently became part of a huge and floating mass of men—and women, although many fewer—who completed their two-year postings to military bases in Japan and what was then West Germany, where they assisted with the de-Nazification process.

Although racial segregation was part of the daily reality on US military bases abroad, as it was at home in the United States, black American servicemen soon realized that the surrounding German society, until recently the racist state par excellence, offered far greater freedom than the segregated South of the US where many of them originated, or indeed the ghettos of the North. Befriending white women and receiving a ready welcome in racially mixed bars and restaurants were totally new experiences for black Americans and made them aware that the institutionalized racism they had left at home was not as normal as they had thought. Their postings therefore had immense impact on them, and many wrote about their experiences in letters to their friends and families across the Atlantic. When they returned to the US, some became politically active and joined the NAACP, thereby infusing the nascent civil rights movement with the cultural and social capital of their overseas experience.[85] The encounters abroad of hundreds of thousands of black American soldiers are crucial to an understanding of the postwar social and political history of the United States,[86] as are the frequently overlooked temporary migrations by such "organizational migrants."[87]

"Xenophobia in the Former GDR—Explorations and Explanation from a Historical Perspective," in *Nationalisms across the Globe: An Overview of Nationalisms in State-Endowed and Stateless Nations*, ed. Wojciech Burszta, 155–70 (Poznan: Wyższa Nikoła Nauk Humanistycznych i Dziennikarstwa, 2005).

84   Pavel Polian, *Against Their Will: The History and Geography of Forced Migrations in the USSR* (Budapest: CEU Press, 2004).

85   Maria Höhn and Martin Klimke, *A Breath of Freedom: The Civil Rights Struggle, African American GIs, and Germany* (New York: Palgrave Macmillan, 2010). More in general on soldiers as migrants, see Rass, *Militärische Migration;* Joshua A. Sanborn, "Unsettling the Empire: Violent Migrations and Social Disaster in Russia during World War I," *Journal of Modern History* 77, no. 2 (2005): 290–324.

86   See also Foley, this volume.

87   Leo Lucassen and Aniek X. Smit, "The Repugnant Other: Soldiers, Missionaries, and Aid Workers as Organizational Migrants," *Journal of World History* 26, no. 1 (2015): 1–39.

Other organizational migrants who crossed cultural borders were at least as important in forging social, cultural, and political changes. They included sailors, missionaries, aid workers, diplomats, skilled technicians, and experts working for large multinational corporations such as Shell or Phillips. Nancy Green's recent study of the American business and diplomatic community in Paris, which numbered approximately 60,000 between the wars, illustrates the volatility of societies and the continuing nature of outside influences.[88] Often equipped with military, economic, and cultural power and prestige, the influence of such migrants on those with whom they temporarily interact is often underrated or simply disregarded, but their movements too are part of migration flows and consequently of migration history. To ignore them obscures the impact of migration in general and propagates the idea that migration is the exception, and—as Gérard Noiriel noted years ago—that societies are defined by long-term stable and static structures.[89]

Seasonal Migrants

The second category of temporary migrants in the CCMR model concerns those who move seasonally, their travels determined mainly by agricultural cycles. Although nowadays Polish and Romanian seasonal migrants are a topic of debate in more than one EU member state, such migrants had previously gone largely unnoticed in migration history, apart from specific cases like the Bracero Program (1942–64) to bring Mexican manual workers into the United States through temporary arrangements, or a similar scheme the Prussian state introduced in the 1880s for Polish agricultural workers in the east of the German Empire.[90] Those examples are only the tip of a much larger iceberg, especially if we consider the millions of seasonal workers who have migrated over the past centuries.[91] Most of them were free to move, especially those who remained within their own countries such as in Spain, France, and Italy, and lived alternately on their small family farms, where their wives and children lived permanently, and periodically in the regions where they earned their money. Nowadays, and in much the same way, Eastern Europeans come to Western Europe to harvest asparagus and strawberries.

By crossing cultural borders seasonal migrants become familiar with market economics. Their ability to earn wages and their exposure to commercialization and new consumption patterns, along with a range of other new cultural experiences, changed

---

88   Nancy L. Green, "Americans Abroad and the Uses of Citizenship: Paris, 1914–1940," *Journal of American Ethnic History* 31, no. 3 (2012): 5–32.

89   Noiriel, *Le creuset français*; idem, *La tyrannie du national*.

90   On *braceros*, see Kitty Calavita, *Inside the State: The Bracero Program, Immigration, and the I.N.S.* (New Orleans: Quid Pro Quo Books, 2010); Foley and Tichenor, this volume. For Poles in late nineteenth-century Prussia, see Stefan Berger, "Building the Nation among Visions of German Empire," in *Nationalizing Empires, ed. Stefan Berger and Alexei Miller, 247–308* (Budapest: CEU Press, 2014).

91   Jan Lucassen, *Migrant Labour in Europe, 1600–1900: The Drift to the North Sea* (London: Croom Helm, 1987).

not only the migrants but also their communities of origin.[92] As money is invested in home communities and boosts conspicuous consumption, social inequality in those communities increases as communal solidarity is eroded, which demonstrates that social changes through cross-cultural migrations can have both positive and negative effects. This is similar to Phil Martin's "migration hump," and the paradox that migration and development beget more migration and more inequalities in the sending and receiving societies, at least in the short to medium terms.[93]

City Dwellers

Urban communities, both within and outside Europe, long relied on continuous immigration from rural areas to exist and grow. But when urban mortality levels declined during the course of the nineteenth century, cities still remained a primary migrant destination. Moving to cities, even temporarily, brought villagers into very different social and cultural environments. In addition to potential employment and sources of income, the public space and institutions in cities offered individuals greater autonomy from their families and allowed them to be less dependent on their kin and less subject to their social control. Women especially found more opportunities to act on their own initiative and achieve far greater agency, albeit within the prevailing gender norms. Urban historians have recently argued along similar lines that the greater public role of women in English and Dutch cities during the early modern period led to a rise in crime rates,[94] while economic historians stress the relationship between gender equality in urban areas and economic growth.[95]

Although these examples concern the early modern period, in the nineteenth and twentieth centuries rural-to-urban migration proved to have a liberating effect in many parts of Europe thanks to the reduced role of patriarchy and to educational and income-earning opportunities. Most recently the enormous volume of migration by men and women alike to Chinese cities has drawn the attention of social scientists, who observe similar cultural changes.[96] The effect is not straightforward and depends on how far

---

92   Leo Lucassen, "Lippische Ziegler unter dem Gesichtspunkt der globalen Migrationsgeschichte," in *Saisonale Arbeitsmigration in der Geschichte: Die Lippischen Ziegler und ihre Herkunftsgesellschaft*, ed. Bettina Joergens and Jan Lucassen, 33–57 (Essen: Klartext, 2017). See also Hazan, this volume.

93   See Martin, this volume.

94   Ariadne Schmidt and Manon van der Heijden, "Women Alone in Early Modern Dutch Towns: Opportunities and Strategies to Survive," *Journal of Urban History* 42, no. 1 (2016): 21–38.

95   Alexandra M. de Pleijt *et al.*, *Gender Relations and Economic Development: Hypotheses about the Reversal of Fortune in Eurasia*, CGEH Working Paper no. 79 (Utrecht: Utrecht University, 2016). See also Tine de Moor and Jan Luiten van Zanden, "Girl Power: The European Marriage Pattern and Labour Markets in the North Sea Region in the Late Medieval and Early Modern Period," *Economic History Review* 63, no. 1 (2010): 1–33.

96   Hong Zhang, "Labor Migration, Gender, and the Rise of Neo-local Marriages in the Economic Boomtown of Dongguan, South China," *Journal of Contemporary China* 18, no. 61 (2009): 639–56.

patriarchal family systems are eroded by urban influences and on the specific urban "membership regime" that establishes gendered and other formal and informal rules concerning migrant access to urban institutions and public spaces.[97]

For the twentieth century we no longer counted migration to cities within states, because we assumed that by then cultural differences between rural areas and cities had become much less significant following continuing processes of national homogenization. We realize, however, that even in the twentieth century considerable cultural differences remained within states. One example is that of southern Italians (*Sudistas*) moving to northern Italy up until the 1970s, or interimperial moves between the Habsburg and Ottoman empires until World War I. One could therefore differentiate depending on the national and regional situation. In other parts of the world, however, especially in large states such as India, Russia, and China, where internal ethnic, linguistic, and religious diversity is far greater, we continued to classify internal movement as cross-cultural and therefore included it in the CCMR model. Moreover, in China, apart from cultural differences between the different parts of the country, the discriminatory *hukou* system means that rural migrants have only limited access to urban institutions, such as schools and housing.[98]

Colonists

A recurrent phenomenon in both the early modern and modern periods in large empires such as China, Russia, and the Ottoman and Habsburg empires, as well as on overseas plantations in the Americas and Oceania, was that people moved as farmers, soldiers, and administrators to areas that were culturally and ecologically different. Such colonizing migrations were often organized and supported by the state, and some migrants were coerced, such as French and British convicts and Russian dissenters.[99] Others saw no option other than to leave for unknown destinations as indentured migrants or redemptioners, to be treated on arrival as virtual slaves until they had repaid the debt incurred for the journey.[100] By far the largest group of coerced colonist migrants were the approximately ten million Africans taken against their will to the Americas to toil on plantations as hereditary chattel slaves. These examples convey the full range of free to unfree migrations within this category, with "free" migrants very much the exception until the mid-nineteenth century. They have in common that they migrated to rural settings, and that in many cases institutions such as states and commercial firms organized both their displacement and their exploitation.

---

97   Leo Lucassen, "Population and Migration," in *The Oxford Handbook of Cities in World History*, ed. P. Clark (Oxford: Oxford University Press, 2013), 664–82.

98   Martin King Whyte, ed., *One Country, Two Societies: Rural-Urban Inequality in Contemporary China* (Cambridge, MA: Harvard University Press, 2010).

99   Nicholas B. Breyfogle, *Heretics and Colonizers: Forging Russia's Empire in the South Caucasus* (Ithaca, NY: Cornell University Press, 2005).

100   Günter Moltmann, "The Migration of German Redemptioners to North America, 1720–1820," in *Colonialism and Migration: Indentured Labour before and after Slavery*, ed. P. C. Emmer, 105–24 (Dordrecht: Martinus Nijhoff, 1986).

Those four types of migrants who form the core of the CCMR approach (organizational migrants, seasonal migrants, city dwellers, and colonists) offer a much more systematic view of the extent and impact of migration in Europe before, during, and after World War II. By far the majority of them were Europeans who moved within their own countries, while many others who did cross national borders did so temporarily. Still others—the bulk of them soldiers—came from abroad as organizational migrants, and although some of them came to the attention of state authorities, most did not and so strengthened and maintained the idea of a static Europe with migration as the exception. That so considerable a proportion of the population experienced at least one cross-cultural move shows that migration was much more pervasive than assumed and that movement was crucial to all kinds of social, cultural, economic, and political changes, at the level of individuals, households, and states.

In the course of the nineteenth and twentieth centuries, however, all such movements were perceived much less as migration but were shifted to the discursive realm of "mobility," while migration was increasingly reserved for foreigners with low skills, and in the CCMR model those migrating to different continents—in particular from the 1960s onward—are recorded under the heading of "immigration." The shift went hand in hand with the "othering" of immigrants in racial and phenotypical terms, first applied to colonial migrants from sub-Saharan Africa and Asia but soon to labor migrants from Turkey and North Africa, most of whom differed in appearance only very slightly from Europeans. From the 1980s onward Islam became the focus of the criticism of immigration and "failed integration," with Muslims perceived en bloc as a static and unchangeable group of people unable or unwilling to accept Western values, which suggested the racializing of religion.[101]

The gradual narrowing of the migration category explains why in postwar "migration states" migrants have become such a contested and polarizing topic and have come to be regarded as a threat to both the socioeconomic and cultural identity and status of the native population.

To what extent did migration dynamics in both Eastern and Western Europe fundamentally change during the twentieth and early twenty-first centuries, and how should we assess the impact of migration on European societies? To answer those questions the "migration state" concept of James Hollifield has proved a useful starting point as it allows us to see the change in the discourse as well as in legislation from emphasis on rights and markets (roughly 1945–90) to security and culture (1990–present), as presented in figure 16.3.

---

101   As argued by Jytte Klausen, *The Islamic Challenge: Politics and Religion in Western Europe* (Oxford: Oxford University Press, 2005); Jennifer Fredette, *Constructing Muslims in France: Discourse, Public Identity, and the Politics of Citizenship* (Philadelphia: Temple University Press, 2014). On the racialization of Muslims, see also Leonie B. Jackson, *Islamophobia in Britain: The Making of a Muslim Enemy* (Basingstoke: Palgrave Macmillan, 2018).

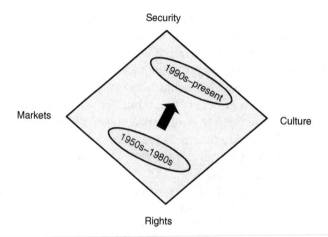

Figure 16.3. Immigration of asylum seekers and *Aussiedler* in Germany, in relation to the general unemployment rate (in %) (1990–2015).

In the literature this broad shift toward a more xenophobic public and political atmosphere is explained by two broad and related structural changes during the postwar period, one of which was institutional and the other demographic. The first is captured in Hollifield's "embedded rights" mechanism, which partly neutralized the power of states to control immigration and thereby produced societal tensions, while the second emphasizes the unprecedented mass immigration of people from separate continents embodying different cultures and phenotypes.

This chapter has put those two developments into a somewhat different and longer-term perspective. Where the "embedded rights" of migrants are the product of a liberal democracy-cum-welfare state, I would add that institutional and demographic dynamics should be seen as parts of a much broader international humanitarian and ethical turn. On the one hand, that turn was directed from below by decolonized states in the global South, while on the other—and especially in Europe and North America—by the increasing awareness of racism caused by raised awareness from the 1960s onward of the ideology that drove the Holocaust. Although the humanitarian and ethical turn was onto a bumpy road and has so far failed to end racism and xenophobia, it did create a brief cultural hegemony, to use Gramsci's tool, that restrained the most overt expressions of racism and discrimination in the name of equality and multiculturalism. No matter how vaguely defined and implemented, it delegitimized policies, like South Africa's apartheid system, that diverged from that ideal. It was no coincidence that the turn to humanitarianism and ethics, which was largely even if not entirely limited to the dominant North Atlantic region, overlapped with the most egalitarian period in large parts of the world and was buttressed by the rise of the concept of the welfare state.[102] Nor was it by chance

---

102   Thomas Piketty, *Capital in the Twenty-First Century* (Cambridge, MA: Harvard University Press, 2014).

that the global shift to neoliberalism, which led to a gradual disassembling of that welfare state and the rise of inequality, coincided with the rise of integration pessimism and the partial return of openly expressed racism.[103]

These developments placed demographic changes in a somewhat different light. Many studies implicitly or explicitly explain the rise of integration pessimism at least partly by the sudden arrival in Western Europe and North America of enormous numbers of immigrants from Africa and Asia since the late 1940s, who not only looked very different but brought with them very different cultural baggage. From the very beginning their arrival caused friction, but since the 1990s the second-generation descendants of migrants from Islamic countries have become the center of a great deal of attention, much of it negative. Discomfort with immigration is strengthened by socioeconomic precarity and religious radicalization of a visible minority, especially noticeable in big cities.

Given the unfortunate timing of that immigration, much of which coincided with unforeseen welfare-state dynamics, we can now conclude that second-generation descendants of immigrants are generally doing much better than could have been expected. Considering the human capital of their parents, many have made impressive steps up the social ladder, while overall the idea of culturally parallel societies is largely refuted by the facts, just as a century ago predictions of failed assimilation and clashes of civilizations did not come true. Nevertheless, integration pessimism has not only lingered and been reinforced by radical politicians at both ends of the political spectrum, it is now being imitated by mainstream parties, which have begun to use migrants and their descendants as scapegoats for growing social inequality and as a reason for retraction of the welfare state. This has greatly stimulated the rise of welfare chauvinism that misleadingly represents welfare as a zero-sum game, depicting immigrants and natives as competitors.[104]

That framing gathered yet more wind in its sails from inequality and precarity, both of which have deepened within European since the 2010s and become a powerful weapon seized by authoritarian radical-right politicians, many of whom are now mainstream and have legitimized xenophobic and racist sentiments that had become unthinkable, let alone unspeakable, during the "ethical revolution." As the antiracist consensus rapidly dissolved, radical and extreme-right political parties seized an opportunity to instrumentalize cultural features of migrants from Muslim countries and lampoon the "political correctness" that ensued from the multiculturalist ideal.[105]

It should be stressed, however, that the political and societal discussion on migration, and the role of the state in controlling or facilitating it, is limited to certain segments of migrant populations. To put it crudely, in general, migrants pop up on the public and political radar only when they are low skilled and, rightly or wrongly, seen as a

---

103   As also argued by Piketty in his *Capital and Ideology*.

104   Crepaz, *Trust Beyond Borders*; idem and Regan Damron, "Constructing Tolerance: How the Welfare State Shapes Attitudes about Immigrants," *Comparative Political Studies* 42, no. 3 (2009): 437–63.

105   Cas Mudde, "Three Decades of Populist Radical Right Parties in Western Europe: So What?," *European Journal of Political Research* 52, no. 1 (2013): 1–19.

threat to the socioeconomic position or cultural status of lower-skilled native workers.[106] In other words, when they seem to threaten the jobs, housing, status, and identity of the native population. In reality such migrants, who postwar were increasingly equated with "coloured" migrants from Africa and Asia, were only a fraction of the total number of people who crossed cultural borders to work, join their families, or find temporary jobs. Higher-skilled migrants, some of them employed by international businesses and organizations, were notably exempted from the problematizing political discourse on migration. The same is true for the many better-off white colonial migrants who settled in postwar Europe, for whom the term "migrants" has always been studiously avoided, to be replaced by new categories that distinguish them from the lower skilled and unwanted. For these "invisible migrants," new terms were invented, such as "repatriates," "returnees," and *Aussiedler* for the ex-colonial migrants, and "expats" for highly skilled migrants.[107] Such conceptual apartheid affirms the self-fulfilling negative framing of migrants and reproduces the idea that migration is a problem in need of a solution.

Ironically, that views of migration can be so myopic is merely confirmed by the words of migration scholars who, for very different reasons, stress the uniqueness of postwar immigration and highlight its differences from earlier immigration, in terms of both migration and integration.[108] Never before, runs the argument, have cities in Europe and the United States been so "superdiverse," with natives now in the minority, such that the settlement process is expected to change fundamentally.[109] Seen from a long-term perspective and considering the highly diverse and enormous scale of immigrations in the past, both in Europe and the US, such forecasts are highly questionable. The diversity seen in seventeenth-century Amsterdam or in New York around 1900 was not so very different from what we are seeing today, and in the long run it did not stop the integration process. Ironically, celebration of "superdiversity" can have the unintended consequence of confirming the fears of influential integration pessimists.[110]

Understanding and defining migration in much broader strokes, and adding internal, temporary, colonization and seasonal migrations to the mixture, helps us to see both optimistic and pessimistic views on current immigration from a longer-term perspective and to better understand the nature of the migration state, which is prisoner of the narrow and statist obsession with "bad migrants."

---

106   On the issue of fear of status loss, see Lamont, "Addressing Recognition Gaps."

107   Andrea L. Smith, ed., *Europe's Invisible Migrants: Consequences of the Colonists' Return* (Amsterdam: Amsterdam University Press, 2003).

108   See, for example, Castles and Miller, *The Age of Migration*.

109   Steven Vertovec, "Super-diversity and Its Implications," *Ethnic and Racial Studies* 30, no. 6 (2007): 1024–54; Maurice Crul, "Super-diversity vs. Assimilation: How Complex Diversity in Majority-Minority Cities Challenges the Assumptions of Assimilation," *Journal of Ethnic and Migration Studies* 42, no. 1 (2016): 54–68.

110   Christopher Caldwell, *Reflections on the Revolution in Europe: Immigration, Islam and the West* (London: Allen Lane, 2009); Thilo Sarrazin, *Deutschland schafft sich ab* (Munich: Deutsche Verlags-Anstalt, 2010); Douglas Murray, *The Strange Death of Europe: Immigration, Identity, Islam* (London: Bloomsbury, 2017).

James F. Hollifield

The Liberal Paradox

ALL COUNTRIES IN THE world face the challenge of managing migration and mobility, a task made infinitely more difficult and complex by the COVID-19 global pandemic. As we can see from various chapters in this book, the dilemmas of migration management are not limited to the principal receiving countries of the "OECD world." But they are especially acute in (erstwhile) liberal democracies where economic pressures push governments to be open to migration, while political, legal, and security concerns argue for greater closure—what I have called a liberal paradox (Hollifield 1992). How can countries be simultaneously open to migration and mobility (for economic and demographic reasons and for purposes of national and human development) and closed to protect sovereignty, security, and the social contract? This chapter explores the liberal paradox through a comparative-historical overview of immigration and citizenship policies in Europe, advancing a political economy framework for understanding the dilemmas of migration governance (see figure 1.2 in the introduction to this volume).

Since the eighteenth century when Adam Smith laid down the precepts of economic liberalism in his treatise on *The Wealth of Nations*, self-regulating markets and laissez faire became the hallmark of what Richard Rosecrance (1986) dubbed the trading state. With Britain's rise to power—which reached its zenith in the Victorian era of the late nineteenth century—and America's dominance of the post–World War II international system, laissez-faire economics and free trade were key to enhancing the wealth, power, and security of the nation-state.[1] The debacle of World War I and its aftermath of isolationism, intense nationalism, protectionism, and Depression only served to reinforce this liberal ideology. After 1945, the victorious Western democracies, led by Britain and

---

1   In this context, it is important to remember that Smith was not worried about high levels of international migration, because as he put it, "*Man is of all sorts of luggage—the most difficult to be transported.*"

the United States, were determined not to repeat the mistakes of the 1920s and 1930s, and they set about constructing a new international order, based on liberal principles of free trade and respect for fundamental human rights.

The problem, however, is that the source of power and authority in international relations continues to revolve around the nation-state. Since the Peace of Westphalia in 1648, the international legal system has been based upon the inviolability of the nation-state. In order for a state to exist in the Grotian tradition of international law, it must have control of a territory, a population, and the capacity for self-governance. Once a state has fulfilled these criteria, it may be recognized as independent and takes on the legal attribute of sovereignty, which Stephen Krasner (1999) wryly describes as "organized hypocrisy." If a state is sovereign, it has a legal personality and the capacity to enter into relations with other states.

Transnationalism, in the form of trade, cross-border investment, and migration, can challenge the sovereignty and authority of the nation-state. Migration in particular represents a challenge, in the sense that the (unauthorized) movement of individuals across national boundaries can violate the principle of sovereignty, which requires a degree of territorial closure (Hollifield 1994, 2004b, 2012; Sassen 1996; Joppke 1998). In every region of the globe—with the partial exception of the European Union—borders are sacrosanct and they represent a fundamental organizational feature of the international system (Andreas and Snyder 2000; Schain 2019). Unlike trade in goods or international financial flows, migration can change the ethnic composition of societies and disrupt what Rey Koslowski (2000) aptly describes as the "demographic boundary maintenance regime." If too many foreigners reside on the national territory, then it may become difficult for a state to identify its population vis-à-vis other states. The national community may feel threatened, and there may be a social or political backlash against immigration. Finally—and this is most important from the standpoint of *political liberalism*—the citizenry or the *demos* may be transformed in such a way as to violate the social contract, and undermine the legitimacy of the government and the sovereignty of the state itself (Walzer 1983). Thus, migration can be seen as a threat to national security, and it can lead to conflicts within and between states (Weiner 1993, 1995). Hence the liberal paradox: the economic logic of liberalism is one of openness, but the political and legal logic is one of closure (Hollifield 1992, 1998, 2004a, 2012). How can states escape from this paradox and manage the dilemmas and trade-offs associated with migration governance?

In order to answer this question, we need to (1) look at the emergence of migration states in Europe in the modern era, (2) review the transformation of Europe from a continent of emigration to one of immigration in the post–World War II era, and (3) look at the rise of rights-based politics and its impact on immigration policy in Europe. In international relations theory, states are defined primarily by their security or military function. The Westphalian state is above all else a *garrison state* (see figure 1.3 in the introduction to this volume). Realists like Hans Morgenthau (1978) and neorealists like Kenneth Waltz (1979) view the state as a unitary rational actor, with the overriding responsibility to maximize power, protect its territory and people, and pursue its national interest (*la raison d'etat*, to use the French expression). However, at least since the beginning of the

Industrial Revolution in Europe, the state has taken on an economic function. Ensuring material wealth and power required states to risk greater economic openness, and to pursue policies of free trade, giving rise to what Richard Rosecrance (1986) calls the *trading state*. As a result, states have been partially liberated from their dependence on territory and the military as sources of power. International relations theory moved away from the narrow realist view of the state, recognizing that in an increasingly interdependent world, power is more diffuse (Keohane and Nye 1977). In this neoliberal view, states are linked together by international trade and finance, forcing them to alter their grand strategies and seek new ways to cooperate. Here I argue that migration and trade are linked closely—two sides of the same coin. Hence the rise of the trading state necessarily entails the rise of the *migration state* (Hollifield 2004a, 2012), where considerations of power and interest are driven as much by migration (the movement of people) as they are by commerce and finance.

European Emigration States

In the eighteenth and nineteenth centuries, Germany—which only loosely could be defined as a state until it was unified by Bismarck in 1870—was primarily a country of *emigration*, with millions of Germans migrating to East Central Europe and to the Americas (Bade 1992; Herbert 2001). Not until relatively late in the nineteenth century did the German economy begin to grow at a sufficient rate to absorb its surplus population and excess labor supply. Strong *supply-push factors* were at work, compelling Germans to go abroad. At the same time, there were powerful *demand-pull forces*, leading German farmers and workers to emigrate to neighboring countries—like France, Switzerland, and the low countries—in search of employment, while many went to Russia or the United States, lured by the promise of cheap land and a new start.

In eighteenth-century Russia, the emigration of Germans was organized by the German-born empress, Catherine the Great, who sought to upgrade Russian agriculture and tame the eastern frontier by bringing in skilled German farmers as pioneers who could teach Russian peasants new farming techniques. For centuries states have been in the business of organizing mass migrations for the purposes of colonization, economic development, and to gain a competitive edge in a globalizing economy.

Once an international market for labor has been created, however, it may be difficult to manage or regulate. Migration can become self-perpetuating because of chain migration and social networks (Massey 1987, 1998). Word begins to spread from one family and one village to another about the possibilities for gainful employment, free land, or striking it rich. At the same time, the transaction costs associated with migration are reduced by kinship networks, which can grow into transnational communities and diasporas and constitute a form of social capital (Morawska 1990; Portes 1996, 1997). As international migration accelerates, states are forced to respond by developing new policies, to manage immigration (in the host country) or to deal with an exodus and potential return migration (in the sending country). Looking at the eighteenth and nineteenth centuries—a period of relatively free migration—many states with open frontiers, like the United States and Russia, were happy to receive immigrants. Whereas overpopulated societies, with a growing rural exodus and burgeoning cities in Europe, were happy to be rid of masses of unskilled and often illiterate peasants and workers (Thomas 1973; Bade 1992; Nugent 1992).[2]

By the end of the nineteenth century and beginning of the twentieth, however, the sending societies in Europe were well into the Industrial Revolution and entering a demographic transition, with falling birth rates and more stable populations. Nationalism was on the rise (Hobsbawm 1990), and it was increasingly important in terms of mobilization for (total) war for states to be able to identify their citizens and to construct new demographic regimes (Koslowski 2000). The need to regulate national populations, for purposes of taxation and conscription, led to passport and visa systems and the concomitant development of immigration and naturalization policies (Torpey 1998). Every person was expected to have one and only one nationality; and nationality, as a legal institution, would provide the individual with a measure of protection in a hostile and anarchic world of nation-states (Shaw 1997; Koslowski 2000; Hollifield 2004b). Countries of emigration, like Germany, tended to opt for nationality laws based upon *jus sanguinis* (blood, kinship or ethnicity), whereas countries of immigration, like the United States and France, developed a more expansive political citizenship based upon *jus soli* (soil or birthplace). The German nationality law of 1913 had a strong ethnic component, and it was designed specifically to accommodate return migration (Bade 1992; Brubaker 1992); whereas birthright citizenship in the United States, as codified in the Fourteenth Amendment to the Constitution, was more inclusive (Brubaker 1989; Schuck 1998). It is important to remember, however, that the Fourteenth Amendment was adopted in the aftermath of the Civil War, and its primary purpose was to grant immediate and automatic citizenship to former slaves (Kettner 1978). Moreover, American immigration policy in the late nineteenth and early twentieth centuries evolved along racial lines, culminating in the Chinese Exclusion Act of 1882 and the National Origins Quota system, enacted in 1924 (Smith 1997; King 2000; Hollifield 2019; Foley and Tichenor, this volume).

Until 1914, international migration was driven primarily by the dynamics of colonization and the push and pull of economic and demographic forces (Hatton and Williamson 1998; Lucassen, this volume), even though many receiving states were struggling to put in place national regulatory schemes to manage the growing international market for labor. Illegal or irregular migration was not recognized as a major policy issue, and there were virtually no provisions for political or humanitarian migration. Efforts to regulate international migration would be rendered moot by the outbreak in 1914 of war in Europe, which stopped economic migration in its tracks. However, war and decolonization fostered the rise of intense and virulent forms of nationalism—often with a strong ethnic dimension—resulting in the displacement of millions.

World War I sparked irredentism, and the redrawing of national boundaries in Europe, which in turn fostered new kinds of migration. Millions of displaced persons, refugees,

---

2   Clearly, inequalities and disequilibria in the international political economy, as well as land/labor/capital ratios, have played an important role in the history of international migration, just as they have in the history of trade (Rogowski 1989). But this type of straight political economy or coalitional approach (Peters 2015) only tells part of the story.

and asylum seekers would cross national boundaries in the twentieth century to "escape from violence" (Zolberg, Suhrke, and Aguayo 1989). Thus, World War I marked a crucial turning point in the history of migration and international relations. States would never return to the relatively open migration systems of the eighteenth and nineteenth centuries, when markets (supply-push and demand-pull) were the dominant forces driving international migration (Thomas 1973). Instead, the twentieth century would be an era of migration restriction, and travel would come to require elaborate documentation. World War I also marked the beginning of the end of the age of imperialism, with struggles for independence and decolonization in Asia and Africa—movements that would eventually result in the displacement of more millions of people.

In the interwar years, the Westphalian system of nation-states hardened and became further institutionalized in the core states of the Euro-Atlantic region, and the system continued to spread around the globe with the creation of new states (or the reemergence of old ones) in Asia, Africa, and the Middle East. Old and new states guarded their sovereignty jealously, and peoples in every region gained a stronger sense of citizenship and national identity. Because of these developments, international migration took on more of a political character, with diaspora and exile politics coming to the fore (Shain 1989; Adamson and Hazán, this volume). Henceforth, crossing borders had the potential of being a political as well as an economic act, and states reasserted their authority with a vengeance. The rise of anti-state revolutionary movements, such as anarchism and communism, not to mention eugenics and "scientific racism," provoked harsh crackdowns on immigration, and the rollback of civil rights and liberties, in the name of national security, national identity, and racial purity (Smith 1997; King 2000; Foley, this volume).

The interwar period was marked by intense protectionism, nativism, atavistic policies, and racism (Eichengreen 1989; Tichenor, this volume). States enacted draconian laws to protect their markets and populations. The international community was not prepared to deal with refugee movements, humanitarian crises, and new forms of political migration. Under international law, states were and still are not required to admit foreigners. However, if they do, they are obliged to treat them in a humane and civilized manner. This concern for the rights of migrants was clearly enunciated in Articles 22 and 23 of the Covenant of the League of Nations, which created a kind of rudimentary human rights law, aimed at protecting peoples in former colonies (Shaw 1997; Hollifield 2004b).

The events of the 1930s and 1940s in Europe radically changed legal norms governing international migration. The Holocaust and World War II led to the creation of the United Nations and a new body of refugee and human rights law. Although states retained sovereign control over their territory, and the principle of noninterference in the internal affairs of states still held, the postwar international order created new legal spaces (rights) for individuals and groups. The 1951 Geneva Convention Relating to the Status of Refugees applied specifically to European states and established the principle of asylum, whereby an individual with a "well-founded fear of persecution," once admitted to the territory of a safe state, cannot be arbitrarily expelled or sent back to the state of his or her nationality. Under international law, the individual is entitled to due process, although no state is compelled to admit an asylum seeker (Goodwin-Gill 1996). If, however, the state is a signatory of the convention, it cannot legally send an individual back to his or her country of origin, if he or she is threatened with persecution and violence. This is the principle of *non-refoulement*.

The United Nations Charter as well as the Universal Declaration of Human Rights, which was adopted by the UN General Assembly in December 1948, reinforced the principle of the rights of individuals "across borders" (Jacobson 1996). Likewise, as a direct response to the Holocaust and other crimes against humanity, the international community in 1948 adopted and signed the Convention on the Prevention and Punishment of the Crime of Genocide. Alongside these developments in international law, we can see a growing "rights-based liberalism" in the politics and jurisprudence of the most powerful liberal states in Europe and North America (more on this below). These liberal developments in international and municipal law fed one another, creating new rights (legal spaces) for migrants at both international and domestic levels.[3]

Why are these legal developments so important? How can they help states in Europe and elsewhere cope with the liberal paradox and manage migration? Unlike trade and financial flows—which can be promoted and regulated through international institutions like the WTO and the IMF—the movement of individuals across borders requires a qualitatively different set of regulatory regimes—ones based squarely on the notion of civil and human rights (Hollifield 2000a). Unlike goods, services, or capital, individuals have wills of their own and can become subjects of the law and active members of the societies in which they reside (Hollifield 1992; Weiner 1995). They also can become citizens of the polity (Koslowski 2000). The question, of course, is how far are states willing to go in cooperating to establish international and regional regimes for the orderly (legal) movement of people (Ghosh 2000; various chapters, this volume, especially Gomes and Geddes), and to what extent would such a regime rely upon municipal as opposed to international law (Hollifield 2000a)?

The last half of the twentieth century has marked an important new chapter in the history of global migration, especially in Europe where a regional migration regime emerged. With advances in travel and communications technology, migration accelerated, reaching levels not seen since the end of the nineteenth century. As noted in the introduction to this volume, in 2019, roughly 272 million people were living outside of their country of birth or citizenship. Even though this figure constitutes a mere 3.5 percent of the world's population, the perception is that international migration is rising at an exponential rate, and that it is spiraling out of control, prompting fears of a "rush to Europe" and "replacement migration" (Smith 2019; Camus 2011). In 2015, roughly 2.4 million people emigrated to the EU from non-EU countries, a year that saw record

---

3   In the 1990s, a debate erupted among migration scholars over the source of migrant rights. Do they arise primarily from domestic-legal sources (Joppke 2001), or do they find their origins in international or regional human rights laws (Soysal 1994; Jacobson 1996)? Obviously, both domestic and international law/institutions play a role, but from the standpoint of international law, states are still the primary source of protection for their nationals (Shaw 1996; Hollifield 2004b), and human rights still depend heavily on the willingness of the most powerful liberal states to promote and enforce them.

numbers of asylum seekers arriving in the EU. It seems that economic and political forces compelling people to move are intensifying, if we are to believe the rhetoric and the polemics surrounding immigration. With more than half the world's migrant population in the global South (see various chapters, this volume), especially those rich in natural resources, like oil, gold or diamonds, the biggest regulatory challenge confronts states like South Africa (Klotz, this volume) or Lebanon and Turkey (Tsourapas and Adamson, this volume), which share land borders with states riven by conflict and civil war. Supply-push forces remain strong, while the ease of communication and travel have reinforced migrant networks, lowering transaction costs and making it easier than ever for potential migrants to gather the information that they need in order to make the life-changing decision about whether or not to move.

To some extent *supply-push forces are constant or rising* and have been for many decades. What is highly variable are demand-pull forces, both in the OECD world and in the wealthier states of the global South, many of which suffer from a shortage of skilled and unskilled labor. The oil sheikdoms of the Persian Gulf are perhaps the best examples (see Thiollet, this volume), but increasingly we have seen labor shortages in the newly industrialized countries (NICs) of East and Southeast Asia as well (Fields 1994; Chung, this volume; Hollifield and Sharpe 2017). Singapore, Malaysia, Hong Kong, and Taiwan, for example, have become major importers of cheap labor from other developing countries in Southeast Asia, particularly the Philippines, Indonesia, and Thailand (see Hirschman and Sadiq, this volume). Taiwan has experienced rising levels of illegal migration from mainland China—which poses a security threat for the island country (again Chung, this volume).

With very few exceptions, however, these developing countries have not evolved elaborate laws or policies for governing migration (Chung 2020). Middle-income states have put in place contract or guest-worker schemes, negotiated with the sending countries, and with no provisions for settlement or family reunification. These types of pure manpower policies leave migrants with few if any rights, making them vulnerable to human rights abuses and arbitrary expulsion (Thiollet, this volume). The only protections they have are those afforded by the negotiating power of their home countries, which may choose to protest the treatment of their nationals (Sadiq, this volume). However, more often than not, the sending countries are unwilling to provoke a conflict with a receiving state over individual cases of abuse, for fear of losing access to remittances, which are one of the largest sources of foreign exchange for many developing countries (Tsourapas, Thiollet, and Sadiq, this volume). Hence, economics and demography (forces of supply-push and demand-pull) continue to govern much of international migration in the developing world, and the liberal paradox is less acute, because there are fewer legal or institutional constraints on the behavior of states vis-à-vis foreign nationals. Summary deportations and mass expulsions are viable options for controlling immigration in non-liberal states (Tsourapas and Thiollet, this volume) but not in liberal democracies, at least not on a massive scale (Ellermann 2009; Wong 2015).

In Europe as we can see, immigration has been trending upward for most of the post–World War II period, to the point that well over 40 percent of the world's migrant population resides in Europe and America, where roughly 11 and 14 percent of the population is foreign born respectively. Postwar migration to the core liberal democracies of Europe, North America, and the Dominions has gone through several distinct phases, which make these population movements quite different from the transatlantic migration of the nineteenth century or economic migrations in the global South today. As pointed out above, the first wave of migration in the aftermath of World War II was intensely political, especially in Europe, where large populations were displaced as a result of the redrawing of national boundaries, irredentism, and ethnic cleansing. Much of the remaining Jewish population in Central Europe fled to the United States or Israel, whereas large ethnic German populations in East Central Europe flooded into the newly created Federal Republic of Germany. The partition of Germany, the Cold War, and the division of Europe contributed to the exodus of ethnic populations seeking refuge in the democratic West. Until the construction of the Berlin Wall in 1961, twelve million German refugees arrived in West Germany.

Once this initial wave of refugee migration had exhausted itself and Europe began to settle into an uneasy peace that split the continent between the superpowers—thus cutting (West) Germany and other industrial states in Western Europe off from their traditional supplies of surplus labor in East Central Europe—new economic forms of migration and migration corridors began to emerge. The massive effort to reconstruct the war-ravaged economies of Western Europe in the 1950s quickly exhausted indigenous supplies of labor, especially in Germany and France. Like the United States, which launched a guest worker (*bracero*) program (1942–64) during World War II to recruit Mexican agricultural workers (Calavita 1992), the industrial states of northwest Europe concluded bilateral agreements with labor-rich countries in Southern Europe and Turkey. These recruitment policies allowed states in Western Europe to recruit millions of guest workers during the 1950s and 1960s to obtain unlimited supplies of labor needed to sustain high levels of noninflationary economic growth (Kindleberger 1967; Miller and Martin 1982; Hollifield 1992; Martin, Abella, and Kuptsch 2006). Together with decolonization, international labor migration would lead to a *second great transformation* in Europe, comparable to the Industrial Revolution of the eighteenth and nineteenth centuries (Polanyi 1944; cf. Messina 1996), and the trading state would evolve into a migration state. Just as in the earlier transformation, rapid marketization would provoke a protective reaction from societies, and new forms of embedded liberalism (Ruggie 1982) would limit states capacity for treating labor (foreign workers) as pure commodities.

The Second Great Transformation of Europe

The transformation of Europe from a continent of emigration to immigration can be traced to three historical developments. First is the crisis of decolonization that led to an unsettled period of mass migrations from roughly 1945 to 1962–63, when national boundaries in Eastern and Central Europe were redrawn and empires in Africa and Asia were dismantled, often through violent processes of rebellion, genocide, irredentism, and civil war (see also Lucassen, this volume). These developments uprooted entire populations and freed up large supplies of labor in Central and Eastern Europe, and eventually in Africa and the Indian subcontinent. The transformation of European and world politics created new migration corridors and new categories of citizens that continue to mark immigration debates: in Germany (the *Aussiedler* or ethnic Germans and *Vertriebene* or displaced persons, along with Jews from the former Soviet Union); in France (the *pieds noirs* or French colonists returning from Algeria and the *Harkis*, who fought with the French Army in the Algerian War, and large numbers of immigrants from North and sub-Saharan Africa); and in Britain (the Commonwealth and later New Commonwealth immigrants, and many immigrants from South Asia). The significance of these movements of populations early in the postwar period should not be underestimated, for it is the aftermath of war and decolonization in the 1950s and 1960s that created new ethnic cleavages and brought an ethnic consciousness to European societies (Ireland 1994). The influx of migrants into these old, established societies changed the cultural landscape. In Germany, for example, traditionally Catholic or Protestant regions were transformed virtually overnight. The absorption of displaced persons in West Germany altered the religious map, mixing up Catholic and Protestant communities and contributing to the formation of new social and political cleavages.

The second wellspring of the transformation of Europe is the set of public policies known as guest worker (*Gastarbeiter*) or rotation policies. Similar to the US *bracero* program that initiated large-scale migration to the US from Mexico (see Foley and Tichenor, this volume), these policies for recruiting ostensibly temporary, foreign workers began as early as 1945 in Switzerland, which came to be viewed as the model for guest-worker programs in other West European countries, notably in neighboring Germany (Hoffmann-Nowotny and Hondrich 1982; Rogers 1985; D'Amato 2014). The central feature of these policies was the concept of rotation, whereby unmarried male workers could be brought into the labor market for a specified (contractual) period, and sent back at the end of this period. They would serve as shock absorbers in the business cycle (*Konjunkturpuffer*) and could be replaced by new workers as needed. This was a rather neat macroeconomic formula for solving what was one of the principal obstacles to continued high rates of noninflationary growth in the 1950s and 1960s (Kindleberger 1967; Hollifield 1992). In fact, it seemed to be working so well in the Swiss case that the newly reorganized Organization for Economic Cooperation and Development (the OECD, which was created from the OEEC) recommended the policy to European states that were experiencing manpower shortages. The Bonn Republic, which had orchestrated the economic miracle (*Wirtschaftswunder*) in the 1950s under the leadership of Konrad Adenauer and Ludwig Ehrhard, forged a consensus in 1959–60 among business and labor groups to opt for a policy of importing labor, rather than offshoring industry, capital, and jobs, as was done in the United States. This was the beginning of the largest guest-worker program in Western Europe, which would bring millions of young Turks, Yugoslavs, and Greeks to work in German industry (Martin 2014). The unlimited supply at first of ethnic German refugees (*Aussiedler*) and displaced persons (*Vertriebene*) from Eastern and Central Europe, including refugees from the German Democratic Republic (*Ubersiedler*), suddenly dried up in 1961, as the last crack in the Iron Curtain was sealed with the construction of the Berlin Wall.

Two fateful turning points in the history of the German guest-worker program are of interest. The first came in 1967–68, following the shallow recession of 1966. It was at this point that the Grand Coalition government (1966–69) rotated some Turks and other guest workers out of the labor market, and back to their countries of origin. This operation was so successful that there was little resistance to bringing the guest workers back in 1969–70, when the West European economies were heating up again. The second fateful turning point in the history of the *Gastarbeiter* program in Germany came in 1973 when the attempt was made to stop recruitment of foreign workers (or *ausländische Arbeitnehmer*, as they came to be called in official parlance), repatriate them, and prevent family reunification. At this crucial juncture, the relatively new liberal features of the Bonn Republic came fully into play to prevent the government and administrative authorities from stopping immigration (especially family reunification) and deporting unwanted migrants. The contours of the German (and European) migration state were coming into view.

Although France is often mentioned as a European country that pursued guest-worker-type policies, this is misleading. The Provisional or Tripartite Government under General de Gaulle (1945–46), as well as the first governments of the Fourth Republic, put in place policies for recruiting foreign labor (*la main-d'oeuvre étrangère*), which were specified in the various five-year plans and implemented by a new immigration office, the *Office National d'Immigration* (ONI). However, the foreign workers were defined from the outset as *travailleurs immigrés ou permanents* (immigrant or permanent workers; see Hollifield 1992). It was the policy of Fourth Republic governments to encourage foreign workers to settle permanently, because immigration was part of population policy, which was itself a reflection of pronatalist views among the policy and political elites. The traditional French preoccupation with depopulation and falling birth rates was a driving feature behind postwar immigration policy (Teitelbaum and Winter 1985) and a central feature of the French migration state. In the 1950s, immigration was viewed as an important asset, especially since most newcomers were from culturally compatible neighboring countries, mainly Italy and Spain. The "admissionist" policies of the 1950s together with the crisis of decolonization and the desire on the part of French authorities not to sever relations with former colonies in North and West Africa (see Charbit, this volume) set the stage for the open-door policies of the 1960s..

As the French economy boomed in the 1960s, authorities rapidly lost control of immigration. Instead of sucking more labor from culturally compatible neighboring countries, such as Italy and Spain (which were beginning to develop economically and going through a demographic transition), the newly independent states of North Africa (Algeria, Morocco, and Tunisia) became the principal suppliers of foreign/immigrant labor. The major exception was Portugal, which continued to provide large numbers of workers for the French labor market. By the end of the decade of the 1960s, however, Algerians were rapidly becoming the most numerous immigrant group. Because of their special postcolonial status (as spelled out in the Evian Agreements, which ended the Algerian War), they had virtual freedom of movement into and out of the former *metropole* of France; and those Algerian nationals born before independence in 1962 were entitled to French citizenship. The result was to create a large undocumented (but not illegal) foreign population in France. The principal "mode of immigration" during this period was immigration "from within," whereby foreigners would enter the country, often having been recruited by firms, take a job, and then a request would be made on their behalf by the sponsoring firm for an adjustment of status (*régularisation*). The ONI, which was created to control immigration, became little more than a clearinghouse for foreign labor (Hollifield 2014). By the early 1970s, the rapid increase in North African immigration convinced the Pompidou government that something had to be done to regain control of immigration. The deep recession of 1973–74, which brought an abrupt end to the postwar economic boom (the *trente glorieuses*, or thirty years of high growth rates), simply confirmed this decision. The new government under Valéry Giscard d'Estaing took fairly dramatic steps, using heavy-handed statist and administrative measures to try to stop immigration (*l'arret de l'immigration*), repatriate immigrants, and deny rights of family reunification (Hollifield 1990). Thus, the French followed much the same logic as the Swiss and the Germans in attempting to use foreign workers as a kind of industrial reserve army or shock absorber (*Konjunkturpuffer*) to solve social and economic problems associated with recession, especially unemployment, treating foreign workers like pure commodities.

Other labor-importing states in Western Europe followed the same guest-worker logic in changing from policies of recruitment to suspension, with a couple of notable exceptions. Britain had never really launched a full-scale guest-worker program, because of the availability of New Commonwealth and Irish labor, and because economic growth rates in Britain were never high enough to justify large-scale importation of foreign labor. Demand-pull in the British case was weak (Hansen 2000, 2014). The Swiss, who had been the first to use a guest-worker or rotation approach to labor migration, were also the first to try to suspend recruitment of foreign labor (officially in 1970). Xenophobic pressures had built up in Switzerland, because of the sheer size of the foreign population relative to the total population (15–20 percent at the time). But the Swiss economy continued to grow throughout the 1970s (demand-pull remained strong), and unemployment was negligible, thanks in part to the efficacy of foreign worker policies that relied heavily on seasonal and frontier workers. For these reasons, the Swiss returned fairly quickly to their rotation policies, making sure that as few of the foreign workers as possible would actually settle and seek naturalization.

As a result, the Swiss were able to ride out the xenophobic backlash against immigration in the 1970s, which coalesced into a national campaign calling for strict limits on the size of the foreign population, the *Nationale Aktion gegen die Uberfremdung von Volk und Heimat* (Hoffmann-Nowotny and Hondrich 1982). Access to badly needed foreign labor was maintained, and Swiss authorities avoided the trap, into which the French and Germans fell, of freezing the foreign population in place. In effect, by attempting to stop immigration, French and German authorities created a large (and more permanent) foreign population, exactly what US authorities did in the 1990s (Massey 2020; Tichenor and Foley, this volume). Workers refused to leave for fear of being denied reentry, and they began to bring their families to join them, which led to an upsurge in family immigration. The Swiss writer Max Frisch famously observed of the guest-worker programs: "We asked for workers, and we got people instead (*Wir riefen Arbeitskräfte, und es kamen Menschen*)." Because of the civil rights (especially due process) guaranteed to individuals under the aegis of liberal constitutions, the foreign guests could not simply be sent home. Rights trumped markets and the guests were allowed to stay (Rogers 1985; Chin 2007).

The development of migration states in Western Europe cannot be fully understood apart from the history of the guest-worker programs. These programs created the illusion of temporary migration, leading some states (especially Germany) to avoid or postpone a national debate over immigration and citizenship policy, and Germany had no viable "national model" or myth around which to organize the debate (see below). This problem was compounded by the statist impulses in 1973–74 to stop immigration and repatriate foreigners, which furthered the "myth of return" and heightened public expectations that governments could simply reverse the migratory process. By taking such a strong, statist stance against further immigration, it was more difficult for French and German governments in the 1980s and 1990s even to discuss an "American-style" legal immigration policy, with green cards, naturalization, and a path to citizenship. Instead, immigration became a highly charged partisan issue, leading to soul-searching debates about national identity and citizenship (Jurgens 2010; Hollifield, Martin, and Orrenius 2014; Wong 2016). The more practical questions of "how many, from where, and in what status," simply could not be asked. The result of trying to slam the "front door" of legal immigration shut led to the opening of side doors and windows (for family members and seasonal workers), and most important of all, the "back door" was left open (especially in Germany) for refugees and asylum seekers. Not surprisingly, many would-be legal and illegal immigrants (as well as legitimate asylum seekers and others) flooded through the side and back doors in the 1980s and 1990s, further undermining the legitimacy of immigration policy across the continent.

The third historical development that led to the second great transformation in Europe is the influx of refugees and asylum seekers, which is a direct legacy of imperialism and colonialism, and of the failed guest-worker policies. Large-scale refugee migrations began in Europe in the aftermath of World War II, and with the advent of the Cold War (see Lucassen, this volume). In fact, it was the beginning of the Cold War in the late 1940s that led to the 1951 Geneva Convention and the creation of the United Nations High Commissioner for Refugees (UNHCR). These were essentially Cold War institutions, created to handle the flow of refugees in Europe from east to west, at a time (the 1950s and 1960s) when there was little doubt as to the meaning of a "well-founded fear of persecution"—the acid test of political asylum and a core principle of international refugee law, which was incorporated into national and constitutional law. In practice, flight from a communist regime was sufficient grounds for the granting of political asylum in most of the countries of Western Europe. The famous Article 16 of the West German Basic Law, which granted almost an unconditional right to asylum for any individual fleeing persecution, was written with the weight of history and with refugees from the East in mind, especially ethnic German refugees (*Aussiedler und Ubersiedler*), although Jews fleeing the Soviet Union also would benefit from German asylum policy.

Refugee and asylum policies in Western Europe functioned rather well for almost three decades from roughly 1950 to 1980 (during most of the period of the Cold War and decolonization). However, with the closing of front-door immigration policies in the 1970s, political asylum became an increasingly attractive mode of entry for unwanted migrants who would come to be labeled "economic refugees." These included not only migrants from former colonies (in Africa and Asia) but an increasing number of refugees from the countries of East Central Europe, including the Romani or Roma (also known as gypsies). As governments across Western Europe struggled to redefine their immigration and refugee policies in the wake of the "oil shocks" and severe economic recessions of the 1970s, which led to a rapid rise in unemployment, the pace of refugee migrations picked up: Tamils, Sikhs, and Kurds were coming to Britain and Germany, Zairians and other sub-Saharan African nationals were coming to France and Belgium at a rate of tens of thousands annually, and Eritreans and Somalis were coming to Italy. One of the first efforts to address this new movement of populations came at the level of the European Community, where, it was thought, national governments could simultaneously reassert control over refugee movements, while avoiding the painful, moral, and political dilemmas involved in limiting the right to asylum (see Geddes, this volume). The Single European Act of 1985 set in motion a new round of European economic integration, which included the consolidation of the single market and the goal of "free movement of goods, persons, services, and capital," the four freedoms, and in effect the establishment of a border-free Europe. To achieve this goal, however, it became clear that European states would have to agree upon common visa and asylum policies (again see Geddes, this volume).

Toward this end, five states (France, Germany, and the Benelux countries) met in the Luxembourg town of Schengen, and in 1985 the Schengen Agreement was unveiled as a prototype for a border-free Europe. The agreement called for the elimination of internal borders, the harmonization of visa and asylum policies, and the coordinated policing of external borders, leading to the construction of a symbolic "ring fence" around the common territory. Schengen, which was enlarged to include Italy, Spain, and Portugal, was followed in 1990 by the Dublin Agreement, which established the principle that refugees must apply for asylum in the first EC member state in which they arrive. But no sooner had the states of Western Europe begun to focus on a common policy for dealing with the refugee and asylum issue than the entire international system in Europe changed, with the breaching of the Berlin Wall, the collapse of communist regimes in East Central Europe and the Soviet Union, and the eruption of civil war in the former Yugoslavia.

The first result of the abrupt end of the Cold War was to raise fears among governments and publics in Western Europe that there would be a flood of (economic) refugees from Eastern Europe—sensational headlines such as "The Russians Are Coming!" were splashed across newspapers. These fears turned out to be unfounded, at least as far as economic migration from Central and Eastern Europe and the Soviet successor states was concerned (Fassmann and Münz 1994). Nonetheless, the euphoria associated with the "triumph of liberalism" over communism and the "end of history" contributed, at least briefly, to a surge in refugee migration. The surge lasted for about four years, from 1989 to 1993, and it placed enormous strains on what were essentially Cold War institutions, namely the Geneva Convention itself and the UNHCR. Governments were forced to reconsider and rewrite sweeping constitutional provisions, which guaranteed the right to asylum, at the same time that new irredentist movements swept the Balkans, Transcaucasia, and other formerly communist territories, leading to civil wars and new refugee migrations across Europe. Population movements in Africa and Asia also increased, placing even more pressure on the entire structure of the international refugee regime. While the decades of the 1990s and 2000s saw modest upticks in asylum seeking, the 2010s were a period of humanitarian crisis with millions of displaced persons fleeing conflicts in the Middle East (Syria and Iraq), Africa (Somalia and Sudan), and South Asia (Afghanistan).

How did European states respond to the second great transformation? The responses have been at three levels. The first is political, in the sense that politicians, especially on the far right, exploited the migration crisis for political gain. The second is a policy-level response, which lurched from one extreme to another, trying to achieve "zero immigration" in the 1990s but recognizing that liberal states have a legal and moral obligation to deal with humanitarian crises that are often the legacy of European colonialism. Liberal and assimilationist policies of amnesty (for irregular migrants) were followed by harsh crackdowns on asylum seekers, and attempts to restrict citizenship and make naturalization more difficult. Finally, emerging from this political and social cauldron is a search for national models of immigration and naturalization, which range from a tempered pluralism and multiculturalism in Britain and the Netherlands to stringent assimilation and republicanism in France, with some northern European social democracies (Sweden and Germany) welcoming ever larger numbers of migrants and asylum seekers (Hollifield 1997b; Bertossi 2011). As a backdrop to these national debates, the legacies of colonialism loomed large; and terrorist attacks by Islamic radicals added fuel to the fire of ethnic conflict.

To cope with such crises, I argue (Hollifield 1997a) that migration states need a national model, which is cultural, historical, legal, and institutional. National models link the struggle for control of immigration with the imperative to integrate newcomers. Even though this concept stresses national differences, we have seen a convergence in immigration policies in liberal democracies (Hollifield, Martin, and Orrenius 2014). The stated objectives of immigration policy in liberal democracies have been to control/restrict/stop immigration and to integrate newcomers through "grand bargain" strategies, bringing together strange bedfellow coalitions (Hollifield, Hunt, and Tichenor 2008). These struggles to integrate newcomers are shaped by (the strength or weakness of) the national model, by the extent to which the model is legitimate in the eyes of the citizenry, and the extent to which it finds expression in law and public policy. Rights are at the heart of European immigration policies. Even though they are hotly contested, I argue that rights are the key to the development of national models in liberal democracies, and they are the cornerstone for the legitimation of immigration and citizenship in liberal states.

Rights-Based Politics in Europe

The postwar international "liberal" order is defined by what I have called a *rights-markets dynamic*, based upon free trade, stable exchange rates, capital mobility, and migration, where migrants and refugees are able to acquire basic civil and human rights (Hollifield 1992, 2000a/b; Hollifield, Martin, and Orrenius 2014; cf. Ikenberry 2012). Citizenship, on the other hand, remains a sovereign prerogative of the nation-state, with the partial exception of the European Union (see Geddes, this volume). The politics of immigration and citizenship in the postwar period are closely linked to the rise of rights-based politics. All states, but especially liberal states, must grapple with the fundamental issues of how many migrants to accept, from which countries, and with what rights (status). By protecting foreigners from the arbitrary power of the state, civil rights–based policies help immigrants to get in, to remain, and to settle, whereas human rights and refugee conventions underscore the rights of asylum seekers, migrant workers, and their families. The Global Compact for Safe, Orderly and Regular Migration (CGM) along with the Compact on Refugees, endorsed by the UN in 2018 and 2017 respectively, are the culmination of decades of struggle to extend rights to migrants and refugees, and to institutionalize these rights in the international legal system. The liberal social democracies in Western Europe especially have been supportive of the push to build a rights-based, global migration regime.

The extension of rights to minorities and foreigners in the decades following World War II is one of the most salient aspects of European and world politics, contributing mightily to the second great transformation of Europe. The creation of new legal spaces for marginal groups, including foreigners, in societies as different as Germany, the United States, and Japan (Thränhardt 1996; Hollifield and Sharpe 2017; Chung, this volume) is directly linked to developments in international politics. The rise of rights-based politics started in earnest with the adoption in 1948 of the Universal Declaration of Human Rights by the international community and the 1951 Refugee Convention. It continued apace with the civil rights struggles of the 1950s and 1960s in the US, through greater European integration and the consolidation of the "four freedoms" in Europe in the 1980s (as noted above), the "third wave" of democratization (Huntington 1991; Hollifield and Jillson 2000), the collapse of communism, and the end of the Cold War in 1989–90.

Rights-based politics took shape at every level of the liberal democratic polity and in the international system and it has been particularly salient in Europe: in legislative acts, partisan and interest group (especially ethnic) politics, and in judicial rulings (Ireland 1994; Schuck 1998; Hollifield 2000b; Joppke 2001; Abraham 2015). Judicial activism—sometimes referred to derisively as "government by judges"—gained many supporters and detractors and helped to spawn a plethora of lawsuits on behalf of immigrants and refugees, and in the process created many human and civil rights advocacy groups (Bonjour 2016). MIPEX scores (figure 17.1) show that rights for foreigners are most advanced in European (social) democracies, especially Sweden (top of the charts). Among the settler societies and nations of immigrants, not surprisingly Canada (the quintessential migration state; see Triadafilopoulos/Taylor, this volume) and Australia are highly ranked, with the United States in the top five, followed by Spain, Italy, and the UK.

Even though the history of rights-based politics in the United States is quite different from Europe (the former more focused on civil rights and the latter on social or economic rights—see the Marshallian trilogy of rights, Marshall 1964; Hollifield 2000b), the impact on immigration and citizenship policies has been much the same—expanded rights for marginal and ethnic groups, including foreigners. These historical developments provoked a rethinking of citizenship in classical liberal theory in the works of scholars who place civil, social, and human rights at the center of a new social contract (for example, Rawls 1971; Walzer 1983; Soysal 1994; Bauböck 1994; Jacobson 1996; Gibney

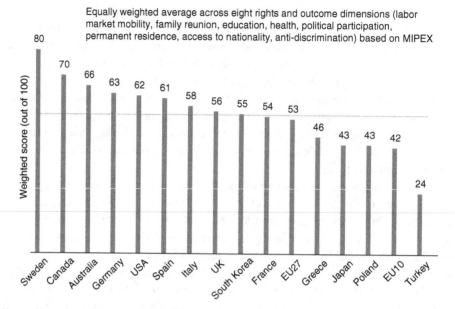

Figure 17.1. Index of immigrant rights.

1999; Carens 1989). Redefining the relationship between individuals, groups, and the state, through a process of political struggle, has had a great impact on the way in which democratic states manage migration and mobility, and it has given rise to new theories of citizenship, focused on multiculturalism and a rethinking of the social contract (Kymlicka 1995; Benhabib 2004; Carens 2000, 2013; Joppke 2017).

It is the confluence of markets and rights that explains the politics of migration, mobility, and citizenship, and the dilemmas of migration governance in the postwar period, giving rise to the liberal paradox. The rights-markets dynamic has weakened the historically close linkage between business cycles and "admissionist" or "restrictionist" immigration policies (Hollifield and Wilson 2011), leading to a more expansive definition of citizenship (Joppke 2010).

On the economic and demographic side, neoclassical push-pull arguments provide a simple and straightforward explanation for increases in immigration. Demand-pull forces in the US and European economies during the 1950s and 1960s were sufficient to stimulate large-scale migrations from the poorer economies of the periphery (Mexico, Turkey, and the Maghreb). As outlined above, these labor migrations were initiated and legitimized by the receiving states in Western Europe through guest-worker (*Gastarbeiter*) programs so prevalent in the 1950s and 1960s, and in the United States through the *bracero* program of contract labor importation (1942–64). However, what started as a market-driven movement of labor from south to north became, in the 1970s and 1980s, a sociopolitical liability as economic growth in Western Europe and North America slowed in the aftermath of 1970s recessions (Hollifield, Martin and Orrenius 2014; Martin, Abella, and Kuptsch 2006).

Stopping immigration, even during periods of sharp economic contraction, proved difficult, in part because of powerful, underlying supply-push forces. Demand-pull migration initiated processes that continued to have unanticipated consequences, from the micro—employers wanting to retain their "guest workers" indefinitely—to the macro level—the increasingly large role of immigration in host-country population and labor force growth, and the dependence of sending-country economies on migrant remittances (Hollifield, Orrenius, and Osang 2006; Massey 2020). Moreover, supply-push migration increased as the populations of peripheral countries like Turkey, Mexico, and the Maghreb (Algeria and Morocco) grew at a rapid pace, even as their economies slowed due to the global recession. Migration networks that developed during the years of expansionary immigration policies in the 1950s and 1960s (the *trente glorieuses*) helped to spread information about job opportunities and modes of entry and residence in the receiving countries (Massey 1987). In the 1980s and 1990s, these transnational social networks, perhaps more than any other factor, helped to sustain migration—especially family reunification in Europe and undocumented migration from Mexico and Central America to the United States—during periods of high uncertainty regarding employment prospects in the sending countries. In the last decades of the twentieth century, the composition of immigration flows shifted from workers to families and refugees, so that family reunification and asylum seeking became the principal avenues of immigration in Europe (figure 17.2). Only in the traditional nations of immigrants did labor migration (skilled and unskilled) retain its prominence, with the notable exception of the United States, which has given priority to family immigration since the 1965 Hart-Celler immigration reform that abolished the system of national origins quotas (see Tichenor and Foley, this volume).

Composition of Migrant Flows in Principal Receiving Countries, 2015

Push-pull forces and the imbalances between economies of the North and South (as well as West and East within Europe) provide necessary but not sufficient conditions for immigration, especially on the scale experienced in recent decades. To explain what Myron Weiner (1993) called the "global migration crisis," we must look beyond macro- and microeconomics, and even social networks, to trends in the political development of the major receiving countries.

In settler societies like the United States, Canada, and Australia, immigration is part of the founding ideal (or myth). However, like all immigrant receiving countries, these states must address key issues, such as how many foreigners to admit, from where, and with what status. "Nations of immigrants" are those that were founded, populated, and built by immigrants in modern times. As a result, immigration is a fundamental part of the founding myth, historical consciousness, and national identity of these countries, and they normally anticipate and welcome large numbers of immigrants (Bertossi 2011). A liberal consensus prevailed in much of the postwar period (Hollifield, Hunt, and Tichenor 2008), until the end of the Cold War and a populist backlash, culminating in the election of Donald Trump in 2016 (Norris and Inglehart 2019).

Since the end of the Cold War, the "liberal trend" reversed, with many OECD governments focused on rolling back civil and human rights for noncitizens in order to stop

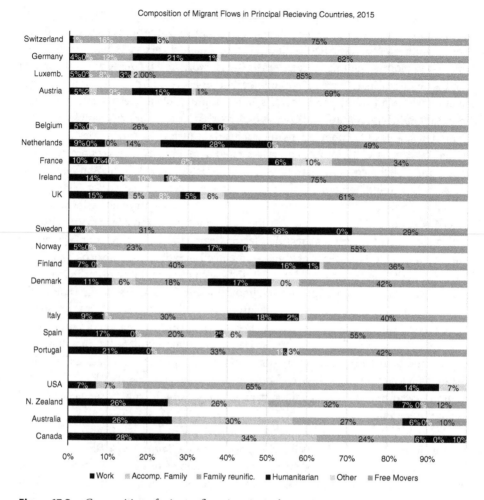

Figure 17.2.   Composition of migrant flows in principal receiving countries, 2015.

asylum seeking and control immigration. Examples include Proposition 187 in California (1994) and the 1996 Illegal Immigration Reform and Immigrant Responsibility Act, which tightened restrictions on legal as well as illegal immigrants. Even earlier, the German decision to amend Article 16 of the Basic Law (see above) to restrict the blanket right to asylum was directly linked to the end of the Cold War and the collapse of the USSR. In France, the Pasqua and Debré Laws of the 1990s and the Sarkozy policies of the 2000s were a challenge to the French republican tradition (Hollifield 2014). Executive authority was strengthened by new and often sweeping powers granted to police and intelligence services in the aftermath of the terrorist attacks of the 2000s to carry out surveillance and identity checks and to detain individuals without charge for extended periods. This trend has accelerated in the 2010s with Brexit, fought largely over the issue of immigration and free movement (Eatwell and Goodwin 2019). The new nativism and nationalism (America First) in the United States propelled Donald Trump to power, further undermining the liberal order.

Martin Ruhs (2013) argued that there is a trade-off between numbers and rights—states with more temporary foreign workers accord them fewer rights, while those with fewer foreign workers give them more rights. According to Ruhs (2013), no state can have both high numbers (open labor markets) and extensive rights for foreign workers. But is this argument generalizable to the liberal and social democracies, since it relies so heavily on evidence from the Gulf (GCC) countries? As we can see from the MIPEX scores (above), European democracies and settler nations of immigrants, including Brazil and Mexico, grant extensive rights to migrants and have high levels of immigration.

The postwar development of rights-based politics in the latter half of the twentieth century gave way to nationalism in the twenty-first century. The French *Front National* (now renamed *Rassemblement National*) is one of the oldest and most widely known of anti-immigrant political parties, but others have emerged in almost every liberal democracy that experienced large-scale immigration (Norris and Inglehart 2019). The backlash is nationalist, nativist, and exclusionary in character. Its principal targets are immigrants and liberal parties and politicians who support the expansion or preservation of civil and political rights for immigrants and ethnic minorities (Brubaker 2017; Foley, this volume). Nationalist, authoritarian, and reactionary populism is widespread in Europe, the United States, and Australia. Canada, where immigration plays a key role in national development strategies, however, is an outlier (see Triadafilopoulos/Taylor, this volume). The passage of Brexit in 2015 and the election of Donald Trump in 2016 have been attributed directly to the failure of Britain and the US to control immigration (Eatwell and Goodwin 2018; Norris and Inglehart 2019). The growth of extreme-right anti-immigrant parties places politicians of the center-right and left under tremendous electoral pressures (Thränhardt 1993; Boswell and Hough 2008; Carvalho and Ruedin 2019).

The dilemmas of migration governance (see figure 1.2 in the introduction) have become more acute in the 2010s. How can liberal societies tolerate the presence of individuals who are members but not citizens—"denizens," to use the term popularized by Tomas Hammar (1985, 1990)? Should not all individuals who are members (more or less permanent residents) of a liberal society be accorded the full panoply of rights (social and political as well as civil) enjoyed by those who are citizens (Joppke 2010; Carens 2013)? This is the paradox or dilemma that most liberal societies face, and it is particularly acute in countries with large, multigenerational resident alien populations that remain outside the social contract—see debates about *Gastarbeiter* in Germany in the 1980s and 1990s, and the DACA and DAPA debates in the US in the 2010s (Martin, Abella, and Kuptsch 2006; Wong 2016). Immigration and citizenship policy cannot be understood strictly in economic or demographic terms; the terms of citizenship, membership in national and local communities, and basic human rights must also be addressed (Brubaker 1989; Carens 2000; Wong 2016).

Demand-pull and supply-push forces and networks that link the sending to the receiving societies are the necessary conditions for emigration to occur, but granting legal status (rights) to foreigners is a sufficient condition for immigration. Migrant rights derive from domestic sources of law (Schuck 1998) and liberal constitutions, and they are protected by international law and human rights conventions—especially in Europe (Joppke 2001; Geddes 2003 and this volume) but also in Latin America (see Gomes and Hazán, this volume). Despite the rise of rights-based politics and incipient international migration regimes (Hollifield 2000a), which check the action of states trying to control migration and limit naturalization, reactionary populist movements and nativist policies increasingly target migrant rights (civil, social, and political) to stop or control immigration (Hollifield 2019).

Legal and constitutional constraints notwithstanding, reforming immigration policies has become a political imperative in most of the OECD world. The principal exceptions are Japan and South Korea (Hollifield and Sharpe 2017; Chung, this volume), where the numbers of immigrants are growing but still relatively small, and Canada, Australia, and New Zealand, where public hostility to immigration has been less pronounced (Triadafilopoulos/Taylor, this volume). The great recession of 2007–9 led to a decline of flows, in the United States where net migration from Mexico turned negative in 2007. Yet despite the moderation in the pace of immigration in the US, the politics of immigration shifted toward control (enforcement) and away from concerns about the integration of a large immigrant population, many of whom are undocumented (Hollifield 2019; Wong 2016). Meanwhile, integration dilemmas were acute in Canada, Australia, and New Zealand—*nations of immigrants*—where sources of immigration, as in the US and Europe, became more diverse (Favell 1998; Bloemraad 2006; Schain 2012).

Immigration and citizenship are highly contested in Europe in the countries of immigration—like France, Germany, the Netherlands, Switzerland, Britain, and the Scandinavian countries—where immigration is not part of the founding ideal as in the *nations of immigrants*. The public are uneasy about the long-term implications of immigration for the maintenance of national cultures, languages, and identities, and right-wing politicians are increasingly hostile to immigration. Debates over Muslim immigration in largely Christian societies have been especially vociferous and divisive in Europe (Kastoryano 1997; Kepel 2017; Roy 2019). Even when foreign workers and their dependents are legal residents—there are millions of settled, legally admitted foreign workers, family members, and free movers in European countries—they are often *unwanted* as a permanent component of the population for noneconomic reasons. These include low tolerance for cultural, racial, and ethnic diversity (Bleich 2003; Vertovec 2007), and fears of crime, terrorism, and overcrowding in major urban areas (Fetzer 2000; Norris and Inglehart 2019).

Public hostility generates strong incentives for officials in Europe and other liberal societies to redouble their efforts at immigration control, by fine-tuning existing control measures (Brochmann and Hammar 1999; Hollifield, Martin, and Orrenius 2014), like employer sanctions (internal control), investing more heavily in border enforcement (external control), and pursuing new experiments to restore at least the appearance of control like so-called foreign trainee programs in Japan and South Korea (Chung, this volume). For this reason, the politics of immigration in many receiving countries have taken on a strong symbolic dimension, including Trump's vow to build a wall along the entire two-thousand-mile, southern border of the United States (Rudolph 2006; Hollifield 2019). Wide gaps exist between policy outputs and outcomes and between public opinion—which in most countries wants immigration reduced—and liberal admissions policies (Hollifield 1986; Freeman 1986, 1995; Czaika and de Haas 2013; Lutz 2019; Hollifield, Martin, and Orrenius 2014).

The Future of Migration in Europe

International migration is likely to increase in coming decades, unless there is some cataclysmic international event, like war or economic depression. Even after bloody terrorist attacks, the liberal democracies remained relatively open to international migration. Global economic inequalities mean that supply-push forces remain strong, while at the same time demand-pull forces are intensifying. The growing demand for highly skilled workers and demographic decline in the liberal democracies create economic opportunities for migrants. Transnational networks have become more dense and efficient, linking the sending and receiving societies. These networks help to lower the transaction costs of migration, and new communications technologies make it easier for people to move across borders and over long distances. Moreover, when legal migration is not an option, migrants have turned increasingly to professional smugglers, and a global industry of migrant smuggling—often with the involvement of organized crime—has sprung up, especially in the first decades of the twenty-first century. Hardly a week passes without some news of a tragic loss of life associated with migrant smuggling (Kyle and Koslowski 2001). A big, unanswered question is whether the global pandemic of 2020 will lead to long-term decline in migration and human mobility, and perhaps the end of liberalism (Hollifield 2020).

Migration, like any type of transnational economic activity (such as trade and foreign direct investment), cannot and does not take place in a legal or institutional void. As we have seen, states have been and still are deeply involved in organizing and regulating migration, and the extension of rights to nonnationals has been an important part of the story of international migration in the post–World War II period. For the most part, rights that accrue to migrants come from the legal and constitutional protections guaranteed to all "members" of society (Carens 2000). Thus, if an individual migrant is able to establish some claim to residence on the territory of a liberal state, his or her chances of being able to remain and settle will increase. At the same time, developments in international human rights law have helped to solidify the position of individuals vis-à-vis the nation-state, to the point that individuals (and certain groups) have acquired a sort of international legal personality, leading some analysts to speculate that we are entering a postnational era, characterized by "universal personhood" (Soysal 1994), the expansion of "rights across borders" (Jacobson 1996), and even "transnational citizenship" (Bauböck 1994).

Others have argued that migrants have become transnational, because so many no longer reside exclusively on the territory of one state (Glick Schiller 1999; Levitt 2001), opting to shuttle between a place of origin and destination. This line of argument gives priority to agency as a defining feature of contemporary migrations; but it often ignores the extent to which structure in the form of state policies shapes the choices that migrants make (Hollifield and Wong 2015). The migration state is almost by definition a liberal state, inasmuch as it creates a legal and regulatory environment in which migrants can pursue individual and household strategies of accumulation.

Regulating international migration, however, requires liberal states to be attentive to the (human or civil) rights of the individual. If rights are ignored or trampled upon, then the *liberal* state risks undermining its own legitimacy and *raison d'être* (Hollifield 1999).

As international migration and transnationalism increase, pressures build upon liberal states to find new and creative ways to cooperate in order to manage migration flows. The definition of the national interest and *raison d'etat* have to take this reality into account, as rights become more and more a central feature of domestic and foreign policy. New international and regional regimes (like the EU) will be necessary if states are to risk more openness, and rights-based (international) politics will be the order of the day.

Some politicians and policy-makers, as well as international organizations, continue to hope for market-based/economic solutions to the problem of regulating international migration. Trade and foreign direct investment—bringing capital and jobs to people, either through private investment or official development assistance—it is hoped, will substitute for migration, alleviating both supply-push and demand-pull factors (Bhagwati 1983). Even though trade can lead to factor-price equalization in the long term, as we have seen in the case of the European Union (Stolper and Samuelson 1941; Mundell 1957; Straubhaar 1988), in the short and medium term exposing developing countries to market forces results in increased migration, as is evident with NAFTA and the US-Mexican relationship (Martin 1993; Massey *et al.* 2002; Martin, this volume). Likewise, trade in services can stimulate more "high end" migration, because these types of products cannot be produced or sold without the movement of the individuals who make and market them (Bhagwati 1998; Ghosh 1997).

In short, the global integration of markets for goods, services, and capital entails higher levels of international migration; therefore, if states want to promote freer trade and investment, they must be prepared to manage higher levels of migration. Many states (like Canada and Germany) are willing, if not eager, to sponsor high-end migration, because the numbers are manageable, and there is likely to be less political resistance to the importation of highly skilled individuals. However, mass migration of unskilled and less educated workers and asylum seekers meets with greater political resistance, even in situations and in sectors, like construction or health care, where there is high demand for basic manpower. In these instances, the tendency is for governments to go back to the old guest-worker models, in hopes of bringing in just enough temporary workers to fill gaps in the labor market, but with strict contracts between foreign workers and their employers that limit the length of stay and prohibit settlement or family reunification. The alternative is irregular or illegal immigration and a growing black market for labor—a Hobson's choice.

As this chapter and the book illustrate, the nineteenth and twentieth centuries saw the rise of the *trading state* (Rosecrance 1986). The latter half of the twentieth century has given rise to the *migration state* (see figure 1.3 in the introduction). In fact, from a strategic, economic, and demographic standpoint, trade and migration go hand in hand, because the wealth, power, and stability of the state is now more than ever dependent on its willingness *to risk both trade and migration*. In launching a modest "green or blue card" program, Germany and the EU sought to emulate the United States and Canada, on the premise that global competitiveness, power, and economic security are closely related to a willingness to accept immigrants (Jurgens 2010). Germans in particular and Europeans in general are (reluctantly) following the American and Canadian examples, in order to enhance their material power and wealth. But in one important respect Germany and

Europe have an advantage over the United States and Canada or Australia: Germany is part of a regional economic enterprise—the European Union—which is not only creating a free trade zone but also an area of free movement.

Now more than ever, *international security and stability are dependent on the capacity of states to manage migration*. It is extremely difficult, if not impossible, for states to manage or control migration either unilaterally or bilaterally. Some type of multilateral/regional regime is required, similar to what the EU has constructed for nationals of the member states. The EU model, as it has evolved from Rome to Maastricht to Amsterdam and beyond, points the way to future migration regimes, because it is not based purely on *homo economicus*, but incorporates rights for individual migrants and even a rudimentary citizenship, which continues to evolve. The problem, of course, in this type of regional migration regime is how to deal with third country nationals (TCNs). As the EU expands and borders are relaxed, the issue of TCNs, immigrants, and ethnic minorities becomes ever more pressing; and new institutions, laws and regulations must be created to deal with them (Guiraudon 1998; Geddes, this volume).

In the end, the EU, by creating a regional migration regime and a kind of supranational authority to deal with migration and refugee issues, allows the member states to finesse, if not to escape, the liberal paradox. Playing the good cop/bad cop routine and using symbolic politics and policies to maintain the illusion of border control help governments fend off the forces of closure, at least in the short run (Rudolph 2006). In the end, however, it is the nature of the liberal state itself, and the degree to which openness is institutionalized and (constitutionally) protected from the "majority of the moment," that determine whether states will continue to risk trade and migration (Hollifield 2004a).

Regional integration reinforces the trading state and acts as a midwife for the migration state. In the EU, migrants are gradually acquiring the rights that they need in order to live and work on the territory of the member states. Regional integration blurs the lines of territoriality, lessening problems of integration and national identity. The fact that there is an increasing disjuncture between people and place—which in the past might have provoked a crisis of national identity and undermined the legitimacy of the nation-state—is less of a problem when the state is tied to a regional regime, like the EU. This does not mean, of course, that there will be no resistance to freer trade and migration. Protests against globalization and nativist or xenophobic reactions against immigration have been on the rise throughout the OECD world, culminating in the election of Donald Trump as president of the United States. in 2016. Nonetheless, regional integration—especially when it has a long history and is deeply institutionalized as it is in Europe—makes it easier for states to risk trade and migration and for governments to construct the kinds of political coalitions that will be necessary to support and institutionalize greater openness.

Even though there are large numbers of economic migrants in Asia, this region remains divided into relatively closed and often authoritarian societies, with little prospect of granting rights to migrants and guest workers. The more liberal and democratic states, like Japan, Taiwan, and South Korea, are the exceptions, but they have only just begun to grapple with the problem of immigration, on a relatively small scale (Hollifield, Martin, and Orrenius 2014; Chung, this volume). In Africa and the Middle East, which have high numbers of migrants and refugees, there is a great deal of instability, and states are fluid with little institutional or legal capacity for dealing with international migration (Tsourapas and Thiollet, this volume).

In conclusion, we can see that migration is endogenous. It is both a cause and a consequence of political and economic change. International migration, like trade, is a fundamental feature of the postwar liberal order. But as states and societies become more liberal and open, migration has increased. Will this increase in migration be a virtuous or a vicious cycle? Will it be destabilizing, leading the international system into greater anarchy, disorder, and war; or will it lead to greater openness, wealth, and human development? Much will depend on how migration is managed by the more powerful liberal states, because they will set the trend for the rest of the globe. To avoid a domestic political backlash against immigration, the rights of migrants must be respected and states must cooperate in building an international migration regime. Even as states become more dependent on migration, they are likely to remain trapped in a liberal paradox for decades to come.

References

Abraham, D. 2015. "Law and Migration: Many Constraints, Few Changes." In *Migration Theory: Talking across Disciplines*, ed. C. Brettell and J. Hollifield, 289–317. New York: Routledge.

Andreas, P., and T. Snyder, eds. 2000. *The Wall around the West: State Borders and Immigration Controls in Europe and North America*. Boulder, CO: Rowman & Littlefield.

Bade, K. J., ed. 1992. *Deutsche im Ausland—Fremde in Deutschland: Migration in Geschichte und Gegenwart*. Munich: C. H. Beck.

Bauböck, R. 1994. *Transnational Citizenship: Membership and Rights in International Migration*. Aldershot: Edward Elgar.

Benhabib, S. 2004. *The Rights of Others: Aliens, Residents and Citizens*. Cambridge: Cambridge University Press.

Bertossi, C. 2011. "National Models of Integration in Europe: A Comparative and Critical Analysis." *American Behavioral Scientist* 55(12): 1561–80.

Bhagwati, J. 1983. *International Factor Mobility*. Cambridge, MA: MIT Press.

———. 1998. *A Stream of Windows: Unsettling Reflections on Trade, Immigration, and Democracy*. Cambridge, MA: MIT Press.

Bleich, E. 2003. *Race Politics in Britain and France*. New York: Cambridge University Press.

Bloemraad, I. 2006. *Becoming a Citizen: Incorporating Immigrants and Refugees in the United States and Canada*. Berkeley: University of California Press.

Bonjour, S. 2016. "Speaking of Rights: The Influence of Law and Courts on the Making of Family Migration Policies in Germany." *Law & Policy* 38(4): 328–48.

Boswell, C., and D. Hough. 2008. "Politicizing Migration: Opportunity or Liability for the Centre-Right in Germany." *Journal of European Public Policy* 15(3): 331–48.

Brochmann, G., and T. Hammar, eds. 1999. *Mechanisms of Immigration Control: A Comparative Analysis of European Regulation Policies*. Oxford: Berg.

Brubaker, R. 1989. *Immigration and the Politics of Citizenship in Europe and North America*. Lanham, MD: University Press of America.

———. 1992. *Citizenship and Nationhood in France and Germany*. Cambridge, MA: Harvard University Press.

———. 2017. "Why Populism?" *Theory and Society* 46: 357–85.

Calavita, K. 1992. *Inside the State: The Bracero Program, Immigration and the INS.* New York: Routledge.

Camus, R. 2011. *Le Grand Remplacement, Introduction au remplacisme global.* Paris: Reinharc.

Carens, J. H. 1989. "Membership and Morality: Admission to Citizenship in Liberal Democratic States." In *Immigration and the Politics of Citizenship in Europe and North America*, ed. R. Brubaker. Lanham, MD: University Press of America.

———. 2000. *Culture, Citizenship, and Community: A Contextual Exploration of Justice as Evenhandedness.* New York: Oxford University Press.

———. 2013. *The Ethics of Immigration.* New York: Oxford University Press.

Carvalho, J., and D. Ruedin. 2020. "The Positions Mainstream Left Parties Adopt on Immigration: A Cross-cutting Cleavage?" *Party Politics* 26(4): 379–89.

Chin, R. 2007. *The Guest Worker Question in Postwar Germany.* New York: Cambridge University Press.

Chung, Erin Arean. 2020. *Immigrant Incorporation in East Asian Democracies.* New York: Cambridge University Press.

Czaika M., and H. de Haas. 2013. "The Effectiveness of Immigration Policies." *Population and Development Review* 39(3): 487–508.

D'Amato, G. 2014. "Switzerland." In *Controlling Immigration: A Global Perspective, 3rd Edition*, ed. J. F. Hollifield, P. L. Martin, and P. M. Orrenius, 308–32. Stanford, CA: Stanford University Press.

Eatwell, R., and M. Goodwin. 2018. *National Populism: The Revolt against Liberal Democracy.* London: Penguin Books.

Eichengreen, B. 1989. "The Political Economy of the Smoot-Hawley Tariff." *Research in Economic History* 12: 1–43.

Ellermann, A. 2009. *States against Migrants: Deportation in Germany and the United States.* Cambridge: Cambridge University Press.

Fassmann, H., and R. Münz. 1994. "European East-West Migration, 1945–1992." *International Migration Review* 28(3): 520–38.

Favell, A. 1998. *Philosophies of Integration: Immigration and the Idea of Citizenship in France and Britain.* New York: St. Martin's Press.

Fetzer, J. S. 2000. *Public Attitudes toward Immigration in the United States, France, and Germany.* Cambridge: Cambridge University Press.

Fields, G. 1994. "The Migration Transition in Asia." *Asian and Pacific Migration Journal* 3(1): 7–30.

Freeman, G. P. 1986. "Migration and the Political Economy of the Welfare State." *The Annals* 485(May): 51–63.

———. 1995. "Modes of Immigration Politics in Liberal Democratic States." *International Migration Review* 29(4): 881–902.

Geddes, Andrew. 1995. "Immigrant and Ethnic Minorities and the EC's Democratic Deficit." *Journal of Common Market Studies* 33(2): 197–217.

———. 2003. *The Politics of Migration and Immigration in Europe.* London: Sage.

Ghosh, B. 1997. *Gains from Global Linkages: Trade in Services and Movement of Persons.* London: Macmillan.

———. 2000. *Managing Migration: Time for a New International Regime.* Oxford: Oxford University Press.

Gibney, M. 1999. "Liberal Democratic States and Responsibilities to Refugees." *American Political Science Review* 93(1): 169–81.

Glick Schiller, N. 1999. "Transmigrants and Nation-States: Something Old and Something New in the U.S. Immigrant Experience." In *The Handbook of International Migration: The American Experience*, ed. C. Hirschman, P. Kasinitz, and J. DeWind, 94–119. New York: Russell Sage.

Goodwin-Gill, G. S. 1996. *The Refugee in International Law.* Oxford: Clarendon.

Guiraudon, V. 1998. "Third Country Nationals and European Law: Obstacles to Rights' Expansion." *Journal of Ethnic Studies* 24(4): 657–74.

Hammar, T., ed. 1985. *European Immigration Policy: A Comparative Study.* New York: Cambridge University Press.

———, ed. 1990. *Democracy and the Nation-State: Aliens, Denizens and Citizens in a World of International Migration*. Aldershot: Avebury.

Hansen, R. 2000. *Immigration and Citizenship in Postwar Britain*. Oxford: Oxford University Press.

———. 2014. "Great Britain." In *Controlling Immigration: A Global Perspective, 3ʳᵈ Edition*, ed. J. F. Hollifield, P. L. Martin, and P. M. Orrenius, 199–219. Stanford, CA: Stanford University Press.

Hatton, T. J., and J. G. Williamson. 1998. *The Age of Mass Migration: Causes and Economic Impact*. New York: Oxford University Press.

Herbert, U. 2001. *Geschichte der Ausländerpolitik in Deutschland: Saisonarbeiter, Zwangsarbeiter, Gastarbeiter, Flüchtlinge*. Munich: C. H. Beck.

Hobsbawm, E. 1990. *Nations and Nationalism since 1780*. Cambridge: Cambridge University Press.

Hoffmann-Nowotny, H-J., and K-O. Hondrich, eds. 1982. *Ausländer in der Bundesrepublik Deutschland und in der Schweiz: Segregation und Integration*. Frankfurt am Main: Campus Verlag.

Hollifield, J. F. 1986. "Immigration Policy in France and Germany: Outputs vs. Outcomes." *The Annals* 485(May): 113–28.

Hollifield, J. F. 1990. "Immigration and the French State." *Comparative Political Studies* 23(2): 56–79.

———. 1992. *Immigrants, Markets and States: The Political Economy of Postwar Europe*. Cambridge, MA: Harvard University Press.

———. 1994. "Entre droit et marché." In *Le défi migratoire: Questions de relations internationales*, ed. B. Badie and C. Wihtol de Wenden. Paris: Presses de la Fondation Nationale des Sciences Politiques.

———. 1997a. *L'Immigration et L'Etat-Nation à La Recherche d'un Modèle National*. Paris: L'Harmattan.

———. 1997b. "Immigration and Integration in Western Europe: A Comparative Analysis." In *Immigration into Western Societies: Problems and Policies*, ed. E. Uçarer and D. Puchala. London: Pinter.

———. 1998. "Migration, Trade and the Nation-State: The Myth of Globalization." *UCLA Journal of International Law and Foreign Affairs* 3(2): 595–636.

———. 1999. "Ideas, Institutions and Civil Society: On the Limits of Immigration Control in Liberal Democracies." *IMIS-Beiträge* 10(January): 57–90.

———. 2000a. "Migration and the 'New' International Order: The Missing Regime." In *Managing Migration: Time for a New International Regime*, ed. B. Ghosh. Oxford: Oxford University Press.

———. 2000b. "Immigration and the Politics of Rights." In *Migration and the Welfare State in Contemporary Europe*, ed. M. Bommes and A. Geddes. London: Routledge.

———. 2004a. "The Emerging Migration State." *International Migration Review* 38: 885–912.

———. 2004b. "Migration and Sovereignty." In *Immigration and Asylum*, ed. Matthew Gibney and Randall Hansen. Los Angeles: ABC Clio, 2004.

———. 2012. "Migration and International Relations." In *The Oxford Handbook of the Politics of International Migration*, ed. M. R. Rosenblum and D. J. Tichenor, 345–79. Oxford: Oxford University Press.

———. 2014. "France." in *Controlling Immigration: A Global Perspective, 3rd Edition*, ed. J. F. Hollifield, P. L. Martin, and P. M. Orrenius, 157–87. Stanford, CA: Stanford University Press.

———. 2019. "The Migration Challenge." In *Governance in an Emerging New World*, ed. G. P. Shultz, 34–53. Stanford, CA: Hoover Institution Press.

———. 2020. "Migration and Mobility in an Age of Pandemic." *Notes on Migration and Inequalities* 4: 22–24.

Hollifield, J. F., V. F. Hunt, and D. J. Tichenor. 2008. "Immigrants, Markets, and Rights: The United States as an 'Emerging Migration State.'" *Washington University Journal of Law & Policy* 27: 7–44.

Hollifield, J. F., and C. Jillson. 2000. *Pathways to Democracy: The Political Economy of Democratic Transitions*. New York: Routledge.

Hollifield, J. F., P. M. Orrenius, and T. Osang 2006. *Migration, Trade and Development*. Dallas, TX: Federal Reserve Bank of Dallas.

Hollifield, J. F., P. L. Martin, and P. M. Orrenius, eds. 2014. *Controlling Immigration: A Global Perspective, 3ʳᵈ Edition*. Stanford, CA: Stanford University Press.

Hollifield, J. F., and M. O. Sharpe. 2017. "Japan as an 'Emerging Migration State.'" *International Relations of the Asia Pacific* 17(3): 371–400.

Hollifield, J. F., and C. J. Wilson. 2011. "Rights-Based Politics, Immigration, and the Business Cycle: 1890–2008." In *High-Skilled Immigration in a Global Labor Market*, ed. Barry R. Chiswick. Washington, DC: AEI Press.

Hollifield, J. F., and T. K. Wong. 2015. "The Politics of International Migration: How Can We Bring the State Back In?" In *Migration Theory: Talking across Disciplines*, ed. C. Brettell and J. Hollifield, 227–88. New York: Routledge.

Huntington, S. P. 1991. *The Third Wave: Democratization in the Late Twentieth Century.* Norman: University of Oklahoma Press.

Ikenberry, G.J. 2012. *Liberal Leviathan: The Origins, Crisis, and Transformation of the American World Order.* Princeton, NJ: Princeton University Press.

Ireland, P. 1994. *The Policy Challenge of Ethnic Diversity: Immigrant Politics in France and Switzerland.* Cambridge, MA: Harvard University Press.

Jacobson, D. 1996. *Rights across Borders: Immigration and the Decline of Citizenship.* Baltimore, MA: Johns Hopkins University Press.

Joppke, C., ed. 1998. *Challenge to the Nation-State: Immigration in Western Europe and the United States.* Oxford: Oxford University Press.

———. 2001. "The Legal-Domestic Sources of Immigrant Rights: The United States, Germany and the European Union." *Comparative Political Studies* 34(4): 339–66.

———. 2010. *Citizenship and Immigration.* Cambridge: Polity Press.

———. 2017. *Is Multiculturalism Dead? Crisis and Persistence in the Constitutional State.* Cambridge: Polity Press.

Jurgens, J. 2010. "The Legacies of Labor Recruitment: The Guest Worker and Green Card Programs in the Federal Republic of Germany." *Policy and Society* 29: 345–55.

Kastoryano, R. 1997. *La France, l'Allemagne et leurs immigrés: Négocier l'identité.* Paris: Armand Colin.

Keohane, R. O., and J. S. Nye. 1977. *Power and Interdependence: World Politics in Transition.* Boston: Little Brown.

Kepel, G. 1988. *Les banlieus de l'Islam.* Paris: Seuil.

———. 2017. *Terror in France: The Rise of Jihad in the West.* Princeton, NJ.: Princeton University Press.

Kettner, J. 1978. *The Development of American Citizenship, 1608–1870.* Chapel Hill: University of North Carolina Press.

Kindleberger, C. P. 1967. *Europe's Postwar Growth: The Role of Labor Supply.* Cambridge, MA: Harvard University Press.

King, D. 2000. *Making Americans: Immigration, Race and the Diverse Democracy.* Cambridge, MA: Harvard University Press.

Koslowski, R. 2000. *Migrants and Citizens: Demographic Change in the European System.* Ithaca, NY: Cornell University Press.

Krasner, S. D. 1999. *Sovereignty: Organized Hypocrisy.* Princeton, NJ: Princeton University Press.

Kyle, D., and R. Koslowski. 2001. *Global Human Smuggling: Comparative Perspectives.* Baltimore, MD: Johns Hopkins University Press.

Kymlicka, W. 1995. *Multicultural Citizenship.* Oxford: Clarendon Press.

Levitt, P. 2001. *The Transnational Villagers.* Berkeley: University of California Press.

Lutz, P. 2019. "Reassessing the Gap-Hypothesis: Tough Talk and Weak Action in Migration Policy?" *Party Politics* 20(10): 1–13.

Martin, P. L. 1993. *Trade and Migration: NAFTA and Agriculture.* Washington, DC: Institute for International Economics.

———. 2014. "Germany." In *Controlling Immigration: A Global Perspective, 3rd Edition*, ed. J. F. Hollifield, P. L. Martin, and P. M. Orrenius, 224–50. Stanford, CA: Stanford University Press.

Martin, P. L., M. Abella, and C. Kuptsch. 2006. *Managing Labor Migration in the Twenty-First Century*. New Haven, CT: Yale University Press.

Massey, D. S. 1987. *Return to Aztlan: The Social Processes of International Migration from Western Mexico*. Berkeley: University of California Press.

———. 1998. *Worlds in Motion: Understanding International Migration as the End of the Millennium*. Oxford: Oxford University Press.

———. 2020. "Immigration Policy Mismatches and Counterproductive Outcomes: Unauthorized Migration to the U.S. in Two Eras." *Comparative Migration Studies* 8(21): 1–27.

———, et al. 2002. *Beyond Smoke and Mirrors: Mexican Immigration in an Era of Economic Integration*. New York: Russell Sage Foundation.

Messina, A. M. 1996. "The Not So Silent Revolution: Postwar Migration to Western Europe." *World Politics* 49(1): 130–54.

Miller, M. J., and P. L. Martin. 1982. *Administering Foreign Worker Programs*. Lexington, MA: D.C. Heath.

Morawska, E. 1990. "The Sociology and Historiography of Immigration." In *Immigration Reconsidered: History, Sociology, and Politics*, ed. V. Yans-McLaughlin. New York: Oxford University Press.

Morgenthau, H. J. 1978. *Politics among Nations: The Struggle for Power and Peace*. New York: Alfred A. Knopf.

Mundell, R. A. 1957. "International Trade and Factor Mobility." *American Economic Review* 47: 321–35.

Norris, P., and R. Inglehart. 2019. *Cultural Backlash: Trump, Brexit, and Authoritarian Populism*. Cambridge: Cambridge University Press.

Nugent, W. 1992. *Crossings: The Great Transatlantic Migrations, 1870–1914*. Bloomington: Indiana University Press.

Peters, M. E. 2015. "Open Trade, Closed Borders: Immigration Policy in the Era of Globalization." *World Politics* 67(1): 114–54.

Polanyi, K. 1944. *The Great Transformation: The Political and Economic Origins of Our Time*. Boston: Beacon Press.

Portes, A. 1996. "Transnational Communities: Their Emergence and Significance in the Contemporary World-System." In *Latin America in the World Economy*, ed. R. P. Korzeniewidcz and W. C. Smith. Westport, CT: Greenwood.

Portes, A. 1997. "Immigration Theory for a New Century." *International Migration Review* 31(4): 799–825.

Rawls, J. 1971. *A Theory of Justice*. Cambridge, MA: Harvard University Press.

Rogers, R., ed. 1985. *Guests Come to Stay: The Effects of European Labor Migration on Sending and Receiving Countries*. Boulder, CO: Westview.

Rogowski, R. 1989. *Commerce and Coalitions: How Trade Affects Domestic Political Alignments*. Princeton, NJ: Princeton University Press.

Rosecrance, R. 1986. *The Rise of the Trading State*. New York: Basic Books.

Roy, O. 2019. *L'Europe est-elle chrétienne ?* Paris: Seuil.

Rudolph, C. 2006. *National Security and Immigration: Policy Development in the United States and Western Europe since 1945*. Stanford, CA: Stanford University Press.

Ruggie, J. G. 1982. "International Regimes, Transactions, and Change: Embedded Liberalism in the Postwar Economic Order." *International Organization* 36(2): 379–415.

Ruhs, Martin. 2013. *The Price of Rights*. Princeton, NJ: Princeton University Press.

Sassen, S. 1996. *Losing Control? Sovereignty in an Age of Globalization*. New York: Columbia University Press.

Schain, M. A. 2012. *The Politics of Immigration in France, Britain and the United States*, 2nd ed. New York: Palgrave-Macmillan.

———. 2019. *The Border: Policy and Politics in Europe and the United States*. New York: Oxford University Press.

Schuck, P. H. 1998. *Citizens, Strangers and In-Betweens: Essays on Immigration and Citizenship*. Boulder, CO: Westview.

Shain, Y. 1989. *The Frontier of Loyalty: Political Exiles in the Age of the Nation-State.* Middletown, CT: Wesleyan University Press.

Shaw, M. N. 1997. *International Law.* Cambridge: Cambridge University Press.

Smith, R. 1997. *Civic Ideals: Conflicting Visions of Citizenship in U.S. History.* New Haven, CT: Yale University Press.

Smith, S. 2019. *La ruée vers l'Europe: La jeune Afrique en route vers le Vieux Continent.* Paris: Grasset.

Soysal, Y. N. 1994. *Limits of Citizenship: Migrants and Postnational Membership in Europe.* Chicago: University of Chicago Press.

Stolper, W. F., and P. A. Samuelson. 1941. "Protection and Real Wages." *Review of Economic Studies* 9: 58–73.

Straubhaar, T. 1988. *On the Economics of International Labor Migration.* Bern: Haupt.

Teitelbaum, M. S., and J. M. Winter. 1985. *Fear of Population Decline.* Orlando, FL: Academic Press.

Thomas, B. 1973. *Migration and Economic Growth.* Cambridge: Cambridge University Press.

Thränhardt, D. 1993. "Die Ursprünge von Rassismus und Fremdenfeinlichkeit in der Konkurrenzdemokratie." *Leviathan* 21(3): 336–57.

Thränhardt, D., ed. 1996. *Europe: A New Immigration Continent.* Münster: Lit verlag.

Torpey, J. 1998. "Coming and Going: On the State's Monopolization of the Legitimate 'Means of Movement.'" *Sociological Theory* 16(3): 239–59.

Vertovec, S. 2007. "Super-Diversity and Its Implications." *Ethnic and Racial Studies* 30(6): 1024–54.

Walzer, M. 1983. *Spheres of Justice: A Defense of Pluralism and Equality.* New York: Basic Books.

Waltz, K. N. 1979. *Theory of International Politics.* Reading, MA: Addison-Wesley.

Weiner, M., ed. 1993. *International Migration and Security.* Boulder, CO: Westview.

———. 1995. *The Global Migration Crisis: Challenge to States and to Human Rights.* New York: HarperCollins.

Wong, T. K. 2015. *Rights, Deportation, and Detention in the Age of Immigration Control.* Stanford, CA: Stanford University Press.

———. 2016. *The Politics of Immigration: Partisanship, Demographic Change, and American National Identity.* New York: Oxford University Press.

Zolberg, A. R., A. Suhrke, and S. Aguayo. 1989. *Escape from Violence: Conflict and the Refugee Crisis in the Developing World.* New York: Oxford University Press.

18   HOW IMMIGRANTS FARE IN EUROPEAN LABOR MARKETS

Pieter Bevelander

INTERNATIONAL MIGRATION within and to Europe has been increasing and, consequently, so has the challenging situation of the economic performance of different categories of immigrants in Europe over the last four to five decades. The economic structural changes, together with a change in immigration to Western Europe since the 1970s by source country and by admission category, has gradually induced lower levels of immigrant economic integration. This native–foreign-born economic integration gap is partly due to a shift away from labor migration and toward family reunification, marriage migration, and refugee migration, and especially toward increased migration from outside Europe—particularly from the Middle East and Africa. The creation of the European Union common labor market has resulted in higher levels of both permanent and temporary internal migration, in particular from the new accession countries to western and southern European countries since the mid-2000s. Southern European countries, once providers of immigrants to labor-demanding European states in the northwest of Europe, have seen a substantial increase in immigration over the last two decades, inducing a dual labor market with natives employed in the primary, and immigrants working in the secondary and informal, labor markets during both the booming economy of the 1990s and early 2000s and the ensuing financial crisis. The substantial increase in the foreign-born population in a number of European countries and the consequent native–foreign-born economic integration gap was conducive to changes in policies—notably stricter immigration, integration, and citizenship policies—with the goal of increasing the labor-market performance of immigrants in general and refugees in particular.

In what follows, immigration to Europe over the last four to five decades is briefly addressed. This is followed by a presentation of the native–foreign-born employment integration gap connected to the change in origin and admission category of migrants, as well as an account of the situation of refugees on the labor market in European countries. The chapter ends with a discussion on the gradual and growing interdependence of European states on international migration (for more on this, see Hollifield and Lucassen, this volume).

Migration to Europe

Migration to Europe can generally be situated within three periods (Castles *et al.* 2014). The first period, from the end of World War II to the oil crisis in the early 1970s, is connected to several booming Western economies that, while flourishing, were also experiencing a shortage of labor and therefore began actively recruiting immigrants from both neighboring and southern European countries (including Turkey), as well as significant migration from former colonies (Lucassen, this volume).

The second period (1975–95) started with the oil crisis of the mid-1970s, which induced economic structural changes toward flexible work organization and teamwork, a gradual outsourcing of manual assembly-line labor production to low-wage countries, and slower general economic growth in many countries compared to earlier decades. Due to the closing of the door to labor migration, the type of migration in and to Europe, especially northwestern Europe—Austria, Germany, Belgium, the Netherlands, Denmark, Sweden, and Norway—became one of marriage and family reunion, together with increased refugee migration.

The third period, starting in the middle of the 1990s, had its roots in a number of events that took place in the earlier period, such as the fall of the Berlin Wall in 1989 and the collapse of the Soviet Union and its allies in the Warsaw Pact. This political change led to an increase in immigration, mainly labor, from eastern European countries such as Bulgaria, Romania, Ukraine, Poland, and the Baltic States to wealthier western Europe. Moreover, the civil war in the former Yugoslavia forced many to seek refuge in other European countries; Sweden, Germany, and Austria, in particular, took in large numbers of refugees from there during the 1990s. This period also encouraged immigrants from various parts of the world to travel to southern Europe and Ireland when the host-country economies boomed. Finally, the establishment of the Schengen Area and the enlargement of the European Union to include the Baltic States, Poland, Slovenia, Hungary, the Czech Republic, Malta, Cyprus, Slovakia, and, later, Bulgaria, Romania, and Croatia, induced substantial labor migration within the EU. The economic crisis of 2008 meant that migration in Europe slowed down for a number of countries and that, in southern Europe, some became emigration countries (Bevelander and Petersson 2014).

Migration and Changing Labor Markets

The increase in unemployment and the fear of social tension and further recession after the first oil-price shock caused a number of western European governments to cease their active recruitment of migrants. As touched upon earlier, structural changes in western European economies following the oil crisis prompted capital exports and investment in the establishment of manufacturing industries in underdeveloped areas like the Gulf states, South Korea, Taiwan, and Singapore in the 1970s and 1980s, leading to both lower rates of GDP growth and a lesser demand for labor. Moreover, the microelectronic revolution reduced the need for low-skilled labor, which was usually the preserve of many immigrants in traditional manufacturing. As a reaction to this new economic situation, immigration policies became more restrictive, thus affecting labor migrants. Even if the idea was that labor migration, especially to those countries which used the guest-worker system, was temporary, the return to the countries of origin of migrants was slow or non-existent. Instead, relatively liberal family reunification policies induced the migration of spouses and marriage migration. The signing by many countries of the 1951 Geneva Refugee Convention has, over time, paved the way for asylum seekers—many of whom came from Asia, Africa, and eastern Europe, especially in the 1980s and 1990s—to be granted residence permits relatively easily. Germany, Sweden, Denmark, Norway, Austria, Switzerland, and the Netherlands all took in larger numbers of refugees.

In this period, southern European countries were in a transitory phase in their migration experience and went from being emigration to immigration countries. The economic upturn of the 1980s and lower birth rates among the native population—i.e., both economic and demographic demand factors—led to labor shortages in Italy, Spain, Greece, and, to a lesser extent, Portugal, turning them from countries generally of emigration into countries of immigration. Migrants came initially from former colonial countries in North Africa, Latin America, Asia, and, a decade later, eastern Europe to fill these labor shortages. In contrast to other European countries, the inflow of immigrants to southern Europe largely consisted of irregular international migrants, flows that the weak governments in the host countries had great difficulty in controlling (Reyneri 2001). Over the decades, as a tool of migration management, the governments of both Spain and Italy have enacted a number of regularizations of undocumented immigrants.

Migration to Europe since the 1990s has included a growing number of humanitarian migrants from Africa and Asia. Armed conflict, as well as limited and failed development strategies, has led to greater inequalities both within and between regions and increased internal and international migration to Europe.

EU migration increased from the middle of the 1990s when the Schengen Agreement—which included all EU members with the exception of the UK and Ireland, and nonmembers such as Switzerland, Liechtenstein, Iceland, and Norway—came into force. Together with the continued growth of the EU, with new member-states joining in 2004, 2006, and 2013, internal migration grew substantially. Since the enlargement of the EU, immigrants from these new accession countries, and especially from Poland, have found employment in the economically more-developed countries of the EU, the UK, Sweden, Germany, Ireland, and the Netherlands. While, before EU enlargement, the dominant feature of migration flows from eastern European countries to other parts of Europe was mainly the temporary and seasonal migration by uneducated males, both permanent and temporary flows of both sexes by, in particular, high-skilled migrants were observable following the enlargement (Burrell 2009).

Fueled by economic growth and employment opportunities in the first decade of the new millennium up to 2008, immigration to and within Europe increased sharply. A number of countries opened their borders to both high-skilled labor and student migration to fill labor shortages in high-tech sectors. Additionally, multinational companies used intracorporate transfers to meet this demand. The demand for low-skilled workers (and, as a consequence, irregular migration) was met through temporary and seasonal regulations. In general, flows of labor migration from outside Europe were relatively low compared to those of family reunion and refugee migration although, for this latter category, some countries have been more open to admitting asylum seekers than others.

Linking international migration to European economies, we see that, gradually, the growing complexities of modern, national labor markets have created a very different kind of labor demand today than that which existed during the 1960s and 1970s (Bevelander 2000). Since the 1990s, the more pronounced expansion of both low- and high-skilled service sectors has generated increasing levels of education and occupational specialization. Currently, western European countries are service economies and, for a growing number, employment is mainly casual labor, often part-time and less secure. Many countries have put more selective labor migration policies in place in order to attract high-skilled migrants and students—on both a long-term and a temporary basis—to their knowledge-intensive economies; the low-skilled, on the other hand, are either kept out or are rerouted through irregular migration and thus have fewer rights (Ruhs 2013).

The 2008 financial crisis and its repercussions for the European economy and migration are difficult to assess and few have done so (however, see Koser 2009 for a historical perspective). Bevelander and Petersson (2014) describe the net migration streams for a number of countries in the years both before and after the crisis; the results show that, following the recession, net migration decreased throughout the EU, with the exception of Germany, the UK, and France. Turkey and the BRIC countries seemed to be less affected by the economic downturn and showed either positive, lower, or similar levels of net migration. However, according to Hatton (2014), the economic slump did not induce a policy backlash, thus making it more difficult for immigrants to move to Europe. He argues that this could be due to EU regulations.

This overview of international migration in Europe over the last five decades is, naturally, somewhat sketchy and does not claim to be complete. It is based on official statistics and does not cover the increase in undocumented migrants in Europe. However, it illustrates an increase in migratory flows after WWII—and especially since the 1980s in Europe—a migration that is now an essential element of European societies, having changed the population composition substantially (see table 18.1 and figure 18.1).

The Economic Integration of Immigrants

From an economic theoretical perspective, international migration can be seen, on the one hand, as the determinant of supply-side selectivity—that is, the characteristics of the migrant. On the other hand, on the demand side are the opportunities and restrictions created by immigration law in the receiving country (Chiswick 2008). Given the large pool of potential individuals who hope to engage in international migration, immigration law and its reinforcement by a particular country influence the actual immigration flow, together with the individuals' ability, schooling, skills, health, occupational status, and, subsequently, employment and earnings prospects, as well as their further inclusion in both the short and the long term. One of the standard suggestions in the economic migration literature is that migrants tend to be favorably self-selected on the basis of their skills, health, and other traits. However, with a growing diaspora, there is a diminishing selection of new emigrants (Ferrie and Hatton 2015). In addition, noneconomic migrants, such as those involved in family reunion and/or refugee migrants, are in a less advantageous position when it comes to their labor-market integration since factors

Table 18.1. International migration stock for Europe, 1990–2015 (% of population).

Country	1990	2000	2010	2015
Germany	7.52	10.98	14.43	14.88
Ireland	6.40	9.13	15.82	15.92
Netherlands	7.93	9.79	11.02	11.70
United Kingdom	6.39	8.04	12.13	13.20
Belgium	8.93	8.31	9.63	12.28
France	10.36	10.57	11.43	12.09
Luxembourg	29.81	32.04	32.12	43.96
Switzerland	20.86	21.92	26.50	29.39
Austria	10.29	12.38	15.20	17.47
Greece	6.10	10.15	11.36	11.34
Spain	2.10	4.07	13.48	12.69
Italy	2.51	3.71	9.71	9.68
Cyprus	5.71	8.49	17.03	16.83
Turkey	2.16	2.03	1.89	3.77
Malta	4.24	5.56	8.03	9.90
Portugal	4.41	6.34	7.21	8.09
Czech Republic	1.07	2.15	3.79	3.84
Hungary	3.35	2.90	4.36	4.56
Poland	2.95	2.14	1.67	1.60
Romania	0.58	0.57	0.77	1.16
Bulgaria	0.24	0.54	1.03	1.43
Croatia	9.95	13.22	13.28	13.60
Slovenia	8.87	8.60	12.36	11.41
Slovak Republic	0.78	2.16	2.71	3.27
Bosnia and Herzegovina	1.24	2.19	1.01	0.91
Macedonia, FYR	4.77	6.25	6.29	6.29
Montenegro	..	..	12.62	13.19
Serbia	1.04	9.05	9.12	9.12
Estonia	24.40	17.83	16.36	15.42
Latvia	24.25	18.14	15.01	13.35
Lithuania	9.45	6.15	5.15	4.73
Denmark	4.58	6.95	9.18	10.10
Finland	1.27	2.63	4.62	5.74
Iceland	3.76	5.65	11.03	11.39
Sweden	9.22	11.31	14.76	16.77
Norway	4.54	6.51	10.77	14.24

Source: Selected countries from Table 3, United Nations, Department of Economic and Social Affairs, Population Division (2019), International Migrant Stock 2019 (United Nations Datrabase, POP/DB/MIG/Stock/Rev.2019).

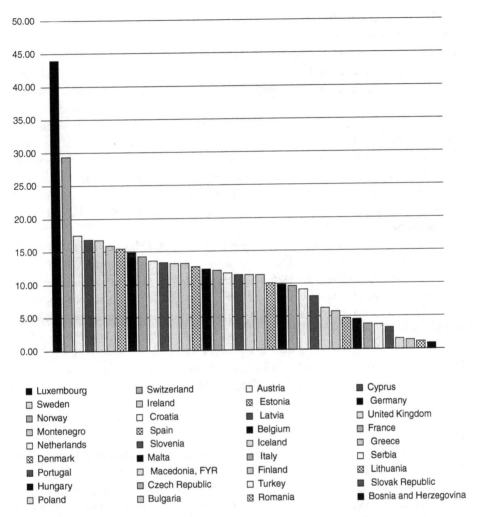

Figure 18.1. International migration stock in 2015 (% of population).

Source: United Nations Population Division, "Trends in Total Migrant Stock."

Legend:
- Luxembourg
- Sweden
- Norway
- Montenegro
- Netherlands
- Denmark
- Portugal
- Hungary
- Poland
- Switzerland
- Ireland
- Croatia
- Spain
- Slovenia
- Malta
- Macedonia, FYR
- Czech Republic
- Bulgaria
- Austria
- Estonia
- Latvia
- Belgium
- Iceland
- Italy
- Finland
- Turkey
- Romania
- Cyprus
- Germany
- United Kingdom
- France
- Greece
- Serbia
- Lithuania
- Slovak Republic
- Bosnia and Herzegovina

other than economic ones are important in their migration decision (Chiswick 2008). For an overview and analysis of refugee immigration in the OECD, see Hatton (2011).

Barry Chiswick's (1978) groundbreaking paper has been both the starting point and the trigger for numerous studies on the labor-market integration of immigrants in host countries. Over subsequent decades, research on this topic has grown massively. Increased migration worldwide, public and political discourse, and better and more available statistical information are key to this increase in research. Most studies still use a standard labor-market supply approach, through which it is hypothesized that the probability of employment, higher earnings, and skills match is determined by the level of human capital (Becker 1992), including formal education, labor-market experience, and skills acquired at work. However, when it comes to migration, some educational qualifications and skills may not be perfectly transferable between countries. These skills could be labor-market information, destination-language proficiency, and occupational licenses, certifications, or credentials, as well as more narrowly defined task-specific skills (Bevelander 2000; Chiswick *et al.* 2005). The lesser the international transferability of the skills, the wider the native-immigrant employment and/or earnings gap. The difficulties in the transferability of credentials are often greater for humanitarian migrants (Hatton 2011).

Aydemir (2011) argues, moreover, that there are many unobservables that make up the quality and relevance of immigrants' human capital and may result in skill transferability problems or a mismatch between demand and supply. The longer their period of residence in the new country, the more migrants will invest, learn more country-specific skills, and adapt to the level of human capital required in the receiving society. The human capital of immigrants will grow over time, as will their employment level and earnings.

Many studies on the economic integration of immigrants in host counties show both differences between groups with the same human capital and other observable characteristics or between different contexts or countries. On this topic, over the most recent decades, social capital propositions (Lancee 2010; Portes and Sensenbrenner 1993; Seibel and van Tubergen 2013), institutional factors like admission status (Luik *et al.* 2016), segmentation of the labor market and over education (Massey and Constant 2005), integration and citizenship policies (Helgertz *et al.* 2014) concerning immigrants, and different kinds of discrimination (Zschirnt and Ruedin 2016) have increased in importance as factors explaining the native-immigrant employment or income gap, as well as differences between immigrant/ethnic groups in host countries.

How Do Immigrants Fare in Europe?

The economic integration of immigrants in Europe has been documented in a number of publications in recent decades (see, for example, Hatton and Williamson 2005; OECD 2017; Zimmerman 2005). In figure 18.2 we depict the employment situation in Europe and other comparable OECD countries. In line with Hatton and Williamson, we find substantial native–foreign-born employment gaps in Denmark, the Netherlands, the Nordic countries, Germany, Austria, and France. Smaller gaps are visible for Canada, Australia, Greece, Spain and the UK. Higher employment rates of the foreign born are found in the US, Portugal, and Italy.

As shown earlier, explanations for the difference between the two groups are many and are a combination of supply- and demand-side factors as well as institutional barriers. Whereas the labor-market integration of immigrants is heavily conditional on the skills they bring with them and the type of labor market they wish to enter, other important aspects like social welfare levels, the structure of the labor market, employment protection legislation, and restrictions to prevent immigrants from taking jobs that require citizenship of the country are also at play. For example, a number of studies argue that unemployment and employment gaps between natives and immigrants in southern Europe are much narrower, since the labor market in these countries is more open to self- and informal-sector employment and therefore also much more precarious (Mottura and Rinaldini 2009; Solé and Parella 2010) and the income dispersion is

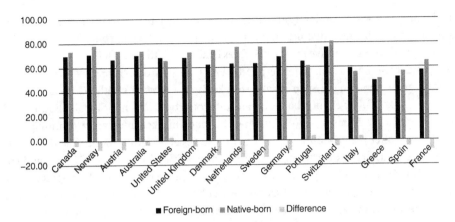

Figure 18.2. Native and foreign-born employment levels, and difference (selected countries).

Source: Based on OECD, Indicators of Immigrant Integration, Settling in (2015), https://www.oecd-ilibrary.org/docserver/9789264234024-en.pdf?expires=1612771137&id=id&accname=guest&checksum=C7A84D25FE1980061DE72B49716F9BFC.

higher (Bergh 2013). Fleischmann and Dronkers (2010), studying unemployment rates among first- and second-generation immigrants in European labor markets, found that immigrant unemployment is lower in countries with a larger segment of low-status jobs. Destination-country integration policies are not found to be significant in this study. Immigrants from Muslim countries seem to have a harder time finding employment. In a study by Rendall *et al.* (2010) that compares the labor-market integration trajectories of immigrant women in western and southern European countries, it shows that immigrant women in western European countries begin with a lower labor-force participation rate relative to native women but, over time, show some convergence. Immigrant women in southern European countries have similar labor-force participation rates relative to native women at the start but these rates do not change over time. The study also argues that the receiving-country context is important for explaining differences in immigrant labor-force participation. Kogan (2006) comes to a similar conclusion when comparing the employment situation for third-country nationals across European Union countries—those going to countries with a greater need for low-skilled labor are less disadvantaged on entering the labor market.

As indicated above, immigration to southern European countries is more recent. Increasing GDP and aging populations triggered growing labor shortages in certain sectors of the economy and induced immigration. In a seminal study for Spain, Amuedo-Dorantes and De la Rica (2006) showed that the labor-market integration of immigrants, measured through employment and occupational assimilation, increased the longer the migrants were in residence. It also showed that there is a large variation in integration by gender, origin, and educational attainment. The author suggests that the slow integration of African immigrants in particular could lead to marginalization and calls for training programs to facilitate their adaptation to the Spanish labor market. In a survey conducted by Corkill (2001), these results are reiterated; by studying Spain and Portugal, he argues that labor-market integration is also dependent on available policies and attitudes toward immigration. Other studies on the labor-market integration of immigrants to Spain show that immigrants have employment levels roughly on a par with those of natives, but do have more difficulties in adjusting to native levels of occupational attainment (Bernardi et al. 2010; Fernandéz and Ortega 2006). Strong segmentation for immigrant women on the Spanish labor market is also shown by Vidal-Coso and Miret-Gamundi (2014), revealing that they are disproportionally employed in house- and care-work (Jerve Ramsøy 2019). Studying the labor-market integration of immigrants in Portugal after the economic crisis of 2008, Esteves *et al.* (2018) found that, during the subsequent austerity regime, immigrants had more difficulty keeping their jobs and endured wage cuts out of proportion with those of the native population. Strategies to cope with the worsening economic situation were either to rely more on family and change their consumption habits or to move to another country. One of largest labor markets in Europe is that in Italy; until the mid-1990s, the share of migrants there was fairly low in international comparison. However, with an increasing demand for low- and semiskilled labor over time as well the enlargement of the EU and increased refugee migration over the last fifteen years, migration has increased considerably. When it comes to the labor-market integration of these immigrants, Venturini and Villosio (2008) find employment differences between natives and immigrants on entry and this situation increases over time. Career prospects are found to be ethnically different, with the lowest levels for African migrants and higher ones for eastern European and Asian immigrants. Other research on Italy looks at the low risk of unemployment for immigrants, on the one hand, and their highly disfavored occupational status on the other (Fullin and Reyneri 2010).

As indicated earlier, European countries that have experienced immigration over many decades also show variations in the labor-market integration of immigrants. The differences between the countries concerning their native–foreign-born economic integration gap can be understood when we acknowledge that the composition of the population in the origin countries also varies. The different immigration histories are important factors to be taken into account; they can affect both the quantity and the quality of the pool of immigrants *vis-à-vis* the demand on the labor market. Compared to other European countries, Switzerland has relatively high employment levels among immigrants (see figure 18.3 and Liebig *et al.* 2012), and this is mainly attributable to the favorable labor-market conditions and the high immigration intake of high-income OECD countries. However, Fibbi *et al.* (2006) and Riano and Baghdadi (2007) show the discriminatory practices of employers in Switzerland toward immigrants from non-OECD countries and youth of immigrant descent. A number of European countries have had considerable immigration flows from Turkey, Morocco, and the former Yugoslavia. Austria, Belgium, Denmark, Germany, France, the Netherlands, and Sweden have these features in common—the groups of immigrants consist of labor migrants, family-reunion migrants, and, to some extent, refugees (Turkey and the former Yugoslavia). The labor-market integration of these groups shows a remarkable similarity. Although employment levels relative to natives can differ—for example, immigrants from the former Yugoslavia have higher employment levels compared to immigrants from Turkey and Morocco in all the European countries. Higher educational levels are one of the reasons for this difference (Bevelander and Nielsen 2001; Zorlu 2013). Furthermore, research dealing with the labor-market integration of immigrants in European countries shows that language skills (Dustmann and Fabri 2003; Yao and van Ours 2015), social-capital acquisition (Cheung and Phillimore 2014; Lancee 2010), job-search methods (Frijters et al. 2005; Seibel and Van Tubergen 2013), and citizenship acquisition (Fougère and Safi 2009; Helgertz et al. 2014) are all correlated with labor-market integration. For Sweden, Bevelander and Nielsen (2001) show that the gradual increase in the employment gap between natives and foreign born on the Swedish labor market (see Bevelander 2000; Rosholm et al. 2006) can be explained by long-term economic and structural changes in the labor market affecting demand rather than by the declining quality of the immigrants.

It is also claimed that generous welfare-state benefits are responsible for this economic integration gap. The argument put forward is that immigrants are attracted to countries that have more generous welfare provisions while, at the same time, having higher hurdles for immigrants to overcome to obtain employment. This could lead to weaker incentives to accept jobs in the secondary labor market, which pay less and do not differ much from being on welfare benefits (Bergh 2013; Hatton and Williamson 2005). On a more aggregate level, Bergh (2013) tested whether welfare-state generosity, intolerance, employment protection laws, lower educational levels of immigrants compared to natives, collective bargaining agreements, and enclaves/segregation can explain the native–foreign-born employment gap. Keeping constant other factors, a strong negative correlation was found between the employment integration of immigrants and collective bargaining agreements or union power in the OECD. Bergh (2013) argues that insiders (natives) can, through collective agreements, bargain for higher wages and keep outsiders (immigrants) from competing for lower wages.

Another factor that could partly explain the native–foreign-born economic integration gap is that not all immigrants arrive as labor migrants. Some migrant categories, such as family-reunion and humanitarian migrants, have other primary reasons to move and their labor-market integration can be delayed or nonexistent due to a number of factors. Figure 18.3 shows the employment levels by reason for migration in Europe and by country. Apart from the wide variation in the employment integration of immigrants in different contexts, the figures show that labor migrants have high employment rates. Except for two countries, Croatia and Slovenia, humanitarian migrants in all countries have considerably lower employment levels compared to migrants who have moved for work. For most countries, family-reunion migrants have employment levels that fall between those of labor migrants and those of refugees. The comparatively lower level of economic integration of the latter and the increase in their numbers relative to labor migrants—in particular, over recent decades—which affects the total level of immigrant economic integration compared to that of natives (see also Dustmann et al. 2017), have been discussed both publicly and in the political arena. A more in-depth discussion of refugee integration in European countries is therefore described in the next section.

Refugee Labor-Market Integration

As mentioned earlier, the increase in the number of people seeking asylum has had a profound effect on European countries that, over the last thirty to forty years, have had to deal with increasing numbers of refugees from around the globe. However, although

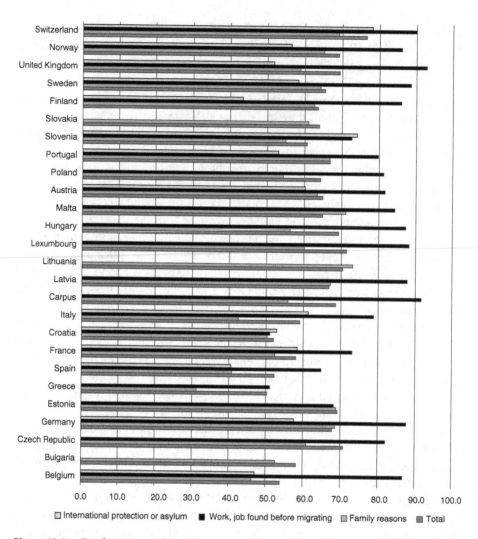

Figure 18.3. Employment rate by reason for migration and by country, ages 15–64 (2014). *Source:* Eurostat.

a large body of literature is available on the economic integration of immigrants in host countries, fewer studies have been conducted on the economic integration of refugees. One obvious question concerns whether or not refugees integrate easily into the host countries' labor markets. Other questions relate to the extent to which refugees are able to reach the same levels of employment as other immigrant groups and the native population, and what the income trajectories of refugees look like in comparison.

A number of studies in the US, Canada, the UK, the Netherlands, Denmark, Norway, and Sweden have specifically focused on the labor-market integration of refugees. The general picture that this research gives is that, compared to other immigrant groups, refugees generally have lower employment rates, particularly soon after their arrival in the host country. However, over time, refugees "catch up" and show similar employment levels to other noneconomic immigrant categories (Bevelander 2011; de Vroome and van Tubergen 2010; Hatton 2011), although they have lower levels compared to economic migrants (Yu *et al.* 2007). Moreover, studies analyzing the income attainment of refugees indicate similar income trajectories for them compared to other noneconomic immigrant groups (Bevelander and Pendakur 2014). Again, refugees lag behind labor migrants in terms of earnings development (Connor 2010).

As refugees, like other noneconomic immigrants, are less favorably selected compared to labor (economic) immigrants (Borjas 1987; Chiswick 2008; Dustmann *et al.* 2017), a number of countries have introduced integration policies that enhance refugee labor-market integration. From a policy perspective, it is important that these policies be effective and lead to higher economic integration. However, it is noteworthy that very few refugee integration policies have been evaluated.

The fact that refugees arrive under different, and often difficult, circumstances, have not primarily migrated for labor-market reasons, and are admitted according to other criteria (noneconomic) appears to affect their labor-market integration. Moreover, as both the migration and the admission processes can be lengthy and cumbersome, health issues and the loss of human capital can hinder individuals' adaption to the labor market of a new country. Whether refugees and family-reunion migrants obtain permanent or temporary residence can also affect their investment in the host language and receiving-country-specific human capital and their labor-market integration process (Dustmann *et al.* 2017; Hainmueller *et al.* 2016). The issue then becomes the extent to which policy hinders or helps in this process.

Research on economic outcomes by category of entry is often quite sketchy due to the lack of availability of the relevant data. In order to assess the labor-market integration of refugees, detailed statistical information relating to immigrant categories is of crucial importance. This is not always easily accessible, given that some countries have very few registered data and that the only reliable sources in other countries are survey information or proxies by country of birth and cohort of arrival.

For example, the national datasets in Scandinavia contain information about entry class whereas, in general, those in North America do not. Thus, quantitative assessments of outcomes by category of entry are much more common in northern Europe than in the United States or Canada. An early study for Sweden by Rooth (1999) shows that refugee integration into the labor market is dependent on individual human capital, investment in human-capital development (in both the source and the host country), and labor-market experience in the host country.

Other studies point to differences in the employment trajectories of government-assisted refugees, asylum seekers, and family-reunion immigrants in Sweden and conclude that these differences are the product of integration policies that vary by entry category. They also point to possible differences in access to social capital and in mobility choice. Government-assisted refugees are often located in municipalities in which housing is available but where employment opportunities are scarce. Asylum seekers often have personal resources and can settle where the job prospects look the most promising. Family-reunion immigrants are likely to draw on the social capital acquired by family and friends who have already settled in the country (Bevelander and Pendakur 2009).

In Sweden, using national data to assess the impact of mobility on economic outcomes for refugees, Rashid (2009) concludes that internal migration generates a positive outcome in terms of higher family income for newly arrived refugee families and is in line with earlier research on the attractiveness of the larger and more diversified labor markets in more densely populated areas and larger cities. This is partly because refugees often move from an area with few jobs to one with greater employment opportunities (Damm 2009; Edin *et al.* 2003). The internal migration of immigrants in general and refugees in particular is thus an important factor when it comes to their obtaining employment. Moreover, it has been shown that choice of city and labor-market situation are important predictors of labor-market integration. Moving to a larger city, for example, is often correlated with the presence of larger coethnic populations and the possibility of accessing ethnic networks (Rashid 2009). These results are in line with the broader literature on the impact of ethnic enclaves on labor-market outcomes (see Bonacich and Model 1980; Breton 1979; Wilson and Portes 1980). In this context, labor-market integration can lead to segmentation and hinder social upward mobility (Borjas 1994).

In addition to national-level datasets, a number of special surveys have been carried out that support the relation between immigrant entry category and economic outcomes. In the case of the Netherlands, de Vroome and van Tubergen (2010) found that host-country-specific education, work experience, language proficiency, and contacts with natives were positively related to the likelihood of obtaining employment and occupational status. In another study on the Netherlands, Bakker *et al.* (2013) showed that postmigration stress or trauma affects refugees' labor-market integration. Survey data from a sample of four hundred refugees in the United Kingdom point to the fact that policies which restrict access to the labor market also have a negative impact on refugees' employment probabilities (Bloch 2007).

Using the *Longitudinal Survey of Immigrants to Canada* to compare the labor-force participation and earnings of differing categories of immigrants two years after their arrival, Aydemir (2011) concluded that refugees have lower participation rates than family-reunion immigrants but that their earnings are about the same. Assessment of economic outcomes in the United States has shown that refugees have lower earnings than other categories of intake, but that this difference can at least partially be explained by differences in language ability, schooling, levels of family support, mental health, and residential area. However, a gap remains even after controlling for these factors (Connor 2010). Studies for Norway and Denmark show that refugees and family members have an initial promising increase in labor-market integration but a subsequent leveling out and even a reverse process after about ten years (Bratsberg *et al.* 2017; Schultz-Nielsen 2017). These studies underscore the heterogeneity within admission class and country-of-origin schooling as explanatory factors for labor-market success.

On the whole, many of the studies, referred to above, on the differences between refugees and economic migrants have concluded that refugees are in a disadvantaged position. However, there are also discrepancies in the results of these studies: some show that refugees perform as well as other noneconomic immigrants, and some that the differences are small, while others argue that the gap is substantial. However, these studies are all based on comparisons between groups in one country, not between countries. In

Bevelander and Pendakur (2014) this problem is overcome by studying the economic integration of noneconomic migrants. Directly comparing two countries and the same refugee groups, as well as admission class, provides additional insights. In their study, asylum seekers who subsequently obtain refugee status, resettled refugees, and family-reunion migrants, all of whom are noneconomic immigrants, are compared in both countries.

The findings of Bevelander and Pendakur's (2014) study show that, after controlling for other variables, the probability of being employed is roughly the same in Canada and Sweden, whereas the difference in earnings between the countries is greater and favors Canada. Additional insights from this study are that differences between intake categories are smaller in Sweden than in Canada. The authors argue that this could be due to the provision of services and programs to all categories in Sweden and only to resettled refugees in Canada. Thus, while the employment rates are comparable across the two countries, Canada may offer greater opportunities for upward earnings mobility than Sweden. Maybe the larger wage dispersion in Canada relative to Sweden could be a possible explanation for this result.

Returning to the question of what we know about how immigrants fare in Europe, the answer is strongly dependent on where the research takes place and who is being studied. Labor migrants, of whom, over recent decades, an increasing share are mobile EU citizens (who can also more easily move back when unemployed), show only narrow native–foreign-born economic integration gaps, whereas these are significantly wider for family-reunion and humanitarian migrants. However, the overall demand for labor in a country and the employment level of natives also affect the economic integration of immigrants, although both will affect the native–foreign-born economic integration gap. This persistent and negative gap, especially in a number of European countries with larger foreign-born populations due to refugee migration, correlates with an increase in the negative sentiments of the native population toward immigrants and asylum seekers. Overrepresented groups with these negative sentiments are poorly educated, male, and from more rural areas (Rydgren 2012). This is connected to the growing influence of far-right populist political parties and their impact on immigration and integration policies, which has led to debates about restricting access to rights and making naturalization more difficult. Criteria for residence have become more restrictive and new conditions have been imposed on the acquisition of citizenship in several countries (Joppke 2010).

The aim of this chapter has been to discuss immigration and the key drivers of immigrant economic integration, mainly through employment in European economies over the last five decades. As Hollifield and Foley (this volume) argue, European countries have gradually become more interdependent on international migration and, with more inclusive policies directed at future citizens, they have also lost the possibility to manage and control migration (Hollifield 2004). Whereas, in the 1950s and 1960s, it was labor migrants from neighboring and European as well as former colonial countries who helped to fill labor demand in the booming industries, the flow gradually shifted in the 1970s to being chiefly humanitarian migration from Africa, Asia, and the Middle East.

Together with internal EU migration since the 1990s, this shift has diversified the population of many European countries and cities. Whereas EU labor migration in general is temporary or circular in nature, that of humanitarian migrants and their families is, to a great extent, permanent because the reason for their movement is to seek refuge; they have few or no options to return to the country of origin. Their incentive to settle permanently and become citizens of the receiving society is therefore considerably greater.

A number of European countries have attained a percentage of the foreign born that is usually associated with immigration countries like the United States, Canada, and Australia. The economic and structural changes in the European economy over the last half decade, induced by globalization, imply a gradual increase in the low-skilled service sector as well as an increased demand for educated workers in production with higher technology content (a so-called skill-biased technology change) due to computerization (Autor et al. 1998).

Additionally, migrants may be hit by the direct and indirect economic consequences of COVID-19–related shutdowns in many European countries during the spring/summer of 2020. They are more likely to hold temporary contracts and tend to be concentrated in sectors more affected by fluctuations in the business cycle (construction, retail services) and exposed to shutdowns (hospitality, domestic services). Migrants may also, to a larger extent, be impacted by COVID/health concerns themselves due to higher proportions working in sectors with high COVID exposure, or their inability to maintain physical distancing: jobs like grocers, cleaners, health care and long-term care home assistance, food processing, etc. Besides, migrants working in the medical and care sector might have an improved position since COVID-19 has emphasized the labor shortages in this sector in some countries and several countries facilitated or fast-tracked recognition of foreign health professionals.

For immigrants to succeed in the labor market, the transferability of skills has become more important and could be a major explanation for the observed persistent native–foreign-born labor-market integration gap in the majority of these European countries. However, to a great extent, this overall immigrant labor-market integration gap is due to initial lower rates of employment, earnings, and the integration of refugees and refugee family members. Upon arrival, refugees have substantially lower employment levels and earnings compared to natives and other immigrant categories—such as labor and nonrefugee family-reunion migrants. The loss and lower transferability of skills as well as institutional factors connected to the asylum procedure are key factors explaining this difference in outcome. Moreover, these lower economic-integration outcomes for refugees are quite similar across countries. Both the increased immigration from Asia, Africa, and the Middle East and the weaker labor-market performance of these immigrants relative to labor migrants and natives have resulted in the segregation and marginalization of large populations in receiving countries, on the one hand, and a growing public and political discontent leading to anti-immigrant and even right-wing political movements and parties in Europe, on the other.

In order to reduce the native–foreign-born economic integration gap and, persuaded by immigrant integration-skeptic tendencies, a number of countries have established harsher immigration, family-reunion, integration and naturalization policies, with a shift away from stressing markets and rights to stressing culture (norms and values) and security (trust) (see Hollifield/Foley, this volume), with the idea that this should increase labor-market integration. However, evaluation of these policies indicates, for example, that fewer individuals have an opportunity to naturalize. What is more, due to the greater difficulties that immigrants have in entering the labor market and obtaining equivalent jobs, the most vulnerable are also stripped of the possibility to reunite with their families, to naturalize, and to obtain the social and formal rights and obligations of the society in which they live.

References

Amuedo-Dorantes, C., and S. de la Rica. 2006. "Labor Market Assimilation of Recent Immigrants in Spain." *IZA Discussion Paper no.* 2104. Bonn: Institute for the Study of Labor (IZA).

Autor, D. H., L. F. Katz, and A. B. Krueger. 1998. "Computing Inequality: Have Computers Changed the Labor Market?" *Quarterly Journal of Economics* 113(November): 1169–213.

Aydemir, A. 2011. "Immigrant Selection and Short-Term Labor Market Outcomes by Visa Category." *Journal of Population Economics* 24(2): 451–75.

Bakker, L., J. Dagevos, and G. Engbersen. 2013. "The Importance of Resources and Security in the Socio-economic Integration of Refugees: A Study on the Impact of Length of Stay in Asylum Accommodation and Residence Status on Socio-economic Integration for the Four Largest Refugee Groups in The Netherlands." *Journal of International Migration and Integration* 15(3): 431–48.

Becker, G. S. 1992. "Human Capital and the Economy." *Proceedings of the American Philosophical Society* 136(1): 85–92.

Bergh, A. 2013. *Labour Market Integration of Immigrants in OECD-Countries: What Explanations Fit the Data?* Occasional Paper no. 4/2013. Brussels: European Centre for International Political Economy.

Bernardi, F., L. Garrido, and M. Miyar. 2010. "The Recent Fast Upsurge of Immigrants in Spain and Their Employment Patterns and Occupational Attainment." *International Migration* 49(1): 148–87.

Bevelander, P. 2000. *Immigrant Employment Integration and Structural Change in Sweden, 1970–1995.* Lund: Lund Studies in Economic History 15.

———. 2011. "The Employment Integration of Resettled Refugees, Asylum Claimants, and Family Reunion Migrants in Sweden." *Refugee Survey Quarterly* 30(1): 22–43.

Bevelander, P., and H. S. Nielsen. 2001. "Declining Employment Success of Immigrant Males in Sweden: Observed or Unobserved Characteristics?" *Journal of Population Economics* 14(3): 455–71.

Bevelander, P., and R. Pendakur. 2009. 'The Employment Attachment of Resettled Refugees, Refugees and Family Reunion Migrants in Sweden." In *Resettled and Included? The Employment Integration of Resettled Refugees in Sweden,* ed. P. Bevelander, M. Hagstrom, and S. Ronnqvist, 227–45. Malmo: Malmo University.

———. 2014. "The Labor Market Integration of Refugee and Family Reunion Immigrants: A Comparison of Outcomes in Canada and Sweden." *Journal of Ethnic and Migration Studies* 40(5): 689–709.

Bevelander, P., and B. Petersson. 2014. "'Crisis, oh that crisis!" The Financial Crisis and Its Impacts on Migration in Europe." In *Crisis and Migration: Implications of the Eurozone Crisis for Perceptions, Politics and Policies of Migration,* ed. P. Bevelander and B. Petersson, 9–24. Lund: Nordic Academic Press.

Bloch, A. 2007. "Refugees in the UK Labour Market: The Conflict between Economic Integration and Policy-Led Labour Market Restriction." *Journal of Social Policy* 37(1): 21–36.

Bonacich, E., and J. Model. 1980. *The Economic Basis of Ethnic Solidarity.* Berkeley: University of California Press.

Borjas, G. J. 1987. "Self-Selection and the Earnings of Immigrants." *American Economic Review* 77(4): 531–53.

———. 1994. "The Economics of Immigration." *Journal of Economic Literature* 32(4): 1667–717.

Bratsberg, B., O. Raaum, and K. Røed. 2017. "Immigrant Labor Market Integration across Admission Classes." *Nordic Economic Policy Review* 520: 17–54.

Breton, R. 1979. "Ethnic Stratification Viewed from Three Theoretical Perspectives." In *Social Stratification: Canada*, ed. J. E. Curtis and W. Scott, 51–72. Toronto: Prentice-Hall.

Burrell, K. 2009. "Migration to the UK from Poland: Continuity and Change in East-West European Mobility." In *Polish Migration to the UK in the New European Union: After 2004*, ed. K. Burrell, 1–19. Aldershot: Ashgate.

Castles, S., H. de Haas, and M. J. Miller. 2014. *The Age of Migration: International Population Movements in the Modern World*, 5th ed. London: Palgrave Macmillan.

Cheung, S.Y., and J. Phillimore. 2014. "Refugees, Social Capital, and Labour Market Integration in the UK." *Sociology* 48(3): 518–36.

Chiswick, B. 1978. "The Effect of Americanization on the Earnings of Foreign-Born Men." *Journal of Political Economy* 86(5): 897–921.

Chiswick, B. R. 2008. "Are Immigrants Favorably Self-Selected? An Economic Analysis." In *Migration Theory: Talking across Disciplines*, ed. C. B. Brettell and J. F. Hollifield, 63–82. New York: Routledge.

Chiswick, B., Y. Liang Lee, and P. W. Miller. 2005. "A Longitudinal Analysis of Immigrant Occupational Mobility: A Test of the Immigrant Assimilation Hypothesis." *International Migration Review* 39(2): 332–53.

Connor, P. 2010. "Explaining the Refugee Gap: Economic Outcomes of Refugees versus Other Immigrants." *Journal of Refugee Studies* 23(3): 377–97.

Corkill, D. 2001. "Economic Migrants and the Labour Market in Spain and Portugal." *Ethnic and Racial Studies* 24(5): 828–44. DOI: 10.1080/01419870020063990

Damm, A. P. 2009. "Ethnic Enclaves and Immigrant Labor Market Outcomes: Quasi-Experimental Evidence." *Journal of Labor Economics* 27(2): 281–314.

de Vroome, T., and F. van Tubergen. 2010. "The Employment Experience of Refugees in the Netherlands." *International Migration Review* 44(2): 376–403.

Dustmann, C., and F. Fabbri. 2003. "Language Proficiency and Labour Market Performance of Immigrants in the UK." *Economic Journal* 113: 695–717.

Dustmann, C., F. Fasani, T. Frattini, L. Minale, and U. Schönberg. 2017. "On the Economics and Politics of Refugee Migration." *Economic Policy* 32(91): 497–550.

Edin, P., P. Fredriksson, and O. Åslund. 2003. "Ethnic Enclaves and the Economic Success of Immigrants: Evidence from a Natural Experiment." *Quarterly Journal of Economics* 118(1): 329–57.

Esteves, A., M. L. Fonseca, and J. Malheiros. 2018. "Labour Market Integration of Immigrants in Portugal in Times of Austerity: Resilience, In Situ Responses and Re-emigration." *Journal of Ethnic and Migration Studies* 44(14): 2375–91. DOI: 10.1080/1369183X.2017.1346040

Fernandéz, C., and C. Ortega. 2006. "Labour Market Assimilation of Immigrants in Spain: Employment at the Expense of Bad Job-Matches?" Working Paper no. 644, University of Navarra.

Ferrie, J. P., and T. J. Hatton. 2015. "Two Centuries of International Migration." In *Handbook of the Economics of International Migration*, ed. B. Chiswick and P. Miller, 53–88. Amsterdam: Elsevier.

Fibbi, R., M. Lerch, and P. Wanner. 2006. "Unemployment and Discrimination against Youth of Immigrant Origin in Switzerland: When the Name Makes the Difference." **Journal of International Migration and Integration** 7(3): 351–66.

Fleischmann, F., and J. Dronkers. 2010. "Unemployment among Immigrants in European Labour Markets: An Analysis of Origin and Destination Effects." *Work, Employment and Society* 24(2): 337–54.

Fougere, D., and M. Safi. 2009. "Naturalization and Employment of Immigrants in France (1968–1999)." *International Journal of Manpower* 30(1/2): 83–96.

Frijters, P., M. A. Shields, and S. Wheatley Price. 2005. *Comparing the Success of Native and Immigrant Job Search in the UK*. https://eprints.qut.edu.au/6838/1/ejfeatures2005.pdf

Fullin, G., and E. Reyneri. 2010. "Low Unemployment and Bad Job for New Immigrants in Italy." *International Migration* 49(1): 118–47.

Hainmueller, J., D. Hangartner, and D. Lawrence. 2016. "When Lives Are Put on Hold: Lengthy Asylum Processes Decrease Employment among Refugees." *Science Advances* 2(1): 1–7.

Hatton, T. J. 2011. *Seeking Asylum, Trends and Policies in the OECD.* London: Centre for Economic Policy Research (CEPR).

———. 2014. "The Slump and Immigration Policy in Europe." In *Crisis and Migration: Implications of the Eurozone Crisis for Perceptions, Politics and Policies of Migration,* ed. P. Bevelander and B. Petersson, 25–47. Lund: Nordic Academic Press.

Hatton, T.J., and J. G. Williamson. 2005. *Global Migration and the World Economy: Two Centuries of Policy and Performance.* Cambridge, MA: MIT Press.

Helgertz, J., P. Bevelander, and A. Teganumataka. 2014. "Naturalization and Earnings: A Denmark-Sweden Comparison." *European Journal of Population* 30(3): 337–59.

Hollifield, J. 2004. "The Emerging Migration State." *International Migration Review* 38(3): 885–912.

Jerve Ramsøy, I. 2019. "Expectations and Experiences of Exchange, Migrancy in the Global Market of Care between Spain and Bolivia." PhD thesis, Malmö University.

Joppke, C. 2010. *Citizenship and Immigration.* Cambridge: Polity Press.

Kogan, I. 2006. "Labor Markets and Economic Incorporation among Recent Immigrants in Europe." *Social Forces* 85(2): 697–721.

Koser, K. 2009. *"The Impact of Financial Crises on International Migration: Lessons Learned."* Research Series no. 7. Geneva: International Organization for Migration.

Lancee, B. 2010. *"The Economic Returns of Immigrants Bonding and Bridging Social Capital."* PhD thesis, Florence. https://hdl.handle.net/11245/1.338106

Liebig, T., S. Kohls, and K. Krause. 2012. "The Labour Market Integration of Immigrants and Their Children in Switzerland." OECD Social, Employment and Migration Working Paper no. 128. Directorate for Employment, Labour and Social Affairs, OECD.

Luik, M.A., H. Emilson, and P. Bevelander. 2016. *"Explaining the Male Native-Immigrant Employment Gap in Sweden: The Role of Human Capital and Migrant Categories."* Discussion Paper no. 9943. Bonn: Institute of Labor Economics.

Massey, D., and A. Constant. 2005. *"Labor Market Segmentation and the Earnings of German Guestworkers."* IZA Discussion Paper no. 774. Bonn: Institute for Labor Economics,

Mottura, G., and M. Rinaldini. 2009. "'Migrants' Paths in the Italian Labour Market and in the Migrant Regulatory Frameworks: Precariousness as a Constant Factor." In *Refugees, Recent Migrants and Employment. Challenging Barriers and Exploring Pathways,* ed. S. McKay, 84–101. New York: Routledge.

OECD. 2017. *International Migration Outlook 2017.* Paris: OECD.

Portes, A., and J. Sensenbrenner. 1993. "Embeddedness and Immigration: Notes on the Social Determinants of Economic Action." *American Journal of Sociology* 98(6): 1320–50.

Rashid, S. 2009. "Internal Migration and Income of Immigrant Families." *Journal of Immigrant and Refugee Studies* 7(2): 180–200.

Rendall, M. S., F. Tsang, J. K. Rubin, L. Rabinovich, and B. Janta. 2010. "Contrasting Trajectories of Labor-Market Integration between Migrant Women in Western and Southern Europe." *European Journal of Population* 26: 383–410.

Reyneri, E. 2001. *Migrants' Involvement in Irregular Employment in the Mediterranean Countries of the European Union.* Geneva: International Labour Organization.

Riano, Y., and N. Baghdadi. 2007. "Understanding the Labour Market Participation of Skilled Immigrant Women in Switzerland: The Interplay of Class, Ethnicity, and Gender." *Journal of International Migration and Integration* 8(2): 163–83.

Rooth, D. 1999. "Refugee Immigrants in Sweden: Educational Investments and Labor Market Integration." PhD thesis, Lund University, Department of Economics.

Rosholm, M., K. Scott, and L. Husted. 2006. "'The times they are a-changin'": Declining Immigrant Employment Opportunities in Scandinavia." *International Migration Review* 40(2): 318–47.

Ruhs, M. 2013. *The Price of Rights: Regulating International Labor Migration.* Princeton, NJ: Princeton University Press.

Rydgren, J. 2012. *Class Politics and the Radical Right.* London: Routledge.

Schultz-Nielsen, M. L. 2017. "Labour Market Integration of Refugees in Denmark." *Nordic Economic Policy Review* 520: 55–85.

Seibel, V., and F. van Tubergen. 2013. "Job-Search Methods among Non-Western Immigrants in The Netherlands." *Journal of Immigrant & Refugee Studies* 11(3): 241–58. DOI: 10.1080/15562948.2013.801727

Solé, C., and S. Parella. 2010. 'The Labour Market and Racial Discrimination in Spain." *Journal of Ethnic and Migration Studies* 29(1): 121–40.

Venturini, A., and C. Villosio. 2008. "Labour-Market Assimilation of Foreign Workers in Italy." *Oxford Review of Economic Policy* 24(3): 518–42.

Vidal-Coso, E., and P. Miret-Gamundi. 2014. "The Labour Trajectories of Immigrant Women in Spain: Are There Signs of Upward Mobility?" *Demographic Research* 13(13): 337–80.

Wilson, K., and A. Portes. 1980. "Immigrant Enclaves: An Analysis of the Labor Market Experiences of Cubans in Miami." *American Journal of Sociology* 86(2): 295–319.

Yao, Y., and J. C. van Ours. 2015. "Language Skills and Labor Market Performance of Immigrants in the Netherlands." *Labour Economics* 34(C): 76–85.

Yu, S., E. Ouellette, and A. Warmington. 2007. "Refugee Integration in Canada: A Survey of Empirical Evidence and Existing Services." *Refuge* 24(2): 17–34.

Zimmermann, K. F., ed. 2005. *European Migration: What Do We Know?* Oxford: Oxford University Press.

Zorlu, A. 2013. "Ethnic Disparities in Degree Performance." *IZA Journal of Migration* 2: 3.

Zschirnt, E., and D. Ruedin. 2016. "Ethnic Discrimination in Hiring Decisions: A Meta-Analysis of Correspondence Tests, 1990–2015." *Journal of Ethnic and Migration Studies* 42(7): 1115–34.

19 THE EUROPEAN UNION

Shaping Migration Governance in Europe and Beyond

Andrew Geddes

THIS CHAPTER EXAMINES the extent to which forms of migration governance beyond the state can shape international migration and also reshape relations between states. It shows how this can happen both through the ordering practices of the European Union related to the borders and boundaries of its member states and through its relations with nonmember states and regions. Particular attention is paid to the oft-used but often ambiguous term "governance." An understanding of governance is developed that emphasizes not only the outputs or outcomes of governance (laws, policies, and the like) but also the understandings and representations of migration that necessarily underpin it. The argument in short is that the EU actively contributes to rebordering, by which is meant that the perceived need to protect the internal European space and its project of market integration has seen limits placed on both free movement for EU citizens and efforts to more tightly regulate the external borders of the EU's member states. These external bordering efforts are particularly focused on migrants from Africa and the Middle East, which suggests that rebordering is also racialized.

In terms of its fit with this volume, the chapter is concerned with understanding the drivers of migration governance, or, put differently, how social and political systems make sense of international migration and, by making sense of it, seek to impose meaning on it. Underlying this is the argument that governance systems—however and wherever organized—play a key role in giving meaning to international migration as a social and political issue. Governance is not just an *ex post* reaction to migration flows, but governance systems through their actions, inactions, and interactions develop the categorizations that organize international migration. This is why "migration governance"—its meaning, practice, and implications—is central to understanding global migration. To this can be added that migration governance is always, everywhere, and necessarily an organizational process (Geddes 2021).

While there is no comprehensive system of global migration governance, and one seems unlikely to develop any time soon, there are many forms of migration governance beyond the state that, crucially, have implications for how "actors" behave. These actors include migrants and refugees but also those who seek to make, shape, or influence migration governance systems and their outputs, laws, policies, and associated practices (such as political leaders, government officials, international organizations, private companies, academic researchers, etc.). To understand global migration, it is necessary to understand how governance systems beyond the state can give meaning to international migration as a social and political issue by influencing the behavior of various types of actor.

This also requires being more specific about the meaning of governance. This is important because governance is a word to which descriptors are often added (such as "multilevel," "multilayered," "deliberative," and "networked"), but which can remain curiously underspecified with more attention devoted to the describers than to the term governance itself. This is an important omission because there are not only practical but also powerful ethical connotations given the frequent references to a need for "good" or "better" governance and the way such normatively loaded terms as "good governance" travel around the world. There are also efforts by both international organizations and academic researchers to measure or index migration governance (Boucher and Gest 2018).

As a case, the EU is distinctive. No other regional organization has the supranational law-making powers possessed by the EU and its institutions, which are independent of its member states. The argument is not that the EU provides a template for other regions—which is highly unlikely—but that the EU has powerful effects on neighboring states and other regions because of the material and ideational power that it projects.

Migration Governance as an Organizational Process

The EU is a distinctive supranational governance system with a legal framework that provides for law-making and enforcement powers held by the EU's four main institutions: the Council of Ministers, which shares law-making power with the directly elected European Parliament; the European Commission, which has the power to make proposals and is the guardian of the EU Treaty framework; and the European Court of Justice, which interprets EU law. The institutional system is a hybrid of combining states and supranational sources of power and authority. In the area of migration it is both hybrid and differentiated with a clear distinction between a Europeanized free movement framework that gives legally enforceable rights to EU citizens (nationals of the twenty-seven member states) and a more state-centered framework for migration of non-EU nationals where the focus is on restricting those forms of migration defined as unwanted by state policies, and admissions policy remains firmly a member-state prerogative (Geddes, Hadj Abdou, and Brumat 2020).

The distinction between free movement for EU citizens and migration and asylum policy for non-EU citizens is fundamental to the effects of EU migration governance. EU migration governance systems play a key role in defining the nature of the challenges they face and the range of possible responses. As already noted, this is necessarily an organizational process. Governance organizations must try to make sense of a complex and highly uncertain situation. To do so, they extract "cues" from their environment as part of their attempt to work out what is going on "out there." Cues are "simple, familiar structures that are seeds from which people develop a larger sense of what may be occurring [and] . . . control over which cues will serve as a point of reference is an important source of power" (Weick 1995, 50).

Whether understood as a crisis of numbers, of security, of trust in political institutions and leaders, as a humanitarian crisis, or perhaps not as a crisis at all, the events of 2015 labeled as the "migration crisis" demonstrate very clearly the complexities of European migration governance. It would, however, be mistaken to attribute causal significance to the crisis without noting that institutional and policy choices were made long before the events of 2015. The crisis increased the focus on migration and the intensity of political debate, but did not lead to a reshaping of institutional and policy choices. Similarly, while the COVID-19 global pandemic led to severe travel restrictions and border closures, the underlying direction of travel in policy was already established and is likely to continue once pandemic-related restrictions ease (Guiraudon 2018).

A significant component of the crisis, however it was understood, or whether understood as a crisis at all, was that it was seen to resonate at both member state and EU levels. It was thus emblematic not only of the ways in which migration governance has evolved in contemporary Europe but also of the meaning of migration governance itself as a social, economic, and political process with implications for the state, for interdependence, and for the future responses to international migration in all its forms.

The EU as Supranational Governance

The EU has developed significant responsibilities for free movement, migration, and asylum. There is a long-standing and politically powerful commitment to intra-EU free movement as a right possessed by EU citizens. EU free movement is enabled and protected by the EU Treaty framework. Within the EU framework, intra-EU movement is defined as "mobility" and not "migration." It has been facilitated by the creation of the Schengen area comprising twenty-six European countries (excluding the UK, Ireland, Bulgaria, Croatia, Cyprus, and Romania while including the non-EU countries of Iceland, Lichtenstein, Norway, and Switzerland) that have abolished passport controls and other types of border control at their mutual borders. EU citizens traveling within the Schengen area are not subject to passport controls or, if resident in another member state, to any integration measures that might be applied to "third country nationals." Article 25 of the Schengen Borders Code allows the temporary reintroduction of border controls for up to thirty days. For example, in 2015, controls were reintroduced to deal with large inflows of people at the borders of Austria, Denmark, Hungary, Norway, Slovenia, and Sweden (Geddes, Hadj Abdou, and Brumat 2020).

While initially envisaged back in the 1950s as a more limited form of free movement for workers, there has been a progressive extension of the categories of people entitled to move freely and, as a right, it is closely associated with EU citizenship created by the Maastricht Treaty in 1993. Free movement was largely a nonissue until the "big bang" expansion of the EU that saw eight Central European countries join the Union. In 2015, there were around 12.5 million "free movers" in the EU (around 1.7 percent of the total population with around 3.7 percent of those being of working age [20–64]). The main countries of destination for EU free movers of working age were Germany (2.7 million), the UK (2.1 million), Spain (1.4 million), and France (circa 950,000). Germans, Italians,

Polish, Portuguese, and Romanians together made up more than half—6.6 million—of all movers in the EU-28/EFTA region (CEC 2020). Opposition to free movement and immigration were the key factors explaining the decision in 2016 by the UK to leave the EU (Dennison and Geddes 2018b). It was very clear in the subsequent Brexit negotiations that the right to free movement as part of the EU's four freedoms (for capital, goods, services, and people) is an inviolable principle.

Since the 1990s there has been a move to develop common migration and asylum policies applied to non-EU nationals, or, in EU jargon, "third country nationals." The key point is that this is a partial framework covering some but not all aspects of migration and asylum policy. While the EU may aspire to a common migration and asylum policy, it does not have one. Instead, it has intensified cooperation on measures to stem flows of those forms of migration it has defined as "unwanted," such as asylum seekers and irregular migrants. The numbers of migrants to be admitted remains strictly a matter for the member states as do integration policies for settled immigrants. The most recent attempt to formulate a strategy for migration and asylum at EU level was the European Agenda on Migration published by the European Commission in 2015, which was designed both to deal with the short-term issue of large inflows across the Mediterranean and to think in the medium to longer term about asylum, irregular migration, and labor migration (CEC 2015). Central to the European Agenda on Migration—and revealing of the limits of European integration—was the plan to relocate asylum seekers from Greece and Italy to other member states in the name of European solidarity. A Council of Ministers decision of September 2015 allocated specific numbers to participating member states. After two years, around 30,000 people had been moved (of which 19,000 went to Germany, who had met its quota of relocated people in full), but this fell way short of the plan to relocate around 100,000 people from Greece and Italy. By October 2017, Hungary had yet to agree to any relocations and Slovakia had agreed to sixteen from its quota of 902.

EU migration and asylum policy has an internal dimension but there is also a developing external dimension to EU migration governance. This initially developed in the 1990s as applicant countries aligned their migration and asylum system with the EU prior to entry. It then developed in what the EU refers to as its "neighborhood," by which it means the fourteen countries that border the EU but are not member states (Algeria, Morocco, Egypt, Israel, Jordan, Lebanon, Libya, Palestine, Syria, Tunisia, Armenia, Azerbaijan, Belarus, Georgia, Moldova, and Ukraine). In 2016, the external governance of migration was extended south to propose "migration compacts" with Senegal, Mali, Niger, Nigeria, and Ethiopia (Reslow 2019).

So far, this chapter has discussed manifestations of regional migration governance, but has had little to say about the terms regionalism and governance themselves. Thus, while it is clear that the state in Europe matters, it is clearly the case that European states (in their varying forms) have been decisively changed by the reordering of political authority associated with European integration and by rebordering that involves the EU.

What Is a Region?

The EU is a form of regional governance, but there are no natural regions. The EU, like all regions, is a political construct that centers on and/or seeks to promote social, political, economic, or organizational cohesiveness (Cantori and Spiegel 1970). The EU is a particular form of regional governance that is unlikely to be replicated elsewhere. As with other regions, however, the EU can be defined as a grouping of states that are geographically proximate leading to perceived common interests derived from location and associated interdependencies. They tend to seek broad-based cooperation on a range of issues, but particularly on trade and economic cooperation.

It is important to be specific about the EU's characteristics. While there are many regional organizations, Hurrell (2007, 241) observes: "The underlying distinctions matter greatly and much regionalist analysis is muddled precisely because commentators are seeking to explain very different phenomena or they are insufficiently clear about the relationship amongst the varied processes described under the banner of 'regionalism'." A reinvigoration of the study of regionalism after 1989 led to a focus on "new regionalism" understood as an "open" rather than protectionist regionalism and defined as "the processes by which actors, public or private, engage in activities across state boundaries and develop conscious policies of integration with other states" (Gamble and Payne 1996, 4).

Regionalism clearly has implications for the role of the state. One element of this has been whether state authority has been "unbundled," to use Ruggie's (1993) term, which would mean that regionalism would lead to a deterritorialization of politics, a diminution of state power, and even the end of sovereignty. This does not seem to have been the case in Europe. Rather, territory in Europe has been "rebundled" as processes such as regional cooperation and integration are suggestive of the simultaneous removal of some boundaries, redefinition of others, and creation of new boundaries (Ansell and Di Palma 2004).

European regional migration governance was initially seen as a way for European states to avoid the domestic political and judicial constraints associated with "rights-based politics" (Hollifield 1992; Guiraudon 2000). For example, in the 1990s, EU cooperation was dominated by the executive branch of national governments with virtually nonexistent scope for any involvement by judicial or legislative authority at either the national or EU level. This then motivated the argument that this was an "escape to Europe" to avoid the constraints of domestic politics that had, for example, allowed the courts to protect the rights of family migrants or constrain more arbitrary uses and abuses of state power in areas such as deportation. Guiraudon (2000) highlighted how EU member states had "venue shopped" to create a new EU setting within which they faced much less significant constraints.

The development of the EU since the early 2000s has to some extent undermined this argument. In those areas of migration policy where the EU has competence, we now see the application of the "Ordinary Legislative Procedure," which means member states in the Council of Ministers (using a majority voting system, not unanimity) share power with the European Parliament. The jurisdiction of the Court of Justice has also been extended so that those areas covered by the treaty are now justiciable (Acosta Arcarazo and Geddes 2013). That said, backsliding by member states, in particular over relocation of asylum applicants post-2015 in the name of EU solidarity, does demonstrate limits on the reach of EU powers (Pech and Scheppele 2017).

Governance

Governance is generally seen as "a signifier of change," by which could be meant change in the meaning, processes, conditions, or methods of governing (Levi-Faur 2012, 7). Peters (2012, 19) recognizes the "ambiguity" of the concept before noting that "successful governance" has four functional requirements: selection of goals, which are then integrated across all levels of the system; goal reconciliation and coordination to establish priorities; implementation; and feedback and accountability as individuals and institutions must learn from their actions. Such definitions are focused on the process of governance and the outcomes of governance systems.

There are, however, perspectives on governance that allow us to think more fundamentally about its meaning and implications for migration governance. In an influential account of governance, Pierre (2000) specified its dual meaning as the conceptual representation of social systems and the empirical analysis of the capacity to manage or steer the effects of change in these systems. Put another way, those actors involved in governance must, first, seek to make sense of what is going on "out there" and then, on the basis of these understandings, think about how to respond to these understandings (to manage or steer them, in the parlance of governance analysis).

We can now apply this to migration governance. The starting point is the basic observation that migration itself is epiphenomenal; it is necessarily a response to structural change in underlying systems that can drive or cause international migration. It is well known that the two core potential drivers of migration are, first, relative inequalities of income and wealth and their impact at household level and, second, the effects of conflict either within or between states. The former then drives migration typical understood as "voluntary" while the latter drives migration seen as "forced." These more immediate economic and political drivers are then influenced by demography, social networks, and the effects of environmental or climate change. The key point about migration governance is that each of these factors is highly uncertain in terms of its own operation but also in terms of its potential effects on migration. This means that it is essential to know more about how key actors in migration governance systems make sense of or understand the operation and potential effects of these drivers. As we will see below, there are data available on potential migration drivers, but this data and other evidence is interpreted in particular organizational and institutional settings that lead to certain understandings of migration that then have a powerful influence on the types of response that develop.

Here is an example of how this can work. As part of a major research project looking at the drivers of migration governance, we interviewed eighty key governance actors both at the EU level and in key member states (for further details see Geddes 2021). We asked them about how they understood the causes and consequences of migration, what they saw as the key risks and uncertainties associated with international migration, and how their organization tried to deal with these risks and uncertainties. Our first round of interviews in Europe and at the EU level were conducted in late 2014 and early 2015. An interesting finding was how the EU migration governance system itself produced an understanding of what was "normal" in terms of migration flows and of an emerging "new normality." A senior official from an EU agency was asked to reflect on the causes and effects of migration and identified important future challenges, which were described as follows:

> Yesterday at this meeting of the US and the Commission and others . . . [they] were re-peatedly mentioning that this will be the new normal. These 250,000–280,000 irregular migrants a year, that's basically what we have to count on in the foreseeable future. Nothing will change in this regard. I tend to agree, because as long as things are going the way they are going on in North Africa, sub-Saharan African countries, Afghanistan, Iraq, what have you, I don't see an end unfortunately to that. (Interview with EU official, Brussels, December 2014)

Whether accurate or not, this view is based on an understanding of the effects on migration of changes in the underlying drivers of migration; in this case, the effects of conflict. These changes are seen as likely to lead to persistently high migratory pressure. Interestingly, in terms of the use of language, the European Commission in June 2016 proposed a new framework for working in partnership on migration with non-EU countries and used the phrase "new normal." The commission paper made a clear link between the framing of the issue (as external migratory pressure) and a set of proposed remedies.

> External migratory pressure is the "new normal" both for the EU and for partner countries. This requires a more coordinated, systematic and structured approach to maximize the synergies and leverages of the Union's internal and external policies. To succeed, it needs to reflect both the EU's interests and the interests of our partners, with clear objectives and a clear way forward on how the objectives will be achieved, in terms of positive cooperation where possible but also the use of leverage where necessary. Such approach will be translated into compacts which will be embedded within the existing and future processes and partnership. (CEC 2016)

The two quotes above develop an understanding of migration that is diagnostic (the problem of external migratory pressures), prognostic (continued, high external migratory pressure), and motivational (the need for strong external governance to counter the problem, as defined). They provide a good example of a push toward rebordering driven by the need to protect or maintain the EU project, as understood. Central to rebordering are representations of the effects of change in underlying social systems and their implications. These representations can then shape the context for action within migration governance systems. This is not to argue that there is a simple transmission mechanism linking ideas to action. What it does show, however, is that international migration is not simply some kind of external shock to these governance systems. Instead, these systems themselves play a key role in constituting international migration as a social and political challenge.

The Multileveling of Governance
The changed role of the state in Europe is often labeled as indicative of the "emergence" of multilevel governance. Multilevelness in Europe involves not only the distribution of authority across levels (substate, state, and supranational) but also the increased role of private actors alongside public actors across each of these levels. The dilemmas

of migration governance are then played out in a system that is pluricentric and that involves more organizations.

Focusing on multilevelness does not mean that the state is written out of the analysis. States remain central to migration governance because it is the borders of states that define international migration as a social and political concern. Levi-Faur (2012) discusses "state-centred governance" that, despite changes in the state (limits on capacity, increased role of private actors), also recognizes their continued centrality. Similarly, Offe (2009) talks about the "resilience" of the state. While states are clearly key actors in migration governance, comparison at the regional level of institutional settings can show how state and nonstate actors potentially operate across multiple levels of governance. This creates the potential for institutionalized modes of coordination to produce decisions at regional level that can be both binding and implemented (Scharpf 1999) or have a more informal character (Börzel 2016).

The field of migration governance in Europe has become very crowded with important implications for interdependence and the future of migration. As Ansell, Levi-Faur, and Trondal (2017, 28) put it: "Governance is not characterized by a move away from organisations, but rather by the entry of new kinds of organizations into an increasingly crowded field." To give an example of how the field is crowded, consider this quote from a European Commission official prompted by an initial reflection on relations with Egypt to then describe cooperation between the EU and countries in the Horn of Africa. Within it, we can see cooperation between the EU and African Union, forms of bilateral and multilateral cooperation, the development of a regional consultation mechanism (the Khartoum process), plus, beneath the surface, a layer of official-level cooperation to support higher-level political meetings:

> That's why the Egyptians like it, with all the meaning. That's why we said, "Listen, why don't we actually use that same venue and occasion to then also bring in our EU Horn of Africa initiative?" Which is what it was initially called and then we turned it into the Khartoum process. "All the people will be there. It's sponsored by you, African Union, and we want you to remain an important role in this." We had signals that everybody would come, including Eritrea. That's actually how it happened. The first formal starting point of the Khartoum, was a senior official's meeting that happened back to back with the African Union conference in Khartoum in mid-October on trafficking and human beings and smuggling. In that senior official meeting we actually brought the draft declaration. We had a first exchange with all delegates on the text and then the ambitions and what it would actually mean, how it would be implemented and all that. Then there were bilateral, very heavy negotiations from October to the end of November in between Khartoum and Rome. We then arrived in Rome where the declaration was endorsed at the ministerial level. Now we are actually starting to, as I said, prepare the first projects. (European Commission official, December 2015)

These complex processes of international migration relations illustrate EU rebordering that aims to make it more difficult for those forms of migration defined as unwanted to get to Europe in the first place. This is a defensive and racialized reaction by European countries to international migration based on understandings of migration (a "new normal," for example) that are produced within governance systems and have the effect of projecting turbulence. This can then lead to a different way of thinking about the European migration crisis and associated "turbulence."

European Migration Governance Projects Turbulence

There are powerful and prevailing understandings of the European migration crisis that often center on the use of maps with ominous arrows pointing toward Europe. Similarly, images of African men in small boats trying to cross the Mediterranean have become ubiquitous representations of migration to Europe, even though they represent merely a small fraction of it. Maps and images can be understood as helping to create "turbulence" in governance systems to which the governance system must then respond, or put another way: "an outcome fulfils some prior definition of the situation" (Weick 1995, 11). This also means that there are important elements of endogeneity within migration governance systems that center on how understandings are developed of the causes and effects of migration. Endogeneity has a further implication, which is that migration governance can be a cause as well as an effect of increasingly turbulent tendencies in governance. This corrects a tendency to see international migration only as an external shock to governance systems when it is entirely plausible that these systems themselves can generate turbulence.

Turbulence can be understood as "the collision of politics, administrative scale and complexity, uncertainty, and time constraints" (Ansell et al. 2017, 1). Governance is becoming quicker as "speed compresses time frames and accelerates activity"; more complex as organizations and institutions become more closely linked to each other "intricately nested and overlapping"; and more conflictual as battles for resources intensify with these conflicts producing more uncertainty—becoming a vicious circle (4). Migration governance exemplifies these tendencies and is not only reflective of turbulence but also generative of turbulence.

Turbulence is linked to complex systems within which interactions are "highly variable, inconsistent, unexpected or unpredictable" (2). That this turbulence is both endogenous and exogenous to organizations means that organizations themselves can play an important role in generating turbulence: "This is particularly relevant for public sector organizations led by a political leadership and accountable to legislatures" (8). Organizations can project turbulence onto their environment. This reinforces the importance of analyzing how actors within these organizations make sense of their roles and also means looking at the role of both formal and informal social networks, habits and routines, learning and sense-making.

It could be the case that turbulence provokes profound institutional change, but it may also lead to reactive modes whereby "decision-makers may tend to replicate structures or procedures that have been perceived as successes in the past" (11). This view is reflected in a quote from a European Commission official:

> It's very much, it goes in cycles . . . we hear the same discussion now that we heard 10 years ago. And we see the same responses now that we saw 10 years ago. It didn't work then so I don't think it will work now. The normal "strengthen the borders", Schengen, controlling,

etc. I just don't think that's the right . . . it's too simplistic I think. (European Commission official, December 2014)

Our interviews also suggest that actors in migration governance systems, particularly at an official level, have concerns about the consequences of interventions because they are unsure of the effects and fear unintended and negative consequences. This ambiguity means that problems and choices can be "decoupled" (Cohen, March, and Olsen 1972) because there are "enduring tensions within organizations which produce ambiguity about what problems, solutions and consequences to attend to at any time, and what actors are deemed efficient and legitimate" (Ansell, Levi-Faur, and Trondal 2017, 45).

Migration governance means dealing with three main forms of ambiguity. First, those arising from competing pressures between, for example, a demand from business for openness and political demands for closure. Yet here too we can see the role played by the interpretation within governance systems of signals from the environment. There is a prevailing understanding that there are high levels of anti-immigration sentiment in Europe driven by negative media coverage and fueling the growth of the radical and populist right. It is true that the immigration issue has become more salient, that media coverage can often be negative, and that there has been a growth in support for the populist and extreme right, but it is also the case that attitudes to Europe have remained relatively stable and also that, perhaps surprisingly, levels of favorability to immigration have actually increased (Dennison and Geddes 2018a). This tension between openness and closure is also reflective of how actors in migration governance systems respond to signals from the political environment. In particular, while the extreme and populist right has tended not to be included in governing coalitions, its views have been co-opted by mainstream parties. This is based as much on understandings by elite actors of public attitudes to migration in Europe that might seem plausible but are not accurate. Instead, a closer look could put a different gloss on the openness versus closure argument. There are actually many people in Europe who fall into what could be called a "persuadable" or "anxious" middle. They have concerns about immigration but deeply resent being labeled as ignorant, or worse, racist, for having these concerns. These people tend to have more conservative values, which means that arguments for migration that focus on the benefits of diversity and mobility as good things in themselves may well not resonate. It is, however, possible that arguments for immigration that are framed in terms of more conservative values (playing by the rules, contributing to the system, fitting in) could be a basis for appealing to this anxious or persuadable section of the population. A problem is that advocates of openness tend to assume that their own liberal and progressive values can be projected onto the rest of the population who do not necessarily share these values and are likely to resent being labeled either implicitly or explicitly as ignorant or racist for not sharing this liberal, progressive worldview. It can be quite startling in the debate about migration governance in Europe how little attention is paid to public attitudes to migration. This is particularly relevant in Europe and in other parts of the world too, such as the United States, where polarization between people or groups with opposed views seems high (Strijbis, Helmer, and de Wilde 2018).

A second ambiguity derives from the inherent complexity of the issues encompassing very different motives for movement, effects of that movement, and diverse social, economic, and political responses. It is hard to pin down what is meant by international migration, which makes it hard to develop a focused policy response. Uncertainty can also induce a fear of making changes because of the potential for a Jenga effect, with one change causing the whole edifice to tumble down.

The third ambiguity is linked more generally to organizations in modern societies and limits on their ability or capacity to respond to their environment. This is not necessarily because they are ignorant of the phenomena (although this is possible) with which they must deal but because there are constraints on time, information and resources, or bounded rationality (Simon 1991).

Decoupling can involve the distinction between what is formally supposed to happen in an organization and what really happens (between "myth" and ceremony," as Meyer and Rowan [1977] put it). This quote from a German government official illustrates the issue—the problem that the implementation of the legislation varies widely:

> A number of different public bodies are involved. Take immigration authorities, for example—we have over 500 immigration authorities in Germany and they implement the legislation very differently on the ground, meaning that they can't make hard and fast plans. Either for refugees or the companies recruiting abroad in terms of how individual immigration authorities approach the statutory provisions. And then you obviously have the interfaces with the Central Placement Office of the German Federal Employment Office for priority check and work permit issues. (German government official, June 2015)

Ambiguity means that decision-making preferences are powerfully driven by interpretations of the effects of external environments, which might be an understanding of the drivers of migration, but could also be an understanding of organizational constraints or the effects of anti-immigration sentiment. Links between decisions and actions may be loosely coupled or decoupled because of "gaps" in the system. This means that the links between problems and choices are interactive rather than linear because they are informed by ongoing evaluations of the effects of actions and by the social context within which these assessments are made. It also means that political and symbolic considerations can play a key role in decision-making that can lead to an emphasis on being seen to do something rather than actions necessarily achieving their intended effects. Big investments in border security and associated technologies—"building a wall"—despite evidence that these might have limited effect or even be counterproductive is an example of the importance of political and symbolic considerations. The overall significance is that reflective action and understandings of history and past experience can create an environment that previously didn't exist. Actions establish boundaries, draw lines, create categories and labels, which is, of course, highly pertinent to migration governance. Such patterns are clearly evident in the United States, as Foley and Tichenor in this volume demonstrate.

Actions are linked to cues that are drawn from the environment. These cues contribute to a larger sense of what is occurring and depends upon their plausibility rather than accuracy. For example, there is heated debate in Europe about the effects of immigration on welfare states. Arguments about negative effects on welfare tend also to be linked to the power of pull factors linked to these welfare states in channeling migration to Europe. For example, then Austrian foreign minister Sebastian Kurz was strongly critical of Germany's more open approach to the refugee crisis, and claimed in March 2016:

> These people don't come to Europe because they want to live on Lesbos. They come here because they want to enjoy the living standards and benefits they are guaranteed in countries like Austria, Germany or Sweden . . . Don't get me wrong, I don't blame these people; I can understand them, because many politicians have triggered false hopes (*The Observer*, March 6 2016).

As noted earlier in the discussion of a "new normal", whether or not this understanding is accurate becomes less important than the wider political resonance it acquires. It expresses a meaning that has developed within the migration governance system that then powerfully influences both the "domestic" response within the EU (deterrence and control) as well as the attempts to externalize the European response to draw in non-EU countries.

This chapter has shown how migration governance beyond the state can shape migration. It does so not only in terms of outputs or outcomes of governance processes but also through the underlying representations of migration that inform these processes. In the EU, an active process of rebordering designed to maintain the integrity of the EU project has led to an increased focus on rebordering that has seen significant effects on neighboring states and regions. This necessarily changes the meaning of state authority in Europe and also means that the EU becomes part of the historical and comparative context that reorders European politics in "multilevel" and "pluricentric" directions.

The EU cannot be understood as a migration state in the terms of the concept developed for this book's framework, but it does fundamentally recast debates about openness and closure in Europe. There is a rights-based framework for intra-EU mobility that is linked to EU citizenship and can be enforced within the EU's legal framework. There are also elements of migration and asylum policy that form the EU legal framework and that are justiciable by the EU's Court of Justice. European and EU politics is also powerfully influenced by the tension between openness and closure, but there is scope to know more about the scope and terms of this debate through more detailed analysis of the formation of and structure of public attitudes to migration. Analyses of migration governance often neglect this more political component of debates about migration in Europe. This is difficult to justify in light of the increased salience of the migration issue across Europe (and in other parts of the world too, obviously). Migration governance cannot be understood as a narrow technical issue of managing and steering migration as though this is somehow detached from the drivers of migration politics, which necessarily includes public attitudes.

Migration and mobility have been, are, and will continue to be central to migration governance in Europe and the EU, but they cannot be understood only as external challenges or threats to the EU and its member states. The EU itself, through its actions and inactions, inclusions and omissions, plays a key role in defining the nature of the challenge and, consequently, the actions that are taken. The EU forms part of a wider system of European migration governance that labels, categorizes, and draws boundaries. The EU itself thus contributes to the definition of international migration both in the domestic settings of its member states and through its international relations. Thus, to understand international migration requires assessment of the role that governance systems play in constituting international migration both as a process and as a set of social, economic, and political concerns. The EU case is distinctive in many ways but exemplifies how this can happen.

References

Acosta Arcarazo, Diego, and Andrew Geddes. 2013. "The Development, Application and Implications of an EU Rule of Law in the Area of Migration Policy." *JCMS: Journal of Common Market Studies* 51: 179–93. http://dx.doi.org/10.1111/j.1468-5965.2012.02296.x

Ansell, Christopher, and Giuseppe Di Palma. 2004. *Restructuring Territoriality: Europe and the United States Compared.* Cambridge: Cambridge University Press.

Ansell, Christopher, David Levi-Faur, and Jarle Trondal. 2017. "An Organizational-Institutional Approach to Governance." In *Governance in Turbulent Times*, edited by Christopher Ansell, Jarle Trondal, and Morten Øgård, 27–76. Oxford: Oxford University Press.

Ansell, Christopher, Jarle Trondal, Morten Øgård, Christopher Ansell, Jarie Trondal, and Morten Øgård, eds. 2017. "Turbulent Governance." In *Governance in Turbulent Times*, 1–23. Oxford: Oxford University Press.

Börzel, Tanja. 2016. "From EU Governance of Crisis to Crisis of EU Governance: Regulatory Failure, Redistributive Conflict and Eurosceptic Publics." *JCMS: Journal of Common Market Studies* 54: 8–31. https://doi.org/10.1111/jcms.12431.

Boucher, Anna, and Justin Gest. 2018. *Crossroads: Comparative Immigration Regimes in a World of Demographic Change.* Cambridge: Cambridge University Press.

Cantori, Louis, and Steven Spiegel. 1970. "The International Relations of Regions." *Polity* 2(4): 397–425. https://doi.org/10.2307/3233994.

CEC. 2015. "Communication from the Commission to the European Parliament, the Council, the European Economic and Social Committee and the Committee of the Regions. A European Agenda on Migration." COM(2015) 240 final.

———. 2016. "On Establishing a New Partnership Framework with Third Countries under the European Agenda on Migration." COM(2016) 385 final.

———. 2020. "Intra-EU Labour Mobility at a Glance: Main Findings of the 2019 Annual Report on intra-EU Labour Mobility." Luxembourg, European Union.

Cohen, Michael D., James G. March, and Johan P. Olsen. 1972. "A Garbage Can Model of Organizational Choice." *Administrative Science Quarterly* 17(1): 1–25. https://doi.org/10.2307/2392088.

Dennison, James, and Andrew Geddes. 2018a. "A Rising Tide? The Salience of Immigration and the Rise of Anti-Immigration Political Parties in Western Europe." *Political Quarterly* 90(1): 107–16. https://doi.org/10.1111/1467-923X.12620.

———. 2018b. "Brexit and the Perils of 'Europeanised' Migration." *Journal of European Public Policy* 25(8): 1137–53. https://doi.org/10.1080/13501763.2018.1467953.

Gamble, Andrew, and Anthony Payne. 1996. *Regionalism and World Order.* Houndmills: Macmillan.

Geddes, Andrew. 2020. *Governing Migration beyond the State.* Oxford: Oxford University Press.

———. 2021. *Governing Migration beyond the State: Europe, North America, South America, and Southeast Asia in a Global Context.* Oxford: Oxford University Press.

Geddes, Andrew, Leila Hadj Abdou, and Leiza Brumat. 2020. *Migration and Mobility in the European Union, 2nd Edition*. London: Palgrave Macmillan.

Guiraudon, Virginie. 2000. "European Integration and Migration Policy: Vertical Policy-Making as Venue Shopping." *Journal of Common Market Studies* 38(2): 251–71. https://doi.org/10.1111/1468-5965.00219.

———. 2018. "The 2015 Refugee Crisis Was Not a Turning Point: Explaining Policy Inertia in EU Border Control." *European Political Science* 17(1): 151–60.

Hollifield, James F. 1992. *Immigrants, States and Markets: The Political Economy of Migration in Europe*. Cambridge, MA: Harvard University Press.

Hurrell, Andrew. 2007. *On Global Order: Power, Values, and the Constitution of International Society*. Oxford: Oxford University Press.

Levi-Faur, David. 2012. "From 'Big Government' to 'Big Governance'?" In *The Oxford Handbook of Governance*, edited by David Levi-Faur, 3–18. Oxford: Oxford University Press.

Meyer, John W., and Brian Rowan. 1977. "Institutionalized Organizations: Formal Structure as Myth and Ceremony." *American Journal of Sociology* 83(2): 340–63.

Offe, Claus. 2009. "Governance: An 'Empty Signifier'?" *Constellations* 16(4): 550–62. https://doi.org/10.1111/j.1467-8675.2009.00570.x.

Pech, Laurent, and Kim Lane Scheppele. 2017. "Illiberalism Within: Rule of Law Backsliding in the EU." *Cambridge Yearbook of European Legal Studies* 19(December): 3–47. https://doi.org/10.1017/cel.2017.9.

Peters, Guy. 2012. "Governance as Political Theory." In *The Oxford Handbook of Governance*, edited by David Levi-Faur, 19–32. Oxford: Oxford University Press.

Pierre, Jon. 2000. *Debating Governance: Authority, Steering, and Democracy*. Oxford: Oxford University Press.

Reslow, Natasja. 2019. "EU External Migration Policy: Taking Stock and Looking Forward." *Global Affairs* 5(3): 273–78. https://doi.org/10.1080/23340460.2019.1604071.

Ruggie, John Gerard. 1993. "Territoriality and Beyond: Problematizing Modernity in International Relations." *International Organization* 47(1): 139–74. https://doi.org/10.1017/S0020818300004732.

Scharpf, Fritz. 1999. *Governing in Europe: Effective and Democratic?* Oxford: Oxford University Press.

Simon, Herbert. 1991. "Bounded Rationality and Organizational Learning." *Organization Science* 2(1): 125–34. https://doi.org/10.1287/orsc.2.1.125.

Strijbis, Oliver, Joschua Helmer, and Pieter de Wilde. 2018. "A Cosmopolitan-Communitarian Cleavage around the World? Evidence from Ideological Polarization and Party-Voter Linkages." *Acta Politica* 55(4): 1–24. http://hdl.handle.net/11250/2582912

CPSIA information can be obtained
at www.ICGtesting.com
Printed in the USA
JSHW031453261221
21515JS00001B/1

9 781503 629578